PAUL BOCUSE'S FRENCH COOKING

TRANSLATED FROM THE FRENCH BY Colette Rossant / EDITED BY Lorraine Davis

Paul Bocuse's

French Cooking

PANTHEON BOOKS / NEW YORK

First Paperback Edition

English translation Copyright © 1977 by Random House, Inc.

All right reserved under International and Pan-American Copyright
Conventions. Published in the United States by Pantheon Books, a
division of Random House, Inc., New York, and simultaneously in
Canada by Random House of Canada Limited, Toronto.
Originally published in France as *La Cuisine du marché* by
Flammarion et Cie, Paris. Copyright © 1976 by Flammarion.

This translation first published in hardcover by Pantheon Books, a division
of Random House, Inc., in 1977.

Library of Congress Cataloging in Publication Data

Bocuse, Paul, 1926–
    Paul Bocuse's French Cooking

    Translation of La cuisine du marché
    Includes index.
        1. Cookery, French.   I. Title.   II. Title:
French cooking.
TX719.B67183   1977   641.5′944   77-76511
ISBN 0-394-75545-6 (pbk.)

Manufactured in the United States of America

Book design by Gayle Jaeger

The publisher wishes to acknowledge a special debt of gratitude to
Phyllis Freeman and Gloria Edwinn, who copy-edited the manuscript
of this book, for their excellent, painstaking work under the
pressures of a demanding schedule.

To my father and Fernand Point,
creators of good cooking

Contents

Paul Bocuse, who may well be the world's greatest chef, is a man of Lyonnaise charm and a captivating Napoleonic air. Recently in discussing his recipes in America, he talked about his book with the assurance of one who holds the title of Meilleur Ouvrier de France Cuisinier (Best Culinary Craftsman in France), awarded him by the President of the French Republic, along with the Légion d'honneur.

Bocuse sees his book first as a novel, to be read for enjoyment. Reading *Paul Bocuse's French Cooking,* he said, should whet your appetite; then, without any specific recipe in mind, go to the market to see what is available. Only then should you choose a recipe. The recipes, he added, although precise, should be considered only guidelines. Bocuse believes that cooking is an art like painting or music. Both imagination and common sense must be employed. Quality is the most important criterion in the choice of ingredients. As he explains in his introduction, in Lyons, Bocuse himself goes to the market every morning to choose his menu for the day. Whatever he finds fresh and in season is what will appear on his table for lunch or dinner.

In following one of Bocuse's recipes, consider first what is available. If one ingredient cannot be found, do not try to replace it with something else unless this is suggested in the recipe. If the missing item is a minor ingredient, proceed without it; if the major ingredients are unavailable, choose another recipe. If the major ingredients are of first quality, the dish will be a success regardless of whether or not you have every one of the seasonings.

Bocuse has great admiration for the United States, where almost everything necessary for fine cooking is available. He thinks that we have the best steaks in the world, that our vegetables, when in season, are of the highest quality. When Bocuse comes to the United States, he always returns to France with a hundred-pound bag of Idaho potatoes, to the great surprise of French customs officials.

Every meal should be a pleasure to make, Bocuse insisted. And since eating a Bocuse dish is a feast in itself, Bocuse recommended that only one recipe in a menu should be taken from his book. If the home cook, therefore, concentrates on one chosen recipe, the rest of the meal should be simplicity *par excellence.* If you make a beautiful leg of lamb, seasoning it and cooking it to perfection, serve it with a simple salad of tomato slices. Or if you devote your efforts to the appetizer—a soufflé or a soup—the rest of the meal may be unadorned, easy to prepare, and very light.

Moreover, French food need not be fattening. French portions are much smaller than those served in America, and if the dish is a rich one, Bocuse suggested, replace your evening dry martini with a glass of white wine; you then would not gain weight and could enjoy your dinner without thinking of calories.

Here are a few points to remember in using the recipes in this book:

Mixed spices
1 tablespoon each: dried
thyme, bay leaf, sage
1/2 teaspoon each:
coriander and mace
1 1/2 tablespoons pepper

Spiced salt
3 1/2 tablespoons salt
1 1/4 tablespoons ground
pepper
4 teaspoons mixed spices
(above)

When a recipe calls for "mixed spices," use the mixture of spices at the left. It can be prepared in advance and stored. Combine the ingredients in a blender or a food processor. When the ingredients are well mixed, rub through a sieve and place in a tightly closed jar.

When the recipe calls for "spiced salt," use the combination at the left. Mix well and store in a tightly closed jar.

Crème fraîche is now being produced in the United States; but if it is unavailable, replace it with heavy cream.

Fresh pork fat can be replaced by salt pork or unsmoked bacon; you may boil these briefly to remove some of the salt.

In all the recipes unsalted butter should be used; salted butter contains more moisture.

Crayfish are rarely available in United States markets; they can be replaced by a small lobster or large prawns. Substitutes for Mediterranean fish and other ingredients are listed in the recipes.

Fresh truffles are difficult to find and very expensive. You can replace them with canned truffles or even canned truffle peels, using the liquid in which the truffles came as flavoring in the sauce or the dish itself.

In numerous recipes Bocuse uses a mortar and pestle. You can blend the same ingredients easily with a food processor or an electric blender, but you must experiment with the timing, and the ingredients should be rubbed through a sieve afterward.

The dough recipes specify rather large quantities. When making any dish that requires a smaller amount, you can either cut down the amounts of the ingredients or follow the recipe as given, use the amount of dough needed, and freeze the remaining dough for future use.

Baking temperatures are indicated; but each cook knows her own oven best. Experiment to discover how to set yours for comparable results.

Wherever oven cooking is specified, the oven should be properly preheated.

Good American beef is also aged more than French beef, and is more tender. Sometimes therefore you may think that Bocuse's cooking times for meat are too long.

Bocuse often stuffs birds in advance and refrigerates them until ready to roast them. You should stuff the bird only when ready to cook it.

In the book, there are numerous recipes for small game birds that usually are not found in United States markets because they are protected by federal laws. Bocuse asked that these recipes be retained in the book, because he hopes that readers will enjoy them, and when traveling in France, recognize these dishes on the menus and be tempted to order them.

Above all enjoy what you are doing; follow the recipes, but don't let them stifle your own imagination.

—Colette Rossant

Every morning—this is a Lyonnaise tradition I find hard to abandon—I go to the market and stroll among the displays. When I shop for produce myself, I know that one peasant has excellent cardoons, that another specializes in spinach, and that one over there brought his delicious goat cheese this morning. Sometimes I do not even know what dish I will make for the noon meal. It is the market that decides. This, I think, is what makes good cooking.

I take the season into consideration in drawing up the menu. When it is time for hare, we cook hare; in the spring, it is spring lamb, then the new vegetables. The calendar also must compose our menu.

In presenting *Paul Bocuse's French Cooking* to the public, I must explain the philosophy of my book. All the recipes in it—simple or complicated—will succeed only insofar as you know how to choose or distinguish, in the market of your city or town, quality ingredients to go into the composition of the dishes you intend to prepare. I dare assert, therefore, that even if you do not achieve total success in your first try at preparing the most prestigious dish, it will not be a total failure insofar as it has excellent products as its base. This is an obvious truth, yet everyone seems to forget it. In fact, for a dish to succeed, the method and the know-how count, to be sure; but the proper choice of foods at the market seems to me just as essential.

But what does one find at the market today? I hear people saying everywhere that one can no longer find good produce. In 1908 the author of a cookbook complained that one could no longer find good produce. And in 1860 the Goncourts asserted that meat had lost its taste! I could quite easily start back in the eighteenth century to draw up a complete catalogue of culinary complaints!

Speaking for myself, at the risk of surprising you, I will say that today we can find the best produce that has ever existed—and find it anywhere, thanks to modern means of transportation, among other things. You must take the time to examine, to shop. The annoying thing is that my contemporaries seem to have lost, little by little, a sense of the unfolding of the seasons, the sense of rite, of ceremonial, brought by each season's characteristics. They want to eat asparagus at Christmas, strawberries on New Year's Day, game at Easter! Can't they remember that good tomatoes are available only in August, that the best cherries are harvested in June, and that the calendar interferes continuously in the preparation of menus?

You must not, therefore, open my book and decide to prepare this or that dish. I would advise you rather to go to your market. There you will see what foods are available; then you should look in the book for a recipe to prepare them. On the other hand, if you leave home with the idea of buying, let us say, sole, and you do not give up that idea, even if you see shining, bright-eyed whiting or a beautiful bream on display, and you return home with sole of inferior quality—then too bad! There is grave risk of forfeiting the meal's success.

The new French cuisine

I have sometimes been criticized for not going to my famous market every day. I have been reproached for being in Japan, in the United States, and so on. I have gone on trips, indeed, but always quick ones—three days here, two days there, rarely more. I think it is essential to go somewhere else to find out what is going wrong at home. The more one travels, the more one realizes that other cooks are not standing still; they are progressing. Their experience should be profitable to others. That is why one must go to see them. After all, the cook's trade makes him part of a brotherhood. It is necessary to have toured France, perhaps many times; and today anyone who wants to progress must go around the world. Each time that I go to another country, I come back with many ideas. In Hong Kong, for example, I realized that they knew how to cook vegetables very well, which meant very quickly. I brought back from there a way of cooking snow peas. I always used to stew them with pork fat and onions, and I realized that cooking snow peas the same way as string beans very quickly in a big pot of salted water resulted in something marvelous. If "the new French cuisine" reflects my compatriots' need to put to the test a return to the sources of our culinary tradition, at the same time it opens new perspectives on what we could do in observing what is happening in our neighboring countries or in those farther away. In brief, "the new French cuisine" is old and it is new.

Journalists come to see me, clients ask me questions. . . . They want to know everything about what we call "the new cuisine." "The new cuisine" at bottom is the true cuisine. But how can one define it more precisely? First of all, as I have said already, by the care one gives the quality of the foods. In this field one must not cheat but always look for what is best, whether it is best as meat, vegetables, etc. This is true for a small roadside diner or for an exceptional restaurant. It is true that to choose whiting or salmon, one must look for the best whiting, the best salmon, which come from the Adour or Brittany or even Ireland. This is true also for the housewife. . . .

One of the principles of "the new cuisine" also is that one must allow foods their proper flavors: it is a question of striving to retain the original taste of the food. In the old cuisine the reasons were more spectacular than culinary. In the new cuisine, everything has a *raison d'être.* Let us take, for example, one of the "Bocuse specialties"—sea perch in a crust, stuffed with a lobster mousse. The perch is baked in the dough, but one does not have to eat the crust; it is there to keep the juices in the perch. One does not have to eat the stuffing in the center, either; it is there to maintain a certain moistness without which the perch has a tendency to dry out. The supporters of the new cuisine follow other rules that I have already mentioned: don't establish a menu in advance, before going to the market in the morning; make up your menu after you know what can be found there. This automatically obliges you to simplify, to lighten your menus. One does not need those depths of sauces, all those marinades, or other doings. Before the Second World War, Fernand Point, who remains my master, had abolished all those sauces, those complicated, overly rich dishes, those garnishes that were the law in nineteenth-century cooking. This simplification of the preparation of the dishes extended also to the cooking time. Fish—as curious as this may seem—should be served pink around the bone. Fish are always overcooked! String beans should be crunchy to the tooth, and pasta must remain firm.

I have not forgotten another maxim of Fernand Point: One can only cook well, he used to say, with love—it is a matter, above all, of promoting around the table friendship and fraternity among men. This seems to me essential: the home cook, as well as the grand chef, must prepare only dishes that he or she loves to prepare. When you prepare a dish, when you roast a chicken, especially if it is a succulent chicken from Bresse, you really must be persuaded that you are making something good and do it with love. I think that cooking is easier and better when it is done for people that one loves. Another point on which I would like to insist: it is always necessary to leave some part of cooking to improvisation. One great orchestra conductor used to say that when he first conducted in public a piece that he had worked on and rehearsed for a long time, he always left a place for imagination and improvisation. The same is true of the home cook, who should realize that one need not follow a recipe to the letter and that at the last minute if one ingredient is not available, it can be replaced with another. If a housewife chooses to prepare a *coq au vin,* for example, but she does not have *lardons* or pork and small onions, she should not worry. If the chicken and the wine are good, if everything is correctly salted and peppered, she can replace the onions with shallots or leeks. Above all, she must not feel herself a slave to the book but must take some initiative—and why not some risks? Even if she does not claim to have any culinary gifts, the mere fact that she has attempted the recipe, has begun the dish, is a sign that she has a feeling for cooking. Therefore, it is permissible to allow oneself a certain margin for maneuver and a margin for fantasy, on condition, to be sure, that you stay in the same style and follow the basic proportions. These are, it seems to me, some of the characteristics of "the new cuisine," and we have been proud to be the ones to make our renewed culinary tradition known on board the planes of Air France, as well as in Japan, where in Osaka I had the honor to teach the cuisine of my country in the biggest hotel school there, Shizuotsuji, to an audience of fifteen hundred students, from a fourteen-year-old apprentice to a professional of eighty-two, who had come there to retrain themselves. I think that I also learned as much there as I taught.

Meals

I find that meals are always too large. In my opinion one

should leave the table feeling a little bit hungry. One hot dish in a meal seems sufficient to me, even for a grand dinner.

At home one cooks just a single hot dish, but cooking it well is sure to satisfy one's guests. These meals with hot hors d'oeuvre, hot fish, hot meat, and a hot dessert are absolutely deadly! Especially since this demands enormous work, and there is nothing sadder for the guests than to see the host or hostess exhausted after a day spent in the kitchen, not able to be at the table with them but obliged to stay at the stove. . . . You must know how to limit your ambition and not compete with chefs. If one wanted to go to a restaurant, one would go there. Look for the simplest recipes—do not arrive at the table smelling of cooking oil. . . . It is better if you serve a cheese soufflé that you know how to do well, followed by a *foie gras,* for example. But, as a general rule, the host or hostess should choose only dishes that can be cooked in advance, in order to be relaxed when he or she sits down to dinner. Allow me to give you one more piece of advice: continue to make the dishes you know how to cook. Perfect two or three dishes and maintain your skills. You make a cheese soufflé superbly or an unforgettable gratin of potatoes. If, in addition, you know how to make creamed chicken or cook a leg of lamb, the battle is won.

Quantities

Fernand Point does not give any proportions or quantities in his cookbook. I think he went a bit too far. In my book the quantities are approximate. If I write "12 onions," this does not mean that the dish will not come out right if you use 9 or 14. The same is true for the flour for flaky pastry. To write "$1/2$ cup flour" does not make much sense. At my town of Collonges we have had the same miller for the last twenty years. We know that 1 pound of his particular flour is necessary to prepare flaky pastry—but, if for one reason or another, we should need one day to go to another miller, we would have to rethink all our recipes that include flour. In this regard, every time one stands in front of a stove, one has to start from zero! Do not, therefore, take what is written here absolutely literally. I will give you the outline of a certain kind of cooking, and you, with your taste, your imagination, your inspiration, will do your own cooking.

I use many of Guérot's recipes, which I find marvelous. Alfred Guérot, one must remember, is one of the great chefs, the most comprehensive chef of the first half of this century. He achieved a synthesis of all the trends in our profession, thanks to his profound knowledge and his writing skill. His recipes are the most perfect in existence; and in this book I use them for the most part. In cooking one invents nothing. There are always the basic ingredients: poultry or meats, vegetables, etc. . . . and on the other hand there is the tradition, to which, to be sure, one must add the margin for innovation that I have been talking about. Therefore I have adapted Guérot's recipes, transformed them . . . and the home cook should do the same with Bocuse's advice.

Cooking times

Perhaps the only thing that one can use directly in a cook-book is the cooking time. And even then, a home cook may have an oven that, when set to heat to 400°, really only heats to 350°. The only instruction of which one can be absolutely sure is that which reads, "Boil for 15 minutes." There doubt is impossible! But in an oven one is never sure of the temperature. If there is one chicken in the oven, it does not cook in the same manner as if there were three. If there are three chickens in the oven, the temperature drops. In general one must be sure that one's oven temperatures are accurate. This is essential.

Wines

I can very well conceive that one could serve champagne throughout a meal: it is simple and delicious. But to find wines that go with each dish is a much more delicate task. Here again I think that the housewife should not be afraid to innovate. One can very easily drink a red wine with oysters; I see no objection to that. Also with game one can serve a Riesling, which is an Alsatian wine, rather fruity and very distinctive; but a great deal of prudence is necessary, and if one is not sure of oneself, it is better to follow the traditional rules. What is most important is the quality of the wine, and for that you must know where and from whom to buy. The best wines have the name of the vineyard's owner on the label. When the wine has the owner's name on the label, that in itself is a sign of quality, but it does not mean that there are no other very good wines. For my part I serve wines quite cool. Beaujolais, in particular. Burgundies are served at 50–54°; white wines, at 46–50°; and Bordeaux, at 59–61°. Many people believe that to "chamber" a wine consists of putting it near the chimney or the radiator. To *chambré* a wine, on the contrary, means to put it in a room in the house where there is no heat! The wine will have all the time it needs to reheat in the glass when you pour it.

Presentation

I have often shocked my listeners when I have said that the presentation is not very important. It is true that today we are far from the culinary art of the beginning of the century, when each dish demanded from the person who prepared it not only cooking knowledge but also the talents of a painter and an architect. Fish, meat, vegetables, sweets had to be presented in the shapes of pyramids, Chinese pavilions, or cathedrals!

Today, when a housewife serves a dish, she should present it without wanting to imitate the corner caterer who has decorated a lobster for his window.

You need only cut the lobster in half and serve it with its *court-bouillon;* and provided the lobster has been cooked at the last moment and cut when it is lukewarm, the guests will eat something admirable. *Grande cuisine* does not mean complicated cooking. . . . *Grande cuisine* can be a poached turkey, a lobster cooked at the last moment, a salad picked in the garden and seasoned at the last minute.

I hope that in these few pages of introduction I have given the essential rules of the art of the new French cuisine. You will find in this book all the details and precise instructions necessary to the success of a simple meal—or a complicated one.

I would like to add that this book owes a great deal to Louis Perrier: he deserves thanks for the effective help that he has given me.

I wish my readers good luck. Do not be discouraged if you cannot create culinary masterpieces immediately. Knowing how to cook—is it a gift one is born with? I do not really know. There is sometimes a sort of predestination: for more than seven generations there have always been cooks in my family. In 1634, my ancestors were millers at Collonges; and, in 1765, part of the mill was transformed into a restaurant. . . . As for me, I started in 1942, in a small restaurant in Lyons, run by Claude Maret. It was during the Second World War, and there was nothing to eat, and one had to get along with the ins and outs of the black market and with difficulties in getting supplies. This background was a great help to me— so much so that I learned nearly everything there is to know in the profession. Since then, times have changed, but I continue to cook. One day, I hope to buy a house in the country. I will build a kitchen according to my own ideas. I will put in a stove and a very beautiful wooden table, and if I still have health and spirit, I will always have four or five seats, and I will serve Bocuse cooking. One will be able to drink water (if necessary) but will be forbidden to smoke! It will therefore be for pleasure and for friendship that I will continue my tasks. . . . One of our moralists has said that the table is an altar that should be set up and decorated to celebrate the cult of friendship. The cook, the host or hostess, should never lose sight of this maxim: if you cook with pleasure and with love, you are certain to succeed with one of those savory dishes from a recipe you find here.

Paul Bocuse

Cooking preparations, simple or complex, are all based on principles that must be faithfully observed if one wishes to succeed in the various steps that result in the realization of the perfect menu.

These rules apply specifically to all the food preparation or handling, the preliminary steps in the process of cooking, of carving, and of the presentation of the dish.

Preliminary steps

Preliminary steps in the cooking of food consist of:
Boning, trimming, cutting, interlarding meat or prepared joints
Eviscerating, cleaning, trussing, barding, stuffing poultry, game, etc.
Peeling, washing, blanching vegetables
Preparing juices, sauces, cooking stocks
Gutting and scaling fish, washing the fillets, etc.
These are the steps prior to cooking.

To trim is to give a piece of meat a neat appearance, to get rid of surface tendons, and to remove the excess fat.

To interlard is to insert small sticks of fat *(lardons)* here and there in a piece of meat. This operation is done with a tool called a larding needle, through slits in the surface of the meat, which are placed in close rows, as regular as possible. The goal is to enrich the flesh by the melting of the fat during cooking. This is the way that one interlards a piece of beef, veal sweetbreads, a rump of veal, a fillet of veal, *grenadins,* a saddle of rabbit or of hare, etc.

To lard is a step similar to interlarding, applied to bigger pieces of meat that are to be braised, with this difference— the *lardons* must be the thickness of a ruler and the length of the piece of meat being prepared. These *lardons* are first seasoned and marinated for 2 hours, then stuck with a larding needle through the thickness of the meat, from end to end following the direction of the grain.

To bard is to protect the fleshy parts, such as the breast, of poultry or game with sheaths of fat fresh lard ¼ inch thick. This prevents the heat of the oven from drying out the meat, and the white meat cooks more slowly than it would otherwise, giving time for the thighs and the other dark meat, which is less sensitive and always slightly firmer, to become tender.

To blanch is a culinary expression without any semantic significance, but one established by professional use; it is equivalent to scalding. When blanching is done at the beginning of cooking, it hardens the external parts of certain pieces of meat, takes away the tartness or the overly strong taste of certain vegetables or softens them. Very often, after blanching, ingredients are cooled in cold water, then drained.

Ingredients are blanched by immersing in boiling water or in cold water heated just to the boiling point. Follow the directions in the recipe.

Cooking methods

There are five cooking methods: *braising, poaching, pot roasting, roasting,* and *broiling*—methods that are all different, as much in the process as in the results, which brings infinite savory resources to French cooking.

Braising   applies primarily to large cuts of meat, nearly always marinated for 5 or 6 hours and often interlarded. In that case the piece of meat is drained, sponged, and browned in butter or any other fat on top of the stove; then it is moistened moderately with marinade and some veal broth or bouillon is added. The pot is tightly closed, and cooking continues very slowly at a simmer.

Poaching   is a barely perceptible simmering in liquid, more or less abundant.

Pot roasting—or cooking in a casserole—must be done over a very low flame with no other liquid than the butter used for the beginning of the cooking and the juice seeping out of the piece of meat being prepared. After the meat is browned, the cooking utensil is kept well covered. One must baste quite frequently; at the end of the cooking time the concentrated juice will be a true essence.

Roasting   can be done two ways—in the oven or on a spit. The second method is certainly superior to the first. In both cases there is a concentration of heat, driving the juices toward the center of the piece of meat and creating a brown exterior crust that retains the juices—which, by an inverse phenomenon, will flow outward and impregnate all the tissues when the roast is no longer submitted to the action of the heat. During roasting, frequent basting with the fat—not the juice of the roast—is recommended.

Broiling   follows the same culinary laws as roasting—quick searing and browning of the exposed flesh by an open fire, driving in and concentrating the juices. The art is in knowing how to coordinate the intensity of the heat, the rapidity of the searing, with the size and thickness of the piece of meat placed on the grill. A piece of grilled meat is turned only once, and with a spatula—never with a fork or a pointed utensil, which would let the juices flow out.

Stewing, sautéing, and frying are fundamental derivatives of these processes. These theories will be found in the proper chapters.

Serving and arrangement

Arranging a dish is the last culinary step, which is a prelude to the eating.

The arrangement is the presentation of a dish with taste, which although elegant must be simple—especially if it is a hot dish—so as to avoid harming the quality and flavor of the food.

Absolute rule: do not sacrifice the substance to the form.

Containers of silver, gold plate, and crystal used for the

presentation of food must be impeccable, big enough without being too big; for example, the edge of a dish must never be covered.

The perfect arrangement is the one that responds to the necessities of serving. One therefore must avoid anything too heavy, which might weigh down the person who carves or serves to the point of interfering with his or her movements.

Carving

It is very difficult to carve well without any knowledge of anatomy; one must learn by observation and research. If you are carving a piece of meat, note the direction of the grain of the meat and always cut perpendicularly to it.

You will notice that when a slice of meat is thus cut correctly, it is easy to chew in the same direction as the grain. On the other hand, if the grain must be chewed at right angles, even tender meat will seem tough.

Seasoning, spices, and condiments

Seasoning   is adding the correct amount of salt—a simple act that is most important in cooking; it requires great subtlety from the tastebuds, and much attention and discernment.

Spices.   Spices used in cooking must, except for very rare exceptions, blend their particular aromas into the general flavor of dishes to which they impart a pronounced flavor. All the spices come from aromatic plants; the following are the principal ones and the most widely used:

Dill, betel, cinnamon, cloves, coriander, laurel or bay leaf, mace, mustard, nutmeg, pepper, thyme, ambergris, anise, Chinese anise, basil, cumin, fennel, juniper, ginger, horseradish, rosemary, sage, paprika, saffron, curry, chervil, tarragon, parsley, vanilla, tea, chocolate, coffee, and zest of lemons, oranges, and tangerines.

These herbs can be replaced by mixed spices—which are easier to use but have the disadvantage of giving a standardized flavor.

[*Editor's note:* Paul Bocuse's formula for mixed spices appears on page x.]

Condiments.   Condiments can be divided into six categories:

Acid condiments: vinegar, verjuice (sour apples or grapes), lemon juice

Pungent condiments: garlic, shallots, scallions, onions, chives, leeks, horseradish, radish

Sugars or sweetening condiments: cane or beet sugar, honey

Fat condiments: oil, butter, fat

Pickled condiments: mustards and all the derivatives, piccalilli, gherkins, onions, tiny melons, capers, green nasturtium seeds, small green tomatoes, cauliflower, etc.—all steeped and preserved in vinegar

Amount to buy

(For 1 person)

Fish and Seafood (before cleaning)

Anglerfish	$^1/_2$ pound
Bass	$^3/_4$ pound
Bouillabaisse (fish for)	1 pound
Bream	$^3/_4$ pound
Brill	$^3/_4$ pound
Carp	$^1/_2$ pound
Char	$^1/_2$ pound
Cod, fresh	$^1/_2$ pound
Cod, salt	5 ounces
Crayfish	14 ounces
Eel	$^1/_2$ pound
Fillet of sole (for 2)	1 pound
Frogs (pieces)	$^2/_3$ pound
Gudgeon	$^1/_2$ pound
Haddock	$^1/_2$ pound
Hake	$^1/_2$ pound
Herring	$^1/_2$ pound
Lamprey	$^1/_2$ pound
Lavaret	5 ounces
Lobster	1 pound
Mackerel	$^1/_3$ pound
Mussels	1 pound
Pike	10 ounces
Red mullet	$^1/_2$ pound
River trout	$^1/_2$ pound
Roach	$^1/_2$ pound
Rock lobster	14 ounces
Salmon, salmon trout	$^1/_2$ pound
Sardines	$^1/_2$ pound
Sea bass	$^3/_4$ pound
Skate	1 pound
Smelts	5 ounces
Sole (for frying)	$^1/_2$ pound
Sturgeon	$^2/_3$ pound
Tuna	$^1/_2$ pound
Turbot	1 pound
Whiting	$^1/_2$ pound

Beef, Veal, Mutton, Lamb, and Pork (for broiling or roasting)

Boned and trimmed	$^1/_2$ pound
Pot roast, stew, and *pot-au-feu*	1 pound

Poultry

Chicken and duck	1 pound
Goose	1 pound
Rabbit	$^3/_4$ pound
Rabbit rump	1 for 2 people
Turkey	1 pound

Game

Hare	7 pounds for 6 people
Lark and ortolans	2 birds

Partridge	1 for 2 people
Pheasant	1 for 4 people
Quail	1 or 2 per person
Roebuck, deer, young wild boar	$3/4$ pound
Saddle of hare	1 for 2 people
Thrush	1 or 2 per person
Wild duck	1 for 2 people
Woodcock	1 for 2 people

Hors d'oeuvre

Hors d'oeuvre form the gastronomic opening of a luncheon menu. They are served, in some form, in addition to the main dish. Presented outside *(hors)*, in addition to the main dish, or work *(oeuvre)*, they should be different from the chief dish; but they should not satisfy one's hunger; they should be varied, delicate, and light.

   Hot hors d'oeuvre are reserved preferably for dinner.

   The list of hors d'oeuvre is unlimited. The culinary combinations within that classification are limited only by the fertility of the maker's imagination. This chapter proceeds, therefore, more through practical examples than by numerous classic definitions.

Cold Hors d'Oeuvre

This group is divided into several categories:
Assorted *charcuteries* (sausages and cold cuts)
Salads
Mollusks and shellfish
Fish
Mushrooms and other vegetables
Cold eggs
Canapés, pastries, etc.

Hot Hors d'Oeuvre

The second group is determined in great part by the second course; hot hors d'oeuvre can, in certain menus, take its place. This group includes:
Mollusks and shellfish
Mushrooms
Mixtures based on vegetables
Soufflés
Toasts
Croquettes
Fritots and *beignets* (fritters made with bits of meat and poultry, such as veal sweetbreads, brains, heart, etc.)
Croustades (shells of pie, pastry, or toasted bread)
Petites bouchées (little puff pastries, baked empty and filled with various mixtures)
Pâtés and turnovers
Ramekins and *paillettes* (puff pastry cut into very thin strips like straws)
Charcuteries (sausages and spiced meats)
This category also includes several butter formulas called compound butters, which are a great help in the preparation of a variety of hors d'oeuvre.

Seasonings for salads

First Method (vinaigrette sauce)
Combine in a salad bowl: salt, pepper, *fines herbes* (parsley,

chives, tarragon, chervil), or other condiments as specified. Pour in 1 tablespoon vinegar, then add 3 tablespoons oil.

Second Method

Instead of the vinegar and the oil, use the juice of 1 lemon and 3 tablespoons cream.

Third Method

Through a sieve rub 2 egg yolks, cooked until firm but not overcooked; if they are too hard they will be very dry instead of creamy; mash the yolks in a salad bowl along with salt, pepper, and a teaspoon of mustard; while mixing well with a hand beater, slowly add 1 tablespoon vinegar, and 3 tablespoons oil. The sauce should be thickened and light. Finish by adding the egg whites cut into very thin strips.

Fourth Method

Cube a strip of fat salted bacon. Sauté the bacon until brown in a frying pan, and pour the bacon and the fat over a salad seasoned with pepper and very lightly salted. Add vinegar that has been warmed quickly in the same frying pan, while it is still hot. This method does not include oil—the bacon fat replaces it.

Fifth Method

The elements that make up the salad are lightly seasoned with salt, pepper, and *fines herbes,* and then bound together with a very light mayonnaise (page 90) flavored with mustard.

Certain mixed salads are classed as hors d'oeuvre as well as salads. On the other hand, some salads are really cold main dishes.

Mixed salads are almost always served in a salad bowl or a crystal bowl. The decorations are chosen from among the ingredients used in the specific salad. Simplicity is a mark of good taste.

Cold hors d'oeuvre

Salade de haricots verts
STRING-BEAN SALAD (For 6 people)

2 pounds young string beans, washed
4 tomatoes, seeded and quartered
1³/₄ ounces fresh truffles
¹/₂ pound white mushrooms
Vinaigrette sauce
¹/₂ cup walnut oil
Scant ¹/₄ cup Beaujolais wine vinegar
2 shallots, finely chopped
Salt and freshly ground pepper

Method. Snap off the ends of the beans and string them; cook quickly in a large quantity of rapidly boiling water. Make sure the beans remain crunchy.

When the beans are cooked, cool them under cold water and drain at once. Pat dry.

Place the beans in a salad bowl; top them with the tomatoes, the truffles, and the mushrooms cut into julienne (matchsticks).

Season at the table with vinaigrette sauce (see above) to which finely chopped shallots are added.

Salade niçoise

1 part boiled potatoes
1 part ripe tomatoes
1 part cooked string
    beans
1 part hearts of lettuce
Oil
Vinegar
Salt and pepper
1 onion, chopped
Pinch chervil

Method. Peel and thinly slice the potatoes. Core, peel, and seed the tomatoes and cut them into quarters. Trim the ends and strings of the beans and cook in salted water. Separate the leaves of the lettuce.

Mix all the ingredients in a salad bowl. Season with the oil, vinegar, salt, and pepper, and spice with a thinly sliced onion, chopped, and a big pinch of chervil sprinkled on the salad just before serving.

Salade Café de Paris

Light-colored lettuce
Salt and pepper
Oil
Vinegar
Cooked chicken breast or
    thighs
Mayonnaise (page 90)
Lettuce heart
1 tablespoon vinaigrette
    sauce (pages 2–3)
Anchovy fillets
Green olives, pitted
Hard-cooked eggs,
    quartered

Method. Separate, wash, and dry the lettuce leaves. Season with salt, pepper, oil, and vinegar; pile into a salad bowl in the shape of a dome. Cover the top with thin slices of cooked breast of chicken arranged in a fan shape—the thighs of the chicken can also be used—and cover with a light layer of mayonnaise. Marinate a heart of lettuce in vinaigrette sauce and place on top of the dome. Arrange anchovy fillets, cut into pieces, green olives, and hard-cooked eggs around the lettuce heart.

Salade de homard ou de langouste

LOBSTER OR ROCK-LOBSTER TAIL SALAD

Prepare a salad with hearts of lettuce; season with vinaigrette sauce (pages 2–3) to which is added the sieved yolk of a boiled egg, just set. Arrange in a salad bowl or a glass bowl, and on top, in the shape of a crown, set the cooked lobster or rock-lobster tail cut into thin slices. Cover the lobster with light mayonnaise (page 90). Decorate the slices with anchovy fillets cut into diamond shapes, capers, and quartered hard-cooked eggs.

Salade demi-deuil

1 part potatoes
1 part truffles
Mustard sauce
1 heaping teaspoon mustard
1 teaspoon vinaigrette
    sauce (pages 2–3)
Salt and pepper
1 tablespoon cream

HALF-MOURNING SALAD

Boil some potatoes; peel and cut them into large dice. Add an equal part of truffles, cooked or raw, cut into large julienne. Season with mustard sauce. Mix with salad in a salad bowl.

Salade de betteraves

BEET SALAD
First Method

Cook very red beets, preferably by baking in a 375° oven for 45 minutes, or in boiling water. Peel the beets and cut them

4

into thick strips or thin slices. Season with salt, pepper, vinegar, oil, and chopped chervil or parsley.

Second Method

Prepare as above but add for each medium beet 1 medium-sized onion that has been baked for 15 minutes in a 325° oven, cooled, and cut into slices.

Third Method

Prepare as above, peel, and cut into thick strips, dice, or thin slices. Season with salt, pepper, lemon juice, cream, and strong mustard.

Proportions for the seasonings: juice of half a lemon, 2 tablespoons cream, 1 teaspoon mustard.

Arrange the beets in a shallow dish or a salad bowl. Just before serving, sprinkle a pinch of chopped chervil on top.

Salade de pommes de terre

POTATO SALAD

2 pounds potatoes with firm yellow flesh
6 tablespoons dry white wine
Salt and pepper
Vinegar
Oil
Chopped parsley
Chopped chervil
1 chopped onion or shallot (optional)

Method. Cook Holland potatoes or a similar kind with firm yellow flesh in salt water. Dry them in a 275° oven. Peel the potatoes while still hot, cut into slices immediately, and marinate, still hot, in dry white wine; then season with salt, pepper, vinegar, oil, and chopped parsley and chervil. A finely chopped onion or shallot may be added.

Salade de tomates

TOMATO SALAD

First Method

Choose well-ripened tomatoes; remove the core and the stem. Plunge the tomatoes into boiling water for 6 seconds; drain, cool under cold water, and peel them. Remove the juice and seeds, and cut into slices about 1/4 inch thick. Place the slices in a shallow dish. Pour vinaigrette sauce (pages 2–3) over them, and sprinkle with a pinch of chopped tarragon. Marinate for a few minutes before serving.

Second Method

Peel the tomatoes as above; squeeze them gently to remove the juice and the seeds and cut into quarters instead of slices. Season in a salad bowl with vinaigrette sauce (page 2–3), chervil, chopped tarragon, and chopped onion; marinate for 1 hour. Transfer to a crystal bowl and decorate with thin onion rings overlapping one another in a crown; add a pinch of chopped chervil in the center. Present the salad at the table; and, before serving, mix one last time, so that the different elements of the salad will be well seasoned.

Salade de concombre

CUCUMBER SALAD

Peel a cucumber and slice in two lengthwise; remove the seeds and cut into very thin slices. Spread slices on a plate, and sprinkle them with salt; mix well and transfer to a bowl. Let stand for 1 hour, so that the cucumber will release its water. Drain well; season with pepper, oil, vinegar, and chopped chervil. Serve in a shallow dish.

Salade de chou-fleur

CAULIFLOWER SALAD

Divide a white firm cauliflower into small florets; peel each stem; wash in water to which vinegar has been added, in order to get rid of the minuscule slugs that may hide in the heads. Boil the cauliflower for 5 minutes, drain; then place again in boiling salted water ($^1/_2$ tablespoon salt per quart of water). Simmer slowly in order to avoid breaking the florets. Drain again and arrange in shallow dishes or small bowls; pour over vinaigrette sauce (pages 2–3) to which mustard and chopped chervil have been added.

After presenting the dish, mix carefully and serve.

Salade de chou rouge ou chou de Milan

RED CABBAGE SALAD OR CABBAGE MILANESE STYLE
First Method

1 small red cabbage
Salt
Garlic cloves
Freshly ground pepper
Bay leaves
Boiled vinegar, cooled
Oil (optional)
Tart apples (optional)

Take the center part of a small red cabbage. Separate the leaves and cut off the rib stalks. Wash the leaves and drain them. Pile the leaves together and slice in thin shreds.

Parboil the shredded cabbage in boiling water for 6 minutes; drain thoroughly. Put into a bowl in layers, sprinkling each layer with a little salt. On top of each layer except the last, place a clove of garlic, a little freshly ground pepper, and a tiny piece of bay leaf. Pour cooled boiled vinegar over all, so that the cabbage is entirely covered. Marinate for 2 days, testing to make sure that the vinegar is covering the cabbage. Cover the bowl, and set in a cool place so that the cabbage can be used in the following different ways:

1. Served as it is
2. Drained and seasoned with 3 tablespoons oil for $^1/_3$ pound cabbage
3. Mixed, after seasoning, with an equal amount of tart apples cut into very thin slices

Second Method

1 cup vinegar
1 red cabbage, shredded
Salt and pepper
Oil

Boil 1 cup vinegar in a saucepan; add the cabbage; boil for an instant, then cool. Drain slightly and just before serving season with salt, pepper, and oil.

Both these methods make the cabbage more tender and more digestible.

Salade de céleri ou rémoulade

CELERY SALAD OR RÉMOULADE

Use the white heart of a celery. Divide each rib into 3- or 4-inch pieces. Cut the pieces lengthwise in thin strips, without completely cutting them apart at one end; soak in cold water for 40 minutes, and carefully drain.

Season with a strong vinaigrette sauce (pages 2–3) made with mustard; or use a dressing made with salt, pepper, mustard, lemon juice, and sour cream or *crème fraîche;* or rémoulade sauce (page 91)

Salade de céleri-rave ou rémoulade
CELERY ROOT SALAD OR RÉMOULADE

1 large or 2 small celery
 root
Salt
Sauce
1 teaspoon mustard
Pinch salt
Pinch freshly ground
 pepper
¹/₂ tablespoon vinegar
¹/₂ cup oil

First Method

Cut the celery root into fine julienne; sprinkle lightly with salt; mix well in a bowl and marinate for 1 hour. Drain and dry the strips for the sauce, put all the ingredients except the oil in a bowl and beat vigorously. Drop by drop, while beating, add the oil. Season the celery root with the sauce. The pieces must be thoroughly coated with the sauce when the mixing is finished. Serve in a shallow dish or salad bowl.

Second Method

Scald the strips of celery root for 5 seconds; drain and let cool. Then season as above.

Third Method

Let the strips of celery root marinate for 30 minutes in lemon juice. Then season with a mayonnaise strongly flavored with mustard or a rémoulade sauce (page 90 or 91).

Salade de boeuf Parmentier
BEEF SALAD PARMENTIER

Mix leftover cooked beef *(pot-au-feu),* diced, with an equal amount of boiled potatoes, thinly sliced; season while hot with salt, pepper, oil, vinegar, chopped onion, and *fines herbes* to taste.

Petits rougets à l'orientale
RED MULLETS ORIENTAL STYLE

12 small mullets from the
 Mediterranean
Salt and freshly ground
 pepper
4 tablespoons olive oil
¹/₂ cup dry white wine
4 tomatoes, peeled,
 seeded, and cut into
 quarters
Sprig thyme
¹/₂ bay leaf
1 garlic clove, crushed
1 pinch saffron
Lemon slices, peeled

Method. Remove the mullet gills, but do not clean the fish; dry them and place them side by side in a lightly oiled ovenproof earthenware dish. Season with salt and freshly ground pepper. Mix the oil, white wine, tomato pulp, and spices and pour over the mullets. Bake in a 425° oven 8 to 10 minutes. Leave in the dish to cool. Serve cold with a slice of peeled lemon on each mullet.

Maquereaux marinés

MARINATED MACKEREL

2 parts dry white wine
1 part vinegar
1 medium-sized carrot
1 large onion, thinly sliced
Thyme
1/2 bay leaf
12 small mackerel, gutted
  and cleaned
Salt
Freshly ground pepper
12 peeled lemon slices

Method. Make a marinade of dry white wine, vinegar, the carrot, the onion, thyme, and bay leaf. Cook for 20 minutes. Arrange the mackerel in an ovenproof earthenware dish; season with salt and freshly ground pepper. Cover the fish with the marinade and bake in a 425° oven for 8 to 10 minutes; cool.

Serve very cold with a slice of lemon on each mackerel.

Harengs marinés

MARINATED HERRING

Prepare like the mackerel.

Note: It is advisable to prepare the fish at least 2 days before serving and keep them in the marinade, well chilled.

Moules au safran

SAFFRON MUSSELS

4 pounds mussels, well
  cleaned
Sprig parsley
Sprig thyme
1/2 bay leaf
Pinch freshly ground
  pepper
Pinch saffron
1 cup dry white wine
1 large onion, finely
  chopped
About 4 tablespoons oil

Method. In a pan combine the mussels, spices, wine, onion; heat rapidly and stir mussels frequently so that they all open. Remove from the heat; drain the liquid into another pan, and reduce it by two-thirds. While it is boiling, add enough oil to make a light emulsion; let it cool. Remove half the shell of each mussel, and set the mussels on a plate or a shallow serving dish; pour the juice and oil mixture over them.

Serve very cold.

Paillettes d'anchois

ANCHOVY PAILLETTES

Make a flaky pastry or puff pastry (pages 382–3), roll out about 1/8 inch thick and about 8 inches wide; prick well with a fork, and bake in 425° oven until golden brown.

After the pastry has cooled, spread a thick layer of anchovy butter (page 18) on it, and cut into very thin strips. Serve with care.

Chou-fleur à la grecque

CAULIFLOWER GREEK STYLE

Divide a firm white cauliflower into small florets; peel the stem of each floret; wash, and put into salted boiling water (1/2 teaspoon salt for each quart of water) for 5 minutes. Drain, rinse in cold water, drain again. Then follow the recipe for artichokes (page 9), adding 3 tomatoes, peeled, seeded, and cut into quarters.

Artichauts à la grecque
ARTICHOKES GREEK STYLE

12 small artichokes
12 small white onions
2 cups water
1 tablespoon salt
Juice of 3 lemons
10 peppercorns
Sprig thyme
1/2 bay leaf
1 celery rib
Pinch dried fennel or
  fennel rib
15 coriander seeds
1 cup oil

Method. Cut off the stems of the artichokes and trim 3/4 inch from the leaves with a scissors; cut the artichokes into quarters and place them, with the onions, in a hot marinade prepared in the following way:

In a saucepan, combine the water, the salt, and the lemon juice. Tie the peppercorns, thyme, bay leaf, celery, fennel, and coriander in cheesecloth and add. Bring to a boil over high heat, and boil 5 minutes; add the oil, the artichokes, and the onions. Cook about 20 minutes at a slow boil. Check whether the artichokes are cooked by pulling off one leaf: if it separates easily, they are done.

Put into a bowl; cool, chill, and serve cold.

Salade de champignons
MUSHROOM SALAD

1/2 pound medium
  mushrooms, firm and
  white
Salt and freshly ground
  pepper
Pinch powdered sugar
1 tablespoon lemon juice
3 tablespoons cream or oil
Fresh herbs and garlic

Method. Carefully wash the mushrooms and wipe dry. Slice them thinly and put into a salad bowl; season with salt, pepper, sugar, lemon juice, cream (or oil); also add fresh tarragon or chervil or chopped fennel or even thyme flowers, crushed garlic, spices, etc. The choice depends on taste and on what is on hand.

Champignons à la grecque
MUSHROOMS GREEK STYLE

Pinch dried fennel or
  fennel rib
Pinch powdered coriander
  or 10 seeds
Small sprig thyme
1/2 bay leaf
10 peppercorns
Small celery rib
1 cup water
Juice of 2 lemons
1 teaspoon sugar
1 teaspoon salt
1/2 pound very small
  mushrooms, firm and
  white
3 tablespoons oil
3 tablespoons dry white
  wine

Method. Tie the herbs and spices in a piece of cheesecloth. Combine water, lemon juice, sugar, salt, and spice bag in a saucepan and boil for 5 minutes. Clean and quickly wash the mushrooms and add. Boil rapidly for 5 minutes. Whip at full boil, add the oil and wine. A light emulsion will form naturally.

Pour into a bowl, and serve very cold.

Poireaux à la grecque
LEEKS GREEK STYLE

Cut the white parts of leeks into pieces 3 to 4 inches long and cook 10 minutes in boiling salted water. Drain, rinse in cold water, and prepare like the artichokes Greek style above.

8 cups small onions
Dry white wine and oil, in
  equal parts
3 large ripe tomatoes,
  peeled, seeded, and
  mashed
Pinch salt
Freshly ground pepper
Garlic clove, grated
Coriander seeds
Pinch saffron

Petits oignons à l'orientale
ONIONS ORIENTAL STYLE

Method. Choose very small onions of equal size. Peel them and put them into a frying pan big enough to hold them easily. Cover the onions with half dry white wine and half oil, then add the tomatoes. Season with salt, pepper, garlic, coriander, and saffron. The saffron should be the dominant seasoning.

Cover, bring to a boil, and simmer until the onions are completely cooked.

Pour into a bowl with the cooking juice, and keep in a cool place until serving time.

Oeufs farcis au paprika
STUFFED EGGS WITH PAPRIKA

Cook eggs until they are just set. Shell them and cut in two, lengthwise.

Place the yolks in a bowl and mash with a fork; mix with an equal quantity of unsalted butter or thick cream. Season this creamy paste with a pinch of salt and paprika to taste. Put the yolk mixture back into the egg-white halves and form them into dome shapes.

Serve on a dish.

6 sweet green or red
  peppers
2 tablespoons finely
  chopped sweet onion
3½ tablespoons unsalted
  butter
18 small Gervais cheeses
1½ tablespoons chopped
  chives
½ ounce fine Hungarian
  paprika
1½ teaspoons cumin
  seeds
Salt and white pepper

Fromage hongrois
HUNGARIAN CHEESE (For 6 people)

Method. Wash, dry, and seed the peppers. Cook the chopped onion in the butter, covered. Cool and mix well with the cheeses. [*Editor's note:* Gervais is a French cream cheese that comes in 2-ounce packages; it may be replaced by an equal amount of cream cheese.]

Mix in the chives, paprika, and cumin, and season lightly with salt and pepper.

Stuff the peppers with this rich preparation.

Serve on a cheese tray.

Hot hors d'oeuvre

Pommes de terre Nantua
POTATOES NANTUA

Bake new potatoes or any similar potatoes about as big as small eggs. Open them like a tobacco pouch, and scoop out the pulp. Replace it with a stew of crayfish tails in a Nantua sauce (page 85).

Place a folded napkin on the serving plate and serve the potatoes on it.

Huîtres à la florentine

OYSTERS FLORENTINE STYLE (For 1 person)

6 oysters
1 handful spinach
2 tablespoons unsalted butter
Salt
Dash grated nutmeg
Pinch sugar (optional)
Grated parmesan or gruyère cheese
Bread crumbs

Method. Shell the oysters and leave them in their juice; clean the shells carefully. At the same time prepare spinach— a good handful for each 6 oysters. Remove the stems, blanch the leaves rapidly for 10 minutes in boiling salted water. Drain, and rinse with cold water; drain again and squeeze to remove all the water.

In a frying pan rapidly heat about 1 tablespoon butter; as soon as it bubbles, add the spinach, seasoning it with salt and a dash of grated nutmeg. Add a pinch of powdered sugar, if it is late in the season for spinach and it is bitter. Stir over high heat 2 minutes. Remove from the flame, and add 1 tablespoon butter.

Arrange the spinach in the center of a heatproof platter. Surround it with the oyster shells, which have been lightly heated. Drain the oysters, remove their beards, and place each on a shell. Sprinkle the oysters and the spinach with grated parmesan or gruyère cheese, mixed with a few bread crumbs to form a crusty *gratin.* Sprinkle with melted butter, and place the dish under a very hot broiler, very close to the flame, for 1 or 2 minutes, just long enough to brown the top.

Place the hot platter on a napkin and serve.

Quiche lorraine

(For 4 people)

½ recipe pastry dough (page 386)
2 ounces smoked bacon, cut into very thin slices
1 tablespoon unsalted butter
2 ounces gruyère cheese, cut into very thin slices
1 tiny onion, chopped
3 eggs
2 cups cream or milk

Method. Roll out the dough, and line an 8-inch pie plate. [*Editor's note:* This quantity of dough is ample for this size quiche. But since this dough freezes very well, you may want to make the full amount of the pastry recipe and freeze what is not needed here.]

Blanch the bacon in boiling water for 2 minutes and then cook slightly in a little bit of hot butter. In the bottom of the crust alternate slices of bacon with slices of gruyère cheese.

Cook the onion, without browning, in the remaining butter. Beat the eggs with the cream or milk and mix in the onion.

Fill the crust with the mixture, which should be lightly salted and peppered, as the bacon and the gruyère are usually rather salty.

Bake 35 minutes in the lower part of the oven at 425°.

Note: Whenever a quiche must be baked in an oven in which the bottom part does not heat sufficiently (this is very common in home ovens), I recommend that you half-bake the crust beforehand, lining it with wax paper, and filling with cherry pits or dry beans kept for this purpose. Be careful not to brown it.

Aubergines provençales

EGGPLANT PROVENÇAL STYLE

4 small eggplants
4 medium-sized tomatoes, peeled, seeded, and crushed
1 tablespoon oil
1 garlic clove, crushed
Salt and pepper
Bread crumbs
Unsalted butter, melted
Tomato sauce (optional, page 77)

Method.   Cut the eggplants lengthwise; fry cut side down 5 minutes; then remove the pulp and chop it coarsely. Retain the shells.

Sauté the tomatoes in the oil. Add the garlic and the pulp of the eggplant; season with salt and pepper to taste. Place the eggplant shells in a buttered ovenproof dish. Fill with the tomato-eggplant mixture. Sprinkle with bread crumbs, and pour some melted butter over the tops. Brown under the broiler.

Serve the eggplants surrounded by a ring of tomato sauce, or pour over 2 tablespoons foamy butter, melted in a frying pan at the last moment.

Risotto aux foies de volailles

CHICKEN LIVERS WITH RICE (For 4 people)

1 medium onion
4 tablespoons unsalted butter
1/2 cup rice
2 cups blond stock (page 73)
6 chicken livers
Salt and pepper
6 large mushrooms
1 shallot, chopped
1 tablespoon veal juice, thickened

Method.   Finely chop the onion and sauté in 4 teaspoons butter until transparent. Add the rice, and heat in the butter. Add the stock, cover, and cook on a low flame for 18 minutes. Then remove the rice from the fire, and carefully add about 4 teaspoons butter. Pour the rice into a bowl.

Cut each liver in two, seasoning with salt and pepper, and sauté over a high flame in the remaining butter. Cook the livers until they are pink; add the mushrooms, quartered, and the shallot. Cook rapidly; then off the flame finish with the veal juice.

Note: Although the rice is well cooked, the grains should remain whole and separate and not be gummy.

Croquettes de volaille

CHICKEN CROQUETTES

1/2 pound leftover cooked chicken
1/4 pound cooked lean ham or tongue
1 1/2 ounces raw truffles (preferably in season)
1/4 pound mushrooms
3 1/2 tablespoons unsalted butter
1 3/4 cups *velouté* sauce (pages 76–7) made with chicken stock
4 eggs
1 cup crumbs from stale bread
About 1/2 cup flour
Oil
Tomato sauce (page 77)

Method.   Dice the chicken, the ham or tongue, and the truffles and mushrooms. In a large frying pan melt the butter rapidly; add the mushrooms and a few seconds later the truffles, and then the chicken *velouté*. By boiling reduce rapidly by half, and add the chicken. Return to a boil, and immediately off the heat add 3 egg yolks. Mix well, and do not permit to boil again. Pour this mixture into a buttered dish, dab the surface with butter, and let cool.

While the meat mixture is cooling, prepare the bread crumbs. Crush the bread, with a pinch of flour, in a cloth; then rub through a medium sieve or a strainer. This gives you freshly made, untoasted bread crumbs.

Beat 1 egg in a bowl.

When the meat mixture is cool, divide into portions of about 1/4 cup. Form each into the shape of a cork by rolling lightly in flour, then in beaten egg, and then in bread crumbs.

(You can replace the fresh bread crumbs with dry bread crumbs, but this is not recommended.)

Fry the croquettes in very hot oil just before serving; they should be crisp on the outside and creamy inside, with a beautiful golden color.

Place on a folded napkin on a plate, and serve with tomato sauce on the side.

Croquettes de coquillages
SHELLFISH CROQUETTES

1 quart mussels
1/4 pound mushrooms
3 1/2 tablespoons unsalted butter
1/4 cup thick béchamel sauce (page 78)
2 egg yolks

Method. Open 1 quart mussels (or other mollusks) that have been well washed and discard those that still contain mud. Remove the shells, cut off the beards, and dice the meat.

Prepare the mushrooms: wash rapidly, drain, and dry; then dice. Melt the butter in a frying pan and cook the mushrooms rapidly over a high flame. Add the diced shellfish and béchamel sauce. Remove from the flame; thicken with the egg yolks, as explained in the recipe for chicken croquettes (above). Finish the dish in the same manner.

Fritots
FRITTERS

Fritters are another way of using leftover fish, shellfish, chicken, meat, giblets, vegetables. They all can be cut into pieces, dipped in a frying batter (page 433), then fried, one at a time, in deep hot oil.

Serve with a dish of sauce or compound butter (pages 18–20) on the side.

Croustade bressane
FILLED PASTRY BRESSE STYLE

1/2 recipe pastry dough (page 386)
Filling
1 part chicken breast, cooked
1 part truffles
1 part mushrooms, coarsely diced
3 1/2 tablespoons unsalted butter, plus extra butter
Madeira or port wine
Cream or béchamel sauce (page 78)

Method. Roll the pastry dough quite thin. Cut with a round or oval pastry cutter to fit the dimensions of the mold chosen (this recipe is suitable for small brioche molds, tart molds, or other individual sizes—or 1 large mold). Line the mold or molds with the dough; prick the dough with a fork. Line with a very good quality wax paper (this will not have a bad odor); fill with dried lentils or other beans, or cherry pits that are specially reserved for this purpose. Bake until lightly browned in a 350° oven. Then remove the beans or other weights and the paper; keep the pastry warm.

Fill the *croustade* a few moments before serving with a mixture of equal parts of chicken breast, truffles, and mushrooms.

Cook the mushrooms first in hot butter, then add the truffles and, depending upon the quantity, 1 or more tablespoons Madeira or port wine, then the chicken, and finally a few tablespoons cream (or béchamel sauce, if you do not have cream).

Boil to reduce rapidly by half, then thicken off the heat

13

with 3½ tablespoons unsalted butter. The mixture should be very creamy. Correct the seasoning, garnish, and serve.

All the garnishes for the *bouchées* (page 390) can be used for a *croustade*.

Rôties galloises
WELSH RAREBIT

Thin slices white bread, toasted and buttered
1 cup beer
Pinch English mustard or ½ teaspoon ordinary mustard
3½ ounces gloucester or cheshire cheese
Dash cayenne pepper
1½ tablespoons unsalted butter

Method.   Toast and butter thin slices of white bread; place in an ovenproof porcelain dish.

Reduce slightly by boiling 1 cup beer mixed with English mustard (if English mustard is not available, ordinary mustard will do); add gloucester or cheshire cheese, cut into small cubes, and cayenne pepper. When the cheese is melted, remove from the flame and add butter. Pour the mixture over the warm toast, covering it completely.

Set in a 475° oven to glaze quickly until the top is a beautiful golden color. Serve immediately.

[*Editor's note:* Cheddar cheese may be substituted.]

Soufflés au parmesan
PARMESAN SOUFFLÉS (For 4 people)

2 cups milk
¾ cup flour
Salt, pepper, nutmeg
2 ounces gruyère or parmesan cheese, grated
2 tablespoons unsalted butter
4 eggs, separated
2 teaspoons milk

Method.   Bring the milk to a boil; when it has cooled slightly, add the flour in small quantities, while stirring, in order to obtain a completely homogeneous and smooth mixture without any lumps. Add salt and a pinch of pepper and nutmeg. Bring to a boil again, stirring constantly. Remove from the heat and to this creamy sauce immediately add the cheese, the butter, and the egg yolks mixed with 2 teaspoons milk.

Beat the egg whites until stiff; delicately fold them into the sauce, taking care that the whites fall as little as possible.

Pour the mixture into 4 well-buttered 3-inch porcelain soufflé dishes, and bake in a 325° oven for 10 minutes.

Serve immediately

Soufflé au jambon
HAM SOUFFLÉ (For 6 people)

1 cup lean cooked ham
2 tablespoons unsalted butter
Pinch paprika
2 cups béchamel sauce (page 78)
3 eggs, separated

Method.   Pound the ham in a mortar with the butter; rub it through a very fine strainer. Stir the ham purée and the paprika into very hot béchamel sauce. Add the egg yolks, then the whites, beaten stiff, being careful that they do not fall. Spoon the mixture into a buttered 1-quart timbale mold or into 6 buttered 3-inch porcelain soufflé dishes. Bake in a 300° oven until set. The mixture will double its volume above the mold. It must be served immediately.

[*Editor's note:* You can grind the ham fine in a meat grinder or chop it in a blender or food processor.]

Laitance de carpe sur toast sauce moutarde

SOFT ROE OF CARP ON TOAST WITH MUSTARD SAUCE

1 soft carp roe or 12 soft
  roe of herring
White wine
Lemon juice or vinegar
Thin slices of toast
1 tablespoon Dijon
  mustard

Method. Rinse the soft roe in cold water, strip off the little black vessels that run along the sides, wash, and dry.

Put the roe into a skillet.

Pour over a little *court-bouillon* made with white wine and water in equal parts and a few drops of lemon juice or vinegar; poach the roe lightly without boiling. As soon as it is cooked, drain and place on thin slices of toasted bread. Reduce cooking liquid and add the mustard. Continue cooking until the mustard sauce has thickened and cover the roe with it.

Beignets de laitances et beignets d'anchois

SOFT ROE BEIGNETS AND ANCHOVY BEIGNETS

12 soft roe or anchovy
  fillets
Dry white wine
Salt and pepper
6 tablespoons oil
Juice of 1/2 lemon
Frying batter (page 433)
Parsley

Method. Slowly poach 12 soft roe in a *court-bouillon* made with equal parts of dry white wine and water, and salt and pepper; cool in the *court-bouillon,* drain, and dry. Marinate the roe for an hour in oil and lemon juice.

Just before serving dip the roe one at a time into a frying batter, and plunge them immediately into hot deep oil to fry. Serve the roe on a napkin, garnished with a bouquet of fried parsley.

After the anchovy fillets have been marinated in oil, dry them, dip in frying batter, and fry like the roe.

Beignets de cervelle

BRAIN BEIGNETS

1 veal brain or 3 lamb
  brains
1/2 tablespoon vinegar
Pinch salt
3 tablespoons olive oil
Juice of 1/4 lemon
Pinch chervil
Salt and pepper
Frying batter (page 433)
Oil
Parsley

Method. Use 1 veal brain or 3 lamb brains; soak in cold water to remove the blood. Remove the surrounding membranes. Make a *court-bouillon* with 1 cup water, 1/2 tablespoon vinegar, and a large pinch of salt. Start the brains in the cold *court-bouillon* and slowly bring to a boil; lower the heat and let it barely simmer for 10 minutes.

Drain; cut the brains into thick cubes (about 1 1/2 inches). Soak for about 20 minutes in a marinade made with olive oil, lemon juice, chervil, salt, and pepper.

Meanwhile, prepare a frying batter; dip the cubes into the batter, and fry one at a time in very hot oil until golden brown.

Serve on a folded napkin on a plate, garnished with a bouquet of fried parsley.

Paillettes au parmesan

CHEESE STRAWS

Method. Make 1/2 recipe flaky pastry. Sprinkle grated parmesan or gruyère cheese onto the pastry board before the

½ recipe flaky pastry (pages 382–3)
2 cups grated parmesan or gruyère cheese
Paprika or cayenne pepper (optional)

last two turns so that the grated cheese will be distributed evenly into the dough.

Roll out the dough and divide into strips 4 inches wide and ⅙ inch thick. Cut the strips crosswise into strips ¼ inch wide. Place them on a cookie sheet and bake in a 450° oven until golden brown.

The *paillettes* can be served as a garnish for various clear soups. They can also be seasoned with a pinch of paprika or cayenne pepper.

Paillettes aux anchois
ANCHOVY CHIPS

Follow the directions for cheese straws above, but do not add cheese. Roll the dough and cut into strips 4 inches wide and ¼ inch thick. Moisten the surface with a bristle or feather brush or cloth dipped into beaten egg. Cut crosswise in 1¼-inch strips.

Cover the tops of the pastry strips with anchovy fillets that have been washed and dried and cut into small rectangles about ¾ inch long. Place them on a pastry sheet and bake for 12 minutes in a 425° oven.

Ramequins au fromage
CHEESE RAMEKINS

1½ cups flour
5 tablespoons unsalted butter
4 eggs
1 cup milk
Pinch salt
Pinch grated or ground nutmeg
Grated gruyère cheese

Method. Prepare a cream-puff pastry (pages 396–7) with 1½ cups flour, 5 tablespoons butter, 4 eggs (save about ½ egg for glaze), 1 cup milk, pinch of salt, pinch of grated or ground nutmeg. Do not add any sugar.

Fill a tablespoon with dough and push the dough onto the pastry sheet with the blade of the knife, leaving about 3 inches between the puffs. Frequently dip the blade in tepid water so that the dough does not stick to it.

Brush the puffs with the reserved ½ beaten egg. Sprinkle with grated gruyère cheese, and then press cheese into the puffs lightly with a knife.

Bake in a 425° oven for about 15 minutes.

Petits pâtés à la bourgeoise
SAUSAGE PASTRIES

Make ½ recipe flaky pastry (pages 382–3) and roll out ⅛ inch thick. Cut the dough with a pastry cutter into circles 2¾ inches in diameter or into 2-inch squares. Place half the circles or squares on a pastry sheet, moisten the edges with a feather brush or cloth dipped in water.

In the center of each piece of pastry, place 1 tablespoon sausage meat. Cover each with a second piece of pastry.

Press lightly all around the edges with your thumb or with a pastry wheel in order to seal the pastry.

Brush tops with beaten egg and score dough with the point of a knife. Bake in a 425° oven for 15 minutes.

Saucisson chaud à la lyonnaise

HOT SAUSAGES LYONS STYLE (For 4 people)

1½ pounds pure pork sausage
2 pounds yellow Belle-de-Fontenay or other spring potatoes, all about the same size

Method. Put the sausage in a saucepan or an earthenware pot. The sausage must be of excellent quality. Cover with 2 or 3 quarts cold water.

Heat on top of the stove just to the boiling point; maintain a constant heat without boiling for 25 to 30 minutes.

Lower heat for a quarter hour to complete the poaching. Peel and steam the potatoes or cook them in salted water and serve with hot sausages and unsalted butter.

This very simple dish, typical of Lyons, is eaten at the beginning of a meal.

Saucisses au vin blanc

SAUSAGES IN WHITE WINE

6 chipolata sausages
Unsalted butter
Croutons, fried in butter
1 tablespoon dry white wine
1 tablespoon veal stock
1 teaspoon tomato sauce or ½ tablespoon fresh tomato pulp

Method. Use the small hot sausages called chipolatas. Cook them in butter in a small frying pan, and place them on rectangular croutons (bread squares) that have been sautéed in the same butter as the sausages; arrange on a hot serving dish. Add dry white wine to the frying pan; boil until reduced by two-thirds, then add veal stock and tomato sauce or tomato pulp. If you are using pulp, let it cook for a few minutes. When this sauce has reduced and is very hot, add 2 pats butter, stirring vigorously off the flame until the sauce is perfectly blended. Keep the sausages very hot, and pour the sauce over them.

Saucisson en brioche

SAUSAGE IN DOUGH (For 5–6 people)

2 pounds uncooked pure pork sausage, about 12″ long
[*Editor's note:* Cotechino may be used.]
1 cup Beaujolais wine
1 recipe ordinary brioche dough (page 379)
1 egg yolk, beaten
Flour
Périgueux sauce (optional, page 82)

Method. Cover the sausage with cold water and cook for 30 minutes, simmering without boiling on a low flame. Leave the sausage to cool in its water away from the heat. Then remove it from the water and strip off the skin. Place in a 475° oven for a few minutes in order to melt more of the fat. Remove the sausage, and drain off the accumulated fat; deglaze the pan with Beaujolais wine, scraping up the concentrated juices, and boil to reduce the wine.

Roll the brioche dough so that it is about 3 inches longer at each end than the sausage and about 6 inches wide.

Brush the sausage with the egg yolk, then roll in flour. Wrap the sausage in the brioche dough, making sure that the dough sticks to the sausage. If necessary, moisten the dough lightly.

Brush the entire surface of the dough with the beaten

egg; decorate with some of the reserved dough or simply with designs made with the point of a knife.

Set the sausage in dough on a cookie sheet, and let the dough rise until it doubles. Bake in a 425° oven for about 30 minutes.

The sausage in dough is served sliced, sometimes accompanied by an excellent Périgueux sauce.

Compound butters

Compound butters are prepared by mixing unsalted butter with substances such as cooked meats, fish, seafood, vegetables, or spices, crushed in a mortar then put through a very fine sieve or cheesecloth.

These butters are used in the preparation of some hors d'oeuvre or to finish a sauce.

In many cases the compound butters are heated, cooked, or simply melted with the complementary ingredients.

This is how to prepare shrimp butter, crayfish butter, lobster butter, etc.

[*Editor's note:* You may experiment with an electric blender or food processor in making these butters; the butter must be extremely cold and hard.]

Beurre d'anchois
ANCHOVY BUTTER

15 anchovy fillets
¾ cup unsalted butter

Rinse the anchovy fillets in water to rid them of salt. Dry them and pound in a mortar with butter. Rub through a fine sieve.

Beurre d'ail
GARLIC BUTTER

8 garlic cloves
1 teaspoon salt
1½ cups unsalted butter

Prepare in the same way but use garlic cloves and salt added to 1½ cups unsalted butter.

Beurre vert pré ou de cresson
GREEN-MEADOW OR WATER-CRESS BUTTER

Chervil
Tarragon
Burnet
Parsley
Chives
Finely chopped water cress
Unsalted butter

Put into boiling water equal parts of chervil, tarragon, burnet, parsley, and chives; boil 1 minute, then rinse under cold water and press well to take the water out. Weigh the herbs, chop fine, and pound in a mortar with an equal weight of unsalted butter. Season, and pass through a very fine sieve. Add to the butter a handful of finely chopped water cress, which should dominate the flavor of the butter.

Beurre de foie gras

First Method

1/4 pound cooked *foie gras*
1/4 pound unsalted
  butter
Dash cayenne pepper

In a mortar mash together *foie gras* and butter. Season, and put through a fine sieve. Add a dash of cayenne pepper.

Second Method

1/4 pound plain cooked *foie
  gras*
1/4 pound unsalted
  butter
1 tablespoon port wine
Pinch salt
Dash cayenne pepper

Put plain cooked *foie gras* through a fine sieve. Heat the butter until soft; when tepid, beat in the sieved *foie gras* and port wine.

  Season with a pinch of salt and a dash of cayenne pepper.

Beurre de Roquefort

ROQUEFORT BUTTER

Mix 5 ounces Roquefort cheese
with 5 ounces unsalted butter.

Beurre d'escargots

SNAIL BUTTER

2 pounds good-quality
  unsalted butter, slightly
  softened
1 1/2 tablespoons coarse
  salt
1/4 teaspoon freshly
  ground pepper
Dash grated nutmeg
3 tablespoons crushed
  garlic
2 tablespoons chopped
  shallots
3 tablespoons sweet
  almonds
1/2 cup finely chopped
  parsley

Method.   Mix in a mortar the salt, pepper, nutmeg, garlic, shallots, and almonds. With the pestle pound these ingredients into a smooth paste. Then add the parsley and the slightly softened butter. Again with the pestle, grind all the ingredients until they are homogenized.

  You may store the snail butter in an earthenware jar in the refrigerator.

Beurre de crevettes

SHRIMP BUTTER

Pound in the mortar equal weights of cooked gray shrimp and unsalted butter. Rub through a fine sieve. To obtain a fine mixture, put the butter through cheesecloth along with the sauce or the soup for which the butter is intended.

Beurre d'écrevisses

CRAYFISH BUTTER

Sauté crayfish in butter. Pound together an equal weight of unsalted butter and the shells and trimmings of the crayfish following the directions for shrimp butter. For 12 crayfish, add 1 teaspoon *mirepoix* (half carrots and half onions, diced very small and slowly cooked until very soft in seasoned butter). Let the creamy parts of the crayfish stick to the shells.

[*Editor's note:* Crayfish are hard to find in the United States; they may be replaced by a small lobster or unshelled large prawns.]

Beurre de homard ou de langouste

LOBSTER BUTTER

Follow the same proportions and directions as above.

Beurre de moutarde

MUSTARD BUTTER

Mix ¼ pound unsalted butter with 1 rounded teaspoon Dijon mustard.

Beurre de paprika

PAPRIKA BUTTER

Mix ¼ pound unsalted butter with a pinch of paprika.

Beurre de raifort

HORSERADISH BUTTER

In a mortar pound 3 tablespoons grated fresh horseradish. Add ¼ pound unsalted butter. Rub the mixture through a fine sieve.

Beurre Bercy

BERCY BUTTER

½ cup dry white wine
½ tablespoon chopped shallots
7 tablespoons unsalted butter
6 ounces beef marrow
1 teaspoon chopped parsley
Juice of ½ lemon
Pinch salt
Freshly ground pepper

Method. Boil dry white wine with shallots until reduced by half. Let the liquid cool, then add the butter, mixing with a whip or a wooden spoon. Dice and poach beef marrow in salted water for 3 to 4 minutes, then drain. Add along with chopped parsley, lemon juice, salt, and freshly ground pepper.

This butter is served lukewarm, with meats or grilled fish.

Beurre d'amandes

ALMOND BUTTER

Drop 4 ounces almonds into boiling water; drain almost immediately and remove the skins. Do this by holding each almond between the thumb and the forefinger and pressing slightly. Pound the almonds in a mortar, adding a few drops of cold water as the almonds are blended into a paste, in order to avoid their becoming oily. Add about half a cup of unsalted butter and mix until smooth.

[*Editor's note:* The almonds may be replaced by any nut you wish.]

Pâtés, terrines, timbales, and pies

¾ pound veal round roast
¾ pound pork tenderloin
1 pound fresh lard or
   unsalted pork fat
2 tablespoons spiced salt
   (page x)
3 eggs
½ cup cognac

1 recipe filling for pâtés
   and terrines (above)
¾ pound veal round roast
¾ pound pork tenderloin
1 pound fresh lard or
   unsalted pork fat
⅔ pound cooked lean ham
Salt, pepper, and mixed
   spices (page x)
1 tablespoon cognac
Thin slices pork fat to line
   the terrine and cover the
   pâté

Filling for pâtés and terrines

[*Editor's note:* In general, a recipe using 2 pounds of meat will fill a 1- to 1½-quart terrine.]

When the filling is to be used for a game pâté or terrine, replace the veal with the meat of the bird or the animal used.

Method. Remove the tendons carefully from the meats and remove the skin from the pork fat. Dice the meat, then chop or grind it fine. Add the salt, then the eggs, one at a time, and then the cognac.

Check the seasoning by poaching a bit of the filling in a little boiling water.

Terrine de veau
VEAL TERRINE

Method. Carefully remove all the tendons and cut meat and lard (or pork fat) into 1-inch dice or strips as thick as a finger. Season with salt, freshly ground pepper, and spices, and mix in a bowl with cognac; marinate for 2 hours.

Line the terrine with the thin slices of pork fat. Combine the filling with the marinated meat; fill the terrine with this mixture.

Or, after lining the terrine, fill with one layer of filling, then one layer of the *lardons* (veal, pork, pork fat, ham, alternating), then another layer of stuffing, etc., until you have used all the ingredients.

Cover the meat with a thin slice of pork fat. Make a hole in the center, and to the right and left of the hole place a small piece of thyme and a bay leaf. Cover and set the terrine in a *bain-marie* (a roasting pan half filled with hot water). Bake in a 425° oven for at least 1½ hours.

The cooking time depends on the shape of the terrine and the nature of the meat used. The terrine is cooked when the juice reaches above the meat to the edge of the terrine and is clear. By that time, the meat juices have been completely transformed into meat essence, which is retained by the meat.

Remove the terrine from the oven. Take off the cover and on top of the pâté put a piece of wood cut to fit the terrine, and on top of this set a heavy object weighing at least ½ pound. [*Editor's note:* You can use a can of food or a brick.]

The pressure of the weight during cooling will produce a homogeneous texture in the meat that would not result without this step. It would be very difficult to slice the pâté, for the meat would crumble into pieces.

On the other hand, if you use too heavy a weight, the fat will be squeezed out and the pâté will not be so well flavored.

To serve, carefully wash off the outside of the terrine and set it on a plate on top of a folded napkin.

Terrine du cordon bleu

This terrine can be made with veal, poultry, or game.

Meat (in proportions as for veal terrine, above)
Salt and pepper
Pinch thyme
Ground bay leaf
Dash nutmeg
2 tablespoons cognac
2 tablespoons unsalted butter
Thin slices pork fat to line the terrine
1 cup meat jelly

Proportions of the ingredients are the same as for the veal terrine, but the preparation is different.

Method. Carefully remove the tendons from all the meats and cut into strips as thick as a finger.

Season with salt, pepper, thyme, bay leaf, and nutmeg. Stir this carefully in a large bowl until it is well mixed. Pour over 1 tablespoon cognac and marinate for 3 hours.

Then drain the meat very well. Reserve the marinade in a bowl.

Heat the butter in a frying pan; when bubbling, add the meat and cook over high heat, stirring with a spatula or wooden spoon until firm.

Remove the meat from the butter with a slotted spoon and place in a bowl.

Pour the reserved marinade into the frying pan; add a second tablespoon cognac and let boil for a minute or two to dissolve (deglaze) the coagulated juices of the meat. Then pour this mixture over the meat in the bowl and let it cool.

Line the terrine with fat as explained in the recipe for the veal terrine (above). Fill with the meats and the stuffing alternately, and pour over some of the marinade that remains at the bottom of the meat bowl. Cook in the same way as the veal terrine in a *bain-marie* in a 425° oven for 1½ hours.

After cooking, let the terrine cool without removing the cover. When it is nearly cold but still slightly tepid, lift the cover and pour in 1 cup good meat jelly made with basic ingredients (veal bones or game bones or the carcass of poultry or other bird, pork rind, and calf's foot, which contains gelatinous elements).

The jelly will penetrate the meat and everything will be solidified when cold.

Terrine de grives

THRUSH TERRINE (For 12 people)

12 fat thrushes
¾ pound fresh goose liver, cut into thin slices
¼ pound fresh lard or unsalted pork fat, diced
Salt, pepper, and mixed spices (page x)
¾ pound veal tenderloin, chopped very fine
6 tablespoons cognac
2 tablespoons goose fat
Melted lard to cover surface of terrine

Method. Pluck the thrushes carefully. [*Editor's note:* The thrushes may be replaced by small squabs.] Singe and clean. Reserve the livers.

In a frying pan with a heavy bottom, melt the lard or pork fat. As soon as it has melted and is hot, add the slices of liver to sear them. After two or three stirs in the frying pan, add the thrush livers; cook for 3 minutes.

Season the mixture with salt, pepper, and a dash of spices. Put into a mortar and let cool; then pound the meat with the pestle until the mixture is well blended. To this stuffing, add the chopped veal and the cognac, and rub through a fine sieve.

Bone the thrushes and stuff each one with a ball of the meat mixture.

Reshape the thrushes and set them in a shallow casserole with 2 tablespoons goose fat.

After seasoning, sear the birds on top of the stove without cooking them too long (about 10 minutes).

Remove the thrushes from the heat and let cool.

In a game terrine large enough to hold the thrushes, put a layer of stuffing on the bottom; place 6 thrushes on top. Add another layer of stuffing. Again add 6 thrushes, and cover them with the remaining stuffing. Smooth the surface and cover the terrine.

Cooking. Place the terrine in a *bain-marie* in a 350° oven. Cook for about 50 minutes. Remove the terrine from the oven and let it cool.

Take off the cover. On top of the meat place a piece of wood on which you set a weight of about ¹/₂ pound in order to press the ingredients together.

Next day remove the wood. Pour over the meat a thin layer of melted lard. When the lard has set, cover with a piece of aluminum foil cut to the size of the terrine. Replace the cover.

The thrush terrine can be eaten right away, but it also can be preserved in a cool place or in the refrigerator for many weeks.

Note: If the mortar is not big enough, pound the ingredients for the stuffing a little at a time.

4 chicken livers
3 tablespoons unsalted butter
¹/₂ cup Madeira
¹/₂ pound lean pork
¹/₂ pound veal
1 pound fresh pork fat
¹/₄ teaspoon coarse salt
4 freshly ground peppercorns
1 teaspoon mixed spices (page x)
¹/₂ cup cognac
1 egg

1 tender chicken, about 3³/₄ pounds
Salt, pepper, spices (as above)
¹/₂ raw *foie gras*, marinated in Madeira and seasoned
2 nice-sized truffles, cut into quarters

6 slices fresh pork fat
¹/₂ cup cognac
Bay leaf
Thyme

Terrine de volaille Paul Mercier
CHICKEN TERRINE PAUL MERCIER
Filling

Method. Sear chicken livers in butter in a small frying pan; off the heat, pour over half the Madeira and let cool. Put the mixture in a bowl. Cut the pork, veal, and pork fat into thick cubes. Add to the liver and mix together. Chop everything in a meat grinder or pound fine in a mortar; then rub the mixture through a fine sieve. Put the purée into a bowl and add the salt, pepper, and spices, the rest of the Madeira, the cognac, and the egg. Mix well with a wooden spoon. Test the seasoning by poaching a small piece of the stuffing in water.

Poultry. Bone the poultry by making an incision in the skin of the back going from the tail to the neck. Cut off the thighs and wings, and carefully cut the flesh from the carcass. Spread the flesh on the table and remove the bones. Season with salt, pepper, spices, and spread on top of it a layer of filling about ³/₄ inch thick. Place the *foie gras* in the middle and surround with the truffles. Cover with another layer of filling and re-form the chicken body over it.

Terrine. Line an oval terrine with thin slices of pork fat. Cover the fat with a layer of the filling about ¹/₂ inch thick. Place the stuffed chicken in the terrine and pour over ¹/₂ cup cognac. Cover with a layer of filling, a slice of pork fat, a bay leaf, and a small piece of thyme. Chop up the carcass, with the bones, quite fine and sprinkle on top. Cover.

Cooking. Place the terrine in a *bain-marie* (a roasting pan two-thirds full of hot water). Bake in a 425° oven for 2¹/₂ hours. When the cooking is done, remove from the oven, uncover, and take out the pieces of the carcass, the thyme, and the bay leaf. Place on the meat a piece of wood and on top of this an object weighing about ¹/₂ pound; during the cooling, this will produce a perfectly homogeneous pâté. Too heavy a weight would squeeze out the fat and hurt the smoothness of the terrine.

When the cooling is completed, remove the weight and the wood. Cover the meat with a layer of lard about 1/2 inch thick and refrigerate. This terrine can be kept for 2 to 3 months in the refrigerator.

Mousse de volaille froide en terrine

COLD CHICKEN MOUSSE

Carefully roast a beautiful 2 1/2-pound chicken, following the directions in the chapter on chicken. Cool, but do not put in the refrigerator.

Then remove the skin and take the flesh off the breast-bone and the thighs, which should give you about 1 1/2 cups of meat.

Pound the chicken flesh in the mortar and rub this purée through a fine sieve; follow the directions for the cold goose-liver mousse (page 272).

Pâté d'anguilles

EEL PÂTÉ

3 pounds river eels
Salt, pepper, and nutmeg
Small amount oil
1 cup white wine
2 tablespoons cognac
7 tablespoons unsalted butter
3 shallots, chopped
1 tablespoon chopped parsley
4 hard-cooked eggs, sliced
Half-flaky dough (page 383) about 1/4 inch thick and the size of the baking dish
1 egg, beaten
1 cup *demi-glace* sauce (page 76)
1 tablespoon reduced fish *fumet* (pages 73–4)

Method.   Skin, wash, and eviscerate the eels. Make an incision along both sides of the bone, and cut them in half lengthwise. Remove the bone. Cut the fillets crosswise into scallops of eel about 3 inches long. Plunge them into boiling salted water. When the water comes back to the boil, remove the eel pieces immediately, rinse them in cold water, and drain. Dry them, and season with 1 tablespoon salt, 1/4 teaspoon pepper, and a dash of nutmeg; add a few tablespoons oil, 1/2 cup dry white wine, and the cognac. Marinate the eel scallops for 2 hours. Drain them reserving the marinade.

Heat 3 1/2 tablespoons butter in a large skillet and cook the shallots briefly; add the eel and cook for 10 minutes; sprinkle with chopped parsley.

In a deep round ovenproof earthenware or porcelain dish put layers of the sliced eel, alternating with layers of the sliced hard-cooked eggs, seasoned with additional salt, pepper, and nutmeg.

Pour over the remaining 1/2 cup white wine and the reserved marinade to cover the eel and the hard-cooked eggs. Add more wine if needed. Cut the remaining butter into small pieces and spread on top. Cover the whole with the dough rolled to fit the dish used.

Brush the dough with beaten egg; with the point of a knife, make a design—flowers or leaves—on the dough, and with a knife make a hole in the center of the dough to let the steam escape. Bake in a 350° oven for 1 1/2 hours.

About 5 minutes before the baking has been completed, finish the *demi-glace* sauce with 1 tablespoon reduced fish *fumet*. When ready to serve, pour the *demi-glace* sauce into the pâté through the center hole.

Pâté chaud de grives ou de mauviettes
HOT THRUSH OR LARK PÂTÉ

The treatment for these two birds is similar. The following recipe can be applied to either.

Pluck, singe, and bone the birds. The boning should begin with an incision in the skin of the back going from the tail to the neck. Stuff them with one of the stuffings given for pâtés or terrines. Reshape birds and truss them with string. Set them in a buttered skillet and bake in a 425° oven: for the thrushes, 12 minutes; for the larks, 8 minutes.

Follow the recipe for the duckling pâté (below) from this point on. Bake in a 325° oven 45 minutes for a pâté of 8 thrushes or of 24 larks.

With the game-bird pâté, serve a salmi sauce (page 303) to replace the Madeira sauce.

Note: Fresh truffles are recommended for these pâtés; but if necessary, one can do without.

Pâté chaud ou froid de caneton
Gaston Richard
HOT OR COLD DUCKLING PÂTÉ GASTON RICHARD

1 plump Nantes duckling, 3–3½ pounds
¼ pound firm white mushrooms
2 pounds stuffing (recipe below)
1 recipe pastry dough (page 386)
1 cup Madeira sauce (page 79)
Truffles to taste
Thyme and bay leaf
1 egg, beaten

Method. Roast the duckling in a 425° oven for 15 minutes; it should be very rare; remove the two wings from the breast; remove the breast skin, and thinly slice the meat. Cut the mushrooms into thin slices and rapidly cook in the same pan used to roast the duckling; they will absorb the seasoning and the juice of the cooking.

Next, butter a 1-quart charlotte mold and line it with the pastry dough, following the technique described for lining a pan (page 390). Cover the dough with a layer of stuffing about ½ inch thick.

For the bottom layer make a bed of sliced duckling and follow with a layer of mushrooms. Slices of raw truffles can also be added. Spread another layer of stuffing, and continue until you have used all the ingredients, finishing with a layer of stuffing.

On the last layer, sprinkle pinches of powdered thyme and bay leaf. Cover the pâté with a sheet of pastry dough, sealing the edges by moistening with water. Brush the pastry with beaten egg, and make some light incisions; then make a hole in the center to allow the steam to escape.

Bake in a 325° oven for 1 hour.

To serve, unmold the pâté on a round plate. Carefully cut the bottom crust of the pâté ½ inch from the edge to preserve the shape; remove carefully. Divide the dough into wedges, one per guest, and set them around the pâté.

Pour 1 tablespoon Madeira sauce on top, and serve the rest of the sauce in a sauceboat.

Just before serving, you can decorate the top of the pâté by placing in the center a nice mushroom cap, cut in the shape of a rose, or fluted, and cooked in butter. Around this put slices of truffles in the shape of a crown and cover with Madeira sauce.

The pâté can be served cold without the sauce.

Stuffing

Method. Remove the rind from the pork fat and dice fat. Brown fat in 3 tablespoons butter in a skillet.

Drain the pork fat with a slotted spoon and reserve on a plate. In the same butter, brown the veal, cut into large dice. Drain also and add to the pork. Still in the same skillet, rapidly sear the veal or pork liver, cut into large dice, to which the duckling liver will be added. Add the chopped shallots, mushrooms, truffles, bay leaf, thyme, salt, and pepper. Return the pork fat and the veal to the skillet. Add the *demi-glace* sauce. Mix and cook everything for 2 minutes. Remove from heat, and baste with the Madeira. Then pour the mixture into a mortar, add the thigh meat of the duckling, cut into cubes, and reduce the mixture into a fine paste by pounding vigorously. Finish the pounding by adding the remaining butter, about 7 tablespoons, and the egg yolks, one at a time.

Rub the mixture through a fine sieve; test the seasoning by tasting a small piece of stuffing poached in salted water; pour into a terrine and smooth with a wooden spoon.

At this point, the stuffing is ready to use.

½ pound pork fat, very fat and fresh
10 tablespoons unsalted butter
½ pound veal round
½ pound veal or pork liver
4 shallots, chopped
1½ ounces mushrooms
4½ ounces raw truffles
Bay leaf, crushed
Pinch thyme
2 teaspoons salt
Large pinch freshly ground pepper
½ cup *demi-glace* sauce (page 76)
Madeira to moisten
6 egg yolks

Timbales

At the time of the famous and talented master pastry cook Antonin Carême, a timbale was a complicated dish composed of ingredients, partly cooked or not, combined in a charlotte mold, poached, and served unmolded.

The timbale may be made individually for each person or in one large mold for 6 to 12 people. The most typical and at the same time most classic is the *timbale à la milanaise.*

Timbale à la milanaise

TIMBALE MILANESE STYLE (For 6 people)

Method. Roll fine unsweetened pastry dough ⅛ inch thick and line a 2-quart charlotte mold, following the method on page 390. Prick the dough with a fork. Reserve remaining dough.

Poach ½ pound macaroni or spaghetti of excellent quality. The poaching is done in the following way: plunge the pasta whole in a large pot of boiling water with ¾ tablespoon salt for each quart. Bring back to the boiling point, stirring the pasta with a wooden spoon to prevent the pieces from sticking together. Reduce the heat and continue cooking, covered and not boiling, maintaining the water at about 160° for about 20 to 25 minutes, depending upon the quality and the origin of the semolina in the macaroni. Make sure that the pasta remains firm.

Drain thoroughly and put back into the saucepan; heat for a few minutes so that the water evaporates from the pasta. Sprinkle with grated cheese, half gruyère and half parmesan if

Fine unsweetened pastry dough (page 386)
½ pound macaroni or spaghetti
¾ tablespoon salt
⅓ pound grated cheese, half gruyère, half parmesan
7 tablespoons unsalted butter
7 tablespoons thick tomato purée
3½ ounces cooked lean ham
Freshly ground white pepper
Financière sauce (pages 158–9)
1 egg, beaten

possible. On top scatter 7 tablespoons butter cut into small pieces. Add the tomato purée and the ham, cut into thin julienne.

Sprinkle 3 or 4 grinds of white pepper on top. Take the saucepan off the fire. While rotating it with one hand, with the other hand stir the pasta with a wooden spoon. This way of stirring the pasta (called *vanner,* ''fan'') prevents its breaking, and the sauce will thicken as the cheese melts.

While the noodles are cooking, prepare a garnish of *financière* sauce, using a thick *demi-glace* sauce with a strong taste of tomato (pages 158–9).

There are two ways to finish the timbale:

1. In the charlotte mold lined with pastry make alternate layers of macaroni and *financière* sauce. When the mold is nearly full, roll out an additional pastry round using the reserved dough. Cover the mold with the round of pastry and seal carefully by moistening the edge of the crust. Decorate the crust and brush with beaten egg; bake in a 325° oven for about 40 minutes.

   Unmold carefully and serve.

2. Cover the pastry in the charlotte mold with wax paper and fill with fruit pits or dried beans; bake in a 425° oven until golden brown.

   Remove the pastry from the oven, empty the timbale, and unmold. Meanwhile keep the pasta and *financière* sauce warm. Brush inside and out with beaten egg. Set the shell in the oven again for a few seconds to dry it and to give it a beautiful golden color.

   In the prepared crust make alternate layers of macaroni and the *financière* sauce.

   Using reserved dough make a cover formed around a wad of paper shaped like a skullcap, of the same diameter as the timbale. Decorate the cover with leaves made of pastry dough. Bake in a 425° oven until golden brown and place on top of the filled crust.

   Serve on a plate with a folded napkin on it.

   Note: This second method is more practical in the home.

Timbales de morilles Antonin Carême

TIMBALE ANTONIN CARÊME (For 6–8 people)

3 cups béchamel sauce (page 78)
14 ounces *godiveau* (about 2 cups)
1³/₄ ounces truffles, finely chopped
2 pounds morels, recently picked
5 tablespoons unsalted butter
³/₄ cup *crème fraîche* or heavy cream
5 egg yolks
2 hard-cooked eggs
Juice of ¹/₄ lemon

[*Editor's note:* Morels are found in the United States in Vermont and Massachusetts, but should be picked only by experts. Dried morels are available; they should be soaked 2 to 3 hours.]

Method. Prepare the béchamel sauce.

Prepare the *godiveau* and mix the truffles with it. [*Editor's note:* Godiveau, a delicate forcemeat, is used for *quenelles* of chicken, veal, or pork; it is never made with fish. Any *quenelles* recipes except those employing fish can be used here.]

Peel the sandy ends of the stems of the morels and wash them thoroughly in several waters; very carefully remove any dirt in the crevices of the honeycomb caps, where the sand is often found.

While cleaning the morels, choose a dozen of the most beautiful ones and set aside, along with about 3½ ounces of the stems.

Cook the rest of the morels in a saucepan with 4 tablespoons butter, a pinch of salt, a pinch of pepper, the juice of ¼ lemon, and 2 tablespoons water. Bring to a boil, cover, and keep boiling for about 7 minutes.

Drain the morels. Reserve 2 tablespoons of the cooking juice and pour the rest into the béchamel sauce. If the morels are large, cut them into halves or quarters. Put them aside.

Add the *crème fraîche* (reserve out 1 tablespoon) to the béchamel sauce; reduce until you have 2 cups.

Now thicken the sauce by stirring in off the heat 5 egg yolks diluted with the remaining tablespoon of *crème fraîche* and 2 tablespoons of the cooking juice from the morels.

The binding is done by pouring a little bit of the béchamel sauce into the egg yolks and mixing with a wire whisk in order to heat them. Then pour the egg mixture in a stream into the sauce while beating it. Set the saucepan on the heat, continuing to beat with the wire whisk. Remove from the heat as soon as the sauce reaches the boiling point. The sauce should be very thick but must not boil.

Add the cooked morels, mix, and let them cool in a bowl.

Line a well-buttered 8-inch *génoise* mold with ¾ of the *godiveau;* the layer should be about ¾ inch thick. Then fill up the mold to ¾ inch from the edge with the morel-béchamel mixture and cover with a layer made with the remainder of the *godiveau.* Smooth the surface and protect it with a round of buttered wax paper.

Set the mold in a pan containing very hot water to about 1 inch from the top and poach in this *bain-marie* in a 325° oven for about 55 minutes.

Remove the mold from the *bain-marie,* let it cool for about 10 minutes, and unmold the timbale onto a round plate big enough to hold a garnish around the edge.

Tourte des gastronomes

GASTRONOMES' PIE (For 6 people)

Half-flaky dough (page 383)
3 sweetbreads, steamed
Madeira
¼ pound white mushrooms, thinly sliced
Salt
Pepper
2½ tablespoons unsalted butter, melted
1 egg, beaten

Method. Prepare 2 rounds of pastry made of half-flaky dough, about 14 inches in diameter and ⅛ inch thick. Place one of the rounds in a 10-inch pie plate or torte pan. Prick the dough with a knife seven or eight times. Brown 3 sweetbreads, cut in half, in a covered skillet. Deglaze with Madeira and reserve the liquid. Put the sweetbreads on the pastry round, keeping them an inch inside of the edge. Sauté the mushrooms quickly in 1½ tablespoons butter, and season with a pinch of salt and pepper. Scatter over the sweetbreads. Spread with 1 tablespoon melted butter.

Moisten the edge of the dough with a cloth dipped in water. Cover the mixture with the second sheet of dough, and seal by pressing with the thumb around the edge and rolling the bottom edge of the dough over the top edge. Brush the top with beaten egg and decorate either by making incisions in the dough with a knife or by making designs cut out of another piece of dough. Make a hole in the center with the point of a knife to allow the steam to escape.

Bake 25 to 30 minutes in a 425° oven.

Serve the dish immediately; on the side serve a sauce made with the deglazing liquid and added Madeira. Put about $1/2$ tablespoon of sauce alongside each portion of pie.

Eggs

In a menu eggs, plain or garnished, are included among the light entrées. Two are generally served for each guest. For the sake of flavor and health, eggs should be eaten very fresh.

The freshness of an egg can be determined by candling or by its weight. A fresh egg of average size weighs not quite 2 ounces. The air chamber, situated in the rounded end of the shell, is barely perceptible; it increases in volume a little bit every day. If you shake a very fresh egg next to your ear, it will make no sound. If the egg is not very fresh, you may hear small muffled noises. Plunged in water, a very fresh egg will sink, a ten-day-old egg will float.

Whether eggs are shirred or soft-boiled; cooked in molds, in the shell, in a cocotte, in a skillet; fried, hard-cooked, or poached—poaching is the method of cooking on which all the preceding ones are based.

On the other hand, scrambled eggs or omelets utilize two quite different methods.

Oeufs sur le plat

SHIRRED EGGS

Apparently simple, this method of cooking eggs involves a technique that must be mastered in order to succeed.

The eggs are cooked just to the point when the white gets a milky look and the yolk is soft-boiled, covered with a light shiny film of white professional cooks call a mirror. Finally, one must be very careful that the eggs do not stick to the bottom of the pan.

Method. For 2 eggs, use 2 teaspoons unsalted butter (a piece the size of a small nut), melted. Put half the butter in a baking dish (for 1 serving) and heat. When the butter begins to bubble, break the eggs one at a time onto a plate so that you can smell them to check their freshness. Slide the 2 eggs into the butter. Pour the rest of the melted butter on top. Season the egg whites with a pinch of fine salt. Bake in a 350° oven for about 4 to 5 minutes.

Watch the coagulation of the egg whites and the shininess of the yolks to obtain the perfect result described above.

Instead of using an oven, one could cook the eggs on top of the stove, continuously basting the tops while they are cooking with the butter in the dish; spoon it up from the side of the frying pan.

Presentation. If the shirred eggs are to be served with a garnish, the garnish should be put in the bottom of the dish before cooking the eggs or added on top of the eggs afterward.

Oeufs au bacon ou au lard maigre

EGGS WITH BACON OR SALT PORK

Cut 2 slices ⅛ inch thick of bacon or lean salt pork, taken from the belly, without skin. Cook them in boiling water for 3 minutes, drain, and brown lightly in a shallow pan with 1 teaspoon unsalted butter. Break 2 eggs on top, and cook them according to the method above.

Oeufs sur le plat au jambon

SHIRRED EGGS WITH HAM

Put a slice of uncooked ham $1/8$ inch thick into 2 cups of cold water. Heat slowly to the boiling point. Drain, then heat in an egg dish with 1 teaspoon unsalted butter; turn once and, 2 seconds later, break in 2 eggs. Cook by the method above.

Oeufs sur le plat à la florentine

SHIRRED EGGS FLORENTINE STYLE (For 6 people)

1 pound spinach
4 tablespoons unsalted
 butter
Salt
Pepper
Pinch grated nutmeg
1½ ounces lean cooked
 ham
6 eggs

In boiling salted water cook the spinach with the stems removed. Drain, rinse, squeeze firmly to get rid of the water. Rub spinach through a sieve. Put this purée in a skillet with 2 tablespoons very hot butter. Season with salt, pepper, and a small pinch of grated nutmeg. Heat rapidly; then mix in off the flame 2 tablespoons butter and 1½ ounces lean cooked ham, diced very small.

Butter 6 individual baking dishes. In the bottom of each put a thin layer of ham, a layer of spinach purée (heated on the stove). Then break 1 egg into each dish; baste with a few drops of melted butter over each egg; add a pinch of salt, and cook in the oven by the method above.

Oeufs sur le plat aux tomates

SHIRRED EGGS WITH TOMATOES

First Method

Peel and seed tomatoes (1 per egg), and simmer in butter. Season with salt and a pinch of sugar. Spread them on the bottom of a buttered dish, then break the eggs on top and cook them to a mirror shine as described above.

Second Method

Cook eggs by the method above and garnish them after cooking with 2 mounds of stewed tomatoes, finishing with butter and salt as in the recipe for shirred eggs Florentine (above).

Oeufs sur le plat au beurre noir

SHIRRED EGGS WITH BLACK BUTTER

Cook the eggs by the basic method above, basting with a thin stream of vinegar and unsalted butter, which have been cooked together until the butter turns light brown.

Butter cooked this way is very flavorful, but not highly digestible. Do not use too much of it.

33

Oeufs pochés

POACHED EGGS

Poached eggs must be absolutely fresh. In poaching, the white coagulates immediately on contact with boiling water, enveloping the yolk and forming an evenly shaped oblong. If eggs are not very fresh, the white spreads while coagulating and the yolk remains uncovered; the form is flat and irregular.

Method. Use the shallow saucepan called a sauté pan (or a deep skillet). Fill it two-thirds full with water, adding 1 tablespoon vinegar for each quart. Bring the water to a boil; break the eggshell, smell for freshness, and drop it into the liquid exactly on the spot where the water is bubbling, so that the yolk remains intact. Continue this operation, breaking at least 8 eggs, one at a time.

Keep the sauté pan on the edge of the flame so that the water simmers very gently.

The cooking, here called poaching, should last $3^{1}/_{2}$ minutes.

Remove the eggs carefully, one by one, with a skimmer, and check the poaching by pressing lightly with your forefinger. The eggs should be very soft. Drain them and plunge them one at a time into a bowl full of cold water to stop the cooking. With your fingers remove the loose ends of egg white and return eggs to the water—the water should be tepid and slightly salted if they are to be served warm; it should be cold if they are to be served cold.

Poached eggs can be served on rice prepared in many different ways and covered with a sauce such as curry, tomato, etc.

One also can serve poached eggs on top of a purée of mushrooms, poultry, asparagus, etc., or on top of chopped fish, shellfish, meat, poultry, or game. The eggs are then surrounded by duchess potatoes (page 358), or covered with a *suprême,* Mornay, béchamel, cream, or hollandaise sauce (see index).

There are a great variety of things that one can do with poached eggs.

A poached egg is an admirable accompaniment to an excellent consommé (a bouillon well degreased and seasoned).

Cold, the poached eggs can be served in an aspic flavored with port or Madeira. They also can top grilled toast or slices of bread spread with a compound butter (pages 18–20).

They can be served cold decorated with tarragon leaves. First drop the leaves into boiling water for a minute, then rinse and pat dry. Or cut ham, tongue, truffles, or sweet peppers into short, narrow strips, place over the eggs, then cover everything with a few spoonfuls of aspic.

You also can serve poached eggs with simple or fancy salads, asparagus tips, Russian salad, etc. In these cases, the eggs are served with a sauce such as a light mayonnaise, with or without the addition of cream.

Finally, the poached eggs can be served with vegetables,

such as sorrel purée (page 349) or spinach with butter, cream, or *velouté* sauce (pages 76–7).

In general, all the garnishes used for poached eggs can be used for soft-boiled eggs and vice versa.

Oeufs pochés à la bordelaise

POACHED EGGS BORDELAISE

Bouchées (page 390)
Sliced marrow
Poached eggs

Method. First prepare small *bouchées*—little flaky puff-pastry patties, baked unfilled—(2 per person) and the same number of slices of marrow about ⅛ inch thick.

Next, poach eggs following the basic method above and drain them carefully.

Into each hot *bouchée* put the following:
½ tablespoon *bordelaise* sauce (recipe below)
1 hot poached egg
1 slice marrow (first poach marrow by placing it in a bowl of boiling salted water for 3 to 5 minutes; then drain). Cover the marrow with 1 tablespoon sauce.

Bordelaise Sauce

2 lumps sugar
3 cups red Bordeaux wine
1 tablespoon chopped shallots
Bouquet garni
Pinch salt
Pinch pepper
1 tablespoon *beurre manié* (2 teaspoons unsalted butter and 1 teaspoon flour)
Half garlic clove
1 teaspoon chopped parsley
2 tablespoons unsalted butter
Veal or beef juice (optional)

In a pan dissolve the sugar and cook to the point of light caramel; add the wine, the shallots, the tiny *bouquet garni*, a big pinch of salt, and a pinch of freshly ground pepper. Cook until the liquid has reduced by one-third. With a fork blend the *beurre manié* in a bowl. Add in little pieces to the boiling wine; it will thicken almost immediately. Beat lightly with a whisk, remove from the flame, and take out the *bouquet garni*. Finish the sauce with half a garlic clove scraped with a knife and the parsley; heat again to the boiling point and then strain the sauce through a very fine sieve or through cheesecloth. Then add about 2 tablespoons butter, and correct the seasoning.

This sauce gains in taste if it is flavored with a little veal or beef juice, or with a little meat extract. If the meat extract is salted, do not salt before reducing the sauce.

Serve the extra sauce, which is very rich, with the eggs.

Oeufs pochés à la florentine

POACHED EGGS FLORENTINE STYLE

1 pound spinach
Salt
4 tablespoons unsalted butter
Pepper
Grated nutmeg
Pinch sugar (optional)
8 poached eggs
Mornay sauce (page 84)
Fresh bread crumbs
Grated gruyère or parmesan cheese

Method. Remove the stems from the spinach, wash well, and cook in boiling water, salted with ¾ tablespoon salt per quart. It must cook rapidly so that the spinach remains green. Drain the spinach and rinse under cold water; drain again, and press firmly to remove the water.

In a skillet heat 2 tablespoons butter; add the spinach, season with salt and pepper and a dash of grated nutmeg—plus a pinch of sugar if the spinach is at the end of the season and a bit bitter. Stir in 2 tablespoons butter off the flame.

Spread the spinach in a shallow ovenproof porcelain dish; place on top 8 poached eggs, hot and well drained, and spread lightly with Mornay sauce. On each egg sprinkle a mixture of equal amounts fresh bread crumbs and grated gruyère or parmesan cheese; baste with a few drops of melted butter, and brown in a 425° oven.

The eggs can also be placed in individual egg dishes, 2 eggs per person, or in small cocottes or ramekins.

Oeufs pochés Henri Quatre

POACHED EGGS HENRY IV

8 artichokes
***Court-bouillon* (page 74)**
Unsalted butter
Salt
Pepper
8 poached eggs
***Béarnaise* sauce (page 89)**
Stewed tomato
3 tablespoons veal juice
Mushroom purée or tomato purée (optional)

Method.   Remove the leaves from the artichokes, dip them in boiling water, remove the chokes, and cook the artichoke bottoms in *court-bouillon.*

In a skillet heat 2 tablespoons butter; add the artichoke bottoms, upside down, and season with salt and pepper. Stew slowly, covered, for 15 minutes, turning them once. Put a pat of butter on the top of each artichoke bottom.

Then place the artichoke bottoms on a very hot platter, and on top of each one put a hot poached egg, well drained. Spread 1 tablespoon *béarnaise* sauce on each egg and on top of the sauce a spoonful of tomato stewed in butter.

In the skillet in which the artichoke bottoms have been stewed, bring lightly salted veal juice to a boil; reduce by half and off the flame incorporate 1 tablespoon butter. Pour this gravy in the dish around the artichokes.

To make this dish richer, the artichoke bottoms can be garnished with a mushroom purée or a thick, buttery tomato purée to which a pinch of chopped tarragon has been added.

Oeufs pochés à l'oseille

POACHED EGGS WITH SORREL

Serve poached eggs on a purée of sorrel, each basted with ¹/₂ tablespoon fatty veal juice.

Oeufs moulés

MOLDED EGGS

Method.   Generously butter small molds, 2 per person, called darioles or baba molds (they are in the shape of small round or oval cups). Carefully break a very fresh egg into each, adding a pinch of salt and a tiny pinch of white pepper. Place the molds in a skillet big enough to hold them easily. Fill the skillet with boiling water until the molds are covered two-thirds up their sides; cover the skillet, and poach for about 10 minutes.

This method of poaching is called *bain-marie.* Since the water must not boil, it is necessary to add 2 to 3 tablespoons of cold water to the skillet whenever you notice that the water is about to boil.

When an egg is correctly poached, the white will have coagulated; and, when you press it with a finger, it will feel about as firm as a soft-boiled egg.

Oeufs moulés Antonin Carême
MOLDED EGGS ANTONIN CARÊME

Cook eggs in molds by the method above; then place each one on a medallion of *foie gras* that has been quickly seared in butter. Then top each egg with a poached oyster, trimmed neatly, and covered with a little cream sauce.

Oeufs à la coque
BOILED EGGS IN THEIR SHELLS

To be really perfect, boiled eggs must be extremely fresh, which means gathered that day.

This condition is essential.

Be sure that the shells have no cracks. Carefully put the eggs into a strainer and plunge it into boiling water; the eggs must be totally submerged.

The instant the water starts boiling again, count 3 minutes; then drain. Immediately put the eggs into a bowl of very hot water, and serve them at once.

Boiled eggs, cooked impeccably, should have a milky white. If the egg is not cooked enough, the inside is cold and the white is sticky; if the egg is overcooked, the white is coagulated and tough and the yolk is partly hard.

Oeufs en cocotte
EGGS IN COCOTTE

This method derives from the boiled egg. The results are excellent. Lightly butter the insides of cocottes (small porcelain ramekins with or without handles), and place them in a skillet with hot water two-thirds up their sides. In each one put a few grains of salt; then break a very fresh egg into each. Bake 8 minutes in a 375° oven.

Remove the cocottes from the skillet, wipe them well, sprinkle a dash of salt on each, and set on a plate on top of a napkin to serve.

Oeufs en cocotte à la crème
EGGS IN COCOTTE WITH CREAM

Place 6 cocottes in a skillet, and pour boiling water about two-thirds up their sides. Boil 6 tablespoons cream with a small pinch of salt, and pour 1 tablespoon cream into each cocotte. Break an egg into each one, and add 2 pats of unsalted butter.

Cover and bake 8 to 10 minutes in a 375° oven.

Remove the skillet from the oven, and take the cocottes out of the hot water; wipe them, and place each one on a plate on top of a folded napkin.

Oeufs en cocotte aux tomates

EGGS IN COCOTTE WITH TOMATOES

Remove the stems and cores of 2 ripe tomatoes. Plunge for 10 seconds into boiling water and peel. Cut in half and press out the juice and seeds.

Dice the tomatoes, and cook in a skillet with 1 tablespoon butter; season with salt and pepper. Cook until the tomatoes have the consistency of jam.

Butter 6 cocottes, and cover the bottoms with the tomato purée. Break an egg into each one and cook in a *bain-marie* in the oven as in the basic recipe above. Remove the eggs from the oven, and put ¹/₂ teaspoon tomato purée and a little chopped parsley on top of each one.

You can add 1 tablespoon finely chopped onion to the tomatoes. In that case, cook the onion in butter, without browning, in the skillet before cooking the tomatoes.

Oeufs en cocotte aux champignons

EGGS IN COCOTTE WITH MUSHROOMS

To prepare mushroom purée with 3¹/₂ ounces clean firm white mushrooms, wash and thinly slice them. Put 2 tablespoons unsalted butter in a skillet and, when it is bubbling, add mushrooms and sauté for 3 minutes, then mash through a fine sieve into a bowl. Add 1 tablespoon cream. Season with a dash of salt.

Butter 6 cocottes, and pour this purée into them; break an egg in each. Cook in the oven in a *bain-marie,* as in the basic recipe above. When you remove them from the oven, pour 1 teaspoon cream over each egg.

Oeufs durs

HARD-COOKED EGGS

Method. Boil water in a pan big enough to hold a strainer with large holes. Put the eggs into the strainer and plunge it into the boiling water. The instant the water starts boiling again, count 9 minutes for eggs of average size, and 10 minutes for large eggs.

Remove the strainer and plunge immediately into cold water; this will make peeling of the eggs easier.

Do not cook them longer than indicated, or the white of the egg will become tough and the yolk very dry.

Oeufs durs à la crème d'oseille

HARD-COOKED EGGS WITH CREAM OF SORREL

Cut into very thin pieces 1 pound young sorrel with the stems carefully removed.

Put the sorrel into a pan with 2½ tablespoons unsalted butter; heat slowly and cook until the juices have completely evaporated. Add 1 tablespoon flour; cook over a low flame 5 minutes, and let cool. While stirring with a wooden spoon, add, little by little, 2 cups boiling milk seasoned with salt and pepper. Bring to a boil, and then simmer for 15 minutes.

Strain the sauce through a very fine sieve, rubbing with a wooden spoon. Bring the sauce back to the boiling point and test the seasoning. As soon as it comes to a boil, off the flame add 4 tablespoons unsalted butter or 2 tablespoons cream. Peel 6 hot hard-cooked eggs and put into a deep dish. Cover them with the simple béchamel sauce that you have made.

Oeufs durs aux oignons dits à la tripe

HARD-COOKED EGGS WITH ONIONS, CALLED À LA TRIPE

3 medium-sized onions
2 tablespoons unsalted butter
1 tablespoon flour
Pinch salt
Pinch freshly ground white pepper
Dash grated nutmeg
2 cups boiling water
2 tablespoons unsalted butter or 1 tablespoon cream
6 hard-cooked eggs

Method.   Cut the onions into julienne; if they are not young onions, soak them in boiling water for 5 minutes, drain, and wipe them. Put the onions into a small pan in which 2 tablespoons butter have been melted; half-cook them, covered, very slowly, without browning them.

Then add 1 tablespoon flour, a pinch of salt, a pinch of freshly ground white pepper, and a dash of grated nutmeg. Cook this white *roux* slowly for 10 minutes; remove from the heat and let cool. Then, with a whisk, mix in 2 cups boiling water, a little at a time. Bring the mixture to a boil while stirring, to avoid lumps. Cook over low heat for 20 minutes. Off the heat add 2 tablespoons butter or 1 tablespoon cream.

At the same time, hard-cook 6 eggs, and remove the shells. Just before serving, add the hot eggs, which have been cut into quarters or thick slices, to the sauce. The sauce may be rubbed through a fine sieve first. In that case, one would also have to rub the onions through the sieve to reduce them to a purée in order to incorporate them into the sauce, which then becomes a *coulis soubise* (a thin onion sauce).

Note: The flour, butter, and milk may be replaced by a béchamel sauce (page 78).

Oeufs durs sur purées diverses

HARD-COOKED EGGS ON VEGETABLE PURÉES

Hard-cooked eggs, like poached eggs, are usually served over vegetable purées, some of the best ones being the purées of asparagus, water cress, chicory, celery, mushrooms, carrots, lettuce, spinach, and chestnuts.

Oeufs mollets

SOFT-BOILED EGGS

Soft-boiled eggs are prepared in the same way as hard-cooked eggs. Place them in a strainer with big holes, and plunge them into boiling water. The instant the water starts boiling again, count 6 minutes for eggs of average size. Remove the strainer and plunge it immediately into cold water. Shell the eggs carefully, and keep them in hot salted water if they are to be served hot.

Soft-boiled eggs can be served in the same way as poached or hard-cooked eggs, except when the latter are stuffed, and vice versa.

Here are some recipes that will supplement those given for poached and hard-cooked eggs.

Oeufs mollets soubise
SOFT-BOILED EGGS SOUBISE

4 large onions
4 tablespoons unsalted butter
8 tablespoons thickened béchamel sauce (page 78)
2 tablespoons cream or 4 tablespoons unsalted butter
8 large mushrooms caps
8 soft-boiled eggs, kept warm in salted water

Method. Dice the onions; cook them in boiling water for 5 minutes, then drain. Put the onions in a small saucepan with 2 tablespoons butter, a pinch of salt, and cook on a low flame, covered. The onions must remain white. After cooking, rub the onions through a very fine strainer into a skillet. Add the reduced béchamel sauce; bring to a boil, and remove from the heat immediately. Add cream or butter; taste. Melt 2 tablespoons butter to coat the mushrooms, and broil or stew them with a few drops of lemon juice. After stewing, the butter may be carefully poured into the onion purée.

Serving. Place the mushroom caps upside down on a hot round plate. On top of each mushroom cap, place a soft-boiled egg and cover with the purée of onion and cream, which will be very rich.

Oeufs mollets béarnaise
SOFT-BOILED EGGS BÉARNAISE

2 tablespoons unsalted butter
8 artichoke bottoms cooked in a white court-bouillon (page 74)
8 soft-boiled eggs
2 cups béarnaise sauce, heated (page 89)

Method. Melt butter in a skillet; add the artichoke bottoms and season with a pinch of salt and one grind of the pepper mill. Cook for 15 minutes on a low flame, turning once; place on a hot serving platter. Pour the butter used to cook the artichoke bottoms over them and place a soft-boiled egg on top of each; cover with the béarnaise sauce. Serve the remaining sauce in a sauceboat.

Oeufs poêlés
PAN-COOKED EGGS

Pan-cooked eggs are a variant of shirred eggs.

For 2 eggs, heat 2 tablespoons unsalted butter in a frying pan until it just reaches a light brown or hazelnut color. Browning the butter first gives the eggs a particularly savory taste.

Continue by following the recipe for shirred eggs (page 32).

Pan-cooked eggs may be served with ham, bacon, smoked pork, or vegetables.

Oeufs poêlés aux tomates
PAN-COOKED EGGS WITH TOMATOES

Peel a very ripe, beautiful tomato; cut it in half, and squeeze out the seeds and juice. In a frying pan heat 1 tablespoon olive oil until it smokes. Place the tomato, cut sides down, in the pan, seasoning with salt and pepper, and cook over a high flame. Turn the tomato halves over carefully with a spatula, and break an egg on top of each. Season with a dash of salt on the egg whites. Cook rapidly in a 350° oven until the tops of the eggs have a mirror shine, and slide them onto a hot plate. Cook 1 tablespoon butter in a small pan until it becomes dark brown (this is *beurre noir,* or black butter). Baste the eggs with this hot butter.

Oeufs frits
FRIED EGGS

Method. Break a fresh egg into a bowl. In a frying pan, heat 1 cup oil; when it is smoking, tip the pan slightly to make the oil collect at one side in a deep pool. Pour the egg into the oil. As soon as the white coagulates in thick blisters, quickly fold the white over the yolk with the help of a wooden spoon dipped in oil, and roll the egg over in the oil; the yolk must be completely enveloped by the white and remain soft. Cook the egg 1 minute; it should have a golden color. Drain on a towel and season with a pinch of salt.

Cook the egg just before serving.

Fried eggs are frequently served on slices of uncooked ham sautéed in a frying pan with 1 tablespoon melted unsalted butter or on slices of lean salt pork or bacon, broiled or sautéed in butter.

The eggs can be accompanied by a garnish of mushrooms sautéed in butter with *fines herbes, champignons de Paris* (white mushrooms), morels, *girolles* (or *chanterelles*), or St. George's mushrooms (small mushrooms that grow in the fields in the autumn and the spring), or with leaf spinach cooked in butter. The eggs also can be served with broiled kidneys, chipolata sausages, broiled or sautéed lamb chops. Fried eggs are part of the classic garnish of chicken Marengo and mock turtle. Tomato sauce, Périgueux sauce, Italian sauce, or other sauces are often served along with the fried eggs.

Oeufs frits à l'américaine
FRIED EGGS AMERICAN STYLE

Serve the fried eggs on a slice of cooked ham, surrounded by broiled tomatoes.

1/3 pound spaghetti or
  macaroni
Salt
Pepper
2 tablespoons tomato
  sauce (page 77) or 2
  tomatoes
2 tablespoons grated
  parmesan or gruyère
  cheese
3 1/2 tablespoons unsalted
  butter
6 fried eggs
6 broiled tomato halves

Oeufs frits à la milanaise

FRIED EGGS MILANESE STYLE

Method.   Boil 1 quart water with 1 teaspoon salt; add 1/3 pound spaghetti or macaroni, and cook covered without boiling for 20 minutes. Drain thoroughly. Pour the macaroni or spaghetti into a bowl, season with salt and pepper, and add 2 tablespoons tomato sauce or 2 tomatoes that have been peeled, the juice and seeds squeezed out, seasoned with salt and pepper, and cooked in 1 tablespoon butter in a small frying pan. Add grated parmesan or gruyère cheese and 2 1/2 tablespoons butter.

Mix well without breaking the noodles.

Pour into a well-buttered 1 1/2-quart timbale mold and lightly press the pasta down with a cloth to pack it. Place the mold in a *bain-marie* half filled with hot water and bake in a 350° oven 18 to 20 minutes. Let stand 5 minutes, then unmold on a hot round plate. Around the timbale, arrange 6 fried eggs and 6 broiled tomato halves alternately. Serve accompanied by tomato sauce.

Omelets

An omelet can be rolled or flat, depending upon your preference and the garnish. A well-made omelet depends more on practice than on advice. This is a skill that is acquired only through experience.

If the omelet is stuffed or garnished, use 3 eggs for 2 people; if it is not, you will need 2 eggs per person.

If you are using more than 8 eggs, it is better to make more than one omelet.

Beat the eggs with a fork just lightly enough to mix the whites and the yolks, but keeping the whites elastic.

If the eggs are beaten too long they will not rise and when they are placed in hot butter, the omelet will be heavy and not taste very good.

Method.   Break the eggs, salt them, and beat them lightly. Do this at the last minute to prevent the eggs from turning brown. In a frying pan set on a very high flame, melt 1 tablespoon unsalted butter for each 2 eggs; when the butter is hot enough it will have a very light brown color.

Pour in the eggs. On contact with the browning butter, the eggs coagulate first at the edges of the frying pan. Quickly, with a fork, fold the edges back to the center repeatedly, to give the omelet an even thickness. When the right consistency is reached (when it is cooked, but *à point,* still very soft), leave the pan on the heat for 2 seconds more; then, with your left hand holding the frying pan, tip it toward the center of the burner and with a fork in your right hand roll half the omelet toward the opposite side; then with your right hand give your left hand a light bang that will shake the whole frying pan. The half-folded omelet will flop over on itself, and it then will be correctly rolled. Quickly place a pat of butter in the frying pan; this will melt to "gild" the omelet. Then turn the omelet upside down onto a long, hot plate. If necessary, correct the shape of the omelet; and rub the top of it with a piece of butter held on the point of a knife; this is called the glazing process.

The omelet, neat and without a wrinkle, is served immediately to the guests who have been waiting for it; it appears before them, golden, appetizing, and fragrant.

Omelets are generally garnished, stuffed, or seasoned with spices.

Omelettes garnies et fourrées

GARNISHED AND STUFFED OMELETS

The garnishes or stuffings for omelets must be prepared before the omelets are made. The recipes for omelets number in the hundreds; here are some of the most common and easy for a home cook. The amounts of garnishes given are for 6 eggs in an omelet.

Omelette aux champignons

MUSHROOM OMELET

Put 1/2 cup mushroom caps, washed rapidly and sliced thin, in an omelet pan; sauté in 2 tablespoons unsalted butter until lightly browned. Pour in the eggs and cook as directed above.

Omelette à l'oseille

SORREL OMELET

Use a dozen leaves of young sorrel, well washed, sponged dry, and cut into thick strips, then wilted in 1 tablespoon unsalted butter in an omelet pan. Add 1/2 teaspoon chopped chervil leaves to the beaten eggs and pour into the skillet with the sorrel. Cook as directed above.

Omelette aux fines herbes

HERB OMELET

Add to the beaten eggs 1 teaspoon chopped fresh parsley and 1 teaspoon chopped chives. Cook as directed above.

Omelette lyonnaise

OMELET LYONS STYLE

Cut 1 medium onion into fine strips; cook with 2 tablespoons unsalted butter in an omelet pan. When the onion is cooked to a golden brown, pour in the beaten eggs. Cook as directed above.

43

Omelette au jambon

HAM OMELET

Mix a scant ¼ cup diced cooked lean ham with the beaten eggs. Cook as directed above.

Omelette au fromage

CHEESE OMELET

Mix a scant ¼ cup grated gruyère cheese with the beaten eggs. Cook as directed above.

Omelette au lard

BACON OMELET

Cut ½ cup lean bacon, with the rind removed, into small cubes. Blanch for 6 minutes, drain, and wipe dry with a cloth. Brown in a skillet in 2 tablespoons unsalted butter.

Pour in the beaten eggs and cook as directed above.

Omelette à la crème

CREAM OMELET

Beat 3 tablespoons heavy cream; as soon as the cream is light and thick (be careful not to turn it into butter by beating it too long), fold in the beaten eggs and pour the mixture into the skillet. Cook as directed above.

Omelette aux morilles

OMELET WITH MORELS

Carefully wash ½ cup of small morels to rid them of sand. Cut them in quarters and sauté, following the recipe for the mushroom omelet (page 43).

Omelette aux truffes

TRUFFLE OMELET

Slice 2 medium-sized raw truffles not too thin, or dice. Heat them rapidly in 2 tablespoons unsalted butter in an omelet pan, and pour in the beaten eggs. Cook as directed above.

Omelette aux tomates

TOMATO OMELET

Remove the stem and the core from a large ripe tomato. Squeeze out the juice and the seeds, and cut the tomato in large dice. Season with salt and pepper and a pinch of sugar, and cook in a skillet with $1/2$ tablespoon oil or 1 tablespoon unsalted butter. When the tomato is reduced, pour it into the beaten eggs, add a pinch of chopped parsley, and cook as directed above.

Omelette aux foies de volaille

CHICKEN-LIVER OMELET

Cut 2 chicken livers into medium dice, season lightly with salt and freshly ground pepper; cook rapidly in 1 tablespoon very hot unsalted butter in a small skillet, just enough to stiffen meat; it should remain pink. Remove the chicken livers from the skillet and keep warm on a plate. To the same skillet, add 1 tablespoon Madeira or port wine; reduce by half; add 2 tablespoons strong veal stock. Again reduce the mixture by half; and off the flame add 1 or 2 tablespoons butter, then add the livers and roll them in this rich sauce.

Make the omelet, following the method on pages 42–3. Before rolling the omelet, garnish the center with two-thirds of the chicken livers, drained of the sauce. Fold the omelet, then turn upside down on a long heated plate. Make a shallow cut lengthwise on top; lightly push open the edges of the cut and coat the inside with $1/2$ tablespoon of the sauce. Finish the omelet by filling the cut with the remaining one-third of the chicken livers. Then pour the rest of the sauce around the omelet.

Omelette chasseur

HUNTER'S OMELET

Prepare the ingredients as in the recipe for the chicken-liver omelet; add 1 small shallot, chopped, and 4 medium mushrooms, diced, cooked over a high flame in the butter used to sauté the livers.

Finish as you would for the chicken-liver omelet.

Omelette aux rognons

KIDNEY OMELET

This omelet is prepared exactly as in the recipe for the hunter's omelet or the chicken-liver omelet. Choose lamb kidneys preferably, about 1 per person; remove the thin outer skin and the inside tubes before coarsely dicing.

Omelette aux pointes d'asperges

OMELET WITH ASPARAGUS TIPS

Remove the tips from a bunch of green asparagus and cut them the size of small peas. Barely cook in salted water; drain, and while still hot, put in a skillet with 2 tablespoons unsalted butter; mix them off the heat. Reserve one-third of the asparagus tips to garnish the omelet, and place the other two-thirds inside the omelet before it is rolled.

Omelettes plates
FLAT OMELETS

These omelets are generally garnished; they are not rolled. When they are finished, they have the same shape as the skillet and are flipped in the same way as crêpes.

Omelette aux noix
WALNUT OMELET

Use 8 eggs and about 20 walnuts. If the walnuts are fresh, it is necessary to remove the thick skin that covers the nut. Chop nuts coarsely and place them in the skillet just at the moment when the butter is bubbling. Immediately pour in the beaten eggs and season. As soon as the omelet is the desired consistency, let it brown for a second. Flip the omelet as you would a crêpe, and cook the other side lightly. Slide the omelet onto a round heated platter.

Note: Use a skillet of the right size, so that the omelet, which will have the same diameter as the bottom of the skillet, will be about 1 to 1¹/₂ inches thick.

Omelette à la savoyarde
SAVOY OMELET

2 medium-sized potatoes, peeled and boiled
7 tablespoons unsalted butter
8 eggs
Salt and pepper
¹/₄ cup grated or thinly sliced gruyère or parmesan cheese
1 teaspoon chopped chervil

Method. Slice the potatoes. Put 3 tablespoons unsalted butter into an omelet pan and cook the potatoes. When they are golden, add 4 tablespoons butter and heat. Pour in 8 beaten eggs, season with salt and pepper, and add a scant ¹/₄ cup grated or thinly sliced gruyère or parmesan cheese, and chopped chervil.

When the omelet is golden on one side, flip it as you would a thick crêpe and brown the other side. Slide the omelet onto a round heated platter.

Omelette Parmentier

Peel 2 medium-sized potatoes, cut evenly into thin slices; wash in cold water, drain, and wipe dry.

In an omelet pan heat 2 tablespoons unsalted butter. When the butter is bubbling, add the potatoes, being careful to separate the slices. Cook the potatoes, turning them frequently so that they are all golden brown and crisp. When the potatoes are cooked, add 4 tablespoons butter and heat. Pour in 8 beaten eggs, season with salt and pepper and 1 teaspoon fresh chopped parsley; finish as for the Savoy omelet.

Omelette aux courgettes

ZUCCHINI OMELET

Peel a medium-sized zucchini, and very thinly slice. Season with salt and pepper. Sauté the zucchini in 1 tablespoon unsalted butter in an omelet pan. When the zucchini is half brown, add 4 tablespoons butter and heat. Pour in 8 beaten eggs, seasoned, and add 1 teaspoon chopped parsley.

Finish the omelet as for the Savoy omelet (page 46).

Omelette André Theuriet

This is a flat omelet stuffed with creamed morels. Flip the omelet onto a heated platter; garnish the ends with asparagus tips cooked in unsalted butter, and place in the center a nice slice of truffle heated in butter.

Omelette au foie gras

GOOSE-LIVER OMELET

Cook diced *foie gras* in unsalted butter in an omelet pan; pour in the beaten eggs, and cook as for the basic flat omelet.

Oeufs brouillés

SCRAMBLED EGGS

Method. In making scrambled eggs properly it is essential to mix the egg whites and yolks absolutely homogeneously so that they are creamy and have no lumps. This can be done in the following way:

Break the eggs into a bowl, season with salt and pepper, and beat moderately as you would for an omelet.

In a saucepan, not too large but big enough for the quantity of eggs used, melt 1 tablespoon unsalted butter per egg; add the eggs and cook slowly, stirring continuously with a wooden spoon. It is best to do this in a *bain-marie* (double boiler). When the eggs are cooked, they should have the consistency of cream; remove from the heat and add, while stirring, 1 tablespoon butter for every 2 eggs.

Scrambled eggs are served in a covered timbale mold, in small *croustades* (shells of bread or flaky pastry), in small cocottes (earthenware or porcelain pots), or simply on a platter surrounded by a garnish. Most of the garnishes used for omelets can be used for scrambled eggs, and vice versa.

Oeufs brouillés au bacon

SCRAMBLED EGGS WITH BACON

Dice ¼ pound bacon, first removing the rind. Blanch the bacon in boiling water for 5 minutes and drain; brown lightly in 1 tablespoon unsalted butter in the skillet to be used to scramble the eggs. Set the bacon aside on a plate and keep warm. Cook the scrambled eggs, following the method above; then add the bacon, mix, and serve.

Oeufs brouillés à la purée de champignons
SCRAMBLED EGGS WITH MUSHROOM PURÉE

Use ¼ pound firm white mushrooms. Clean the mushrooms and wash them quickly, drain, and wipe dry. Slice very thin. Add the mushrooms immediately to a skillet in which 2 tablespoons unsalted butter have been heated. Sauté for 3 minutes over a high flame. Season with a pinch of salt and a few drops of lemon juice. Turn the mushrooms into a very fine sieve above a bowl and pound them through with a pestle.

In the skillet used to cook the mushrooms, cook the eggs by the method above and finish the cooking by adding the mushroom purée.

Oeufs brouillés aux pointes d'asperges
SCRAMBLED EGGS WITH ASPARAGUS TIPS

Boil and stew green asparagus tips in unsalted butter. Carefully mix them into the scrambled eggs and, just before serving, place a bouquet of asparagus tips on top of the eggs.

I have divided soups into two main groups: clear soups and thick soups.

There are many varieties of each.

In the first group you will find bouillons and consommés, with and without garnishes.

The second group includes soups that are thickened by mashing the basic element, purées, for example, or by adding one or more thickening ingredients: a *roux*, cooked rice, bread cooked in the soup, egg yolks, cream, etc.

All soups should be served at the boiling point in hot soup plates (this is essential for a soup to be appreciated).

Le pot-au-feu

STOCK POT

Le pot-au-feu, from which one gets the meat stock, is one of the fundamentals of cooking. Apart from the numerous soups of which it is the main ingredient, it provides a reserve of bouillon used in many cases as the stock to make sauces or certain improvised culinary preparations.

The bouillon set aside should always be put through a strainer or a fine sieve (since vegetables, carrots especially, cause rapid spoiling, this will keep the soup fresh longer). Then it should be boiled. Let it cool without covering it in a glazed tureen or an earthenware or enameled container, placed where there is good circulation of air, in order to shorten the cooling period.

A *pot-au-feu* should be prepared with a sufficient quantity of meat to allow for at least two meals.

(For 12 people)

Method. Place the rib bones at the bottom of a soup kettle, so the meat will not touch the bottom and will not get stuck to it. On the bones, place the beef shin, the beef shank, the chuck, and the oxtail. Finally add the veal shin and the lamb neck. Fill the kettle with cold water so that the meat will be completely covered. Do not add any salt at this time; only after skimming the soup. Cook, uncovered, over a very high flame; otherwise the soup will not be clear.

While this is cooking, peel the vegetables. The leeks must be washed well to get rid of their sand. Prepare the *bouquet garni,* wrapping the herbs together in the green leaves of the leeks. Tie a slice of carrot at either end of each marrowbone in order to seal them.

Skim the soup after 20 minutes of cooking. Carefully tip the kettle slightly so that the scum rises to one side. Reduce the flame, and cook slowly for another 20 minutes. Skim a second time, then season with coarse salt (about 3/4 tablespoon per quart of water) and add a few black peppercorns wrapped in cheesecloth. Slip some slices of truffle under the skin of the chicken and truss it (page 238). Add to the pot. Add the *bouquet garni* and the onions stuck with 4 cloves each. (For a good brown color, cut 1 onion in half and bake in a pan in a 475° oven for 30 minutes; it will color the soup.)

Ingredients:

1/2 pound beef rib bones
3 pounds beef shin
1 pound beef shank
1 pound beef chuck
1 pound oxtail
1 pound veal shin
1 pound lamb neck
1/2 pound leeks
Bouquet garni
1/2 pound carrots
5 marrowbones, cut into
  1 1/2-inch pieces
Coarse salt
Black peppercorns
Truffles
1 3-pound roasting
  chicken
1/2 pound onions
Cloves
1 whole head garlic
2 celery hearts
1/2 pound turnips
1 fennel
1 parsnip
1 pound top part of the
  rump steak, quite juicy
3 large tomatoes

Add the garlic and all the vegetables except the tomatoes; tie the leeks together. Skim again; remove the parsnip after 15 minutes. Then simmer for 40 minutes, skimming from time to time.

Remove the vegetables as they are cooked (test them with a needle—it will pierce them if they are cooked), lifting them carefully with a skimmer and keeping them warm on the side of the stove in a covered pot, basted with about 2 ladlefuls of soup. Remove the chicken when it is tender, and keep it warm in another covered pot in the same manner as the vegetables.

Let the meats cook for another 30 minutes, skimming from time to time; then remove the veal shin and the lamb neck. Let the other meats cook on a very low flame for about an hour. Tie string around the rump steak. To help in removing it from the kettle, tie one end of string to the rump steak and leave a long end to tie to the handle of the kettle. Add the rump steak, the marrowbones, and the tomatoes. Skim again. Cook for 12 to 15 minutes, depending on the thickness of the rump steak. Remove the meat and the marrowbones (when the carrot slices are removed, the marrow should be intact inside); return the chicken and the vegetables to the soup to reheat.

In the center of a large serving platter put the beef shins and surround them with the other meat and the chicken. Then add the vegetables. Pour some soup, which will be served on the side, into a soup tureen. There can be three meals from this pot, all served in soup dishes:

1. Serve the broth with toasted bread, grated cheese, freshly ground pepper, coarse salt, and red wine (optional).
2. Serve the chicken, carved, surrounded by the veal shins and the oxtail, along with the bouillon or with a sauce made with 1 tablespoon wine vinegar, 4 tablespoons walnut oil, salt, pepper, and 2 tablespoons snipped chervil.
3. Serve the beef shins with a little bit of lamb, a little bit of beef chuck, vegetables, and the bouillon.

Note: If you have a large number of guests, you can supplement this dish with a turkey, pheasants, partridges, pork hock or loin (fresh or salted), and a leg of lamb (cooked like the rump), some cabbage and cauliflower (cooked separately in salted water).

Soupe à la jambe de bois
WOODEN LEG SOUP

Here is the recipe for the soup á la *"jambe de bouâ"* as Henry Clos-Jouve has told me to prepare it and as it has been made in Lyons for a very long time: [*Editor's note:* This recipe is delightful reading; it takes an experienced cook to use it.]

"Take an earthenware soup pot or a copper one. Clean well. Place in it a beautiful beef loin that you will cover with cold water, adding salt, onions, cloves, and anything else that will give it flavor. Let simmer very slowly on a low flame. Skim the soup well. Once the soup is very clear, add leeks, turnips, celery. Add 2 or 3 veal shins, a shoulder of pork, turkey, partridge, a juicy leg of lamb, and a juicy beef rump. Half an hour before serving, add a couple of large chickens and, moments later, a pork sausage larded with truffles and pistachio nuts. When all are cooked, set one shin bone right across the stew pot so that everyone will recognize the 'Wooden Leg Soup.' One should serve a Beaujolais wine, and don't be skimpy with it. *Bon appétit!''*

Petite marmite
(For 6 people)

2 pounds beef shin
1 small hen, 2–2¹/₂ pounds
2 quarts bouillon
¹/₂ pound carrots (core removed)
¹/₂ pound turnips
1¹/₄ cups leeks, white part only
¹/₄ cup celery, sliced
Small marrowbones
Slices toasted bread
Grated gruyère cheese

Method.   Cube beef shin, blanch, and drain.

Place in an 8-quart earthenware kettle. Brown a small hen in a 450° oven for 15 minutes. Put the hen into the kettle.

Cover with bouillon and 1 pint cold water. Slowly bring to a boil, and remove the scum as it rises to the surface.

Add the carrots (do not use the hard, strong-tasting centers) and turnips cut into the shape of fat olives, leeks cut into pieces 2¹/₂ inches long, and celery. Cook steadily at a simmer for 4¹/₂ hours.

Serve in the pot, with small marrowbones poached in a little bit of the soup, tiny slices of toasted bread, and grated gruyère cheese.

Note: If the boiling has been done carefully and slowly, you should lose very little liquid through reduction, having about 2 quarts of soup. And no additional salt will be needed.

Consommés

1¹/₂ pounds lean round of beef, the fat completely removed
Chicken giblets
¹/₂ carrot
3 leeks, white part only
1 egg white
2¹/₂ quarts meat stock

A consommé is a meat stock, lightly salted, its flavor heightened by adding meat juices and spices.
(For 2 quarts of consommé)

Method.   Chop the meat and giblets very fine; cut the carrot and the leeks into tiny cubes. In a soup kettle combine the chopped meat, vegetables, and egg white; mix well. Add the meat stock, cold or tepid, stirring with a wooden spoon.

Bring slowly to a boil, continuing to stir constantly. As soon as the soup starts to boil, reduce the heat and keep the soup at a simmer, partially covered, for 1¹/₄ hours.

After that the bouillon is enriched by the juices of the meat and the aroma of the vegetables; it now has more body because of these added ingredients and has become consommé. Strain it through cheesecloth that has been soaked beforehand in tepid water and wrung out.

After this last step the consommé should be absolutely clear because of the albumin of the meat and the egg white.

Consommé de volaille

CHICKEN CONSOMMÉ

This consommé is distinguished by the very clear and characteristic flavor of chicken that is obtained by adding to the ingredients of the ordinary consommé 1 very small whole broiler, 2 giblets, and the carcass of another chicken, finely chopped.

Proceed exactly as for the consommé above.

The small chicken can be used later to make delicious dishes, hot or cold: chicken croquettes, chicken salad, etc.

Consommé printanier

SPRING CONSOMMÉ

To the basic consommé add cooked carrots and turnips, taken from the *pot-au-feu* vegetables and cut into tiny sticks about 1 inch long and 1/8 inch thick, or made into tiny curls with a spoon, or cut into the shape of tiny olives. Add an equal part of tiny peas and string beans cut into small diamond shapes and cooked in a little bit of soup. Complete the soup by adding a pinch of chervil.

Consommé Colbert

This is a *consommé printanier* (recipe above) to which a small poached egg is added for each guest.

Consommé Célestine

This consommé is slightly thickened with tapioca and garnished with a crêpe, made without sugar, cut into very fine strips.

Consommé à la royale

This consommé is thickened lightly with tapioca and garnished with custard (recipe below), made with no sugar and cut with a pastry cutter into decorative shapes, such as diamonds, squares, or stars.

Royale for Soups

4 eggs
1 cup milk
1 cup bouillon, degreased
  completely
Salt
Pinch grated nutmeg

Beat the eggs and strain them through a very fine strainer. Add the milk and the hot soup, which should not be boiling, and the salt and nutmeg. Pour into a cake tin or flat biscuit pan, and bake in a 325° oven in a *bain-marie* like a flan, being careful not to let the water of the *bain-marie* boil, which would cause tiny holes in the cream.

Let cool, unmold, and cut into even strips, and then cut each strip into small decorative shapes: squares, stars, diamonds. When putting the pieces of custard into very hot consommé, be careful not to break them.

Consommé aux profiteroles

Garnish the soup with tiny *profiteroles* (the size of hazelnuts) of cream-puff pastry made with the addition of gruyère or parmesan cheese and baked in a very hot oven.

Consommé brunoise

¹/₂ pound carrots (cored)
¹/₂ pound turnips
2 leeks, white part only
Small celery rib
2 tablespoons stock
Chervil (optional)

Cut into small bits: carrots, turnips, leeks, and celery. Mix everything together, blanch, and drain.

Cook over a very low flame in a small frying pan with 2 tablespoons stock. Use 2 teaspoons of the vegetables to garnish each portion of consommé. A couple of leaves of chervil may be added at the end.

Croûte-au-pot

Garnish the consommé with carrots, turnips, and leeks from a *pot-au-feu.* Cut the vegetables in the shape of an olive and simmer in a little bit of degreased stock. With the soup serve grated gruyère cheese in a small serving dish and on a plate covered by a folded napkin place crusts of toasted French bread without the soft centers.

One could add one-quarter of a small cabbage, cooked in a couple of tablespoons of fat stock.

Consommé froid

COLD CONSOMMÉ

Cold consommé is generally served in a cup, very cold, which does not mean iced. The soup should be like a very fluid jelly, which means half jelled, or like a thick syrup.

For the consommé to have this consistency, it must be very rich in meat juices or, if one wishes to economize, one will have to add a thickening ingredient such as tapioca.

However, I do not advise the use of starch, which dilutes the flavor of the different concentrated juices in the consommé. I would advise, however, the very light use of tapioca, which does not have the same drawback. One can also help compensate for a lack of natural jelling by the addition of an envelope of gelatin; however, tapioca seems to me more natural, tastier, and therefore preferable.

Since raw tomatoes are 90 percent water, adding them to a consommé dilutes its flavor. To avoid this, use tomatoes that have been cooked beforehand and reduced to a thick purée.

Consommé de volaille

CHICKEN CONSOMMÉ

Into a quart of boiling chicken consommé made

from the basic recipe for consommé, put 4 tablespoons tapioca; mix and cook very slowly for 15 minutes.

Put through a fine strainer, let cool, and serve in a cup.

Consommé au fumet de céleri

CELERY-FLAVORED CONSOMMÉ

Proceed as for the chicken consommé, and, when the tapioca has been assimilated into the consommé, add one-half heart of celery. Cook slowly for 25 minutes. Finish as above.

Consommé au fumet d'estragon

TARRAGON-FLAVORED CONSOMMÉ

Follow the same procedure as for the celery-flavored consommé, replacing the celery with a sprig of tarragon. Cook for only 15 minutes.

Consommé madrilène

First Method

6 ripe tomatoes
1 quart consommé
Tarragon
Garlic clove
4 tablespoons tapioca

Choose beautiful ripe tomatoes; cut them in half and squeeze to remove the juice. Force through a very fine sieve. Add this purée to the consommé; put in a small sprig of tarragon and a garlic clove. Thicken with tapioca, and cook slowly for 40 minutes. Strain through a napkin and let cool.

Second Method

1 quart chicken
 consommé
6 ripe tomatoes
4 tablespoons tapioca

Proceed as directed above for the chicken consommé and add, for 1 quart consommé, a cooked purée made from beautiful ripe tomatoes. Thicken with tapioca, and cook slowly for 25 minutes. Strain through a napkin and let cool.

Whether you use the first or the second method, the consommé must be absolutely clear.

Note: It is not necessary to add tapioca for thickening if the consommé is sufficiently rich in meat juices and in natural gelatinous ingredients.

Consommé aux oeufs pochés

CONSOMMÉ WITH POACHED EGGS

In ordinary consommé or a chicken consommé, serve 1 poached egg for each guest.

Consommé julienne

1 quart consommé
1 carrot (core removed)
1 turnip
1 leek, white part only
Celery
1 tablespoon fresh peas

Into the consommé put the outer part of 1 carrot, 1 whole turnip, the white of 1 leek, and a little celery, all cut into julienne, and cook. Toward the end of the cooking, add 1 tablespoon fresh peas.

To serve this very good consommé, add 1 tablespoon of these vegetables for each guest.

Consommé aux quenelles de volaille

CONSOMMÉ WITH CHICKEN QUENELLES

In chicken consommé, poach tiny *quenelles* (pages 192–3) the size of small olives, made with chicken and cream.

Consommé aux truffes

TRUFFLE CONSOMMÉ

In chicken consommé, cook finely diced raw truffles for 2 minutes. Add a little bit of port wine just before serving.

Soups

The basis for soups is one or more vegetables puréed or minced or cut into julienne—this means cut into quarters and then into very thin slices, about $\frac{1}{16}$ of an inch.

Whenever a carrot is among the ingredients or used alone, I recommend peeling it thinly or scraping it, cutting it in half lengthwise, and removing the core, which is tough and has a very strong flavor. Mince the outer part of the carrot, blanch, and rinse, These steps are not necessary when the vegetables are very young.

On the other hand, a turnip should be peeled quite deep; it has a thick skin that can be seen by cutting through it.

In general, you need $1\frac{1}{4}$ pounds vegetables for every $1\frac{1}{2}$ quarts water.

When the vegetables are ready to be used, it is important to proceed in the following manner in cooking them.

Set the soup kettle on the stove with unsalted butter; when the butter is very hot, add the vegetables. Stew very slowly on the corner of the stove, or on the burner on a very low flame, to make the vegetables sweat their juices and to allow the flavor of the butter to soak into the vegetables.

Then add the water, the salt, and the stock; bring to a boil, and simmer only for as long as indicated in the recipe.

To cook it longer than necessary will hurt the flavor of the soup. Before starting to cook the soup, gauge the time it will take so that it will be ready at the desired serving time.

Oxtail clair

CLEAR OXTAIL SOUP

3 pounds oxtail
3 onions
3 medium-sized carrots
6 tablespoons unsalted butter

Method. In the butter brown oxtail cut into pieces, onions, and carrots cut into quarters.

Then transfer the meat and vegetables to a soup kettle; add a *bouquet garni,* a celery rib, Madeira and cognac. Slowly

Bouquet garni
Celery rib
¼ cup Madeira
¼ cup cognac
3½ quarts consommé
Carrots and turnips
Celery heart

reduce, covered, on a low flame. Then pour in the consommé and 2½ cups water. Cook very slowly for 4 hours; the soup should barely simmer.

Strain soup through cheesecloth, reserving some of the best pieces of oxtail, 1 per guest, to add when ready to serve. Garnish each serving with 1 tablespoon carrots and turnips, cut into the shape of small olives, and a celery heart, each cooked separately in a little consommé.

Serve very hot.

Soupe à l'ail
GARLIC SOUP

2 cloves
Sprig sage
1½ tablespoons salt
Pinch pepper
20 garlic cloves
20 slices French bread
**Grated gruyère or
  parmesan cheese**
Few drops olive oil

Method. In a saucepan, combine 2 quarts water, cloves, sage, salt, pepper, and garlic.

Bring to a boil and cook slowly for 15 minutes.

Slice the French bread; put slices on a cookie sheet and cover each with a large pinch of grated gruyère or parmesan cheese; sprinkle with a few drops of olive oil and brown in a 475° oven.

Place the bread in a soup tureen; taste the soup and correct the seasoning if needed. Then pour the very hot soup through a fine strainer onto the bread.

Serve immediately.

Soupe ardennaise
ARDENNES SOUP

2 medium potatoes
6 endives
2 leeks, white part only
5 ounces unsalted butter
1 quart water
1 pint milk
**½ French bread or the
  equivalent quantity of
  white bread**
½ tablespoon salt

Method. Clean the vegetables, peel the potatoes. Cut the endives and the whites of the leeks into julienne, and the potatoes into very thin slices. Heat 3½ tablespoons butter in a saucepan. Add the vegetables, and stew slowly, covered, for 15 minutes. The vegetables must be softened but not browned. Add the water and salt. Simmer 45 minutes. Add the milk at the end of the cooking time.

Cut the French bread into thin slices; brown lightly in a 425° oven and place in a soup tureen with the rest of the butter.

Correct the seasoning of the soup. Pour the boiling soup over the bread just before serving.

Soupe auvergnate
AUVERGNE SOUP

3 carrots
2 medium turnips
1 small cabbage
4 leeks
3½ ounces lentils
2 pounds salted pig's head
Slices bread

Method. Wash and peel the vegetables; remove the cores from the carrots; soak the lentils for 2 hours in cold water and drain.

In a saucepan cover the pig's head and the vegetables with 4 quarts water, and cook on a low flame for 3 hours.

To serve, remove the pig's head and vegetables and arrange on a platter. Pour the soup into a soup tureen in which slices of bread have been placed.

57

Soupe aux truffes Élysée

TRUFFLE SOUP ÉLYSÉE (For 1 person)

2 tablespoons *matignon:*
  equal parts carrots
  (without cores), onions,
  celery, mushrooms, all cut
  into tiny dice and stewed
  in unsalted butter
1³/₄ ounces fresh raw
  truffles
³/₄ ounce fresh *foie gras*
1 cup strong chicken
  consommé
2 ounces flaky pastry
  (pages 382–3
1 egg yolk, beaten

Method.   Into each individual ovenproof soup bowl (called *gratinée lyonnaise*) put 2 tablespoons *matignon,* 1³/₄ ounces truffles cut into irregular slices, ³/₄ ounce *foie gras* also cut into irregular slices, and 1 cup strong consommé.

Brush the edges of a thin layer of flaky pastry with egg yolk, and cover the soup bowl with it, tightly sealing the edges.

Set the soup bowl in a 425° oven. It will cook very fast. The flaky pastry should expand in the heat and take on a golden color; that is a sign that it is cooked.

Use the soupspoon to break the flaky pastry, which should fall into the soup.

This is the way that M. and Mme. Valéry Giscard d'Estaing enjoyed this truffle soup, created for them, during that marvelous lunch that gathered the finest cooks in France at a superb reception, the day when the president of the French Republic awarded me the Cross of the Légion d'honneur as Ambassador of French Cooking, on February 25, 1975.

Soupe fermière

FARMER'S SOUP

2 carrots
4 leeks, white part only
¹/₄ head cabbage
2 medium turnips
2 medium potatoes
5 ounces unsalted butter
2 quarts stock or water
1 tablespoon salt
¹/₂ French bread or the
  equivalent quantity of
  white bread

Method.   Wash, peel, and remove the cores from the carrots; use only the outer portion.

Shred the leeks and the cabbage finely; peel the other vegetables and cut them into very thin slices. Heat 3¹/₂ tablespoons butter in a saucepan; add all vegetables except the potatoes, and stew slowly for 15 minutes.

When the vegetables are softened, add the stock or water. Simmer just at the boiling point for 25 minutes; then add the potatoes, and cook for another 20 minutes.

Cut the bread into very thin slices, brown in a 425° oven, and place in the soup tureen with the remaining butter. Just before serving, correct the seasoning of the soup and pour it over the bread. Cover the bread completely, so that it will soften.

Soupe de courge

PUMPKIN SOUP (For 6–8 people)

1 6–8 pound pumpkin
1 cup toasted croutons
3¹/₂ ounces grated
  gruyère cheese
Salt and pepper
3 quarts cream

Method.   Cut the top out of the pumpkin to give it the shape of a soup tureen. Set the top aside.

Remove all the pumpkin seeds. In the interior make alternate layers of toasted croutons and grated gruyère. Add salt and pepper and fill with the cream. Close the "soup tureen" with its pumpkin top as tightly as possible.

Place the prepared pumpkin in a 425° oven. It will take about 2 hours to cook.

To serve, present the pumpkin tureen before your guests. Remove the cover. With a spoon, scoop out the pumpkin meat. Mix it into the soup with a ladle to make the soup richer. If necessary, correct the seasoning.

Soupe savoyarde

SAVOY SOUP

1³/₄ ounces unsalted pork fat
4 leeks
1 onion
1 celery rib
2 medium potatoes
Salt
2 cups milk
¹/₄ loaf bread
Grated gruyère or parmesan cheese

Method. Remove the skin from the pork fat; dice fat and melt in a heavy saucepan. Add the leeks, the onions, and the celery cut into julienne. Slice the potatoes thinly and add. Stew for 15 minutes, stirring from time to time. Pour in 1 quart water, salt lightly, and cook 35 minutes; add the milk, and return to a boil for a second.

Cut the bread into thin slices and place them on a cookie sheet or roasting pan; sprinkle them with grated gruyère or parmesan cheese and brown in a 425° oven.

Put the bread into the soup tureen, and just before serving pour in the boiling soup.

Soupe nîmoise

NÎMES SOUP

3¹/₂ tablespoons unsalted butter
3 leeks, white part only
²/₃ pound cabbage
1 celery heart
3¹/₂ ounces pearl barley or rice
Pinch crushed basil
1 tablespoon salt
Grated gruyère cheese

Method. Heat the butter in a casserole. Add the vegetables, cut into thin strips, and stew them slowly, letting them soften; stir from time to time. Add the barley, the basil, the salt, and 2 quarts water. Cook 45 minutes.

If the barley is replaced by the rice, first cook the soup for 15 minutes; then add the rice and continue cooking for 30 minutes.

Serve with a dish of grated gruyère cheese.

Gratinée lyonnaise

(For 4–6 people)

1¹/₂ pounds yellow onions
5 ounces unsalted butter
2 tablespoons flour
Salt and freshly ground pepper
1 small *bouquet garni*
¹/₂ pound French bread
9 ounces grated gruyère cheese
4 egg yolks
1 tablespoon old Madeira

Method. Mince the onions. Sauté them in the butter in a heavy frying pan until brown, but without burning them.

Then sprinkle on the flour and stir a few times, so that the flour will form a *roux*. Put it in a soup kettle with 2¹/₂ quarts water.

Add salt, pepper, and the *bouquet garni*. Cook over a low flame for about 40 minutes.

Discard the *bouquet garni*. Rub the onions and the stock through a sieve or a food mill.

In an ovenproof soup tureen, put the bread cut into very thin slices and lightly dried in the oven (over each layer of bread sprinkle grated cheese, using about half of it). After correcting the seasoning, pour the stock over the bread. Cover the surface with the remaining grated cheese.

Set the soup tureen in a 425° oven. Under the heat, the cheese will melt and the surface of the *gratinée* will take on a beautiful golden color.

Put the 4 egg yolks into a bowl and dilute them with the Madeira.

59

Pour the mixture into the soup tureen, stirring quickly with a ladle to thicken the soup and obtain a perfect mixture. This is called *touiller* the *gratinée*.

Note: In Lyons this soup is very popular; it is usually eaten at night at a family dinner, or by friends after a show.

Soupe ménagère
HOME-STYLE SOUP

3 carrots
2 turnips
4 medium leeks
3 potatoes
1/2 pound cabbage
1/3 pound celery
1/2 pound salt bacon
1/4 loaf bread

Method.   Wash and peel the vegetables; discard the cores from the carrots and cut the vegetables into large pieces. Put into a soup kettle with 2 1/2 quarts water and the bacon. Cook 1 1/2 hours.

Remove the bacon, and cut it into tiny pieces. Put the bacon into a soup tureen together with the bread cut into thin slices; correct the seasoning, and pour the soup over the bread.

Soupe à la normande
NORMAN SOUP

1 pound carrots (cores removed)
1/2 pound potatoes
1/2 pound leeks, white part only
2 tablespoons rice
2 quarts stock or water
Salt
Toasted bread slices
Unsalted butter

[*Editor's note:* This soup can be made in any quantity, using 1 1/4 pounds vegetables for every 1 1/2 quarts water.]

Method.   Cut the carrots and the potatoes into very thin slices and the leeks into thin strips. Stew the carrots and the leeks in stock or water and salt to taste. Cook for an hour, then add the potatoes and a couple of teaspoons of rice. Continue the cooking for 30 minutes. Put the soup through a food mill off the flame, and pour into a soup tureen with slices of toasted bread. Serve with unsalted butter.

Soupe paysanne
PEASANT SOUP

1 pound leeks, white part only
6 tablespoons unsalted butter
Core of 1 cabbage
2 quarts stock or water
Salt
1 pound potatoes
Toasted bread slices
Unsalted butter

Method.   Cut the leeks into julienne and sauté in butter as you would an onion for soup. When this is lightly browned, add the hard core of a cabbage, cut into thick julienne and blanched. Stew. Add the stock or water; salt to taste. Cook for an hour. Then add the potatoes, and continue the cooking for 30 minutes. Mash the potatoes coarsely and pour the soup into a tureen lined with slices of toasted bread. Serve with unsalted butter.

Potée bourguignonne

6 ounces half-salted pork
1 1/2 pounds raw garlic sausage
Core of 1 cabbage
1 pound potatoes, quartered
Coarse-textured white or rye bread slices

This is the same as the recipe for *petite marmite* (page 52), with the addition of the following: a good piece of half-salted pork, a raw garlic sausage, the core of a cabbage, and some potatoes cut into quarters. The potatoes should be added just a half hour before serving.

Put the meat and vegetables on a platter. Pour the stock over white bread and serve on the side.

Soupe à l'oseille

SORREL SOUP

Proceed as for the leek and potato soup (page 69), replacing the leeks with sorrel. Sorrel takes only a few minutes to cook.

Soupe minestra

MINESTRONE SOUP

4 ounces fresh pork fat or bacon
1 medium-sized onion, chopped
2 leeks, white part only, diced
1 carrot (core removed), diced
1 medium-sized turnip, diced
1 celery rib, diced
Core of 1 small cabbage, diced
Salt and pepper
Pinch sugar
1½ quarts stock or water
2 tomatoes
1 cup fresh peas
Handful string beans
1 large potato, diced
¼ pound noodles or spaghetti
Garlic clove
Pinch basil
Pinch chervil

Method. In a casserole melt 2 ounces fresh pork fat or bacon cut into tiny dice; add an onion, chopped; the white of 2 leeks cut into tiny dice. Sauté until golden. Add the carrot, turnip, celery rib, cabbage—everything cut into tiny dice. Season with salt, pepper, and sugar. Mix well, cover, and stew for 15 minutes. Pour in lightly salted stock or water (about ¾ tablespoon salt per quart of stock).

Bring to a boil, and simmer for 30 minutes.

At this point, add the tomatoes, skinned, seeded, and diced; the peas; the string beans cut into 1-inch lengths; the potato; and the noodles or spaghetti broken into pieces.

Let the soup simmer for an hour.

Just before serving, bring it to a boil; add remaining pork fat, ground and mashed with a garlic clove, basil, and chervil.

Garbures

There are many versions of this delicious soup, which is typical of the cooking of the province of Béarn. Although they have different names, they are all variations of this recipe.

Garbure béarnaise

10 ounces turnips
10 ounces carrots
1 medium-sized cabbage, sliced, core removed, parboiled, and drained
12 ounces string beans
1 cup dried white beans, cooked in water with a *bouquet garni*
6 ounces fresh pork fat
Piece of *confit d'oie*
2 quarts water
Salt and pepper
Toasted bread slices
Grated gruyère cheese

Method. In an earthenware pot place fresh vegetables of the season—turnips, carrots, cabbage, string beans, white beans—and pork fat and *confit d'oie* (goose meat cooked in goose fat or lard and preserved, page 268). Cover the vegetables and the meat completely with water. Bring to a boil, and simmer for 3 hours.

Halfway through the cooking time, taste and correct seasoning, adding salt if necessary. When the 3 hours are up, pour off the soup and reserve it.

In an ovenproof dish arrange layers of the vegetables, the fat, and the *confit d'oie* cut into pieces; on top place slices of toasted bread; sprinkle them with grated gruyère cheese and freshly ground pepper. Moisten with a couple of tablespoons of the fatty broth from the soup and set in a 325° oven to simmer and brown for 15 minutes. Serve the broth in a soup tureen or in its earthenware cooking pot, along with the dish of vegetables and *confit d'oie*.

Note: In Crécy, *garbure* is made with carrots; in Limoges, with chestnuts; farmer's *garbure* is a very thick peasant soup; *fréneuse,* with turnips; *dauphinoise,* with potatoes and pumpkin; etc. All derive from the recipe above and are generally served with slices of bread fried in butter covered with a thick coat of vegetable purée made from the soup, then sprinkled with cheese and browned under the broiler. These slices are placed in the serving tureen before the soup is poured in.

Garbure à l'oignon
ONION GARBURE

This is onion soup thickened with a large potato, mashed and spread on slices of toasted bread and copiously sprinkled with grated cheese and pieces of butter, then baked in a 350° oven until a golden crust is formed, about 25 minutes.

Soupe cultivateur
FARMER'S SOUP

Use all the vegetables in season, cut into coarse dice, stewed with diced unsmoked bacon without the rind. Cover with white stock or water, salted to taste, and cook 1 hour.

Halfway through the cooking time, add potatoes, fresh peas, and string beans cut into pieces.

Pour into a soup tureen on slices of bread with pieces of butter.

Bortsch à la russe
RUSSIAN BORSCHT

$^1/_2$ pound beets
1 medium-sized leek, white part only
1 onion
$^1/_2$ pound core of cabbage
1 celery rib
1 fennel rib
Unsalted butter
$6^1/_2$ cups stock or water
$1^1/_2$ pounds short ribs of beef
1 small duckling or giblets of 2 ducks
$^1/_2$ cup beet juice
$^1/_2$ cup sour cream

Method.   Thinly slice all the vegetables except the fennel. Mix the rest together and season with a pinch of salt; stew in butter in an earthenware pot large enough to hold the soup.

Pour over $6^1/_2$ cups stock or water; add salt or more water as needed. Bring to a boil. Scald the short ribs in boiling water and add to the soup. Skim the soup, and cook very slowly for $2^1/_2$ hours. Then add the duck browned in butter or, for the sake of economy, the giblets of 2 ducks. Add the fennel, and continue cooking for 40 minutes.

Drain the beef and the duck or giblets.

Cut the beef into large dice and remove the bones and membranes; slice the breast of the duck; and return both to the boiling soup. Off the flame pour in a mixture of $^1/_2$ cup beet juice and $^1/_2$ cup soup cream.

Panade

A *panade* is made with coarsely diced bread, sometimes fried in butter, and cooked in milk, which may be diluted with water.

The soup is then thickened with egg yolks mixed with cream or milk, To this soup one may add shredded sorrel or lettuce or spinach or water cress.

The soup has the consistency of a cream soup or *velouté.* Generally hard bread or stale bread is used.

Panade au céleri
CELERY PANADE

This is a variation of the *panade,* flavored with celery or celery root.

Fish soups

3 pounds white fish
4 medium onions, minced
3 garlic cloves, crushed
2 cloves
1 bay leaf
15 fennel seeds or 1 fresh
   fennel rib
2 ripe tomatoes, peeled,
   squeezed to remove the
   juice and seeds, and
   chopped
2½ tablespoons salt
Pinch pepper
½ cup dry white wine
2¼ cups oil
8 slices bread
Garlic clove (optional)
1 tablespoon chopped
   fresh parsley or chervil

This is a basic recipe for 8 servings. Preferred fishes are carp, weever [a European fish which could be replaced by whiting], gurnet [which could be replaced by red mullet], or John Dory [a fish quite similar to porgy].

Method. Cut the fish into pieces and put them into a soup kettle that will sit firmly on the burner. Add the vegetables and spices, the white wine, and 3 quarts water; bring to a rolling boil; add the oil. Boil rapidly for 15 minutes.

While this is cooking, slice the bread and place it on a cookie sheet; coat the slices lightly with oil, and toast them in the oven. If you like the taste, rub the bread with a clove of garlic. Put the bread into a soup tureen; you may strain the soup if you wish. Pour the soup into the tureen just before serving, and garnish with a tablespoon of chopped fresh parsley or chervil.

If the soup has been strained, the pieces of fish may be served on the side.

Soupe d'écrevisses
CRAYFISH SOUP

Method. Carefully wash the rice and cook rapidly in two-thirds of the stock. While the rice is cooking, put the carrot and the onion into a frying pan with a pat of butter, and cook slowly without letting them brown. Add the parsley, thyme, and bay leaf; raise the heat; add the crayfish, the salt, and the pepper. Sauté quickly on high heat; the crayfish will get red at once. Moisten with the cognac, flame, and put out the flame immediately by pouring in the white wine. Cook for 8

½ cup raw rice
1 quart white stock
5 ounces unsalted butter
2 tablespoons diced carrot,
  core removed
2 tablespoons diced
  onion
1 sprig parsley
1 sprig thyme
1 bay leaf
20 crayfish, about 1½
  ounces each
Salt and pepper
Cognac
White wine
Stock or *crème fraîche* or
  heavy cream
Pinch red pepper

4 quarts mussels
1 bottle Pouilly-Fuissé
3 shallots, chopped
3½ tablespoons chopped
  parsley
7 tablespoons unsalted
  butter
1¼ cups olive oil
⅔ pound onions, minced
⅔ pound leeks, cut into
  strips
6½ pounds Mediterranean
  fish, or other fresh fish
3 pounds tomatoes,
  seeded and cut into
  pieces
3½ tablespoons chopped
  fresh fennel rib
2 garlic cloves, chopped
½ bay leaf
1 sprig thyme
Saffron
Salt and pepper
1½ cups cream
Croutons
Grated cheese

minutes. Remove 10 crayfish, take out the flesh, and reserve in a small amount of stock. Put the shells, along with everything else, into a mortar; rinse the frying pan with a few tablespoons of reserved stock and add to mortar.

Pound the mixture to a fine paste; mix in the very hot rice, and pound again, working on the texture until it has the consistency of cream.

Strain into a fine sieve, rubbing through until nothing is left but the crushed shells. Put this into a saucepan and bring to a boil adding some stock or *crème fraîche,* until it has the consistency of a thick soup. Then off the fire add the remaining butter. Correct the seasoning, and add a pinch of red pepper.

Serve the soup with the reserved crayfish tails cut in pieces. The color of the soup should be a pinkish red, the same as the crayfish after they have been cooked.

[*Editor's note:* Crayfish are hard to find in the United States; they may be replaced by a small lobster or unshelled large prawns.]

Soupe de moules

MUSSEL SOUP (For 10 people)

Method. Boil the mussels with ¼ of the white wine, the shallots, parsley, and butter until they open. Heat the olive oil in an 8- to 10-quart soup kettle; add the onions and the leeks, and cook over a low flame for 5 minutes. Then pour in 4 quarts water, the remaining wine, and the liquid the mussels cooked in; add the fish, the tomatoes, the herbs, and the seasonings, and cook for 40 minutes.

Then put the stock through a very fine strainer, rubbing all the ingredients to extract the juice and the flesh of the fish. Pour the stock into a smaller kettle and bring to the boiling point. At the last moment, add the mussels and the cream. Cook for 2 minutes.

Serve in a soup tureen, with croutons made of toasted bread, and grated cheese on the side.

Thick soups

Under this general heading, I will differentiate according to the thickening ingredient—soups with special thickenings, *veloutés,* creams, and purées.

Purées are almost always made with one vegetable or a combination of more than one.

Some vegetables, such as turnips, carrots, cauliflower, pumpkin, etc., require a supplemental thickening ingredient, such as beans, lentils, etc., or a starch, such as potatoes, rice, *beurre manié,* etc.

Poultry purées are thickened by adding rice; game soups, by adding lentils. Shellfish soups are thickened with rice or croutons. The croutons, toasted or fried in butter, are then simmered in the very hot soup and become a satiny thickening ingredient.

An excellent soup is noteworthy for the velvety sensation on the palate. To prevent the flour or starch from separating from the soup liquid, it is often necessary to add a small quantity of a thickening ingredient such as *beurre manié*—equal parts of unsalted butter and flour mixed—or by a *mitonnade* —croutons simmered in hot soup; for example, with a purée of lentils or split peas or fresh peas or beans, this prevents the purée and the stock from separating in the soup plate when the soup is served.

Fresh vegetables used for a soup should be sliced very thinly, then stewed with 1/4 pound butter for every 1 1/2 pounds of vegetables. Dried vegetables are an exception to this rule; they are soaked for 2 or more hours before cooking.

Each vegetable should be blanched and rinsed.

Each recipe will explain the technique.

Liquids used are stock, milk, or water.

The proportions are 1/3 purée to 2/3 liquid.

Essential advice.   Let the soup stand after it has been cooked and seasoned; the longer it stands, the richer the flavor and the better the soup.

Therefore, it is important to calculate the length of the cooking time and to begin the soup early enough to be ready before the time it is to be served. The soup is "finished" at the last minute with unsalted butter or cream, about 5 1/2 tablespoons per quart. This last step must be done off the flame; the soup is then very hot but not boiling. Absolute principle: a buttered soup must not boil; if it does, the flavor of the butter will be altered and it will lose its nutritional value.

VELOUTÉ SOUPS

Butter, flour, and a liquid are the ingredients of *veloutés.* They are thickened with egg yolks and cream, and a purée of poultry, game, fish, shellfish, or vegetables is added to flavor the soup.

The method of preparation is always the same.

Melt the butter in a saucepan; add an equal amount of flour; mix together and cook slowly for 15 minutes, stirring frequently with a wooden spoon. Be careful not to let this mixture, which often is improperly called a *roux,* become brown; it should remain a very light color. Cool to avoid curdling, then while beating vigorously, pour in small quantities of the boiling liquid ingredients (meat, poultry, game, or fish stocks, or milk). Bring to a boil, beating continuously, and place on a very low flame; simmer gently for 35 minutes.

During the cooking a skin forms on the surface of the *ve-*

louté; this must be removed from time to time along with any other impurities that come to the surface. After it has cooked, strain the *velouté* through a sieve and bring it back to a boil. The purée called for in the particular soup is then added, and, off the flame, the thickening ingredients, egg yolks and cream, which first must be diluted with a small quantity of the *velouté* to avoid cooking the yolks. The soup must be constantly beaten and heated for a few seconds to a temperature of 185°. Do not let it boil.

This soup should be creamy and have the characteristics of a very light sauce.

Note: To thicken the soup, take the *velouté* off the flame so that it is no longer boiling. Separate the egg whites from the yolks. Put the yolks in a bowl, 3 yolks per quart of soup; and 1/2 cup *crème fraîche.* Be sure to remove the stringy whites. Mix yolks and cream together, stirring constantly with a small whisk, and little by little add a cup of the soup. Then beat the soup in the pot and pour the egg-cream mixture in. Raise the heat until the yolks begin to cook, then remove soup from the heat just before the boiling point. Finish the soup by adding, for each quart of soup, 7 tablespoons of butter cut into small pieces. Taste, correct the seasoning if necessary, and serve.

CREAM SOUPS

Cream soups are prepared in the same way as *veloutés;* the only differences are that, instead of stock, slightly salted milk is used. The thickening is also different; to finish the soup, only thick, fresh cream is used, instead of egg yolks.

Crème d'Argenteuil ou d'asperges
CREAM OF ASPARAGUS

1¹/₃ pounds white asparagus
5 cups cream
Seasoning

Peel and cut up thick white asparagus; then boil in salted water for 8 minutes. Drain, then add 1 quart cream, and continue cooking.

When the asparagus is tender, pour the soup into a fine sieve, rubbing through the pieces of asparagus, which must be puréed in order to be incorporated into the soup.

Set the soup on the stove, and bring to a boil; then keep warm in a *bain-marie* (double boiler) until you are ready to serve it. Add 1 cup very fresh cream just before serving. If the soup is too thick, thin it with boiling milk. Correct the seasoning, and pour into a hot tureen.

Crème de céleri
CREAM OF CELERY

1¹/₄ cups rice flour
2 cups cold milk
1¹/₂ quarts stock
1 celery heart
1/2 cup *crème fraîche* or heavy cream

Mix the rice flour with cold milk. Vigorously heat the stock to the boiling point and pour in the mixture. Parboil the celery heart and add. Cook slowly for 2 hours. Put in a sieve and rub the celery through. Finish the soup with *crème fraîche.*

Crème Germiny
CREAM OF SORREL (For 5 generous cups)

7 ounces sorrel
5½ tablespoons unsalted butter
4½ cups meat stock
10 egg yolks
1 cup *crème fraîche* or heavy cream
Pinch chopped chervil or chervil leaves
Croutons, fried in butter
Pinch cayenne pepper (optional)

Method. This soup is one of the most delicate of all cream soups. It is very simple to make, but it needs the attention that is required to make a custard cream, from which it derives.

Remove the stems of the sorrel, and chop. Soften the sorrel in 2 tablespoons butter in a saucepan; then add excellent meat stock. Bring to a boil.

While the soup is boiling, combine the egg yolks and the *crème fraîche* in a bowl. Mix well, stirring with a spatula, and very slowly pour into the sorrel soup, off the flame. If you are not very experienced, put the soup on a very low fire or in a *bain-marie* (double boiler). Cook as you would a custard sauce, stirring the soup continuously until it becomes creamy, without letting it boil. As soon as it has reached the proper consistency, remove from the flame and add 3½ tablespoons butter and a pinch of chopped chervil or chervil leaves. Pour immediately into a soup tureen in which there are some croutons fried in butter.

This soup should be completed just before serving; it should not be allowed to stand. Correct the seasoning, and add a pinch of cayenne pepper, if you wish.

Bisque d'écrevisses
CRAYFISH BISQUE

¾ cup raw rice
1 quart white stock
2 tablespoons diced carrots, core removed
2 tablespoons diced onion
10 tablespoons unsalted butter
Bouquet garni
20 crayfish, 1½ ounces each (see *Editor's note*, page 20)
½ cup cognac
1 cup dry white wine

Method. Wash the rice carefully and cook it quickly in two-thirds of the stock. Meanwhile cut the carrot and the onion into tiny dice *(mirepoix)* and cook slowly, without letting them brown, in a pat of butter in a frying pan.

Add the *bouquet garni.* Raise the flame and add the crayfish to the *mirepoix;* add salt and pepper. Sauté rapidly; the crayfish will turn red immediately. Moisten with the cognac, ignite, and extinguish immediately by pouring in the white wine; cook for 8 minutes. Pour over the rice and serve.

Crème de homard
CREAM OF LOBSTER

Prepare a lobster of about 1 to 1¾ pounds as for lobster *à l'américaine* (page 143). Crush the lobster in a mortar and rub it through a very fine sieve; then put it through cheesecloth.

Add the lobster to 3 cups cream soup (page 66). Correct the consistency by adding *crème fraîche* or heavy cream.

Crème de cresson et d'oseille
CREAM OF WATER CRESS AND SORREL

Follow the directions for a *velouté* soup (pages 65–6). After the cream and egg yolks have been incorporated, add the water cress, half a bunch per quart of soup. Cook for 5 minutes and rub through a sieve. The sorrel is added to the soup just before serving, about 1 teaspoon per serving, finely shredded and wilted in unsalted butter.

Finish the soup with a pinch of chervil and small croutons fried in butter.

Velouté princesse

2 quarts *velouté* soup (pages 65–6), made with chicken
Chicken breast
1/2 cup cream
12 tablespoons unsalted butter
6 egg yolks
Cream
Asparagus tips

Method. Prepare the *velouté* soup, using stock made with a tender hen.

Remove the meat from the chicken breast and skin it; pound in a mortar with the cream and 7 tablespoons butter. Rub through a very fine strainer and reserve in a bowl.

In another bowl thicken the soup with the egg yolks, following the *velouté* recipe.

Note: Just before serving, correct the seasoning and add remaining butter to the soup along with the purée of chicken and some reserved cream. Garnish with tips of green asparagus, cooked in salted water (pages 314–15).

PURÉED SOUPS

Potage Parmentier

2 leeks, white part only
6 tablespoons unsalted butter
1 pound mealy potatoes, peeled and cut into quarters
1 quart stock or water
Milk
1 tablespoon *beurre manié*
2 tablespoons *crème fraîche* or heavy cream
Croutons, fried in butter
Pinch chervil leaves

Method. Wash and slice the leeks, and cook slowly in 2 tablespoons butter. Add the potatoes. Pour over 1 quart stock or water; if water is used, salt to taste. Cook 25 minutes. Strain through cheesecloth, pushing the leeks through. Return the purée to the saucepan, and add enough milk to thin the soup to the desired consistency. Bring to a boil, adding the *beurre manié* in small pieces. Finish the soup off the flame with the *crème fraîche* and 4 tablespoons butter.

Serve with small croutons fried in butter and a pinch of chervil leaves.

Purée de pois

PEA SOUP

1/2 pound split peas
1 1/2 quarts water
2 1/2 teaspoons salt
2 1/2 teaspoons sugar
2 ounces pork fat
2 tablespoons diced carrot
1 onion, finely diced
Parsley
Small leek
Sprig thyme
1/2 bay leaf
Stock or milk
Pat *beurre manié*
Unsalted butter
Croutons, fried in butter
Pinch chervil leaves

Method. Wash 1/2 pound split peas, pick them over, wash in several changes of water until it becomes absolutely clear; soak for 2 or 3 hours in cold water.

By washing the peas carefully, you remove the smell of the burlap sacks and the dust that has a tendency to remain. [*Editor's note:* You may use presoaked peas; follow directions on the package.]

In a saucepan combine the drained peas with 1 1/2 quarts water, 2 1/2 teaspoons salt, and 2 1/2 teaspoons sugar. Bring to a boil, and skim carefully. Add a *mirepoix* made with 2 ounces lean pork fat diced, scalded, and sautéed with 2 tablespoons diced carrot and 1 finely diced onion. Add a *bouquet garni* made of a few sprigs of parsley, a small leek, a sprig of thyme, and $1/2$ bay leaf. Cook for 2 hours, then squeeze through cheesecloth. Return to the saucepan and thin to the proper consistency by adding stock or milk. Bring to a boil and add a pat of *beurre manié*. Finish with some unsalted butter added off the flame.

Serve with small diced croutons fried in butter and a pinch of chervil leaves.

Note: The thickening with the *beurre manié* prevents the pea purée from separating from the cooking water or stock or milk and sinking to the bottom of the bowl after the soup is served. The same results can be obtained by adding croutons fried in butter and simmered in the hot soup.

Potage Dubarry ou crème de chou-fleur
CAULIFLOWER PURÉE

1¼ pounds cauliflower
10 tablespoons unsalted butter
²/₃ pound new potatoes, peeled and quartered
1 quart milk
1¼ cups stock or water
1 tablespoon salt
Boiling milk, water, or *crème fraîche* or heavy cream
Pinch chervil
Croutons, fried in butter

Method.   Clean and parboil the cauliflower. Rinse and drain. Put in a saucepan with 7 tablespoons melted butter; stew for 20 minutes. Add the potatoes, milk, stock or water, and salt. Cook slowly for 20 minutes.

Put through cheesecloth, passing all the vegetables through. Put the purée into a saucepan, bring to a boil, and off the flame add boiling milk, water, or *crème fraîche* to give it the proper consistency.

Add remaining butter to the soup just before serving. Add a pinch of chervil leaves and croutons diced small and fried in butter.

Potage poireaux et pommes de terre
LEEK AND POTATO SOUP

5–6 medium-sized leeks, white part only
4 tablespoons unsalted butter
1 quart stock or water
Salt
1 pound mealy potatoes
Slices bread

Method.   Wash and cut the leeks into strips; stew in butter; pour over the stock or water. Check the seasoning, and add salt if necessary. Simmer slowly for 1 hour, then add the potatoes, peeled and cut into very thin, even slices. Continue cooking for another 20 minutes.

Pour into a soup tureen containing slices of bread dried in the oven and spread with butter.

Potage cressonnière

WATER-CRESS PURÉE
First Method

Follow the recipe for the potage Parmentier (page 68), using a handful of water cress instead of leeks. Garnish with a couple of leaves of parboiled water cress.

Second Method

Wash a bunch of water cress carefully. Cut it up coarsely and stew in 3 tablespoons unsalted butter for a few minutes. As soon as the water cress is wilted, add ½ pound mealy potatoes, sliced, and pour over 1 quart stock or water. If using water, add salt to taste.

Cook for 20 minutes. Put through cheesecloth or a very fine strainer, and return to the saucepan. Bring to a boil, and correct the consistency of the soup with boiling milk.

Add butter or cream off the flame.

Its subtle variety of sauces is the fundamental heritage of the French cuisine.

The importance of this key chapter will not escape my readers. I will limit it, however, to the basic repertoire for a home cook, avoiding overly complicated recipes that require long cooking experience and basic general preparation that is difficult to achieve with domestic resources.

Sauces are classified into two principal categories: white sauces and brown sauces.

Some sauces are made with a *roux* (page 75)—brown, light in color, or white—combined with milk or specially prepared stock; others are made by using egg yolks and butter, cream, or emulsified oil; and finally, some are made with a strong broth, fat or lean.

The white béchamel and *velouté* sauces and the brown sauce called *espagnole* are the basic sauces that have given rise, each in its own respective group, to a host of other sauces, some of which are listed on the following pages.

In preparing these sauces, the first is made with a white *roux* and milk; the second, with a light-colored *roux* and white juices or stock; and the third, with a brown *roux* and dark-colored juices or stock.

In home cooking the juices or stock can be replaced in part by bouillon; but the sauce will not have the same rich flavor.

Juices or cooking stocks

In the soup chapter I have included the recipe for the classic *pot-au-feu* from which light- or dark-colored stock is obtained.

Jus ou fond brun
BROWN STOCK

2 pounds veal meat
$1/2$ pound bones
1 medium carrot
2 medium onions
$1/4$ pound bacon rind
3 quarts water
Bouquet garni
$1/2$ teaspoon salt

To prepare this use veal meat and bones: shin, rump, neck, shoulder, or short ribs.

Method.   In a buttered or greased roasting pan, spread the meat, cut into cubes, and the bones, broken into small pieces; brown in a 375° oven. Stir frequently until the meat is well browned.

Meanwhile, peel and slice the vegetables and put them into a soup kettle. Cover them with the bacon rind; then put the browned meat and bones on top. Let the pot stand for 10 minutes at the side of the stove or over a very low flame to allow the vegetables to sweat their juices. Pour 1 cup boiling water into the roasting pan and stir to dissolve the substances that have stuck to it; then pour this water into the soup kettle, bring to a boil, and reduce by half. Do this last step again, adding another cup water. Be careful to turn off the heat when the liquid has thickened and it is reduced to 1 tablespoon. This procedure is called *faire tomber à glace* (reducing to a glaze).

Then add 2¹/₂ quarts water, the *bouquet garni,* and the salt. Slowly bring to the boiling point. Skim, and place the soup kettle on a low flame and cook very slowly, partially covered, for about 5 hours.

Then strain the stock through a very fine sieve into a bowl. Let it stand 15 minutes; then carefully remove the fat, which can be used for other dishes. When the stock is cool, strain it through cheesecloth into another bowl. Discard the sediment at the bottom of the bowl.

The stock made in this way will be clear, well flavored, and have a beautiful amber color.

In old French cooking, this stock was called *blond de veau* (blond veal)—a tasty expression.

Jus ou fond blanc
WHITE STOCK

White stock is prepared exactly like brown stock except that since the brown color is not desired, the meat is not browned.

The clarity that is characteristic of a white stock is obtained by boiling the soup slowly and watching it carefully.

Fond de volaille brun ou blanc
BROWN OR WHITE CHICKEN STOCK

To the appropriate recipe above add 1 hen or the giblets of 4 chickens. For a white stock do not brown the ingredients.

Fond de gibier
GAME STOCK

Use the cheaper cuts of large game, a roebuck, for example, or use a hare or a rabbit of about 2 pounds, plus a partridge, an old pheasant, or several carcasses.

Add a medium-sized carrot, a medium-sized onion, a sprig of sage, a few juniper berries, and a *bouquet garni.* Follow the recipe for brown stock (above) to brown the meat and bones and to cook the vegetables.

Brown the game in the oven, following the recipe for brown stock, then add 1 cup dry white wine and 2¹/₂ quarts water. Cook very slowly for 4 hours.

Fond de poisson dit fumet de poisson
STRONG FISH STOCK

For this recipe use any fish with white flesh easily available in markets, such as hake, whiting, brill, etc. However, none of

1 quart water
2 pounds white fish or sole
  backbones
2 large onions, thinly
  sliced
2 sprigs parsley or parsley
  root
2 tablespoons mushroom
  peels or cooking juice
Juice of 1/4 lemon
1 teaspoon salt
Mixed spices (page x)

these equals the backbones of sole, which are the only ones that can produce a "real" fish stock.

Method. The procedure is very simple.

In a deep pot, put the fish or sole backbones into cold water. After the water starts to boil, add the onions, a couple of sprigs of parsley or a parsley root, mushroom peels or their juice, lemon juice, and salt. Never forget that fish stock is almost always intended to be reduced for use in sauces or to be combined with butter or cream when a *roux* or egg yolks will not be added. That is why no salt or very little is added to a fish stock.

Bring to a boil, skim the stock, add the spices, reduce the flame, and boil slowly for 30 minutes. Strain through a cloth into a bowl and keep cool.

Courts-bouillons

Blanc pour cuissons diverses
WHITE COURT-BOUILLON FOR VARIOUS DISHES

1 quart water
1/2 tablespoon salt
1 tablespoon flour
2 teaspoons vinegar or
  juice of 1/2 lemon
1 onion, stuck with 1 clove
1 medium-sized carrot,
  quartered
Bouquet garni
2 tablespoons veal or beef
  kidney fat, chopped
  (optional)

The culinary expression *blanc* refers to a *court-bouillon* made from water, salt, flour, and vinegar—or, in certain cases, lemon juice.

Method. Mix the water, salt, flour, and vinegar or lemon juice before putting them over the heat. Then slowly bring to a boil.

Add a garnish of vegetables, such as onion and carrot, and a *bouquet garni.*

When this *court-bouillon* is to be used to cook giblets, it is advisable to add fat from a veal or beef kidney, which will melt during the cooking to form a protective coating to block out the air, which would darken the stock.

Cook the stock for 30 minutes; strain it through a fine sieve, and let it cool. Use it when required for a recipe.

The white stock, or *blanc,* is used for cooking variety meats, and also for cockscombs or cock's kidneys, or certain vegetables such as artichoke hearts, cardoons (a vegetable in the artichoke family), oyster plant or salsify, etc. The fat in that case is omitted.

Cuisson ou blanc pour champignons
WHITE COURT-BOUILLON FOR MUSHROOMS

1/2 cup water
1 teaspoon salt
3 tablespoons unsalted
  butter
Juice of 1/2 lemon
1/2 pound mushrooms,
  quickly washed

Method. Bring the water to a boil; add the salt, butter, and lemon juice. Return this to a high boil and add the mushrooms. Boil rapidly for 5 minutes, then pour into a glazed earthenware pot and cover with a piece of buttered paper to prevent any contact with air.

Roux: brown, blond, white

The *roux* is the thickening element of the sauce, except for such emulsified sauces as hollandaise, *béarnaise,* etc., in which the *roux* is replaced by egg yolks. The *roux* must be cooked with care and attention.

In all three cases, the proportions are identical: for ¼ pound butter, use 1 cup flour.

Method.   Melt the butter and cook it until it is clarified, that is, when the moisture in the butter has evaporated. Add the flour, and blend it into the butter with a spatula or wooden spoon.

Heat the mixture slowly and cook very gently to allow the active element of the flour—the starch—to change and to turn into dextrin, a soluble substance that has the property of thickening a liquid.

Stir frequently and, if you want a brown *roux,* continue cooking until it reaches the desired color. Cook the *roux* less for a blond (or light-colored) *roux,* and even less for a white *roux.*

Any *roux* must be cooked for at least 15 minutes.

The *roux* can be prepared in advance and kept in a cool place in an earthenware pot.

A *roux* is always used cold; in order to avoid lumps when mixing it with a boiling liquid, follow these directions:

Put the *roux* into the saucepan in which the sauce or soup will be cooked. Dilute the *roux* by adding a small amount of boiling liquid (juice, stock, bouillon, or milk) and mix with a whisk; the result should resemble a paste. When the mixture is very smooth, begin the first step again, adding liquid and at the same time heating slowly to the boiling point until the flour absorbs the entire quantity of liquid specified.

Note: In making brown sauces, we recommend that you use the method called *torréfaction* (roasting) of the dry flour. This thickener is less perishable and very simple to make: Spread the flour on a cookie sheet, and brown it in a 325° oven. Store the browned flour in a tightly sealed jar, so that it is ready for use at any time. Dilute it with cold stock and then bring to a boil.

Sauces mères or mother sauces

When the *roux* has been combined with liquids, as described above, if it is a brown *roux* and if the liquid ingredient is col-

¼ cup diced fresh pork fat
  or lard
1 medium carrot, finely
  diced
1 medium onion, finely
  diced
1 sprig thyme
Piece bay leaf
10 tablespoons cooked
  brown *roux*
2 quarts veal stock or
  brown bouillon, lightly
  salted
½ cup dry white wine
1 cup thick tomato purée

ored, it produces a sauce called *espagnole* (Spanish); if the *roux* is blond or light in color, and if the liquid ingredient is a white stock, the sauce is called a *velouté;* if the liquid ingredient is milk, the sauce is then called a béchamel.

Sauce espagnole
ESPAGNOLE OR BROWN SAUCE

Method. Melt the pork fat or lard in the pot in which you are going to cook the *espagnole* sauce. Add the diced vegetables *(mirepoix)* and seasonings and heat slowly until lightly browned.

Drain off the melted fat or lard, add the *roux,* the stock or other liquid (following the recipe for the *roux*), and then add the white wine.

Cook on a low flame and simmer for 2 hours, skimming frequently to remove the impurities and the fat that accumulate on the sides of the pot where the sauce is not bubbling (this step is called *dépouiller*).

If the *roux* has not been prepared in advance, it should be cooked first, in the same pot in which the sauce will cook. Then brown the *mirepoix* in a small frying pan, and add. Then deglaze the frying pan by pouring in the white wine and stirring up the brown drippings on the bottom; add the flavored wine to the sauce, and continue cooking for 2 hours as above.

At this point, strain the *espagnole* sauce through fine cheesecloth, then return it to the stove and add 1 cup thick tomato purée.

Cook very slowly for another hour, and skim off any impurities frequently.

If the *espagnole* sauce will not be used for a while, strain it through a fine sieve into a glazed earthenware bowl and stir it very frequently *(vanner)* with a wooden spoon until it is completely cool; this prevents the formation of a thick skin and consequently of lumps.

Demi-glace
RICH BROWN SAUCE

The *demi-glace* sauce is a derivative of *espagnole* sauce, in which the sauce has been reduced to two-thirds of its volume and then returned to the desired consistency by adding a rich veal stock that is very spicy. This explains why the basic sauces and the stocks with which they are made should always be salted very lightly.

Finish the *demi-glace* sauce off the flame by adding Madeira wine.

Sauce velouté ou sauce blanche
VELOUTÉ OR WHITE SAUCE

This sauce is made by mixing a blond *roux* (page 75) with a white stock or white bouillon, about ½ cup *roux* for 1 quart stock.

Proceed following the recipe given for the *roux;* cook slowly for 1½ hours, and skim as directed for *espagnole* sauce.

The consistency and flavor of this sauce should fit the description *velouté* (velvety), which is given to this sauce correctly because of its special character.

Sauce tomate
TOMATO SAUCE

½ cup pork fat or lard
1 medium-sized carrot, finely diced
1 medium-sized onion, finely diced
Sprig thyme
½ bay leaf
2 tablespoons unsalted butter
1 tablespoon flour
3 pounds very ripe tomatoes, juice and seeds removed
4 garlic cloves
Pinch salt
Pepper
1 cup white stock (page 73)
2 sugar cubes
1 scant tablespoon wine vinegar

Method. Prepare a *mirepoix* with pork fat or lard, a carrot, an onion, thyme, a bay leaf, and butter. Mix together and sauté until lightly browned in the pan in which the sauce will be made. Sprinkle with 1 tablespoon flour. Mix and cook gently like a blond *roux*. Add the tomatoes, garlic, salt, a little pepper, white stock and—finally—2 sugar cubes, melted until they are beginning to take on a light caramel color. Deglaze with wine vinegar.

Bring to a boil while stirring. Then cook gently, covered, in a 275° oven for at least 1½ hours.

Strain, then bring to a boil again and remove any sediment that may have accumulated in rubbing through the sieve; pour into a glazed bowl and store until ready to use. Dab the surface with a generous tablespoon of unsalted butter to prevent a skin from forming.

Sauce allemande appelée aussi sauce parisienne
ALLEMANDE OR PARISIAN SAUCE

1 quart *velouté* sauce (pages 76–7)
5 egg yolks
Pinch crushed pepper
Pinch grated nutmeg
4 tablespoons cooking juice from mushrooms
½ teaspoon lemon juice
8 tablespoons unsalted butter

Just as *demi-glace* sauce is a derivative of *espagnole* sauce, *allemande* sauce (literally German sauce, although, in fact, there is nothing German about its origin, just as *espagnole* sauce owes nothing to Spain) is a derivative of *velouté* sauce.

The *allemande* sauce is a *velouté* sauce that has been thickened with egg yolks. To thicken *allemande* sauce properly, proceed in the following manner:

Method. Bring the *velouté* sauce to a boil; reduce until it reaches the consistency of light cream, stirring constantly with a wooden spoon. The sauce should become shiny and should coat the wooden spoon evenly. At the same time in a bowl, put the egg yolks, a pinch of crushed pepper called *mignonnette,* a pinch of grated nutmeg, cooking juice from mushrooms, lemon juice, and 2 tablespoons unsalted butter.

With a whisk, beat the egg-yolk mixture, pouring some of the *velouté* sauce into it, by tablespoons. Then, off the flame, slowly pour the thickening ingredients into the sauce with your left hand while your right hand beats the *velouté* vigorously. Put the sauce back on the stove and heat it slowly to the boiling point, continuously whipping.

Remove from the flame immediately, and strain the sauce

through fine cheesecloth into an earthenware pot. Continue stirring until the sauce is completely cool.

Just before using the sauce, correct the seasoning, and off the flame mix in the remaining butter. After this sauce has been thickened, it should not be boiled except to preserve it.

Sauce suprême

1 quart *velouté* sauce (pages 76–7)
1 quart chicken stock, reduced to 1 cup
1³/₈ cups *crème fraîche* or heavy cream
¹/₄ pound unsalted butter

This very fine sauce is derived from *velouté* sauce, to which is added rich chicken stock and *crème fraîche* or heavy cream.

Method. In a skillet combine the *velouté* and reduced chicken stock. Bring this to the boiling point on a high flame, stirring continuously with a wooden spoon. Little by little, as the sauce is reduced, add ⁷/₈ cup *crème fraîche*. Continue this reduction until the mass of the *velouté*, the stock, and the cream have reduced to one-third their original volume. At that point, strain the sauce through cheesecloth, correct the seasoning, and finish by stirring to prevent a skin from forming, while adding ¹/₂ cup *crème fraîche* and unsalted butter.

This sauce is noted for its lightness, brilliance, and flavor.

Sauce béchamel
BÉCHAMEL SAUCE

1 quart milk
2 ounces lean white veal
Unsalted butter
1 minced onion
Sprig thyme
Pinch crushed pepper
Pinch grated nutmeg
Pinch salt

Method. Prepare a blond *roux* and, for each ¹/₂ cup, add 1 quart milk. Bring to a boil, being careful to stir continuously in order to obtain a perfectly smooth sauce. Then add 2 ounces lean white veal, diced and stewed in butter with minced onion, thyme, pepper, nutmeg, and salt.

Cook slowly for an hour. Pour the sauce through a sieve taking care not to dislodge the particles that stick to the sides of the saucepan, which generally get somewhat browned during the cooking time; strain the sauce into a glazed earthenware bowl.

Film the surface of the sauce with butter to avoid forming a skin and consequently lumps.

For reasons of economy or time, the veal can be omitted entirely. Obviously, the flavor of the sauce will not be so rich,

This sauce can also be prepared by replacing the veal with white-fleshed fish.

Sauce au beurre
BUTTER SAUCE

8 tablespoons unsalted butter
¹/₃ cup flour
1¹/₂ cups very hot water
Pinch salt
Few drops lemon juice (optional)
2 egg yolks

Method. Make a blond *roux* with 4 tablespoons butter and ¹/₃ cup flour. Cook the *roux* for 15 minutes, let it cool; then add very hot water, whipping the mixture vigorously to obtain a smooth paste. Add a pinch of salt and, if the main recipe calls for it, lemon juice. Bring to a boil, remove from the flame, and add 4 tablespoons or more unsalted butter. This sauce should be creamy, and can be finished with a little more lemon juice. Finally, thicken the sauce with 2 egg yolks, as in the recipe for *allemande* sauce, but do not bring to a boil.

Note: The butter and the flour can be mixed without cooking a *roux:* stir the flour into softened butter and moisten with water that is nearly boiling. Bring to a boil, then remove from the flame to add the final butter. The result is equally excellent.

Plain brown sauces

Jus lié
THICKENED JUICE—GRAVY

1 quart brown veal stock (page 72)
1 teaspoon cornstarch or, preferably, 1 teaspoon tapioca, mixed with cold veal stock

Method.   Bring the veal stock to a boil and cook until reduced by three-fourths; then thicken with 1 teaspoon cornstarch mixed with a little cold veal stock. Boil 2 to 3 minutes; keep warm.

The sauce should be clear and smooth, and have the consistency of the juices left in a casserole after a piece of veal has been braised and sweated its juices.

The use of cornstarch or arrowroot (a very fine starch) as a thickening agent is a culinary trick that gives an appetizing appearance but it is detrimental to the flavor. It is better to use tapioca instead of starch, in the quantity specified. The tapioca must be cooked at least 15 minutes barely bubbling so that the gravy remains clear.

Sauce bordelaise

2 tablespoons unsalted butter
1 teaspoon chopped shallots
1 cup very good red Bordeaux wine
Pinch crushed pepper
Small piece bay leaf
Sprig cultivated or wild thyme
1 cup *demi-glace* sauce (page 76) or *espagnole* sauce (page 76)
2 ounces beef marrow, very fresh

Method.   In a saucepan, heat 1 tablespoon butter; when the butter is very hot, add the shallots; brown lightly. Add the wine and spices, bring the sauce to a boil, and reduce rapidly until 2 tablespoons remain. Add the *demi-glace* sauce and boil for 15 minutes. Strain the sauce through a very fine sieve; bring to a boil again, correct the seasoning, and set aside until ready to serve. Poach the marrow in a bowl of lightly salted hot water for 3 to 5 minutes. Drain and set aside. When ready to serve, warm the sauce slightly. Off the flame, add the rest of the butter to the sauce, stirring continuously with a wooden spoon while adding the marrow.

Sauce madère
MADEIRA SAUCE

Follow the recipe for madeira sauce with mushrooms (page 80), but use mushroom trimmings or stems and strain them through cheesecloth before the sauce is "finished," that is, before adding the Madeira and the butter.

½ pound mushrooms, small and very white
4 tablespoons unsalted butter
2 cups *demi-glace* sauce (page 76) or–though not as good–*espagnole* sauce (page 76)
½ cup very good Madeira

Sauce madère et champignons

MADEIRA SAUCE WITH MUSHROOMS

Method. Clean mushrooms by removing the sandy bottoms of the stems and washing rapidly; do not let mushrooms stand in water or they will get brown.

Heat 4 teaspoons butter in a skillet. When the butter is very hot, the color of a filbert, add the mushrooms, drained, and sauté rapidly over a high flame; then add the *demi-glace* sauce. Boil the wine to reduce it slightly; then off the flame add the reduced Madeira, slightly cooled, to the sauce, and the rest of the butter while stirring.

Correct the seasoning before serving.

1 salmon head
¾ cup vegetable *brunoise*
2½ cups red wine
1½ cups *bordelaise* sauce (page 79)
¼ cup mushroom stems
¼ pound unsalted butter
1 tablespoon anchovy butter or 1 teaspoon anchovy paste (optional)

Sauce genevoise

Method. Gently cook a salmon head, covered, for 15 minutes, with vegetable *brunoise* (*mirepoix* that has been sautéed in butter and oil). Drain off the fat and add very good red wine. Boil to reduce the sauce to ½ cup, add *bordelaise* sauce without the marrow, and mushroom stems. Cook slowly for 15 minutes, skim, strain through cheesecloth. Bring the sauce back to a boil; then off the flame, add butter. To enhance the sauce, 1 tablespoon anchovy butter or 1 teaspoon anchovy paste could be added.

9 tablespoons butter
1 medium-sized onion, finely chopped
1 cup very dry white wine
1½ cups *demi-glace* sauce (page 76) or *espagnole* sauce (page 76)
½ cup chopped or sliced *cornichons*

Sauce charcutière

Method. In a skillet melt 1 tablespoon butter; when the butter is very hot, add the onion. Brown slowly, then pour in the very dry white wine. Reduce the mixture until 2 tablespoons remain; add the *demi-glace* or *espagnole* sauce. Cook slowly for 15 minutes; then, just before serving, off the flame add 8 tablespoons butter and the *cornichons* (small sour pickles), stirring continuously.

½ pound mushrooms
4 tablespoons unsalted butter
6 shallots, chopped
1 cup dry white wine
2 generous cups *demi-glace* sauce (page 76) or *espagnole* sauce (page 76)
1 teaspoon chopped parsley
Juice of ¼ lemon

Sauce gratin

Method. Clean and wash the mushrooms quickly and drain immediately. In a skillet, heat 1 tablespoon butter until light brown; add the shallots and cook slowly. Then add the mushrooms, finely chopped at the last moment, to keep them from turning brown. Cook the mushrooms on a very high flame, stirring constantly to keep them from exuding their juices. Add the white wine and reduce it almost completely. Then add the *demi-glace* or *espagnole* sauce.

Simmer over a low flame for 10 minutes. Finish the sauce off the flame by adding the remaining butter and, at the last minute, 1 teaspoon chopped parsley and the juice of ¼ lemon.

This sauce should be quite thick.

Sauce piquante

1 medium-sized onion,
  finely chopped
2 large shallots, finely
  chopped
5 tablespoons butter
3 tablespoons red wine
  vinegar, reduced to 2
  teaspoons
1 1/2 cups *demi-glace* sauce
  (page 76) or *espagnole*
  sauce (page 76)
2 medium-sized
  cornichons, chopped
Freshly ground pepper

Method.   Finely chop 1 medium onion and 2 shallots. Heat 1 tablespoon butter in a skillet, add the onion and shallots, and cook slowly until they begin to soften; when lightly browned, add the reduced wine vinegar and 1 1/2 cups *demi-glace* or *espagnole* sauce.

Cook slowly for 15 minutes, and off the flame add 4 tablespoons butter. Finish the sauce by adding the *cornichons* and a few turns of the pepper mill.

Sauce Robert

This is a *sauce piquante* (recipe above) to which 2 teaspoons mustard and a pinch of powdered sugar are added just before the butter.

Never let the mustard boil.

Sauce à l'estragon
TARRAGON SAUCE

1 cup dry white wine,
  reduced to 1/2 cup
Sprig tarragon
1 1/2 cup *demi-glace* sauce
  (page 76), *espagnole*
  sauce (page 76), or
  thickened stock
4 tablespoons unsalted
  butter
1 teaspoon chopped
  tarragon leaves

Method.   Add the tarragon sprig to the reduced wine, and let stand for 10 minutes. Then add 1 1/2 cups *demi-glace* sauce, *espagnole* sauce, or thickened stock. Reduce the sauce by one-third, strain through cheesecloth or a very fine sieve, then off the flame add the butter.

Season with 1 teaspoon chopped tarragon leaves.

Sauce chasseur
HUNTER'S SAUCE

4 tablespoons unsalted
  butter
2 tablespoons oil
1/4 pound mushrooms,
  white and firm
1 teaspoon chopped
  shallots
3 ripe tomatoes or 3
  tablespoons tomato
  purée
2 generous cups dry white
  wine
1 cup *demi-glace* sauce
  (page 76) or *espagnole*
  sauce (page 76)
Large pinch each chopped
  chervil and tarragon

Method.   In a skillet heat the butter and the oil, add the mushrooms finely sliced or chopped; brown on a high flame. At that point add the shallots and heat for a few seconds. If you are using fresh tomatoes (which are preferable), remove the stems and the skin around them, the seeds, and the juice; chop coarsely and add to the sauce after adding the shallots. If you are using tomato purée, first add the white wine and reduce by one-half. Finally add the *demi-glace* or *espagnole* sauce and tomato purée.

Off the flame, just before serving, finish the sauce by adding the rest of the butter, the chervil, and the tarragon.

Sauce diable
DEVILED SAUCE

Follow the recipe for *sauce charcutière* (page 80), but omit the pickles and replace the onion with 3 shallots. Strain the sauce through cheesecloth and spice it heavily with freshly ground pepper or a pinch of cayenne pepper, which I do not like as much. It is, in fact, not an aroma but a fire that burns the palate.

Sauce italienne
ITALIAN SAUCE

4 tablespoons unsalted butter
¼ pound very white mushrooms, chopped
1 teaspoon chopped shallots
½ cup dry white wine
1 tablespoon thick tomato purée or 3 ripe tomatoes
1 cup *demi-glace* sauce (page 76) or *espagnole* sauce (page 76)
Scant ¼ cup finely diced lean ham
Juice of ¼ lemon
Chopped parsley

Method. In a frying pan heat 1 tablespoon butter; add chopped mushrooms and brown lightly; add shallots and white wine. Reduce the mixture to 2 tablespoons; add tomato purée or the ripe tomatoes, peeled, seeded, and chopped. Reduce the mixture again, and add the *demi-glace* or *espagnole* sauce and the ham.

Boil slowly for 10 minutes; off the flame add 3 tablespoons butter and lemon juice. Correct the seasoning, and finish the sauce with a pinch of chopped parsley.

Depending upon one's taste or the use intended, you will find that this sauce is also very good with a pinch of chopped tarragon.

Sauce Périgueux

Prepare a Madeira sauce (page 79); finish by adding, for 2½ cups sauce, 3½ ounces chopped truffles. If you are using canned truffles, add the juice in which they come. If they are fresh, chop them raw, then sauté quickly in hot butter for a few seconds, and pour the truffles and butter into the Madeira sauce.

Sauce périgourdine
PÉRIGORD SAUCE

This sauce is the same as the one above, but the truffles here are sliced extremely thin instead of being chopped.

Sauce au vin rouge
RED WINE SAUCE

1 large onion, diced
1 medium-sized carrot (core removed), diced
4½ tablespoons unsalted butter
2 garlic cloves, crushed
2 cups very good red wine
Pinch salt
Pinch sugar
2 cups *demi-glace* sauce (page 76) or *espagnole* sauce (page 76)

Method. Stew the *mirepoix* of the onion and carrot in 1 tablespoon butter for 20 minutes, stirring often; do not let the mixture brown. When the *mirepoix* is well cooked, add the garlic. Heat the mixture for a minute and pour in the red wine. Season with a pinch of salt and a pinch of sugar. Reduce the sauce to two-thirds, then add the *demi-glace* or *espagnole* sauce, and cook slowly for 20 minutes. Strain through cheesecloth, pushing the vegetables through. Bring the sauce back to a boil; finish off the flame by adding at least 3½ tablespoons butter.

Sauce au vin de porto

PORT WINE SAUCE

Follow the recipe for Madeira sauce (page 79), replacing the Madeira wine with port. Finish this sauce by adding the juice of a very ripe and very sweet orange and the juice of $1/2$ lemon.

Sauce rouennaise

ROUEN SAUCE

2 generous cups
  ***bordelaise* sauce**
  (page 79)
3 raw duck livers
1 tablespoon cognac or
  fine champagne brandy
3$1/2$ tablespoons unsalted
  butter or 1$3/4$ ounces
  purée of *foie gras*
Freshly ground pepper

Method. Prepare *bordelaise* sauce without marrow. Rub the duck livers through a very fine sieve into a bowl and dilute with a little *bordelaise* sauce. Heat the sauce. When it is hot but not boiling, add the duck livers, stirring continuously until it reaches the boiling point.

Remove from the heat and strain through cheesecloth; the livers should then be completely incorporated into the sauce, giving it a creamy appearance. Finish by adding the cognac or fine champagne brandy and 3$1/2$ tablespoons unsalted butter or 1$3/4$ ounces purée of *foie gras*.

Correct the seasoning. Spice with a couple of turns of a pepper mill.

Sauce poivrade

PEPPER SAUCE

1 medium-sized carrot
  (core removed), very
  finely diced
2 medium-sized onions,
  finely diced
1 celery rib, finely diced
1 tablespoon unsalted
  butter
2 generous cups game
  marinade
3$1/4$ cups *demi-glace* sauce
  (page 76) or *espagnole*
  sauce (page 76)
Game trimmings or
  carcasses
1 teaspoon gooseberry
  jelly (optional)
1 teaspoon Dijon mustard
  (optional)
Freshly ground pepper

[*Editor's note:* This sauce is usually served with game.]
Method. Cook the carrot, onions, and celery rib in the butter until they are lightly browned.

Pour over 2 generous cups liquid drained from the marinade in which the game has steeped. Reduce by two-thirds and add the *demi-glace* or *espagnole* sauce, and the carcasses or trimmings from the game.

Cook covered, on a low flame, for 3 hours.

Strain through cheesecloth, forcing the remains of the vegetables and the game trimmings through.

Deglaze the meat juices from the pan in which the game has roasted and add its juices. Off the flame add 1 teaspoon gooseberry jelly and 1 teaspoon Dijon mustard. These additions are optional. Do not let the mustard boil.

Season this sauce with freshly ground pepper.

Sauce à la moelle

MARROWBONE SAUCE
For Vegetables

This sauce is prepared in the same way as *bordelaise* sauce (page 79), but the red wine is replaced by white wine and the quantity of marrowbone is doubled. Half the marrow should be diced and added to the sauce, while the other half should be sliced and added to the vegetables.

This sauce can also be served with poached eggs or soft-boiled eggs (which are the ideal "poached" eggs) or with broiled fish.

Sauce portugaise
PORTUGUESE SAUCE

1 large onion
2 tablespoons oil
1½ pounds ripe tomatoes
3 garlic cloves, crushed
Pinch salt
Pinch pepper
Pinch sugar
Bouquet garni
Unsalted butter

Method. Finely chop the onion; brown lightly in the oil; add beautiful ripe tomatoes, peeled, seeded, drained, and coarsely chopped; garlic, salt, pepper, sugar, and the *bouquet garni.*

Cook slowly for 30 minutes.

Correct the seasoning and if the sauce is not to be used to deglaze the pan juices of the dish it will accompany, off the flame add a generous quantity of unsalted butter before serving it.

Sauce duxelles

1 teaspoon chopped shallots
1 tablespoon unsalted butter
¼ pound white mushrooms
½ cup dry white wine
¾ cup *demi-glace* sauce (page 76) or *espagnole* sauce (page 76) or veal stock with tomato sauce
Unsalted butter
1 teaspoon chopped parsley

Method. In a skillet lightly brown the shallots in 1 tablespoon butter. Add ¼ pound firm white mushrooms, cleaned, washed quickly, and finely chopped.

Cook until dry on a high flame, then add the wine and cook until it evaporates. Add *demi-glace* or *espagnole* sauce or a good veal stock; if you use veal stock, finish the sauce with 2 tablespoons very thick and concentrated tomato sauce.

Cook for a few minutes, reducing the sauce by one-third.

Off the flame add a generous quantity of unsalted butter and chopped parsley; correct the seasoning.

Note: For certain dishes, the *duxelles* is used without any liquid ingredients. Follow the instructions in the recipe.

White sauces

Sauce Mornay

2 generous cups béchamel sauce (page 78)
1¾ ounces grated gruyère cheese
2 egg yolks
1 tablespoon cream or milk
2 or 3 tablespoons cream
2 tablespoons unsalted butter

Method. Bring the béchamel sauce to a boil. Add the grated gruyère cheese. Boil, stirring until the cheese is completely melted. Take the pan off the flame so that it stops boiling, and thicken the sauce with the egg yolks mixed in a bowl with 1 tablespoon cream or milk. Heat gently, stirring quickly with a sauce whisk, until it reaches the boiling point.

Finish the sauce off the flame with 2 or 3 tablespoons cream and 2 tablespoons butter.

This sauce should be thick enough to cover completely the food with which it is served; although it looks thick, it must be creamy and flavorful.

When the sauce is to accompany a fish, add some of the cooking juice, reduced.

Sauce Nantua

2 generous cups béchamel
sauce (page 76)
1 cup *crème fraîche* or
heavy cream
3½ tablespoons crayfish
butter (page 19)

Method. Prepare 2 cups béchamel sauce, add the *crème fraîche*. Reduce rapidly, stirring with a spatula until it reaches the proper consistency—slightly thickened. Off the flame finish the sauce with the crayfish butter. Beat the sauce well and correct the seasoning.

Sauce cardinal

Follow the recipe above and finish the sauce with lobster butter (page 20) replacing the crayfish butter. This sauce is better if it is stronger than the Nantua sauce. To do this add 1 cup strong fish stock (pages 73–4) reduced to about 1 tablespoon. One can also add 1 tablespoon truffle juice, when truffles are used to garnish the dish.

Sauce aux câpres commune

CAPER SAUCE

Mix a butter sauce (page 78) with very fine capers, about 3 tablespoons for 2 generous cups of sauce. Do not let the sauce boil after adding the capers.

Sauce crème

CREAM SAUCE

4½ cups béchamel sauce
(page 78)
1 cup *crème fraîche* or
heavy cream
½ cup cream
3½ tablespoons unsalted
butter
Few drops lemon juice

Method. In a saucepan, mix the béchamel sauce and *crème fraîche*. Bring to a boil, then reduce the sauce on a high flame, stirring constantly with a spatula, until 3¼ cups sauce remain.

Strain through cheesecloth; bring back to a boil, then off the flame add ½ cup cream, butter, and lemon juice. Keep it hot in a *bain-marie* (double boiler), but see that it does not boil any more.

Sauce au vin blanc

WHITE WINE SAUCE
For Fish

2 cups *velouté* sauce with
fish stock (page 76)
½ cup fish stock (pages
73–4)
½ cup dry white wine
reduced to 1 tablespoon
2 egg yolks
2 tablespoons *crème
fraîche* or heavy cream
2 tablespoons cooking
juice from mushrooms
¼ pound unsalted butter

Method. Prepare 2 cups *velouté* sauce made with concentrated fish stock, mixing in ½ cup fish stock and ½ cup dry white wine reduced to 1 tablespoon; thicken with 2 egg yolks mixed with 2 tablespoons *crème fraîche* and 2 tablespoons cooking juice from mushrooms. Strain the sauce through cheesecloth; pour into a saucepan and, stirring constantly, heat to the boiling point; add the butter off the flame.

Sauce crevette
SHRIMP SAUCE

Use 2 generous cups white wine sauce (page 85) and add $\frac{1}{4}$ pound shrimp butter (page 19). This sauce should have a pale rose color, which can be obtained by adding a little bit of colored butter—crayfish or lobster or rock lobster—or a little reduced tomato purée.

Sauce Joinville

Prepare white wine sauce (page 85), and enrich it with the addition of as much butter as possible, consisting of half shrimp butter (page 19) and half crayfish butter (page 19). Finish the sauce with 1 tablespoon truffles, cut into julienne, for each cup of sauce.

Sauce Chantilly ou sauce mousseline commune

Prepare 2 generous cups butter sauce (page 78), and add, to finish it, 4 tablespoons *crème fraîche* or heavy cream, whipped until firm with 1 tablespoon milk. Be careful not to beat too long, or the cream may turn into butter.

Sauce normande
NORMAN SAUCE

Use 2 generous cups *velouté* sauce (page 76) made with strong fish stock (pages 73–4); add 1 cup cooking juice from mushrooms and $\frac{1}{2}$ cup liquid in which oysters have poached. Reduce the sauce by one-third, then thicken with 4 egg yolks mixed with 3 tablespoons *crème frâiche* or heavy cream. Strain through cheesecloth and place over the flame; heat to the boiling point, stirring continuously. Off the flame, immediately incorporate $\frac{1}{4}$ pound unsalted butter by beating vigorously.

Sauce soubise

$\frac{1}{2}$ **pound onions, finely chopped**
$5\frac{1}{2}$ **tablespoons unsalted butter**
2 generous cups béchamel sauce (page 78)
2 tablespoons *crème fraîche* or heavy cream

Method. Cook the onions for 1 minute in boiling water; drain, rinse, drain well, then stew slowly for 20 minutes in a frying pan with 2 tablespoons butter. The onions must not brown. Add the béchamel sauce. Cook slowly, covered, for 20 minutes; then strain through cheesecloth, pushing through the onions to make a purée. Bring to a boil again and finish the sauce with the *crème fraîche* and $3\frac{1}{2}$ tablespoons butter stirred in off the flame.

Sauce soubise tomatée

Prepare a soubise sauce as above and mix with thickened tomato purée, 2 parts sauce to 1 part tomato purée.

Sauce hollandaise commune

Use 2 generous cups either butter sauce (page 78) or béchamel sauce (page 78) thickened with 3 egg yolks mixed with 2 tablespoons cooking juice from mushrooms or with 1 tablespoons water to which a couple of drops of lemon juice have been added. Then off the flame add unsalted butter. The more butter you add, the finer this sauce is. It should be thick and creamy.

Sauce aux herbes
HERB SAUCE

Use 2 generous cups butter sauce (page 78); season just before serving with 2 tablespoons parsley, chervil, tarragon—all chopped, parboiled, rinsed, and dried.

Sauce Smitane

1 large onion, finely chopped
3 tablespoons unsalted butter
1 cup dry white wine
2 generous cups *crème fraîche* or heavy cream
Pinch salt
Lemon juice

Method.   Boil the onion for 1 minute, drain, rinse, drain, then stew slowly for 20 minutes in a frying pan with 1 tablespoon butter. Stir frequently and do not let brown. Add the wine, and boil until wine has evaporated. Add the *crème fraîche* and salt. Bring to a boil, reduce rapidly by one-third. Strain the sauce through a double layer of cheesecloth. Bring back to a boil; then off the flame add 2 tablespoons butter cut into tiny pieces; stir the sauce, and flavor with lemon juice so that it has a slightly tart taste.

Sauce Bercy

For Fish

2 teaspoons chopped shallots
1 cup dry white wine
1 cup strong fish stock (pages 73–4)
3¼ cups *velouté* sauce (page 76)
¼ pound unsalted butter
Freshly ground pepper
Pinch chopped parsley

Method.   Cook the shallots in 1 teaspoon butter for 15 minutes without browning; add wine and strong fish stock. Reduce by one-third and add *velouté* sauce made with strong fish stock.

Bring to a boil, and boil for 10 minutes; finish the sauce off the flame by adding ¼ pound butter. Spice the sauce with freshly ground pepper. Just before serving, add a large pinch of freshly chopped parsley.

Sauce au cari
CURRY SAUCE

Method.   Finely chop the onion; cook slowly, covered, in but-

87

1 medium-sized onion
1 tablespoon unsalted
  butter
Sprig thyme
1/2 bay leaf
Pinch mace
3 tablespoons flour
1 1/2 tablespoons curry
  powder
3 1/4 cups white stock (page
  73) or strong fish stock
  (pages 73–4)
4 tablespoons *crème
  fraîche* or coconut milk

ter. Add thyme, bay leaf, a pinch of mace. Sprinkle with flour
and curry powder. Cook for 10 minutes, stirring frequently.

Add the white stock or strong fish stock, if the sauce is
for fish. Simmer for 30 minutes; strain the sauce through
cheesecloth, squeezing all the ingredients firmly, and bring to
a boil. Finish the sauce with the *crème fraîche* or, if you have
it, coconut milk.

Note: Curry sauce can be made by using a simple local
method: Prepare a very rich poultry stock to which has been
added a very strong veal stock; season well with stewed onions and imported curry powder. After cooking, strain through
cheesecloth and thicken with arrowroot.

Emulsified rich sauces

Sauce hollandaise

1 tablespoon white wine
  vinegar
3 tablespoons water
Pinch crushed white
  peppercorns
3 egg yolks
1/2 pound excellent quality
  unsalted butter

Method. In a small saucepan combine the vinegar, 1 tablespoon water, and pepper; reduce this mixture, called *gas-
trique,* to 1 teaspoon.

Cool the mixture; then add the egg yolks and 2 tablespoons cold water. Mix together with a whisk, and heat slowly,
beating continuously and being careful to scrape up the sauce
on the bottom of the pan—so that all the egg yolks are incorporated.

For an inexperienced cook it is advisable to place the
saucepan in a double boiler over water that is very hot but not
boiling. The egg yolks will take longer to cook, but the success of the sauce is more certain. In fact, one is trying to form
a thickening element for the butter—an extremely smooth
support—and, if you use too much heat or cook the yolks too
fast, they will solidify into small lumps and lose their thickening property and smoothness.

Therefore this first step, the most difficult one, consists of
emulsifying the yolks by submitting them to a progressively
increasing heat, which will make the sauce very thick, smooth,
and creamy.

When the egg-yolk emulsion reaches the consistency of
very thick cream, incorporate the butter, melted or cut into tiny
pieces, bit by bit, whipping vigorously, and add a pinch of salt.

If you notice that the sauce is getting too thick and solid,
from time to time, while you are whipping the sauce (which is
called *monter une sauce,* making a sauce mount), add a few
drops of tepid water. This method is preferable to suddenly
adding extra liquid to lighten the sauce when it is finished.

This is the way that a hollandaise sauce becomes savory,
somewhat thickened, but still light. Correct the seasoning
and keep warm in a double boiler over very low heat.

Too much heat will cause the yolks to separate from the
butter. Then the sauce has become *tourné*—curdled.

If this happens, heat 1 tablespoon water in a saucepan, then, beating continuously, add small quantities of the sauce that has separated.

You may omit the vinegar mixture, depending on your taste and what the sauce will be used for.

If the vinegar is not used, the sauce is seasoned—acidulated—with a few drops of lemon juice.

These techniques and the use of first-quality butter are sure guarantees of success: the sauce is really delicious.

As an economy measure, one can add to this sauce one part, more or less, of butter sauce (page 78). This practice is not recommended; however, it lowers the price of the sauce and keeps it from being too sensitive to high heat.

Sauce mousseline

This is a hollandaise sauce, made as above, to which beaten heavy cream, about one-third part, is added.

Sauce béarnaise
(For 6 people)

½ pound unsalted butter
3 medium shallots
3 tablespoons white wine vinegar
2 sprigs tarragon
¼ teaspoon chopped chervil
Pinch salt
Pinch crushed peppercorns
4 egg yolks

Method. In a small saucepan melt 1 tablespoon butter. Add the shallots, finely chopped. Cook slowly for 10 minutes; add vinegar, 1 sprig tarragon, pinch of chervil, and the salt and pepper. Reduce the mixture to about 2 teaspoons. Then proceed exactly as for hollandaise sauce (page 88), heating the yolks until they have thickened.

Strain the finished sauce through cheesecloth. Add a pinch of finely chopped tarragon and chervil, and keep warm in a double boiler. This sauce should be much thicker than a hollandaise; that is why more egg yolks are required. The sauce should have the consistency of mustard.

Just as with the hollandaise sauce, one part of butter sauce can be used, but then the *béarnaise* loses much of its fine taste.

Sauce Choron

Make a *béarnaise* sauce, and add very concentrated tomato purée equal to one-fourth the total amount of the *béarnaise.*

Sauce maltaise

Make hollandaise sauce and add the juice of blood oranges and a few drops of curaçao liqueur.

Cold sauces

Sauce mayonnaise

The "mother sauce" *par excellence* of a number of cold sauces, mayonnaise deserves a detailed technical explanation.

The concept is simple and very old; culinary researchers have found clear references to it in the works of Apicius, which does not mean that there are not even more ancient sources. Mayonnaise is easy to make under certain conditions.

It originated in the south and is sensitive to the cold. Since it is made with a fluid ingredient that is quite inert, it requires strong beating to be savory and light.

The cook, therefore, should be careful of the temperature of both the container in which the mayonnaise will be made and the oil, and should observe the following instructions:

Method. Remove the stringy white from the egg yolks and put them in a bowl with salt, pepper, and vinegar or lemon juice. Mix with a whisk to give more body to the yolks. Then add the oil, drop by drop in the beginning, continuously whipping the mixture. If the mixture thickens too much, dilute with 1 teaspoon vinegar (or water if the sauce is tart enough). Continue adding oil at a faster speed as the volume of the sauce increases.

It is important in making mayonnaise to produce a creamy sauce thick enough so that as you incorporate air in it, you can obtain the maximum lightness while it remains very smooth and oily.

As in making hollandaise sauce, the oil, a fat and fluid ingredient, adheres to the egg yolks, which serve as a thickening agent; but this association takes place slowly and requires vigorous mixing, which increases the temperature of the mass and its area.

I do not hesitate to recommend the substitution of a wooden spoon or a spatula for the whisk for home use in beating to increase the volume of the mayonnaise sauce. It will progress much more slowly, but the success—the flavor and results—will be much greater.

Finally, when the mayonnaise is finished, it will be less liable to separate if you add a few teaspoonfuls boiling wine vinegar.

Mayonnaise that is separating can be fixed easily by reversing the errors that one has made in preparing it: either the oil is too cold or it has been poured in too fast—one or the other. The remedy is to put 1 tablespoon warm water in a bowl; then beat vigorously while adding, little by little, the mayonnaise that has curdled.

6 egg yolks, at room
   temperature
$^3/_4$ tablespoon fine salt
Large pinch freshly ground
   white pepper
$1^1/_2$ tablespoons wine
   vinegar or lemon juice
$5^1/_4$ cups oil, at room
   temperature

Sauce verte
GREEN MAYONNAISE

Prepare 1 quart mayonnaise (above). Then pound in a mortar or chop a large handful spinach, washed clean and trimmed, mixed with a sprig of tarragon and a good pinch of chervil. Put the herbs in cheesecloth and squeeze the juice into a small double boiler, and heat.

The action of the heat will make the herb juices separate into solid and clear parts.

When the green substances are sufficiently solidified, strain everything through cheesecloth. This green paste will then be mixed with the mayonnaise to turn it green. Finish the sauce with pinches of chervil, parsley, chives, and tarragon—all very finely chopped.

Sauce rémoulade

1 quart mayonnaise (page 90)
2 tablespoons capers
6 *cornichons*
Fines herbes (parsley, chervil, tarragon, chives)
1 teaspoon anchovy purée (optional)

Method. Mix mayonnaise with 2 tablespoons capers and 6 *cornichons* (small sour pickles), finely chopped, plus the *fines herbes,* and, depending upon your taste, 1 teaspoon anchovy purée.

Sauce tartare

This has the same ingredients as rémoulade sauce above, but instead of anchovy purée, use 2 tablespoons Dijon mustard.

Sauce Vincent

To 1 generous cup green mayonnaise (above), add 12 leaves young sorrel, finely chopped, and 3 hard-cooked egg yolks, rubbed through a fine sieve. Finish the sauce with 1 teaspoon chopped chervil and tarragon.

Sauce gribiche

3 hard-cooked eggs
Salt
Pepper
1 teaspoon mustard
2 tablespoons vinegar
1 cup oil
1 teaspoon chopped chervil
1 teaspoon chopped tarragon
1 teaspoon capers
3 chopped *cornichons*

Method. Put the egg yolks into a bowl with the salt, pepper, and mustard. Mash them well; then add to this paste the vinegar and then the oil, drop by drop, as in making mayonnaise. Keep the sauce constantly creamy by adding small amounts of vinegar or tepid water, if necessary. Finish the sauce by adding the chopped herbs, the capers, the *cornichons,* and the white of 1 hard-cooked egg, diced very finely. Correct the seasoning.

This sauce is a mayonnaise in which the egg yolks are cooked instead of raw.

Sauce mayonnaise à la crème

CREAMY MAYONNAISE

To mayonnaise (page 90) made with lemon juice instead of vinegar, add one-quarter part whipped heavy cream.

Correct the seasoning.

1/2 tablespoon salt
Pinch freshly ground
  pepper
2 tablespoons capers
1 teaspoon chopped
  parsley
1 teaspoon chopped
  tarragon
1 teaspoon mustard
1 onion, finely chopped
2 tablespoons vinegar
5 tablespoons oil

8 garlic cloves
2 egg yolks
Pinch salt
1 1/4 cups oil
Juice of 1/2 lemon

1 pound white bread
1 teaspoon mustard
2 tablespoons vinegar
3 tablespoons finely grated
  fresh horseradish
Pinch salt
3 tablespoons sugar
1 1/4 cups *crème fraîche* or
  heavy cream

1 large onion, finely
  chopped
2 shallots, finely chopped
3 tablespoons olive oil
1 cup dry white wine
2 cups tomatoes
Salt
Freshly ground pepper
1/2 cup olive oil
Juice of 1/2 lemon

Sauce ravigote

Method.   In a bowl combine salt, a pinch of freshly ground pepper, slightly crushed capers, chopped parsley, chopped tarragon, mustard, and the onion; while beating vigorously with a whisk, pour in, little by little, the vinegar and oil.

When the sauce accompanies a calf's head or calf's feet, add 3 tablespoons of the warm cooking liquid from the veal.

Sauce aïoli

AÏOLI OR GARLIC SAUCE

Method.   Crush the garlic in a mortar; mix the egg yolks into the garlic paste, then add the salt. Add the oil, drop by drop, mixing continuously with the pestle. Keep the consistency creamy by adding a few drops of lemon juice from time to time (the lemon juice forms the acid element in the sauce) and tepid water.

Sauce andalouse

ANDALUSIAN SAUCE

To 1 quart mayonnaise (page 90) add 1 1/3 cups very thick tomato purée and 2 sweet green peppers cut into very thin strips.

Sauce raifort

HORSERADISH SAUCE

Method.   Remove crusts from the bread, soak it in milk, and squeeze dry. In a bowl, dilute the mustard with the vinegar; mix in the horseradish, salt, sugar, and bread. Thin this paste with the cream.

Sauce portugaise froide

COLD PORTUGUESE SAUCE

Method.   Cook the onion and shallots slowly in a skillet with 3 tablespoons olive oil. When they are transparent, pour over the wine and boil to reduce almost completely.

Add the tomatoes, peeled, seeded, and chopped—do not squeeze out the juice. Season with salt and freshly ground pepper; cook and reduce until mixture has reached the consistency of a fairly thin purée. Off the flame thicken the sauce by beating in 1/2 cup olive oil; add the lemon juice. Correct the seasoning.

Sauce rouennaise froide

COLD ROUEN SAUCE

2 cups *bordelaise* sauce
(page 79)
1 duck liver or 2 chicken
livers
Pinch salt
Freshly ground pepper
1 tablespoon champagne
brandy or cognac
¼ cup gelatinous veal
stock
2 tablespoons sherry

Method.　Prepare 2 cups *bordelaise* sauce.

Meanwhile, sauté the liver of a small duck or 2 chicken livers and rub through a fine sieve. Season with a pinch of salt and a little bit of freshly ground pepper. Then dilute the liver purée with fine champagne brandy or a good cognac.

Add ¼ cup gelatinous veal stock to the *bordelaise* sauce and reduce the mixture, over high heat, to about 1¼ cups; correct the seasoning.

Off the heat thicken the sauce with the liver purée, first adding a couple of tablespoons of the reduced sauce to the purée and then pouring the liver mixture into the sauce. Mix well with a whisk while pouring in the liver mixture. Strain through cheesecloth, forcing the liver through.

When the sauce is tepid, season with 2 tablespoons sherry.

Sauce chaud-froid blanche

WHITE CHAUD-FROID SAUCE (For 2 generous cups)

2½ cups blond *roux*
(page 75)
3½ cups white chicken
bouillon, heavily
seasoned (page 73)
3¼ ounces peels or stems
of mushrooms
Alternate: instead of the
preceding, 6 cups *velouté*
sauce (page 76)
1¼ cups *crème fraîche* or
heavy cream
1¼ cups white jelly (page
95)

Method.　Prepare the *roux* with the butter and flour in equal parts, thin with the chicken bouillon; bring to a boil, add the mushrooms, and cook slowly for 1 hour. Skim carefully from time to time.

As an alternative replace the ingredients above with an equal quantity of a good *velouté* sauce.

In a saucepan combine ⅞ cup *crème fraîche* and the cooked sauce.

On a high flame reduce the sauce, stirring constantly with a spatula. Then add the jelly.

When the sauce has been reduced to 2 cups, remove it from the heat and add the remaining *crème fraîche*. Strain through cheesecloth into a glazed earthenware bowl. Let it cool, stirring frequently to prevent the formation of a skin and consequently lumps. Before the sauce jells, use it to coat the dish for which it was made.

Sauce chaud-froid brune

BROWN CHAUD-FROID SAUCE

Reduce 2 cups *demi-glace* sauce (page 76) seasoned with Madeira; add small quantities at a time of a good, slightly salted jelly (page 95).

When the mixture is reduced by half, strain it through cheesecloth into an earthenware bowl and let it cool, following the directions for the *chaud-froid* white sauce above. Use it before it has jelled.

This sauce can be flavored with port, sherry, Marsala, etc.

Marinades

Marinades are used to preserve meats, to soften meat fibers, and to penetrate meat with the aromatic ingredients with which the marinades are made.

Marinade crue

UNCOOKED MARINADE
For Meat or Game

1 medium-sized carrot
2 onions
4 shallots
1 celery rib
2 garlic cloves
Few sprigs parsley
Small sprig thyme
1 bay leaf
Pinch crushed pepper
2 cloves
4¼ cups white wine
2 cups vinegar
1 cup oil

Method. Slice the carrots, onions, shallots, and celery very thinly. Place half these vegetables in the bottom of a bowl large enough to hold the pieces of meat to be marinated—so that the marinade will cover the pieces entirely, like a bath. Add the meat, then the rest of the vegetables, and the spices. Add the white wine, vinegar, and oil, which will remain on the surface and, therefore, prevent the air from touching the ingredients in the marinade; this will prevent spoilage.

Keep in a cool place, turning the pieces of meat frequently in the marinade. The length of the marination depends upon the quantity of the meat and the temperature of the air. The process is more rapid in the summer than in the winter. For very large pieces of meat, the marination can be as long as 5 to 6 days in the winter, 24 to 48 hours in the summer.

Marinade cuite

COOKED MARINADE

The ingredients are the same as for the uncooked marinade.

Method. Heat the oil in a saucepan and brown the vegetables slightly. Add the white wine, vinegar, and spices; and cook slowly for 30 minutes.

Let cool completely before pouring over the meat that is to be marinated.

Storing marinades. In order to keep the marinade from spoiling, especially in the summer, it is necessary to add .035 ounces of boric acid for each 4¼ cups of marinade.

It is also necessary to bring the marinade to the boil every 3 to 4 days. In this case, add 1 cup wine, since the boiling will reduce the amount of alcohol in the mixture.

Note: Red wine can be substituted for white wine for certain preparations.

Brines

Brine is a solution of sea salt, sugar, saltpeter, and water used to preserve foods by salting.

In salting meat use 2¹/₃ ounces powdered saltpeter for 2 pounds sea salt. Put the meats coated with the saltpeter and the salt in a wooden bowl or tub. Do not leave any spaces. Add 1 sprig thyme and 1 bay leaf for each 2 pounds of salt. Tightly seal the tub.

The meats put down in salt must be extremely fresh, without any deterioration. The most favorable period to salt any meat at home is the months of December, January, and February. Salt the animals or parts of the animals 24 hours after killing, which means when the flesh is cool and has become firm.

Saumure liquide
PRESERVING IN BRINE

5 quarts water
5 pounds sea salt
5¹/₄ ounces saltpeter
1¹/₂ cups sugar
12 peppercorns
12 juniper berries
Sprig thyme
1 bay leaf

Method. Place all these ingredients in a saucepan and bring to a boil. Then check the strength of the salt solution with the help of a peeled potato plunged into the brine. If the potato floats, add a bit more water until the potato starts to sink. If the potato sinks to the bottom of the pot immediately, add some salt or reduce the liquid so that the strength of the saline solution keeps the potato nearly at the surface.

Let the brine cool, then pour into the bowl in which the meat will be marinated.

When the pieces of meat are placed in the brine, they should be completely submerged.

Jellies and aspics

Jelly is obtained by melting the gelatinous substances found in certain meats: veal shin, pig's feet, calf's feet, bacon or pork rind.

Jelly can also be made by adding powdered gelatin to a cooking stock (veal or chicken stock, bouillon, etc.). The second method is not recommended, but it can sometimes be used in the summer when the heat makes it difficult to prepare certain cold dishes that are completely encased in jelly.
(For 4¹/₂ cups jelly)

¹/₂ pound veal shin
¹/₂ pound veal bones, cut into small pieces
¹/₂ pound beef shin
1 calf's foot, boned and parboiled 1 minute
2 ounces fresh pork rind
3 tablespoons diced carrot
3 tablespoons diced onion
1 leek, white part only
1 celery rib
Sprig thyme
¹/₂ bay leaf
5¹/₄ cups water
³/₄ tablespoon salt

Method. Proceed exactly as for the veal stock (page 72), lightly browning the ingredients if you are making a light-colored jelly, and avoiding the browning if the jelly is to be white. The total cooking time will be 6 hours.

Add poultry, or the carcass of poultry, for poultry jelly. The addition of poultry greatly enriches any jelly stock.

It is important to check the consistency of the jelly before clarifying it. Pour ¹/₂ tablespoon jelly stock into a bowl, and put it in a cool place. After it has cooled for a few minutes, the consistency of the jelly can easily be tested. Then one can tell if it is necessary to add powdered gelatin.

To clarify jellies. In a saucepan with a flat bottom combine 1/2 pound lean beef, a pinch of tarragon, and a pinch of chervil—all coarsely chopped.

Add 1 egg white, beaten with a whisk, and a little at a time pour in the jelly stock, barely tepid and completely degreased. Degreasing is essential in order to have a clear jelly.

Bring to a boil slowly, stirring constantly.

As soon as the stock starts to boil, lower the heat and simmer for 35 minutes. Then strain through a linen napkin, dampened and wrung out.

Jellies are usually flavored with wine or liqueur: Frontignan (a very heavy type of muscatel wine), port, Madeira, sherry, Marsala, etc., which is added to the tepid jelly—1/2 cup per 5 cups jelly. (If wines such as champagne or Alsatian or any other sauternes are used, the proportions are 1 cup wine per 5 cups jelly.) Adding wine reduces the gelatinous quality of the jelly so that powdered gelatin must be added.

Fish

Fish offers about the same food value as land animals; it is easily digestible, especially lean fish (sole, whiting, etc.). Fish is rich in phosphorus, and it is an excellent nutritional source.

But the fish must meet one important condition: it must be absolutely fresh.

In fact, fish flesh decays so quickly that if it is not fresh, it can easily cause digestive upsets and food poisoning.

Therefore, one must know the obvious signs of spoilage in fish.

Fresh fish flesh is firm; its smell is clean. The fish's eyes should not be sunken in the socket and should be very bright. The scales should be shiny, brilliant. The gills should be bright red. If the fish has been caught and killed very recently, its body will be contracted into a semicircle, the head turned toward the tail.

Cooked fresh fish tastes good, and the flesh resists the teeth slightly. If it is not fresh, it tastes insipid and soft; its smell is dubious.

Preliminary preparation

Before beginning any specific recipe, you must eviscerate the fish and scale it. Remove the dorsal, belly, and caudal fins. Avoid pricking yourself while preparing the fish, because the sting of certain fish is painful and sometimes dangerous. When the scaling of a fish is difficult, as it would be for a tench (European carp), if you first soak it for a few seconds in boiling water, the task will be easier.

This is how to do this first step successfully. First remove the gills; then scale the fish, using a knife with a strong blade, scraping against the direction in which the scales grow. Then make a short incision in the fish's belly to enable you to remove the entrails. Remove the line of blood that has coagulated along the backbone. Finally, cut off the fins and trim the tail with strong scissors. Wash the fish inside and out in running water, wipe dry with a cloth, and keep in a cool place.

Methods of preparing fish

1. Cooking in a *court-bouillon*, with or without seasoning
2. Braising (cooking very slowly with a small amount of liquid on a bed of aromatic vegetables and spices)
3. Poaching (cooking in liquid—white or red wine, the cooking juice from mushrooms, a strong fish stock, known as a *fumet*, etc.)
4. Broiling
5. Frying
6. *À la meunière* (with flour, foaming butter, and lemon juice)
7. *Au gratin* (with crumbs, often with cheese)
8. *Au bleu* (thrown live into a *court-bouillon* with vinegar or wine)

Fish may be served hot or cold, whole or sliced.

In French a slice is called a *darne;* a big piece of fish that includes the head is a *hure.*

Cooking in court-bouillon

After the fish has been gutted, scaled, and washed, inside and out, place it in a pot large enough and long enough to hold it comfortably. If it is a big fish and it is whole, lay it on the rack of a *poissonière* or a *turbotière* (a fish poacher with a removable rack) and pour in one of the cold *courts-bouillons* (page 101) to reach 2 inches above the fish. Bring rapidly to a boil; then immediately reduce the flame. The fish should then poach at a gentle simmer. If it continued to boil vigorously, the fish would lose its shape and break into pieces.

When fish is cut into slices, they should never be less than $1\frac{1}{3}$ to $1\frac{1}{2}$ inches thick; I suggest dropping them into the *court-bouillon* after it has started boiling, in order to keep the fish from losing its juices and flavor.

Braising fish

Braising is usually used for whole or large pieces of fish; the fish is often larded with small pieces of pork fat, truffles, *cornichons,* carrots, etc., cut into small sticks about $\frac{1}{4}$ inch wide.

The pot should always be the same size as the fish. The bottom should be buttered thickly and covered with the usual seasonings: carrots, onions, shallots, mushrooms, all sliced very thin. Then season the fish on both sides and place it on top of the vegetables. Cover to three-fourths of its thickness with 1 part white or red wine and 1 part strong concentrated fish stock. Bring it to a boil on a high flame and continue cooking in a 425° oven, partially covered so that the liquid can evaporate very slowly, somewhat reducing the stock. The fish should be basted very often.

As the stock reduces, it becomes more flavorful; the frequent basting gives the fish a brilliant coating that takes on a nice golden-brown color and a pleasant taste. One says then that the fish is *glacé,* glazed.

When the fish is cooked, drain it carefully and place on a serving platter, covered with a glass bell or any other utensil to keep it warm.

The vegetables cooked with the fish are then strained through cheesecloth, degreased, reduced if necessary, and finished according to the recipe chosen.

Poaching fish

This method is one of the simplest and most satisfactory. Thickly butter a fish kettle exactly the same size and shape as the fish to be cooked.

In the bottom of the pot sprinkle the condiments or the ingredients specified in the recipe you have chosen, season lightly, then place the fish on top. Cover the fish with wine or concentrated fish stock, in the proportions given in the recipe. Cut a piece of butter into pieces about 1 teaspoon each and spread them on the fish. Bring to a boil, then cook in a 450° oven, basting often.

When the fish is cooked, it is usually drained; the cooking juices are used as the main ingredient in making the sauce to accompany the fish. Follow the chosen recipe to finish the dish.

Broiling fish

For broiling, fish should be small or medium-sized. Broiling a big fish presents technical difficulties that only an experienced cook can surmount.

If the fish is medium-sized, make shallow incisions on either side crosswise to help the heat penetrate the flesh and to make the cooking easier.

The heat of the grill (charcoal, gas, electricity) should be adjusted according to the thickness of the fish.

A fish that is heated too quickly on the surface, struck suddenly by excessive heat, does not cook inside. A protective coating is formed by the action of the heat. This coating burns, but it serves as a screen to block the heat from penetrating.

A whole fish that tapers toward the tail should be exposed to the heat so that it will cook evenly. This is the art of good cooking.

Frying fish

The ideal oil for frying is one that can get as hot as 575° without burning.

There should be enough oil so that the fish can be plunged into it, as in a bath. It must be totally immersed.

The temperature of the oil as it heats can be judged by the smoke it releases.

The temperature must always be governed by the thickness of the fish.

Fried fish must be seared; it sears more evenly if it is small. If a medium fish is seared too quickly, it will stop cooking. As with grilled fish, a protective coating forms that keeps the heat from penetrating.

On the other hand, when you plunge the fish into the smoking oil the temperature of the oil will drop. Be careful at this step to restore the temperature quickly—raising the heat, if necessary. [*Editor's note:* Caution—do not spill the oil.]

After each use strain the oil through a cloth to remove the remaining particles of the flour, bread crumbs, etc., used to coat the fish before it is plunged into the hot oil.

Poissons à la meunière ou au gratin
FISH À LA MEUNIÈRE OR AU GRATIN

See recipes for trout *à la meunière* (page 110) and sole *à la meunière* (page 131).

Courts-bouillons

The *court-bouillon* is the liquid in which the fish will be completely immersed. These are the different types of *court-bouillon*.

White court-bouillon

For Turbot or Brill

3¹/₂ quarts water
1 cup vinegar
3 tablespoons salt
4 slices lemon, peeled and seeded

Mix the ingredients together and pour this cold *court-bouillon* over the fish, which should be barely covered. The turbot can be replaced by halibut, the brill by gray sole.

Court-bouillon with vinegar

3¹/₂ quarts water
1 cup vinegar
3 tablespoons salt
2 medium-sized carrots
2 big onions, thinly sliced
Some sprigs parsley
Sprig thyme
¹/₂ bay leaf
Pinch crushed peppercorns, added 10 minutes before the *court-bouillon* is finished

Bring to a boil and simmer for 40 minutes; strain through a fine sieve. Cool before pouring over the fish to be cooked.

Court-bouillon with white wine

Use the same proportions as for the *court-bouillon* with vinegar, but omit the vinegar and replace half the water with dry white wine. Cook as above.

Court-bouillon with red wine

Follow the recipe for the *court-bouillon* with vinegar, but replace the water with 3¹/₂ quarts good red wine. Simmer for 40 minutes on a low flame.

Fresh-water fish

Anguille

EEL

To be tasty, the eel is submitted to a barbarous treatment: it must be skinned alive. To lessen its pain, grab it by the tail with the help of a dishcloth; and, as one would do with a rope, strike the eel's head violently on the table or any other hard surface in order to stun it. Then make two or three incisions in the skin around the head. Free the cut skin with a butcher's hook and fold it back on the eel's body; with your hand always covered by the dishcloth, which keeps the slimy skin from sliding, pull the skin off in one motion. Gut the eel by making an opening in its belly; be certain to remove the coagulated blood from the backbone. Remove the fins, and wash the eel under running water.

Matelote d'anguille à la bourguignonne dite meurette

EEL STEW BURGUNDY STYLE, CALLED MEURETTE

1¹/₂–1³/₄-pound eel
¹/₄ cup onions, thinly sliced
¹/₄ cup carrots, thinly sliced
Garlic clove
Bouquet garni
Salt
Freshly ground pepper
Red wine
20 small onions
Pinch sugar
20 small mushrooms
Beurre manié
¹/₄ pound unsalted butter
¹/₂ tablespoon anchovy
  butter
Crayfish *à la nage* (page 142)
Croutons, fried in butter

[*Editor's note:* A *matelote* is a fish stew cooked in red or white wine. It is also called a *pochouse* or *meurette* according to which district the recipe comes from.]

Method. Skin, gut, and wash the eel, and cut it into pieces 2³/₄ to 3¹/₂ inches long.

Thickly butter a frying pan and cover the bottom with a layer of thinly sliced onions and carrots (about ¹/₄ cup each); heat slowly, covered, for 15 to 20 minutes.

Add a crushed garlic clove and a *bouquet garni.* Season with salt and freshly ground pepper. Add the pieces of eel and cover with a good red wine.

Bring rapidly to a boil and cook, covered, boiling slowly for 20 minutes.

Remove the pieces of eel and put them into a bowl; over them pour the cooking liquid, strained through a very fine sieve.

Eel cooked in this way can be kept in a cool place, in its cooking liquid, which will jell when cold; or the fish can be used later for various recipes.

If the eel is served in a *matelote,* it should be garnished in the following manner:

Peel about 20 small onions, blanched and drained, and cook them in butter, covered, in a skillet. Season with salt and a pinch of sugar.

The onions should color slowly as they are cooking; when they are finished, they should be perfectly golden. The onions are then "glazed," because they are coated with the onion juice, which becomes slightly caramelized when the sugar melts.

When the onions are cooked, add about 20 small, firm, white mushrooms; sauté everything for a few seconds, then pour just enough cooking liquid from the eel in the skillet to cover the pieces. Bring to a boil, then add the pieces of eel. Bring to a boil again for 3 to 4 minutes; and thicken with *beurre manié,* ³/₄ tablespoon for each 2 cups cooking liquid. (The *beurre manié* is made with 4 parts butter to 3 parts flour.)

Thicken the sauce by putting the *beurre manié* by teaspoonfuls into the skillet. Give the skillet a slight circular movement while the butter is dissolving, and the sauce will thicken and coat the pieces of eel and their garnish.

Correct the seasoning and finish the sauce off the heat by adding $^1/_4$ pound butter.

You may add, at the same time, $^1/_2$ tablespoon anchovy butter, made with unsalted anchovies pounded with an equal amount of butter and squeezed through very fine cheesecloth.

Place the eel on a hot serving dish, garnish with crayfish cooked *à la nage* and croutons cut into diamond shapes and fried in butter.

Anguille en pochouse

EEL STEW POCHOUSE

The eel is prepared as for the *matelote à la bourguignonne,* except for the addition of $^1/_4$ pound pork fat—blanched and rinsed, if the fat is salted—for an eel of $1^1/_2$ to $1^3/_4$ pounds. Cut the fat into *lardons* (small pieces) and soften them in the skillet where the onions and mushrooms will be cooked later. Follow recipe above.

Anguille à la crème

EEL WITH CREAMED CRAYFISH SAUCE

1$^1/_2$–1$^3/_4$-pound eel
Salt
12 live crayfish
1 quart milk
4 tablespoons unsalted butter
2 dozen mushrooms
Freshly ground pepper
1 tablespoon cognac or champagne brandy
2 tablespoons dry white wine
1$^1/_2$ cups *crème fraîche* or heavy cream
Beurre manié
Croutons, fried in butter
Pastry shell as for *vol-au-vent* (optional)

Method. Skin, gut, and wash the eel; cut it into large pieces. Sprinkle the pieces with salt and let them marinate for $^1/_4$ hour; then cook like a *matelote* with white wine (page 102).

[*Editor's note:* The crayfish may be replaced by a small lobster or 12 unshelled large prawns.]

Wash 12 live crayfish and soak in 1 quart milk for 2 hours to purge them; sauté them in butter in a frying pan on a high flame; add 2 dozen firm, white mushrooms; season with salt and freshly ground pepper. Cook 2 or 3 minutes; then add cognac or fine champagne brandy and wine. Boil 5 minutes; remove the crayfish and the mushrooms separately. Reserve the cooking liquid.

Remove the crayfish tails and add them to the mushrooms, along with the pieces of eel. Put them all in a frying pan. Crush the heads and the shells of the crayfish in a mortar and put this mixture into a frying pan with the cooking liquid from the crayfish. Add the cooking liquid from the eel. Bring to a boil and reduce by one-third; then add 1 cup *crème fraîche,* bring to a boil, and strain through cheesecloth into the frying pan containing the eel, crayfish tails, and mushrooms. Bring to a boil, and thicken with *beurre manié,* 1 tablespoon for each $^1/_2$ cup sauce (follow the recipe for the *matelote à la bourguignonne,* page 102). The sauce should be thicker than for the *matelote.*

Correct the seasoning, and finish the sauce off the heat with $^1/_2$ cup *crème fraîche,* which will thin it.

103

1¹/₂–1³/₄-pound eel
3 tablespoons unsalted
  butter
2 medium-sized onions,
  finely diced
Celery rib, white part only
Dry white wine
Salt
Freshly ground pepper
¹/₄ pound sorrel leaves
¹/₄ pound water cress
2 ounces white nettles
1 teaspoon chopped
  parsley
1 teaspoon chopped
  chervil
Pinch sage
Pinch savory
Pinch fresh mint
4 egg yolks
2 tablespoons *crème
  fraîche* or heavy cream

Pike
Court-bouillon with vinegar
  (page 101)
3 shallots, finely chopped
2 tablespoons vinegar or
  ¹/₂ cup muscadet wine
Pinch salt
Pinch freshly ground
  pepper
14 ounces unsalted butter

Place on a very hot serving platter and garnish with heart-shaped croutons fried in butter.

This dish can also be served in a *vol-au-vent* shell (page 388).

Anguille à la flamande dite au vert
EEL FLEMISH STYLE

Method. Cut the eel into 2¹/₂-inch pieces. Brown the pieces in butter in a frying pan. Then add the onions and celery.

When these ingredients are lightly browned, immediately add dry white wine to cover the pieces of eel. Season with salt and freshly ground pepper. Tie in a piece of cheesecloth sorrel leaves, cut into strips, water cress, white nettles, chopped parsley, chopped chervil, sage, savory, and fresh mint. Put in the pan. Bring to a boil and boil rapidly for 15 minutes.

In a bowl beat 4 egg yolks with 2 tablespoons *crème fraîche.* Remove the pieces of eel, being careful not to break them, and keep warm and covered.

Thicken the cooking liquid with the egg yolks and cream, as in making sauces and soups (page 66).

Place the pieces of eel in the sauce and coat them well by shaking the frying pan. Correct the seasoning, and serve hot or cold.

Brochet à la nantaise
PIKE NANTES STYLE

Method. Put a pike in a vinegar *court-bouillon.* As soon as it starts to boil, skim the *court-bouillon* and place the fish kettle over the lowest possible flame and poach the fish for 20 to 25 minutes.

While it is poaching, very slowly cook the shallots in butter in a frying pan. Add 1 tablespoon water, 2 tablespoons vinegar or ¹/₂ cup muscadet wine, pinch of salt, and pinch of freshly ground pepper. Reduce by two-thirds.

Keep the sauce simmering and, without boiling, add, piece by piece, 14 ounces butter cut into small bits. With a sauce whip beat the mixture vigorously, without stopping. The butter, whipped like cream, will become very foamy and white. This is why the sauce is also called *beurre blanc* (white butter).

Drain the pike and place in a heated plate on a napkin; serve the white butter on the side as soon as it is ready. This preparation must not wait.

Note: Different regional methods can be used to make an excellent white butter. One of these methods is recommended for its simplicity. To the reduced sauce described above add 1 cup pike *court-bouillon,* reduce it by two-thirds on a high flame; then while it is at full boil, add the butter cut into pieces. While melting, the butter is mixed into the strongly reduced sauce and through the action of the boiling forms an emulsion by itself. Beat the sauce while it is melting and remove from the flame when the sauce is thickened.

Brochet braisé aux champignons
BRAISED PIKE WITH MUSHROOMS

2-pound pike
Salt
Pepper
Mushrooms
1 cup port or sherry
1 cup white veal stock
  (page 72)
1/2 pound unsalted butter
1 cup *crème fraîche* or
  heavy cream
1 tablespoon champagne
  brandy

Method. Gut and clean the pike. Wash it very carefully, season with salt and pepper on all sides, and place in a fish kettle the same size as the fish, on a bed of very tiny white mushrooms.

Pour in 1 cup port or sherry and an equal quantity of white veal stock; on top, scatter 1/4 pound butter cut into small pieces.

Cook in a 425° oven for 30 minutes. Do not cover the fish kettle, and baste frequently. At the end of the cooking time the pike should be perfectly golden.

Remove the fish to a serving platter, surround it with the mushrooms, well drained, and keep hot. Reduce the fish liquid by half in a skillet, add 1 cup *crème fraîche,* reduce again slightly. Then off the flame add 1/4 pound butter and fine champagne brandy. Correct the seasoning, and pour the sauce over the pike; the sauce should be a light ivory color.

Note: If it is more convenient, the veal stock may be replaced by an equal quantity of strong sole stock.

The pike cooked in a *court-bouillon* may be accompanied by various sauces: hollandaise sauce (pages 88–9), butter sauce (page 78), ravigote sauce (page 92), etc.

Brochetons "Tatan Nano"
YOUNG PIKE (For 4 people)

4 small pike, 4 1/2 to 5
  ounces each
24 frogs' legs
1/4 recipe *court-bouillon*
  with vinegar (page 101)
1/4 pound unsalted butter
1 egg white and 2 egg
  yolks
1/2 cup *crème fraîche* or
  heavy cream
Salt and pepper
1 1/2 tablespoons chopped
  shallots
3 tablespoons chopped
  mushrooms
1/2 cup white wine
1/4 pound spinach
Velouté sauce (page 76)

Method. Scale, trim, clean, and remove the gills of the young pike. Make an incision in the backs to remove the bones. Use the back of a tablespoon to push the flesh aside and remove the very fine bones that are an unpleasant characteristic of this fish. Gut the fish through the incision.

Bone the frogs' legs carefully (it is important to have frogs that have not been kept on ice, because the water swells the flesh).

With the pike bones and the frog bones, make the *court-bouillon.* Before adding the liquid, cook the flavoring vegetables in 1 tablespoon butter. Reduce to make about 1 cup *fumet.*

Pound the frog flesh together with the white of egg; rub through a fine sieve to eliminate the tendons. As in making fine *quenelles* (page 106), beat, over ice, with the cream and season highly. As usual, poach one to test.

Stuff each small pike with this filling. To close the incision, press the edges together; they are gelatinous and will stick easily.

Place the stuffed pike in a buttered pan on a bed of chopped shallots and half the chopped mushrooms. Pour over 1/2 cup white wine and the *fumet.* Season again, cover with buttered wax paper, and braise over a low flame. When cooked, drain the pike on a cloth, remove the skins. Trim again. Envelop each fish (except for the head) in blanched and seasoned spinach.

105

With the fish cooking liquid make a *velouté* sauce, beaten with butter and thickened with egg yolks and cream to produce a smooth sauce that will glaze the fish; to ensure this, use the technique for a *sabayon,* beating the egg yolks in a double boiler until they emulsify with the liquid. Here the liquid beaten with the yolks is cream.

Arrange the pike on a serving platter. On top of each fish make a stripe of minced mushrooms. Strain the sauce through a double cheesecloth and coat the fish with it. Glaze in a 475° oven or under the broiler until golden brown.

Quenelles de poisson ou farces

FISH QUENELLES OR STUFFING

Fish *quenelles* (or stuffing) are generally made with the flesh of whiting or pike and nearly always with white-fleshed fish.

These *quenelles,* like veal, chicken, or game *quenelles,* are of two kinds: fine and ordinary

Fine *quenelles,* or *mousselines,* are not much different from chicken *mousselines* (page 273). Both are composed of cream and egg whites, in addition to the flesh.

One must, however, be somewhat vague about the proportions of the ingredients; one cannot insist on mathematical precision. The stiffness of the stuffing depends on the albumin in the flesh used. Since the percentage of albumin in the flesh varies with each fish—according to size, age, or species—the number of egg whites added must vary. The function of the egg whites is to solidify the cream incorporated and to compensate for the variable composition of the flesh. Therefore, it is essential to experiment with the amount of egg whites in order to attain the maximum degree of fineness.

Ordinary *quenelles* are a mixture of fish flesh, *panade,* and eggs. They can be refined by adding butter or cream.

Quenelles de brochet à la lyonnaise

PIKE QUENELLES LYONS STYLE

(For 80 *quenelles* weighing about 3½ ounces each)

9 cups milk
4 pounds unsalted butter
5¼ pounds flour, sifted
4 pounds pike meat
½ cup salt
1 teaspoon freshly ground pepper
1 teaspoon grated nutmeg
12 egg whites
50 eggs

Three important steps are necessary to make the *quenelles:* preparing the *panade,* combining the mixture, and poaching.

Making the panade. In a saucepan with a thick bottom bring the milk to a boil, add 14 ounces butter and the sifted flour, and whip vigorously. As soon as the mixture is well thickened, turn the heat very low and, stirring constantly with a wooden spoon, "dry" the *panade.* After this step has been completed (about 20 minutes), set the *panade* in a cool place.

Combining the mixture. With a pestle pound the pike meat in a mortar, together with the salt, pepper, and nutmeg. When the meat becomes a paste, strain it through a fine sieve.

106

Return to the mortar, work in the egg whites, and then the cooled *panade*.

When these are well mixed, add the whole eggs. When they have been incorporated smoothly, finish by adding the remaining butter, softened.

Before poaching, cool the *quenelle* mixture to make it firmer.

Poaching the quenelles. Bring to a boil 6 gallons salted water. With the help of a special *quenelle* spoon, mold the *quenelles,* which should be ovals weighing about 3$\frac{1}{2}$ ounces each. Poach them, 20 at a time, in hot, but not boiling, water.

After about 15 minutes, when the *quenelles* have been poached, if they are not to be used immediately, plunge them into a bowl of fresh water until they are completely cool. Drain and set aside in the refrigerator. *Quenelles* can be prepared later as one needs them, with cream, *à la Nantua* (page 85), or *au gratin.*

Quenelles de brochet
PIKE QUENELLES
Old Method

Method. Make a *panade* by stirring the ingredients with a wooden spoon without stopping until it boils, in the same way as a frangipane. Cool.

If you are using kidney fat in the pike forcemeat, remove the skin, fibers, and sinews, and chop fine. Otherwise, chop the fat and marrow fine. Pound the pike meat in a mortar until it becomes a smooth paste. Mix in the chopped fat and the seasonings. Pound again until the ingredients are completely mixed. Add the egg whites one by one (more or less maintaining the consistency). Incorporate the cooled *panade* and strain the mixture through cheesecloth. Spread it $\frac{3}{4}$ inch thick in a dish, and place in the refrigerator until the next day.

Make the *quenelles* by hand on a table sprinkled with flour: with the tips of your fingers, roll the mixture into pieces the size of a nut, or roll the entire mixture into the shape of a sausage the thickness of a finger, and cut it into sticks about 3 inches long.

Poach in boiling salted water, keeping the water at a low boil for 7 or 8 minutes. The *quenelles* are done when they resist slightly when pressed. Drain the *quenelles* well; arrange them in an ovenproof earthenware dish coated with a light Mornay sauce (page 84), and cover them with more of the sauce. Sprinkle grated gruyère cheese mixed with a pinch of fine bread crumbs. Moisten with a little melted butter and place in a 425° oven for 8 to 10 minutes.

Serve immediately, piping hot. This delicious dish is the great specialty of restaurants and caterers in Lyons.

Note: The beef fat can be partially or totally replaced by unsalted butter, which is preferable.

Panade
1$\frac{1}{4}$ cups sifted flour
4 egg yolks
3$\frac{1}{2}$ tablespoons unsalted butter, melted
1 cup hot milk seasoned with pinch salt and pinch nutmeg

Pike forcemeat
$\frac{1}{2}$ pound beef kidney fat or $\frac{1}{4}$ pound fat and $\frac{1}{4}$ pound beef marrow
$\frac{1}{2}$ pound pike meat, bones and skin removed
$\frac{3}{4}$ tablespoon salt
Pinch pepper
Pinch nutmeg
3 egg whites
Mornay sauce (page 84)
Grated gruyère cheese
Fine bread crumbs

Laitance de carpe

SOFT ROE OF CARP

The soft roe of carp is very delicate and can be prepared poached or *à la meunière* or as a garnish for eggs, fish, etc. For family use, we advise using the recipe for trout *à la meunière* (page 110), suitable for most fresh-water or sea fish.

Carpe à la juive

JEWISH CARP

4-pound carp
2 large onions
3 shallots
3¼ cups oil
2 tablespoons flour
3 garlic cloves, crushed
Bouquet garni
White wine
Strong fish stock (pages 73–4) or white veal stock (page 72) or water
Salt
Freshly ground pepper
Chopped parsley

Method.　Gut the carp and clean carefully. If the carp has soft roe, reserve it. Slice the carp.

Finely chop the onions and shallots; cook them in 1 cup oil heated slowly in a skillet big enough to hold all the pieces of carp flat. Place the fish slices on the onion and sauté for a few minutes in the hot oil, then turn them. Sprinkle with flour, mix carefully, and cook for 5 minutes without browning. Add the garlic and the *bouquet garni.* To the height of the fish pour in liquid consisting of half white wine and half strong fish stock or white veal stock or water. Add 4 tablespoons oil. Season with salt and freshly ground pepper, and cook slowly, covered, for 20 minutes.

Drain the pieces of carp and set them, side by side, on a long fish-shaped platter. Boil the cooking juice to reduce by two-thirds. Remove the *bouquet garni,* and off the flame incorporate 2 cups oil into the reduced sauce, as in making mayonnaise. Correct the seasoning, pour the thickened sauce over the carp, and let cool. The sauce will then jell.

Serve with chopped parsley sprinkled on at the last moment.

Féra

LANDLOCKED SALMON

The landlocked salmon belongs to the group of salmon that is caught almost exclusively in the Swiss lakes. The most famous is the one from Lake Geneva; its flesh is fat, white, and very delicate. [*Editor's note:* Landlocked salmon can be found on this continent in eastern Canada and New England. It can be replaced by other salmon.]

The simplest preparation is the best for landlocked salmon. Scale, gut, wash, and wipe the salmon. Rub with a little oil and season with salt and pepper on both sides. Roll the fish in flour; shake it to remove the excess.

Heat an ovenproof earthenware platter with a good-sized piece of butter in it. When the butter sizzles, put in the salmon and bake in a 450° oven.

Turn the fish once and baste frequently during cooking. When it is done, the fish will be covered with a light golden coating produced by the mixture of the oil and the flour.

Serve in the platter used for the cooking. Squeeze a few drops of lemon juice on the fish and sprinkle over it 1 teaspoon chopped parsley, blanched and still damp. Baste with a few teaspoons of butter lightly browned. Serve immediately while the butter is still foaming after contact with the moisture in the parsley.

Goujon
GUDGEON

The gudgeon is one of our best river fishes, especially if it comes from running water with a stony bottom.

The only proper way to cook this fish is by frying.

Goujons frits
FRIED GUDGEON

[*Editor's note:* This is a European fish, for which other small river fish can be substituted.]

Choose small fish; gut them with the point of a knife, wash, wipe, and soak them in a little bit of milk. Drain and roll in flour, one at a time, with your hand. When they are all prepared, put into a frying basket and plunge them into very hot oil.

Cook 3 to 4 minutes. Drain on a cloth and sprinkle with salt.

Arrange the fish on a serving platter in bunches, accompanied by bouquets of fried parsley and lemon quarters. Serve immediately, very hot and crisp.

Omble chevalier

This is a first cousin of the *lavaret* and the *féra;* it is even rarer than the latter. It lives in the very deep waters of the Savoy and Swiss lakes. It is prepared in the same way as a salmon trout. The flesh is pale rose and aromatic.

[*Editor's note:* Also known as char in the trout family, it can be replaced by other trout.]

Perche
PERCH

The small perch is an excellent frying fish, cooked in the same way as gudgeon (above).

When the perch weighs 2 to 4 pounds, it is cooked like a river trout (page 110) because it has about the same flavor.

[*Editor's note:* The American equivalents are perch, black bass, and perch trout.]

Truites de rivière à la meunière
RIVER TROUT À LA MEUNIÈRE

Remove the gills and the intestines of the trout. Wash and wipe them. Rub them with salt and pepper mixed with 1 tablespoon oil, and roll them in flour. Shake well. Melt a large piece of butter with a little bit of oil in a frying pan, and put the fish in.

As soon as the fish touches the hot fat, it will be seared. This must be done carefully and very quickly to prevent the fish from sticking to the pan, but the fat must not be too hot, or a solid crust will be formed by the coating of the oil and flour that will prevent the heat from penetrating, and the inside of the trout will not cook properly.

The cooking must be done very quickly. The fish must fry slowly but the fat must not be boiling hot.

When the trout is cooked on one side, turn it with a spatula, and continue cooking on the other side.

When the fish is golden and slightly crusty, place it on a very hot platter, squeeze a couple of drops of lemon juice on top, and cover with a pinch of parsley, coarsely chopped, blanched, and drained—this last step is done at the last minute—and pour over the cooking butter enriched with extra butter, lightly browned. The heat of the brown butter and the dampness of the parsley create a foaminess and a pleasant smell that remain when this delicious fish is presented without delay.

Mousse chaude de truite de rivière au coulis d'écrevisses
HOT RIVER TROUT MOUSSE WITH CRAYFISH SAUCE

1¼ pounds trout fillet
1 heaping tablespoon salt
15 turns of a pepper mill
4 egg whites
4 cups heavy cream
Unsalted butter

[*Editor's note:* Crayfish are almost unavailable in the United States, but they can be replaced by a small lobster or unshelled large prawns.]

Method.   Pound the trout in a large mortar with the seasonings until well puréed; beat in the egg whites. When the mixture is smooth, rub through a sieve into a bowl. Set the bowl into a larger bowl of cracked ice and beat in the cream.

Butter a large savarin mold or a 7- to 9-inch ring mold. Pour in the mousse and set the mold in a *bain-marie;* bake in a 325° oven for about 45 minutes.

Crayfish Sauce

2 pounds red crayfish
7 tablespoons butter
½ cup cognac
4¼ cups *court-bouillon* with vinegar (page 101), made with the trout bones
½ cup heavy cream
***Beurre manié* (1 tablespoon unsalted butter creamed with 1 tablespoon flour)**
Salt and pepper

Method.   Cook the crayfish rapidly in boiling water. Shell the tails, reserving both meat and shells. Pound the shells in a mortar. To increase the redness, return the crushed shells to a skillet and sauté with half the butter. Add the cognac and cook until reduced by half. Add the *fumet,* which should be highly seasoned. Cook over low heat for a few minutes, thickening slightly by adding bits of the *beurre manié.* Correct seasoning, then add the cream, and simmer briefly. Strain the mixture through a fine sieve. Keep it hot.

To serve.   Stew the crayfish tails in the remaining butter for a few minutes, season, and add a little sauce to moisten them. Unmold the mousse on a round silver or porcelain platter. Fill the center with the crayfish. Serve the extra sauce in a sauceboat, along with a bowl of rice pilaf (page 371).

Variation. You can also use individual ring molds. For a richer dish you can sprinkle sliced truffles on top and border the plate with decorative shapes of flaky pastry (pages 382–3).

Truites au bleu
BLUE TROUT

This recipe is very simple and one of the best, but it calls for live trout.

A few minutes before serving the trout, fish them from the pond. Stun them by hitting their heads on something hard. Remove the gills and the intestines with the point of a knife. Do not wash or dry the trout; this would remove their coating, which makes them blue. Plunge them immediately into a rapidly boiling *court-bouillon* that contains a great deal of vinegar, about ½ cup per quart of water.

Cook 7 to 8 minutes for a fish of about 5 to 6 ounces.

Drain the trout, which now have a bluish tint. Arrange them on a napkin placed upon a hot platter, and serve them garnished with boiled potatoes in their skins and a butter sauce flavored with a few drops of lemon juice.

Blue trout can also be served cold with ravigote sauce (page 92) or oil or a very light mayonnaise (page 90).

Lavaret

The *lavaret,* a member of the salmon family, lives mainly in the very deep waters of Lake Bourget and Lake Annecy.

All the recipes for river trout (page 110) can be used for *lavaret.*

Salt-water fish

Barbue
BRILL

Brill is of the same family as sole or halibut and is one of the finest fish in the sea. All the recipes for sole or halibut can be used for brill. A medium-sized fish is best.

Filets de barbue grillés Saint-Germain
BROILED BRILL FILLETS SAINT-GERMAIN

Gut and skin a medium-sized brill, and remove the fillets in the following way:

Make an incision in the back flesh of the brill through to the bone following the dorsal fin from the head to the tail. Bring the incision in a circle around the fillets, starting at the small bones at the end of the backbone. Then with the point of a flexible knife, starting with the dorsal fin, slide the blade, flat, under each fillet, cutting and pulling the knife toward you.

The bones and the head will be used to make a fish *fumet* or a soup.

Check the fillets to see that no bone or gristle remains. Dry the fillets and season with salt and pepper mixed with a drop of olive oil. On one side of each fillet, sprinkle a few very fine bread crumbs, making them stick by pressing lightly with the flat blade of a knife. Moisten the bread crumbs with a few drops of melted butter. Set the fillets on a glowing charcoal grill, with the breaded sides to the flame.

Adjust the distance from the coals according to the thickness of the fillets. For example, since the end of the fillet toward the tail is thinner, the heat at that end should be lower, which means that part of the fish should be farther away from the coals. If gas or electricity is used, put the thinner part of the fish farther away from the flame. Thus it will cook evenly, and the thinner part will not dry out.

When the fillets are cooked on one side, turn them over carefully with a spatula.

When the second side has cooked, arrange the fillets on a long, hot serving platter, sprinkle with the juice of $1/2$ lemon, then surround with a garnish of small tomatoes, seasoned and grilled. A tablespoon of rice—cooked creole style, as a pilaf, or in salted water and then finished with unsalted butter—can be added to the tomatoes.

Finally serve with it a sauceboat of *béarnaise* sauce (page 89).

A simpler way of cooking the fillets is to put them in a frying pan with butter, *à la meunière* (page 110). A whole brill can also be broiled. In this case, remove only the black skin and carefully scrape the scales from the white skin. Cooking it this way requires more care, but the dish will be even more delicious because of the bones, which contain juices that will enrich the flesh during the cooking.

Bouillabaisse

(For 6 people)

This dish is strictly Provençal, from Marseilles in particular. It has its origins in the eating customs of the fishermen who cook certain fish in the same way on their boats as a *pot-au-feu* with fewer different ingredients.

Southern taste, on the one hand, and the refinements contributed by professional cooks, on the other, have combined to make this a divine dish.

Some people add shellfish such as mussels or cockles, etc. We do not advise using these shellfish. The taste of mussels is too strong, and the shells often leave sand at the bottom.

3 pounds freshly caught
fish (live, when possible),
including hog fish,
whiting, red mullet,
weever, John Dory,
conger eel, lobster
Slices bread rubbed with
garlic
Flavorings
4 tablespoons finely
chopped onion
1 medium-sized leek, white
part only, finely chopped
1/2 cup olive oil
2 tomatoes, peeled,
seeded, and
chopped—do not
remove the juice
1 tablespoon grated garlic
Large pinch coarsely
chopped parsley
Sprig each thyme, laurel,
savory
1 fennel rib
Dash anise
Pinch saffron
1 tablespoon unsalted
butter

Method. Clean, scale, gut, and trim the fish. Make an unsalted *fumet* (pages 73–4) with the heads of the fish used or, if available, the bones of sole and brill, and a halibut head.

Place the onion and leek in a saucepan with 2 tablespoons oil. Heat slowly, stirring frequently, until they are both cooked but not brown. Then add the fish (except the lobster). Add all the flavorings and sprinkle with a large pinch of salt (about 1/2 tablespoon) and a pinch of freshly ground pepper. The anise and the saffron are the essentials; the saffron must dominate the soup.

Pour in the *fumet* to cover. Sprinkle over the butter cut into pieces, and the rest of the oil.

Start cooking over a high flame. As soon as the liquid boils, add the live lobster cut into pieces. Cook on a high flame for 15 minutes. Meanwhile, take the slices of bread that have been rubbed with garlic, sprinkle them with a few drops of oil, and broil in the oven.

As it boils, the fish stock (enhanced by the savory juices of the fish used), the oil, and the butter (forming an emulsion) will mix and thicken to the consistency of a creamed soup.

It is essential to serve this dish, with its rare succulence, as soon as it is cooked. If it is forced to wait, the natural thickening that forms the charm of this dish will rapidly disappear.

Drain the fish carefully, and arrange the pieces on a serving platter. Pour the boiling soup into a soup tureen over the slices of bread.

Last and very important: Before pouring the soup over the bread, correct the seasoning and the condiments, which are the key to the character of the bouillabaisse.

We have said that the saffron, with its flavor and its golden color, must be the dominating note, but to this must be added the fennel and the anise according to the palate of the cook, if he is skilled in the art of tasting and has a precise notion of the fine flavor characteristic of this dish.

Since fennel and anise can sometimes be hard to find, a drop of absinthe may be added, but very sparingly.

Cabillaud à la ménagère

FRESH COD HOME STYLE

Scale and wash a fresh cod. From the center cut a piece about a foot long. Thickly butter an ovenproof earthenware dish big enough to contain the fish and its garnish. Put in the fish, well seasoned with salt and pepper on both sides, and surround it with small new potatoes and small new white onions. If you cannot get young vegetables, first blanch, drain, and season them with salt. Moisten the fish with melted butter and cook in a 425° oven, basting frequently with additional melted butter, which can be supplemented without any harm—quite the opposite—with a tablespoon of olive oil.

The onions should constitute one-quarter of the total garnish, and the vegetables should be placed around the fish, which must lie flat on the bottom of the dish, so that it is constantly in the cooking butter and browns evenly.

Just before serving on the cooking platter, sprinkle the fish with a pinch of freshly chopped parsley and add, on the side, a lemon cut into quarters, to be squeezed over the fish when it has been served on hot plates.

Cod also can be poached or broiled, cut into slices 3/4 inch thick, and served with any of the sauces given in recipes for fish prepared this way.

Colin
HAKE

The hake should occupy an important place in family cooking. Abundant in all French markets in all seasons, it is one of the cheapest fish available. [*Editor's note:* Hake is seldom sold under that name in the United States; it is usually called haddock or cod.] Hake has little waste and few bones and possesses a white, delicate flesh; it can be cooked by any method: served hot or cold, whole, in pieces, or in slices *(darnes);* poached, fried, broiled, cooked in a skillet, in a frying pan, or *à la meunière* (page 110). Seasoned properly, it is always delicious.

The flesh of hake is nourishing, easily digestible, and would be suited to meals for those who do physical labor or brainwork or are invalids.

Colin à la portugaise
HAKE PORTUGUESE STYLE (For 6 people)

1¼ cups raw rice
2 pounds very ripe
  tomatoes
1 large onion
14 tablespoons unsalted
  butter
3-pound hake
Salt
Freshly ground pepper
6 tablespoons olive oil
2 garlic cloves
1 cup dry white wine
Pinch freshly chopped
  parsley

Method.   Cook 1¼ cups rice in salted water for three-quarters of its cooking time. Remove tops, skins, and seeds from the very ripe tomatoes—do not remove juice—and chop coarsely. Chop the onion and soften in 2 tablespoons butter in a frying pan.

Cut the hake into 6 slices weighing about ½ pound each. Season generously on both sides with salt and freshly ground pepper. Place the fish in a frying pan with 6 tablespoons butter and 6 tablespoons olive oil. Add the other ingredients: the onion, the garlic cloves, crushed, the tomatoes, the rice, and the white wine.

Cover the frying pan, raise the heat, and cook for 10 minutes; remove the cover and continue cooking for 8 to 10 minutes; the resulting evaporation will reduce part of the tomato juices and the white wine. Take off the flame, and remove the fish slices to an oval or round dish. Cut the remaining butter into pieces and add to the frying pan, shaking the pan to mix; the butter will blend into the rice and tomatoes. Correct the seasoning, and pour the mixture over the slices of hake.

Sprinkle on top a pinch of freshly chopped parsley.

Note: The rice and tomatoes and the cooking juices should be slightly thickened but not dry.

Daurade
GILTHEAD BREAM

[*Editor's note:* Gilthead bream can be replaced by carp, since *daurade* is not found in the United States.] The gilthead is protected by a thick layer of scales that must be removed completely in cleaning. When you gut the fish, if you find roe or soft roe, leave it in place. If the fish is to be served whole, leave the head on.

There are many species of gilthead. The best (sparoid fish), which lives in the Mediterranean, has a pearly transparent bulge between the eyes. It should not be confused with the gilthead that is native to the China Seas.

Small *daurades* can be cooked in the same way as red mullet: broiled, fried, *à la meunière* (page 110), etc.; medium or large, they can be cooked in a frying pan, poached, stuffed as for a shad, *au gratin* like a sole, with white wine or red wine, *à la Bercy* (below), *à la dieppoise, à la portugaise* (page 114), etc.

Daurade farcie
STUFFED GILTHEAD (For 6 people)

3-pound *daurade*
¹/₂ pound unsalted butter
4 shallots, chopped
¹/₂ pound mushrooms
Salt
Pepper
Pinch rosemary
2 cups dry white wine
1 large tomato
¹/₂ cup fine dry bread crumbs
1 egg, beaten

Method. Prepare a *daurade* of about 3 pounds. Slowly melt ¹/₄ pound butter in a frying pan, and add the chopped shallots; do not let brown. It will take 15 to 20 minutes until the shallots are cooked. Then raise the heat under the pan and add the mushrooms, carefully washed and chopped. Cook rapidly until dry, season with salt and pepper and rosemary; pour over 1 cup dry white wine; add the tomato, peeled and seeded. Reduce quickly over a high flame. Finish off the heat with ¹/₂ cup very fine dry bread crumbs and the beaten egg; mix in thoroughly and correct the seasoning.

If the *daurade* contains soft roe or roe, add it to the mixture; then stuff the mixture inside the fish through the gills. Place the fish on a thickly buttered ovenproof dish; season with salt and pepper; pour over 1 cup dry white wine, and sprinkle on 1 tablespoon fine bread crumbs and ¹/₄ pound butter cut into small pieces.

Bake in a 375° oven, basting frequently, for 40 minutes.

Daurade Bercy
GILTHEAD BERCY

Choose a *daurade* for 5 or 6 people: clean, gut, scrape, and wash it; gash lightly crosswise every ³/₄ inch on the back and both sides. Season with salt and pepper and place in a gratin dish with the bottom thickly buttered and sprinkled with 2 shallots, chopped, and a large pinch of chopped parsley. Add dry white wine to one-third of the height of the fish and baste with 6 tablespoons melted unsalted butter. Cook in a 350° oven for 25 to 30 minutes, basting frequently with the cooking liquid. Place the *daurade* on a long serving platter and keep warm, covering with a glass bell or a shallow dish so that the fish does not dry out or cool.

If there is too much cooking liquid, reduce it to the quantity needed to serve with the fish. Stir in, off the heat, ¼ pound unsalted butter cut into small pieces.

This thickened cooking liquid provides the sauce. Correct the seasoning, and pour it over the fish. Place for a few minutes in a 425° oven or under a heated broiler, electric or gas, and the sauce will take on a pretty golden color. Serve immediately.

If you do not have a sufficiently hot oven or a broiler, you may omit the last step.

This recipe can be made more economically by replacing the ¼ pound butter with 3½ tablespoons butter mixed with 1 teaspoon flour. Sprinkle this butter mixture, called *beurre manié,* little by little into the cooking liquid while it is boiling, reduced or not; stir for a few seconds, and pour over the *daurade* when the sauce has been thickened by the simple melting and cooking of the *beurre manié.*

Éperlans

SMELTS

Always buy small smelts and fry them on a skewer or deep fry and serve in bunches exactly like gudgeon (page 109).

Large smelts can be prepared like whitings; they are very similar, except that they have an excessive number of bones for their size. This makes them difficult to eat.

Esturgeon

STURGEON

This is a migratory fish that, like the salmon, lives by turns in fresh or salt water. Sturgeon are found mainly in the large rivers of Russia and, in limited quantities, in the Gironde. They can reach a very large size.

Sturgeon eggs, after special treatment, become caviar; the fish's flesh is firm, oily, and of secondary quality.

Although sturgeon is rarely found in French markets, it is quite cheap. The recipes for sturgeon are the same as for braised veal.

Fricandeau d'esturgeon

STURGEON FRICANDEAU

Cut a piece of sturgeon, with its skin removed, into slices about 1½ inch thick, interlarding with pork fat as for an ordinary *fricandeau.* Cover the bottom of a well-buttered frying pan with sliced carrots and onions; place the slices of sturgeon on top and braise them for around 1 hour.

Serve the fish with the braised vegetables and a garnish of small onions or olives, or of vegetables: spinach, sorrel, zucchini, mashed potatoes *au gratin,* or sautéed mushrooms (*cèpes, girolles,* morels, etc.).

Haddock ou aiglefin fumé

SMOKED HADDOCK

This fish is sold smoked in markets.

Whole or in fillets, haddock is generally cooked by poaching in water with some milk added. Cooking time, starting from the boiling point, is 8 to 10 minutes for each 2 pounds.

Serve drained, on a hot platter placed on a napkin, accompanied by a sauceboat of melted butter and by steamed potatoes.

Hareng

HERRING

This is a very popular fish because of its abundance and low price.

Eaten very fresh, herring is excellent but difficult to digest. Serve it for luncheon menus.

It can be prepared by broiling, frying, or *à la meunière* (page 110), accompanied by a spicy sauce such as mustard sauce, or it can be cooked in a marinade and served cold.

The soft roe of herring is a delicacy used for garnishes or for special dishes, for example, soft roe *à la Villeroy* (breaded and fried, and covered with a very reduced *allemande* sauce, page 77).

Smoked herring is broiled or marinated in fillets and served as an hors d'oeuvre.

It is very simple to prepare herring: Gut the fish through its gills, without removing the soft roe or the roe, rub it vigorously to dry it (which removes the scales), and on each side of the back make small slashes to allow the heat to penetrate easily, which will make it cook more quickly. Season with salt and pepper mixed with a few drops of oil and cook on a grill, or roll the fish in flour and cook in a frying pan in very hot butter.

Harengs frais marinés

FRESH MARINATED HERRINGS

Clean and gut the herrings and macerate in salt (a small handful of salt for a dozen herrings) for 6 hours.

Drain the fish, wipe, and place in an oval earthenware dish, lined with thinly sliced onions and carrots, a couple of sprigs of parsley, a sprig of thyme, 1 bay leaf, 3 crushed peppercorns, and 2 cloves.

Moisten just to the top of the herrings with a mixture of half dry white wine and half vinegar; cover the fish with a second layer of onions and carrots, chopped, and cover with a sheet of wax paper.

Bring slowly to a boil, cover the dish, and cook for 15 minutes. Cool, and keep fish in cooking liquid until serving time.

Limande—Limande-sole
DAB

[*Editor's note:* This fish, which is not available in the United States, can be replaced by plaice.]

This is a flat fish that, if necessary, can be substituted for sole without, however, quite equaling its taste or its fineness.

The flesh of the dab is crumbly, stringy, and not so delicate as sole.

All the recipes for sole and brill can be used for this fish.

Lotte de mer ou baudroie
ANGLERFISH

[*Editor's note:* This is a fish not found in the United States; it can be replaced by other fish fillets or steaks.]

The anglerfish must be skinned before it can be eaten.

Its flesh, white and firm, is usually added to bouillabaisse or other fish soups.

It is generally prepared in the same way as fresh codfish or hake.

Escalopes de lotte sautées
SAUTÉED SCALLOPS OF ANGLERFISH

Fillet of anglerfish
Salt
Freshly ground pepper
1 egg, beaten
1 tablespoon oil
Pinch salt
Fine bread crumbs
1/4 pound unsalted butter
1 tablespoon olive oil
Juice of 1/2 lemon
1 teaspoon chopped parsley
Tomato sauce (optional)

Method. From the thick part of an anglerfish fillet, cut 6 scallops, 3/4 inch thick. Flatten them slightly, season with salt and freshly ground pepper, dip in an egg beaten with 1 tablespoon oil and a pinch of salt, and roll in very fine bread crumbs.

To make the bread crumbs adhere to the fish, press lightly with the flat part of a knife blade.

Heat 1/4 pound butter and 1 tablespoon olive oil in a skillet and place the scallops in it side by side. When they are half cooked and golden, turn them and cook the other side.

Arrange fish on a serving platter; squeeze juice of 1/2 lemon over the tops and sprinkle with chopped parsley, blanched and moistened with the cooking butter. If there is not enough butter, add another piece cooked in the skillet until light brown.

A sauceboat of tomato sauce (page 77) can be served on the side.

Filets de lotte frits
FRIED FILLETS OF ANGLERFISH

The scallops are prepared as for the sautéed anglerfish; then soak them in milk, flour well, and plunge into very hot oil.

Drain the scallops and serve on a napkin placed upon a hot platter; garnish with fried parsley and lemon quarters.

Foie de lotte

ANGLERFISH LIVER

Anglerfish "liver," actually the soft roe of anglerfish, is much prized by gastronomes.

The preparation is usually the same as for the soft roe of various other fish; it takes a little longer to cook. We suggest the recipe called *au plat* (below).

Foie de lotte au plat

ANGLERFISH LIVER AU PLAT

Season ¹/₂ soft roe of an anglerfish with salt and pepper. Meanwhile, quickly heat ¹/₄ pound unsalted butter on an ovenproof earthenware serving platter. Place the roe in the butter; as soon as it stiffens, set the platter in the oven, protected on top by a piece of buttered wax paper. Continue cooking, basting frequently.

The soft roe will absorb part of the butter, and it will brown lightly. Add more butter so that the bottom stays well buttered.

Serve the soft roe in the cooking platter and squeeze the juice of ¹/₂ lemon over the top.

Loup de la Méditerranée en croûte

SEA BASS IN PASTRY (For 6–8 people)

6-pound sea bass
Chopped chervil
Chopped tarragon
Salt
Pepper
Flaky pastry dough (recipe below)
Egg yolk
Melted butter or *beurre blanc*

The Mediterranean sea bass, with flesh that is very fine, white, and of exquisite taste and aroma, can be cooked many different ways: poached, braised, served whole cold; but it is when sea bass is grilled with fennel that it has the most admirers—unless it is when it is prepared in pastry.

Method. Buy a nice, very fresh sea bass; gut it carefully, and remove the skin without hurting the meat; leave the head and the tail intact.

Cut the fish along the back to the backbone. In this long cavity, place freshly picked chervil and tarragon, chopped, salt, and pepper; close the fish. Do the same thing on the belly.

Next, roll out 2 thin sheets of flaky pastry dough the length of the sea bass. Place the fish on top of one of the sheets of pastry, cover it with the other sheet of pastry. Seal the dough by pressing all around the fish to enclose it completely and follow its original shape.

With a very sharp knife, cut off the excess dough, leaving enough to simulate the fins. Make a few lines lengthwise on the fins and tail, and with the remaining dough simulate the gills. Do the same for the eye.

Glaze the dough with an egg yolk, and to make it look more like a fish, reproduce the scales by pressing the dough with a little mold in a half-moon shape. This careful work demands much patience and a certain dexterity.

Place the sea bass thus prepared on a cookie sheet, in a 425° oven. When the dough is firm, reduce the heat to 350°, so that it cooks evenly, inside as well as outside, without burning the dough. It will take 1½ hours to cook.

To serve place the sea bass on a long platter and carve in front of the guests. Accompany it simply with melted butter or *beurre blanc.*

Variation. Before it is wrapped in dough, the sea bass can be stuffed with this excellent lobster mousse:

Lobster Mousse

½ pound raw lobster meat
Coral
¾ tablespoon salt
Freshly ground pepper
Dash grated nutmeg
1 cup heavy cream
¼ pound pistachios
Truffles

In a mortar pound the lobster meat. Add the coral seasoned with salt, a turn of the pepper mill, and finely grated nutmeg.

Rub the lobster meat through a very fine sieve into a bowl. Set the bowl on ice, and beat into the lobster 1 cup very heavy cream and then the pistachios and truffles.

Flaky Pastry Dough

5 cups sifted flour
¾ tablespoon salt
1 cup water
¾ pound unsalted butter

Place the flour on a pastry board, making a well in the middle for the salt and water. Mix and knead the flour with the water until the dough is smooth and elastic. Roll into a ball and let stand for 20 minutes. Roll the dough out evenly into a sheet about 8 inches square. On top place the butter, which has been kneaded in the same way until it has the same consistency as the dough.

Fold the ends of the dough over the butter so as to enclose it completely.

Let it stand again for 10 minutes; then give the dough two "turns." Each "turn" consists of rolling the dough, on a marble slab with a rolling pin, into a rectangle 24 inches by 8 inches and ½ inch thick. Fold the pastry crosswise in three, forming a square again. The second turn is given by rolling the dough, with a rolling pin, in the opposite direction and folding in three.

The purpose of turning and rolling is to distribute the butter evenly in the pastry and to ensure that it expands evenly during the cooking.

Finally, give the dough two more pairs of turns, letting it stand 10 minutes between each pair of turns. The flaky dough is ready to be used and cut after having had 6 turns, which means handled 3 times, 2 turns each time.

Loup au varech à la façon de Michel Guérard

SEA BASS IN SEAWEED À LA MICHEL GUÉRARD

3–3½-pound sea bass
2 handfuls fresh seaweed
Salt
Pepper
1 cup dry white wine

Method. In a long, shallow ovenproof dish, place one-third of the seaweed. Gut, clean, and season the sea bass; place it on top and cover completely with the remaining seaweed. Pour white wine over it.

Cover the dish with a piece of aluminum foil. Place it in a preheated 400° oven. It will take about 30 minutes to cook.

Serve the sea bass accompanied, on the side, by the following sauce:

In a bowl combine 1 tomato, seeded and finely chopped; 1 sweet pimiento, cut into small dice; 2 tablespoons chopped

Sauce
1 tomato
1 sweet pimiento
2 tablespoons chopped
fines herbes
Salt
Pepper
Juice of 2 lemons
½ cup olive oil

fines herbes, consisting of parsley, chervil, tarragon, basil, and chives.

Mix, season with salt and pepper, and thin with the lemon juice and olive oil.

The chives can be replaced with a little bit of chopped onion or shallot.

The sea bass can also be cooked in this way in a fish kettle, covered, over a low flame.

Maquereau

MACKEREL

Like herring, mackerel is very abundant in the spring, and it is an economical food, but it is difficult to digest. It is also simple to prepare: gut the fish through the gills and rub it vigorously to dry it. Cut off the fins and make a couple of slashes in the back.

Maquereaux grillés

BROILED MACKEREL

Choose medium-sized mackerels. Bread and season with salt and pepper mixed with 1 tablespoon melted butter or oil. Place on a very hot grill. Regulate the intensity of the flame according to the thickness of the bodies, which are spindle shaped, in order to cook them evenly. When the fish are half cooked, turn them over and complete cooking. Place the fish on a long platter and serve with a sauceboat of maître d'hôtel butter—a mixture of butter with fines herbes, vinegar or lemon juice, and salt and pepper.

If the mackerels are very large, they can be cooked more easily by slitting them down the back without separating the two halves. Pour on some seasoned melted butter and place the opened fish on the grill, searing the inside first; then turn and cook the skin side. Close the fish to serve.

Note: The thin end of the fish can be protected by sliding a slice of potato or any other vegetable between the tail and the flame. Do this after the mackerel has been seared.

Maquereaux au beurre noir

MACKEREL WITH BROWN BUTTER

Prepare a court-bouillon with 1 quart water, 2 teaspoons salt, ½ cup vinegar, and a few crushed peppercorns. Since this court-bouillon is cold, plunge the mackerel into it, and slowly bring to a boil; turn the heat as low as possible and poach for 10 to 15 minutes, depending upon the thickness of the fish, which should all be about the same size.

Drain the fish and place them on an ovenproof plate; dry for a few seconds in the oven. Sprinkle with chopped parsley and a few drops of vinegar or lemon juice and some unsalted butter cooked in a frying pan until brown. This last step is done just before serving.

1 large mackerel
Salt
Pepper
Strong fish stock (pages
 73–4)
Dry white wine
Unsalted butter
3 pounds spinach
Cream
1 cup Mornay sauce (page
 84)
Grated cheese
Pinch bread crumbs

Filets de maquereaux à la florentine

MACKEREL FILLETS FLORENTINE STYLE (For 6 people)

Method. Clean and fillet a large mackerel. Begin by half loosening the fillet from the side of the head while the fish is lying flat. Then detach the fillet, starting from the tail, with the blade of the knife placed flat, resting lightly on the backbone. Do this on each side.

Place the fillets on an ovenproof serving platter. Season with salt and pepper and moisten with a mixture of half strong fish stock and half dry white wine, covering the fish halfway. Sprinkle a few pieces of butter on top. Cook covered in a 375° oven for 8 to 10 minutes.

Meanwhile, prepare spinach in butter or cream, either puréed or whole, and 1 cup of Mornay sauce, slightly thickened.

Just before serving, spread the very hot spinach on a long platter and place the carefully drained mackerel fillets on top. Pour the remaining cooking juice from the fillets into the Mornay sauce without spoiling the consistency of the sauce. Coat the fillets and the spinach with the Mornay sauce and sprinkle with grated cheese mixed with bread crumbs. Pour some melted butter over and brown under the broiler.

Merlan

WHITING

The flesh of the whiting is very delicate and easy to digest, and is particularly good for invalids.

Because its flesh is very fragile, it is better to cook whiting whole. Gut it through the gills; since there are few scales, it is enough to scrape it lightly and dry vigorously.

The best recipes for whiting are: fried, *à la meunière* (page 110), *au plat* (page 119), and *au gratin*—although most of the recipes for white-flesh fish are applicable. (See the recipes for sole, pages 129–35.)

Merlan au plat

WHITING AU PLAT

Split the whiting down the back, open it flat, and season with salt and pepper. Set on an ovenproof dish, thickly buttered, and moisten with 2 tablespoons white wine; on top sprinkle a few pieces of butter and the juice of ¼ lemon. Start cooking on the stove and continue in a 375° oven, basting very often.

It will take 10 to 15 minutes to cook; at the end the white wine and the butter should be almost totally absorbed by the fish, which is glazed by the syrupy consistency of the liquid.

Merlan frit

FRIED WHITING

Clean and gut 1 medium-sized whiting, make 5 or 6 slashes on each side, and dip in milk and then in flour.

Just before serving, plunge into very hot oil. Follow the advice given on frying (page 100).

If fish is seared too quickly it does not cook inside. On the other hand, if the oil is not hot enough, the fish boils instead of frying. This requires attention; the size of the fish must also be considered.

Drain and wipe the fish in a cloth. Sprinkle lightly with salt, and serve immediately so that it has a golden crusty coating.

Whiting is generally accompanied by fried parsley and lemon quarters.

Mostelle

The *mostelle* is in the whiting family; but it is of higher quality. It lives in the waters of the Mediterranean Sea and is too delicate to be shipped. It is eaten only in the coastal regions. [*Editor's note:* This Mediterranean fish is not found in the United States; whiting can be substituted.]

Because of its fragility and its fineness, *mostelle* can be prepared only *au plat.*

Slit the fish down its back. Remove the bone. Season on both sides and place on a thickly buttered ovenproof earthenware dish big enough to hold it easily. Sprinkle a few pieces of unsalted butter on top, and cook in the oven, basting frequently with the cooking butter. The *mostelle* is a glutton for butter and must be cooked while the guests are sitting at the table; it cannot wait. Just before serving, sprinkle a few drops of lemon juice on top. Ah, this is a royal treat!

Morue

COD

Choose cod that is very dark on the back and silver on the belly, and thick, with white flesh and short fibers.

Discard flat fish and dry or yellow fish.

Before cooking, wash the cod under cold running water, brushing the fish on both sides. Cut the fish into pieces of about ¼ pound each and soak in cold water for at least 24 hours to desalt it before cooking. The water should be changed several times.

The cooking is very simple.

Drain the pieces after desalting. Roll each one up, with the skin on the outside, and tie with string.

Place the pieces of fish in a frying pan and cover with cold water. As soon as the water starts to boil, put the pan on the lowest possible heat. Skim off the foam. Cover, and poach for 15 to 18 minutes, depending upon the thickness of the cod.

The cooked cod is now ready for various culinary preparations, especially the most succulent of all:

Brandade de morue aux truffes

BRANDADE WITH TRUFFLES

Into the *brandade,* prepared as described below, mix truffles cut into large dice and heated in unsalted butter. Pile in a dome shape and arrange some slices of truffle in the center and a ring of fried croutons around the edge.

Brandade de morue à la ménagère

BRANDADE HOME STYLE (For 6–8 people)

1 pound very white salt cod
1–1¹/₂ cups olive oil
1 crushed garlic clove
¹/₂ cup cream or milk
¹/₂ cup cooked potato pulp
Pinch white pepper, very finely ground
Salt
Juice of 1 lemon

Method.   Desalt the cod in fresh water for 24 hours. Change the water several times.

Poach the desalted cod in water. To do that, place the fish, cut into several pieces, in a saucepan with 4 quarts water. Bring to a boil. As soon as the water boils, turn the heat as low as possible and poach the fish for 10 to 12 minutes.

Drain the pieces of cod. Remove the black and white skin and the bones. Break the flesh into fine flakes.

In a heavy-bottomed saucepan heat ¹/₂ cup oil. Add the cod and the crushed garlic clove.

Work the mixture quickly with a spatula or a wooden spoon until the fish is reduced to a fine paste. Then lower the heat. Continue to beat the paste without stopping, adding the rest of the oil and the cream or milk.

Then add the hot potato pulp and mix well. The potato should be boiled in the skin or steamed. Season with white pepper and, if necessary, add salt. Then mix in the lemon juice well. When finished, the *brandade* should be a smooth paste, light, and very white.

Serve the hot *brandade* on a platter in the shape of a dome. Surround with tiny bread croutons cooked golden in oil or butter.

Morue à la lyonnaise

COD LYONS STYLE

3 medium-sized onions
¹/₂ tablespoon unsalted butter
2 tablespoons oil
3 medium-sized potatoes
1 pound cod
Pinch freshly ground pepper
Pinch chopped parsley
¹/₂ tablespoon vinegar

Method.   In a frying pan slowly cook the onions, cut into julienne, with ¹/₂ tablespoon butter and 2 tablespoons oil. Cook 3 potatoes in salted water, peel, and cut into slices. When the onions are cooked but not brown, add the potatoes and sauté the mixture to brown lightly.

Poach the cod; remove the skin and bones, flake and dry over a low flame just long enough to evaporate the cooking water. Add to the mixture in the frying pan and sauté for a few minutes on a high flame. Correct the seasoning and add a pinch of freshly ground pepper.

Just before serving, stir freshly chopped parsley into the mixture. Pile onto a serving platter and add vinegar to the cooking pan; bring rapidly to a boil, and pour over the cod.

Raie
SKATE

Preferably buy a *raie* called *bouclée,* which can be recognized by growths shaped like buttons scattered over its skin.

Wash the skate under running water and scrub with a brush to remove the slimy matter that covers it. Then remove the fins and cut them into pieces about ½ pound each and place them in a skillet along with the central part of the tail and the two sides of the head, where there are two fleshy parts called the cheeks.

Cover with water, salt to taste, and add ½ cup vinegar for each quart of water. Bring slowly to a boil; skim; and as soon as the water boils, lower the heat and poach for 15 minutes.

Drain the skate carefully. Remove the skin on both sides and arrange on a serving platter; it can be served using the following recipe.

Raie au beurre noir
SKATE WITH BROWN BUTTER

Prepare the skate as directed above. While it is still very hot, season it with salt and freshly ground pepper. Sprinkle crushed capers and a pinch of chopped parsley on top. Baste it with hot browned butter and with a splash of vinegar that has been poured for just a second into the hot frying pan used for browning the butter. Serve steamed potatoes on the side.

Rougets (rougets-barbets)
RED MULLETS

The red mullet is notable for the two wattles fixed to the lower jaw; the back is red, the sides and belly a silver pink, and the tail scalloped. The flesh is white, fine, and very delicate.

This delicious fish lives at the bottom of the Mediterranean, where it feeds on small marine plants that grow on the rocks. It is also called the sea woodcock. The only way to cook red mullet that is worthy of it is on the grill, while it is still very fresh.

Preparation is very simple: wipe, remove the gills, but do not gut the fish.

When the red mullets are cooked following the method for broiling fish on page 100, place them on a very hot serving platter and serve, on the side, a sauceboat of *maître d'hôtel* butter (pages 161–2).

On the table, in the presence of the guests, detach and remove the heads. Open the mullets down the back. Carefully scoop out the insides and mix with the *maître d'hôtel* butter. Remove the bones and spread the *maître d'hôtel* butter on the flesh of the fish. Season the fish with a few drops of lemon juice and one turn of a pepper mill; then serve this divine dish.

6 small red mullets
sautéed as above
1 onion, coarsely chopped
6 tomatoes
1 garlic clove
Pinch chopped parsley
1/2 cup pitted black olives
Pinch salt
Freshly ground pepper
Few drops lemon juice

Rouget à la provençale
RED MULLET PROVENÇAL STYLE

The mullet *à la provençale* is a hot variation of the mullet *à l'orientale* (page 127).

Proceed as for mullet *à l'orientale* until the mullets have been placed in the ovenproof platter in which they will be served. Then add the onion to the oil and cook it slowly until it is just light brown. Add the tomatoes, peeled, seeded, with the juice reduced, and the garlic clove coarsely chopped, chopped parsley, black olives, salt, and pepper. Simmer for 10 minutes and pour over the mullets. Finish the cooking in a 325° oven for 10 minutes. Serve hot, with a few drops lemon juice. This dish can also be served cold.

Rougets de la Méditerranée —
Sauce au pistou

MEDITERRANEAN RED MULLETS WITH PISTOU SAUCE
(For 4 people)

8 Mediterranean red
mullets, about 1/2 pound
each
2 cups white wine
1 cup water (preferably
bottled Evian water)
3 1/2 tablespoons chopped
carrots
3 1/2 tablespoons chopped
onions
3 1/2 tablespoons coarse
salt
1 tablespoon parsley
leaves
1 tablespoon sliced celery
1 tablespoon chopped leek
1/2 bay leaf
Small sprig thyme
2 teaspoons peppercorns
2 cloves
2 coriander seeds
4 slices orange
4 slices lemon

Pistou sauce

1 cup olive oil
1 1/2 tablespoons chopped
basil
2 teaspoons chopped
parsley
1 teaspoon chopped
tarragon
1 teaspoon chopped
chervil
1 teaspoon chopped
chives
1 garlic clove, crushed
Juice of 1 lemon
2 teaspoons salt
3 turns of a pepper mill

For this delicious dish you will need very fresh red mullets, which can be distinguished by their bright eyes and beautiful red color.

Method. Prepare a *court-bouillon* with all the ingredients listed. (Evian water is very good and does not have the taste of chlorine; use it unless you have a spring near you.) Bring the mixture to a boil, and boil for 15 minutes. Add the mullets to the saucepan; return to a boil. Lower the flame immediately and poach for 15 minutes.

Mix all the ingredients for the pistou sauce, and serve with the fish. Keep in a cool place. In the summer these mullets can be eaten cold.

Small red mullets
Salt
Pepper
Flour
Oil
Slices of peeled lemon
Chervil leaves

2 pounds ripe tomatoes
2 tablespoons oil
Salt
Pepper
Garlic clove
Pinch sugar
Pinch saffron
Fennel stalk
Sprig thyme
1/2 bay leaf
Few grains coriander
Pinch chopped parsley

Rouget à l'orientale
RED MULLET ORIENTAL STYLE

The red mullet is a noteworthy addition to the collection of cold dishes and, treated *à l'orientale,* it is a very choice hors d'oeuvre or a cold dish (depending upon the rest of the menu).

Method. Season small red mullets with salt and pepper. Roll them in flour and brown them rapidly in a frying pan in a little bit of oil, as for *à la meunière.*

Place the fish in an oiled ovenproof dish and cover them with a *fondue* of tomatoes, prepared in the following manner.

Tomato *Fondue*

Skin and seed ripe tomatoes, retaining the juice. Cut into coarse pieces and put into a frying pan where a little oil is heating. Season with salt and pepper and add a crushed garlic clove and sugar; cook slowly until the liquid in the pot is reduced by three-fourths.

The tomato *fondue* used for the mullets will be seasoned further with saffron, a fennel stalk, thyme, and bay leaf, crushed to a powder, coriander, and chopped parsley.

Continue cooking the mullets covered with the *fondue.* Bring to a boil on top of the stove; then place, covered, in a 325° oven for 8 to 10 minutes.

Cool and garnish to taste with thin slices of peeled lemon. Place a chervil leaf in the center of each lemon slice; serve mullets at room temperature or slightly chilled.

Sardines

Fresh, unsalted sardines are rarely found in the inland markets. Their flesh is delicate and cannot be shipped.

Along the Mediterranean Sea, where the sardines are especially fine, they are eaten as soon as they have been caught, usually broiled and accompanied by fresh butter.

1 pound large fresh sardines
2 tablespoons olive oil
2 large onions
1/2 cup dry white wine
6 tomatoes
Salt
Pepper
Anchovy butter (optional, page 18)

Sardines antiboises
SARDINES ANTIBES STYLE

Method. Scale, gut, and wipe large fresh sardines.

Heat olive oil in a skillet; when it smokes, add the sardines and brown them rapidly on both sides. Set aside on a plate.

Then slowly cook the onions cut into julienne in the oil used for the sardines; do not let them brown. Moisten with wine. Reduce by two-thirds, then add the tomatoes, peeled, seeded, drained, and coarsely chopped; season with salt and pepper and simmer to reduce by half.

Pour the sauce in a *gratin* dish. Place the sardines on top and put in a 425° oven for 5 minutes. Serve with a sauceboat of anchovy butter. This last step is optional.

Saumon
SALMON

The salmon first lives in large rivers, then swims to the sea, and returns to the rivers to reproduce. It often reaches a very large size—6 or 7 feet.

Choose a medium-sized fish, which means that the fish is adult but not old.

Salmon is cooked by either of two methods: whole or cut into slices about ³/₄ inch thick, called *darnes.* I advise you to cook the fish whole except in two cases: if you are broiling it or cooking it *à la meunière* (page 110).

The whole salmon is generally cooked in a *court-bouillon* (page 101) and served hot, with a hollandaise sauce, *mousseline* sauce, cream sauce, shrimp sauce, *genevoise* sauce, etc., or cold with a mayonnaise sauce, green sauce, ravigote sauce, etc. (see index).

Salmon can also be poached, grilled, or braised, following the recipes indicated for large fish.

One can also make an excellent fish pastry called *coulibiac.*

Coulibiac de saumon
HOT SALMON IN PASTRY

1 recipe firm unsweetened brioche dough (pages 376–8)
³/₄ pound salmon, backbone removed, cut into ¹/₄-inch slices, seasoned, and sautéed in butter until firm
3¹/₂ tablespoons chopped mushrooms and 1 medium-sized onion, chopped, stewed until soft in the salmon butter, cooled, then sprinkled on the salmon
3¹/₂ ounces of thick semolina cooked in white stock (page 73)
1 hard-cooked egg, coarsely chopped
¹/₂ pound fresh vésiga (the dorsal marrow of the sturgeon) or 1¹/₂ ounce if dried, soaked for 5 hours, and cooked in water or in white stock for 3 hours, and then chopped
Melted unsalted butter

Method.   Roll the brioche dough into a rectangle; on top place layers of the ingredients listed as explained for a pâté Pantin (pages 191–2). Fold the dough so that it encloses the fish and the seasonings, moistening the edges so that the pastry will stick together. Turn upside down onto a cookie sheet; let stand at room temperature for 20 minutes, covered with a cloth. Brush the dough with melted butter; make a couple of slashes in it, and in the center make a small hole to allow the steam to escape.

Bake in a 425° oven for about 35 minutes. Before serving, pour a couple of tablespoons of melted butter through the hole.

Note: The grains of the cooked and seasoned semolina should remain separated from one another, like rice, while becoming very soft.

Saumon cru Renga-Ya
RAW SALMON RENGA-YA

Japanese cooking was my inspiration for this recipe. Just before serving cut the salmon into scallops of about ¹/₄ pound each.

Place the salmon scallops on very cold plates; salt them, and give them a turn of a pepper mill. Pour on each a tablespoon of olive oil, the juice of a quarter lemon, and a pinch of chives. A tablespoon of caviar can be placed in the middle.

Serve with thin slices of hot broiled bread.

Escalope de saumon à l'oseille des frères Troisgros

SALMON SCALLOPS WITH SORREL À LA TROISGROS
(For 8–10 people)

1 cup dry white wine
1 cup Noilly Prat dry white vermouth
1 cup strong *fumet* (pages 73–4)
6 tablespoons chopped shallots
2 cups cream
¼ pound sorrel cooked in salted water and drained
Salt
Pepper
3 pounds fresh salmon cut into very thin scallops
½ cup oil

Method. In a saucepan, reduce the white wine, the vermouth, the *fumet,* and the chopped shallots.

When the liquid becomes syrupy, strain it through a fine sieve. Add the cream, and reduce again to thicken. Season. Then add the well-drained sorrel.

Salt and pepper the salmon scallops. Place them in a skillet with the hot oil. Do not let them dry out; a few seconds is enough to cook each side.

To serve, place the salmon scallops on warm plates; cover with the sorrel sauce or serve it on the side.

As a garnish make a fish-shaped ornament of flaky pastry.

Sole

The sole is the finest of all the flat fish. Its flesh is white, firm, delicate, and easy to digest.

To clean the sole remove its two skins, the black and the white; the latter is easily scraped off when the sole is served whole. However, this rule has some exceptions.

Cut the head off on the bias at the beginning of the fillets. Trim the end of the tail. At the tail end lift the black skin by scraping with the point of a knife. Grasp this thin end of the skin with the corner of a dish towel and pull sharply. The skin usually will detach itself in one pull. If the sole is not to be prepared in fillets, scrape the scales off the white skin. Otherwise, remove the white skin in the same way as the black one.

Using strong scissors, cut off the lateral fins. Make a small incision above the intestines and remove them. Wash the sole under running water and dry it with a cloth.

To aid in serving, just before cooking the fish make a slash on the right and left sides of the backbone, which will guide the point of the serving knife.

When the sole is to be prepared in fillets, and the two skins have been removed, cut a circle with the point of the knife around the edges of each fillet. Detach the fillet by sliding the blade of a thin, flexible knife between the bones and the fillet, starting from the backbone and cutting close to the bones so as not to leave any flesh.

Then slightly flatten the fillet with a mallet (or the side of a cleaver) that is a little damp in order to tenderize the flesh.

Finally, if the sole is to be served whole and made with a sauce, just before cooking cut the short bones that extend from the fins off the edges of the fillets.

This need not be done when the sole is fried or broiled; its purpose is to avoid the annoyance of the numerous short bones that too often can mix into the sauce or the garnish as one serves the sole.

Certainly the fillets lose some of their attractiveness, but on the other hand, it is easier to eat the fish, the sauce, and the garnish since they are free of bones.

The bones, as well as the head, are always used to make a strong sole stock, which will be used to baste the fish while it is cooking.

Before cleaning, a sole for two people should weigh about 12 to 14 ounces; a fillet should average about 9 ounces net weight. Use 2 fillets per person.

Sole frite

FRIED SOLE

Clean the sole, remove the black skin, and scrape the white one.

Soak the fish in milk, roll in flour, shake off the excess, and plunge into a large saucepan of hot oil. Follow the basic instructions for frying (page 100); the cooking time for a sole of about 1/2 pound will be 8 to 10 minutes. Then the fish will be crusty and golden when served.

When the sole is drained from the oil, pat it quickly with a cloth, sprinkle it with salt, and place it on a plate with quarters of lemon and a bouquet of parsley plunged in very hot oil for a second and then salted to taste. Serve without delay.

Sole grillée

BROILED SOLE

Prepare the sole as above; in addition, with the point of a knife make a few diamond-shaped slashes in the white skin. Season with salt and pepper and dip into unsalted melted butter or a little oil. Place on a very hot grill, with the white skin side down. Adjust the heat of the flame according to the thickness of the sole, and place the thin tail end farther from the heat so that it does not cook more rapidly than the opposite end and dry out.

Cook for 3 minutes; then slide a spatula between the grill and the sole and lift and rotate the fish about 3/4 inches, as a wheel turns on its axis. The second cooking time is 3 minutes (we are still talking of a fish about 1/2 pound). Slide the spatula, a second time, under the sole and turn the fish over with a rapid movement. The white skin will be golden and ornamented with a nice diamond pattern left by the crossed bars of the grill.

Moisten lightly with a few drops of melted butter while

cooking the second side of the sole, and sprinkle with a little salt, which will penetrate the flesh while it melts.

Serve the sole with the diamond pattern up, accompanied by grilled tomatoes, grilled mushrooms, and melted butter in a sauceboat, or *maître d'hôtel* butter, anchovy butter, or a *béarnaise* or Choron sauce (see index).

Sole meunière

Sole
Salt and pepper
Oil
Flour
5¹/₂ tablespoons unsalted butter
1 tablespoon olive oil
Lemon slices and juice
1 teaspoon chopped parsley

Method.   Prepare the sole as above, leaving the well-scraped white skin on.

Season with salt and pepper mixed with a few drops of oil; then roll in flour.

Cook, white skin side down, in 2 tablespoons very hot butter and 1 tablespoon olive oil. Use a skillet, preferably an oval one, in order to avoid using excess butter, which often burns; the skillet should be almost the same size as the fish.

Cook very quickly; when the sole touches the very hot butter, it will be sufficiently seared so that it will not stick to the skillet. The cooking butter should not boil.

After 5 or 6 minutes, turn the sole with a spatula and continue cooking until it is done.

Place the fish on a very hot serving platter. Garnish the edges with a row of thin lemon slices, halved, with their skins cut in points like wolf's teeth.

Squeeze a few drops lemon juice onto the sole; sprinkle with chopped parsley, blanched at the last moment and still damp. Add 3¹/₂ tablespoons butter to the cooking butter in the pan and heat until it turns brown. Pour over the sole.

When the very hot butter touches the damp parsley, it produces a rich foam, which will still cover the sole when it is placed on the table in front of the guests.

Sole au champagne

SOLE WITH CHAMPAGNE

Sole
Strong sole stock
Champagne
Unsalted butter
Salt

Dress the sole by cutting the short bones that form the ends of the fins off the edges of the fillet. With the bones and the head make a strong sole stock using champagne instead of the usual wine.

Thickly butter a long ovenproof dish the size of the fish; sprinkle with a pinch of salt, and place on it 1 or 2 sole with the white skin side underneath.

Moisten, just to the top of the sole, with equal parts of dry champagne and strong sole stock. Sprinkle a few pieces of unsalted butter on top, and cover with a piece of buttered wax paper. Bring to a boil on top of the stove, then place in the oven to poach the fish slowly. The fish is cooked when the fillets can be detached easily from the backbone. This takes about 12 to 15 minutes.

Drain the fish with a spatula, and place it on a very hot serving platter; cover with another dish to keep it moist while

Cooking juice from sole
Unsalted butter
Flour

the sauce is being prepared. The sauce can be thickened in various ways.

First Method

Place the dish used for cooking the sole on the stove, and boil to reduce the stock until you have just enough to sauce 1 or 2 sole. Then add to the boiling sauce a mixture of 3 parts butter to 2 parts flour (by weight). The butter will melt immediately and thicken the sauce. Off the flame finish the sauce by adding $3\frac{1}{2}$ tablespoons butter. Correct the seasoning. Add the juices in the serving platter that have drained from the sole. Pour the sauce on the fish.

Second Method

Cooking juice from sole
3 tablespoons fish *velouté*
  page 76) or béchamel
  sauce (page 78)
1 egg yolk
1 tablespoon cold strong
  fish stock (pages 73–4),
  milk, or cooking juice
  from mushrooms
Unsalted butter

Pour the cooking juice from the sole into a small saucepan. Boil to reduce the stock two-thirds, then add (for 1 sole) 3 tablespoons fish *velouté* or béchamel sauce; stir the mixture. Bring to a boil, and thicken with 1 egg yolk beaten with cold strong sole stock, milk, or mushroom juice. Be careful not to cook the yolk; it should not boil but the sauce should thicken to the consistency of cream. Finish by adding butter off the flame, as in the method above. Serve in the same way.

Third Method

Cooking juice from sole
1 egg yolk
1 tablespoon cold strong
  sole stock, milk, or
  cooking juice from
  mushrooms
· $\frac{1}{4}$ pound unsalted butter

Reduce the cooking liquid by two-thirds. Remove from the flame and thicken with 1 egg yolk mixed with cold strong sole stock, milk, or mushroom juice. Cook without boiling on a low flame or in a double boiler, stirring with a whisk as for hollandaise sauce. Correct the seasoning. Off the flame finish with $\frac{1}{4}$ pound butter. Serve as in the two methods above.

This sauce should have the consistency of light cream.

Sole Bercy

(For 2 people)

1 shallot
Unsalted butter
Salt
Pepper
Dry white wine
Cooking juice from
  mushrooms or strong
  sole stock
1 teaspoon chopped
  parsley
Few drops lemon juice

Method.   Thickly butter an ovenproof dish; on the bottom sprinkle a chopped shallot. Heat the dish slowly on the stove; cook the shallot without browning for about 10 minutes.

Season the sole on both sides with salt and pepper. Place on top of the shallot, the white skin side up, and moisten with dry white wine and the cooking juice from the mushrooms or strong sole stock—by halves, or thirds if you have all three. The liquid should just reach the top of the fish. Sprinkle pieces of butter over it. Bring to a boil on the stove, and continue to poach in a 325° oven for about 10 minutes. Baste frequently.

Place the sole on a serving platter; cover with another platter to keep warm while you finish the sauce.

Pour the liquid from the sole into a small saucepan. Boil to reduce rapidly, until only 4 tablespoons of very syrupy liquid are left. Off the flame shake the saucepan in a circle to blend in 4 tablespoons butter, cut into small pieces, which will thicken in the cooked sauce. Add 1 teaspoon freshly chopped parsley, and squeeze in a few drops of lemon juice. Correct the seasoning; then cover the well-drained sole entirely with the sauce.

If you have a very hot oven, or a gas or electric broiler, place the sole under the broiler for a few seconds. The sauce will get a beautiful golden color. This last step must be done very quickly without letting the sauce boil, or the two main ingredients—the cooking liquid and the butter—will separate immediately. (This is called, improperly, "turning.")

This procedure, which is the simplest and the most delicious of all, can be utilized in many recipes for fish. Only the condiments and the garnishes will change.

To succeed, it is necessary to understand the method; and you need only remember this: the thickening of the cooking liquid and the butter is possible only if the liquid is sufficiently strong, which means that the juices of the fish in the sauce are sufficiently concentrated to support, to bind, or to make an emulsion of the oily components, which, by their nature, do not have the same density.

In making an extreme reduction of the fish stock you will note that little by little a gray-colored liquid is formed, which first has the consistency of a sugar syrup and then finally solidifies. This extract is called fish glaze and constitutes the thickening substance and the flavor of the sauce.

For reasons of economy or practicality, one may apply, to this classic recipe, one of the three methods for the sole with champagne (pages 131–2). In all three cases the cooking stock called *à la Bercy* is added to the prepared sauce or used to make it.

Sole aux champignons ou sole bonne femme
SOLE WITH MUSHROOMS

This recipe is identical to the preceding one.

The only change is the addition of 4 or 5 white mushrooms (for 2 people), finely chopped and spread on the chopped shallot after it is cooked.

Proceed, then, as for sole Bercy.

Sole aux moules dite marinière
SOLE WITH MUSSELS MARINIÈRE (For 2 people)

1 pint mussels
1 tablespoon dry white wine
1 tablespoon unsalted butter
Sole, prepared as for sole with champagne (pages 131–2)

Method.   Clean the mussels, making sure that no sand is left. Boil with dry white wine and butter until they open.

Drain the cooking liquid and strain it through cheesecloth into a bowl. Remove the mussels from their shells and clean them. Add to the liquid.

Meanwhile, prepare a sole as for the sole with champagne, moisten it with the cooking liquid from the mussels, and poach as in the recipe. Finish the sauce in the same way, adding the mussels, which have been heated in a little bit of their cooking juice and drained well.

Place the sole on a serving platter and cover with the sauce.

The hot mussels, well drained, can also be placed around

the sole on the serving platter and covered with sauce at the same time as the fish.

I advise you not to reduce the mussel stock too much. If this stock is concentrated excessively, it becomes coarse and has too strong a flavor.

Sole à la bourguignonne
SOLE BURGUNDY STYLE (For 2 people)

12 small onions
Unsalted butter
12 small mushrooms
Sole prepared as for sole
  Bercy (pages 132–3)
6 tablespoons red wine
  with pinch sugar
4 tablespoons strong sole
  stock
Croutons, fried in butter

Method. In a saucepan cook the onions slowly in butter until brown. When the onions are nearly cooked, add the mushrooms.

Prepare a sole as for sole Bercy. Place the onions and the mushrooms around the sole in the cooking dish. In a skillet bring 6 tablespoons good red wine (sweetened with sugar) to a boil, and reduce the liquid to 1 tablespoon. Then add 4 tablespoons strong sole stock. Moisten the sole with the reduced fish stock, and continue the recipe as for sole Bercy. Arrange the sole on a platter and pour the sauce over, without putting under the broiler. On top place some diamond-shaped croutons fried in butter.

Sole normande
NORMAN SOLE

Sole
Unsalted butter
Pinch salt
Sole stock
1 tablespoon dry white
  wine
1 tablespoon cooking juice
  from mushrooms
Norman sauce (page 86)
Poached mussels
Shrimp tails
Poached oysters
Mushrooms stewed in
  butter with lemon juice
Truffles
Gudgeons rolled in
  bread crumbs and fried
Crayfish cooked in
  ***court-bouillon* (page 142)**
Fleurons

Method. Place the sole in a buttered ovenproof dish, season with salt. Mix sole stock with 1 tablespoon dry white wine and 1 tablespoon mushroom juice. Pour over to reach the top of the fish. Dot with 1 tablespoon butter cut into small pieces; cover with buttered wax paper, and poach slowly in a 325° oven without boiling.

Drain the cooking liquid; reduce to 2 tablespoons, and incorporate into a Norman sauce.

Put the sole on a long hot platter big enough to hold it and the garnish. Surround it with bearded, poached mussels, shrimp tails, poached oysters, and mushrooms stewed in butter with a few drops of lemon juice. Coat the dish with the Norman sauce, and place a row of sliced truffles on top, and at either end of the platter a handful of gudgeons, rolled in bread crumbs and fried, and 1 crayfish, cleaned and cooked in a *court-bouillon,* per guest. Around the edge, arrange a row of *fleurons* made of flaky pastry.

Sole meunière à la niçoise
SOLE MEUNIÈRE NICE STYLE

2 ripe tomatoes
1 tablespoon unsalted
  butter
Pinch salt
Pinch sugar
Small garlic clove
Sole prepared as for *à la*
  ***meunière* (page 131)**

Method. Remove the cores and skins of the tomatoes and squeeze them to remove the seeds and the juice. Cut into quarters and sauté in a skillet with the butter, salt, sugar, and a piece of crushed garlic the size of a pea.

Reduce the mixture slightly; taste it. Place a sole prepared *à la meunière* on a serving platter and a "bouquet" of the tomato mixture at either end.

Note: Zucchini, eggplants, and cucumbers mix deliciously with tomatoes cooked as a garnish. If two vegetables are used, arrange a bouquet of each alternating at either end of the serving platter.

Sole aux tomates ou à la portugaise

SOLE WITH TOMATOES OR PORTUGUESE STYLE

Use the same method of preparation as for sole Bercy and replace the mushrooms with 2 beautiful ripe tomatoes, skinned, seeded, coarsely chopped, and stewed in 1 tablespoon butter.

Thon braisé à la ménagère

BRAISED TUNA HOME STYLE (For 6 people)

1 slice fresh tuna, about 2$^1/_2$ pounds
3$^1/_2$ tablespoons chopped onion
$^3/_4$ cup olive oil
Salt and pepper
$^2/_3$ pound tomato pulp
1 cup white wine
Small *bouquet garni* (bay leaf, thyme, rosemary, and parsley)

Method. Soak the tuna in cold water for about 1 hour to remove the blood.

In a saucepan with a heavy bottom sauté the chopped onion in the olive oil without letting it brown. Salt and pepper the slice of tuna, and place it on the onion and continue cooking. Turn after 5 minutes.

Add the tomato, the white wine, and the *bouquet garni*. Season.

Cover the saucepan and simmer on a low flame for about 30 minutes. When the tuna is cooked, set it on a serving dish. Just before serving, cover the fish with the sauce, which should be very thick.

Accompany the dish with a mold of creole rice (page 370).

Thon grillé

BROILED TUNA

Cut a piece of tuna into $^3/_4$-inch slices, season with salt and pepper, and marinate for about 1 hour with 1 onion, minced, a couple of sprigs of parsley, a sprig of thyme, 1 bay leaf, 1 tablespoon oil, 1 tablespoon white wine, and the juice of $^1/_2$ lemon.

Just before broiling, drain and wipe the fish, moisten with a few drops of oil, and place slices on a very hot grill. Follow the instructions for broiling a fish (page 100).

Serve accompanied by a rémoulade sauce (page 91), tartar sauce (page 91), or mayonnaise (page 90).

Turbot et turbotin

TURBOT

[*Editor's note:* European turbot is not available in the United States. It may be replaced by halibut.]

The turbot is one of the best flat sea fish, with white and

savory flesh. The best turbot comes from the Pas-de-Calais and the North Sea.

A 2-to-6-pound turbot is called a *turbotin*.

For a small turbot or *turbotin*, use the recipes for brill and sole. For a large turbot follow the more complicated recipes of the *grande cuisine* or simply poach it.

Turbot ou turbotin poché

POACHED TURBOT

Cook the turbot in a fish kettle, an indispensable utensil that has a rack that enables you to drain the fish without breaking it.

First gut and scrape the turbot, remove the fins, and wash it. Then make an incision along its back (brown side) the length of the backbone and place the fish (white side up) on the rack of the fish kettle. Cover with cold water, adding 1 cup milk and $1\frac{1}{2}$ tablespoons salt for each 2 quarts water; place on the fire. As soon as the liquid starts to boil, skim, lower the heat, and simmer very gently. It will take about $\frac{1}{4}$ hour for each 2 pounds of fish, depending on its thickness.

It is not very difficult to serve the fish, despite its shape and size. Drain by lifting the rack out of the liquid and slide the fish onto a serving platter or a wooden plank covered with a napkin. Serve the turbot with potatoes boiled in their skins and one of the following sauces: melted butter, hollandaise, *mousseline,* caper, *béarnaise, maître d'hôtel* butter, white wine, shrimp, etc. (see index).

The meat of the turbot is extremely gelatinous, almost gummy, and does not lend itself to being served cold.

Turbot leftovers can be served in scallop shells or used in other recipes.

Coquilles Saint-Jacques

[*Editor's note:* French scallops are larger than those in the United States and are sold unshelled. They contain a roe or coral, and their meat is eaten as well as their muscular sections. The only part sold in the United States is the edible muscle, and more scallops per serving must be allowed.]

Preliminary steps.   Scrub the outside of the scallop shells with a brush and place them in a very hot oven until they part slightly. Slide the blade of a knife between the flat shell and the muscle, and open them. Discard the flat shells.

With the blade of a flexible knife do the same to separate the muscle from the concave shell.

Remove the membranes and the fringes that surround the muscle and then the red part, called the coral. Wash the muscle and the coral carefully under running water.

Scrub the insides of the concave shells with a brush and set them aside for further use, either to serve the scallops or to fill with other fish.

Ragoût de coquilles Saint-Jacques
aux truffes fraîches

SCALLOP RAGOÛT WITH FRESH TRUFFLES (For 1 person)

3–5 scallops in their shells
¹/₄ cup excellent
  ***demi-glace* sauce**
  (page 76)
3¹/₂ tablespoons minced
  fresh truffles
3¹/₂ tablespoons steamed
  spinach leaves
Unsalted butter
Salt and pepper

Method.   Open the scallop shells. Discard the parts that are not edible. Poach the meat in simmering *demi-glace* sauce with the minced truffles; 5 to 8 minutes is sufficient to cook them.

Drain the cooked spinach leaves. While hot, season with butter, salt, and pepper.

To serve, place the spinach on a hot plate and cover with the ragoût of scallops with truffles.

Note: If the scallop shells are large, they can be used instead of plates.

Coquilles Saint-Jacques à la ménagère

SCALLOPS IN SHELLS HOME STYLE (For 6 people)

12 scallops in their shells
18 tablespoons unsalted
  butter
¹/₂ pound white mushrooms
1 tablespoon flour
2 egg yolks
Fine bread crumbs
Court-bouillon
1 cup water
¹/₂ cup dry white wine
Sprig thyme
¹/₂ bay leaf
1 medium-sized onion
Pinch salt
Pinch pepper

Method.   Prepare scallops in their shells as above. Poach the cleaned scallops for 4 minutes in a *court-bouillon* made with: 1 cup water, ¹/₂ cup dry white wine, a sprig of thyme, ¹/₂ bay leaf, 1 medium-sized onion, finely minced, a pinch of salt and pepper.

Drain the scallops and slice them about ¹/₈ inch thick. Melt 3¹/₂ tablespoons butter in a frying pan, and add ¹/₂ pound white mushrooms, cleaned and sliced very thin. Cook rapidly. Then add the scallop slices, mix well, and keep hot, covered.

In a frying pan melt 7 tablespoons butter, add 1 rounded tablespoon flour, and cook slowly like a *roux* for 10 minutes. Cool the *roux*. Strain the *court-bouillon* through cheesecloth, and add the hot liquid in small quantities to the cooled *roux*, stirring until the sauce is smooth. Bring to a boil, stirring with a whisk, and cook for 1 minute.

Thicken the sauce, off the heat, with 2 egg yolks diluted with 2 teaspoons *court-bouillon.* Continue to beat while heating; remove from the heat when the mixture approaches the boiling point.

Do not let the sauce boil or the yolk will cook and form small lumps. Add 7 tablespoons unsalted butter and correct the seasoning.

Plunge 6 of the concave scallop shells into boiling water, drain and wipe them, and put 1 tablespoon of the sauce on the bottom of each shell; then, on top, add the meat of about 2 scallops with the mushrooms and, finally, 2 pieces of coral. Cover with the sauce, and sprinkle over some fine bread crumbs, moistened with a few drops of melted butter. Brown in a very hot oven.

Serve on a platter on top of a folded napkin

Huîtres

OYSTERS

There are many recipes for oysters in the section on hot hors d'oeuvre; here are a few more that can be useful to complete menus.

However, for those who like them, good-quality *marennes, belons,* or *cancales* [different types of oysters], eaten raw, make a dish incomparable in its natural simplicity.

Huîtres frites en brochettes

OYSTERS FRIED ON SKEWERS

Remove the oysters from their shells, stiffen them by heating for 2 minutes in their juice together with the juice of 1 lemon. Drain on a cloth and roll in beaten egg, then in fine bread crumbs; place 6 oysters on each skewer, leaving a little space between them. Plunge into very hot oil for 2 minutes. Serve with fried parsley and a lemon quarter per skewer.

Huîtres au gratin

OYSTERS AU GRATIN

Detach each oyster from its shallow shell, leaving it in the concave one. Sprinkle on top some chopped *fines herbes,* the juice of 1 lemon, and a pinch of fine bread crumbs; moisten with melted butter. Bake in a 425° oven for 3 to 4 minutes.

Serve in the shell.

Moules

MUSSELS

Mussels must always be carefully scraped, one by one, with a knife, to remove all the grassy filaments that hold them onto the rocks (or to the cork, when they are cultivated mussels); then test them by a light pressure of the thumb and the forefinger, trying to slide the two shells against each other; they always separate when they are filled with mud. Discard the muddy ones; then wash the rest several times under running water, turning them vigorously, and drain.

The mussels are then ready to cook.

Moules à la marinière
MUSSELS À LA MARINIÈRE

**2 quarts mussels
1 medium-sized onion
7 tablespoons unsalted
  butter
1/2 cup dry white wine
3 sprigs parsley
Pinch freshly ground
  pepper**

Prepare the mussels as explained above. Chop the onion very fine. In a saucepan big enough to hold the mussels in their shells, cook the onion very slowly in 3½ tablespoons butter without letting it brown.

When the onion is transparent, which should take 15 to 20 minutes, moisten with dry white wine, add the mussels, then 3 sprigs of parsley, chopped, and a pinch of freshly ground pepper. Cover the saucepan tightly, place over high heat, and let the mussels boil rapidly for a few minutes, until they open.

Remove the mussels with a slotted spoon and keep them warm in a covered soup tureen. Pour the liquid into another saucepan; be sure not to pour out the broth at the bottom of the pot, which will contain sand, despite careful cleaning. Boil to reduce the liquid by half, if you like it strong; less, if you prefer a more delicate flavor. Add the remaining butter, then pour the liquid over the mussels, sprinkle a pinch of chopped parsley on top, and serve.

Note: The mussels à *la marinière* must be cooked at the last moment, and the guests must wait for them. Mussels prepared in advance and kept warm darken, dry out, and lose their flavor.

Court-bouillon pour crustacés
COURT-BOUILLON FOR SHELLFISH

**3 quarts water
1 quart white wine
1 cup vinegar
3 tablespoons salt
15 crushed peppercorns
1 bay leaf
2 sprigs thyme
1 celery rib
Several sprigs parsley
1 onion, sliced**

Method. For 4 quarts *court-bouillon,* place all the ingredients in a saucepan and cook for 20 minutes before using.

Crabes ou tourteaux
CRABS

Cook the crabs in a *court-bouillon* prepared as above for 30 minutes; after letting them cool in the *court-bouillon,* remove the crab meat and the coral. This step must be done very carefully so that no cartilage is left in the meat.

With this meat, you can prepare many delicious dishes.

Bouchées de crabe
CRAB IN PASTRY SHELLS

Fill small shells made of flaky pastry (pages 382–3) with the cooked crab meat (recipe on page 140) mixed with some of the sauce that will accompany the crabs: an *américaine* sauce, a well-spiced tomato sauce, a cream, Mornay, or curry sauce, etc. (see index). Extra sauce should be served in a sauceboat.

Crabe en pilaf
CRAB WITH RICE

Line the bottom and the sides of a buttered shallow mold with a thick layer of hot cooked rice; fill with the cooked crab meat (page 140) mixed with some of the sauce that will accompany the dish, and then cover with another layer of rice. Pack down and keep warm.

Just before serving unmold and accompany with a sauceboat of curry sauce or *américaine* sauce, etc.

Crabe à la parisienne

Fill the shell of a crab with a salad made with one part cooked crab meat (page 140) and one part cooked vegetables, all diced very small: carrots, turnips, potatoes, string beans. Bind the vegetables and crab with a well-seasoned mayonnaise; and sprinkle a pinch of chopped parsley and chopped hard-cooked egg on top.

Gratin de queues d'écrevisses
Fernand Point

FRESH-WATER CRAYFISH AU GRATIN À LA FERNAND POINT
(For 4–6 people)

4 pounds live crayfish
6 tablespoons unsalted butter
3¹/₂ tablespoons chopped onions
3¹/₂ tablespoons chopped carrots
¹/₄ cup cognac
2 cups dry white wine
1 teaspoon tomato purée
Small *bouquet garni,* with several sprigs tarragon
Salt, pepper, cayenne
2 tablespoons flour
1 cup cream
3¹/₂ tablespoons truffles, cut into julienne
¹/₂ cup hollandaise sauce (page 88)

[*Editor's note:* Crayfish are hard to find in the United States; they may be replaced by a small lobster or unshelled large prawns.]

Method. Plunge the crayfish into boiling water for 5 minutes. Drain immediately, remove the tails and claws, and shells. Pound the shells in a mortar.

In a saucepan, sauté the pounded shells in 1 tablespoon butter; add the onions and carrots, cut into a fine *mirepoix.*

Flame half the cognac and pour it over the mixture. Pour in the white wine and a little water to moisten. Add the tomato purée and the *bouquet garni.* Season with salt, pepper, and a dash of cayenne.

Cook on a very low flame for about 20 minutes. Then rub the mixture through a very fine sieve and thicken with *beurre manié* made with 2 tablespoons flour and 3 tablespoons butter to make a sauce.

Stew the tails and claws in 2 tablespoons butter. Deglaze the pan with the remaining cognac. Add the cream and the

141

crayfish sauce. After adding the truffles, bring to the boiling point for a few minutes; then off the heat mix in the hollandaise sauce.

Correct the seasoning, and combine the crayfish and the sauce in individual ovenproof porcelain *gratin* dishes.

Place under the broiler to brown lightly.

This dish, of very fine quality, must be served immediately.

Écrevisses à la nage

CRAYFISH IN COURT-BOUILLON (For 12 people)

1 carrot
2 medium-sized onions
2 shallots
2 cups dry white wine
1 tablespoon salt
Pinch pepper
Bouquet garni (1 bay leaf,
  2 sprigs thyme, 1 celery rib,
  2 sprigs parsley)
Crayfish
1 quart milk

Method. Thinly slice the carrot, onions, and shallots; place them in a saucepan with 2 cups water, 2 cups dry white wine, salt, pepper, and the *bouquet garni.* Simmer until the vegetables are completely cooked.

Wash the crayfish and soak in 1 quart milk for 2 hours to purge them. Bring the *court-bouillon* to a boil and plunge the crayfish into it; cook for 8 to 10 minutes.

Heap the crayfish in a crystal bowl; reduce the cooking liquid by half and pour over the crayfish. Serve tepid or cold.

Écrevisses à la bordelaise

CRAYFISH À LA BORDELAISE

24 crayfish
1 medium-sized carrot,
  core removed
1 onion
2 shallots
12$\frac{1}{2}$ tablespoons unsalted
  butter
Pinch salt
Sprig thyme
Bay leaf
$\frac{1}{2}$ cup cognac
1$\frac{1}{2}$ cups white wine
3 tablespoons tomato
  purée
Pinch chervil
Pinch tarragon

Method. For 24 crayfish, finely dice the carrot, onion, and shallots. Stew the vegetables slowly in 2 tablespoons butter; add 3$\frac{1}{2}$ tablespoons more butter, the clean washed crayfish, salt, sprig of thyme, and a bay leaf. Sauté on a high flame until the crayfish are bright red. Pour over $\frac{1}{2}$ cup cognac, 1$\frac{1}{2}$ cups white wine, and 3 tablespoons tomato purée. Cook covered for 8 to 10 minutes.

Spoon the crayfish into a bowl, and keep warm.

Boil to reduce the sauce by half; and finish by adding off the heat 7 tablespoons butter, a pinch of chopped chervil and a pinch of chopped tarragon.

Pour the sauce over the crayfish.

Crevettes

SHRIMP

Shrimp must be cooked alive, preferably in sea water; if that is not available, the water should be heavily salted, with 2 tablespoons of sea salt, a sprig of thyme, a bay leaf, and 10 crushed peppercorns for each quart of water.

Plunge the shrimp into the boiling water for 3 minutes. Drain them and cool.

Unshelled shrimp are used as garnishes for fish and their sauces.

Homard a l'américaine

LOBSTER À L'AMÉRICAINE (For 3–4 people)

1½–1¾-pound live lobster
4 tablespoons oil
Salt
Freshly ground pepper
1 medium-sized onion, chopped
2 shallots, finely chopped
¼ garlic clove, crushed
1 cup dry white wine
1 cup *fumet* (pages 73–4) or water
2 tablespoons plus 2 teaspoons cognac
2 medium-sized tomatoes, peeled, seeded, and chopped, or ½ cup tomato purée
3 sprigs tarragon
Dash cayenne pepper
7½ tablespoons unsalted butter
Pinch chervil
Pinch tarragon
Chopped parsley

For this dish it is necessary to have a live lobster.

Method. Cut the lobster in the following way:

Hold the lobster with your left hand, the tail and the claws stretched out; cut the claws off close to the body and crack the shells; cut the tail into 5 or 6 pieces; slit the head in half lengthwise and remove the little sac close to the head that contains sand and the intestinal tract. In a bowl set aside the creamy part, the green part called tomalley, and, if it is a female, the coral. This must be done rapidly.

In a skillet, heat the oil very quickly. Place the pieces of lobster in the very hot oil, season with salt and freshly ground pepper. Sauté until the shells become red. Remove the pieces of lobster, set aside, and keep warm. Add the onion to the oil and cook, stirring constantly, without letting it brown. When the onion is nearly done, add the shallots, finely chopped, and the garlic. Cook briefly and drain off the oil. Pour in the white wine, the *fumet* (or water if you do not have fish stock), and 2 tablespoons cognac; add the tomatoes, or tomato purée, a bouquet of tarragon, and a dash of cayenne pepper. Place the pieces of lobster on top and cook, covered, for 20 minutes.

Remove the pieces of lobster, place them in a bowl, and keep warm. Remove the tarragon from the cooking liquid; boil to reduce by half, and thicken with the reserved creamy parts of the lobster, mixed with 3½ tablespoons unsalted butter, a pinch of chervil, and a pinch of tarragon. As soon as the liquid boils, remove from the heat; add the remaining butter and cognac.

Pour the sauce over the lobster and sprinkle with chopped parsley.

Rice pilaf (page 371) may be served with the lobster and sauce.

Note: More and more often the lobster meat is removed from the shells. This procedure is recommended since it makes serving easier and the guests do not soil their fingers.

Homard thermidor

LOBSTER THERMIDOR

Live lobster
Salt and pepper
Few drops oil
Melted unsalted butter
Sauce
3½ tablespoons unsalted butter
2 tablespoons flour
1 cup milk, salted
1 egg yolk
2 tablespoons cream
1 teaspoon strong mustard
Mornay or hollandaise sauce (optional, page 84 or 88)

Method. Cut a live lobster in half lengthwise. Remove the sac and intestinal tract. Crack the claws and season the flesh with salt and pepper and a few drops of oil.

Place the 2 halves of lobster, shells down, in a roasting pan, and bake in a 425° oven for 15 minutes. Baste from time to time with a little melted butter.

Prepare a sauce in the following manner: make a *roux* (page 75) with 3½ tablespoons butter and 2 tablespoons flour. Cook without letting it brown for 15 minutes; pour in the milk, bring to a boil, and boil for 1 minute. Thicken off the heat with 1 egg yolk diluted with 2 tablespoons cream; add the mustard.

Remove the lobster meat from the shells and slice it; mix

with some of the sauce, then replace in the shells. Cover with the remaining sauce or, even better, with Mornay or hollandaise sauce; brown in the oven.

Homard au porto

LOBSTER WITH PORT WINE

1 lobster, cooked in *court-bouillon* (see page 140)
6 tablespoons unsalted butter
¹/₂ cup port
1 cup cream
Salt
1 egg yolk
Dash cayenne pepper

Method. Cut up a lobster that has been cooked in *court-bouillon.* Heat the pieces slowly in 4 tablespoons unsalted butter in a skillet. Moisten with the port; let wine evaporate for a few minutes, then add the cream, salt lightly, and boil 4 to 5 minutes. Remove the pieces of lobster, take the meat from the shell, and place the meat in a dish. Thicken the sauce, without boiling, with 1 egg yolk and 2 tablespoons butter; add a dash of cayenne pepper. Pour the sauce over the lobster.

Homard à la crème

LOBSTER WITH CREAM

1 lobster
7¹/₂ tablespoons unsalted butter
4 teaspoons cognac
¹/₂ cup white wine
1¹/₂ cups cream
Salt
Dash cayenne pepper
20 small truffle slices

Method. Cut up a lobster as for lobster *à l'américaine* (page 143). Sauté pieces rapidly in 4 tablespoons butter; moisten with cognac and white wine; boil to reduce the wine. Then add the cream and season with salt and cayenne pepper.

Cook, covered, for 15 minutes.

Remove the lobster and take the meat from the shells; mix it with truffle slices.

Boil the sauce to reduce by one-third, and off the flame add the remaining butter. Place the lobster and the truffles in a dish and pour the sauce on top.

Navarin de homards

LOBSTER STEW (For 4 people)

6 small potatoes
¹/₂ pound very tender string beans
¹/₄ pound carrots cut to resemble cloves of garlic
¹/₄ pound turnips cut to resemble cloves of garlic
¹/₄ pound fresh shelled green peas
2 live female lobsters, 1¹/₂ pounds each
9 tablespoons unsalted butter
3 shallots, finely chopped
6 small white onions
Salt and pepper
1 cup dry white wine
1 cup chicken consommé (page 54)
Tarragon
Chervil

Method. Put the potatoes and string beans into separate pans of boiling salted water and blanch; make sure that they remain firm. Also blanch the carrots and turnips, starting with cold salted water. Drain, rinse in cold water, drain again.

Put the green peas into boiling salted water and cook at a simmer for 4 to 6 minutes. Drain, rinse in cold water, drain again.

Plunge a knife into the lobster at the center of the point where the tail and body join. This will kill the lobster instantly. Slice off the tail and cut it into 4 sections. Split the body lengthwise; remove the small pouch of membrane at the top, which contains the stomach, and the intestine, which runs down the center. Reserve the coral. Break the claws.

In a saucepan heat 7 tablespoons butter and brown the pieces of lobster in it for 3 to 4 minutes. Add the shallots and onions, and stir them briefly. Add the blanched vegetables, salt, and freshly ground pepper. Cook about 5 minutes, stirring to blend the ingredients thoroughly. Add the wine and the consommé. Cover and cook for about 10 minutes.

Remove the pan with the lobster from the fire, and pour the cooking juices into another saucepan. Keep the lobster warm, and start to reduce the juices. Meanwhile blend the reserved coral with an equal amount of butter (1–2 tablespoons). After the juices have reduced for about 15 minutes, add the butter-coral mixture, and bring to the boiling point. Then add the tarragon and the chervil.

Pour the sauce over the lobster, bring to the boiling point again, continuing to stir, and cook for another 5 minutes. Serve immediately.

Mayonnaise de homard
LOBSTER MAYONNAISE

Cook the lobster in *court-bouillon.* Let it cool; remove the flesh from the shell, and cut the tail meat into slices. Season with salt and pepper, and moisten with a few drops of vinegar and oil.

Cover the bottom of a salad bowl with chopped lettuce, top with the lobster meat. Coat the lobster with mayonnaise; and decorate with anchovy fillets, quartered hard-cooked eggs, capers, and, in the center, the heart of a small lettuce.

Just before serving, after presenting the dish, mix everything well so that the chopped lettuce and the heart will be seasoned.

Langoustes et langoustines
ROCK LOBSTER

Rock lobster is cooked exactly like lobster.

Note: Shellfish that are going to be served cold and cooked in *court-bouillon* should always be cooled in the cooking liquid. Drain them after they are completely cold. When they are removed from the *court-bouillon,* make an incision in each shell, next to the head. The shellfish then can be placed on their heads, and the *court-bouillon* that has penetrated inside the shells will drain out.

La langouste grillée aux deux sauces
BROILED ROCK LOBSTER WITH TWO SAUCES (For 2 people)

1½-pound or 2¾-pound live rock lobsters
3½ tablespoons melted unsalted butter
Salt and freshly ground pepper
Sprigs parsley
Choron sauce (page 89)
Américaine sauce (page 143)

Method. Plunge the rock lobster into a large kettle of boiling salted water for 2 or 3 minutes to kill it and stiffen the meat.

Remove the lobster; split in half; salt and pepper the meat, and brush with melted butter.

Cook the rock lobster (meat up) under a moderately hot broiler. Cooking time is about 15 minutes (do not let meat dry out).

Serve the rock lobster on a heated plate on a napkin or pleated paper. Decorate with sprigs of parsley.

Serve with a timbale of creole rice (page 370)

Choron sauce and *américaine* sauce are served on the side in sauceboats.

Lobster may be prepared in the same way.

145

Escargots

SNAILS

In France vine snails and *petit-gris* are the two species that are eaten.

Snails that are already "sealed" for the winter are preferable; if they are not, you must starve them for a few days.

Wash the snails several times under running water, until the slimy part is completely gone. Blanch them by plunging into boiling water for about 5 minutes.

Drain, rinse, pull the snails from their shells, and remove the black ends.

Place the snails in a saucepan; cover them with half white wine, half water; season each quart of cooking liquid with 1 medium-sized carrot, 1 onion, 2 shallots thinly sliced, a *bouquet garni* made with a dozen parsley sprigs, a sprig of thyme, a bay leaf, a pinch of crushed pepper, 1 teaspoon salt. Bring to a boil and skim, then simmer for 3 hours. Pour into a bowl and let the snails cool in their liquid.

Meanwhile, wash the empty snail shells and boil them in a saucepan of water for ½ hour. Drain, rinse them, and dry.

Note: It is important not to put salt in the water in which the snails are being purged. Their gastronomic quality will suffer.

Escargots à la bourguignonne

SNAILS BURGUNDY STYLE
Special Butter (for 50 snails)

¾ tablespoon garlic
2 tablespoons very finely chopped shallots
1½ tablespoons finely chopped parsley
¾ tablespoon salt
Pinch freshly ground pepper
½ pound unsalted butter

Crush the garlic, add the shallots, parsley, salt, pepper, and butter. Mix well.

Snail preparation.   In each shell place a scant teaspoon of the special butter; insert a cold, drained cooked snail, which will push the butter to the bottom of the shell. Seal the shell by adding more butter.

Arrange the snails on an ovenproof dish; sprinkle each snail with water and a pinch of fine white bread crumbs; bake in a 425° oven for 8 minutes.

Escargots à la mode de Chablis

SNAILS CHABLIS STYLE

The snails are prepared in the same way as snails Burgundy style (above). However, instead of putting the teaspoon of butter in the shell use ½ teaspoon white wine that has been reduced with chopped shallots, then replace each snail in the shell and continue as in the recipe above.

Escargots à l'alsacienne

SNAILS ALSATIAN STYLE

Follow the same method as for the snails Burgundy style (above), with this slight difference:

146

Although the snails must be covered, they should be cooked in less liquid. Add a couple of fresh pork rinds and a piece of veal shin to the liquid before putting the snails in it, in order to produce a savory and gelatinous stock.

After the snails have cooled in their cooking liquid, replace them in their shells, surrounded with some of the jellied stock mixed with the special butter. Finish, as for snails Burgundy style, by sprinkling a pinch of fine white bread crumbs on each snail, just before placing them in the oven.

Grenouilles sautées à la bordelaise

SAUTÉED FROGS' LEGS À LA BORDELAISE (For 1 person)

12 frogs' legs
Flour
2 large tablespoons
  unsalted butter
Pinch salt
Pinch freshly ground
  pepper
1 chopped shallot
1 teaspoon fine white
  bread crumbs
Pinch chopped parsley

Sprinkle the frogs' legs with flour, shake well, and place in a skillet with 2 tablespoons hot butter. Sauté over a high flame and brown lightly. Season with salt, pepper, the shallot, and at the last minute sprinkle with fine white bread crumbs. Add chopped parsley, and serve.

Grenouilles frites

FRIED FROGS' LEGS (For 2 people)

24 frogs' legs
Juice of 1/2 lemon
Oil
1 teaspoon chopped
  parsley
1 garlic clove, crushed
Pinch salt
Pinch freshly ground
  pepper
Frying batter (page 308)
Bouquet fried parsley

Marinate 24 frogs' legs for 1 hour in lemon juice, a little oil, chopped parsley, garlic, salt, and pepper.

Dip the legs, one at a time, in frying batter and plunge them one at a time into the very hot oil.

Drain the legs when they are golden, and serve on a napkin placed upon a hot platter. Decorate with a bouquet of fried parsley.

Grenouilles à la lyonnaise

FROGS' LEGS LYONS STYLE

Proceed as for the sautéed frogs' legs *à la bordelaise* (above), replacing the shallot and the bread crumbs with onions cut into strips and cooked in butter.

At the last minute, just before serving, splash some vinegar into the hot skillet and pour over the frogs' legs.

Sprinkle with chopped parsley.

Grenouilles à la poulette

FROGS' LEGS Á LA POULETTE (For 2 people)

Method. Poach 24 frogs' legs in a small amount of white wine, mixed with a few drops of lemon juice and melted but-

147

24 frogs' legs
White wine
Few drops lemon juice
2 tablespoons unsalted
  butter
Salt
Pepper
1 onion
Bouquet garni
$1/4$ pound white
  mushrooms, sliced
3 egg yolks
$1/2$ cup cream
Chopped parsley

ter. Season with salt and pepper, 1 onion cut into julienne, and a *bouquet garni.* As soon as the liquid comes to a boil, add $1/4$ pound sliced white mushrooms. Cook slowly, covered, over a low flame.

Drain the frogs' legs and mushrooms and keep warm. Reduce the cooking liquid, and strain through double cheesecloth. Thicken with 3 egg yolks and $1/2$ cup cream.

The sauce must be quite thick; be sure the cooking liquid is sufficiently reduced before adding the thickening ingredients.

After the sauce has thickened, add the frogs' legs and mushrooms and $3^1/2$ tablespoons unsalted butter. Mix well, correct the seasoning, and pour, very hot, into a dish.

Sprinkle with freshly chopped parsley.

Meats and variety meats

Beef

Knowing how to recognize good-quality meat and to choose the right piece for roasting or broiling or boiling or braising or simmering is the key to success in cooking a dish.

These are the chief characteristics of good-quality meat:

1. The color is a strong purplish red; the texture is firm, uniform, and slightly elastic to the touch.
2. It is plentifully streaked with fine fat veining; the meat is then called "spotted" or "marbled."
3. It is covered with a thick layer of white or light yellow fat.
4. The flesh is springy.

Beef from a female has a finer grain than that from a male; meat from an old bull is a dark brown-red; all meat that is lean, limp, pale, or very dark red is of inferior quality.

Most desirable cuts

The choice cuts of meat come from the filet of the loin and the ribs.

The filet comes from between the top of the haunch and the first rib; it is the back of the animal.

The filet is divided into four parts: the tenderloin and the sirloin in the center; the round or rump near the tail; and the rib eye, near the chuck or shoulder.

The filet can be roasted whole or in large pieces; however, the four parts of the filet are usually cooked differently.

The filet is the tenderest, the most sought-after, and the most expensive part of the animal.

Whole or in large pieces, with the tendons removed and larded, or barded, it is an excellent roast. The roasting time in an oven is: 15 minutes per pound; on a spit over coals: 25 minutes to sear the meat; then the roast is allowed to "rest" until time to serve. (See instructions below for roasts.)

These are the cuts into which beef filet can be divided:

Filets grillés: Slices cut crosswise to the grain of the meat, 1 to 2 fingers thick (filet steaks from the back of the sirloin)

Châteaubriants: Slices cut crosswise to the grain of the meat, 2 to 3 fingers thick (filet steaks from the tenderloin portion of the porterhouse)

Coeurs de filet: Slices cut crosswise to the grain, 1 to 2 fingers thick (filet steaks from the back of the tenderloin)

Tournedos: Slices cut crosswise to the grain of the meat, 2 fingers thick (filet steaks from the front of the tenderloin)

Filets mignons: Slices cut parallel to the grain of the meat about 1 finger thick (front end of the tenderloin)

The short loin, boned, can be roasted like the filet, whole or in thick slices (same cooking time). It is sold with the bone in for broiling under the names of porterhouse steak or T-bone steak.

The rumpsteak and sirloin are cooked in the same way as the other pieces of meat.

The ribs of beef come between the eighth and the last

vertebrae. This cut can be roasted whole or in thick slices, preferably not boned, which will make it more flavorful. Cooking time in an oven: 15 to 18 minutes per pound; on a spit over coals: 20 to 22 minutes. [Times do not include "resting" period; see instructions for roasts.]

Cut in slices crosswise to the grain of the meat, the ribs can be broiled like steak.

ROASTS

In roasting, broiling, or sautéing a piece of meat, poultry, or game, the cooking is done by concentrating the heat, which penetrates, little by little, toward the center. This heat drives the juices inward, and creates a brown coating that keeps them from escaping. This initial process is followed by an opposite phenomenon.

When the heat has penetrated the meat, the meat should be removed from the direct action of the naked flame (if it is cooked on a spit) or of the radiant heat (if it is cooked in an oven) and permitted to rest. This allows the imprisoned interior juices, which have been forced inward, to move slowly toward the surface, up to the brown coating. As the juices penetrate the tissues and the cooking finishes, the meat acquires a nice pink color.

The brown coating now becomes slightly softer and thinner; it is scarcely more than a brown outline around the red or white slices of meat from which pink or golden pearls of fatty juice escape.

Methods of roasting

Roasts can be cooked in the oven or on a spit, which, though too seldom used nowadays, is far superior to the oven, because the open air causes moisture to evaporate. The meat browns more delicately, and it is more flavorful if you use certain woods, such as stems from a grapevine, which transfer their aroma to the roast.

An oven is an enclosed environment, which means that roasting is carried out in a humid atmosphere, which in part destroys the function of browning.

The size of the meat determines whether the grill or the oven should be blazing or only very hot in order to produce searing.

When the browning has taken place, the intensity of the heat is reduced by adding less wood to the grill or by moving the meat away from the heat or by using some other protective measure, such as a screen.

The piece of meat being roasted should always lie on a rack to prevent it from bathing in the fat or cooking juices. The meat should be basted frequently with this fat, not with the juice. In cooking on a spit, use a drip pan to gather the fat and the juice.

One can determine whether a roast of any kind, except poultry, is correctly cooked by touching, which necessitates a

151

certain experience. If you do not have this experience, consult the recommended cooking time, according to the weight of the meat and the information given on pages 150–1 or in the individual recipes. Then insert a very fine needle into the meat. The puncture will let a few drops of juice escape. If the meat is red (beef and mutton), it has cooked enough if the juice is pale pink.

Fully cooked white meats (veal, lamb, pork) will lose a few drops of colorless juice. Game is usually cooked lightly rare; when it is done, its juice should be pale pink, as for red meats.

To test whether poultry is cooked, tilt it over a plate; when the juices that run from the inside are completely clear and colorless, the poultry is cooked.

Roasting juices

Except when otherwise indicated in a recipe, a roast should always be served with its cooking juices.

If one has carefully followed the cooking method for roasting, the juice gathered in the drip pan or in the roasting pan should be sufficient.

While roasting in an oven, carefully regulate the intensity of the heat; if it is too high, it will reduce the juices and cause *pinçage,* an overbrowning, which makes them bitter. The cooking butter will burn also.

This can be avoided by sliding something under the roasting pan or by pouring one or two tablespoons of water or white bouillon into the roasting pan.

The roasting juice can be degreased partially or not at all; do not forget that much of the flavor is retained by the fat.

Serving and carving roasts

Generally, a roast is served simply on a very hot, long platter and lightly sprinkled with one or two tablespoons of the roasting juice. The remaining juice is served in a sauceboat.

The vegetables accompanying the roast form a garnish, either served in a vegetable bowl or placed around the roast. In that case, they should be arranged tastefully; for example, in large clusters at either end of the platter or around the roast, alternating in small clusters. The garnish should be placed inside the serving platter, never on the edge. The platter used should therefore be ample but not excessively large.

For grand and impressive dinners, it is the custom to decorate a large piece of roasted meat with silver or silver-plated *hâtelets* (skewers topped with emblems), on which are artfully placed certain ingredients—crayfish, mushrooms, truffles, cockscombs, etc.—related to the accompanying garnish.

The carving consists of cutting very thin slices perpendicular to the grain of the meat. One can understand the reason for this principle by thinking of how the meat is chewed. If one is presented with a piece of meat cut against the grain, the teeth will sink in without any resistance. If the slice has been cut along the grain of the meat, the grain will present an obstacle to the teeth. Tender meat therefore will seem tough.

Preparing the meat for roasting

Before roasting there are particular ways of preparing tenderloin, loin roast, rib roast, veal roast, leg of lamb, poultry, game, etc.

A tenderloin of beef must have its fat and tendons removed; then it is larded or barded.

A loin roast must have its tendons removed. This is done after lifting the fat that covers the tendons; then the fat is put back into place where the tendons have been removed.

Ribs of beef must be lightly trimmed, which means that the bones are sawed off to shorten them. Or all the bones may be removed. When this is done, the meat is rolled and tied with a string, not too tightly, just enough to hold the meat. It is important never to tie the piece of meat too tightly. During cooking, the tissue swells and needs some space. The strings should be cut two-thirds of the way through the cooking.

Veal roast should be larded when it is cooked.

The bone end of a leg of lamb is removed to facilitate carving. If the meat is larded with garlic, the cloves should be inserted between the membranes; always avoid cutting the meat to slide in a garlic clove.

Poultry and feathered game are trussed and very often barded.

Larding and Barding

The purpose of larding meat—inserting five or six tiny sticks of fresh pork fat into the exterior of a piece of meat—is to nourish the meat with the fat melting during the cooking.

To bard a piece of meat is to cover it with a layer of fat to protect it from too high a heat coming from an open grill or an oven and, at the same time, to nourish it with the melting fat.

BROILED OR GRILLED MEAT

To broil or to sauté a piece of meat, generally small, means cooking it over an open fire, on a grill, under a broiler, or in a skillet.

For broiling, the heat should be intense, whether it be hot coals, charcoal, coke, gas, or electricity. How intense it should be depends on the size, especially the thickness, of the meat to be cooked.

All the rules for roasting discussed above should be observed.

The grill should be preheated, by the glowing coals or other heat, above or below the meat. Brush the meat with melted butter and place it on the hot grill. After a few minutes, rotate the meat with a spatula (this movement is a quarter turn from the original position; the bars of the grill sear the meat, forming a checkerboard pattern). When the meat is done on one side, turn it over with a spatula and season with salt, which will melt when mixed with the meat juices that will appear on the top of the meat and penetrate slowly into the meat's tissues. Give the second side a quarter turn also, and when it is cooked, place it on a serving platter, with the side that was cooked last on top. This side is then seasoned.

To obtain perfectly cooked red meats—such as beef or lamb—it is necessary to cook them rare and to let them stand a few minutes before serving. During this resting time, the concentrated juices that were driven inward spread to the outer parts of the meat. Like roasted meat, grilled meat should be perfectly cooked and pink all the way to the brown surface. If the meat is not allowed to rest, it will be soft, much too raw in the center, and have a thin black crust on both sides.

Sautéed—pan-broiled—meats are cooked by the same method but in a skillet; then the skillet is deglazed (this is the melting of the juices that have solidified), producing juices to be served with the cooked meat.

BRAISED MEATS

A piece of braised meat requires a lot of attention, even to the minutest details. Braising meats is, among the various culinary steps, one of the most difficult in which to succeed perfectly.

The best meats to braise come from animals three to six years old for beef; and one to two years old for lamb.

Younger animals are not suitable for braising (contrary to the case in roasting meat). Older animals are stringy and dry; the long cooking period in braising accentuates this fault.

Beef for braising should always be larded when the pieces come from the leg or the chuck. When it is a cut of meat from the sirloin, larding is not necessary, if the animal is of good quality, for this part is sufficiently marbled with its own fat.

All the cooking phenomena explained in the section on roasts also occur in braising. After reading and following all the advice given concerning roasts, the reader will have no difficulty in proceeding with the recipes for braising.

I will add, however, that in "the old cooking," the recipes for braising were different from those we use today; reasons of economy and the pressures of time have obliged cooks virtually to abandon that extremely rich and tasty method. Years ago a piece of braised meat was cooked so long that it was impossible to slice it with a knife. The meat was really so soft that it absorbed all the juices and the liquid used for braising; it became so tender, literally melting, that it was served with a spoon *(une cuiller)*—the only utensil with which one could manage it.

Gourmets who are able to follow this old method of braising should not hesitate to do so, for nothing equals it in flavor.

MEAT COOKED IN A FRYING PAN

Cooking a piece of meat or poultry in a frying pan is a method essentially belonging to home cooking, very simple, and, after all, one of the best.

It consists of cooking a piece of meat with butter in a utensil of appropriate size and finishing it slowly, preferably in the oven, covered. Almost no evaporation takes place, and the sweating of the meat forms a juice that is fatty, syrupy, and exquisite.

FRIED MEATS

For all frying one should use only strong, deep round or oval utensils, just big enough and filled only halfway with fat or oil.

The ideal frying medium is absolutely pure peanut oil.

One can use animal fat, which can reach a high temperature without burning, although it burns at a lower temperature than vegetable oil.

Beef kidney fat is one of the best of all animal fats, but it does not tolerate high temperature. Mutton fat is truly bad and is not advisable. Pork fat can be used, but it is better to keep it for recipes in which it is used for flavoring.

Butter burns at 266°; it cannot be used for deep frying.

Animal fats, when very hot, reach 356°—above that, they smoke lightly.

Lard can go up to 482° before burning.

Vegetable oils start to burn at 572°.

The proper heat for frying can be gauged in the following ways:

1. Medium hot: a parsley leaf thrown in starts to fry.
2. Hot: a slightly damp ingredient thrown in makes the fat sizzle.
3. Very hot: an ingredient thrown in makes the fat smoke and starts to smell.

After each use, it is important to strain the frying oil through cheesecloth, to remove all the impurities left by the food that has fried in it.

If these residues remain in the oil, they will burn and break down the frying fat and finally produce a smell harmful to the foods being fried in the future.

Store the frying fats in earthenware pots or in a terrine.

Roast sirloin, tenderloin, loin roast, rib roast, and rump roast

On a menu, one usually finds a sirloin, a tenderloin, or a loin, roasted or braised.

Only the presentation of the meat is different.

In the beginning of the section on roasts, I described the method of preparation and cooking. (See pages 151–3.)

Any of the vegetable garnishes, without exception, can accompany any of these cuts of meat.

We will limit ourselves to some typical examples.

Boneless beef tenderloin
Lardons of fresh pork fat
1 medium-sized carrot
1 large onion
Salt
Unsalted butter
1 cup veal stock, white
  stock, or water

Filet de boeuf Richelieu
FILET OF BEEF RICHELIEU

Method. Remove the fat and the tendons from a piece of boneless beef tenderloin, trimming it by removing the *chaîne*—the sinewy fibers along the sides of the filet from one end to the other.

Lard the filet with *lardons* of fresh pork fat about 1³/₄ inches long and about as thick as a large match.

To do this, put the filet of beef on a dish placed upside down on a table, with the edges of the meat hanging down slightly around the dish. Hold the meat with the left hand; with the right hand insert the larding needle just below the surface of the filet, following the grain of the meat. Leave the *lardon* in the meat, with its two ends extending outside.

Place the *lardons* in a row about ³/₄ inch apart. The rows follow one another, at even intervals, so that the *lardon* of each row will come out slightly behind the preceding one and form a checkerboard pattern.

The purpose of the larding fat is to nourish the filet and to provide it with the benefit of constant basting during the cooking time.

To hold the filet together, tie the meat every 2¹/₂ inches with a string, tightened slightly.

At the bottom of a roasting pan place 1 medium-sized carrot and 1 large onion, thinly sliced; place the filet of beef on top; season with salt on all sides, and moisten with melted butter; place in a 425° oven. Cook following the directions given for roasts (pages 151–3).

Baste frequently, and be careful not to let the vegetables at the bottom of the roasting pan or the juices that escape from the filet brown too much.

If you have a big enough pan, the best cooking method is to pan broil it, still keeping the meat rare. In both cases the cooking time is 12 to 15 minutes per pound [not including "resting" time].

When the meat has finished cooking (check whether it is done by probing with a needle if you do not have the experience to do it by touch), place the filet in a roasting pan and keep it hot while resting, which is the second cooking phase.

Into the roasting or braising pan pour 1 cup good veal stock (page 72) or white stock (page 73) or, if you do not have either, use water; simmer for 5 minutes, then strain through a fine sieve and keep warm.

Garniture Richelieu

Braised lettuce
Mushroom purée
Stuffed mushrooms
Stuffed tomatoes
Potatoes
Chopped parsley
1 cup Madeira

This consists of braised lettuce stuffed with mushroom purée; stuffed mushrooms; stuffed tomatoes; potatoes cooked in butter (see each of these recipes in the chapter on vegetables)—all in sufficient quantity so that each guest has all four vegetables.

Presentation. Place the filet of beef on a fairly large platter, then surround it, alternately, with one portion of lettuce, one mushroom, one tomato, and potatoes. Finish the dish by sprinkling chopped parsley on the potatoes. Off the flame add

1 cup Madeira to the blood that has escaped from the meat during the resting time. Mix in a stream of cooking juice and moisten the meat lightly with it. Serve with the remaining juice in a sauceboat.

Serving. Place very hot plates on the table while the meat is being carved; serve one slice of filet, one of each vegetable, a teaspoon of meat juice, poured on the plate but not on the meat, which should keep its beautiful light pink color; finally, sprinkle on each slice a dash of ground sea salt.

The filet of beef Richelieu can be simplified. Without changing the cooking method, limit the garnish to one, two, or three of the vegetables; this remains, however, a dish of high style. One then changes the name by substituting the name of the garnish, for example: beef with braised lettuce, etc.

Filet de boeuf sauce madère et champignons à la ménagère

BEEF TENDERLOIN WITH MADEIRA SAUCE AND MUSHROOMS HOME STYLE (For 8 people)

This recipe is essentially a dish cooked in the home. It can frequently be used as a base when domestic culinary resources do not include the concentrated stocks generally required in *grande cuisine*.

3 pounds beef tenderloin, cut from the center
¼ pound fresh pork fat
4 tablespoons butter

Method. Prepare the filet—trim it, remove the tendons, lard it, tie it, and roast or pan broil it following the recipe for filet of beef Richelieu above.

To serve place the meat on a long platter; remove the strings, and surround it with beautiful mushroom caps taken from the vegetable garnish.

Madeira Sauce

This will take 1½ hours to prepare and cook.

1 small carrot, diced
1 medium-sized onion, diced
7 tablespoons unsalted butter
3 tablespoons flour
Scant cup dry white wine
1 quart veal stock or juice (page 72), lightly salted
2 tablespoons thick tomato purée
Sprigs parsley
Sprigs thyme
½ bay leaf
½ pound mushrooms
½ cup Madeira

Method. Cook the carrot and the onion slowly in a saucepan big enough to hold the sauce, with a piece of butter as big as 2 walnuts (about 4 tablespoons). When the vegetables are light brown, add the flour; mix well, and cook this *roux* slowly, stirring constantly, until it turns dark brown; cool. Dilute the *roux* by slowly pouring in the white wine; then add the veal stock or juice, reserving about ½ cup. Add the tomato purée, parsley, thyme, and the bay leaf.

Bring to a boil, stirring with a whisk to avoid lumps, and simmer for 45 minutes.

Add the trimmings from the filet, lightly browned, along with 4 or 5 mushroom stems, cleaned and chopped.

While it is simmering, from time to time skim off the fat and the skin that forms. This is necessary to remove the impurities from the flour and the fat and finally to clarify the sauce, leaving only the starch from the flour, which makes a fine, light thickening.

After 45 minutes of simmering, strain the sauce through a fine sieve into another saucepan, pressing the vegetables vigorously; bring the sauce slowly to a boil and continue to clarify it by skimming. As needed, add 1 to 2 tablespoons of the remaining stock in order to help clarify the sauce.

This second step will take 30 minutes.

The mushrooms. The mushrooms must be firm and very white. Cut off the sandy ends and quickly wash the mushrooms twice, without letting them soak. Drain immediately, and wipe dry.

Reserve a few whole mushroom caps to garnish the filet; cut the rest into quarters.

Heat the remaining butter in a skillet big enough to hold the sauce as well as the mushrooms. When the butter is quite hot and has a hazelnut color, toss the mushrooms in; stir over a high flame until lightly browned.

Remove the mushrooms from the fire. Strain the sauce through a cloth and add to the mushrooms. Bring to a boil, and simmer 5 minutes; remove again from the heat, correct the seasoning, and keep warm without boiling until ready to serve.

Just before serving, add the Madeira and the cooking juices from the meat to the sauce. Do not let this sauce boil, for this would make the aroma of the Madeira evaporate, and its alcohol, together with the bloody meat juices, would combine into black lumps.

The Madeira sauce by now should be reduced to $2\frac{1}{2}$ cups—to about half of the liquid ingredients used—because of the purifying, clarifying, and evaporation.

Obviously if you have among your kitchen stocks some *demi-glace* sauce (the recipe can be found on page 76), it will make a far more flavorful sauce. In that case, the recipe for the mushrooms remains the same, but they will be moistened with $2\frac{1}{2}$ cups *demi-glace* sauce instead of the sauce just described. Finish the sauce with the Madeira and cooking juices, following the instructions above.

Filet de boeuf bouquetière

FILET OF BEEF WITH VEGETABLE GARNISH

Lard the filet; roast it or pan broil it following the method given for filet of beef Richelieu (pages 156–7).

To garnish surround the beef with small bunches of different vegetables: carrots, turnips (cooked following the instructions for glazing, pages 309–10), string beans and peas (with butter sauce), potatoes cut in the shape of olives and browned.

Filet de boeuf à la financière

FILET OF BEEF À LA FINANCIÈRE

Lard a beef tenderloin and roast or pan broil it. At the same time prepare a Madeira sauce made with *demi-glace* sauce (page 76), which is preferable, or made by the recipe on pages 157–8; and add the following garnish:

Small mushrooms sautéed in butter; sliced truffles;

cockscombs and kidneys cooked in a *court-bouillon* made with white stock (page 101); and for each 2 cups, $\frac{1}{2}$ tablespoon flour and the juice of half a lemon or 1 tablespoon vinegar; veal *quenelles* (pages 192–3) or a piece of sweetbread, braised but not browned and cut into slices $\frac{1}{4}$ inch thick.

Filet de boeuf Saint-Germain

FILET OF BEEF WITH PEA PURÉE (For 15 people)

6$\frac{1}{2}$–8-pound beef
  tenderloin
Pea purée (see below)
Glazed carrots (see below)
Potatoes, cooked (see
  below)
Béarnaise sauce (page
  89) or Valois sauce

Method. Trim the beef tenderloin; cut off the rump end, the sinewy sides, and the rib end. Broil the rump as filet steaks; make the rib end into *filets mignons;* and use the *chaîne,* or sides, to make minute steaks or *carbonade à la flamande* (pages 171–2).

Lard the filet and roast it or pan broil it in a skillet.

Place the filet on a platter and garnish it with 15 timbales filled with a purée of fresh peas, along with glazed carrots, and potatoes cooked in butter (see below).

Serve accompanied by the cooking juices and a sauceboat of *béarnaise* sauce or Valois sauce (*béarnaise* with added meat glaze).

Pea Purée

2 pounds peas
Spinach
$\frac{1}{4}$ pound unsalted butter
2 tablespoons heavy
  cream
Pinch sugar
5 whole eggs
6 egg yolks

Bring 3 quarts of salted water to a boil in a large saucepan and add 2 pounds shelled fresh peas; cook rapidly over a high flame. Before peas are completely cooked, add a handful of spinach (the spinach is used to give the purée a strong green color); boil for 5 minutes, remove from the heat, and drain. Rub the peas and spinach through a fine sieve. Place the purée in a bowl, whip it vigorously with a wooden spoon to make it very smooth, and add $\frac{1}{4}$ pound unsalted butter and 2 tablespoons heavy cream. If the peas are not sweet enough, add a pinch of sugar. Beat together 5 whole eggs and 6 yolks and, without stirring too much, add the eggs to the purée.

Generously butter 15 small cylindrical *dariole* or *baba* molds; fill to about $\frac{1}{4}$ inch from the top with the prepared purée. Bake in a *bain-marie* (a roasting pan half full of hot water). It should not be permitted to boil; watch it constantly and add 1 to 2 tablespoons cold water if you see any sign of boiling in the *bain-marie* water.

Test for doneness as for a *crème renversée* (page 414); the purée should be a little firmer to the touch.

Keep warm in the *bain-marie* while waiting to unmold; unmolding will be easier if you let the purée rest for a few minutes after it is cooked.

Glazed Carrots

Bunch of carrots
Pinch salt
Pinch sugar
6 tablespoons unsalted
  butter

Choose a bunch of new carrots, peel as thinly as possible. If carrots are small, leave them whole; if not, cut into halves or quarters and trim the ends slightly to give the pieces the shape of large garlic cloves.

Wash the carrot pieces and place in a skillet big enough to hold them in one layer; pour in water to go halfway up; add a pinch of salt, a pinch of sugar, and a piece of unsalted butter as big as 2 walnuts (about 4 tablespoons); bring to a boil, and cook slowly without a cover so that the liquid will have evaporated almost completely when the carrots are cooked.

Then the juices of the vegetables, the butter, the sugar, and the moisture will have formed a syrupy mixture.

Off the fire add 2 more tablespoons butter and stir gently; the carrots will be coated with a shiny glaze and be very tender.

Potatoes Cooked in Butter

Use 2 pounds new potatoes no bigger than walnuts; peel and cook in 3 tablespoons butter, with a pinch of salt, in a covered skillet. They should be lightly browned and very tender.

Serving. Place the filet of beef on a large platter; remove the strings and baste with a little of the cooking juices. At either end of the platter, in a semicircle, arrange the timbales of puréed peas; and along either side of the beef alternate the carrots and the potatoes, piled in pyramids.

Top each pile of potatoes with a little chopped parsley.

2 pounds new potatoes
3 tablespoons unsalted butter
Pinch salt
Chopped parsley

Boeuf à la ficelle

BEEF ON A STRING (For 6 people)

Method. Heat 3 quarts water in a large soup pot, adding the vegetables and seasonings.

After 5 minutes of boiling, plunge in the beef, tied by a string to the handle of the kettle; this will help in removing the meat.

After skimming well, continue to cook at a gentle boil. Allow about 10 to 15 minutes for each pound; as for roast beef, the meat should remain rosy red inside.

Serve the meat surrounded by the vegetables and accompanied by tomato sauce (page 77) seasoned with tarragon and chives; you can also serve the meat simply with coarse salt, *cornichons,* and small pickled onions. It can also be eaten with a rémoulade sauce (page 91).

After lightly buttering the broth, serve it with small bread croutons and grated parmesan cheese.

Note: The top part of the rump or ribs of beef or a leg of lamb can be prepared in the same way.

4 pounds filet of beef, trimmed and tied
1/2 pound carrots, cut into sticks
1/2 pound turnips, cut into sticks
6 leeks, white part only
2 celery hearts
3 tomatoes, peeled, seeded, and quartered
1 onion, stuck with 3 cloves
1 sprig each parsley, chervil, and tarragon
2 tablespoons coarse salt
1 teaspoon peppercorns
Croutons
Grated parmesan cheese

Hamburger ou steak haché

CHOPPED STEAK

Method. Chop the onion fine; cook it slowly in a skillet with 1 tablespoon butter, but do not let brown.

Prepare chopped steak as in the recipe for steak tartare (page 161) season with salt and freshly ground pepper, and mix in the cooked onion.

Shape the steak into a hamburger, cook it on both sides in 1 tablespoon butter in the same frying pan used for the onion (be sure that all the bits of onion have been removed, or they will burn). The hamburger is done when a drop of blood forms on the cooked upper surface.

Place the meat on a serving platter; put 1 tablespoon butter in the frying pan with 1 tablespoon veal stock; bring to a boil, and boil for 2 minutes. Pour over the steak.

1 medium-sized onion
3 tablespoons unsalted butter
1/2 pound beef filet
Salt
Freshly ground pepper
1 tablespoon veal stock (page 72)
Poached egg (optional)

If you wish, you may slide a poached egg on top of the steak.

Steak tartare

Take ½ pound of beef filet from the sirloin, remove the sinews and fat; chop fine, and season with salt and freshly ground pepper. Shape the chopped meat into a disk about 1¼ inches thick; place on a serving plate, and make a hollow in the center with the back of a teaspoon dipped in cold water; place the yolk of a raw egg in the hollow.

Serve with a bowl of very hot consommé and surround with three relish dishes: one with capers, one with very finely chopped onions, and one with chopped parsley.

Steak aux oeufs au miroir

STEAK WITH GLAZED EGGS

Prepare chopped steak, as described in the recipe for steak tartare above; cook in unsalted butter in a skillet until pink; place on a serving platter and cover with 2 eggs, cooked in the frying pan or the oven until the yolks are glazed (see the recipe for shirred eggs, page 32). The glaze can also be obtained by spooning some of the very hot cooking butter over the yolks.

Pour 2 tablespoons veal stock into the frying pan used for the cooking, reduce by half, and surround the steak with the juice.

Châteaubriant

BONED PORTERHOUSE STEAK

For this, use a piece of meat cut from the thickest part of the beef filet, the fat and the tendons removed.

A *châteaubriant* [sometimes spelled *châteaubriand*] should not weigh more than ¾ to 1 pound, so that it can be evenly broiled.

Broil following the methods in the section on broiling (page 153), and serve accompanied by *maître d'hôtel* butter (below) or another compound butter and with puffed fried potatoes (page 356), arranged in bunches at one end of the platter, and, at the other end, a bunch of water cress; or serve with Pont-Neuf potatoes (page 355), matchstick potatoes (page 355), or sautéed potatoes (page 361), or any other vegetable.

However, the classic garnish for a *châteaubriant* is puffed fried potatoes accompanied by *maître d'hôtel* butter or *béarnaise* sauce (page 89).

Maître d'Hôtel Butter

Mix ingredients together until creamy; serve in a sauceboat; the heat of the *châteaubriant* will melt the butter.

To serve the *châteaubriant* cut it on the serving platter,

161

¼ pound unsalted butter
1 teaspoon chopped fresh
** parsley**
Large pinch salt
Couple of turns of the
** pepper mill**
Juice of ¹/₂ lemon

after showing it to your guests. The meat should be cut on a bias. Each slice is served on a heated plate, with some puffed fried potatoes (or any other garnish) placed beside it along with a few sprigs of water cress. A teaspoon of *maître d'hôtel* butter and some of the meat juice, which will escape as it is sliced, are added on the plate but not on the meat. The guests may season the meat with some sea salt and a pinch of pepper, both ground from mills, which are usually placed on the table.

Coeur de filet sauté ou grillé
SAUTÉED, GRILLED, OR BROILED FILET STEAKS

These are slices of filet of beef, of about 5 to 7 ounces, cut from the center part of the filet, with the tendons and the fat removed.

Cook them in a skillet as for *tournedos* or on a grill as for the *châteaubriant*.

The garnish and the sauces for the other two steaks can be used.

Filets mignons

This cut permits the use of the rib end of the filet, which is too thin to be cut for *tournedos.*

The end piece is trimmed, which means the tendons and the fat are removed, then sliced into thinner steaks with the grain of the meat.

Preparation of *filets mignons* is simple: flatten them lightly with a mallet or the flat side of a cleaver or big kitchen knife; season with salt and freshly ground pepper and press in lightly with the flat part of a knife blade; dip the steaks in melted butter and immediately into fine bread crumbs, pressing the bread-crumb coating on with the blade of a knife. With the back of the blade, make a grid pattern on both sides of the meat; place the meat on a hot grill or under a broiler, pouring on some melted butter. Cook it rare.

Serve with vegetables and a sauceboat of *maître d'hôtel* butter (page 161) or a *béarnaise* (page 89) or Choron sauce (page 89), or Valois sauce (page 159), etc.

Never pour a liquid sauce on the *filets mignons,* such as meat juice, Périgueux sauce, Madeira sauce, etc., which would immediately make the bread crumbs soggy. If you wish to use one of these sauces or juices, serve it on the side in a sauceboat and pour ¹/₂ tablespoon on the plate next to the grilled meat, not on top.

Tournedos et médaillons
TOURNEDOS AND MEDALLIONS OF BEEF

The medallion is a sort of *tournedos.* They are both broiled or sautéed and garnished the same way. All the recipes for *tournedos* are applicable to medallions.

The steaks are cut from the center of the filet just before the rib end (which is the thinnest part of the filet).

This part of the filet must be trimmed, and the tendons, fat, and sinewy sides removed. The *tournedos* are cut about 2 to 2½ inches thick and each steak is encircled by a thin band of fresh pork fat (or bacon) as high as the steak, tied tightly in place with a piece of string so as to thicken the steak slightly, giving the *tournedos* the appearance of a thick disk.

Preparation of the tournedos. If the *tournedos* is broiled, follow the recipe given for the *châteaubriant* and serve with one of the garnishes listed (page 161).

I prefer, however, to sauté *tournedos;* this method allows for the deglazing of the pan and produces juices or sauces with a better flavor.

Tournedos à la béarnaise

Prepare and sauté 6 *tournedos* as in the recipe below. In butter fry slices of bread (croutons) the same size as the steaks, about ¾ inch thick. Arrange in a circle on a hot round platter, and top each with a *tournedos.*

In the center put a garnish of small new potatoes, cooked in butter and lightly browned, or of château potatoes (pages 361–2) or potato balls (page 362), sprinkled with a pinch of chopped parsley.

Surround each *tournedos* with a border of *béarnaise* sauce (page 89) and, in the center, pour ½ teaspoon of the cooking juice, deglazed with a good veal stock and buttered lightly off the heat.

Serve the remaining *béarnaise* sauce in a sauceboat.

Tournedos à l'arlésienne
TOURNEDOS ARLES STYLE

2 tablespoons oil
7 tablespoons unsalted butter
6 *tournedos,* ¼ pound each, wrapped in fresh pork fat and tied
Salt and pepper

Method. In a skillet, heat 2 tablespoons oil and 2 tablespoons butter; when the butter sizzles, place the *tournedos* in the skillet. The oil and the butter must be very hot (smoking) in order to sear the meat. Cook, covered, for 4 minutes; turn the steaks with a spatula, so as not to prick them; season with salt and freshly ground pepper on the turned side (see discussion of broiling, page 153), and cook the other side for the same length of time.

One minute before the meat is finished, remove the strings and the pork fat; turn the *tournedos* on their sides and roll them in the cooking butter to seal the sides that were protected by the fat.

Place the steaks on a plate, turning them flat; season the second sides and keep warm. While waiting, the *tournedos* will finish cooking.

Prepare the garnish of tomatoes, eggplants, and onions so that it will be ready when the *tournedos* have finished cooking.

163

Garniture

6 tomatoes of equal size
2 medium-sized eggplants
1 tablespoon flour mixed
  with pinch salt
Oil for frying
2 large onions
$^1/_2$ cup milk
Chopped parsley

1 cup veal stock (page 72)
$^1/_2$ cup Madeira wine

6 sautéed *tournedos*
Croutons, fried in butter
$^1/_2$ cup dry white wine
$^1/_2$ cup veal stock (page 72)
1 tablespoon unsalted butter

3 shallots
1 tablespoon unsalted butter
$^1/_2$ cup dry white wine
$^1/_4$ pound unsalted butter
$^1/_2$ pound marrow
$^1/_2$ tablespoon chopped parsley
Pinch salt
Pinch pepper
Juice of $^1/_4$ lemon

Tomatoes

Cut off the tops and press to remove the seeds and the juice; season the insides with salt and pepper; and cook in 3 tablespoons butter, covered, in a skillet.

Eggplants

Peel the eggplants; slice very thin; sprinkle with a pinch of salt and 1 tablespoon flour, well mixed; shake off excess flour, and fry eggplant slices in very hot oil. When slices are a nice golden color, drain on a cloth and salt lightly; they should be very crisp.

Onions

Slice the onions and separate into rings; dip into a bit of milk, then sprinkle with flour, shake well, and plunge for 3 minutes into the hot oil, after cooking the eggplant. As soon as the rings are golden, drain on a cloth and salt lightly.

Presentation.   Arrange the tomatoes in a circle on a hot round platter; on top of each tomato, place a *tournedos* and, on top of the meat, some fried onion rings. Place the fried eggplants in a dome in the center, and sprinkle with a pinch of chopped parsley. Pour 1 tablespoon of the following sauce into the bottom of the platter.

Sauce

In the skillet, combine the cooking juices from the tomatoes and the veal stock; boil to reduce rapidly to three-fourths, and off the heat add the Madeira, the juice that gathered in the plate from the *tournedos,* and the remaining butter; shake the skillet to mix, and serve in a sauceboat.

Tournedos Bercy

Method.   Place the *tournedos* on round croutons, $^3/_4$ inch thick and $2^1/_2$ to 3 inches in diameter, fried in butter. Pour $^1/_2$ cup dry white wine into the skillet used to cook the meat, and reduce by three-fourths; add an equal amount of veal stock, and reduce to two-thirds; finish the sauce off the heat by adding 1 tablespoon butter, mixing it into the sauce by shaking the skillet.

Pour the sauce over the *tournedos,* and on top of each steak place 1 teaspoon of creamed Bercy butter (below).

Bercy Butter

Chop the shallots fine; cook them slowly with 1 tablespoon butter, without browning. When the shallots are very soft, add $^1/_2$ cup dry white wine, boil to reduce to 3 tablespoons; add off the heat to the hot skillet used to cook the shallots: $^1/_4$ pound butter; diced marrow, poached for a few minutes in nearly boiling salted water and then well drained; chopped parsley; salt, pepper, and the lemon juice; mix well to produce a thick creamed butter.

This butter can be served on the side in a sauceboat.

Tournedos sautés à la bordelaise

Arrange 6 sautéed *tournedos* on a hot round platter; on top of each steak, place a substantial slice of marrow, poached in nearly boiling salted water. Deglaze the skillet with ¹/₂ cup *bordelaise* sauce (page 79); finish the sauce off the heat with 3 tablespoons butter. Pour some sauce on the meat, and on the marrow put pinches of chopped parsley; serve very hot.

Tournedos Choron

6 slices stale bread
6 tablespoons unsalted
  butter
6 *tournedos,* ¹/₄ pound
  each
2 tablespoons oil
1 cup Choron sauce (page
  89) with 3 parts *béar-
  naise* sauce (page 89)
  to 1 part tomato purée
6 artichoke bottoms,
  cooked in white
  court-bouillon (Bresse
  style, page 312)
2 bunches green
  asparagus tips *à l'an-
  glaise* (page 351)
2 pounds large potatoes
6 tablespoons veal stock
  (page 72)

Method.   With the 6 slices stale bread, prepare the croutons (page 163) and fry them in 4 tablespoons butter; place on a round platter and keep warm.

Cook the *tournedos* in the oil and 2 tablespoons butter, following the instructions for sautéing (page 154).

Place the steaks on the croutons, arranged in a circle, and pour on each a border of Choron sauce.

Between the *tournedos,* intersperse the 6 artichoke bottoms, seasoned with salt and pepper and stewed on both sides in butter for 15 to 20 minutes; garnish the artichoke bottoms with small bunches of asparagus tips cooked *à l'anglaise* (boiled in a large quantity of salted water, then drained and coated lightly, off the heat, with unsalted butter). Correct the seasoning.

Fill the center of the dish with the potatoes, cooked following the recipe for Parisian potatoes (page 362).

Deglaze the skillet with 6 tablespoons veal stock, reduce by half, and pour a few drops on each *tournedos* in the center of the circle of Choron sauce.

Tournedos sautés aux champignons

TOURNEDOS SAUTÉED WITH MUSHROOMS

Sauté 6 *tournedos;* arrange in a circle on a round heated platter. In the center, place a garnish of small mushrooms in the shape of a dome and, on each steak, a beautiful fluted mushroom cap.

Mushroom Garnish

From ¹/₂ pound small, very white mushrooms, cleaned and washed, choose 6 nice caps and flute them; this means, use a vegetable knife to make parallel cuts in the skin to form a rosette. If the other mushrooms are larger than marbles, cut each one into 2 or more pieces; in the skillet where the *tour-nedos* were cooked gently heat ¹/₄ pound butter so that the meat juices left in the skillet will not burn. Add the mushrooms, cook on a high flame for 5 minutes and add ¹/₂ cup dry white wine. Reduce by two-thirds; then add 1 cup *demiglace* sauce (page 76), or 2 cups good veal stock (page 72). If using veal stock, reduce by half; add about 1 tablespoon butter off the heat. Correct the seasoning, then place the fluted mushrooms on the *tournedos* and the other mushrooms in the center.

Coat the *tournedos* with the sauce, and finish the dish with chopped parsley on the fluted mushrooms.

Tournedos chasseur
TOURNEDOS HUNTER'S STYLE

Follow the same recipe as for *tournedos* with mushrooms, cutting the mushrooms into slices. Just before adding the butter to the sauce also add ¹/₂ teaspoon each chopped tarragon and chopped parsley.

Do not boil the sauce after adding the herbs.

Tournedos Clamart

3 large potatoes, baked
Salt and pepper
9 tablespoons unsalted butter
6 *tournedos,* ¹/₄ pound each
2 tablespoons oil
6 small tarts made with unsweetened very fine dough (pages 386 and 391–2), baked but not browned
2 cups green peas cooked *à la française* (page 352)
¹/₂ cup sherry
1 cup veal stock (page 72)

Method.   Cut the baked potatoes in half; remove the pulp, place in a bowl, season with salt and pepper, and mix with a fork, adding 3 tablespoons butter. With this paste, make 6 patties the shape and size of the *tournedos* and brown them in a skillet in butter. Turn them carefully with a spatula. Arrange in a circle on a round platter and keep warm.

Cook the *tournedos* in 2 tablespoons oil and 2 tablespoons butter and place them on the potato patties.

Around the steaks put the small tart shells (baked in a 325° oven between two molds so that they keep their shape, or lined with wax paper and filled with dried beans). Fill each tart with the green peas coated with 2 tablespoons butter.

Deglaze the skillet with the sherry and the veal stock, reduce by two-thirds; add 2 tablespoons butter off the heat, and serve in a sauceboat. Do not pour the sauce on the serving platter; it would destroy the crispness of the potatoes.

Tournedos Henri Quatre

6 slices stale bread
2 tablespoons oil
6 *tournedos,* ¹/₄ pound each
1¹/₂ pounds large potatoes
¹/₄ pound unsalted butter
6 artichoke bottoms, cooked in a *blanc* (page 306)
1 cup *béarnaise* sauce (page 89)
Dash chopped chervil and tarragon

Method.   Prepare the *croutons* (page 163). Brush the steaks with the oil and broil them. Peel the potatoes and cut into ovals the size of a filbert; sauté in butter.

Slice the artichoke bottoms, and place them in a skillet in 3 tablespoons sizzling butter. Brown lightly.

Place the *tournedos* on the croutons, pour a circle of *béarnaise* sauce on each, and alternate the steaks with clusters of potatoes and artichoke bottoms. Correct the seasoning of the vegetables. Finish the dish with a dash of chopped chervil and tarragon on the potatoes.

Serve the remaining *béarnaise* sauce on the side.

Tournedos à la moelle
TOURNEDOS WITH MARROW

6 *tournedos*, ¹/₄ pound each
6 slices beef marrow
¹/₂ cup *bordelaise* sauce (page 79)

Method.   Broil the *tournedos.*

Poach marrow for 5 minutes in a pan of nearly boiling salted water.

Place the *tournedos* on a round platter and put a slice of marrow on each piece. Coat with the *bordelaise* sauce, slightly reduced and buttered off the heat.

Tournedos forestière

6 slices stale bread
10 tablespoons unsalted
   butter
1¼ pounds mushrooms
   (morels, *cèpes*, *girolles*,
   etc.)
4 tablespoons oil
6 *tournedos*, ¼ pound
   each
Chopped parsley
½ cup veal stock
   (page 72)

Method. Prepare 6 croutons in 4 tablespoons butter (page 163)

Clean and wash the mushrooms carefully, do not let them stand in water; drain well and wipe dry. If they are medium-sized or a little large, slice them.

Heat the oil in a skillet; as soon as it smokes, add the mushrooms, season with salt, and cook over a high flame for 5 minutes, stirring frequently. Drain and place 3 tablespoons butter in the skillet; heat until sizzling; add mushrooms and brown lightly. Correct the seasoning with salt, if needed, and add a couple of turns of the pepper mill.

Cook the *tournedos;* place them on the croutons, arranged in a circle, and in the center put the mushrooms; sprinkle with a pinch of chopped parsley.

On the *tournedos,* pour sauce made by deglazing the skillet with the veal stock, adding the remaining butter.

Serve very hot.

Note: If you like, you can add 1 teaspoon chopped shallots to the mushrooms at the last minute.

Entrecôte à la bordelaise

[*Editor's note: Entrecôte* is the part of the meat between the bones of the beef ribs; it can be replaced with a rib steak.]

Grill the *entrecôte.* After it has been turned, and when the second side is half cooked, completely cover the steak with slices of beef marrow about ⅛ inch thick, which have poached for 5 minutes in nearly boiling salted water.

As soon as the meat is cooked, carefully remove the *entrecôte* with a spatula and place on a long, hot serving platter. Sprinkle the marrow with a pinch of Bonnefoy sauce (a *bordelaise* sauce, page 79, made with white wine).

Note: Entrecôte, porterhouse steak, and rumpsteak, broiled or sautéed, are accompanied by fried potatoes: puffed, Pont-Neuf, matchstick, etc. (page 355).

Côte de boeuf à la moelle au vin de Brouilly

RIB OF BEEF WITH MARROW AND WINE (For 2 people)

1 2-pound beef rib
Salt and freshly ground
   pepper
¼ pound unsalted butter
½ tablespoon chopped
   shallots
1 bottle Brouilly wine
1 tablespoon *beurre manié*
   made with equal
   quantities of butter and
   flour
¼ pound marrow

Method. Salt and pepper the rib of beef. In a heavy-bottomed skillet, cook the meat in melted butter, browning it on both sides. For rare meat the cooking time is 5 minutes a side.

Remove the meat to a serving platter and keep warm.

In the cooking butter, sauté the shallots without browning them. In order to deglaze the pan and make the sauce, add the Brouilly to the skillet and let it boil until reduced by half.

Thicken the sauce with the *beurre manié*, and after correcting the seasoning, add the remaining butter in order to make the sauce more velvety.

Serve the rib of beef covered with slices of marrow, poached for 5 minutes in lightly salted water.

¹/₂ pound fresh pork fat
Salt, pepper, and mixed
  spices (page x)
¹/₂ cup cognac
3¹/₂ pounds flank steak or
  rumpsteak
Chopped parsley
Chopped thyme
Crushed bay leaf
2 cups white wine
2 calf's feet
2 ounces fresh pork rind
4 tablespoons unsalted
  butter or pork, chicken, or
  veal fat
1 medium-sized carrot,
  quartered
1 large onion, quartered
Bouquet garni **(10 parsley**
  sprigs, bay leaf, sprig
  thyme)
5 garlic cloves
1 quart lightly salted veal
  stock (page 72)

1 pound carrots
20 small onions
2 tablespoons unsalted
  butter

The rib of beef can be served coated with the sauce or the sauce can be served in a sauceboat.

Note: It is better to cream the butter and add it at the last moment to any sauce made with wine; it will eliminate the acidity and improve the flavor.

Boeuf à la mode

(For 6 people, 2 meals—one hot and one cold)

Method.   This dish must marinate for at least 5 hours before it is cooked, and it must cook for 5 hours. Cut ¹/₂ pound pork fat into pieces the width and length of a pencil; place them in a shallow dish, season with salt and pepper and a dash of spices; add 2 tablespoons cognac, mix, and let macerate for 20 minutes, turning them from time to time.

Just before using the fat, sprinkle it with chopped parsley. With a larding needle introduce the pieces of fat into the meat by pushing the larding needle through in the direction of the grain of the meat. The pieces of fat should form a checkerboard pattern in each slice of meat when it is carved. Season the meat with salt and pepper and a pinch of thyme and crushed bay leaf, and place it in a bowl just big enough to hold it, so that when the remaining cognac and the white wine are added, the meat will be completely covered; let it marinate in the wine and cognac in a cool place for 5 hours, turning it from time to time to let the spices penetrate the meat.

Cooking.   Have the butcher bone the calf's feet; retain the bones. Blanch the feet (place them in cold water and boil for 10 minutes), rinse, and tie them in cheesecloth. Break the bones into tiny pieces.

Plunge the pork rind into boiling water, rinse, and tie in a bundle.

Drain the meat from the marinade, wipe carefully, and tie it with string—not too tightly, just enough to hold the meat together. Put the butter or the fat in a saucepan big enough to hold the meat; heat well, and brown the meat on all sides. Add the carrot and the onion and brown lightly. Add the calf's feet, the bones, the pork rind, the *bouquet garni*, and the garlic. Pour over the marinade and enough stock so that the meat is covered. Bring just to a boil, cover, and continue cooking, preferably in a 325° oven, slowly and evenly without interruption. Too-rapid boiling clouds the stock, makes it insipid, and gives it an unpleasant taste. This dish should simmer, not boil. The stock will then blend with the meat juices and the gelatinous ingredients of the pork rind and the calf's feet, and it will become rich and flavorful. Cook for 4 hours.

Garnish

While this is cooking, prepare the carrots and the onions for the garnish. Cut the carrots into pieces the size of a walnut, rounding the edges. If they are old carrots, remove the cores, which are always hard and have a very strong taste. Plunge the cored carrots into boiling water for 15 minutes. If they are new carrots, omit the last two steps.

Peel the small onions and brown with 2 tablespoons butter in a skillet or a frying pan.

At the end of 4 hours remove the meat, the calf's feet, the pork rind, and the large carrot and onion from the saucepan; strain the stock through a fine sieve, let it stand for 5 minutes, and then remove the fat from the surface.

Cut the calf's feet and pork rind into pieces ½ inch square.

Place the meat in a saucepan just big enough to hold the meat and the garnish and add the calf's feet, the pork rind, the carrot pieces, the small onions, and the stock. Bring to a boil, cover, and cook for 1 hour, as slowly as before. A larding needle should now penetrate the meat easily.

To serve, lift the meat carefully and place on a serving platter, remove the string; surround the meat with the carrots, the onions, the calf's feet, and the pork rind. Pour over just enough stock to moisten them.

At the end of the cooking time, if the recipe has been carefully followed, the stock should be syrupy and reduced to about 2 cups.

To serve this cold, see recipe, page 175.

Boeuf à la bourguignonne

BEEF WITH BURGUNDY (For 6 people)

3 pounds flank steak or rumpsteak
⅓ pound fresh pork fat, with rind removed and reserved
½ cup cognac
¾ cup good red Burgundy wine
1 calf's foot
7 tablespoons unsalted butter
2 tablespoons flour
1 quart stock
***Bouquet garni* (sprigs parsley, sprig thyme, 1 bay leaf)**
1 pound mushrooms
½-pound slab lean bacon, cut in ¼-inch slices
2 dozen small onions, peeled

Method. This dish will take 5 hours to cook. Lard the meat with the pork fat, and place it in a marinade of the cognac and wine for 3 hours.

Have the butcher bone the calf's foot; retain the bones. Plunge it into boiling water for 10 minutes, rinse, and tie it in cheesecloth; break the bones into tiny pieces. Plunge the pork rind into boiling water and rinse.

Drain the meat, wipe dry, and brown 4 tablespoons butter as for the *boeuf à la mode* (page 168). When the meat is well browned, remove and set aside on a plate; add the flour to the butter and brown the mixture slowly, stirring constantly.

Dilute with the marinade and the stock. Bring to a boil, stirring with a whisk, and place the meat in the sauce, which should just cover the meat. Add the *bouquet garni,* the calf's foot, the bones, the pork rind, and the stems of the mushrooms, well cleaned. Cover, and cook very slowly in a 325° oven for 4 hours.

Plunge the bacon slices into boiling water for 5 minutes, drain, and wipe dry. Brown in a frying pan with the remaining butter; remove to a plate, and in the same pan with the butter, brown the onions.

After 4 hours, remove the beef and the calf's foot; then strain the sauce through a fine sieve. Dice the calf's foot thickly and return to the pan with the beef; add the bacon, the onions, the mushroom caps, quartered, and the strained sauce. Bring to a boil, and continue cooking in the oven, covered, very slowly—at a simmer—for 1 hour.

At the end of this time the sauce should be reduced to 3 cups. If more remains, boil the sauce until it is reduced to this point.

Beef

To serve place the meat on a round, deep platter, surround with garnishes, and pour the sauce over.

Cuisse de boeuf rôtie au feu de bois
LEG OF BEEF COOKED OVER CHARCOAL (For 80 to 100 people)

1 beef leg, about 80–100 pounds
Salt and finely ground pepper
1 pound crushed garlic cloves

Method. Choose, preferably, a beef leg from the Charolais region, carefully aged. The day before cooking trim it as you would a veal leg (saw the knuckle and remove the end).

Pierce the flesh deeply with a larding needle every 4 inches. In each hole, place a pinch of salt and finely ground pepper mixed with crushed garlic. Also salt and pepper the surface of the meat, rubbing it in with your hand so that the seasoning penetrates the flesh.

Cooking. In a big fireplace with a spit prepare a fire with aromatic wood. When the logs are partly burned and the heat is strong, place the beef leg (threaded on the spit) in the hearth about 4 inches from the coals. Start the roasting jack to turn the spit. The cooking time for a leg of 80 to 100 pounds is 8 hours of steady cooking.

During this long time the fire will need more wood; the leg should be basted frequently with the juice and the fat that collect in the drip pan. To prevent the leg from drying out it can also be basted with melted butter during the cooking.

Before serving it let the leg stand for 1 hour in a warming oven at a low temperature.

After this magnificent roast has been shown to the guests, carve it in front of them. When sliced, the flesh should be pink and slightly bloody.

Serve with potatoes in their skins, cooked in the embers, along with the following:

Garnish (For 10 people)

2 pounds white onions
2 1/2 quarts olive oil
2 pounds fresh tomatoes, seeded and cut
1 pound green or red peppers, diced small
1 head garlic, crushed
Salt, pepper, paprika, cayenne
Bouquet garni

Chop the onions fine; sauté in the olive oil, in a large skillet, without letting them brown.

Add the tomatoes, the peppers, and the garlic.

Season with salt and pepper, paprika, cayenne, and add the *bouquet garni;* cook slowly for 3/4 hour, covered; remove the *bouquet.*

Note: In Mexico this garnish is very popular served with a leg of beef.

Daube de maître Philéas Gilbert
(For 6 people)

1/2 pound fresh pork fat
Salt, pepper, mixed spices (page x)
Pinch thyme and bay leaf
1 teaspoon chopped parsley
3 1/2 pounds beef flank, round, and chuck, in equal parts
1/2 cup cognac
1/2 bottle red Burgundy wine

Method. This dish must marinate for at least 3 hours before it is cooked, and it must cook for 5 1/2 hours.

Cut the fresh pork fat into *lardons* (strips) as thick as a finger and 2 1/2 inches long; season with salt, pepper, and a dash of spices or a pinch of thyme and a bay leaf; sprinkle with 1 teaspoon chopped fresh parsley and marinate for 1 hour.

Cut the meat in 3-ounce cubes, and lard them with 4 *lardons,* using a larding needle and piercing the meat in the direction of the grain; season the meat with a pinch of salt, pepper, and spices, mixed well; place the meat in a bowl, add

170

2 shallots, chopped
Sprigs parsley
1/4 pound fresh pork rind
1 calf's foot, bones
  removed and reserved
1/2-pound slab lean bacon
4 large onions
4 garlic cloves
4 medium-sized carrots
4 tablespoons unsalted
  butter or fat
Bouquet garni
2 cups lightly salted stock
Flour-and-water dough to
  cover

the cognac, the red wine, the shallots, and a couple of parsley sprigs cut into pieces. Marinate for 2 hours.

Place the pork rind and the boned calf's foot in cold water; blanch for 5 minutes, rinse and cut into small cubes. Break the calf's foot bones into tiny pieces. Cut the bacon into large dice and blanch. Coarsely chop the onions, mince the garlic with the point of a knife, mix well, and put between two plates to prevent the onion from browning when the air touches it; slice the carrots.

Drain and wipe the pieces of meat.

Heat the butter or the fat in a skillet; when it sizzles, add the meat, 5 or 6 pieces at a time, so that each piece browns on all sides.

Use an ovenproof earthenware terrine (a tripe terrine for example) large enough to hold the quantity of meat that is going to be cooked. At the bottom of the terrine, place the calf's foot bones; on this bed of bones, put one-third of the meat; then half the carrots (with their cores removed, if they are not new carrots) cut into pieces; half the onions, the calf's foot, pork rind, and one-third remaining *lardons;* sprinkle with a good pinch of salt, add another layer of meat. Then add the other half of the condiments—carrots, onions, calf's foot, pork rind, and another third of the *lardons;* then a pinch of salt, a *bouquet garni,* and a third layer of meat. Finish by pouring in the marinade and the stock, which should reach 1/2 inch above the last layer of meat. Cover this with the remaining *lardons.*

Place a cover on the terrine, and seal it with dough made from flour and water, to prevent too-rapid evaporation during the cooking.

Place on the lowest possible heat. When it starts to boil continue cooking for 5 1/2 hours in a 325° oven so that it simmers slowly and evenly.

The ideal heat is a baker's oven, after bread has baked. Don't pass up the chance of cooking the meat that way, if you can.

After taking the dish out of the oven, let it stand for a few minutes before serving so that the grease can be removed; remove the *bouquet garni,* correct the seasoning, and present.

Carbonade à la flamande

(For 6 people)

1 1/2 pounds beef, chuck or
  boned short ribs
Salt and pepper
3 tablespoons fat
4 tablespoons unsalted
  butter
3 large onions
2 tablespoons flour
3 cups beer
3 cups bouillon
1 teaspoon sugar
1 tablespoon vinegar
Bouquet garni

Method. Cut the meat into small 2-ounce pieces, and season with salt and pepper.

Heat the fat and the butter in a skillet; as soon as it is smoking, brown the meat on all sides, remove, and put aside on a plate.

Then chop the onions fine and brown them lightly in the fat used to brown the meat.

Remove the onions and stir in the flour over a low flame until the *roux* has a dark gold color. Pour in the beer and the bouillon; add a pinch of salt, a pinch of pepper, the sugar, and the vinegar.

Bring to a boil, stirring, and simmer on a very low flame for 15 minutes.

In an earthenware casserole or tripe terrine large enough to hold all the meat, place the meat and the onions in layers. Put the *bouquet garni* in the center.

Strain the sauce through a very fine sieve onto the meat; cover and seal tightly with a ribbon of dough made from flour and water; cook in a 375° oven for 3 hours, until the meat is cooked and the sauce reduced and slightly thickened.

Take out of the oven; remove the cover and the *bouquet garni*. Let stand for 6 minutes, and skim off the fat. Correct the seasoning of the sauce, and serve in the cooking pot.

The *carbonade* can also be served on a deep platter. In that case, strain the sauce through a very fine sieve, rubbing through the onions to make a purée.

Mix well, then heat and pour over the meat, which should be kept hot and covered so that it does not dry out during the last step.

Estouffade de boeuf

BRAISED BEEF (For 6 people)

½ pound fresh pork fat
5 tablespoons unsalted butter
1½ pounds beef chuck
3 medium-sized onions, quartered
½ tablespoon salt
Pinch of ground pepper
2 tablespoons flour
2 garlic cloves, crushed
2 cups good red wine
4 cups veal stock (page 72) or lightly salted bouillon
Bouquet garni
½ pound mushrooms

Method. Cut the pork fat into large cubes, blanch, drain, and brown with 2 tablespoons butter in a saucepan just big enough to hold the meat and the stock.

Remove the pork fat, and in the same butter, half brown the meat cut into 3- to 4-ounce pieces. Add the onions and continue cooking until everything is browned.

Sprinkle with salt, pepper, and flour. Mix well, and brown lightly, stirring constantly. Be careful that the onions do not brown too much or they will give the sauce a bitter taste.

Add the garlic, stir again for a few seconds, just long enough for the heat to bring out the perfume of the garlic; then add the red wine. Boil to reduce the wine by two-thirds, then pour in just enough veal stock or bouillon to cover the pieces of meat; bring to a boil, stirring, and finish by adding the sautéed pork fat and the *bouquet garni.* Cover the saucepan and cook slowly in a 325° oven for 3 hours. The dish should barely simmer.

Clean the mushrooms, wash rapidly, and cut into quarters; sauté with remaining butter for 5 minutes over a high flame in a skillet as big as the one previously used. Remove from the heat as soon as the mushrooms start to brown.

Remove the meat from the oven, and place the meat and pork fat on top of the mushrooms. Let the sauce stand in the original meat pan for 5 minutes, remove the fat, and correct the consistency of the sauce by adding liquid or boiling to reduce it; by this time it should be lightly thickened and reduced so it will half cover the meat and the garnishes. Correct the seasoning, and strain the sauce through a very fine sieve onto the *estouffade,* rubbing it through with a wooden spoon.

Bring to a boil, and simmer on a very low flame for another 15 to 20 minutes.

Place in a deep serving platter and serve with a bowl of potatoes cooked in their skins.

Note: The garnish may be completed by adding to the mushrooms 1 pound tomatoes, peeled, seeded, drained, and cut into pieces. Be careful: raw tomatoes make the sauce more liquid because of the water in the pulp. When finishing the sauce, that important detail must be taken into account.

The *estouffade,* an exquisite dish of the old cuisine, can also be made with white wine.

SHORT RIBS AND BRISKET

The short ribs and the brisket are usually reserved for a *pot-au-feu.* They are served accompanied by the traditional vegetable garnish and the condiments of the *pot-au-feu:* coarse salt ground at the table with a salt mill, *cornichons,* horseradish with cream, and mustard.

Other vegetable garnishes can be served: sauerkraut, braised cabbage, Brussels sprouts, red cabbage, stuffed cabbage, rice cooked in fat, purées of fresh or dried beans.

Very often, especially when the dish is left over and served cold, it is accompanied by a strongly spiced, somewhat acid or peppery sauce such as *piquante,* hunter's, or Robert (page 81).

The short ribs and the brisket can also be pickled and salted (i.e., corned) and served with pasta, such as noodles, macaroni, spaghetti, or lasagna.

Plat de côtes salé
CORNED SHORT RIBS (For 6 people)

4 pounds beef short ribs or
  brisket
2 handfuls sea salt
2 tablespoons saltpeter,
  crushed
Sprig thyme
1 bay leaf
Pinch pepper
2 medium-sized carrots,
  quartered
2 large onions, quartered
  and stuck with 2 cloves
Bouquet garni
3/4 pound fresh noodles or
  1/4 pound dry noodles
Pepper, nutmeg, salt
1 cup grated gruyère or
  cheshire cheese
3 1/2 tablespoons unsalted
  butter

Method. The short ribs should be thick, well marbled, and have a heavy coating of white or pale yellow fat. Have the butcher saw the rib bones so that the meat can be carved easily and each guest can have a piece of meat with a bone.

In a bowl mix the sea salt with the saltpeter.

With a larding needle, pierce the meat; rub it all over with the salt and saltpeter. Sprinkle some of the salt on the bottom of an enamel baking dish big enough to contain the meat, put in the meat, and pour the rest of the salt mixture on top. Break up the thyme and the bay leaf and place on the salt along with the pepper.

Place the meat in a cool place for 10 to 12 days in the winter, 6 to 8 days in the summer or if the weather is humid. Every two days, turn the meat. [*Editor's note:* It may also be refrigerated.]

To cook, drain the meat and rinse it in cold water. Place in a saucepan, cover with cold water, and add the carrots, the onions, and the *bouquet garni.* Bring to a boil, and cook very slowly, as you would a *pot-au-feu* (pages 50–1), for 3 hours. It need only simmer very slightly as long as it continues to cook steadily; a sudden stop might spoil the flavor.

If the noodles are fresh, poach them for 15 minutes before serving by plunging them into a saucepan of boiling water.

Remove from the heat as soon as the water starts to boil again; cover and cook without boiling for 10 minutes; drain thoroughly. [*Editor's note:* Or follow package directions for dried noodles.]

While the noodles are very hot, put them into a heated skillet, give a couple of turns of the pepper mill, a dash of grated nutmeg, a pinch of salt, if needed—taste the noodles, taking into account the saltiness of the cheese—the grated gruyère or cheshire, and the butter cut into pieces. Mix well with a fork until the cheese has coated the noodles.

Remove the short ribs from the saucepan and put on a long heated platter; place the noodles at either end or serve separately in a bowl. In that case, pour a ladle of the cooking bouillon on the meat.

Boeuf en miroton

(For 6 people)

6 large onions
4 tablespoons unsalted butter or chopped fresh pork fat
1 heaping tablespoon flour
2 tablespoons vinegar
2 generous cups bouillon or veal stock (page 72)
1 teaspoon thick tomato purée or 3 tomatoes, peeled, seeded, drained, and cut into pieces
2 garlic cloves, crushed
Pepper
1½ pounds boiled beef
1 teaspoon chopped parsley
1 tablespoon bread crumbs
Melted butter

Method.   Cut the onions into thin strips, boil for 5 minutes to remove the bitterness, drain, and wipe dry.

In a saucepan or an earthenware pot heat the butter, add the onions and cook on a low flame, stirring often with a wooden spoon.

When the onions are golden, add the flour and continue to brown slowly. When the *roux* is browned, add the vinegar and let it cool. Gradually pour in the hot bouillon or stock, nearly at the boiling point, whisking it into the flour in the same way as for a sauce, to prevent lumps from forming; complete by adding the tomato purée or tomatoes and the crushed garlic; give the sauce a couple of turns of the pepper mill. Bring to a boil, then simmer for 20 minutes.

Fifteen minutes before serving cut the beef into slices ¼ inch thick; arrange on a fireproof earthenware dish; correct the seasoning of the sauce, then pour it over the beef, covering it completely. Heat on the stove to the boiling point; then sprinkle with the chopped parsley and bread crumbs, pour on a few drops of melted butter, and place in the oven to brown.

Note: One teaspoon mustard or grated horseradish or some sliced *cornichons* can be added to the sauce. In that case, do not let it boil after adding one of these ingredients. Finish the dish in the following way: dilute these condiments with vinegar and add to the sauce off the heat; then add the beef to the sauce, cover the pot, and keep it warm without letting it boil.

The *miroton* is served in a heated dish and sprinkled with chopped parsley. The edges of the dish can be decorated with sliced *cornichons.*

The *miroton* can be served with various garnishes:
1. Surround the meat with quartered, hot hard-cooked eggs.
2. Serve the meat with a platter of sliced eggplant and onions, fried very crisp in oil.
3. Surround the meat, before the final browning, with a circle of boiled potatoes, cut up and moistened with the sauce.

COLD BEEF

A sirloin roast, ribs of beef, sirloin steak, roast filet of beef should all be pink inside when cooked.

The presentation is simple: trim the meat, removing the tendons, the skin, and the fat or burned parts; coat the meat with a thin layer of jelly spooned on when half set. Place the meat on a serving platter big enough for the garnish, if it will be arranged around the meat, or for the size of the meat, if the garnish is to be served separately. In the latter case, surround the meat with jelly chopped or cut into decorative shapes and placed in the inside rim of the platter.

The garnish is nearly always a vegetable salad—mixed or not. The vegetables are cooked and cooled without being rinsed, well drained, seasoned, and bound with one of the following sauces: vinaigrette (pages 2–3), rémoulade (page 91), or light mayonnaise (page 90). If the salad is to be molded or placed in mounds around the meat, the mayonnaise should be made with 1 part half-set jelly for each 4 parts sauce.

It is not necessary to add jelly when the garnish is presented in a salad bowl.

Filet ou contre-filet froid ménagère
COLD FILET OF BEEF OR SIRLOIN ROAST HOME STYLE

This recipe requires a piece of meat cooked in a skillet and cooled naturally and not refrigerated. Trim it and slice evenly into ¼-inch slices.

Moisten with the juices from the bottom of the pan, well degreased, strained through cheesecloth, and half set; spoon a little on each slice.

Reshape the meat as a roast, and place on a serving platter surrounded with chopped jelly or water cress.

Serve with a vegetable salad.

Daube froide
COLD DAUBE

The leftovers of *daube* Philéas Gilbert (pages 170–1), cooled in the cooking pan, make an excellent cold dish for a summer lunch.

The gelatinous elements in the calf's foot, the pork rind, and the beef muscle are sufficient to jell the meat, which can be cut into slices like a pâté in a terrine.

Boeuf à la mode froid
COLD BOEUF À LA MODE

This dish, which is very pleasant in the summer, is an exquisite way to serve leftovers of *boeuf à la mode* made according to the recipe on pages 168–9 and intended for two meals.

Method.   Remove the garnish and the braising juices from the meat, and boil them for 2 or 3 minutes. Pour through a strainer and reserve the carrots, onions, and calf's feet on a plate. Discard the pieces of pork rind, which lose their tenderness when cold.

If necessary, add some veal stock or some bouillon to the braising juices if there is is not enough sauce to cover the beef and the garnish when they are placed in a mold. Add 2 or 3 envelopes of gelatin, presoaked in cold water and brought to a boil to dissolve.

To test whether the jelly is strong enough, put 2 teaspoons of it on a plate and cool. The jelly should be firm enough to cut with a knife without being rubbery. A jelly that is too gelatinous is not appealing. Correct the seasoning, taking into account that, when it is cooled, the salt is less strong and that a properly salted hot dish seems tasteless when eaten cold.

Use a charlotte mold of the size needed, or any container of a similar shape, and pour in a little of the sauce prepared as directed above. Let it jell, then artistically arrange some of the carrots and the onions, then the beef, which must not touch the sides of the mold. Place the remaining carrots, onions, and calf's feet around the beef; then pour in the rest of the sauce.

The jelly must not overwhelm the garnish; be careful not to add too much veal stock or bouillon. Refrigerate the mold, which should not be served until the next day.

To serve dip the mold in hot water for a second, wipe, and turn upside down on a cold platter; remove the mold. Decorate the edges of the jellied meat with some *cornichons.*

This dish can be simplified in the following way:

Cut the meat into even slices, place them in a shallow dish, overlapping the slices. Around them place carrots, onions, and calf's feet; cover with the braising sauce with or without gelatin, and cool until the sauce has set.

Since this dish will not be unmolded, the braising juices will probably be sufficiently stiff without the addition of extra gelatin (test it first as directed above). The dish will be more flavorful since gelatin diminishes its savor.

Note: This preparation can be braised following the old method called *à la cuiller* (page 154). This procedure is not economical, but it reaches the heights of perfection.

Veal

Good-quality veal is almost white or rather a very pale pink. The fat is clearly white, thick on the loin or the breast. The meat and the fat are very firm.

These superior qualities are found exclusively in animals two or three months old that are fed on their mothers' milk and grain and never allowed to graze.

Inferior-quality meat is red, soft, and often lean. If the meat is flabby and gelatinous, the animal was only a few weeks old and killed prematurely.

Parts of the animal

A side of veal includes three main parts:

The veal leg, the shoulder, and, between the two, the loin and ribs. If the entire loin is used in one piece, it is called a saddle of veal.

The leg can be cut into three pieces: the rump, the round, and the knuckle. Except for the knuckle, these are the choice pieces for roasting, braising, or using in scallops or cutlets, *grenadins* (small thick scallops), and *paupiettes* (thin scallops).

A roast cut across the thick part of the leg is called a round roast. This way of cutting veal is rarely used today.

The top part of the rear leg next to the tail is called the rump or butt.

The shoulder is used to make ragoûts or roasts.

The loin, or the rack, and the ribs are roasted or braised; they are also cut into chops. Next to them is the third portion: the riblets, the breast, and the neck. The neck is used in ragoûts; the riblets and the breast also make excellent ragoûts or sautés and are used cut or whole for braising.

The variety meats are: the head, the liver, the fat, the lung, the heart, the sweetbreads, the brains, the tongue, and the feet.

Quasi de veau bourgeoise

VEAL RUMP OR BUTT POT ROASTED (For 12 to 15 people)

1 calf's foot
1/2 pound fresh pork rind
1 pound veal bones
1 medium-sized carrot, sliced
2 large onions, sliced
10 tablespoons unsalted butter
4–5-pound veal rump
Salt and pepper
Bouquet garni
2 fresh tomatoes when in season

Method. Have the butcher bone the calf's foot; retain the bones. Plunge it with the pork rind into boiling water for 10 minutes; rinse. Break the extra veal bones and the bones of the calf's foot into tiny pieces, and brown them in the oven with the carrot and onions.

Generously butter the bottom of a casserole, braising pan, or ragoût pot with a tight cover. In it place the meat seasoned with salt and freshly ground pepper. Spread the rest of the butter over the meat. Place the pan in a 325° oven, uncovered. Brown the meat slowly on all sides. Be careful that the butter does not burn.

When the meat has browned, remove it from the pan; add to the pan the bones and the browned vegetables, the pork rind, the calf's foot, the *bouquet garni,* and the crushed tomatoes. Return the meat, and cover tightly. Continue cooking for 2 1/2 hours in a 325° oven, basting frequently with the meat juices. If the cooking is done slowly, the liquid from the meat is turned into vapor by the oven's heat. This steam, imprisoned under the tight cover, condenses and falls in drops on the meat, moistening and basting it before running down into the butter and the flavorful gelatinous ingredients that escape from the bones, the calf's foot, the pork rind, and the vegeta-

177

bles—which, in turn, will form a light-colored broth, fragrant and syrupy, ample enough to sauce the veal.

If in spite of your care, it cooks too rapidly because of a sudden rise in the oven temperature and the juice reduces and threatens to *tomber à glace*—which means to become thick and caramelize at the bottom of the pan, where it could burn and give the dish a bitter taste—moisten the bones with 1 cup veal stock (page 72) or bouillon or, if you have neither, 1 cup water.

When the cooking is over, remove the cover; place the meat, round side up, under the broiler for a few minutes, basting it several times. The juice, which is now very rich, will give the meat a shiny glaze when it is ready to be served.

Strain the juice and serve it in a sauceboat without removing the fat; it should be rich, light in color, and slightly syrupy.

Generally, the veal rump is served with a vegetable as garnish. The best ones are indicated below:

Bouquetière: glazed carrots, turnips (trimmed very small), peas, string beans, and cauliflower (both cut very small), served with butter or hollandaise sauce (page 88); *bourgeoise:* glazed carrots and oinons; spinach, chicory, endive, sorrel; *jardinière:* tiny peas, celery, and carrots, mixed together; different types of noodles; lettuce, eggplant, zucchini, small onions, etc.; purées of mushrooms, potatoes, celery, sorrel, etc.

Presentation. At the table the veal rump is carved in very thin slices, cut crosswise against the grain. You will know if the meat is correctly cooked as soon as you start to carve: it will look very white and moist, and pearls of slightly pink, very clear juice will appear. If the meat is overdone, it will look dry and be unsavory.

Although the bones at the bottom of the pan have cooked for 3 hours and are nearly dry, they have not as yet yielded up all the tasty ingredients they contain. Place them in a small saucepan with a carrot and an onion, sliced, then moisten with 1½ quarts water and a large pinch of salt. Bring to a boil and simmer for 3 hours; this will make a stock that can be used later in other dishes.

If the calf's foot has not been used with a vegetable garnish, it can be served as a hot hors d'oeuvre with a vinaigrette sauce (pages 2–3).

The pork rind, cut into strips, is an excellent addition to beans and to carrots prepared *à la bourgeoise*.

Fricandeau

VEAL RUMP OR TOP ROUND

The *fricandeau* is a cut of meat from the upper part of the leg, cut parallel to the meat grain and about 2½ to 3 inches thick.

Pound the slice of meat to break the meat fibers and lard with unsalted pork fat as you would do with a filet of beef.

The *fricandeau* is cooked in the same way as the rump. Only the cooking time is different, depending on its thickness.

The *fricandeau*, fed by the pork fat, can also be braised

until it is so tender that it is served with a spoon. This dish, obviously expensive, is extremely succulent, whether hot or cold.

The garnishes for the rump can be used for the *fricandeau*.

Rouelle de veau
VEAL ROUND ROAST

The round roast of veal, a cut 2$\frac{1}{2}$ to 3 inches thick, comes from the center of the leg; it is one section of the three main parts of the leg: the rump, the round, and the knuckle.

This cut need not be larded; it is cooked in the same way as a *fricandeau*—pot roasted or braised.

The round is served with a purée of sorrel or spinach or chicory or with a *fondue* of tomatoes.

Carré de veau
VEAL RIB ROAST

The veal rib roast is made up of ribs with the tips trimmed. We advise also removing the backbones so that they will not interfere with the carving.

Remove the tendons, surround the veal with fresh pork fat, and lard it with additional pork fat on the top side, as you would a filet of beef. Pot roast it whole like a rump roast.

It can be served with any vegetable garnish.

Selle de veau
SADDLE OF VEAL

The saddle combines in one splendid piece the two halves of the veal loin. It is cut from the part of the animal between the rump and the bottom ribs.

The kidneys are removed, but most of the fat is left; the rib tips are cracked and folded so as to cover and protect the tenderloin.

Slices of fresh unsalted pork fat are wrapped around the meat and held in place with strings.

The saddle is cooked in the same way as the round roast. It must be basted often. When the meat is nearly cooked, the pork fat is removed so that the surface of the meat can be well basted with the juice and take on a nice golden color. It takes about 3 hours to cook in a 325° oven.

The meat is carved in very thin slices, the knife placed flat on the filet and turned toward the bone.

All the garnishes for the *fricandeau* and the round roast can accompany a saddle of veal. A saddle of veal is usually served for grand dinners; it is an imposing, succulent main course that is cooked in a special way; for example, a saddle of veal Prince Orloff, one of the most celebrated recipes of the *grande cuisine*.

179

**Saddle of veal
2 pounds onions
1/2 pound unsalted butter
Pinch salt
Large pinch sugar
1 1/2 quarts béchamel
sauce (page 76)
1/2 cup heavy cream
Dash grated nutmeg
1 slice *foie gras,* poached
in port
1 slice truffle
Grated parmesan or
gruyère cheese
Artichoke bottoms cooked
in white stock
Green asparagus tips or
tiny peas
Truffle slices**

Selle de veau prince Orloff
SADDLE OF VEAL PRINCE ORLOFF

Method. Trim the saddle as explained above, and pot roast according to the principles outlined for pot roasting a veal rump (pages 177–8).

Peel the onions, slice, and boil for 5 minutes; drain, wipe dry, and cook slowly with 7 tablespoons butter, salt, and sugar.

Also prepare 1 1/2 quarts béchamel sauce and reduce it until thick. Mix half the sauce with the onions, and use the other half for a Mornay sauce. Continue cooking the onions until they are completely softened and well mixed into the béchamel. Strain the onion sauce through cheesecloth into a saucepan, boil for 2 minutes, and finish, off the heat, with about 1/4 pound butter and 1/2 cup heavy cream—using enough of each to give this *soubise* purée the consistency of a firm *crème fraîche.* Correct the seasoning. A dash of grated nutmeg will add an agreeable touch.

Remove the saddle of veal, perfectly cooked and golden, from the braising pot. Place it with the bone tips underneath on an ovenproof platter. Strain the juice through a very fine sieve and keep it warm.

Carve the saddle in the following way:

With the point of a knife make two deep incisions, continuing in straight lines 1/4 inch from the outside edges of the two filets. Do the same on each side of the backbone with the knife just grazing it; then carefully detach the filets from the bones.

Cutting slightly on the bias, make slices 1/8 inch thick.

With the *soubise* purée cover the two cavities made in the saddle and replace the sliced filets, each slice separated by 2 tablespoons of purée, a slice of *foie gras* poached in port, and a beautiful slice of truffle heated or cooked 2 minutes in the meat juice that was set aside.

Finish by mixing the remaining *soubise* purée into the Mornay sauce, which must be very creamy, and cover the surface of the saddle. Sprinkle with grated parmesan or gruyère cheese, moisten with melted butter, and place under a hot broiler or in a 425° oven to brown very quickly.

Presentation. Place the saddle carefully on a long serving platter. All around put a garnish of small artichoke bottoms cooked in a white stock, steamed, seasoned, and then lightly browned in butter in a skillet. On each artichoke bottom place a small mound of green asparagus tips, boiled, and coated with butter or cream in the skillet where the artichokes were cooked. Tiny peas can be substituted for the asparagus. On each mound place a slice of truffle heated with the artichokes for a few seconds before removing them. This truffle-flavored butter will then be absorbed by the asparagus.

Serve the juice from the roasting pot in a sauceboat; 1/2 tablespoon poured on each slice is sufficient for each guest.

Thus prepared and served, a saddle of veal Prince Orloff makes a very grand appearance.

Côtes de veau

VEAL CHOPS (For 6 people)

The ribs and loin are usually used as veal chops. It is preferable to sauté the veal chops rather than to broil them, because that makes them more juicy.

A veal chop weighing 1/2 pound is enough for 2 people; if cut any thinner, the meat will dry out while cooking. Remove the end of the rib bone and the backbone that often comes with the chop.

No matter what garnish is chosen to accompany the chop, follow this method:

In a skillet heat 2 tablespoons unsalted butter and slowly brown 3 veal chops placed flat in the skillet; when they are cooked on one side, turn them and season the browned surface with salt and freshly ground pepper.

Continue cooking for a total cooking time of 15 to 18 minutes.

Place the veal chops on a round heated platter, the seasoned surface underneath; sprinkle the top side with salt and pepper and cover with a glass bell or a plate to keep them warm while making the sauce or the garnish.

Côtes de veau à la ménagère

VEAL CHOPS HOME STYLE

Prepare veal chops and sauté in a small skillet as above; when they are half cooked, surround them with small onions and small new potatoes (or potatoes cut like large olives and three-quarters cooked in butter, seasoned, and well browned). Cover tightly until completely cooked. At the last moment, for each chop add 1 tablespoon veal stock, bouillon, or water.

Deglaze the meat juices for 1 minute; sprinkle with a pinch of chopped parsley. Place the skillet on a round platter to serve.

Côtes de veau aux champignons

VEAL CHOPS WITH MUSHROOMS (For 2 people)

1/2-pound veal chop, sautéed in 2 teaspoons unsalted butter
2 ounces very small mushrooms
1 tablespoon dry white wine
1 tablespoon veal stock, bouillon, or water
1 tablespoon unsalted butter
Pinch chopped parsley

Sauté the veal chop following the recipe above and place it on a platter.

Add the mushrooms to the cooking butter. Brown lightly, season with a pinch of salt, and add dry white wine; reduce by half; add veal stock, bouillon, or water; bring quickly to a boil and finish the sauce off the heat with 1 tablespoon butter. Add the juice that has escaped from the chop while it was standing, mix, and pour over the chop.

Sprinkle with a pinch of chopped parsley.

181

Veal

Escalopes de veau

VEAL SCALLOPS

The scallops are slices of veal about ¹/₂ inch thick cut from the filet, the rib, or the leg; they are always cut against the grain. Their average weight is 4 to 5 ounces.

Since they are thin, veal scallops must be sautéed on a high flame. They are often breaded, but this is not essential. If the meat is breaded, it is better not to moisten them with meat juice or sauce when serving; this would make the bread crumbs soggy, and breaded scallops should be crisp.

Escalopes panées au beurre noisette

BREADED VEAL SCALLOPS WITH BROWN BUTTER (For 6 people)

6 veal scallops, ¹/₄ pound each
Salt, paprika (or pepper)
1 egg
6¹/₂ teaspoons oil
¹/₄ pound stale bread grated into fine crumbs
8 tablespoons unsalted butter
Juice of ¹/₂ lemon

Method. Flatten the scallops with a mallet or the flat side of a cleaver. This breaks the fibers of the meat and spreads out the scallops, which should then be ¹/₈ inch thick; season with salt and paprika (or pepper) on both sides. Beat 1 egg in a plate with a pinch of salt and ¹/₂ teaspoon oil. Dip the scallops in the egg mixture, then coat them with bread crumbs on both sides; press the bread crumbs down with the blade of a knife to make them stick.

Combine 4 tablespoons unsalted butter and 6 teaspoons oil in a skillet big enough to hold the scallops without overlapping. Heat the oil-butter mixture and arrange the scallops so as to sear them well; brown the scallops until the bread crumbs are golden brown on both sides and finish cooking for a few minutes on the lowest possible heat. The total cooking time will be 8 minutes.

Place the veal scallops on a heated platter. Pour the oil out of the skillet and put in 4 tablespoons butter; brown it lightly. Squeeze the juice of ¹/₂ lemon on the scallops and pour the butter over. The breaded scallops must be crisp. The guests should wait for them, not the scallops for the guests. This applies to all the following recipes based on this one.

The best vegetable to accompany this dish is potatoes, boiled and then sautéed, or even better, sautéed raw potatoes. The potatoes can be replaced by artichoke hearts, sliced and sautéed raw.

Escalopes de veau à la viennoise

VEAL SCALLOPS VIENNESE STYLE (For 6 people)

6 veal scallops, ¹/₄ pound each
1 large lemon, sliced
6 pitted olives
12 anchovy fillets marinated in oil
2 teaspoons capers
1 hot hard-cooked egg
4 tablespoons unsalted butter
2 teaspoons chopped parsley

Method. Prepare 6 veal scallops as explained in the previous recipe and garnish them the following way:

Place the scallops on a serving platter, and on top of each put 2 slices of peeled lemon with the seeds removed; on top of the lemon slices, place a pitted olive.

Around the lemon slices, place the anchovy fillets, and around the plate small bunches of capers and the white of the hard-cooked egg, chopped.

Pour the lightly browned butter on the scallops.

182

To serve the scallops, after having shown them, place on hot plates; mix the capers, the white of the hard-cooked egg, and the butter, and pour 1 tablespoon on each scallop. Sprinkle with chopped parsley.

Accompany by sautéed potatoes, parboiled or not, well browned.

Escalopes de veau à la milanaise
VEAL SCALLOPS MILANESE STYLE

Prepare in the same way as the breaded veal scallops with brown butter but add to the bread crumbs 1 ounce grated parmesan or gruyère cheese.

Place the veal scallops around a plate of macaroni *à la milanaise* (pages 368–9). Serve with a buttery light tomato sauce.

Grenadins
(For 6 people)

1¹/₂-pound veal filet or boned rib roast
¹/₄ pound fresh pork fat
Salt and pepper
¹/₄ pound unsalted butter
1 medium-sized carrot, very thinly sliced
1 large onion, very thinly sliced
4 fresh pork rinds, blanched and drained
¹/₂ cup dry white wine
2 cups veal stock (page 72) or lightly salted bouillon, if the meat is to be braised
Bouquet garni (few sprigs parsley, sprig thyme, ¹/₂ bay leaf)

A scallop is called a *grenadin* when it is small and thick, larded with tiny sticks of fresh pork fat, and pot roasted or braised like a miniature *fricandeau*.

Method. Cut the *grenadins* 1¹/₄ inches thick; lard them with the pork fat cut into small short sticks, and season with salt and pepper.

Heat the butter in a skillet, and brown the *grenadins* slowly on both sides; remove and reserve on a plate. In the same pan soften and brown the carrot and the onion. Do this over very low heat. Do not raise the flame; this would burn the butter and caramelize the meat juices.

Add the pork rinds, then the *grenadins* placed side by side on top of the other ingredients.

Cover, and steam in a 325° oven for 15 minutes. If the *grenadins* are pan broiled instead of being put in the oven, continue cooking uncovered for 10 minutes, basting frequently with the meat juices. Be careful not to let the juice reduce too much. Add a couple of tablespoons lightly salted veal stock or water if it begins to reduce.

If you are cooking them in the oven, braise them after steaming; moisten them with white wine, reduce the liquid by two-thirds, then add the veal stock to cover and the *bouquet garni*. Cook in a 425° oven for 40 minutes to reduce the sauce by two-thirds. Toward the end of the cooking time, remove the cover, and baste very often in order to glaze the surface of the *grenadins* and brown the pork fat. Glazing gives the *grenadins* a shiny coat of reduced sauce and heightens their flavor.

Set the *grenadins* in a circle around the garnish chosen. Correct the seasoning of the sauce, strain it through a very fine sieve, and pour it over the meat.

Paupiettes de veau

STUFFED VEAL ROLLS OR BIRDS (For 6 people)

Paupiettes are veal scallops cut very thin from the rump or the round. They are seasoned with salt, pepper, and nutmeg. They are filled with a stuffing, the type determining the name of the dish, rolled like a crêpe, wrapped in a layer of very thin pork fat held in place by a string, then braised.

This dish requires 2 hours for preparation and cooking.

Stuffing

¼ pound veal
Salt, pepper, nutmeg
1 medium-sized potato,
** boiled**
Milk
4 tablespoons unsalted
** butter**
1 egg
***Crème fraîche* or béchamel**
** sauce (page 78)**
¼ pound mushrooms
2 shallots, chopped
1 teaspoon chopped
** parsley**

Remove the sinews from ¼ pound veal and pound in a mortar with a pinch of salt, a pinch of freshly ground pepper, and a dash of nutmeg. Place in a bowl.

Slice the boiled potato thinly; place in a small saucepan, half cover with hot milk, and boil for 10 to 15 minutes in order to reduce the milk and reach the consistency of a firm paste. Pour into the mortar, and while the potatoes are still hot, pound until it forms a dough; add the veal and 2 tablespoons of butter, mix well, and then add 1 egg. Add a little *crème fraîche* or béchamel sauce to produce the proper consistency.

Rub the stuffing through a strainer into a bowl, and smooth the mixture with a spatula. Wash and clean the mushrooms, wipe dry, and chop fine. Put a piece of butter the size of a nut (2 tablespoons) in a skillet; brown lightly, add the mushrooms and shallots, and cook over a high flame for about 5 minutes. Add to the mixture in the bowl. Finish the stuffing with 1 teaspoon chopped parsley, and season to taste.

6 veal scallops, ¼ pound
** each**
6 slices fresh pork fat, cut
** very thin**
Unsalted butter
1 small carrot, thinly sliced
1 onion, thinly sliced
Few pork rinds
Bouquet garni
1 cup dry white wine
1 cup veal stock (page
** 72) or lightly salted**
** bouillon**

Assembling the paupiettes. Pound the veal scallops to ¼-inch thickness, sprinkle with a dash of salt, then spread ⅙ of the stuffing on each one; roll the meat like a crêpe, wrap each with a slice of pork fat, and tie with a string.

Use a flameproof baking dish that is deep and rather narrow, because the *paupiettes* will be standing in it on end. First butter the dish generously; heat it, add the carrot and the onion, and brown. Place the pork rinds on top of the carrot and onion, then the *paupiettes,* side by side, and place the *bouquet garni* in between.

Cover and bake for 15 minutes in a 325° oven to condense and evaporate the juices in the meat; in professional jargon this is called *faire suer la viande* (to sweat the meat).

Add the white wine and boil to reduce it completely over a high flame; then add stock or bouillon to cover the meat. Bring to a boil, cover with buttered wax paper and then with a lid, and simmer in the oven for 1¼ hours.

During the cooking, baste more and more frequently, as the juices reduce.

To serve carefully remove the *paupiettes;* cut off the strings, take off the pork fat, and place the veal rolls in a circle on a heated round plate; in the middle, place the garnish. Strain the juice through a fine sieve and pour over the *paupiettes.* If the juice is not thick enough, boil to reduce it to the right consistency before straining.

The best garnishes to accompany the *paupiettes* are: mushrooms in cream (page 322) or with béchamel sauce (page 78), cucumbers sautéed in butter, tomato *fondue* (page

127), noodles or spaghetti *à la milanaise* (pages 368–9), small potatoes *dauphine* (page 203); they should be served on the side so that the meat juice does not soak into them), boiled asparagus tips or peas coated with butter, artichoke bottoms sliced and sautéed in butter, a purée of mushrooms, etc.

Médaillons ou noisettes de veau
MEDALLIONS OR NOISETTES OF VEAL

These pieces of veal, taken from the filet, weigh about ¼ pound each. They are served one per guest and have a shape and delicacy to warrant their two names.

The medallions or *noisettes* correspond to the beef *tournedos*. The recipe for veal medallions is the same as for veal chops and they are served like a *tournedos*. All the sauces or garnishes for one or the other can be used for medallions.

Médaillons de veau à l'estragon
VEAL MEDALLIONS WITH TARRAGON (For 6 people)

6 veal medallions, ¼ pound each, cut from the *filet mignon* or loin
4 tablespoons unsalted butter
3 tablespoons olive oil
Salt and pepper
½ cup dry white wine
1 cup good veal stock (page 72)
1 tablespoon chopped fresh tarragon
Fresh tarragon leaves

Method. This will take 15 to 18 minutes to prepare and cook. In a large skillet combine half the butter and all the oil. When the fat is smoking, sear the medallions moderately on both sides, seasoning with salt and pepper as directed for the veal chops and the scallops. Cook slowly for 10 to 12 minutes.

Remove the medallions and keep warm between two plates; pour out the butter-oil mixture and replace with the white wine; reduce by two-thirds, then add the veal stock; reduce to the quantity needed for sauce and remove from the heat immediately.

Return the medallions to the skillet and sprinkle with 1 tablespoon chopped tarragon; cover and let stand for 5 minutes without boiling on the side of the stove (boiling would toughen the meat and destroy the aroma of the tarragon).

Place the veal medallions on a round hot platter; decorate the top of each with 4 or 5 tarragon leaves, blanched in boiling water. Add the rest of the butter to the juice; correct the seasoning, and pour over the medallions.

Médaillons de veau à la compote d'oignons
VEAL MEDALLIONS WITH ONION STEW

8 slices veal filet, ¼ pound each, cut into medallions ½ inch thick
Salt, pepper, flour
8 tablespoons unsalted butter
¼ cup Madeira wine
⅓ cup dry white wine
3 cups *crème fraîche* or heavy cream
2 tablespoons fresh Périgord truffles cut into julienne

Method. Salt and pepper the veal medallions and flour them lightly. In a shallow saucepan with a heavy bottom sauté the veal pieces in 7 tablespoons butter; keep them tender.

When they have cooked and lightly browned, arrange on a serving platter; cover with buttered wax paper and keep the platter warm.

Deglaze the saucepan with the Madeira and the white wine, let reduce by three-fourths; add the *crème fraîche,* correct the seasoning, reduce again over heat to produce a smooth sauce.

Briefly stew the truffles in 1 tablespoon butter (especially if they are raw); add to the sauce.

To serve, under each medallion place a portion of stewed onions and coat the whole dish with the excellent sauce.

The medallions can also be served individually, one on each plate; this method allows the food to keep its heat.

Onion Stew

Chop the onions fine, season lightly with salt and pepper, and stew in butter in a covered saucepan. Halfway through the cooking add the vinegar and continue cooking for a couple of minutes. Add the cream, stirring. Cook covered until tender.

3 pounds onions
Salt and pepper
7 tablespoons unsalted
 butter
2 tablespoons wine
 vinegar
1/2 cup cream

Médaillons de veau sautés chasseur

VEAL MEDALLIONS HUNTER'S STYLE (For 6 people)

This will take 25 minues to cook.

Method.   Clean and rapidly wash the mushrooms twice, drain, and wipe dry. Cut into very thin slices.

Lightly flatten the veal medallions, season with salt and pepper. In a skillet heat the oil and one-third of the butter. Add the veal and brown on one side; turn over, continue cooking until done, then remove and keep warm. This step requires 10 to 12 minutes.

In the butter where the meat was cooked, cook the shallots until golden; add the mushrooms and sauté them on a high flame, then add the white wine, reduce nearly entirely. Add the tomatoes and the sauce or the stock; boil to reduce for 5 minutes. If veal stock is used, thicken with a dash of cornstarch diluted with cold water or with 1/2 tablespoon *beurre manié.*

To finish the sauce, off the heat add the chopped herbs and butter; taste to correct the seasoning, and add the juice that has escaped from the veal medallions while standing. Place the medallions in a circle on a heated round platter, cover with the mushrooms and the sauce. Sprinkle a pinch of chopped parsley on top.

1/4 pound very white
 mushrooms
6 veal medallions,
 preferably cut from the
 filet
Salt and pepper
3 tablespoons olive oil
3 1/2 tablespoons unsalted
 butter
2 shallots, finely chopped
1/2 cup white wine
1 tablespoon tomato purée
 or 2 fresh tomatoes,
 peeled, seeded, drained,
 and cut into pieces
1 cup *espagnole* sauce
 (page 76) or *demi-glace*
 sauce (page 76) or a
 good veal stock (page
 72)
Large pinch each chopped
 chervil, parsley, and
 tarragon

Poitrine de veau farcie et braisée

BRAISED STUFFED VEAL BREAST (For 6 people)

This dish requires 3 1/2 hours for preparation and cooking.

Stuffing

Heat 1 tablespoon of the butter in a skillet and very slowly cook the onion, finely chopped.

Clean, quickly wash, and immediately drain the mushrooms; chop and add to the onion; dry over a high flame for 3 to 4 minutes; remove to a bowl.

Dice the pork and the pork fat, chop them separately, and pound them together with the spiced salt in a mortar so that the ingredients are well mixed into a fine stuffing.

This mixture can be made in a bowl with a wooden spoon if you do not have a mortar and pestle, but the lean meat and the fat will never be completely mixed.

1 tablespoon unsalted
 butter
1/2 onion, finely chopped
1/2 pound mushrooms
1/2 pound lean pork
2/3 pound fresh pork fat
Pinch spiced salt
 (page x)
1 egg
1 teaspoon chopped
 parsley
Big pinch chopped
 tarragon
1 tablespoon brandy

One can also use sausage meat bought in a pork store; but one is never sure whether proportions are correct unless it is ordered specially.

Mix together the pork stuffing and the *duxelles* (the chopped cooked onion and mushroom); then add the egg, the parsley, the tarragon, and the brandy. Work the mixture with a wooden spoon in order to obtain perfect blending.

Test the seasoning by poaching a little ball of the stuffing (as big as a hazelnut); taste, and correct the seasoning, if necessary.

Preparing the breast. Bone the breast; slit it horizontally through the center without cutting the ends or the third side so that the cut forms a pocket. Season the inside with a pinch of spiced salt, and fill with the stuffing, making an even layer; sew the opening with thick thread.

In an ovenproof casserole in 2 tablespoons butter lightly brown the sliced carrot and onion and the bones cut into tiny pieces. On top place the pork rind cut into little pieces, the veal knuckle, the *bouquet garni,* and then the veal breast; spread over the remaining butter. Place in a 325° oven for 15 minutes.

Moisten with the white wine, boil to reduce nearly totally, then add the lightly salted bouillon, veal stock, or water so that it barely covers the meat. Bring to a boil, cover the veal breast with buttered wax paper; put on the lid, and simmer for at least 2 hours.

At the end of 2 hours, remove the cover, the paper, and the bones. The braising juice should be reduced by two-thirds; if it is not, raise the heat until it has reduced, and during the next 20 minutes baste the veal breast frequently with it. This last step will give the surface of the meat a brilliant coating with a beautiful golden color.

Place the veal breast on a long platter, remove the sewing threads and pour over the meat juice strained through a fine sieve.

In a bowl serve the chosen garnish, which can be celery ribs, braised and simmered with the veal breast during the final cooking; braised sauerkraut, cooked the same way with a couple of slices of *foie gras;* braised lettuce, spinach, chicory, sorrel; small new carrots, glazed; any fresh or dry bean purée, etc.

Jarret de veau à la ménagère
VEAL KNUCKLE HOME STYLE (For 4 people)

Method. Season the veal knuckles with the salt and pepper. In a saucepan, preferably oval, brown the meat on all sides in butter. Then add the diced onion, the sliced carrots, and after these are browned, the tomatoes.

Moisten with the dry white wine and the veal stock. Add the *bouquet garni,* and cook covered in a 325° oven or simmer on top of the stove for about 45 minutes.

Serve the veal knuckles in a shallow dish surrounded by the vegetables and coated with their juice; only the *bouquet garni* is removed.

---

1 veal breast
Pinch spiced salt (page x)
1 medium-sized carrot, sliced
1/2 onion, sliced
7 tablespoons unsalted butter
1 pork rind
1/4 pound veal knuckle
Bouquet garni
1/2 cup dry white wine
2 cups lightly salted bouillon or veal stock (page 72) or water

---

4 milk-fed veal knuckles, about 3 pounds
Salt and pepper
5 tablespoons unsalted butter
1 large onion, diced
1/4 pound new carrots, sliced
2 ripe tomatoes, seeded and crushed
1/4 cup dry white wine
1 cup veal stock (page 72)
Small *bouquet garni*

This dish can also be accompanied by fresh noodles with butter.

Jarret de veau aux petits pois printaniers
VEAL KNUCKLE WITH SPRING PEAS

1 veal knuckle, sliced 2½ inches thick
Salt
Unsalted butter
½ cup dry white wine
Bouillon, barely salted, or water
2 generous cups tiny peas
2 lettuce hearts, cut into shreds
12 small white onions
Pinch salt
½ sugar cube
Small *bouquet garni* or sprig savory

Method. Have the butcher cut a veal knuckle into slices 2½ inches thick. Season with salt and brown in butter in a skillet. Moisten with ½ cup dry white wine; boil to reduce nearly completely; then add a little bit of barely salted bouillon or water, half covering the slices, and cook slowly, covered, for 2 hours.

In a saucepan mix together the peas, the lettuce hearts, and the onions; add a pinch of salt and ½ of a sugar cube; mix well, add 2 tablespoons water and a small *bouquet garni* or a sprig of savory.

Bring to a boil on a high flame; lower heat and simmer, covered, for 5 minutes; then add to the veal knuckle slices, without the *bouquet garni.* Continue cooking for ½ hour, basting frequently; watch the sauce carefully, it should be thick while still covering the peas.

Correct the seasoning, and place the slices of veal knuckle in a shallow dish, surrounding them with the peas coated with the syrupy juice of the veal.

Tendron de veau
VEAL RIBLETS

The riblets are the extreme end of the breast, the part where the ribs meet. The bones look more like cartilage; they are very gelatinous and give the cut its name: *tendron* means "gristle"; it is indispensable in a *blanquette de veau.*

The simplest and most delicious way to prepare this meat is by braising; it is served with a vegetable garnish.

Tendron de veau braisé
BRAISED VEAL RIBLETS

Cut veal riblets in pieces of about ¼ pound each; they should be thicker than they are wide. Heat some butter in a skillet that will hold all the pieces side by side; brown on both sides on a low flame.

Remove the meat and put aside; in the same skillet, brown a few slices of carrots and onions. Season the riblets with salt and pepper and place on top of the vegetables; cover, and stew slowly in the butter in a 325° oven for 1 hour.

Then moisten with dry white wine; boil to reduce the wine nearly completely, add a good veal stock lightly salted, covering the riblets halfway. Continue cooking, uncovered, in the oven for 1 hour, basting very often. Add more stock if necessary.

At the end of the cooking time, strain the juice through a fine sieve; it should be thick and golden like a syrup; the riblets then should be extremely soft and tender.

Cooled in the cooking juices, which will jell, the riblets make an excellent cold dish to serve with a vegetable salad.

Fricassée de veau à l'ancienne
OLD-FASHIONED FRICASSEE OF VEAL (For 6 people)

9 tablespoons unsalted butter
2 pounds milk-fed veal, one-third riblets, one-third end chops, one-third shoulder, cut into large cubes
Salt and pepper
1 medium-sized carrot, quartered
1 onion, quartered and stuck with a clove
2 tablespoons flour
White bouillon or water
Bouquet garni (5 sprigs parsley, sprig thyme, 1 bay leaf)
12 small onions
¹/₄ pound mushrooms
Juice of ¹/₄ lemon
2 egg yolks
1 cup *crème fraîche,* light cream, or milk
Dash grated nutmeg

Method. In a skillet heat 4 tablespoons butter; add the veal, seasoned with salt and pepper, and the carrot and onion. Stew slowly for 15 to 20 minutes, stirring from time to time.

Sprinkle with the flour, mix well, and cook over a low flame for 10 minutes, like a *roux,* but without letting it brown.

Moisten with barely salted white bouillon just covering the meat; if one is using water, salt lightly. Bring to a boil, stirring to thicken the sauce smoothly, and simmer in the oven or over a low flame on top of the stove for 2 hours with the *bouquet garni.*

Blanch the small onions, drain, and stew in about 2 tablespoons butter in a skillet until they are cooked. They must remain white; watch them carefully.

Clean the mushrooms and wash them rapidly in water, drain, and wipe dry. Cut off the stems and put them to simmer with the meat; quarter the caps, sauté them in a skillet with 1 tablespoon butter for 2 minutes on a high flame; season with a pinch of salt and squeeze in a few drops of lemon juice. When the onions are cooked, add the mushrooms to the onions. Cover the skillet and set aside.

Place the egg yolks in a bowl with 3 tablespoons white bouillon (or milk or light cream), 1 tablespoon butter in pieces, and a dash of grated nutmeg. Mix well.

When the meat is cooked, remove from the heat, and with a skimmer and a fork, take out the pieces of meat, reserving them separately. Place the mushrooms and the small onions over the veal, cover, and keep warm.

Thickening the sauce: Place the skillet with the vegetable garnish over a high flame and reduce the liquid by half, stirring with a wooden spoon; when it reduces, it will become very thick. Add just enough *crème fraîche,* light cream, or milk to give the sauce the smooth consistency and subtle flavor characteristic of this delicious dish.

Remove the skillet from the flame, and slowly mix 1 cup of the sauce into the egg-yolk mixture, stirring rapidly with a sauce whisk.

Squeeze the rest of the lemon juice into the egg yolks and sauce, and add the mixture in a stream to the sauce in the pan, whipping it with a whisk continuously so that the egg yolks start to cook without losing their thickening and enriching qualities.

If for any reason the sauce cools off too much, preventing the melding of the yolks and the sauce, put the pan back on the flame and, while stirring with a whisk, blend the yolks and start them cooking. An inexperienced hand often can overdo this step; then the egg yolks harden into small granules and no longer play the delicate culinary role that the experienced cook tries to give them.

189

As a supreme finishing step one can also add to the perfectly thickened sauce a tablespoon or so of butter cut in small pieces; beat into the sauce with a whisk. Correct the seasoning.

Strain the sauce through double cheesecloth, pressing the quartered carrots and onions lightly; pour the sauce over the veal and garnish, which have been kept warm. Spread carefully with a spatula, so that the meat is well coated with the sauce; serve on very hot plates with creole rice (page 370) or boiled potatoes in their skins.

Also place around the fricassee small croutons in the shape of hearts, made of white bread and fried in butter, or some *fleurons,* small semicircular shapes cut with a fluted mold, made of flaky dough or the trimmings of flaky dough and well browned in the oven.

Blanquette de veau

This uses the same ingredients as the old-fashioned fricassee of veal above.

Method. Cook the veal in a seasoned *court-bouillon,* which is used to moisten the *roux.* The sauce is made velvety by egg yolks and cream. The total cooking time is 2½ hours.

Sauté de veau Marengo

SAUTÉED VEAL MARENGO (For 6 people)

Method. This will take 2 hours to prepare and cook. In a skillet, heat 3½ tablespoons butter and the oil; when the mixture is smoking, add the pieces of veal and the carrot and the onions. Season with salt and freshly ground pepper; cook on a high flame until browned.

Sprinkle the meat with the flour, mix well, and brown the flour slightly; add the crushed garlic, heat for a second, then add the white wine; reduce by two-thirds. Then add the tomato purée or the fresh tomatoes, the *bouquet garni,* and the veal stock, bouillon, or water. If one is using water, salt lightly. Bring to a boil, stirring with a spatula; cover and simmer on a low flame, or in the oven, for 1 hour.

Unless the onions are new ones, scald them, drain, and wipe dry; cook until glazed in a skillet with 1 tablespoon butter.

Clean the mushrooms, wash carefully and quickly, and drain. Put the stems in the skillet with the veal. Quarter the caps, if they are large or medium-sized, and "turn" them (page 234). Add the peels to the veal. Do not cut the mushrooms if they are small. Prepare a second skillet or a saucepan and heat 1 tablespoon butter; add the mushrooms and stir over a high flame until they are browned; remove from the heat and add to the small onions.

When the veal is half cooked, remove the pieces of meat from the pan and place them in the second skillet on top of the mushrooms and the glazed onions. Let the sauce stand

5½ tablespoons unsalted butter
2 tablespoons olive oil
2 pounds veal: one-third veal riblets, one-third shoulder, one-third neck, cut into large cubes
1 carrot, quartered
2 medium-sized onions, quartered
1½ tablespoons flour
2 garlic cloves, crushed
½ cup dry white wine
1 pound fresh tomatoes, peeled, seeded, and quartered, or 1 cup tomato purée
Bouquet garni (sprig parsley, sprig thyme, ½ bay leaf)
2 cups veal stock (page 72) or bouillon, barely salted, or water
12 small onions, peeled
¼ pound mushrooms
Juice of ¼ lemon
6 croutons, cut into heart shapes and fried in butter
1 teaspoon chopped fresh parsley

for a few minutes until the fat comes to the surface and you can remove it easily. Degrease the sauce; strain through a very fine sieve onto the meat, rubbing the vegetables through. Correct the seasoning, and simmer until completely cooked, about 20 minutes.

To serve, squeeze lemon juice over the veal, put it into a dish or a deep serving platter; place the croutons around and sprinkle some chopped parsley on top.

Pâté Pantin du maître Ferdinand Wernert
PÂTÉ PANTIN À LA MASTER CHEF FERDINAND WERNERT
(For 10 people)

Dough

3³/₄ cups flour
1 tablespoon salt
11 tablespoons unsalted butter
1 egg
1 cup water or more, depending upon the quality of the flour

Make the day before; after 12 hours it loses its elasticity; keep it firm; give it four turns, as explained for flaky dough (page 383).

Garnish

From the rump or top round cut 8 pieces 6 inches long and ⁵/₈ inch thick.

Cut the fresh pork fat into 2 large bards, 8 inches wide and 12 inches long, or into 4 bards, 6 inches long, and 8 *lardons* the same length as the pieces of meat.

1 pound veal, rump or top round
1¹/₂ pounds fresh pork fat
¹/₂ pound uncooked lean ham
1¹/₂ tablespoons spiced salt (page x)
Pinch thyme
Pinch bay leaf, crushed to powder
¹/₂ cup cognac or other brandy
³/₄ pound pork tenderloin
2 eggs, beaten

Cut pieces of ham the same size. Combine the meat and the *lardons* in a shallow dish; season with the spiced salt, thyme, and powdered bay leaf; mix well, so that the meats will be permeated by the spices, and pour the cognac over. Marinate until ready to be used, stirring from time to time.

Stuffing

Cut the pork tenderloin, the remaining veal, pork fat, and ham into large cubes; season with spiced salt, thyme, and powdered bay leaf, then grind finely with a meat grinder or use a hand chopper. Pound the meats in a mortar and mix vigorously, adding the beaten eggs, and any cognac that was not absorbed by the meat while it was marinating.

If you do not have a meat grinder or a mortar, use a hand chopper and mash the meats together in a bowl with a wooden spatula.

To be sure the seasoning is correct, poach a ball of stuffing in boiling water and taste it.

Method. Roll out three-quarters of the dough to which the last two turns have been given, making a rectangle 14 inches long and ¹/₈ inch thick; place it on a pastry sheet.

In the center of the dough, place a bard of pork fat and spread a layer of the stuffing on top, then a layer of veal, then pork fat, then ham, then a second layer of stuffing; continue the same way until you have used up all the meats, arranging them symmetrically; finish with a layer of stuffing and cover it with the final bard of pork fat.

Moisten lightly with a wet cloth or pastry brush all around the edges of the dough, lift the two long sides of the rectangle of dough up over the top of the pork fat, so that the two edges of dough meet. With a rolling pin, roll out the two ends of the dough and lift them up so that their moistened edges meet the top dough and stick, pressing lightly with your fingers.

191

Brush the whole surface of the pâté with a wet brush or cloth and place on top a rectangle of dough of the same size (first slit the dough all around with a knife, so that it will puff up while cooking).

Pinch the edges together with a pastry wheel or with your thumb and forefinger; brush the surface with 1 tablespoon beaten egg; decorate the top surface with designs incised in the dough; finally, with the point of a knife make two 1/4-inch openings in the center of the decorated dough and insert in each a little piece of buttered paper rolled like a chimney to allow the steam to escape from the liquid ingredients.

To bake, place in a 400° oven. When the dough is golden brown, protect the pastry by covering it with good-quality white paper, lightly dampened, which, while it is heating, will not let out a bad odor that could be transmitted to the pâté.

The pâté is done after 1 hour more in the oven when some juice comes out of the chimneys and, little by little, solidifies to form a meat glaze. This is an infallible sign. Total baking time will be about 1 1/4 hours.

The pâté is ready to be served hot, tepid, or cold; if served cold, it is harder to cut.

Note: This recipe can be enriched with truffles, *foie gras*, poultry, or game. It is one of the most remarkable of gourmet concepts; in it cooking and baking are combined superlatively.

Quenelles de veau au beurre
VEAL QUENELLES WITH BUTTER (For 1 pound of forcemeat)

Panade

1 cup water
Pinch salt
2 tablespoons butter
1 scant cup sifted flour

Combine in a saucepan the water, a pinch of salt, 2 tablespoons butter; bring to a boil. Add the flour off the flame, and mix until smooth. Put back on a high flame, stirring constantly to evaporate part of the water. The dough will pull away from the sides of the pan in one ball when it is dry enough. Let it cool on a plate.

Forcemeat

1/2 pound veal rump or round
7 tablespoons unsalted butter
1 tablespoon salt
Pinch pepper
Dash grated nutmeg
2 eggs, beaten

Dice the veal and chop fine in a meat grinder or with a hand chopper. Place the chopped meat in a mortar and pound vigorously, adding the cold *panade;* pound until the two are blended; add 7 tablespoons butter, and continue to work the mixture with the pestle until all the ingredients are completely mixed. Add the salt, pepper, nutmeg; then little by little work in the beaten eggs.

With the pestle rub the meat through a fine sieve over a bowl. Mash the sieved meat for a while with a wooden spatula, put it in a cool place or refrigerate, covering the surface with a round of white paper to protect it from the air until ready to use.

Method. With a tablespoon pack the stuffing into a pastry bag fitted with a simple tube 1/4 inch in diameter. Close the bag and press to push the stuffing through the tube onto a shallow baking dish. Regulate the pressure on the pastry bag to produce little sticks about 3¼ inches long; put them about 2 inches apart.

Fifteen minutes before serving, cover the *quenelles* with boiling salted water; place in a 325° oven to cook so that the water barely simmers.

The *quenelles* are done when they float in the water and resist when pressed lightly with a finger.

These *quenelles* are used for certain garnishes of *vol-au-vent, bouchées à la reine,* etc., or are served alone for entrées accompanied by a sauce such as a light Mornay (page 84).

Note: This recipe can be refined by adding some *crème fraîche,* which makes the *quenelles* more delicate. In that case, use less *panade* or eliminate entirely; increase the number of egg whites. To be sure of the right consistency, it is advisable to test the mixture by poaching a little ball of it before shaping the *quenelles.*

Le veau froid

COLD VEAL

Veal loin, rib roast, filet, round, rump, or *fricandeau,* whether roasted, braised, or cooked in a skillet, can be served cold like roast beef.

If veal is to be served cold, it is best to cook it in a skillet. One should not forget that the stock, well degreased and strained, makes a marvelous jelly to serve with the meat.

Serve with a garnish of cold vegetables, seasoned like a salad, such as a *macédoine* of vegetables coated with mayonnaise sauce (page 90).

Mutton and lamb

The full-grown sheep has deep-red flesh—dense, firm, and fat—called mutton. The legs are plump; the saddle is wide and fat. The fat is well distributed, abundant, very white, and hard.

Spring lamb, in France called *pré-salé* (salt-meadow) lamb, is a young sheep not fully developed; its flesh is much tenderer and tastier than the adult animal's; its flesh is pale red.

Salt-meadow lamb gets it name from the unrivaled meadowlands along the English Channel and the Atlantic Ocean; the richest ones are in the Coutances region in Normandy.

Baby or milk-fed lamb is an animal that has not yet been weaned and has never grazed. Its flesh is pale pink, nearly white. The most famous baby lamb comes from Pauillac.

These are the essential qualities, immediately visible in good lamb.

Lamb meat is not very palatable in the summer during the shearing time; the flavor is strong and increases during cooking.

[*Editor's note:* In the United States, meat called lamb is usually from a sheep less than a year old; meat from a one-year-old sheep is called yearling mutton; meat from a sheep two years or older is called mutton. Yearling mutton or mutton is rarely found in retail stores. Milk-fed lamb is also seldom available except by special order. Recipes for mutton may also be used for lamb.]

Lamb cuts

Baby lamb, spring lamb, and mutton are butchered in the same way.

The parts in greatest demand are: the leg, the saddle, and the ribs and loin; then come the shoulder, the breast, and the neck; finally the variety meats or organ meats.

The two back legs are called the hindquarters. The two back legs and the saddle are called the baron or hind saddle. The hindquarters and the baron are cuts to be served at great feasts. They are nearly always roasted. The saddle includes two filets and on the underside, protected by the top of the loin, two *filets mignons* or tenderloins. Sliced $1^{1}/_{4}$ to $1^{1}/_{2}$ inches thick, this cut will make mutton chops or lamb chops—the first cut from the half saddle and the second from the entire saddle.

The rack or ribs and the loin are divided into first-cut chops and second-cut chops.

All these cuts can be roasted, pot roasted, boiled, sautéed, or broiled depending on their size and the recipe chosen.

The shoulder can be roasted or pot roasted. It also is used for ragoûts.

The neck is used for ragoûts, as is the breast, which can also be used for various small dishes.

Baby lamb can be prepared like mutton; but because of its delicate flesh, there are some special recipes for it.

How to carve a leg of lamb

Hold on tightly to the leg bone.

First Method

Hold the bone with your left hand and lift it slightly, with the other end on the platter rump side down.

With your right hand, cut parallel to the bone, slicing from right to left. The slices should be thin. When you reach the bone, turn the leg of lamb on the opposite side and slice the rump, with the blade on a bias, toward the bone.

Second Method

Hold the leg of lamb as above but keep the sharp edge of the blade always perpendicular to the bone. The carving is also done in two steps. In both cases, the bone will be completely clean.

194

Important: Since the juice is very fatty, the serving plates must be burning hot. Without this essential step, the fat would congeal rapidly and this delicious dish would lose a great part of its gastronomic value.

Gigot de mouton rôti

ROAST LEG OF LAMB

To carve the leg more easily, I recommend boning the sirloin end.

It is an excellent practice to insert garlic cloves in the leg, according to one's taste; do not, however, pierce the muscles with the point of a knife but insert the garlic between the muscles and the bone or on the sides of the rump.

Place the leg on a rack in a roasting pan; coat with butter, season with salt, and place in a 375° oven.

Cooking time: 10 minutes per pound [for searing; meat must "rest"].

Baste frequently. At the end of the cooking, add 6 tablespoons hot water to deglaze the pan juices, without letting them boil. Let the roast stand in a hot place, in a warming oven for example, before serving.

Serve the lamb juices in a sauceboat without degreasing them.

If the leg of lamb is very fat, it is preferable to remove some of the fat before cooking it.

A leg of lamb should be cooked rare, although the heat should reach the bone.

Gigot de pré-salé rôti

ROAST LEG OF SPRING LAMB

This can be given the same preparation and cooked for the same length of time as the leg of lamb.

A leg of lamb or a leg of spring lamb can also be roasted on a spit. Increase the searing time by 5 minutes for each pound. On the side serve the juices gathered in the drip pan.

The garnishes for a roast leg of lamb are: string beans or lima beans; potato purée, new potatoes cooked and browned in butter, potatoes *à la sarladaise* (sliced boiled potatoes with thinly sliced truffles, page 363), etc., or any fresh or dried beans.

Gigot bouilli à l'anglaise

BOILED LEG OF LAMB ENGLISH STYLE

Method. Trim the leg, shorten the shank bone, and remove the sirloin bone; place in a braising pan with sufficient boiling water to cover it completely.

Add to the cooking water: 1 scant tablespoon salt for each quart of water, the carrots, turnips, and onions; the *bouquet garni;* potatoes; and a celery rib. As soon as the

195

Leg of lamb
12 small carrots
4 turnips
4 onions, quartered, one
stuck with a clove
Bouquet garni
4 large potatoes
1 celery rib
8 tablespoons unsalted
butter
5 tablespoons flour
2–3 teaspoons capers

1 quart cooked white
beans
1 medium-sized onion,
chopped finely
1 tablespoon unsalted
butter or fatty lamb juice
1/2 cup dry white wine
1 cup thick tomato sauce
(page 77) or 2 cups fresh
tomatoes, peeled,
seeded, and chopped
2 garlic cloves, crushed
1 teaspoon chopped
parsley

water starts boiling again, lower the flame so that it barely simmers. From that point, calculate the cooking time at 15 minutes per pound.

To serve drain the leg of lamb and present it alone on a serving platter. Remove the carrots and the onions from the braising pan (with a skimmer and with infinite care) and serve in a bowl; in another bowl serve the turnips, mashed with 1 tablespoon butter, a pinch of salt, and a pinch of freshly ground pepper. Also in a sauceboat serve English butter sauce prepared in this way:

Make a *roux* with 7 tablespoons butter, 5 tablespoons flour; let it brown, then moisten with the cooking liquid from the leg of lamb, to make a moderately thick sauce; cook slowly for 10 minutes, strain, and add 2 to 3 teaspoons capers.

Gigot rôti aux haricots à la bretonne
ROAST LEG OF LAMB WITH DRIED WHITE BEANS

Roast the leg of lamb following the classic method (page 195) and serve with its own juice—not degreased, even if it is quite fatty—along with a bowl of lima beans *(flageolets* or *soissons* or *suisses)* Breton style.

Lima Beans Breton Style

First, cook the beans, fresh or dried.

Then, for 1 quart cooked lima beans prepare 1 cup Breton sauce: Cook the onion very slowly with 1 tablespoon butter or lamb juice. When the onion is golden, add the dry white wine (reduced by two-thirds), and the tomato sauce or fresh tomatoes. Simmer for 10 minutes, add the garlic and chopped parsley. Away from the flame make 2 or 3 turns of the pepper mill over the sauce.

Drain the beans and mix them with the sauce to coat them lightly. If the lamb juice is very fatty, the excess fat can be added to improve the flavor of the beans.

Note: The beans may be served as a purée, but in the recipe above, to thicken the beans does not mean to give them the consistency of a purée, even a soft one; the juice or the sauce must be slightly thickened, like the sauce of braised veal. The beans should remain very juicy which excludes both extremes; they should be neither dry nor literally bathing in their own juice.

Double, baron et selle
HINDQUARTERS, BARON, AND SADDLE

The hindquarters, the baron, and the saddle are prepared in the same way as the leg of lamb. The same vegetable garnishes can be used.

The cooking time for the saddle is easy to determine. Cooking time: 10 minutes per pound [for searing; the roast must "rest"].

To test for doneness: Plunge a trussing needle into the marrow; let it stay for 1 minute; remove, and place it immediately against the back of your hand. If the needle is cold, the meat needs more cooking; if it is quite warm, the meat is done (let the meat rest for 10 minutes in a warm oven); if it is clearly hot, the saddle is overdone.

How to carve a saddle of lamb

Before placing the meat in the oven, trim the thin hindquarter flank, fold it under the saddle over the tenderloin strips, and tie in place with a string.

When the saddle of lamb is removed from the oven, place it on a platter, the cut end facing the carver. He should make a deep incision releasing the tenderloin from right to left.

The carving knife should be held flat in a position that will enable the carver to cut from right to left along the loin, cutting thin slices the length of the saddle. When one tenderloin strip is carved, turn the platter around in order to carve the second one the same way.

Then turn the saddle over, free the thin hindquarter flank, and cut out the tenderloin strips.

As recommended for the leg of lamb, the serving plates should be very hot to prevent the fat from congealing.

If the cooking juice is too lightly salted, sprinkle a dash of ground sea salt on each slice of meat; it gives a better flavor.

The juice must be served very hot; never pour the juice on top of a rare slice of lamb; pour 1 tablespoon on the plate next to the slice of meat, which will keep its good color and all its flavor.

Selle d'agneau de pré-salé des gastronomes

SADDLE OF SPRING LAMB GASTRONOME STYLE (For 12 people)

1 saddle of lamb, about 5 pounds
Veal bones
Salt and pepper
6 tablespoons unsalted butter
1 cup good veal stock, barely salted (page 72)

Method.   Trim the saddle, that is, remove the membrane over the fat covering the meat; score the fat, forming a checkerboard pattern with the point of a knife—this is to allow the heat to penetrate the meat. Remove the two balls of fat that surround the kidneys; trim the two thin hindquarter flanks and fold over the tenderloin strips to protect them and to make the saddle stand firmly. Tie them in place with five pieces of string. Do not tie the saddle too tightly, however, as the meat must be allowed to expand as it cooks.

Cook by pot roasting: At the bottom of a braising pan just big enough to hold the meat place either a rack or veal bones broken into tiny pieces (which are better). Place the saddle on top with the fat side up; season with salt and pepper and moisten with 6 tablespoons melted butter or good veal fat or fresh pork fat. Roast in a 425° oven, turning three times; finish by basting frequently. The fat will give the saddle a nice golden color.

The cooking time is estimated at 10 minutes per pound for searing. When the meat should be done, probe the marrow by inserting a trussing needle; if after 1 minute inside the marrow, the needle is just warm when placed against the back of your hand, the meat is done. Remove it from the hot oven, place on a platter, and let stand for 15 minutes in a warm oven.

Pour 1 cup veal stock into the braising pan and boil for 5 minutes to dissolve (deglaze) the solidified juices on the bones and in the pan.

Strain the juices into a small deep saucepan; and after waiting a few minutes, remove the fat that floats to the top. Taste the sauce, and correct the seasoning by adding salt or water, whichever is needed.

Garnish

12 truffles, all medium-
  sized
1 cup champagne *brut*
1/2 cup cognac
Cayenne pepper
12 tablespoons good veal
  stock, barely salted
  (page 72)
12 cock kidneys
1 cup white bouillon
1/2 tablespoon flour
1/2 teaspoon vinegar or
  juice of 1/4 lemon
1 teaspoon port or Madeira
  wine
24 chestnuts
1 celery rib
4 1/2 tablespoons unsalted
  butter
Mushroom purée made
  with 1 pound mushrooms
  (page 323)
12 small unsweetened tarts
  (page 389)

While the saddle is roasting in the braising pan, prepare the garnish. To reduce the amount of work before a big dinner and to be able to give more care and attention to the final details, it is essential to make certain preparations the night before or several hours before serving time: make a white bouillon for the cock kidneys; scrub the truffles and macerate in the cognac in a tightly sealed jar; peel the chestnuts; clean the mushrooms; and make the tart crusts; so that during the braising of the saddle, only these steps will remain to be done:

Cooking the truffles. In a small saucepan with a tight cover place the whole uncooked truffles, the champagne, the cognac from the maceration, a pinch of salt, and a dash of cayenne pepper. Bring to a boil on a high flame for 5 minutes. Remove from the heat; drain the truffles, place in a bowl, cover, and keep warm.

To the remaining champagne, add 4 tablespoons veal stock, and boil to reduce to 3 tablespoons; return the truffles to the saucepan and coat them by rolling them in the reduced juice, which should be totally absorbed by the truffles.

Cooking the kidneys. Prick the cock kidneys with a needle to prevent them from bursting; poach them in a white bouillon made with 1 cup white stock or salted water, 1/2 tablespoon flour, and 1/2 teaspoon vinegar or the juice of quarter of a lemon. Plunge the kidneys, which have been well soaked in fresh water, into the white bouillon and remove the saucepan from the heat without letting it boil. Simmer for 5 minutes.

Reduce 1/2 cup veal stock almost completely; drain the kidneys and roll carefully in that reduced liquid, which can be flavored, off the heat, with 1 teaspoon port or Madeira.

Preparing the chestnuts. Place the chestnuts in a 425° oven for 5 to 6 minutes or plunge into deep hot oil or boiling water for 2 minutes (page 345); peel. Boil in white stock to cover with a celery rib for 20 minutes very slowly, so that the chestnuts will remain whole when cooked and slightly firm.

When they are done, drain and brown (as you would glazed small onions) with 1 tablespoon butter in a skillet big enough so that they fit in one layer on the bottom of the skillet.

The mushrooms. Make a mushroom purée, using 3 1/2 tablespoons butter.

The tarts. Make the tarts with unsweetened dough and place in small molds; cook them between two molds to keep their shapes, and fill with the mushroom purée.

Serving. Place the saddle on a long platter big enough to hold the garnishes around the meat without covering the edges, which should remain bare. Place the garnishes around the meat, alternating 1 tart with the purée of mushrooms and 1 cock kidney, a truffle, and 2 chestnuts.

Pour 1 to 2 tablespoons cooking juice over the saddle and serve the rest of the juice, very hot, in a sauceboat.

Carving. To reduce the carving time at the table and to make it easier, the saddle can be carved in the kitchen, the slices put back in their places, and the tenderloin strips re-shaped carefully.

Do not forget to put very hot plates on the table just before serving.

Carré d'agneau de pré-salé ou filet rôti

RIB OR LOIN ROAST OF SPRING LAMB

The rib roast includes all the rib chops. The bones should be trimmed to the length of ordinary lamb chops and the ends cleaned. The chine bones must be removed to facilitate the carving; the membrane covering the layer of fat must also be removed.

Cooking time for the rib roast: 12 minutes per pound at 425° or higher [for searing; the meat must "rest"].

The loin roast is made up of half the saddle, cut length-wise along the spinal cord.

To roast remove the covering membrane; trim the hind-quarter and bone it completely; season the inside with salt and pepper and reshape; hold in place with string.

Cooking time for the loin roast: 7$^{1}/_{2}$ minutes per pound at 425° [for searing; the meat must "rest"].

To serve, remove most of the fat; deglaze with a little bit of bouillon, veal stock, or water to dissolve the solidified juices sticking to the roasting pan; serve the juices in a sauce-boat with the chosen garnish.

All the garnishes for the leg of lamb, the saddle, and lamb chops can be used with the rib roast and the loin filets.

Note: It is preferable to cook the loin with the bone in; the flavor will be better, but it is more difficult to carve.

Filet d'agneau de pré-salé Parmentier

LOIN ROAST OF SPRING LAMB PARMENTIER

Trim and bone the loin, place on a large pan, and roast in butter. As soon as the meat is golden, surround it with 2 large potatoes diced into $^{3}/_{4}$-inch cubes, washed (to remove the starch and to prevent their sticking to one another), and carefully dried. Sprinkle with a pinch of salt. Continue cooking in a 425° oven, stirring the potatoes from time to time. Baste the meat often. To serve, place the meat on a long heated platter, with the potatoes at each end in a bouquet; sprinkle the potatoes with a pinch of chopped parsley.

Deglaze the roasting pan with 2 tablespoons veal stock and pour over the meat.

199

Cuts from the ribs and loin of mutton or spring lamb

The ribs and loin are cut into chops.

The mutton loin, cut into slices 2 inches thick, gives the mutton chops or English-cut chops; the sirloin chops next to them are seasoned with salt and pepper, the thin part rolled over itself toward the inside and fastened with a skewer.

The spring lamb loin, cut the same way, makes lamb chops.

The best way to cook lamb chops or mutton chops is to broil them. When the meat is nearly cooked, turn the fatty part of the chop toward the flame in order to broil it as well. Remove the skewer from the sirloin mutton chops, and expose the inside of the hindquarter to the flame to sear it.

Let the meat rest in a warm oven for a few minutes; serve with a bouquet of water cress (trim the stems and gather together into a tight bunch so that the stems do not show) and with an additional vegetable as garnish.

All vegetables served with mutton or lamb, broiled or sautéed, are suitable for the chops. However, green vegetables coated with butter are usually preferred, such as string beans, peas, lima beans, asparagus tips, artichoke hearts. Also potatoes, usually fried: puffed, Pont-Neuf, matchstick, straw, chips, etc., or puréed (pages 355–6, 357).

Côtelettes d'agneau à la parisienne

SPRING LAMB CHOPS PARIS STYLE

Broil the chops, place them on a platter, and garnish with broiled tomatoes and mushrooms.

Broiled Tomatoes

If the tomatoes are large, cut them in two crosswise; if they are medium-sized, cut off the top part and the stem. In both cases, squeeze them carefully to remove the juice and the seeds.

Season with salt and pepper inside, cover with oil or melted butter, and place under a very hot broiler. Turn them over halfway through the cooking.

Broiled Mushrooms

The mushrooms should be large and regular in shape. Remove the stems; wash the caps, wipe, and cover with oil or melted butter; season and place under the broiler, top side up first, under a medium flame.

Turn the caps over halfway through the cooking and in each stem cavity place a pat of butter, which will soak into the mushroom during the second part of the cooking.

Arrange the lamb chops in a semicircle, overlapping; in the center place a bouquet of water cress and on the outer edge alternate the mushrooms and the tomatoes.

Note: The mushroom stems can be used to make *duxelles.*

Côtelettes d'agneau panées, sautées ou grillées

BREADED LAMB CHOPS, SAUTÉED OR BROILED
Sautéed
Dip the lamb chops (rib or loin) in an egg, beaten and seasoned, then in bread crumbs. Press lightly to make the bread crumbs adhere.

Heat some clarified butter (page 75) in a skillet and place the chops in it; cook slowly so that the browning of the bread crumbs and the cooking of the chops are completed at the same time. When the chops are turned the first time, sprinkle them with a pinch of salt; do this a second time on the other side after the chops are cooked.

Broiled
Brush the chops (rib or loin) with oil or melted butter, season, and sprinkle with very fine bread crumbs, white or light brown. Sprinkle again with a few drops of melted butter. Place on a very hot grill or under a broiler, and broil at a gentle heat; it is sufficient to push aside the coals or to lower the flame.

Garnish. For sautéed chops, serve with a fine purée of potatoes or fresh peas. For broiled chops, serve with fried potatoes.

Côtelettes de mouton sautées aux cèpes

SAUTÉED MUTTON CHOPS WITH CÈPES

3¹/₂ tablespoons olive oil
6 mutton chops
1 pound *cèpes*
2¹/₂ tablespoons unsalted butter
Pinch chopped parsley
Dash grated garlic
Pinch freshly ground pepper
2 tablespoons reduced white dry wine
2 tablespoons spicy tomato sauce

Method.   Heat 2 tablespoons olive oil in a skillet; when the oil is smoking, place in one layer 6 mutton chops, trimmed, lightly flattened, and seasoned.

Halfway through the cooking turn the chops over and finish cooking.

Place the chops in a circle on a heated round platter with paper frills on the bones. Garnish the center with the *cèpes* sautéed in 1¹/₂ tablespoons oil and 1¹/₂ tablespoons butter. Brown them well and at the last minute complete the seasoning with a pinch of chopped parsley, a dash of grated garlic, and a pinch of freshly ground pepper.

Deglaze the skillet with dry white wine (reduced) and spicy tomato sauce.

Off the heat add 1 tablespoon butter, and pour over the chops.

Côtelettes de mouton Pompadour

MUTTON CHOPS POMPADOUR
Method.   Sauté the chops; place them in a circle on a round, heated platter, and put a paper frill on the end of each bone.

In the center, form a pyramid of potato croquettes rolled in balls in big as walnuts and fried just before serving (recipe below). In butter stew 1 artichoke bottom per guest for 15 minutes. Arrange them in a circle around the chops.

Garnish with a purée of lentils or any other dried or fresh vegetable, buttered well. Deglaze the skillet with a few table-spoons of veal stock or *demi-glace* (page 76) or Périgueux sauce (page 82) flavored off the heat with Madeira; serve in a sauceboat.

Potato Croquettes

1 pound potatoes
7 tablespoons unsalted
  butter
4 egg yolks
Salt and nutmeg
1 whole egg, beaten
Bread crumbs

Peel the potatoes, cook them in salted boiling water until the pressure of your finger makes a dent; do not wait until they fall apart. Drain the potatoes well and replace them in the saucepan; leave them for a few seconds on very low heat so that the dampness evaporates.

Turn the potatoes into a sieve and press them through to form a purée; the sieving of the pulp should be done by press-ing, not rubbing, which makes the pulp stringy and chewy.

Reheat the pulp in a casserole and beat in the butter vig-orously, using a wooden spatula. When well beaten, potatoes will still be white; still beating, incorporate the egg yolks and a little nutmeg. Add more salt if needed.

Turn the mixture out on a buttered plate, butter the top to keep a crust from forming, and let stand until cool. Divide in pieces the size of a walnut; roll them on a lightly floured table; dip in beaten egg, roll in bread crumbs, patting to make the crumbs adhere.

Plunge into very hot deep fat for a few minutes; drain. The outside should be crusty. Arrange and serve.

Côtelettes de mouton à la Champvallon

MUTTON CHOPS CHAMPVALLON (For 6 people)

6 first-cut loin mutton
  chops
4 tablespoons unsalted
  butter
Salt and pepper
2 large onions, peeled and
  sliced into thin strips
2 generous cups bouillon
  or white veal stock (page
  72)
Bouquet garni
6 medium-sized yellow
  potatoes, peeled,
  washed, dried, and
  thinly sliced
2 garlic cloves, grated
Pinch chopped parsley

Method. This will take 1½ hours to prepare and cook. In a skillet big enough to hold the chops in one layer, heat the but-ter. When it bubbles, add the chops; sprinkle each chop with a pinch of salt and a dash of pepper; brown slowly to avoid burning the butter; then turn over, season a second time, and brown again.

Remove the chops and place on an ovenproof earthen-ware platter that has been rubbed with garlic.

Put the onions in the skillet. Brown them, stirring fre-quently; pour over half the bouillon or veal stock, boil for 5 minutes, and pour over the chops, spreading the onion on top. If the bouillon does not quite cover the lamb chops, add more as needed. Bring to a boil, insert the *bouquet garni* be-tween the chops, cover, and cook in a 400° oven for 30 min-utes.

Spread the potatoes over the chops; add the remaining bouillon, bring to a boil, and continue cooking in a 400° oven, covered, for 20 minutes more.

Then remove the cover, sprinkle the grated garlic on the potatoes, and baste with the juice. Continue cooking uncov-ered in the oven for another 20 minutes, basting often with the juice, which will reduce and thicken slightly. When the cooking is finished, the cooking juice should be largely ab-sorbed by the meat and the potatoes, which will be very soft;

the top of the vegetables will be covered with a *gratiné* surface with a beautiful dark golden color.

Sprinkle the dish with a pinch of chopped parsley, and serve on the cooking platter.

Noisettes de pré-salé à la dauphine
NOISETTES OF SPRING LAMB À LA DAUPHINE

Prepare the *noisettes* cut from the boned loin of a spring lamb in slices 1½ inches thick. Trim the meat and flatten it slightly; sauté in butter in a skillet. Season the meat on both sides while cooking. The center should be pink.

Place the meat in a circle on a large round platter over croutons fried in butter (the bread slices should be the same size as the meat and ¼ inch thick).

Around the edge, like a string of big pearls, place croquettes of potatoes *dauphine* (recipe below).

Deglaze the skillet with 2 tablespoons dry white wine, reduce nearly completely, then add ½ cup good veal stock (page 72); reduce again by one-third, and add butter off the heat; pour a moderate amount over the *noisettes*. Serve the remaining juice in a sauceboat.

Potatoes *Dauphine*

Mix together 2 parts potato croquettes (page 202) with 1 part batter for unsweetened soufflé fritters (pages 435–6).

Form into large sausages on a lightly floured table and cut them into pieces as big as walnuts. Roll each piece in the shape of an egg and dip it in an egg beaten with salt and pepper and a few drops of oil, then in bread crumbs. Roll each croquette between your palms so that the bread crumbs will stick.

Place the croquettes in a frying basket and plunge at once into very hot oil for 7 to 8 minutes. Shake the frying basket carefully so that the croquettes move in the oil or fat.

Drain on a paper towel, sprinkle with salt, and serve.

Épaule d'agneau de pré-salé rôtie
ROAST SHOULDER OF SPRING LAMB

The meat of a shoulder of lamb is tough; only the shoulder of a very young lamb can be roasted. Mutton or lamb shoulder should be braised or stewed.

The shoulder of a young lamb can be roasted with or without the bone. In boning, the butcher lifts out the blade bone; then, without slitting the shoulder, the central bone is easily removed; at the end, the leg bone, which is sawed near the stump, remains.

Season the meat inside with salt and pepper, roll it like a sausage, and tie it with string, leaving a long loop at the end, which serves as a handle, like the end of the bone in a leg of lamb. [*Editor's note:* In the United States, boned lamb shoulder is sold already rolled and tied.]

203

For better flavor we advise against boning. Naturally the carving is not so easy; therefore cooking the meat in this way is suitable only for a family dinner or when the number of guests warrants cooking the whole shoulder.

Place the shoulder on the rack of a roasting pan; season, and baste with melted butter. Cook in a 425° oven, basting frequently. Watch the bottom of the roasting pan so that the meat juices do not burn.

Cooking time will be about 15 minutes per pound [to sear; the meat must "rest"].

Deglaze the roasting pan with 3 to 4 tablespoons bouillon or water. Serve this juice after correcting the seasoning, without degreasing it.

Épaule de pré-salé boulangère

SPRING LAMB SHOULDER WITH POTATOES (For a whole shoulder)

1 young lamb shoulder, boned or not
4 teaspoons unsalted butter
3 medium-sized onions
4 large baking potatoes

Method. Prepare the shoulder as you would for roasting; brown it quickly in a 450° oven in an ovenproof earthenware dish that holds the meat easily.

Peel the onions and the potatoes; dry them. Cut the onions into julienne and thinly slice the potatoes; sprinkle with salt.

Remove the shoulder from the pan and spread the onions, then the potatoes, in thin layers, on the bottom of the pan; place the shoulder on top, pour over some melted butter, and continue cooking until done in a 425° oven.

Serve in the cooking pan. Remove the strings carefully, if the shoulder has been boned.

Note: The onions and the potatoes will brown slightly and will absorb the butter and the lamb juice. If the garnish sticks to the pan, this is not a problem; it can be loosened with a serving spoon at the table.

Épaule de mouton braisée aux navets

BRAISED LAMB SHOULDER WITH TURNIPS

3½ tablespoons unsalted butter
15 small onions, peeled
1 pound turnips
Pinch sugar
1 lamb shoulder, boned, seasoned, and tied with a string
1 cup dry white wine
2 cups lightly salted bouillon
Bouquet garni
Garlic clove

Method. Heat the butter in an oval saucepan or pot and brown the onions slowly; remove them.

Peel the turnips thickly, quarter them lengthwise, and trim to look like big walnuts. Place them in the same butter, sprinkle with a pinch of sugar, and brown. Then set aside with the onions.

Place the lamb shoulder in the pot and brown it; moisten with the white wine, reduce the wine almost completely, then add the bouillon, covering the shoulder. Add the *bouquet garni* and garlic, bring to a boil, and cook, covered, in a 425° oven for 2 hours.

As the braising juices reduce, baste more frequently.

After the meat has cooked for 2 hours, add the onions and turnips. If the juices have reduced too much to cover the garnish, add a little bit of bouillon or water to avoid an overly salty dish.

Simmer, covered, for 25 to 30 minutes. Baste often.

Serve the shoulder in a shallow dish, surrounded by its garnish, and moistened with the braising juices—there should be just enough to serve with the meat.

Épaule de mouton farcie à la mode du Berry
STUFFED SHOULDER OF LAMB À LA BERRY

1 lamb shoulder, boned
Stuffing
1 medium onion, chopped
2 tablespoons unsalted butter
½ pound good sausage meat
1 garlic clove, grated
1 egg
1 teaspoon chopped parsley
2 slices white bread, soaked in bouillon and squeezed
Salt, pepper, mixed spices (see page x)
Garnish
3 leeks, white part only
2 celery ribs
Bouquet garni
1 onion stuck with a clove
2 medium-sized carrots, peeled
1 pound celery root, peeled and quartered
3 large baking potatoes, peeled
7 tablespoons unsalted butter
Salt and pepper

Method.   Cook the onion in 2 tablespoons butter. Combine in a bowl with the sausage meat, the grated garlic, the egg, the chopped parsley, the squeezed bread, and the salt, pepper, and spices. Mix well, and spread the stuffing on the shoulder where the bones were. Roll the meat to enclose the stuffing and tie with a string.

Place the shoulder in a braising pan; add water to reach halfway; add salt—2 teaspoons per quart of water, or to taste—pepper, and spices.

Bring to a boil, and add the following from the garnish: the leeks, celery ribs, *bouquet garni,* the onion stuck with the clove, and the carrots.

Cook slowly for 1¼ hours; then surround the shoulder with the pieces of celery root; simmer for another 25 minutes, and add the potatoes.

When the potatoes are cooked (they should be firm), drain all the vegetables and rub them through a fine sieve into a skillet; dry this purée over a high flame, stirring constantly with a spatula. When the purée has thickened, add the butter, off the heat. Add salt and grind in 3 or 4 peppercorns. Correct the consistency, if necessary, with a couple of tablespoons of the cooking juices.

To serve, place the meat on a long serving platter, remove the string, and pour over a little bit of the cooking juices. Accompany the meat with a sauceboat of the cooking juice and the vegetable purée in a bowl.

Poitrine et épigrammes d'agneau
LAMB BREAST AND CHOPS (For 6 people)

1 pound breast of lamb
1 cup dry white wine
1 onion, sliced
1 carrot, sliced
Bouquet garni
Salt
1 egg
Bread crumbs made from 4 slices white bread
6 lamb chops
2 tablespoons unsalted butter, melted

Method.   In a skillet, combine the lamb breast, the white wine, the vegetables, and the *bouquet garni.* Add enough water to cover the meat and the vegetables. Add salt and bring to a boil. Simmer, covered, for 40 minutes. Before the 40 minutes are up, check the meat; it has cooked enough when the bones can be detached easily.

Then drain the breast and place it flat on a plate; remove the bones. Lay the breast on one half of a dish towel and cover the meat with the other half. Place on a cookie sheet and put a weight of about 2 pounds on top. Let the meat cool under the weight.

After the meat is completely cooled, cut into pieces to resemble a lamb chop, 1 per guest. Dip each piece first into egg beaten with a little bit of oil and a pinch of salt, then into bread crumbs. Press the bread crumbs on the meat with a knife blade, so that they stick.

Lightly flatten and season the lamb chops and bread in the same way, or pour some melted butter over them and roll in bread crumbs.

Pour some melted butter on the pieces cut from the breast and the chops and broil them under a low flame.

Place in the shape of a crown on a round platter, alternating the breast pieces and the chops.

In the center, in the shape of a pyramid, place a *jardinière* garnish—carrots and turnips—or green peas, asparagus tips, a vegetable purée, braised chicory, etc.

Ragoûts, sautés et navarin
LAMB STEWS AND SAUTÉED DISHES

The breast, the neck, the lower ribs, and the shoulder are the parts of the lamb or mutton best suited to be sautéed or to make stews and the *navarin* (stew with potatoes and turnips).

Navarin
LAMB STEW WITH POTATOES AND TURNIPS (For 6 people)
Classic Recipe

2 pounds lamb or mutton breast, neck, lower ribs, and shoulder, in equal parts.
Oil or unsalted butter
1 large onion, peeled and quartered
1 medium-sized carrot, peeled and quartered
Salt and pepper
Pinch sugar
2 tablespoons flour
2 garlic cloves, crushed
2 tablespoons tomato purée or 3 fresh tomatoes, peeled, seeded, and chopped
Bouquet garni
3/4 pound small potatoes, peeled
24 small onions
1/4 pound lean bacon

Method.   Have the shoulder and lower ribs boned and cut into pieces of about 2 ounces; have the breast and the neck cut the same way but not boned.

In a skillet brown the meat in very hot oil or butter with the onion and the carrot, seasoned with salt and pepper.

When the meat is well browned, drain off some of the fat; sprinkle the meat with a pinch of sugar, and stir over a high flame, just enough so that the sugar caramelizes—it will give the *navarin* a nice color. Then add the flour, mix, and brown for a few minutes.

Add the crushed garlic to the meat, and mix well for a few seconds to heat it; cover the meat with water. Add the tomato purée or the fresh tomatoes and the *bouquet garni*.

Bring to a boil, and simmer in a 325° oven, covered, for 1 hour.

After 1 hour, pour the meat into a strainer placed on top of a bowl; take out the meat, removing the bones and skin, and separate from the vegetable garnish; place the meat in a clean skillet. Sprinkle the potatoes on top—if they are too large, cut and trim them to the size of a small egg. Brown and glaze the onions. Cut the bacon into small pieces, blanch, and brown it. Add the onions and bacon to the meat.

Degrease the sauce, which has been allowed to stand; taste and correct the seasoning. Pour the sauce over the meat and potatoes. If there is not enough sauce, add some water.

Bring to a boil again, cover, and simmer in the oven for 1 hour more.

Serve the stew in a round dish.

**12 small onions, browned
and glazed**
**20 pieces cored carrots,
cut to resemble large
olives**
20 small turnips
Unsalted butter
20 small new potatoes
1 cup fresh green peas
**Handful string beans, cut
on diagonal 1¹/₂ inches
long**
Chopped parsley
Dash chervil

**3 pounds lamb shoulder,
breast, neck, and lower
ribs, in equal parts**
Salt and pepper
**2 tablespoons curry
powder**
**5 tablespoons unsalted
butter**
1 large onion, chopped
2 tablespoons flour
Bouquet garni
¹/₂ pound apples
1 banana
**¹/₂ cup *crème fraîche* or
heavy cream**
**³/₄ cup raw rice, prepared
according to the recipe
for Indian rice (page 370)**

Ragoût de mouton printanier
LAMB STEW WITH SPRING VEGETABLES

Method. This stew is the same as the *navarin;* only the garnish is different.

Follow the preceding recipe until the meat has been cooking for an hour. Then garnish with the following spring vegetables: onions, carrots, and turnips. Stew all the vegetables in butter for 15 minutes; add the new potatoes.

Moisten with the sauce, bring to a boil, and cook in the oven for 25 minutes; add the green peas and string beans.

Continue cooking slowly in the oven for 30 minutes.

Serve in a bowl, sprinkled with chopped parsley and a dash of chervil.

Cari de mouton aux reinettes
LAMB CURRY WITH APPLES (For 6 people)

Method. Have the shoulder and the lower ribs boned and cut into 2-ounce pieces.

Season the meat with salt, pepper, and curry powder and mix well so that all the pieces of meat are impregnated with the spices. In a skillet heat 2 tablespoons butter and sear the meat in it.

When the lamb is half browned, sprinkle the chopped onion on top and continue browning, stirring very often. As soon as the onion starts to brown, sprinkle the meat with the flour; stir again to coat the meat, and brown lightly.

Be careful not to burn the onion during this last step.

Cover the meat with water, add the *bouquet garni,* bring to a boil, stirring the stew with a wooden spatula. Cook in a 325° oven for 2¹/₂ hours.

Peel and quarter the apples, removing the seeds and core.

Peel the banana and cut into 3 pieces.

Brown the apples and the banana in 3 tablespoons butter in a skillet big enough to hold the stew. Take the stew out of the oven, remove the pieces of meat, and add to the apples and the banana.

Cool the sauce and degrease it, and reduce by one-third; pour in enough *crème fraîche* to bring it back to its original amount and to thicken it. Correct the seasoning, and strain the sauce over the meat through a very fine sieve.

Shake the skillet with a rotating motion to coat the meat and the garnish with the sauce.

Serve in a shallow dish with a bowl of the Indian rice on the side. There should also be enough sauce to cover the Indian rice.

Note: The dish can be improved by replacing the water for moistening with coconut milk. This milk is obtained from the grated pulp of the coconut, fresh or dry. Grate or pound pulp in a mortar, and macerate for 1 hour in enough tepid water to moisten. Pour the water and pulp into a dish towel or double cheesecloth spread over a bowl and squeeze to extract the milk.

3 pounds lamb shoulder, lower ribs, breast, and neck, in equal parts
3 large mealy potatoes, peeled, quartered, and thinly sliced
3 large onions, peeled and finely chopped
Salt and pepper
Bouquet garni
12 small new potatoes
12 small onions
2 celery ribs, white part only
Pinch crushed sage
Chopped parsley

Ragoût de mouton à l'irlandaise

IRISH STEW (For 6 people)

Method. This will take about 2¹⁄₂ hours to cook.

Bone the shoulder and the lower ribs, cut them, along with the breast and the neck, into 2-ounce pieces.

Place the potatoes and onions on a plate with the *bouquet garni.*

In a skillet big enough to hold the stew, sprinkle one-third of the onion and one-third of the sliced potatoes. On this layer place half the pieces of meat. Season with salt and freshly ground pepper. Add the *bouquet garni;* then place on the meat the second third of the onion and the second third of the potatoes. Cover with the remaining meat; season with salt and pepper, and finish with a layer of the remaining onion and potatoes. Add more pepper; this stew should be spicy.

Cover with hot water just to the top of the meat and vegetables. Bring to a boil, cover, and cook slowly and evenly in a 275° oven for 1¹⁄₂ hours.

Peel the new potatoes; if they are not very small, about the size of large walnuts, then cut them in two lengthwise and trim to give pieces the shape of long olives; leave them in cold water until adding them to the stew.

After 1¹⁄₂ hours remove the stew from the oven; the potatoes and the onions should then be completely disintegrated. If some pieces remain, rub them through the strainer. Add the small onions, the celery cut into sticks, and the raw potatoes; push them down into the stew sauce and sprinkle with a pinch of sage. If the sauce is too thick because it has reduced or because of the mealy potatoes, add some hot water.

Bring to a boil, correct the seasoning. Over the stew, place a piece of buttered wax paper the size of the saucepan; cover, and continue cooking in the oven for 45 minutes.

Test the potatoes; when they are cooked, serve in a very hot shallow platter; sprinkle a pinch of chopped parsley on top.

Note: If one wishes a smoother sauce, take out the pieces of meat and place them in a clean skillet. Rub the sauce through a fine sieve, pressing the vegetables with a pestle. Reheat the stew quickly.

The stew should be served steaming, and the plates on the table should also be very hot.

Baron, gigot, carré ou quartier d'agneau de lait rôti et persillé

BARON, LEG, LOIN, OR HINDQUARTERS OF BABY LAMB ROASTED WITH PARSLEY

The meat of baby lamb has little taste; flavor must be added to it during the cooking.

Roasted with parsley is, for us, the best way.

Method. Season the meat with salt and pepper; place it on a rack in a roasting pan. Baste generously with melted butter, and put it in a 325° oven for about 20 minutes. While the meat is roasting, it must be basted frequently with the cooking butter.

Meanwhile, prepare a mixture of 1 tablespoon chopped parsley mixed with 2 tablespoons fresh bread crumbs as big as peas.

After the meat has been cooking for 15 minutes, sprinkle the bread-crumb mixture on top of the meat; baste with melted butter, and raise the heat so that the bread crumbs turn golden brown.

Serve very hot, basted with the cooking butter.

On the side serve a bowl of sautéed potatoes sprinkled with chopped parsley.

Sauté d'agneau de lait printanier
SAUTÉED MILK-FED LAMB WITH SPRING VEGETABLES

Cook separately the spring vegetables: carrots, turnips, small onions, peas, and string beans.

The carrots and the turnips should be trimmed to the shape of an olive or chopped; cook them following the recipe for glazed vegetables (pages 309–10); prepare the peas the French (page 352) or English way (page 351), and cook the string beans in water.

Meanwhile, cut a piece of lamb in 3- to 4-ounce pieces and sauté in unsalted butter in a skillet big enough to lay them flat.

Season with salt and pepper and cook slowly, covered; turn the pieces of meat when they are browned on one side. Season again.

When the meat is cooked, place on a round platter; turn the vegetables over in the cooking butter, add 2 or 3 tablespoons of a good veal stock, bring to a boil, pour over the lamb, and serve.

COLD LAMB AND MUTTON

Carré, gigot, baron, selle, épaule
LOIN, LEG, BARON, SADDLE, SHOULDER

All these cuts of meat can be served cold after they have been roasted, accompanied by their jelly, a vegetable salad, a green salad, or condiments (cornichons, etc.) and with a cold sauce (pages 90–93).

Pork

Pork meat is fat, firm, and nearly white because all the blood is drained from the carcass after butchering. Pork is difficult to digest but, on the other hand, combines easily with other ingredients. It is too rich a food for young children. In general, when the meat is red, flabby, and not very fat, the animal is old or mediocre or comes from bad stock. Absolutely never buy such meat, especially if the pork is to be used for salting, which is the case with numerous parts of the animal. The cuts of pork most often used fresh are the ribs and loin, the tenderloin, the chops, and the ham. The spareribs, breast, and knuckles are placed in a salting tub for 2 to 3 days to make salt pork.

The blood, fat, intestines, stomach, feet, liver, and skin of the pig are used in making blood sausage, other pork sausages cooked or raw, cervelat, pigs' feet rolled in bread crumbs or with truffles, and *andouillettes, pâté de foie,* head cheese, etc.

Ham

Salting.   The best period for salting a ham is the cold season (December 15 to January 15); this is also the time when pigs are usually fat, especially if they have been fed with corn, chestnuts, potatoes, and grain mixed with milk products.

The animal is killed by bleeding in cold dry air, cooled for 24 hours, then skinned and cleaned.

The ham is cut from the back leg from the base of the spine to above the knee. To prepare it remove the bone of the rump, where flies could easily have laid their eggs as long ago as the summer, giving birth to tiny worms and altering the meat.

The pork shoulder can be prepared in the same way.

The salting mixture.   This must be prepared during dry weather. In a very clean bowl, mix $1/2$ pound sea salt, finely crushed with a rolling pin or a wine bottle, $1/4$ pound brown sugar, and $1^3/4$ ounces saltpeter.

Salting or curing.   *First step:* Place the ham, skin side down, on a very clean table. Hold the bone with your left hand; with your right hand massage the ham up and down with the salt mixture so that it penetrates the meat. Do the same for the skin side; then start again on the other side and cover all the sides of the ham, until you have used up all the salt.

The nice pink color of the ham depends upon this first step; it is therefore very important. The care and the time spent are always repaid in the end by success.

Second step: Place the ham, skin side down, in a salting tub made of wood or earthenware and extremely clean. The dimensions of the salting tub should be close to the size of the ham to avoid wasting salt.

Cover the ham with 1 pound sea salt. Cover the salting tub with a cloth and then with its cover. Let stand for 2 days;

then turn the ham, using a special fork. Never use your fingers. Cover again with 1 pound sea salt. Let stand again for 2 days.

Two days later remove the ham, set it on a platter in a cool place, and cover with a dish towel. Empty the salting tub into a very clean saucepan and add 2 quarts cold water, $1/4$ pound sugar, 2 bay leaves, a large branch of thyme, a branch of rosemary, 4 sage leaves, 25 peppercorns, 25 coriander seeds, 6 cloves, 12 juniper berries, a clump of parsley with its roots well washed, 1 tablespoon crushed cinnamon bark; a pinch each of marjoram, nutmeg, savory, mace, and cumin.

Boil for 3 minutes. Remove from the heat. Cover and let cool.

Replace the ham in the salting tub and pour in the brine, well cooled and strained through a cloth.

The quantity of brine specified above should be enough to allow the ham to soak completely immersed, if the salting tub is the right size.

Turn the ham over every 2 days. If it is not covered completely by the brine, it will have to be turned every day.

It will take 20 days to cure a ham from a pig of 180 to 200 pounds.

If the ham is not going to be kept for several months, this length of time can be reduced by half; then the ham must be eaten, cooked, as soon as it is taken out of the salting tub and without removing the salt.

Smoking. A salted ham can be preserved smoked or not. In both cases, it must be dried by being suspended in a dry airy place.

The smoking is done in a fireplace. The ham is hung quite high; underneath the leaves and stems of aromatic and resinous plants are burned: oak, bay, juniper, genista, vine shoots, etc.

After 6 months of drying, the ham can be sliced very thin and can be eaten raw.

After the ham has soaked for 20 days, it can be served cooked at any time after it is removed from the brine. However, it is necessary to soak the ham in water for 6 to 12 hours, depending upon the length of the drying. The longer the ham is dried, the more the flavor of the meat becomes concentrated and therefore salty.

Cooking. Weigh the soaked ham to determine the cooking time. Scrub it well and wash it in cold water; place in a stew pan or a braising pan and immerse in cold water. Add a large handful of hay, tied in a bunch. Bring to a boil, and reduce the heat to a simmer. The poaching should be done at a temperature of 175°, 20 minutes per pound.

Let the ham cool completely in the cooking liquid unless it is to be served hot; then drain it and prepare, following the recipes below:

Presentation. *First method:* Remove the skin and trim the excess fat, which can be used in cooking cabbage or sauerkraut; sprinkle the ham with superfine sugar and place in a very hot oven or under a broiler. This step must be done quite quickly; the sugar melts, caramelizes, and covers the layer of fat with a shiny, amber-colored coating. The meat has a more appetizing appearance and is also more flavorful.

Second method: Glaze by braising the ham. Thirty minutes before the ham is completely poached, take it from the pot and remove the skin; trim off the excess fat, and place ham in a braising pan. Baste it with 2 cups Madeira, port, Frontignan, Banyuls, sherry, or Marsala.

Place the braising pan, covered, in a 275° oven and let cook for 1 hour.

Baste often. Then sprinkle the ham with superfine sugar and continue cooking as above.

Hams served hot are usually accompanied by a vegetable garnish and by Madeira (page 79) or *demi-glace* sauce (page 76) flavored with the essence of the well-degreased cooking stock.

Among the best vegetables to serve with ham are: braised sauerkraut, spinach, endives Flemish style, braised celery (pages 320–1), cucumbers with Mornay sauce (page 84) or *à la jardinière,* Alsatian noodles, green peas *à la* Clamart, braised lettuce (page 343–4), etc.

Chausson Lucas-Carton
TURNOVER LUCAS-CARTON

¾ pound braised ham from the part close to the knuckle (which is more gelatinous and softer), with some of the fat left on
1 fresh truffle
3 tablespoons unsalted butter
¼ pound fresh *foie gras*
¼ pound firm, white mushrooms, chopped
2 tablespoons port wine
1 recipe *brioche* dough (pages 376–8)
Salt, freshly ground pepper, mace
1 egg, beaten
½ cup *demi-glace* sauce (page 76)

Method. Cut the ham into pieces. Slice the truffle thickly and heat in butter in a skillet. Cut the *foie gras* into 2 or 3 slices and sear in the same butter. Remove and add the mushrooms. Sauté rapidly and moisten with 2 tablespoons port, then reduce almost completely and off the heat coat with 1 tablespoon butter. Roll the dough ¼ inch thick into an oval shape; prick several times with a fork; on one half of the dough (the other half will be folded as a cover), spread alternating layers of the ham, the truffle, the *foie gras,* and the mushrooms.

During these various steps, the truffle, the *foie gras,* and the mushrooms should be seasoned with a pinch of salt, freshly ground pepper, and just a dash of mace.

Fold the other half of the dough over the ham and the other ingredients, first moistening the edges with beaten egg; seal well by pressing lightly with your fingers to fasten the bottom layer to the top one.

The turnover is now shaped like a semicircle. Place it on a cookie sheet. Brush the top with beaten egg. Decorate the top with small designs cut out of dough in a diamond shape. With the back of a knife blade draw leaf veins on them, and arrange them like leaves; brush them with beaten egg and bake in a 400° oven until golden brown, at least 30 minutes.

Degrease the *demi-glace* sauce and reduce; flavor off the heat with 1 tablespoon port and 1 tablespoon butter per guest. Add a dash of freshly ground white pepper.

The intense flavor of this sauce must be modified by the harmonious richness and the aroma of the port and the freshness of the butter, added off the heat, both uncooked.

Serve this dish as soon as it comes from the oven, accompanied by a sauceboat of *demi-glace* sauce.

Note: This delicious turnover can also be made with flaky pastry dough (pages 382–3).

The turnover should be served as is, as a hot hors d'oeuvre, or as a main dish accompanied by morels sautéed in butter and covered with *crème fraîche* flavored with port.

Mousse froide de jambon
COLD HAM MOUSSE

1 pound cooked lean ham
1 cup *velouté* sauce (page 76), very cold
1 cup jelly made with pale Madeira (pages 95–6)
2 cups thick *crème fraîche* or heavy cream

Method. Cut the ham into tiny cubes and pound in a mortar until completely crushed. Add the very cold *velouté* sauce a little at a time.

Put this purée in a very fine sieve, made of horsehair if possible, and with a pestle rub it through into a bowl. Place the bowl on top of crushed ice, then work the purée vigorously with a wooden spatula, adding, little by little, two-thirds of the jelly, half melted; then correct the seasoning and add the *crème fraîche,* half whipped.

Pour the remaining half-melted jelly in a 1½-quart mousse mold, and coat the mold by rotating it on a bed of ice, in order to make the jelly set. Fill the mold with the mousse and refrigerate.

Unmold on a silver platter by dipping the mold for a second in hot water. (Dry the mold to avoid getting stains on the silver platter.) Place the platter upside down on top of the mold and, with a quick movement, turn the platter and the mold right side up. Lift off the mold. The mousse will appear pink under the shiny transparent layer of jelly. Serve immediately.

Jambon au foin
HAM IN HAY

6-pound smoked ham, lightly cured
½ pound excellent hay, fresh or dry
Sprig thyme
2 bay leaves
6 cloves
10 juniper berries

Method. The night before using the ham, soak it in cold water to remove the salt, after having sawed the knuckle and removed the end of the bone.

Place the ham in a kettle, cover it completely with cold water, add the hay and the seasonings.

Put the kettle on the stove and, without letting it come to a boil, simmer, keeping a constant temperature of 175° to 195° (as a rule, allow 15 minutes per pound).

Remove the skin when the ham is cooked.

Ham cooked in hay can be served hot or cold.

Jambon chaud garni de légumes divers
HOT HAM WITH VEGETABLES

Cold poached ham is very often served reheated with a vegetable garnish and the thickened pan juices or a brown sauce.

Prepare the chosen vegetable garnish and place it, piping hot, on a very hot platter. Cut slices of ham as thin as possible and serve several slices per guest rather than one thick slice of ham, which is not pleasant to eat, and place the slices on top of the very hot vegetables, cover with a glass bell or a shallow dish, then serve. The heat from the vegetables concentrated under this improvised cover will be sufficient to heat the ham.

Be sure to give each guest a very hot plate.

Ham served this way is always accompanied by a little *demi-glace* sauce (page 76) or some thickened veal stock (page 72) flavored with Madeira, sherry, port, etc.

Andouillettes et andouilles, boudins blancs et noirs, saucisses

ANDOUILLETTES, ANDOUILLES, WHITE SAUSAGE, BLOOD SAUSAGE, OTHER PORK SAUSAGES

All these sausages are usually bought already prepared at a delicatessen.

The cooking is therefore always brief. The sausages may be grilled or sautéed.

Accompaniments: puréed potatoes, puréed green or dried peas, puréed lentils or white beans; fresh vegetables or various dried ones; sautéed potatoes, rice prepared in various ways; cauliflower, cabbage, Brussels sprouts, braised leeks or celery, etc.

Andouilles sautées aux oignons

PORK SAUSAGE SAUTÉED WITH ONIONS

First, cut 1 medium-sized onion per guest into julienne and cook slowly in butter in a skillet.

Then cut a piece of fresh pork sausage in slices 1/2 inch thick and brown them in another skillet. Add the sausage to the onions; raise the heat, and cook rapidly for 2 minutes, adding a pinch of freshly ground pepper, and a splash of vinegar; off the heat, finish the dish with a pinch of chopped fresh parsley. Serve very hot with sautéed or fried potatoes.

Boudins blancs grillés purée mousseline

BROILED WHITE SAUSAGE WITH PURÉE MOUSSELINE

Plunge white pork or chicken sausages into boiling water. Immediately move the pot off the heat to stop the boiling; then lower the heat, and maintain a temperature of 200°. Poach for 12 minutes. Drain and cool.

Prick each sausage with a pin; wrap it in buttered white paper and place it on a grill. Broil under a low flame.

Serve with a potato purée *mousseline* (page 360).

Boudins noirs aux pommes reinettes
BLOOD SAUSAGE WITH APPLES

For each guest, use a piece of blood sausage and an apple.

Peel the apple, remove the core, cut into quarters, and cook in butter in a skillet until the apples are brown and tender. Spice the apples with a dash of salt and a small pinch of powdered cinnamon.

Make shallow slashes in the sausage skin to let the heat penetrate, and brown in a skillet in butter. When the sausage is cooked, add the apples; simmer 4 to 5 minutes, so that the ingredients flavor one another as they touch.

Serve very hot.

Saucisses au vin blanc
SAUSAGE WITH WHITE WINE (For 1 person)

2 fresh pork sausages
2 tablespoons unsalted butter
Slice of bread ⅛ inch thick
1 tablespoon white wine
1 tablespoon veal stock (page 72)
½ teaspoon *beurre manié* made with equal parts of flour and butter

Method.   This will take 15 minutes to cook. Thickly butter a skillet or a shallow baking dish and place the sausages in it; baste with melted butter and place in a 225° oven to cook slowly.

Butter the slice of bread and brown it in the oven.

Remove the sausages from the skillet and keep them warm; pour the white wine into the same skillet, reduce nearly totally; add the veal stock and thicken with *beurre manié.* Bring to a boil, and turn off the heat.

Place the slice of bread on a hot plate and put the 2 sausages on it; pour over the sauce, adding butter off the flame at the last minute.

Échine de porc, petit salé d'échine aux choux farcis
SALTED PORK LOIN WITH STUFFED CABBAGE

During the cold season, lightly salt a piece of pork loin. Rub it vigorously with crushed, spiced salt (page x). Place it on a plate and cover it with sea salt. The next day remove the sea salt and again rub with spiced salt. Place in a clean earthenware pot with 1 sprig of thyme, 1 bay leaf, and 1 tablespoon sugar; cover completely with salt. Cover the pot with a dishcloth, and put it in a cool place. Let stand for 8 days; if the salt does not cover the meat completely as it dissolves, turn the meat over with a fork every day. Do not touch the meat with your fingers.

After 8 days, drain the meat, wash, and cook in cold water that has been slowly brought to the boiling point; add a carrot cut into quarters and an onion stuck with a clove. Cook the meat following the directions for time and method given for poaching a ham (page 211).

Serve on a round platter surrounded with stuffed cabbage leaves about the size of apples (page 333). On the side serve

215

boiled potatoes and a sauceboat of the bouillon in which the pork cooked.

Carré et filet de porc frais

FRESH PORK LOIN AND TENDERLOIN

We will give two methods of cooking a pork loin or tenderloin.

First Method

Do not bone the loin but saw every 1¼ inches along the backbone to make the carving easier. Two hours before roasting season with salt and pepper.

Place the meat in a metal or earthenware roasting pan, baste with melted lard, and roast in a 375° oven. Baste and turn the meat often until completely cooked. Rare pork is undigestible and even dangerous. Cooking time: 25 to 30 minutes per pound, depending on the thickness of the meat.

Second Method

Follow the preparation explained above, then place the loin in a kettle or braising pan with carrots, an onion studded with 3 cloves, a head of garlic, the white of 2 leeks, 1 celery rib—as one would do for a *pot-au-feu.* Pour over cold water 2 fingers above the meat.

Add 1 tablespoon salt for each quart of water. Bring to a boil, skim, lower the heat, and simmer, continuing to poach the meat at 175°, without ever letting the water boil.

Note: If the cooking liquid will not be used because of its strong taste, the loin of pork can be placed directly in boiling liquid, rather than starting in cold water.

The cooking time is the same as in the first method.

When the loin is poached, drain and place in a roasting pan with 2 to 3 tablespoons smoking lard; baste the meat with the hot lard and place it in a 425° oven to brown quickly.

Serve with Robert (page 81) or *piquante* sauce (page 81) or with a tablespoon of veal stock (page 72) to which has been added some of the fat used to brown the pork.

Côtes de porc

PORK CHOPS

Pork chops must be at least ¾ to 1¼ inches thick. If the chops are thinner, they will be dry when cooked. Pork chops are served broiled or sautéed.

Broiled. Before placing on the grill, coat the chops with unsalted butter or melted lard, season with salt and pepper, and sprinkle with bread crumbs.

Sautéed. Cook in a skillet over a low flame. The chops should brown slowly and not dry out.

Deglaze the skillet for the accompanying sauce, generally a spicy one—Robert (page 81) or *charcutière* (page 80)— and serve with vegetables: a potato purée (pages 357–8), potatoes *dauphine* (page 203), or sautéed potatoes (page 361); applesauce, etc.

Choucroute à la strasbourgeoise

SAUERKRAUT WITH PORK STRASBOURG STYLE (For 6 people)

4 pounds very white
sauerkraut
4 large slices fresh pork
fat, cut very thin
1 large carrot, peeled and
sliced
1 onion stuck with a clove
Bouquet garni
Juniper berries
¹/₂ pound goose fat or lard
1 pig's knuckle from a
fresh ham
1 pound smoked bacon
1 slice poached ham per
guest
2 pounds smoked pork loin
1 large garlic sausage
2 cups white Alsatian wine
or dry white wine
1 quart light bouillon
1 frankfurter per guest

Method.   Three hours before cooking the sauerkraut, soak, wash, drain, and squeeze it by handfuls to remove all the water. Spread the handfuls of sauerkraut on a cloth; grind some peppercorns over them and mix well.

Blanch the pork fat by boiling briefly, drain, and rinse; trim the edges.

Line the sides and the bottom of a deep saucepan or braising pan with the slices of pork fat. Over them place one-third of the sauerkraut and then add half the carrot, the onion, *bouquet garni,* juniper berries tied in cheesecloth, and one-third of the goose fat or lard. Add the second third of the sauerkraut, the remaining carrot, the pig's knuckle, and the second third of the goose fat; then add the bacon, the slices of ham, the pork loin, the sausage pricked with a pin, and finally the remaining sauerkraut, with the remaining goose fat spread on top.

Pour over enough white wine and bouillon to immerse the sauerkraut.

Bring to a boil, top with greased white paper, then cover with the lid. Place in a 425° oven. The cooking must proceed slowly and continue until the liquid has been almost totally absorbed.

After 35 minutes, remove the sausage carefully. An hour later, the bacon; an hour and a half later, the loin—and reserve.

Twenty minutes before serving, place the frankfurters in boiling water and poach them for 10 minutes without letting the water boil.

Remove the sauerkraut from the oven, remove the paper; top the sauerkraut with the bacon, the sausage, and the frankfurters.

Cover and let stand for 10 minutes.

Presentation.   Remove all the meats that will accompany the sauerkraut, this time including the pig's knuckle, and keep hot on a covered plate.

Remove the vegetables and stir the sauerkraut with a fork.

Pile the sauerkraut in the shape of a dome on a long wide platter. Overlap the slices of ham in a straight line on top of the sauerkraut, alternating with slices of bacon, thick slices of sausage, and slices of pig's knuckle; finally, surround the dish with the frankfurters placed on the edges of the platter.

On the side serve a bowl of very creamy potato purée (pages 357–8) or steamed potatoes (page 357).

This dish must be served very hot, on hot plates.

COLD PORK

Porc rôti froid avec salade de chou vert ou rouge

COLD ROAST PORK WITH A SALAD OF GREEN OR RED CABBAGE
Whether the meat comes from a leftover roast or is specially cooked for the purpose, cold pork should be carved in very thin slices just before serving.

Arrange the slices on a round platter, in a circle, overlapping them. Decorate with *cornichons* cut into different shapes.

Serve with a green cabbage salad—the heart should be firm and white—or red cabbage cut into thin shreds and soaked in boiling vinegar. Just before serving, mix in some sweetened chopped apples.

Cold pork can also be served with a vegetable salad: potatoes, cauliflower, string beans, lima beans, mixed vegetables, etc. . . . or *cornichons,* capers, etc.

All cold sauces made with a mayonnaise base are excellent accompaniments.

HOME-MADE SAUSAGES AND COLD CUTS

Rillettes de porc

POTTED MINCED PORK
Remove the ribs, the gristle, and the skin from a fresh pork belly. Rub vigorously on all sides with 7 tablespoons sea salt, crushed very fine and flavored with bay leaf, thyme, mace, cinnamon, sage, marjoram, basil, nutmeg, cloves, and pepper. Wrap the meat in a dish towel, and soak the meat in that mixture for 2 hours.

Cut the meat into 1¼-inch squares. Melt 5 tablespoons pork fat in a casserole, add the pieces of meat, and fry slowly, browning them on all sides but keeping the fat clear and white.

With a skimmer remove the pieces of fat that have turned golden, drain the melted fat into a container. Chop the pieces of fat, and return them, along with 1 cup water, to the pan where the meat is frying. Cook very slowly for 7 to 8 hours, stirring often and maintaining the level of liquid by adding more water as the water in the pan evaporates.

At this point in the cooking the water should be almost totally reduced; remove from the heat, and season with 1 teaspoon paprika. Add the drained fat to the purée of cooked meat and fat, and mix well until the meat is completely cold and is a fine smooth paste that gives the impression of being well cooked and blended—these qualities result from the slow cooking.

Divide the *rillettes* among medium-sized earthenware pots of about 2 cups each; pack down to avoid pockets of air, and cover with a ¹⁄₈-inch layer of melted lard. To preserve the *rillettes* for a long period of time, when you have filled the pots, heat them in a *bain-marie* for 25 minutes. While cooling, stir each pot often to keep the contents perfectly homogeneous.

Cover with fat and aluminum foil.

Pâté de foie de porc

PORK LIVER PÂTÉ

½ pound ham fat or fresh
  pork fat
½ pound lean pork meat
  or veal, the tendons
  removed
1 pound pork liver
3½ tablespoons salt
Pinch mixed spices
  (page x)
2 shallots, finely chopped
1 medium-sized onion,
  finely chopped
1 tablespoon cognac
½ pound bread soaked in
  milk and squeezed
1 tablespoon chopped
  parsley
3 eggs
4 slices fresh pork fat
1 bay leaf
Sprig thyme
Flour-and-water dough

Method. Cut the ham or pork fat, the lean pork or veal, and the liver into ³⁄₄-inch cubes. Place all these ingredients on plates and season with the salt and the spices.

In a skillet partially melt the pork fat. Brown slightly, then add the liver; sauté, and as soon as the liver is seared, sprinkle with the shallots and onion; sauté again for a few seconds, then add the meat; sear quickly, remove from the heat, and pour on the cognac. Mix to dissolve the juices that have stuck to the skillet. Empty everything into a bowl and let cool.

Chop everything, either with a chopper or with an electric meat grinder, not too fine. Add the bread, the chopped parsley, and the eggs. Work the mixture with a wooden spatula until it is blended.

Check the seasoning by poaching a small ball of pâté in boiling water or in the oven. Correct the seasoning, if necessary, with added salt and spices.

Line the bottom and sides of a pâté terrine or mold with 3 slices of pork fat. Fill a 1½- to 2-quart terrine with the chopped meat, cover with the fourth pork fat slice, and top with the bay leaf and thyme. Cover and seal with a layer of dough made with flour and water.

Note: The terrine or mold should be just big enough to be filled with the chopped meat.

Cooking. Place the terrine in a roasting pan half filled with hot water; keep it at the same level by adding more boiling water during the cooking.

Place in a 300° oven for about 1 hour. The pâté is done:

1. When the fat that rises to the surface is clear (if it is cloudy, the pâté is not yet cooked).
2. When the fat is clear, meat juices collect on the edges of the terrine. When this juice becomes meat glaze, the pâté is cooked.
3. When a thin larding needle, inserted into the pâté and removed after 2 minutes, is clearly hot against your hand, the pâté is completely cooked.

Remove from the oven, and take off the cover. Cool for 15 minutes. Then cover with a piece of white paper or foil the size of the terrine and top with a piece of wood the same size. Place a weight (about 1 pound) on it. Let cool completely under the weight. In choosing the weight, be guided by the fact that its purpose is to compress the ingredients of the pâté while it is being cooled without squeezing out the fat that is still liquid. If there has been no pressure, the pâté will break when cut; if there is too much pressure, the fat will be squeezed out of the pâté which will become dry and lose all its flavor and smoothness.

Wash the outside of the terrine and present it on a long platter on top of a napkin. Cut slices ⅛ inch thick at the table.

Fromage de tête de porc
HEAD CHEESE

1 small pig's head, about 6–8 pounds
Seasoned sea salt (page x)
1 pound fresh pork rind
2 large carrots
2 large onions each stuck with 1 clove
1 small garlic head, peeled
Large *bouquet garni*
Salt and pepper

Method. Singe the head and scrape carefully; remove the brain and the tongue, then cut the head in two. Cut each half in two. Rub each piece and the tongue with crushed seasoned sea salt.

Repeat salting step 5 times; place the pieces of head, tongue, and the pork rinds in a bowl. Sprinkle lightly with a layer of salt, cover with a cloth, and let cure for 4 days in a cool place.

Then remove the meat and the salt from the bowl; wipe each piece. Place the meat with the tongue, the rinds, the carrots, the onions, the garlic, and the *bouquet garni* in a pan big enough to hold everything without any empty spaces; cover with water.

Bring to a boil slowly; remove the scum as it rises to the surface. Reduce the heat, and simmer, covered, for 3 hours. The water should barely quiver.

After the meat is cooked, drain the pieces of head, the tongue, and the rinds. Let cool, then remove all the bones. Reserve the flat part of the ears. Cut the meat, the tongue, and the thick part of the ears into ¾-inch cubes and place in a bowl.

Check the saltiness of the meat, and add more salt if necessary. Spice with a couple of turns of the pepper mill, and add ½ cup of the cooking juice strained through a very fine sieve. (Taste beforehand for seasoning.) Mix everything well.

Line a terrine with the pork rinds, or use a salad bowl, which is wider at the top and can be unmolded easily. First pour in one-third of the mixture of meat and cooking liquid; on top, spread half the flat parts of the ears; then a second third of the meat and the remaining ears; finish with the remaining meat.

Cover the mold with a round piece of white paper or a piece of foil and top with a piece of wood the same size. On top of the wood, place a weight of about 1 pound.

Let cool for 24 hours.

The head cheese can be served unmolded or in the terrine. We advise leaving it in the terrine if it is not going to be eaten in one meal. To keep the edges from drying out, protect the cut side with a piece of foil.

Variety meats

The French word *triperie* includes:

For beef: The liver, heart, lungs, tongue, kidneys, brain, spinal marrow (called in French *amourette*), cheeks, feet, and belly

For veal: The liver, heart, lungs, kidneys, spinal marrow, sweetbreads, intestinal lining, head, feet, and brain

For lamb and mutton: The kidneys, liver, brain, tongue, sweetbreads, and feet

For pork: The liver, kidneys, brain, feet, head, blood, stomach, and intestines

Most of the recipes below can be used for any of these various parts of any of these four animals. This applies to the liver, heart, lungs, kidneys, spinal marrow, and brain.

The cooking time for some—such as the sweetbreads and the tongue—is determined by their size. There are special recipes for the feet, depending on whether they come from an ox, a calf, a lamb, or a hog. The same is true for the belly, stomach, heart, liver, lungs, and head.

Pork blood and intestines are mainly used for pork sausages.

Cervelle de mouton, de veau, de porc

LAMB, VEAL, OR PORK BRAIN

1 lamb, veal, or pork brain
1 quart water
3/4 tablespoon salt
1 tablespoon vinegar or juice of 1/2 lemon
1/2 bay leaf
Sprig thyme
1 medium-sized carrot, chopped, cooked for 25 minutes, cooled, and drained
1 medium-sized onion, chopped, cooked for 25 minutes, cooled, and drained

Method. Soak the brain for 12 hours in cold water, changing the water often. Remove the membranes and the coagulated blood that surround the brain and soak again until the brain is very white.

Unless you are using a recipe calling for uncooked brains, poach the brain in a *court-bouillon* made with 1 quart water, flavored with salt, vinegar or lemon juice, bay leaf, thyme, carrot, and onion.

Place the brain in the cold *court-bouillon,* bring slowly to a boil, skim, and poach without boiling on a very low flame for 10 to 15 minutes, depending on the weight.

If the brain is not going to be used immediately, keep in the *court-bouillon.*

Cervelle au beurre noir ou noisette

BRAINS IN BROWN BUTTER

When the brains are poached and warm, cut into slices 1/8 inch thick, and place flat on a hot plate; season with a pinch of salt, a dash of freshly ground pepper, and a pinch of freshly chopped parsley; moisten with *beurre noir* (black or dark brown butter) or with *beurre noisette* (hazelnut-colored or light brown butter) cooked in a frying pan just before serving.

Add a splash of vinegar to the very hot frying pan after the butter has been removed, and pour quickly over the brains.

221

Cervelle à la meunière
BRAINS À LA MEUNIÈRE

Use raw brains, soaked and with the membranes removed. Cut into slices about ⅛ inch thick, season with salt and pepper, then sprinkle with flour.

Meanwhile, heat 2 tablespoons unsalted butter in a skillet or a frying pan; sear the slices of brains, brown on both sides, and cook slowly for 5 minutes.

Place the slices on a hot plate, squeeze a quarter of a lemon over them, sprinkle with some chopped parsley, and baste with the cooking butter, adding extra butter, if necessary.

Beignets de cervelle sauce tomate ou Orly
BRAIN FRITTERS WITH TOMATO SAUCE (ORLY STYLE)

Cook the brains in a *court-bouillon*, and cut into large dices or slices. Salt and pepper, dip in a light frying batter, and plunge one at a time into very hot deep oil.

When the dough is crisp and golden, drain the fritters, pat dry, sprinkle with a pinch of salt, and place in a pyramid shape on a round platter on top of a folded napkin.

On top of the pyramid, place a bouquet of parsley, fried for a second in the hot oil; around the base place a lemon cut in half.

On the side serve a sauceboat of tomato sauce (page 77).

Sweetbreads can be prepared the same way.

Cervelle sautée à la niçoise
SAUTÉED BRAINS NICE STYLE

Follow the recipe for brains *à la meunière* (above). Place the slices in a circle on a round hot plate and cover them with stewed tomatoes Provençal style.

Stewed Tomatoes Provençal Style (For 1 person)

1 tablespoon olive oil
1 large tomato per serving, peeled, seeded, drained, cut into pieces
Salt, freshly ground pepper
½ garlic clove, crushed
Pinch parsley chopped with a tarragon leaf
6–8 small black cured olives, pitted
1 tablespoon unsalted butter

In a skillet heat the olive oil; when it is smoking, add the tomato. Season with salt and freshly ground pepper. Cook for 10 minutes. Then add the garlic, parsley, and tarragon and olives. Heat for 2 or 3 seconds; then off the heat add 1 tablespoon butter. Correct the seasoning of the stew, which should be a little thick; it should leave a taste of tomato and fresh butter on the palate. The flavor should be slightly piquant.

Amourette de boeuf ou de veau
SPINAL MARROW OF BEEF OR VEAL

Veal marrow is finer than beef marrow.

Method. Soak the marrow in water for at least 12 hours,

changing the water several times. Remove the membrane and the cords that surround it, being careful not to crush the central substance, which resembles brains.

Poach the marrow for 5 minutes in a *court-bouillon* made with salted water, 1 tablespoon vinegar per quart of water, 1 sprig of thyme, and 1 bay leaf. Place the marrow in cold water, then slowly bring to a boil, cool, and leave in the cooking liquid. *Amourette* is prepared in the same way as brains.

Le foie

LIVER

Beef liver is often stringy, always mediocre; pork liver is usually used in terrines and pâtés; lamb liver is used with the heart and lungs; only calf's liver has true culinary value.

Foie de veau à l'étuvée
STEWED CALF'S LIVER (For 6 people)
A Burgundian Specialty

20 large *lardons* of fresh pork fat
Salt and pepper, mixed spices (page x)
Chopped parsley
3 pounds calf's liver cut from the thickest part
1 veal or pork caul
2 tablespoons unsalted butter
Pork rind
1/4 pound onions, peeled and quartered
1/2 pound carrots (core removed), peeled and quartered
***Bouquet garni* (10 sprigs parsley, sprig thyme, 1/2 bay leaf)**
2 garlic cloves
1 tablespoon cognac

Method. Prepare the *lardons,* cutting them as thin as a ruler and the length of the liver; place them on a plate, season with salt and pepper, a pinch of chopped parsley, and a pinch of spices. Mix well. Marinate for 15 minutes, and insert *lardons* in the liver with a larding needle as you would for *boeuf à la mode* (pages 168–9).

Season the liver with salt and pepper and spices and wrap in the caul. Hold the caul in place with string.

In a saucepan or an earthenware pot or a tripe terrine just big enough to hold the liver, heat the butter and brown the liver; it must be seared to keep it from releasing its juice, which would make it stew. Turn over with a skimmer, so as not to prick the meat, and brown on all sides.

When the caul is golden, place the pork rind under the liver; around the liver add the onions, the carrots, the *bouquet garni,* and the garlic—everything sprinkled with a pinch of salt and a dash of pepper. Cover tightly.

Heat slowly. When you hear a light frying sound from inside the pan, place the pan in a 250° oven.

This dish can also be stewed on top of the stove or over charcoal; in that case, use a deep cover on top in which you also place hot coals (this is called a *doufeu*).

This is the oldest and the best way of stewing.

Cook for 3 hours. Halfway through the cooking add the cognac.

Since the pan is tightly closed, the steam cannot escape; and since it cooks very slowly, there is hardly any reduction of the juices from the meat and the vegetables. When the cooking is finished, the liver should still be bathed halfway in its juice.

To serve, place the liver on a plate and remove the string and what is left of the caul. Remove the *bouquet garni* and rub the vegetables through a strainer. Put this purée in a small saucepan. Degrease the cooking juices. Mix the juices into the purée until it has the consistency of a light *coulis* (a tomato sauce, for example).

If the steaming was properly done, the purée should absorb all the juice.

Pour the sauce on the liver and serve very hot.

Note: This dish is delicious served cold. In that case cool the liver in the sauce and remove to slice it.

Brochettes de foie de veau

CALF'S LIVER ON SKEWERS

Method. Clean the mushrooms, wash them, and remove the stems; peel the curved cap of each mushroom and the sides of the stem. Reserve the caps. Chop the stems and the peels very fine and add to the shallots, which have been chopped and softened in 2 tablespoons butter in a skillet. Dry quickly over a high flame.

Moisten with dry white wine, boil to reduce almost totally; add the tomato purée and veal stock. Reduce by one-third, and thicken with *beurre manié* made with 1½ tablespoons butter and 1 teaspoon flour well mixed with a fork.

As soon as the *beurre manié* has melted in the boiling sauce, remove from the heat, correct the seasoning, and add the chopped parsley.

Remove the pork rind and cut the fat into 1¼-inch squares, ⅛ inch thick. Place in cold water and bring to a boil. Blanch for 5 minutes and drain.

Cut the liver into 1¾-inch squares, ¾ inch thick.

Preliminary cooking. Heat the oil in a skillet; as soon as it is smoking, add the mushroom caps cut into slices ⅛ inch thick. Sear them, season with a pinch of salt, then sauté on a high flame for 1 minute, and with a slotted spoon remove to a plate.

Reheat the oil, and sear the liver squares; season with salt and pepper, and sauté on a high flame just long enough to stiffen them; drain the liver, and remove to a plate.

Do the same for the squares of pork fat, but let them brown slightly.

Stringing on skewers. In a bowl, combine the liver, the pork fat, the sliced mushroom caps, and the sauce prepared with the mushroom stems *(duxelles).* Mix well, so that the meats are thoroughly coated with the sauce.

On metal skewers, string one piece of liver, one piece of pork fat, and one slice of mushroom cap; continue doing this, ending with a piece of liver.

Roll each skewer in fresh bread crumbs and set aside on a plate.

Cooking on the grill or broiling. Fifteen minutes before serving, sprinkle the food on the skewers with unsalted melted butter and place on a medium-hot grill or under a broiler. Turn them on all four sides until the bread crumbs are golden brown. Serve on the skewers accompanied by a sauceboat of tomato sauce or *maître d'hôtel* butter.

½ pound large, firm, white mushrooms
2 shallots
2 tablespoons unsalted butter
2 tablespoons dry white wine
2 tablespoons tomato purée
1 cup veal stock (page 72)
Beurre manié
1 teaspoon chopped parsley
½ pound lean salt pork fat
1 pound calf's liver
4 tablespoons oil or chicken fat
2 tablespoons fine bread crumbs
Tomato sauce (page 77) or *maître d'hôtel* butter (page 161)

Foie de veau grillé Bercy

BROILED CALF'S LIVER BERCY (For 6 people)

6 slices liver, ³/₄ inch thick (3¹/₂ ounces each)
4 tablespoons unsalted butter
Salt, pepper, and flour
3¹/₂ ounces beef marrow, soaked
1 shallot, finely chopped
¹/₂ cup dry white wine
¹/₂ cup veal stock (page 72)
Beurre manié made with 2¹/₂ tablespoons flour and 7 tablespoons unsalted butter
Chopped parsley
Juice of ¹/₄ lemon

Method. Brush the slices of liver with 3 tablespoons melted butter; sprinkle with salt, pepper, and flour. Shake off the excess flour, and sprinkle each slice with a few drops of melted butter; place under a very hot broiler or over burning coals.

After 2 minutes give each slice a quarter turn; the bars of the grill will sear a square design into the liver. In another 2 minutes turn the liver over; after it has cooked for 2 minutes on the second side, give it a quarter turn also. Remove the liver slices from the grill and place them on a serving platter. Cover with a glass bell, keep warm, and let stand.

Cut the marrow into very thin slices with a knife dipped in hot water. Place in a saucepan of boiling salted water and poach for 5 minutes without boiling.

Heat 1 tablespoon butter in a small skillet, add the shallot, and cook slowly without letting it brown; moisten with white wine and boil to reduce to 2 to 3 tablespoons, then add the veal stock and reduce by half. Add the *beurre manié;* then the marrow, well drained; a pinch of salt; a pinch of pepper; chopped parsley; and the lemon juice.

Heat slowly, shaking the saucepan so that the sauce thickens as the *beurre manié* melts.

Drain the liver juice from the platter; add it to the sauce, and pour the sauce over the liver slices. Sprinkle with chopped parsley and serve with a bowl of steamed potatoes.

Foie de veau sauté à la lyonnaise

SAUTÉED CALF'S LIVER LYONS STYLE (For 6 people)

4 tablespoons unsalted butter
6 slices liver
Salt and pepper
Flour
4 large onions
1 tablespoon vinegar
Chopped parsley

Method. Heat half the butter in a skillet or frying pan; meanwhile, season the liver with salt and freshly ground pepper; flour the meat and shake off the excess; sear in the butter when it has turned a light brown color. Cook on a high flame for 2 minutes; turn the slices, and cook for another 2 minutes; remove to a serving platter. Cover and keep warm.

Heat the remaining butter in the same skillet; when it is hot, add the onions cut into fine julienne or chopped fine; cook over moderate heat until brown, stirring constantly. When the onions are well softened, add the vinegar, without boiling, and the juice drained from the liver on the platter. Shake the skillet until all the juices sticking to the bottom of the pan have dissolved, and pour the onions and the juice over the liver. Sprinkle with chopped parsley.

Note: Pork liver can be cooked the same way.

Gras-double de boeuf

BEEF TRIPE

The tripe or the stomach of beef is usually bought cooked. If it is not, soak in water, scrub carefully, wash again, and blanch in boiling water for 25 minutes.

225

Drain the tripe, rinse, and scrape with a knife to remove any traces of scum or odor.

Cook the tripe for 6 hours in salted water, using 1 tablespoon salt per quart of water. The water should be boiling slowly. To the cooking liquid, add 2 carrots cut into pieces, 2 onions each stuck with 1 clove, a *bouquet garni* made largely of thyme and bay leaf, and 1 garlic head.

When the tripe is cooked, remove from the heat, let cool in the liquid, then drain. Roll up the tripe and refrigerate until ready to use.

Gras-double à la lyonnaise

TRIPE LYONS STYLE (For 6 people)

4 large onions
4 tablespoons oil
2 tablespoons unsalted butter
1³/₄ pounds cooked beef tripe (above)
Salt and pepper
Chopped parsley
1 teaspoon vinegar

Method. Cut the onions into fine julienne; heat the oil in a skillet big enough for the tripe to be placed flat. As soon as the oil is smoking, add the onions and cook them slowly, stirring often. Toward the end of the cooking, raise the heat to brown the onions well.

Lift the onions onto a plate with a slotted spoon, leaving the oil in the skillet; add the butter.

Cut the tripe into large strips, about ¹/₄ inch thick. Heat the butter and the oil, and sear the tripe. Taste a piece to see if there is enough salt, and correct the seasoning. Add some freshly ground pepper. Sauté the tripe on a high flame to brown it slightly. When it is light brown, add the onions, sauté, and mix well; finish by adding chopped parsley.

Place the tripe in a bowl, and pour the vinegar into the hot skillet; pour over the tripe. Add another pinch of chopped parsley and serve on very hot plates.

Langue de boeuf ou de mouton

BEEF OR LAMB TONGUE

Beef tongue is served fresh or salted ("purple tongue"). It should always be soaked in water for 2 to 3 hours. Remove all inedible parts and the skin. It is easy to remove the skin if the tongue is placed first in a kettle of cold water and boiled for 20 minutes.

Place the tongue in a bowl, and as soon as it is cold, cover it with a large handful of sea salt; let it macerate for 24 hours before cooking it. Turn the meat from time to time when the salt starts to dissolve.

Langue de boeuf braisée à la bourgeoise

BRAISED BEEF TONGUE

Follow the recipe for *boeuf à la mode* (pages 168–9), but instead of larding the tongue, wrap it in one or more pieces (bards) of pork fat.

LAMB TONGUES WITH LENTIL PURÉE (For 6 people)

6 lamb tongues
1/4 pound pork rind, blanched
1 carrot, thickly sliced
1 medium-sized onion, thickly sliced
Bouquet garni
1 cup dry white wine
2 cups bouillon or lightly salted veal stock (page 72)

Method. This dish will take 2 1/2 hours to cook.

Soak the tongues in cold water for 2 hours, changing the water several times.

Pick over the lentils to remove small stones or any other debris. Wash lentils, and soak in tepid water for 2 hours. [*Editor's note:* Or use the presoaked variety, following directions on the package.]

Place the tongues in a saucepan, cover with cold water, and boil for 8 minutes. Remove with a slotted spoon and plunge into a bowl of cold water. When cold, drain, cut off the larynxes, and remove the skins. Set aside on a plate.

Drain the soaked lentils and place in a saucepan, cover with water, and boil for 5 minutes; drain again.

Choose a skillet big enough to hold the tongues in one layer. In the skillet melt a couple of *lardons* cut from the salt pork fat for the lentils; then add the carrot and the onion and brown. Remove the vegetables and reserve. Put in the tongues to coat quickly with fat. Remove them; return the slices of carrot and onion to the bottom of the skillet, add the *bouquet garni;* cover with the blanched pork rind, then place the tongues on top.

Pour over the white wine, and boil to reduce by two-thirds; then cover with the bouillon or veal stock.

Place a piece of buttered wax paper cut the same size as the skillet on the tongues, cover, and cook in a 300° oven for 2 hours.

Lentil Purée

2 cups dried lentils
1 onion stuck with 1 clove
1 small carrot, cut in half
1/2 head garlic
Small *bouquet garni*
1/3 pound salt pork fat
2 tablespoons unsalted butter
Peppercorns

Put just enough water in a saucepan to cover the lentils. Add 1/2 tablespoon salt per quart of water, the onion stuck with the clove, the carrot, the garlic, the small *bouquet garni,* and the pork fat cut into 6 slices. Bring to a boil and add the blanched lentils, skim, and lower the heat; simmer over the lowest possible flame for 1 3/4 to 2 hours. [*Editor's note:* Or follow directions on the lentil package.]

When the lentils are cooked, drain, remove the garnish, and rub the lentils through a very fine sieve. (When starchy foods are cold, it is harder to put them through a sieve.) Pour the purée into a saucepan, and reduce over a high flame, stirring with a wooden spatula. When the purée has thickened, return it to the proper consistency by adding some braising juice from the tongues. Butter off the flame and crush a few peppercorns over the top; do not boil.

Presentation. By now the juice in which the tongues are cooking has been reduced through evaporation. At the last minute uncover the tongues, baste with their juice, and raise the oven heat to its highest temperature. The juice will caramelize slightly and cover the tongues with a shiny coating. The result is an attractive and tasty glaze.

Pile the lentil purée in the shape of a dome in a shallow dish, then add the tongues, the tips up and the glazed side showing.

Baste each tongue with a tablespoon of the braising sauce, strained through a very fine sieve.

In a circle at the base of the tongues place 6 slices of salt pork fat.

On the side, in a sauceboat, serve the remaining sauce, after correcting the seasoning.

Note: This dish can be served cold accompanied by mayonnaise or a sauce made from mayonnaise, such as *tartare* sauce (page 91).

Rognons de veau, de mouton, de porc
VEAL, MUTTON, LAMB, OR PORK KIDNEYS

Mutton, lamb, veal, or pork kidneys should not boil; they should always be broiled, sautéed, or cooked in a skillet, very quickly, just before serving.

The principle of cooking kidneys is always the same.

When kidneys are broiled, place them, slit open, on a very hot grill over glowing coals or under a very hot broiler.

When kidneys are sautéed, place them in a skillet large enough so that the pieces of kidney will lie flat and will be seared as soon as they come in contact with the hot butter.

Veal kidneys are usually pan broiled; place them in a hot earthenware or metal pan where very hot butter will sear them. Do not cook them over very high heat, because then the kidneys will be dry. Mutton or lamb kidneys should be pink when cooked, veal or pork kidneys should be pale brown.

Rognons de mouton grillés
BROILED LAMB KIDNEYS (For 6 people)

12 lamb kidneys
Salt and pepper
¹⁄₄ pound *maître d'hôtel* butter (page 161)

Method. Split the kidneys lengthwise two-thirds of the way through; remove the thin membrane that covers them; open the kidneys and put crosswise on skewers, 2 on each; brush with melted butter, season with salt and pepper, and place on a very hot grill over half-burned charcoal. Turn after 3 minutes; cook them until slightly pink. Place on a long hot platter; in the center of each kidney, put 1 teaspoon *maître d'hôtel* butter and, at each end of the platter, the garnish preferred.

Usually fried potatoes are used: straw, Pont-Neuf, puffed, matchstick, etc. (pages 355–6).

Rognons de mouton grillés vert-pré
BROILED SPRING LAMB KIDNEYS

Broil and serve as directed above in the recipe for broiled lamb kidneys; garnish one end of the platter with straw potatoes (page 355), the other end with a bouquet of water cress.

Rognons sautés au madère

SAUTÉED KIDNEYS WITH MADEIRA

**2 lamb kidneys or ½ veal
kidney per serving
2½ tablespoons unsalted
butter
7 tablespoons *espagnole*
(page 76) or *demi-glace*
sauce (page 76) or
thickened veal stock
(page 72)
½ cup Madeira
Salt and pepper**

Method. Cut the lamb kidneys in two lengthwise, remove the membrane, and cut each half in two diagonally. Veal kidneys should be diced. Remove the tubes and the fat. On a plate, season with salt and freshly ground pepper.

Heat 1 tablespoon butter in a skillet; as soon as the butter "sings," sear the kidneys; sauté rapidly over a high flame. During this step, do not let the kidneys stew, or they will harden. Brown lightly and place on another plate.

In the skillet, boil the Madeira to reduce by half; add the *espagnole* or *demi-glace* sauce. Bring to a boil for 2 minutes; off the flame add 1½ tablespoons butter to thicken the sauce. Serve very hot in a bowl. Instead of the *espagnole* or *demi-glace* sauce, you can use lightly salted veal stock; boil to reduce by half, and thicken with a pinch of cornstarch or 1 tablespoon butter mixed with 1 tablespoon flour.

Rognons sautés aux champignons

SAUTÉED KIDNEYS WITH MUSHROOMS

Sauté the kidneys as described above, replacing the Madeira with white wine; then in the cooking butter used for the kidneys, for each serving, sauté 4 mushrooms, quartered, with a pinch of salt; add the mushrooms to the kidneys. Finish the sauce and thicken as directed above for the sautéed kidneys with Madeira.

Rognons de veau ou de mouton au riz pilaf

VEAL OR LAMB KIDNEYS WITH RICE PILAF (For 6 people)

**13 tablespoons unsalted
butter
2 large onions, finely
chopped
1 pound Carolina rice or
any other good-quality
rice
4¼ cups bouillon or white
stock (page 73)
3 veal kidneys or 6 lamb
kidneys
Chopped parsley
Madeira sauce (page 79)**

Method. In a skillet, heat 7 tablespoons butter; when the butter "sings," add the onions, and cook slowly without letting them brown. Wash the rice several times until the water is clear. Washing is the only way to get rid of the smells or dust of the bag in which the rice comes. [*Editor's note:* Clean boxed rice need not be washed.]

When the onions are soft, add the rice. Stir the rice over a low flame until it is completely coated with butter.

Add the hot bouillon or white stock.

Cook in a 325° oven, covered, without stirring for 18 to 20 minutes.

Remove from the oven; cut 3 tablespoons butter into small pieces, scatter over the rice, and mix in with a fork.

While the rice is cooking, remove the skins and tubes from the kidneys. Slice and sauté in 3 tablespoons butter, following the recipe for sautéed kidneys with Madeira above.

Presentation: Pack the rice in a ring mold and unmold on a round platter. In the center place the kidneys and sprinkle with chopped parsley. Pour the Madeira sauce around the rice.

229

Note: Rice cooked this way can be varied by adding condiments or garnishes that are listed in the section on rice (pages 369–72).

Rognons de veau à la moutarde
VEAL KIDNEYS WITH MUSTARD (For 6 people)

3 veal kidneys
Salt and pepper
1 shallot, finely chopped
7 tablespoons unsalted
  butter
1 tablespoon cognac or
  fine champagne brandy
4 tablespoons thick *crème
  fraîche* or heavy cream
1 teaspoon Dijon mustard
Pinch chopped parsley
Juice of ¼ lemon

Method.   Remove the membrane and fat from the kidneys and season with salt and freshly ground pepper.

Cook the shallot in a small skillet in 1 tablespoon butter without browning.

Heat 4 tablespoons butter in an earthenware saucepan, and brown the kidneys quickly on all sides. Place in a 425° oven for 12 minutes; remove while the kidneys are still clearly pink.

Put the kidneys on a plate, cut into slices ⅛ inch thick, replace in the saucepan; baste with 2 teaspoons of the cognac or champagne brandy; flame while stirring.

Remove the kidney slices from the saucepan and add to the shallot in the skillet. Cover and keep warm.

While the pot in which the kidneys cooked is still very hot, add the *crème fraîche,* boil to reduce by half; then off the heat season with the mustard and a few turns of the pepper mill. The mustard should not boil.

Pour the contents of the skillet—the kidneys, the shallot, and the juice from the kidneys—into the saucepan. Cut the remaining butter into small pieces and sprinkle on top along with the chopped parsley, then the remaining cognac or brandy; mix well, so that all the ingredients are coated with the thickened sauce.

Correct the salt, squeeze in the lemon juice, and serve on very hot plates.

The kidneys should be cooked until half done if the cooking is to be continued after they have been flamed with the cognac (optional).

Ris de veau
SWEETBREADS

Sweetbreads is not a common dish in France because of its high price; but it belongs to *haute cuisine*, of which it is one of the most delicate and characteristic dishes.

The preliminary preparations do not vary: sweetbreads must be soaked in water for at least 5 to 6 hours, and the water changed several times.

Scald by placing in a saucepan of cold water and slowly heating to the boiling point, stirring from time to time with a wooden spoon, until the outer tissues stiffen. Drain, and rinse under running water.

Trim the sweetbreads, which means separating the round lobes from the long lobes and removing the filaments of fat and the cartilages.

From this point on, the preparation differs, depending upon the recipe used.

Ris de veau aux écrevisses et aux pois gourmands

SWEETBREADS WITH CRAYFISH AND TINY GREEN PEAS
(For 6 people)

6 sweetbreads from young calves
¼ cup chopped onions
¼ cup chopped carrots
7 tablespoons unsalted butter
¼ cup vermouth
¼ cup dry white wine
2 cups white stock (page 73)
Salt and pepper
Bouquet garni
2 cups *crème fraîche* or heavy cream
¼ pound fresh mushrooms, washed and sliced
14 ounces shelled crayfish (see Editor's note, page 64)
¾ ounce truffles, cut into julienne
1⅓ cups tiny green peas

Method.   Soak the sweetbreads in water for 24 hours. Blanch briefly, rinse, and trim.

Stew the chopped onions and carrots in 3 tablespoons butter in a saucepan. Place the sweetbreads on top. Moisten with the vermouth, white wine, and white stock. Season with salt and pepper. Add the *bouquet garni,* cover, and cook very slowly for 20 to 30 minutes.

Remove the sweetbreads. Strain the sauce through a fine sieve. Boil to reduce nearly to a glaze.

Add the *crème fraîche* and the mushrooms. Reduce again until the sauce thickens and becomes very smooth.

Correct the seasoning; then add the sweetbreads, the shelled crayfish, and the truffles.

Cook the green peas in salted water, then sauté in the remaining butter and season; place in a shallow dish. Arrange the sweetbreads on top, covering them generously with the sauce along with the crayfish, the truffles, and the mushrooms.

Serve immediately on hot plates.

Note: The green peas can be replaced with spinach cooked in butter.

Ris de veau poêlé

BRAISED SWEETBREADS

6 sweetbreads
Fresh pork fat for larding
1 large onion, sliced
1 medium-sized carrot, sliced
Fresh pork rind cut into pieces
Salt
Small *bouquet garni*
Melted unsalted butter
Veal stock (page 72)
2 croutons, fried in butter

Method.   Soak, scald, and trim the sweetbreads as described on page 230. Wrap in a dish towel and place on a plate; cover with a piece of wood with a 4-pound weight on top. Leave under that weight for at least an hour. Using a thin larding needle, lard the sweetbreads with several rows of fine-cut fresh pork fat as directed for the filet of beef Richelieu (pages 156–7).

Choose a skillet that is just large enough to hold the sweetbreads. Butter the bottom of the skillet well and put in it 1 large onion, sliced, and 1 medium-sized carrot, sliced.

Heat slowly over a low flame until the vegetables begin to brown. Add the fresh pork rind, and place the sweetbreads on top, the larded side up, and sprinkle with salt.

Finish by filling any empty spaces with the trimmings of the sweetbreads and adding a small *bouquet garni*.

Baste with melted butter and cook, covered, in a 300° oven for 25 to 30 minutes, depending upon the size of the sweetbreads.

It is important to baste often with the cooking butter and the juice that escapes from the sweetbreads.

If the sauce boils down too rapidly, add a few tablespoons of good veal stock and cover the skillet.

As the cooking proceeds and the basting becomes more frequent, the sauce will become syrupy and caramelize, coating the sweetbreads with a tasty glaze. To give this glaze a beautiful shiny golden color, remove the cover for the last few minutes of cooking.

The cooked sweetbreads should not fall apart; the meat should remain firm and should not squash when sliced.

To serve, place the sweetbreads on 2 croutons of bread fried in butter, and arrange on a heated round platter; baste the sweetbreads with 1 tablespoon of the cooking juice, strained through a very fine sieve. Too much juice would soak the croutons.

Serve the remaining juice in a sauceboat.

If the braising was properly done, the juice will be quite reduced but there will be enough to serve with the sweetbreads. This golden, fat, and naturally thickened juice is delicious in itself.

Accompany the dish with a vegetable: green peas *à la française* or green peas cooked in butter; asparagus tips coated with cream; mushrooms, *cèpes,* morels, *girolles;* spinach; string beans; braised vegetables; lettuce, endives, celery; purées of various vegetables; truffles; rice pilaf; noodles; braised or sautéed tomatoes; or else a *financière,* Nantua, or Périgord sauce (see index).

Ris de veau braisé à blanc
SWEETBREADS BRAISED À BLANC

A "white" braising of sweetbreads uses the same recipe as above, but without browning the ingredients: the sweetbreads are cooked, covered, in a 275° oven.

This recipe is used when the sweetbreads are accompanied by a garnish thickened with a white sauce, such as *velouté,* cream, or béchamel sauce; or if the sweetbreads are going to be served in a *vol-au-vent,* a timbale, or as *bouchées* (puff pastries), etc., with a white sauce.

Ris de veau grillé maréchal
BROILED SWEETBREADS (For 6 people)

1³/₄–2 pounds sweetbreads
12 small artichoke bottoms
11 tablespoons unsalted butter
Salt and pepper
1 bunch green asparagus
6 medium-sized truffles
1 tablespoon cognac or fine champagne brandy
¹/₂ cup mushroom purée (page 323)

Method. Soak, scald, rinse, and trim the sweetbreads as described on page 230.

Cook the artichoke bottoms in a clear stock, drain, and stew in 3 tablespoons butter in a skillet. Season with salt and pepper.

Cook the asparagus in a large kettle of boiling water, the tips tied in a small bouquet, and the tender part of the stalks cut into small dice. Drain and stew in 2 tablespoons butter in a skillet; remove the asparagus tips and place them on a plate; off the heat coat the remaining asparagus with 1 tablespoon butter. Season with salt and pepper.

Cut the truffles into thick slices and sauté rapidly in 2 tablespoons very hot butter. Season with salt and pepper. Moisten with the cognac or champagne brandy and cook to reduce almost completely. Off the heat, add 1 tablespoon butter.

Split the sweetbreads in half, brush with 1 tablespoon melted butter, season with salt, and broil under a low flame.

Place the sweetbreads on a hot round platter, arranging them in the shape of a cross; between each two arms of the cross put 3 artichoke bottoms; garnish the center ones with the truffle slices, those around them with the diced asparagus, on top of which place the asparagus tips. Inside the cross, pile the mushroom purée. Baste the sweetbreads with 1 tablespoon melted butter.

Escalopes de ris de veau sautées
SAUTÉED SLICED SWEETBREADS

Prepare the sweetbreads as described on page 230; slice each into 3 or 4 pieces, season with salt and pepper, dust with flour, and sauté in very hot butter in a skillet as you would for veal scallops. Place in a circle on a round platter with a vegetable garnish in the center. With 2 tablespoons veal stock dissolve the meat juices sticking to the bottom of the skillet, and pour these juices, mixed with the cooking butter, over the sliced sweetbreads.

Tête de veau
CALF'S HEAD (For 12 people)

1 young calf's head, whole, not boned
1 lemon
10 quarts water
6 tablespoons flour
1 cup white vinegar
2 carrots
2 medium onions stuck with 4 cloves
1 garlic head
Bouquet garni
Salt and pepper

Method. Trim and clean the calf's head. Soak in water for 24 hours. Drain and rub with lemon on all sides: snout, cheeks, ears, etc.

Prepare a *blanc:* fill a big kettle with 10 quarts water; mix the flour with some of the liquid and add it with all the other ingredients.

Place the calf's head in this richly flavored liquid. Bring to a boil. Cook about 2 hours on a low flame.

The calf's head is served accompanied by various sauces: vinaigrette, green, *gribiche, tartare,* rémoulade, etc. (see index).

Pieds de mouton
MUTTON FEET

In France, mutton feet (also called "trotters") are usually bought already blanched. First singe the feet and with the point of a knife detach the small woolly tufts between the two parts of the hoofs.

Mutton feet are cooked exactly the same way as calf's head and feet, which means in a *blanc*, but with a little less flour. Place the feet in the stock when it starts to boil.

Let simmer for 2½ to 3 hours. The feet are cooked when the main bone comes away from the skin easily without breaking it.

Let the feet cool in the cooking liquid and drain in a sieve.

233

Separate those from old animals and those that are not fully cooked. Cook them again.

Be sure to remove the bones while the feet are still hot, without breaking them; place the feet in a bowl with the cooking stock, strained through a fine sieve. Keep refrigerated; the cooking liquid will jell and preserve the feet for several days.

Pieds de mouton à la poulette

MUTTON FEET POULETTE (For 1 person)

4 or 5 mutton or lamb feet
2 ounces firm, white mushrooms
Pinch chopped parsley
4 tablespoons water
1 tablespoon unsalted butter
Juice of ¼ lemon
Pinch salt

Method. Cook the mutton feet following the recipe above; cool them in a little of their cooking liquid, drain on a plate, and remove the small bones—without spoiling the shape of the feet, if possible.

Place the feet in the cooking liquid again, and heat to the boiling point. The feet are then ready to be used.

Preparing and cooking the mushrooms. Clean the bottoms of the mushroom stems; wash in two different waters without letting them stand. Do this step quickly, so that the mushrooms do not turn brown.

Cut off the stem close to the cap and "turn" the cap. This means peeling it in such a way that it seems to have been cut in one motion (as one peels an apple in one long strip). After first removing the peel in a thin shaving, begin incising at the center with a sharp knife in your right hand, turning the cap with your left; continue cutting a spiral groove around the cap and finish at the edge. The mushroom cap will form a decorative rosette. Reserve the stems and peels to be used later.

As the mushroom caps are "turned," place them in a hot bouillon made with water, butter, lemon juice, and salt. When the mushrooms are all in the bouillon, cover the saucepan, raise the heat, and boil for 3 minutes; drain and place the mushrooms in a bowl, covered with a piece of buttered paper cut so that it will rest flat on the mushrooms; reserve the cooking liquid.

Poulette Sauce (For 1 quart sauce)

10 tablespoons unsalted butter
4 tablespoons flour
1 quart white bouillon
Mushroom stems and peels and cooking liquid from the caps
4 egg yolks
Dash nutmeg
Juice of ¼ lemon
Chopped parsley

Method. Melt 4 tablespoons butter in a 2-quart saucepan. When it bubbles, add the flour, mix, and cook slowly, without letting it brown, for 10 minutes. Stir often with a wooden spoon.

Let the mixture cool; then slowly add the boiling bouillon and most of the mushroom cooking liquid to the *roux*. As you slowly pour the liquid, mix with a whisk while the sauce thickens, to avoid lumps. As soon as the sauce comes to a boil, add the mushroom stems and peels; reduce the heat and simmer very slowly for 30 minutes. From time to time, remove the scum and the impurities that come to the surface at the edges of the saucepan.

Note: The same quantity of *velouté* sauce (page 77) could replace the sauce above.

Strain the sauce through a very fine sieve into a skillet, and off the heat thicken with the egg yolks as follows.

Place the yolks, with their white strings removed, in a bowl with a few tablespoons of the reserved mushroom cooking liquid, 6 tablespoons butter, and a dash of grated nutmeg.

While mixing the egg yolks with a whisk, to keep them from cooking, slowly add a ladleful of the boiling sauce. When the mixture is smooth, pour it all back into the sauce, while beating with the whisk. Heat the sauce slowly to the boiling point.

Remove from the heat and enrich with additional butter. Correct the seasoning.

Finishing the feet with the poulette sauce.   Drain off the cooking liquid from the feet and wipe them dry with a cloth; place in a skillet. Reheat the mushroom caps and their stems in a little of their cooking liquid, then drain, scatter them over the feet, and cover with sauce—about 3/4 cup of sauce for 5 feet. Squeeze the lemon juice over the top.

Heat everything together to coat the feet and the mushrooms with sauce; when everything is well mixed, sprinkle with a pinch of freshly chopped parsley and serve on a very hot plate.

Pieds de mouton sauce rémoulade
MUTTON FEET WITH RÉMOULADE SAUCE

Cook the mutton feet in a white stock, then carefully drain, bone completely, and coat with a rémoulade sauce made with a generous quantity of mustard and seasoned with finely chopped raw onion.

Place in a bowl and sprinkle with chopped chervil and parsley.

Pieds de porc
PIGS' FEET

Pigs' feet can be prepared like a calf's head (page 233) and braised like mutton feet (pages 233–4). They are, however, usually prepared by a recipe that is designed for them and that makes a delicious dish.

Pieds de porc grillés sauce rémoulade
BROILED PIGS' FEET WITH RÉMOULADE SAUCE

Method.   Use front feet, which are better than hind feet. Singe or scald them and scrape.

Wrap each foot in a strip of cloth tied firmly with string to keep the foot from losing its shape during cooking.

Place the feet in a braising pan, cover with cold water, and add vegetables and seasonings as for a *pot-au-feu* (pages 50–1), adding also 1 quart dry white wine for each 10 quarts of water. Add salt.

Bring to a boil, skim, cover, simmer very slowly, either in the oven or on top of the stove, for 10 hours.

Let the feet cool in the cooking liquid, drain, and remove the strips of cloth. Dip the feet in melted butter, then in fresh bread crumbs.

To serve the feet, sprinkle with melted butter and broil slowly in a broiler or over coals.

Accompany with a bowl of sautéed potatoes or potatoes *mousseline* (page 360) and a sauceboat of rémoulade sauce (page 91). Serve on very hot plates.

Pieds de porc grillés sauce béarnaise
BROILED PIGS' FEET WITH BÉARNAISE SAUCE

Use the same method and garnish as for the broiled pigs' feet with rémoulade sauce (above). Instead of rémoulade sauce use a *béarnaise* sauce (page 89).

This chapter includes turkeys and guinea hens, ducks and geese, squabs, and chickens—which form the most important group, consisting of roasting chickens and capons, the chickens called *à la reine* (queen), spring chickens, and the very young pullets.

These inhabitants of the chicken coop are succulent when they are roasted.

Roasting chickens and capons are often on the menu of a grand dinner, preceding the main course.

Frying chickens are preferable sautéed; they make a remarkable entrée. Spring chickens and very young chickens are best cooked in a casserole or broiled.

Of the chicken giblets, the wings, the neck, and the gizzard are used for light entrées; the liver, the combs, and the kidneys are used for certain garnishes.

Roasting chickens and capons may be roasted, poached, or braised. They are the leaders of the group because of the particular methods used and care taken in their raising.

These chickens weigh from $2^3/_4$ to 6 pounds, sometimes more. They are distinguished by their size, their whiteness, and the fine grain of their skins; their necks and feet are large, their spurs elongated.

Whether roasted, poached, or braised, roasting chickens and capons are prepared in the same way.

Draw, singe, and remove the pinfeathers buried in the skin; truss the birds. There are two ways to truss a chicken, depending upon the way it is going to be cooked: roasted, poached, or braised.

In the first two cases the feet are singed or blanched, their skin removed and spurs shortened. During the cooking, the feet are held close to the breast by the trussing.

In the third case, the feet, trimmed the same way, are then folded back on the thighs, and the first joints, with the exterior tendons severed, are tucked into the breast skin through incisions made on the sides. The feet are thus fastened to the thighs on either side of the breast.

If the chicken is going to be poached, rub the breast with a quarter of a lemon to keep it white; and cover the breast with a piece of fresh pork fat.

If the chicken is going to be studded with truffles, to facilitate this step, it is necessary to firm the meat by dipping the breast and the thighs in boiling bouillon or white stock for a few seconds.

Very young chickens are ready to appear on a menu when they are 7 to 10 weeks old. They are generally roasted or broiled.

The "spring" chicken is one that is 4 to 5 months old; it is usually cooked in a casserole, broiled, or roasted; it is sometimes sautéed.

The chicken called *à la reine* is one that has been force fed and is in between the age of a spring chicken and that of a roasting chicken; it is used for *suprêmes* of chicken and is usually sautéed. This bird also can be roasted, baked in a casserole, or braised.

3³/₄-pound roasting chicken (about 3 pounds drawn)
1 pound truffles
2 tablespoons Madeira
1 tablespoon cognac
2 tablespoons oil
Sprig thyme
¹/₂ bay leaf
Salt and pepper
Mixed spices (page x)
1 pound fresh pork fat or lard
¹/₄ pound raw *foie gras* (if unavailable, add ¹/₄ pound extra pork fat)
2 slices fresh pork fat for barding
Melted butter or chicken fat

Poularde de Bresse truffée rôtie

TRUFFLED ROAST CHICKEN (For 6 people)

Method. Before cooking the chicken, stuff it.

Scrub and wash the truffles carefully (they will lose about 3¹/₂ ounces in this process); peel and retain the peels. From the largest truffles cut a dozen thick slices, place in a bowl, and add 1 tablespoon Madeira; the truffles should soak in it for a little while.

Cut the remaining truffles in quarters and marinate in the cognac, the remaining Madeira, oil, thyme, bay leaf, a pinch of salt, a few turns of the pepper mill, and a dash of mixed spices.

Skin the pork fat and cut into small pieces, removing any membranes; pound in a mortar. When completely crushed, add the *foie gras* and work the mixture into a fine paste. Put the mixture into a pot and heat gently to soften the fat so it will go through a fine sieve easily.

Strain into a bowl and add the quartered truffles, the truffle peels (finely chopped), and the remaining marinade and 1¹/₂ tablespoons salt, 3 peppercorns, and a dash of mixed spices. Remove the thyme and the bay leaf, and mix well to obtain a smooth paste.

The chicken should be drawn entirely through the neck. Lift the breast skin and slide the slices of truffles set aside between the skin and the meat. Put the stuffing into the chicken, fold the neck skin over the hole, and truss and bard the bird.

To roast the chicken, cover with buttered white paper to protect the breast. Place the bird in a roasting pan on a rack so that it will not rest in the melted fat. Brush with melted butter or chicken fat and place in a 350° oven.

The cooking should be slow, at an even temperature, and the chicken should not be basted, but it should be turned from time to time. It will take 1¹/₂ hours to cook (it is a long roasting time because the stuffing was not previously cooked).

Ten minutes before the end of the cooking time, remove the paper and the barding and let the bird brown lightly; during this time, baste it with the melted fat coming from the stuffing.

Test the chicken for doneness by pricking with a trussing needle at the thickest point of the thigh. If the juice runs clear and white, the chicken is cooked; if the juice runs pink, let the bird stand for a few minutes in a low oven, protecting the breast with the fat removed earlier.

Serve with the juice of the chicken, partly degreased.

Poularde poêlée châtelaine

BRAISED CHICKEN (For 6 to 8 people)

Method. Clean the chicken, season it inside and out, truss, and bard it. Place in a casserole with 2 tablespoons melted butter.

Cover and cook for 40 to 50 minutes in a 325° oven or

3³/₄-pound chicken
2 slices fresh pork fat for
 barding
4 tablespoons unsalted
 butter
50 chestnuts
2 cups bouillon or veal
 stock (page 72)
1 celery rib

3³/₄-pound chicken
10 carrots, cut and
 trimmed in the shape of
 olives
10 small turnips, cut and
 trimmed in the shape of
 olives
10 small onions
6 leeks, white part only,
 cut into pieces 2¹/₂ inches
 long
Bouillon or blond veal
 stock (page 72)
Coarse salt

simmer on top of the stove. Keep an eye on it, turning the chicken on its sides and its back, but rarely on its breast.

Since there is almost no evaporation, the juice that collects in the bottom of the pan will be rich, fat, and golden.

Slowly broil the chestnuts, or fry them; peel and poach in a little bouillon or clear veal stock. Flavor the stock with a small celery rib and the remaining butter. The chestnuts should still be slightly firm when removed from the heat.

Fifteen minutes before the end of the cooking time remove the bard and the trussing, and place the poached chestnuts around the chicken.

Simmer, uncovered. Baste often, carefully, to avoid breaking the chestnuts. The breast will brown slightly.

Place the chicken on a long platter and arrange the chestnuts around it, like a necklace of large pearls. Baste with the chicken juice.

Poularde au gros sel

CHICKEN WITH COARSE SALT

Method. Draw, singe, and truss the chicken; place in a saucepan just big enough to hold it easily. Add the carrots, turnips, onions, and leeks.

Cover with bouillon or blond veal stock; bring to a boil, skim, and poach, covered, on a very low flame.

Drain the chicken, and place on a round platter; arrange the vegetables in small bouquets as a garnish.

On the side in a sauceboat serve the bouillon, which, if the saucepan used for poaching was of the correct size, will be very well flavored because of the limited quantity of liquid used.

On the side serve a dish of coarse salt.

Poularde pochée à l'estragon et au riz

CHICKEN WITH TARRAGON AND RICE

Poach the chicken as in the recipe above, but use only one-third of the vegetables.

Place the chicken on a round platter with these side dishes:
1. A sauceboat of the bouillon in which you have cooked 1 teaspoon tapioca until completely softened. Let a few leaves of tarragon steep in this bouillon, lightly thickened by the tapioca. Strain through cheesecloth.
2. A dish of rice pilaf (page 371).

Poularde de Bresse au riz sauce suprême

CHICKEN WITH RICE AND SUPRÊME SAUCE

Method. Poach the chicken, following the recipe for chicken with coarse salt (above). The cooking juice should be about 5 cups, made with 1 onion and a *bouquet garni*.

3³/₄-pound chicken
5 cups cooking juice
1 medium-sized carrot
1 onion stuck with a clove
Bouquet garni
¹/₂ pound rice
7¹/₂ tablespoons unsalted
  butter
1 tablespoon flour
¹/₂ cup thick *crème fraîche*
  or heavy cream
¹/₂ teaspoon lemon juice
Dash grated nutmeg

Wash ¹/₂ pound rice in cold water, changing the water several times until it is quite clear; place the rice in a saucepan and add enough cold water to cover generously; boil 5 minutes, stirring from time to time; drain, wash again in tepid water to remove the starch, which would make the grains stick together, and cook in a 425° oven for 15 minutes.

When the rice is cooked, separate the grains with a fork, adding 2¹/₂ tablespoons butter.

Sauce

In a saucepan, melt 1¹/₂ tablespoons butter; mix in the flour; cook 10 minutes without browning.

Let the mixture cool; then add, stirring, ³/₄ cup very hot stock from the poaching. Bring to a boil, stirring with a whisk until the sauce is at the boiling point; simmer 10 minutes slowly.

Strain the sauce through a very fine sieve or a double cheesecloth into a skillet; raise the heat, and boil to reduce the sauce by half, stirring with a wooden spoon. The sauce will be too thick; give it the proper consistency by adding *crème fraîche* or heavy cream. Off the heat season the sauce with lemon juice and grated nutmeg. Correct the salt, if necessary, and finish the sauce by adding remaining butter. The sauce should be very white and creamy.

To serve. *First method:* Pile the rice on a long footed platter (like a cake stand). Remove the pork fat and the strings from the chicken, leaving the breast exposed, and place on top. Cover the breast with a coating of the finished sauce.

Serve the remaining sauce in a sauceboat.

Second method: Present the chicken bare on a serving platter, after removing the pork fat and the strings. Baste the bird with 1 tablespoon of the poaching stock.

Serve the rice on the side in a bowl and the *suprême* sauce in a sauceboat.

Poularde pochée princesse

POACHED CHICKEN WITH ASPARAGUS, ARTICHOKES, AND TRUFFLES

Follow the above recipe but do not make the rice.

To the *suprême* sauce add pieces or slices of truffles, stewed in butter, and add butter to the sauce also. If you use canned truffles, add the truffle juice to the sauce.

Serve as above; around the chicken, place artichoke bottoms, cooked in white stock and stewed in butter, then topped with steamed asparagus tips coated with butter or with a spoonful of *suprême* sauce.

Suprêmes de volaille, filets et côtelettes de volaille

SUPRÊMES OF CHICKEN, CHICKEN FILLETS, AND CHICKEN CUTLETS

These names are literary cooking terms and have little to do with the anatomy of the bird. They are all synonyms, designat-

241

ing the same part of the chicken—the fleshy and tender tissues that cover the left and right sides of the breastbone. *Suprême* is used for a roasting chicken; fillet and cutlet for the chicken *à la reine* and the plump spring chicken.

Whatever the name, this part, which is very tender, is taken from the carcass in three steps: (1) First remove the wing, then the skin covering the breast; (2) make a deep incision in the flesh through to the bones of the carcass, cutting along the breastbone on the right and left sides; (3) place the knife blade in the wing joint and, sliding it close to the carcass, remove the fillet and the *filet mignon,* which means the entire fleshy part of the breast, in one piece; the bones will be clear of any flesh if this step has been done carefully.

Each of the two *suprêmes* from a large chicken consists of three parts: the *filet mignon,* which is clearly separate, and the fillets, cut into two or three parts on the bias to produce heart-shaped pieces; flatten them slightly.

The fillets taken from a chicken *à la reine* or from a spring chicken remain whole, but without skin or bones.

The cutlets are made by keeping part of the wing bone attached. The name cutlet is also given to chopped raw chicken or finely diced chicken thickened and reshaped to look like a cutlet.

Because of the extreme delicacy of this cut of chicken, the three basic cooking methods take very little time:
1. Season the chicken breast with salt and pepper; dust with flour, carefully shaking off the excess. Place the chicken pieces, side by side without squeezing them, in a skillet with some hot melted butter. Sear and brown quickly on both sides; do not raise the heat suddenly.
2. Dip the pieces of chicken breast in melted butter, season with salt and pepper on both sides; place in a thickly buttered skillet; squeeze a few drops of lemon juice on top; cover, place in a 425° oven for 5 to 8 minutes, depending on the thickness.
3. Dip the pieces of chicken breast in melted butter, season, roll in fresh bread crumbs, sprinkle with a few drops of melted butter or melted chicken fat, and grill or broil at a high temperature.

It is important that the chicken *suprêmes* be cooked only minutes before serving them. This dish cannot wait. Furthermore, these pieces should never be boiled.

This way of serving chicken is not so expensive as one might imagine. The carcass is used to make or to enrich consommés or soups; the giblets and the back can be made into a stew or sautéed; the legs can be broiled or poached and diced for various uses such as cutlets, *rissoles* (filled pastry turnovers), croquettes (page 12), etc.

Poularde de Bresse truffée mère Brazier
CHICKEN WITH TRUFFLES MÈRE BRAZIER (For 4 people)
Method. Prepare the chicken as usual, which means pluck, singe, and draw it; slide the truffle slices under the skin (4

3¹/₂–4-pound roasting chicken
8 large slices of truffle
¹/₂ lemon
Salt and pepper
1 medium onion stuck with cloves
4 leeks, white part only
¹/₂ pound new carrots
¹/₄ pound white turnips
1 celery rib

around the breast and 2 under the skin of each thigh). Then rub the chicken on all sides with the lemon; truss it.

Put 2 quarts water in a kettle; add salt and pepper. Add the onion, the leeks, the carrots, the turnips, and the celery rib.

Bring to a boil; plunge in the chicken; lower the heat, and simmer.

Chicken must be poached without great haste. Allow 30 to 40 minutes for a 3¹/₂-pound chicken.

The chicken is served with the bouillon and the vegetables—carrots, turnips, leeks—and a rice pilaf (page 371). Serve coarse salt on the side.

Volaille de Bresse sautée au vinaigre
CHICKEN SAUTÉED WITH VINEGAR (For 4 people)

3-pound roasting chicken, drawn, and cut into 8 pieces
10 tablespoons butter
Salt and pepper
4 shallots, chopped
1 cup good wine vinegar

Method. Heat 7 tablespoons butter in a skillet big enough to hold the pieces of chicken. Season the pieces with salt and pepper; brown lightly. The butter should remain light in color.

Cover, and continue cooking in a 425° oven for about 20 minutes.

When cooked, place the pieces of chicken on a platter, cover, and keep warm.

Sauté the chopped shallots without letting them brown in the butter in the skillet. Deglaze with the wine vinegar. Boil to reduce by half and beat 3 tablespoons butter into the sauce. Pour the sauce on the pieces of chicken, carefully coating them.

Poularde de Bresse truffée en vessie
Joannes Nandron
CHICKEN WITH TRUFFLES IN A BLADDER JOANNES NANDRON (For 4 people)

4-pound roasting chicken
8 large slices of truffle
¹/₄ pound veal from the *filet mignon*
5¹/₂ tablespoons heavy cream
Salt and pepper
3¹/₂ tablespoons cooked diced carrots
3¹/₂ tablespoons cooked diced turnips
3¹/₂ tablespoons cooked diced celery root
3¹/₂ tablespoons cooked green peas
3¹/₂ tablespoons cooked sliced string beans
White part of a cooked leek
1 pork bladder soaked in salted water
1 tablespoon Madeira
10 quarts white chicken bouillon

One can add to the ingredients 3¹/₂ tablespoons of diced truffles and *foie gras* and also the chicken liver, diced.

Method. Carefully draw the chicken and bone the body, leaving the wings and the legs. Slide the slices of truffle under the skin on the breast and the thighs.

Veal forcemeat. In a blender, chop ¹/₄ pound veal from the *filet mignon,* seasoned with salt and pepper. Place the meat in a bowl; set the bowl in a larger bowl of ice; and add, beating with a wooden spoon, 5¹/₂ tablespoons heavy cream. Mix in the cooked, cut-up vegetables. Correct the seasoning.

Stuff the cavity with the vegetable and veal mixture. Insert the leek in the center.

Close up the chicken, sewing the openings and trussing to return it to its original shape.

Turn the pork bladder inside out, and place the stuffed chicken inside, adding a pinch of salt and pepper and the Madeira. Close the bladder very tightly, tying it twice with string.

To cook, plunge the chicken in the bladder into a kettle of hot white bouillon, prepared with the giblets and the carcass of the boned chicken (page 242).

The chicken will be poached without boiling, at a slow simmer for 1½ hours.

Present the chicken on a platter, and remove it from the bladder in front of the guests.

Carve by first cutting away the wings and the legs. To serve, give each guest a piece of chicken and some of the stuffing.

Optional: The chicken can be accompanied by an excellent *suprême* sauce (page 241) and a rice pilaf (page 371).

Suprême de volaille Françoise
CHICKEN BREAST FRANÇOISE (For 1 person)

¼ pound green asparagus tips
6½ tablespoons unsalted butter
1 *suprême* (large chicken breast)
2 tablespoons *crème fraîche* or heavy cream
Salt and pepper
Dash nutmeg

Method. In salted boiling water, cook the asparagus with the tips tied in a small bunch and the tender part of the stems cut into pieces ½ inch long. Drain immediately and stew in a skillet with 1 tablespoon butter. Season with a pinch of salt. Just before serving, remove the asparagus stems to a hot plate and coat with 1 tablespoon butter.

Untie the asparagus tips and baste them with ½ tablespoon melted butter.

Ten minutes before serving, season the chicken breast with salt and freshly ground pepper, dust lightly with flour, and place flat in a skillet, just large enough to hold it, in which 2 tablespoons butter are bubbling. Baste the breast with melted butter, cover tightly, and cook in a 450° oven. Cooking time will be 5 minutes, or more, depending upon the weight of the chicken breast.

Pile the asparagus stems onto a hot round platter, topping them with the asparagus tips. Place the chicken on the platter and coat it with the juices from the skillet, deglazed with the *crème fraîche.*

Note: The deglazing is done in the following way:

After the chicken breast has been removed to the platter, pour the *crème fraîche* into the skillet; bring to a boil quickly; season with a pinch of salt, a turn of the pepper mill, and a dash of grated nutmeg. After boiling for a few seconds, the cream, liquefied by the heat, reduces slightly and thickens. At this point, remove from the heat and finish the sauce, without letting it boil, by adding 2 tablespoons butter. Correct the seasoning and pour the sauce over the chicken.

Suprêmes de volaille Antonin Carême
CHICKEN BREASTS ANTONIN CARÊME (For 4 people)

Potatoes Anna (pages 362–3)
4 raw truffles, cut into julienne
4 *suprêmes* (large chicken breasts)
Salt and pepper
6–7 tablespoons unsalted butter
¼ cup port wine
4 tablespoons *crème fraîche* or heavy cream

Method. Prepare potatoes Anna in a pan the diameter of a dessert plate, mixing in the raw truffles cut into large julienne. The potatoes should be no more than 1 inch deep.

Make 5 incisions on the surface of each of 4 chicken

breasts and insert pieces of raw truffle. Season with salt and pepper, and cook the breasts following the preceding recipe.

To serve, unmold the potatoes Anna on a hot round platter; place the chicken breasts on top; deglaze the chicken juices with the port wine and the *crème fraîche;* boil to reduce by half. Finish the sauce off the heat with 1 tablespoon butter. Baste the chicken breasts with 3 or 4 tablespoons butter, cooked until it is light brown. Serve the rich sauce from the deglazing on the side, in a sauceboat.

Côtelettes de volaille, volailles sautées ou fricassées, poulets sautés

CHICKEN BREASTS, PIECES OF CHICKEN SAUTÉED OR FRICASSEED, SAUTÉED CHICKENS

1 large frying chicken, cut up
3¹/₂ tablespoons unsalted butter or 1¹/₂ tablespoons unsalted butter and 2 tablespoons oil
Salt and pepper
Deglazing liquid: wine, spirits, cooking juice from mushrooms, chicken or veal stock, etc.

The best chicken to use is the chicken *à la reine* (large frying chicken), fleshy and tender.

It is cut up in a traditional and logical way:

First remove each thigh and drumstick, in one piece. Remove the thighbone by breaking it off at the joint to the shinbone, which will be cut off at the joint of the foot. Remove the foot at this joint and take off the claws; broil the feet or boil them a few seconds, then remove the skins by rubbing with a dishcloth while they are still warm.

Cut the wing tip at the joint, and remove the wing from the bird by inserting the blade of a knife in the joint of the upper bone located just where the neck begins. With your left hand on the thigh of the chicken, cut nearly up to the thigh, slicing off a third of the breast.

Cut the breast and the back apart with one crosswise blow with a meat cleaver or chopper through the middle. The breastbone with the white meat is thus separated from the carcass, which is then cut into two pieces. Trim any small bones that will hinder serving. Thus cut, the chicken will be in seven pieces, not including the giblets and the neck.

Method. The cooking method is the same, regardless of the sauce or the garnish.

Choose a skillet big enough to hold the pieces of chicken in one layer without squeezing them; the skillet must be neither too big nor too small.

Heat 3¹/₂ tablespoons butter or 1¹/₂ tablespoons butter and 2 tablespoons oil.

Place the pieces of chicken in the very hot butter, season with salt and pepper, and brown lightly on both sides. The butter must keep its light brown color; the browning must be done carefully.

Cover and continue cooking in a 425° oven. Remove the wings and the white meat after 8 to 10 minutes. Cook the legs, which are thicker and firmer, 5 to 8 minutes more.

When cooked, place the pieces of chicken on a plate, cover, and keep warm.

Then deglaze the skillet. During the cooking, the juices coming from the meat will stick, nearly solidified, to the bottom of the skillet, where they will form particles of light chicken glaze. They must be dissolved so that they can be used to make the sauce, which has a distinctive character and flavor.

First drain off most of the fat used for browning the chicken; pour in the skillet a liquid specified in the recipe chosen: wine, spirits, cooking juice from mushrooms, chicken stock, or veal stock, etc.

Boil to reduce, following the recipe, and add the sauce or stock.

Simmer the pieces of the carcass in it, for 3 to 4 minutes, along with the feet, neck, wing tips, gizzard, and thighs; then, without letting them boil, add the wings and the breast.

Place the pieces of chicken on a very hot long or round platter in the following order: the carcass in the middle; to the right and to the left, the feet and the wing tips; at either end, the neck and the gizzard (reserve the liver for other garnishes or entrées); on top, the breast; then the legs, crossed; and, to finish, the wings.

Pour the sauce, correctly seasoned, over the chicken to coat it completely.

Note: If the chicken is going to be poached, the method is the same but the browning is omitted. Instead, sear the meat in hot butter and cook it, covered, in a 325° oven. The deglazing for the sauce is done the same way but usually with *crème fraîche* or heavy cream, *velouté* (page 77), *allemande* (page 77), or béchamel sauce (page 78).

Volaille de Bresse aux écrevisses
CHICKEN WITH CRAYFISH (For 4 people)

3-pound chicken
24 crayfish *à la bordelaise* **(page 142)**
4 tablespoons unsalted butter
3¹/₂ tablespoons chopped shallots
3¹/₂ tablespoons carrots (core removed), chopped as for a *mirepoix*
2 tablespoons cognac
¹/₂ cup dry white wine
¹/₄ pound tomatoes, coarsely chopped
1 garlic clove, crushed
Chopped parsley and tarragon

Method. After singeing the chicken, draw and cut into eight pieces following the recipe for sautéed chicken (pages 245–6).

Meanwhile, prepare the crayfish *à la bordelaise,* removing the shells of 20 of the crayfish tails and reserving the sauce.

In a heavy skillet, heat 3 tablespoons butter. When the butter is hot, add the pieces of chicken, seasoned with salt and pepper. Brown the pieces of chicken lightly, turning them to brown evenly on all sides.

Add the *mirepoix* made with the shallots and the carrots. Cover the skillet, and place in the oven or on top of the stove on a low flame for about 15 minutes to half cook the chicken.

Boil the juice to reduce slightly, then degrease if necessary. Deglaze with the cognac and the white wine. Reduce again and add the chopped tomato and the garlic. Finish cooking the chicken, covered.

When the chicken pieces are cooked, remove to a plate. Again, boil the juices to reduce slightly, and add the *bordelaise* sauce from the crayfish. Boil for a few minutes; thicken with 1 tablespoon butter or 2 tablespoons heavy cream.

To finish, put the pieces of chicken back into the sauce, adding also the 20 crayfish tails.

To "marry" the different flavors, let the dish simmer for a few minutes, and correct the seasoning, if necessary.

To serve, place the pieces of chicken and crayfish on a shallow serving platter, coat them with the sauce, and sprinkle over the chopped parsley and tarragon.

Garnish with 4 beautiful crayfish in their shells.

Poulet sauté aux champignons

SAUTÉED CHICKEN WITH MUSHROOMS

1 large frying chicken, cut up
1 tablespoon oil or 1 tablespoon unsalted butter
¹/₄ pound mushrooms, cleaned, washed, and thinly sliced
1 tablespoon flour
Salt and pepper
¹/₂ cup dry white wine
1 cup veal stock (page 72) or 1 cup bouillon and 2 tablespoons tomato purée
2 tablespoons unsalted butter

Method. Follow the instructions for sautéed chicken (pages 245–6). When the chicken has been cooked and removed from the skillet, the skillet is ready to be deglazed.

Add oil or butter to the skillet; heat, and add the mushrooms. Sauté the mushrooms quickly on a high flame, and as soon as the juices have evaporated completely, sprinkle with the flour; season with salt and pepper, mix, and brown lightly. Moisten with white wine; boil to reduce by half, and add 1 cup veal stock or 1 cup bouillon and 2 tablespoons tomato purée. Stir carefully into the flour.

Bring to a boil, and boil 5 minutes; add the pieces of carcass and the legs; simmer 5 more minutes. Remove from the heat, and add the breast and the wings; coat the chicken with the sauce and the mushrooms; remove to a platter.

Finish the sauce by boiling to reduce it, if it is too thin; correct the seasoning, and add 2 tablespoons butter; stir well, and do not boil.

Sprinkle with a pinch of chopped fresh parsley.

Note: If you have *espagnole* sauce (page 76) or *demiglace* sauce (page 76), use one of them as the moistening liquid and do not add flour.

Poulet sauté à la Marengo

CHICKEN MARENGO (For 6 to 8 people)

1 chicken sautéed with mushrooms
Crushed garlic clove
¹/₂ cup dry white wine
1 cup tomato sauce (page 77)
¹/₂ cup veal stock (page 72)
Unsalted butter
1 dozen mushroom caps
6–8 small fried eggs
6–8 crayfish
6–8 croutons, fried in butter
6–8 thick slices truffle
Juice of ¹/₄ lemon
Pinch chopped parsley

Method. Follow the directions above for sautéed chicken with mushrooms for the first steps. Cook a crushed garlic clove in the butter for 1 second before deglazing the skillet.

Deglaze the skillet with wine; boil to reduce by two-thirds; moisten with tomato sauce and veal stock. Season with the cooked garlic clove.

Bring the sauce to a boil, first with the carcass and the legs; then follow the steps given in the recipe for sautéed chicken; and finish off the heat by adding butter. Correct the seasoning.

The presentation is done the classic way: Garnish the platter with mushroom caps, sautéed with the chicken and set aside, then coated with the sauce at the last moment; small fried eggs; crayfish (the claws turned back and stuck in the tails) cooked in a *court-bouillon* or sautéed in butter; heart-shaped croutons fried in butter; and thick slices of truffle, cooked in the sauce for 2 minutes before finishing.

Squeeze lemon juice over the dish, and sprinkle with parsley.

Note: It is easier, especially when given the variety of garnishes used here, to correct the seasoning of the sauce after having placed the chicken on the platter. This makes it possible, in this case, to simmer the mushrooms and the slices of truffle in the sauce for a few minutes and add the butter off the heat afterward.

Poulet sauté chasseur

SAUTÉED CHICKEN HUNTER'S STYLE

Proceed as for the chicken sautéed with mushrooms (page 247), making these changes:
1. Before sprinkling with the flour, add 1 teaspoon finely chopped shallots.
2. Before moistening with the white wine, add 1 tablespoon cognac; ignite for 2 seconds, then snuff out the flame with the cover of the skillet.
3. With the moistening liquid, add a large ripe tomato, peeled, seeded, and coarsely chopped.
4. With the butter, add ¹/₂ teaspoon each of chopped tarragon and chervil.

Note: The flour can be omitted if you have *espagnole* (page 76) or *demi-glace* sauce (page 76), with the fat removed. These sauces replace the liquid used with the flour as a thickening ingredient, and produce a better result.

Poulet sauté aux morilles ou aux cèpes

SAUTÉED CHICKEN WITH MORELS OR CÈPES

1 chicken sautéed with mushrooms (page 247)
1 tablespoon oil
¹/₂ pound morels or *cèpes*
1 teaspoon finely chopped shallots
Salt and freshly ground pepper
¹/₂ cup white wine
6 tablespoons veal stock (page 72)
2 tablespoons unsalted butter
Pinch chopped parsley

Method.   Follow the recipe for sautéed chicken with mushrooms up to the deglazing of the sauce.

After removing the chicken from the skillet, add 1 tablespoon oil and the morels or *cèpes,* cleaned very carefully (the undersides of the caps generally contain a great deal of sand); sauté over a high flame for 3 minutes; sprinkle with shallots, and season with salt and freshly ground pepper.

Place the pieces of chicken, except the breast and the wings, on the morels; cover, and stew in a 425° oven for 5 minutes.

Remove from the oven, and moisten with wine; boil to reduce almost completely, add veal stock, boil 2 minutes; add the breast and the wings, but do not let boil; finish off the heat by adding butter while stirring. Correct the seasoning, and pile on a platter. Sprinkle chopped parsley over all.

Poulet sauté printanier

SAUTÉED CHICKEN WITH SPRING VEGETABLES

Prepare and sauté the chicken following the classic method (pages 245–6).

Deglaze the skillet with 4 tablespoons veal stock.

Place the chicken on a platter and surround it with spring vegetables: carrots, turnips cut in olive shapes, onions cooked in butter and glazed, peas and string beans steamed and coated with butter.

Pour over the reduced juices.

Poulet sauté à l'estragon
SAUTÉED CHICKEN WITH TARRAGON

Sauté the chicken according to the basic instructions (pages 245–6). Place the bird on a platter; deglaze the skillet with $1/2$ cup dry white wine. Boil to reduce by half; add $1/2$ cup veal stock (page 72). Bring to a boil for 3 minutes, and off the heat correct the seasoning and add a pinch of chopped chervil and tarragon to the nearly boiling juice.

Baste the chicken with this juice, which should be thick.

With this dish, serve a bowl of small Parisian potatoes, lightly browned in butter (page 362).

Poulet sauté lyonnaise
SAUTÉED CHICKEN LYONS STYLE

1 chicken sautéed with mushrooms (page 247)
12 small onions
$1/4$ cup dry white wine
4 tablespoons veal stock (page 72)
Chopped parsley

Method. Cook the chicken in butter as for the sautéed chicken with mushrooms. Cook the onions in salted water.

After the breast and the wings have been removed, add the onions to the legs and the pieces of carcass, which should cook longer.

Simmer for 5 minutes.

Place the chicken on a platter; surround it with the onions, which will now be well soaked in the fatty juice of the chicken and lightly browned.

Deglaze the skillet with $1/4$ cup dry white wine. Boil to reduce by two-thirds, and moisten with veal stock. Correct the seasoning. Bring to a boil and immediately pour the sauce over the chicken.

Sprinkle the onions with chopped parsley.

Poulet sauté à la portugaise
SAUTÉED CHICKEN PORTUGUESE STYLE

1 chicken sautéed in half oil and half butter
1 onion, finely chopped
2 garlic cloves, crushed
$1/2$ cup dry white wine
3 large ripe tomatoes, peeled, seeded, coarsely chopped
Salt and pepper
Pinch chopped parsley
$3^1/2$ tablespoons unsalted butter

Method. Sauté the chicken using half oil and half butter.

When the wings and the breast are cooked, remove the pieces of chicken from the skillet. To the cooking butter add the onion; soften it slowly, then brown lightly. Add the garlic; heat for a second, then moisten with white wine; reduce almost completely; add the tomatoes. Be careful not to leave any seeds in the tomato pulp, and season with salt and pepper; add the chicken carcass and the legs and cook, covered, in a 425° oven for 7 to 8 minutes.

Remove the pieces of chicken.

If the sauce at the bottom of the skillet is not sufficiently reduced, raise the heat for a few seconds. Correct the seasonings.

249

Season with a pinch of freshly ground pepper and chopped parsley, added to the sauce off the heat. Coat the pieces of chicken with the sauce and place on a platter. Finish the tomato sauce, which should no longer boil, by adding the butter.

Cover the chicken with the sauce, and sprinkle with a pinch of chopped parsley.

Poulet sauté aux truffes
SAUTÉED CHICKEN WITH TRUFFLES

1 chicken sautéed in butter (pages 245–6)
$^1/_4$ pound raw truffles, quartered
1 cup champagne
2 tablespoons Madeira
$3^1/_2$ tablespoons unsalted butter

Method.   Sauté the chicken in butter.

In the second part of the cooking, along with the legs and the carcass, add the truffles.

Place the chicken on a platter, leaving the truffles in the skillet. Deglaze with the champagne. Boil to reduce by two-thirds. Off the heat finish the sauce with Madeira and butter. Mix the truffles into the sauce and pour over the chicken.

Poulet de Bresse au sel
ROASTING CHICKEN COOKED IN SALT (For 4 people)

$3^1/_2$-pound roasting chicken
Pepper
$8^1/_2$ pounds sea salt

Method.   Prepare the chicken for roasting and remove the feet. Pepper it lightly.

Line the bottom and the sides of a braising pan with aluminum foil. Spread a generous layer of sea salt on the bottom. Place the chicken, breast down, in the center of the pan. Cover the chicken completely with salt, and fold over the foil on top to enclose the chicken.

Place the braising pan in a 450° oven for $1^1/_4$ hours.

To serve, place the chicken in the foil on a platter. Remove the foil.

In front of the guests, break the block of salt. If the cooking instructions have been observed, the chicken should be golden brown.

Seasoned by the iodine in the sea salt, the chicken has an incomparable flavor, and its meat is succulent.

Volaille de Bresse à la broche
CHICKEN ROASTED ON A SPIT (For 4 people)

Choose a roasting chicken weighing about $3^1/_2$ pounds. Carefully draw and truss (page 238). Season inside and outside with salt and freshly ground pepper.

Put the chicken on a spit, and brush with $3^1/_2$ tablespoons melted butter. Place over a hot wood fire with glowing red coals. At regular intervals baste the chicken with the juice that collects in the drip pan.

For a chicken of this size, allow about 45 minutes' cooking time.

If the advantage of cooking a chicken on a spit is to be appreciated fully, the chicken should be eaten as soon as it is finished.

Serve the concentrated juice from the drip pan in a sauce-boat.

Note: One can slide truffle slices under the skin of the chicken before trussing it.

Poulet de Bresse en soupière

CHICKEN IN A SOUP TUREEN (For 4 people)

3-pound chicken
2 hearts lettuce, quartered
1/4 pound fresh green peas, shelled
1/4 pound young string beans
1/8 pound spring turnips, cut into sticks
1/4 pound young carrots, cut into sticks
4 small white onions
7 tablespoons unsalted butter
Salt and pepper
Pinch sugar
Flaky pastry (pages 382–3)

Method. Prepare the chicken (draw, singe, trim, and truss); place it in a large, ovenproof soup tureen with feet, called a *soupière à gratinée lyonnaise.*

Surround the chicken with the vegetables. Add the butter, and season with salt and pepper and a pinch of sugar.

Cover the soup tureen tightly with a thin layer of flaky pastry.

Place the soup tureen in a preheated 425° oven; 5 or 10 minutes later, cover the pastry with aluminum foil, so that it will not brown too much during cooking.

Cooking time is 1¾ hours in the heated oven, plus ¼ hour with the heat turned off.

To serve, place the soup tureen in front of the guests. Remove the pastry cover by cutting through the dough with the point of a knife. The steam that escapes is very agreeable.

Carve the chicken in the usual way. Serve a portion to each guest, accompanied by the excellent vegetables and a piece of the pastry cover.

Fricassée de poulet vallée d'Auge

FRICASSEE OF CHICKEN AUGE VALLEY STYLE

6½ tablespoons unsalted butter
3-pound spring chicken
Salt and pepper
1½ tablespoons flour
2 cups white bouillon
Bouquet garni
12 small onions
12 medium mushrooms, washed and quartered
Juice of ½ lemon
2 egg yolks
Dash grated nutmeg
¼ cup *crème fraîche* or heavy cream
Croutons

Method. In a skillet just big enough to hold the chicken, heat 2 tablespoons butter. Add the chicken, cut into pieces—the thighs separated from the drumsticks, the breast cut into three parts, the carcass into four; the wing tips, the neck, and the gizzard will be added.

Season with salt and freshly ground pepper.

Cook over medium heat to sear the meat. Do not brown. Stir often with a wooden spoon.

Sprinkle with flour, mix, and cook for a few minutes without letting the flour brown. Moisten by adding the bouillon and stirring it into the flour until the liquid reaches the boiling point. Add the *bouquet garni.* Cover, and simmer slowly for 35 minutes.

If you have no bouillon, replace it with water. In that case, you must flavor the liquid with 1 medium-sized carrot cut into quarters and 1 onion stuck with a clove. Add salt as needed.

While the chicken is simmering, cook the small onions, barely covered with water, with 1 tablespoon butter and a few grains of salt. Also cook the mushrooms for 4 minutes in 1 tablespoon boiling water, ½ tablespoon butter, the lemon juice, and a pinch of salt. Remove the mushrooms to a bowl.

Prepare the thickening ingredients: Place the yolks in a bowl; add 2 tablespoons of the cooking juice from the mushrooms, 1 tablespoon butter in bits, and a dash of grated nutmeg. Beat the *crème fraîche* into the egg yolks.

When the chicken is cooked, remove the pieces from the sauce and place them in another skillet; sprinkle the onions and mushrooms, both drained, on top.

Slowly pour 1 ladleful of the sauce into the mixture of egg yolks and cream, stirring with a whisk. Then do the opposite, adding the egg yolks and cream to the sauce. Heat for a minute, and remove from the heat just as the sauce reaches the boiling point; it should not boil.

Off the heat finish the sauce by stirring in the 2 tablespoons remaining butter. Correct the seasoning.

Strain the sauce through cheesecloth onto the chicken. Turn the chicken over in the sauce to coat it well, and place it on a hot round platter.

Around the chicken and vegetables arrange the bread croutons, cut into heart shapes and fried in butter.

Note: This recipe can be used for a young hen. The cooking time will be longer accordingly. The garnish can be supplemented with about 15 tiny carrots cooked following the recipe for glazed vegetables (pages 309–10), coated with the chicken sauce, and served on the side or mixed with the mushrooms and onions.

Coq au vin à la bourguignonne

CHICKEN WITH BURGUNDY (For 8 to 10 people)

4-pound chicken
Salt and pepper
$1/4$ pound lean pork fat
$3^1/_2$ tablespoons butter
12 small onions
$1/4$ pound mushrooms, washed
1 tablespoon flour
2 garlic cloves, crushed
2 quarts red Burgundy wine
Small *bouquet garni*
2 cups lightly salted bouillon or water
The chicken blood kept liquid with a little bit of vinegar, or 3 tablespoons pork blood
3 tablespoons cognac

Method.   Cut the chicken as for the sautéed chicken (page 245). Put the pieces, including the giblets but not the liver, on a plate, and season with salt and freshly ground pepper.

Cut the pork fat into *lardons* and place them in a skillet; cover with cold water and blanch for 5 minutes; drain and wipe dry.

In an earthenware pan heat the butter and brown the *lardons* slowly along with the small onions. When they are both golden, drain and set aside on a plate.

In the same butter and over high heat, cook the washed mushrooms, cut into quarters if they are too large. Brown the mushrooms slightly and add them to the onions and pork fat.

In the same butter sauté the pieces of chicken; then sprinkle the chicken with flour, mix well, and let brown, uncovered, in the oven.

After 5 minutes, remove from the oven, add the garlic, stir for 1 minute, and pour over the Burgundy wine. Heat to the boiling point, stirring continuously. Add the *bouquet garni,* the onions, the *lardons,* and the mushrooms. Add bouillon or water to cover. Cover the pan, and cook 45 minutes in a 350° oven.

Remove from the oven and drain the liquid from the chicken into a fine sieve.

If the sauce is too thin, having reduced too little during

the simmering, boil to reduce rapidly to the proper consistency before draining. Clean the earthenware pan.

After the liquid has been strained, return the chicken and the liquid to the earthenware pan; bring to a boil, correct the seasoning, and thicken as directed below.

Cut the chicken liver into large cubes, season with a dash of salt and pepper, sear rapidly in a skillet with 1 tablespoon butter; place in a sieve and rub through with a pestle. Combine the liver purée with the chicken or pork blood and dilute with the cognac.

Remove the pan with the chicken from the heat to stop the boiling; pour a little bit of very hot sauce, in a stream, into the bowl with the blood, stirring well with a whisk; then add all the liver and blood mixture to the chicken pan, shaking it in a circular movement to mix the sauce and the purée so that the sauce thickens without boiling; the heat of the saucepan will cook the blood and the liver.

Correct the seasoning again, and pour the chicken and sauce into a shallow dish or serve in the cooking pot. The pot is better, for this delicious dish should remain warm.

The thickened sauce should be very smooth.

This dish can be served with bread croutons cut into heart shapes and fried, and placed on top.

Coq au fleurie
COCK WITH FLEURIE WINE

It is preferable to use a grain-fed rooster or cock. If you are in the country, collect the cock's blood as it is killed. Before the blood coagulates, add $^1/_2$ cup wine and 1 tablespoon vinegar.

Method. Prepare the chicken in the usual way, cutting the bird into several pieces (legs and wings in four). Marinate the chicken in a bowl with the Fleurie wine. To flavor the marinade add: a carrot, an onion, a *bouquet garni* with some extra thyme, garlic, and peppercorns. For the marinade to be effective, the bowl must be kept in a cool place for a minimum of 24 hours.

In a skillet heat 1 tablespoon lard. Season the pieces of cock with salt; sauté quickly in the hot fat. When the pieces are browned on all sides, moisten with a little cognac, ignite, then cover the skillet to put out the flame.

Sprinkle the chicken with flour. After mixing well, place in a 425° oven for a few minutes. Add the carrot and onion, sautéed in butter, and the *bouquet garni*.

Moisten with the wine used for the marinade, bring to a boil, and stir well. Simmer, covered, on a very low flame.

Depending upon the age of the cock, cooking time will be 45 minutes to 1 hour.

When the cock is cooked, remove the pieces to another saucepan. Add glazed onions, *lardons,* and mushrooms.

Thicken the sauce in the first pan with the cock's blood or with pork blood, as for the royal hare Senator

1 grain-fed rooster or cock, with its blood (or pork blood)
$^1/_2$ cup wine
1 tablespoon vinegar
1 bottle Fleurie wine
1 carrot
1 onion, sliced
Bouquet garni with extra thyme
2 garlic cloves, unpeeled
10 peppercorns, crushed
1 tablespoon lard
Cognac
1–2 tablespoons flour
20 small onions, lightly glazed
$^1/_4$ pound pork fat, cut into *lardons,* blanched and slightly browned
1 pound small mushrooms, sautéed in butter
Croutons browned in butter

Couteaux (page 285) and after correcting the seasoning, strain the sauce onto the cock.

Serve the cock with croutons cut into points and browned in butter.

Poulet en cocotte à la bonne femme
CHICKEN IN A CASSEROLE

1 large frying chicken
3¹/₂ tablespoons unsalted butter
1³/₄ ounces lean salt pork fat, cut into *lardons* and boiled 10 minutes
10 very small onions, boiled 5 minutes
20 potatoes, cut the size and shape of olives, boiled briefly
Chopped parsley

Use a casserole big enough to hold the chicken and its garnish; this should never be overpowering, and it should be able to rest completely on the bottom of the pan, around the chicken, and cook in the juice of the chicken.

Method. Heat the butter in the casserole; add the chicken, seasoned, and cook it, covered, turning and basting often.

When the chicken is half cooked, surround it with the *lardons,* onions, and potatoes. Continue cooking in a 425° oven to brown the vegetables lightly. Season, taking into account that salt pork has been used. Sprinkle with chopped parsley just before serving.

Poulet de grain grillé à la diable
DEVILED SPRING CHICKEN

Prepare the spring chicken by slipping the feet and the drumsticks into incisions made in the skin on either side. Cut the connective tissue at the leg joints to make it lie flat when the heat touches it.

Split the chicken from neck to tail down the back, open it out, and flatten it slightly; season with a pinch of salt; place on a roasting pan, baste with melted butter, and roast in a 350° oven for 10 minutes.

Then brush with mustard slightly diluted with water; sprinkle with bread crumbs, baste with melted butter, and finish cooking in the broiler.

Serve with water cress, matchstick potatoes, Pont-Neuf potatoes, etc. (page 355), and with a sauceboat of deviled sauce (page 81).

Volailles rôties
ROAST CHICKEN

The chickens to cook by this method are called roasting chickens, frying chickens, or spring chickens.

Roasting in the oven and on a spit are the two different ways of cooking: they were discussed previously (pages 250–1).

The method is the same for all the chickens; only the cooking time varies, depending on the size and the weight of the chicken.

In the oven. Place the chicken, seasoned inside and out with a pinch of salt, on a roasting pan with a rack; baste it with melted butter. The chicken should be kept on its side as much as possible and basted often with the cooking butter—not with the cooking juice, which will remain at the bottom of the pan, because it is heavier.

If the cooking has been done carefully and slowly, the juice and the butter that have collected in the pan should be sufficient to sauce the chicken. If not, add 1 or 2 tablespoons hot water before finishing the cooking.

On a spit. The amount of glowing coals is based on the size of the chicken. Basting is done with the juice that collects in the drip pan with the fat.

The juice is the proper sauce for the chicken.

Roast chickens are usually served with a bunch of water cress, and the cooking juice, not degreased, is served on the side.

Poulet de grain grillé à l'américaine
BROILED SPRING CHICKEN AMERICAN STYLE

Follow the recipe for deviled chicken (page 254); place the chicken on a large long platter; on top place 6 slices of broiled smoked bacon, and 6 small tomatoes and 6 mushroom caps, both broiled. Serve with a sauceboat of deviled sauce (page 81).

Les volailles froides
COLD CHICKEN

Whether roasted or poached, any chicken that is going to be served cold should be kept in a refrigerator with the temperature set between 46° and 50°.

If a cooked chicken is kept too cold, it becomes hard, tasteless, and unpleasant to eat.

I would advise leaving the chicken to cool on a plate in a room other than the kitchen, if possible.

Serve the cold chicken like other cold meats, following the recipes given concerning garnishes and sauces.

Mayonnaise de volaille
CHICKEN MAYONNAISE

Shred one or more hearts of lettuce—the quantity needed for a given number of guests; salt this julienne and sprinkle with a few drops of vinegar. Mix and arrange in a dome in a crystal bowl or salad bowl.

Over it place pieces of chicken, skin removed, and cut into scallops. Spread over it a generous coating of mayonnaise (page 90). Decorate with designs made with red beets, tomatoes, capers, *cornichons,* pitted olives, quarters of hard-cooked eggs, anchovy fillets, marinated herrings, and in the center an opened heart of lettuce.

When ready to serve, mix the sauced and seasoned dish with the mayonnaise.

Mousse de volaille
CHICKEN MOUSSE

Follow the recipe for ham mousse (page 213). Use a light-colored aspic, the color of champagne.

Poularde pochée à la gelée
POACHED CHICKEN IN JELLY

Place a large hen or a large spring chicken in a deep saucepan just big enough to hold it. Cover the chicken with a white veal stock, rich in gelatinous substances, well spiced and clear (page 72).

Bring to a boil, remove the scum, cover, and poach at a simmer.

Place a bouquet of fresh tarragon in a bowl deep enough so that the chicken can be completely immersed in the cooking stock as it cools. Then place the chicken in the bowl, and pour the boiling cooking liquid over the top.

When the chicken has cooled, carve it following the advice given in the discussion of roasts (page 238); arrange the pieces of chicken in a crystal bowl, and through cheesecloth pour over the chicken stock, now lightly flavored with the tarragon.

If the poaching has been done correctly, the chicken stock should be clear and well flavored but not sufficiently stiff that it would be possible to unmold the dish as a whole.

This is the right consistency.

Keep refrigerated until ready to serve.

Dinde farcie aux marrons
TURKEY STUFFED WITH CHESTNUTS

Small turkey, 4–5 pounds drawn
Turkey giblets

Preparing the young turkey. Remove the wing tips; singe the bird and pull out the pinfeathers; draw the bird by first cutting through the skin of the neck down the back; loosen the skin and without disturbing it cut the neck off at the base. Work through this hole to eviscerate the turkey: detach and remove the wishbone, which blocks your finger from reaching inside the bird completely. Slide your finger inside in order to break all the membranes holding the organs: lungs, gizzard, heart, and liver.

Remove the organs one by one, being careful not to break the gall bladder, attached to the liver. Also remove the intestines, if they were not removed when the bird was killed, as they generally are.

Remove the tendons of the drumsticks, following the explanation above.

Trim the giblets: remove the pocket of bile and the stringy membranes from the liver; cut the liver into six pieces, season with salt and pepper and a dash of thyme and bay leaf crushed to a powder; assemble the pieces on a plate. Cut the two meaty pieces from the gizzard and remove the gristle. Place with the heart and the lungs alongside the liver. Add the neck.

Preparing the stuffing. Cut the ham or pork tenderloin into cubes; chop it very fine with the pork fat (rind removed); season this mixture with the spiced salt; add the heart, the lungs, and the two pieces of the gizzard—all finely chopped.

Cut the lard into small pieces, removing any membranes or fibers; mash with a pestle, and put this paste into a skillet; heat it very slowly to soften the mass and then rub immediately through a very fine sieve.

In another skillet melt 2 tablespoons of this strained pork fat. When it is smoking, add the pieces of liver; sear quickly and drain on a plate while still rare. As soon as the liver is cold, chop fine and place in a bowl.

In the same skillet place 1 tablespoon of the strained pork fat and heat it; as soon as the fat is hot, brown the chopped shallots and add the finely chopped ham or pork mixed with the turkey giblets. Stir continuously with a wooden spatula, leaving the skillet on a high flame for a few minutes—as long as necessary to half cook the stuffing.

Just before removing from the heat, add 1 tablespoon of excellent cognac or fine champagne brandy, ignite, and cover immediately.

Set aside to cool almost completely.

When this stuffing is tepid, pour into a container with the liver. Add the remaining strained pork fat and mix well with a spatula to blend the mixture. The best result can be obtained by using a mortar and pestle.

Place the mixture in a bowl and refrigerate.

Before using, test the seasoning by poaching 1/2 tablespoon stuffing in salted water. Correct, if necessary.

Preparing the chestnuts. Slash the skins of the chestnuts and plunge them for a few minutes into boiling oil or broil them in the oven. Remove the skins while the chestnuts are still hot; both layers will come off easily.

Place the peeled chestnuts in a deep saucepan with a celery rib; add bouillon to cover. Cook, letting the bouillon boil gently; stop the cooking when the chestnuts are still firm. Avoid crushing them.

Drain the chestnuts when they are tepid; add them to the stuffing, and mix well, taking care not to break the chestnuts.

Stuffing and braising the turkey. Once the turkey has been cleaned, the legs carefully singed or blanched and their skin and tendons removed, it is ready to be stuffed.

First season the cavity with salt and pepper through the hole made in the neck; then insert the stuffing and the chestnuts. Fold over the neck skin; and truss the turkey with two strings, the first one passing through the wing tips and holding the neck skin in place; the second one crossing the turkey at the level of the thigh and drumstick joints (which are folded toward the wings), then crossed over the legs at the joints of the feet. Then bard the bird with the 2 pieces of pork fat.

Place the prepared turkey in a braising pan, laying it on

Stuffing
Salt and pepper
Thyme
Bay leaf
3/4 pound fresh ham or pork tenderloin
3/4 pound fresh pork fat
3/4 tablespoon spiced salt (page x)
3/4 pound lard
2 shallots, peeled and chopped
1 tablespoon cognac or fine champagne brandy

1 3/4 pounds chestnuts
1 celery rib
Bouillon

2 large pieces fresh pork fat

its side; brush it with some pork fat specially set aside for the purpose, add the neck, sprinkle with a pinch of salt, and cook slowly in a 325° oven, covered.

Calculate the weight of the turkey plus the stuffing, and cook 20 minutes per pound.

Turn the bird often. Toward the end of the cooking remove the cover and then the pork fat so that the turkey will take on a beautiful golden color.

Remove the trussing strings and serve along with the cooking juice, slightly degreased.

Note: The ingredients for the stuffing are completely cooked, or nearly so, before being put into the turkey. This method has the advantage of allowing you to cook the turkey without adding any time (or very little) to the total cooking time because of the stuffing. This makes it possible to braise the turkey like an unstuffed bird, and to stop the cooking at just the right moment to obtain perfectly tender meat.

If the turkey were stuffed with raw ingredients, the cooking time would have to be increased and the turkey would become dry; turkey flesh becomes very crumbly when it is cooked too much. Furthermore, in spite of all, the chestnuts would remain completely raw.

Dinde de Crémieu truffée
TURKEY WITH TRUFFLES

Here, for winter, is my paternal grandfather's recipe, as it has always been made in my family. [*Editor's note:* Poultry must be kept very cold; this recipe may be better read than cooked.]

"Take a turkey of 4 to 6 pounds. Stuff it with 1 pound sausage meat and the same amount of sliced truffles. Slide some truffle slices under the skin before trussing the bird. Wrap your turkey in wax paper and enclose it in a potato sack. In the soil of your garden, dig a hole, not too deep, and bury the turkey. The cold and the humidity of the earth will allow the aroma of the truffles to come out fully. Two days later, prepare a *court-bouillon* with carrots, celery, onions, leeks, cloves, salt, pepper, a veal shin, and an oxtail cut into pieces. Poach your turkey for 1½ hours. Serve with vegetables and a rice pilaf."

Pigeonneaux aux petits pois
SQUABS WITH GREEN PEAS

General rules. Draw the squab but never remove the liver, which does not have a gall bladder.

Truss the birds by the method called *en entrée:* fold the legs and slide the ends of the drumsticks through incisions made in the sides of the breast. Tie them with a string, crossing the squab first at the wings and then around the legs.

Method. Remove the rind from the pork fat, cut into small

¼ pound fresh lean pork
  fat
4½ tablespoons unsalted
  butter
12 small white onions
3 squabs
4 cups green peas
Small *bouquet garni*
Pinch sugar

dice, place in cold water, and boil 5 minutes to blanch. Drain, wipe dry, and brown in a skillet with 1 tablespoon butter.

Drain the fat cubes with a skimmer and set aside on a plate.

In the same butter brown the onions until golden. Drain the onions with a skimmer and add to the pork fat.

Replace the onions in the skillet with the squabs, and brown them on all sides, cooking, covered, for 12 minutes. Remove and keep warm between two plates.

Return the onions to the same skillet, add the pork fat and the fresh green peas, the *bouquet garni,* and a pinch of sugar. Add 2 tablespoons water and cook, covered, on a high flame.

As soon as the peas are nearly cooked, which will take 15 to 20 minutes if they were recently picked, add the squabs, just to heat them. Do not let the birds boil.

Place the squabs on a shallow round platter; remove the *bouquet garni,* and off the heat add 3½ tablespoons butter to the peas; mix well, taste, and pour the garnish on the squabs. Serve immediately.

Note: The juice from the cooking should be reduced to a syrupy glaze; however, it must be sufficient to baste the peas.

Pigeonneaux en salmis

SALMI OF SQUAB

1 medium carrot (core
  removed), finely diced
1 medium onion, finely
  diced
2 shallots, finely diced
9 tablespoons unsalted
  butter
Salt and pepper
Pinch grated nutmeg
¼ pound mushrooms
1 cup good red wine
3 young squabs, killed by
  smothering to keep the
  blood in the meat
1 tablespoon cognac
Croutons

Method.   Stew the carrot, the onion, and the shallots in a skillet with 1½ tablespoons butter; season with salt, pepper, and nutmeg. When the vegetables are cooked, add the mushroom stems, cleaned, washed, and finely chopped. Moisten with the red wine; and cook slowly until the wine is reduced by half.

Roast the squabs in 3 tablespoons butter in a 450° oven for 12 to 15 minutes, depending upon their weight. They should be rare. Remove the squabs to a plate; in the same pan sauté the mushroom caps, whole if they are small and in quarters if they are medium or large, for 2 minutes. Season with a pinch of salt.

Cut the squabs into five pieces: the two legs, the two wings, and the breast. Remove the skin, and replace the pieces of squab in the skillet where the mushroom caps have just been browned.

Remove the livers from the carcasses and put on a plate; with a fork mash them with 3½ tablespoons butter.

Chop the carcasses into large pieces, along with the necks and the gizzards; place them in a duck press to extract all the blood and collect it in a bowl.

Mix the blood with the chopped vegetables cooked in wine; heat nearly to the boiling point. Stir with a whisk, but do not let boil.

Baste the pieces of squab with the cognac, ignite, and smother the flames right away.

Strain the vegetable, wine, and blood mixture (the *brunoise* sauce) through a fine sieve, rubbing the vegetables through. Pour on the squab.

Heat together, stirring, without letting the sauce boil. The

259

thickening will occur through the coagulation of the blood as it is heated.

Off the heat add the livers mixed with the butter. Spice with freshly ground pepper.

Place the squabs on a very hot platter and surround with bread croutons cut into heart shapes and fried in butter.

Pigeon en bécasse à l'assiette

SQUABS ON A PLATE (For 4 people)

4 squabs
Salt and pepper
7 tablespoons unsalted
  butter
2 tablespoons fine
  champagne brandy
1 cup white chicken stock
  (page 73)
1³/₄ ounces purée of *foie
  gras*
1³/₄ ounces fresh *foie gras,*
  finely diced
³/₄ ounce truffles, cut into
  julienne
4 bread croutons

Method.   After cleaning the squabs, season them; roast in 7 tablespoons butter in a covered pan in a 450° oven for 12 to 15 minutes.

When the squabs are cooked, remove them and keep warm.

Deglaze the pan with the brandy. Moisten with the white stock. Boil for a few minutes without reducing very much. Thicken the sauce by beating in the purée of *foie gras,* the diced *foie gras,* and the truffles.

On each plate place a large crouton browned in butter. On top place a squab, cut in half.

Pour over the sauce and serve immediately.

Note: Wood pigeons and doves can be cooked in the same way.

[*Editor's note:* Fresh *foie gras* (goose liver, not pâté) from France is available at specialty shops in large cities in the United States; it is very expensive.]

Canards et canetons

DUCKS AND DUCKLINGS

The French duck farmer offers two specimens, both of equal quality, but quite different from a culinary point of view: the Rouen duck and the Nantes duck. The swamps, furthermore, are full of wild ducks in varieties as numerous as they are decorative and delicious. I will talk about wild ducks in the game chapter. Here I will write only about the products of the duck farmer.

Canard rouennais

ROUEN DUCK

The Rouen duck is the largest of French ducks and can be compared to a Long Island duck.

The Rouen duck is killed in a unique way. The breeder smothers the bird, which allows the blood to remain distributed throughout the meat; this gives the duck its brown color and special taste.

However, this method has the drawback of hastening the spoilage of the meat during warm weather. It is, therefore, important to be sure that the duck is very fresh if it is going to appear on a summer menu. One can become quite ill from eating duck meat that has gone bad.

There are two ways to cook a *rouennais* duck that produce a superb but simple salmi, the best that one can imagine.

I, however, prefer the recipe that is a specialty of Normandy. I call it Rouen Duck from the Hôtel de la Couronne, to celebrate the famous restaurant of the brothers Dorin.

Le canard rouennais de l'Hôtel de la Couronne

ROUEN DUCK FROM THE HÔTEL DE LA COURONNE

1 *rouennais* duck, 3 pounds drawn
Salt and pepper
Duck liver and 3 additional livers, cut into large dice, seasoned
1³/₄ ounces fresh pork fat
2 shallots, finely chopped
1 tablespoon calvados or cognac
1³/₄ ounces fresh bread crumbs soaked in milk and squeezed
Spiced salt (page x)
2 tablespoons cognac

Choose 1 *rouennais* duck, weighing about 3 pounds drawn.

Method. Draw the duck through the neck and set aside the liver. Season the inside with salt and pepper.

Besides the duck liver, prepare 3 additional livers (chicken livers can be used), and mix well. Set aside on a plate.

Grind the pork fat. Melt 1 tablespoon of the fat in a skillet and stew the shallots in it. When the shallots are cooked, add the 3 additional livers; reserve the duck liver for later. Sear the livers on a high flame, keeping them rare; moisten with calvados or cognac, ignite, and smother the flame at once.

Pour the contents of the skillet into a sieve and rub the hot rare livers through it into a bowl.

Mix that purée with the remaining ground pork fat and the bread crumbs soaked in milk and squeezed.

Correct the seasoning.

Season with the spiced salt, and put the stuffing in the duck. Fold the bird's legs and truss.

Roast the duck in a 450° oven or on a spit over a hot fire for 18 to 20 minutes. The duck should be rare.

Carve immediately, first removing the legs, which will be very rare.

Turn the cut sides of the duck legs toward the grill to finish the cooking, and continue to carve. Remove the wings and then slice the breast. Place the slices on a hot round platter in the shape of a fan.

Open the carcass, remove the stuffing, and pile it at the base of the fan, crossing the legs on the edges of the stuffing. Cover the platter with another plate or a glass bell to keep it warm.

Quickly chop the carcass and place it in a duck press to extract the juices; add 2 tablespoons cognac to the bloody juice collected in a bowl. Coat the breast slices with the following *rouennaise* sauce.

Rouennaise Sauce

4 tablespoons unsalted butter
¹/₂ teaspoon finely chopped shallots
Dash powdered bay leaf and thyme
1 cup good red wine
¹/₄ cup *demi-glace* sauce (page 76)

Stew the shallots in 1 teaspoon butter. Add the bay leaf and thyme. Moisten with red wine and cook, reducing by two-thirds. Mix this reduced sauce with *demi-glace* sauce, and boil for 5 minutes; rub the reserved duck liver through a sieve, and add it to the sauce off the heat. Add the bloody juice gathered from the duck press. Heat slowly, without letting the sauce boil.

Strain through a double layer of cheesecloth, and complete the sauce by adding the remaining butter.

Correct the seasoning and coat the duck slices and the stuffing generously with the sauce.

Caneton rouennais en salmis
SALMI OF ROUEN DUCKLING

Roast the duckling in a 450° oven for 16 to 18 minutes maximum.

After taking the duck from the oven, let it stand for 5 minutes.

Thickly butter a long platter, then sprinkle with 1 teaspoon chopped shallots, a dash of nutmeg, and a couple of turns of the pepper mill.

Heat the platter in order to brown the shallots.

Carve the duck—first the legs, placing them back on the grill, the cut part to the flame; then carve the wings and slice the breast. Place the duck slices flat on the heated platter.

Chop the carcass, crush it in a duck press, and collect the juice in a bowl; pour 3 or 4 tablespoons good red wine on the carcass during the pressing to help to bleed it. To the blood and wine add the raw duck liver, which has been puréed by rubbing it through a very fine sieve.

Sprinkle the slices of duck with some pieces of butter, baste them with 1 tablespoon of cognac, ignite, and smother the flames immediately. Coat the duck with the bloody juice from the press mixed with the puréed liver; heat in the platter, shaking to mix, and, without letting the sauce boil, place for a second in a 450° oven; serve, adding the legs to the dish.

Note: The thickness of the sauce results from the coagulation of the blood in the juice and the puréed liver; the difficult part of this dish is to heat this juice very slowly, without allowing it to boil, until it has the consistency of a thick smooth sauce.

Steaks de canard
DUCK STEAKS (For 2 people)

2 duck breasts
Salt and pepper
1/4 pound unsalted butter
1 tablespoon chopped shallots
1 tablespoon old armagnac brandy
1 cup red Burgundy wine

Method. Trim the two duck breasts. Season with salt and pepper.

In a skillet, sear the duck breasts in 1 tablespoon butter; brown them on both sides without cooking too much, because duck meat must remain pink, almost bloody.

When the breasts are cooked, place them on a serving platter and slice.

In the skillet stew the shallots; deglaze the juices with the armagnac and Burgundy.

Boil to reduce the sauce by half, and thicken with the remaining butter,

Correct the seasoning.

To serve, coat the duck steaks with the excellent sauce and garnish with small glazed onions and turnips, St. George's mushrooms (small spring or autumn mushrooms) sautéed in butter, and fresh spinach.

Canard Claude Jolly, création Michel Guérard

DUCK CLAUDE JOLLY, CREATED BY MICHEL GUÉRARD

**Duck livers
Salt and pepper
Port wine
Cognac
Duck stock
Cornstarch
Gelatin
Duck slices
1/2 veal stock, 1/2 red
  Bordeaux wine**

Foie gras with pepper.   Remove the membranes from the duck livers.

Marinate the livers for 2 days with salt, pepper, port wine, and cognac. Tie them in a dishcloth and cook in a duck stock with some port wine for about 10 minutes, depending on their size, and let cool.

Reduce the stock in which the duck livers have cooked; thicken it slightly (for 2 quarts of reduced stock, use 1 table-spoon cornstarch and 4 envelopes gelatin). Chill.

Let the gelatin stiffen somewhat until you can coat the livers with a first layer of jelly. Sprinkle coarsely ground pepper over the first layer. Finish the glaze with more jelly.

Duck slices.   Cook ducks (killed so their blood remains in the meat) in a broth of 1/2 veal stock, 1/2 red Bordeaux wine, for about 30 minutes.

Degrease the slices of duck and let them cool.

Glaze the duck slices with the same jellied stock used for the livers.

On a plate, serve the slices of duck with a slice of duck liver coated with the jelly.

[*Editor's note:* This recipe was cooked for the President of the French Republic, Valéry Giscard d'Estaing, on February 25, 1975; it is included here to document the menu on pages 488–9.]

Caneton nantais

NANTES DUCKLING

The word *caneton* means young duck, and the ducklings of Nantes are a renowned breed. The preparation is always the same, regardless of the recipe or the garnish. Unless they are cooked *en chemise*, which generally means poached, they should be roasted or braised. Avoid any method that would produce boiling, which would dry out the tender part — the breast. These recipes are especially designed to reveal their savor and texture.

Caneton poêlé à l'orange dit à la bigarade

BRAISED DUCKLING WITH ORANGE

Method.   Season the cavity of a duckling with salt and pepper. Using 2 tablespoons butter, braise the duckling very slowly as for duckling with turnips (page 264). Cook the bird slightly rare, so it will be just pink after it has stood for 10 to 15 minutes.

While the duckling is cooking, remove the rind of an

1 duckling
Salt and pepper
6½ tablespoons unsalted
  butter
3 oranges
2 cubes sugar
2 teaspoons vinegar
Juice of ¼ lemon
1–2 tablespoons veal stock
  (page 72)
Pinch tapioca

orange (the thin orange coating), leaving the bitter white part of the skin; cut the rind into fine julienne and boil 5 minutes; drain and wipe dry. Set aside on a plate. Peel 2 oranges, detach the sections, and remove the membranes; place the sections in scallops around the edge of the platter where the duck will be placed.

Rub the rind of another orange with the cubes of sugar. Then cook the sugar in a small saucepan until it is a light caramel color; add 2 teaspoons vinegar; reduce almost completely, to a thick syrup.

Squeeze the orange into a bowl and combine with the lemon juice. Strain it through cheesecloth.

When the duckling is cooked, place it in the center of the orange sections. To the braising juice add 1 or 2 tablespoons of veal stock; through cheesecloth placed over the saucepan strain the juices into the caramelized sugar. Add a pinch of tapioca, and boil for a few minutes to cook the tapioca completely; this will give the sauce its slightly syrupy consistency. Then off the heat add the orange rind and the orange and lemon juices; thicken with the remaining 3½ tablespoons butter. Correct the seasoning, and coat the duckling with sauce. In a sauceboat, serve the remaining sauce.

Note: Do not reduce the braising juice too much; if that happens, correct by adding veal stock.

Caneton aux navets
DUCKLING WITH TURNIPS

1 duckling
4 tablespoons unsalted
  butter
15 small onions, peeled
  and boiled for 5 minutes
1 tablespoon chicken fat
1 pound turnips, cut and
  trimmed to look like small
  eggs
Pinch salt
1 teaspoon sugar
1 tablespoon flour
½ cup dry white wine
Veal stock (page 72),
  lightly salted bouillon, or
  water
Salt and pepper
1 garlic clove, finely
  chopped
Tiny *bouquet garni*
  (parsley, sprig thyme, and
  ¼ bay leaf)
Chopped parsley

To prepare the duckling, singe, draw, and season it inside with salt and pepper, trussing it around the legs, and barding it.

Method. Brown the duckling slowly on all sides in a skillet with 2 tablespoons butter. When it is golden brown, cover and continue cooking for 25 minutes.

It is important to stop the cooking when the juice, drained from inside the duck onto a plate, is a clear pink color.

In order for the duck to be tender and juicy, the meat should be somewhat undercooked. Slightly pink beads should form on the meat as the duck is carved.

If the breast slices have a dark color, the meat will be hard and dry.

Following the recipe and cooking the duck medium rare are the two essential conditions for the success of this delicious but unappreciated dish.

While the duck is cooking, prepare the garnish.

In a skillet, heat 2 tablespoons butter and brown the onions. Drain them and set aside on a plate.

Add 1 tablespoon chicken fat to the butter, and sauté the turnips. Season with a pinch of salt. When the turnips are lightly browned, sprinkle with the sugar, which will darken the turnips to a deep gold when it caramelizes. (If the turnips are old, boil them well before browning them.)

Sprinkle the turnips with the flour; brown for 2 minutes, then moisten with white wine; boil to reduce by two-thirds;

then cover the turnips with veal stock, lightly salted bouillon, or water. Season with salt and pepper; add the onions, garlic, and the *bouquet garni*. Simmer until completely cooked.

When the duck is cooked, place it on a hot shallow platter. Remove the *bouquet garni,* and put the turnips and onions into the saucepan used to braise the duck.

The vegetables should have cooked down into a rich, light mixture that, combined with the drippings from the duck, will make enough sauce to serve with the duck and the turnips.

Shake everything together to deglaze the bottom of the duck pan, correct the seasoning, and place the vegetables in heaps to the left and right of the duck; pour the remaining sauce over the duck.

Sprinkle chopped parsley on the turnips.

Caneton aux olives
DUCKLING WITH OLIVES

Prepare and braise the duckling as in the recipe above. When it is cooked, put it on a platter. Pit and boil $1/4$ pound green olives for 2 minutes to remove the brine taste; drain and wipe dry. Simmer in the braising juice (there will be enough if the recipe has been followed carefully; if it has reduced too much, add 1 or 2 tablespoons veal stock, bouillon, or water). Off the heat stir 2 tablespoons unsalted butter into the braising juice and the olives. Pour over the duck.

Caneton aux petits pois
DUCKLING WITH GREEN PEAS

1 braised duckling
4 cups fresh green peas *à la française* **(page 352)**
$1/4$ pound lean fresh pork fat (rind removed), finely diced, blanched, and browned
2 tablespoons unsalted butter
Seasoning

Method. Braise the duckling following the recipe for duckling with turnips (page 264). Place the duckling on a platter. Into the braising juice, put the green peas and pork fat.

Simmer the peas in the braising juice for 5 minutes; off the heat stir in the butter; correct the seasoning, and pour the peas and juices over the duck.

Note: Peas prepared by this method should not be soaked in juice; it should be lightly thickened and give a syrupy coating made smooth by the addition of the butter.

Pintades et pintadeaux
GUINEA FOWL AND HENS

January and February are the best months for guinea hens.

The young guinea hen, roasted, braised, or cooked in a saucepan, should have pink flesh when done. Its meat, once cooked, cannot wait. Cook just in time to serve.

The guinea fowl should be braised with cabbage. It would be dry if roasted, whereas braised, it is delicious (see *chartreuse* of young partridges, pages 293–4).

Oie
GOOSE

Generally, a fat goose is cooked in the same way as a turkey or a duck. The preceding recipes can be used.

If the goose is no longer young, do not hesitate to make a stew. Cooked that way, with turnips, chestnuts, onions, horseradish, rice, potatoes, kohlrabi, or rutabagas, the goose will always be appreciated.

Oison farci à la fermière
STUFFED GOSLING FARM STYLE

1 gosling, 3 pounds drawn
2 slices white bread,
  crusts removed
Milk
4 tablespoons unsalted
  butter
2 shallots, finely chopped
1 medium-sized onion,
  finely chopped
Gosling liver
2 chicken livers
Salt and pepper
1 tablespoon cognac
4 tablespoons ground
  fresh pork fat
1/2 teaspoon chopped
  parsley
2 sage leaves, chopped
1 egg
Dash grated nutmeg
3–4 tart green apples,
  peeled, quartered,
  seeded, and chopped
2 tablespoons veal stock
  (page 72) or water

Method. Choose a gosling from the first hatching, well developed and weighing about 3 pounds drawn. Draw through the neck, following the instructions for the small turkey (page 256), and make this stuffing:

Soak 2 slices of white bread, crusts removed, in milk.

Meanwhile, in 1 tablespoon butter in a skillet slowly cook the shallots and an onion. When the shallots and the onion are cooked but not browned, add the gosling liver and the chicken livers. Heat quickly for 3 seconds to sear; season with salt and pepper. Moisten with cognac, ignite, and smother the flame immediately with the lid.

Pour the contents of the skillet into a strainer and rub the livers, shallots, and onions through onto a plate; set the purée aside.

Squeeze the bread, which has been soaking, and add it to the liver purée.

Place the purée in a bowl; add the pork fat, parsley, sage leaves, egg, nutmeg, salt, and pepper. Mix well with a wooden spatula.

Sauté the apples in 3 tablespoons butter in a skillet until they are half cooked. Add to the purée in the bowl.

When the mixture is smooth and the seasoning corrected, season the gosling inside and stuff it. Truss and bard the bird. Place in a roasting pan.

Season the gosling with salt, and baste generously with melted butter. Cook in a 425° oven for 60 minutes, basting frequently with the cooking butter.

To serve, add 2 tablespoons veal stock (preferably) or water to the cooking butter. Boil for 2 minutes to deglaze the pan, and serve the juices without degreasing.

L'oie du réveillon
CHRISTMAS EVE GOOSE

1 plump goose, less
  than 1 year old

Preparing the goose. Singe the goose, clean, draw through the neck, and reserve the liver after removing the gall bladder. Collect the excess fat, including the fat that surrounds the intestines.

60 chestnuts
Consommé
2 celery ribs
3¹/₂ tablespoons unsalted butter

Preparing the chestnuts. Broil the chestnuts in the oven or plunge them in very hot oil; peel.

Divide the chestnuts in two batches. Take the batch that are less attractive and cook them, covered, in a *court-bouillon* made with consommé and 1 celery rib.

Place the more beautiful chestnuts in a skillet big enough to hold them all without crowding. Sprinkle these chestnuts with the white part of a celery rib, finely chopped, and moisten with consommé just to cover. On top sprinkle 3¹/₂ tablespoons butter, cut into small pieces.

When the first batch of chestnuts are cooked but still firm, drain them. Uncover the second batch a few minutes before they are fully cooked, and boil to reduce the consommé until the reduced liquid mixed with the butter and the natural sugar released by the chestnuts becomes a thick syrup. This step must be done carefully so that the chestnuts will not crumble.

Start cooking the best chestnuts 35 minutes before serving; those in the first batch should be cooked when the recipe is begun, for they will be used for stuffing the goose.

7 ounces fresh pork fat
¹/₂ pound fresh ham
7 tablespoons goose fat
Goose liver
Salt and pepper
12 chipolatas or other small sausages
6 small pigs' feet, truffled
7 ounces small firm white mushrooms
2 medium-sized onions, peeled and chopped
2 shallots, peeled and finely chopped
1 tablespoon cognac
1 egg, beaten
1 tablespoon spiced salt (page x)
¹/₂ teaspoon fresh chopped parsley

Preparing the stuffing. Cut the pork fat into small pieces and remove all the membranes. Pound it in a mortar and place it on a plate in a warm place to soften. Then rub through a fine sieve. Set aside.

Chop the fresh ham fine and set aside.

Cut the goose liver into large dice. Set aside.

In a skillet melt 2 tablespoons goose fat. When the fat is smoking, quickly sear the goose liver. Season with salt and pepper. Keep the liver rare; drain. Place on a plate.

In the same fat, on a high flame, brown the following, one at a time, and place on the plate:
1. The sausages, which have first been cooked for 2 seconds in nearly boiling water to firm the skin
2. The truffled pigs' feet
3. The mushrooms, cleaned, quickly washed, and seasoned with a pinch of salt
4. The chopped onions and shallots; cook them slowly

Add 3 tablespoons goose fat to the skillet; and, when it is hot, add the ham with the shallots and onions, and stir for 5 minutes with a spatula over a high flame. Pour in the cognac, ignite, and smother the flame immediately with the lid. Remove from the heat.

Pound the goose liver in a mortar; when it becomes a paste, first add the pork fat and mix well, then the ham with the shallots and onions. Finish with 2 tablespoons of raw goose fat, the beaten egg, the spiced salt, and the chopped parsley. Check the seasoning of the stuffing by poaching a teaspoon of it and tasting.

Place the stuffing in a bowl and carefully mix into it the mushrooms and the second-choice chestnuts. Stuff the goose, alternating layers of stuffing with layers of sausage and the truffled pigs' feet. Truss and bard the bird.

Pork fat for barding

Braising. In a braising pan, brown the goose very slowly in melted butter or goose fat. Cover the pan and braise, basting often, for 1¹/₄ hours. Then remove the bard and the

267

truss and return to the oven for the final 10 to 15 minutes of cooking. Because the goose is cooked slowly, the juices that escape should be sufficient. If they are too reduced, add a couple of tablespoons of water.

Presentation.   Place the goose on a long platter and surround it with the cooked first-choice chestnuts.

Pour a little bit of the cooking juice on the goose and serve the remaining juice, degreased, in a sauceboat.

Confit d'oie et rillettes d'oie

PRESERVED GOOSE AND POTTED GOOSE MEAT

Confit d'oie is easy to prepare. It is an excellent food that can be stored a long time.

This dish is part of French regional cooking; it is a specialty in Languedoc, Gascony, and the Béarn.

Method.   Bleed a fat goose, pluck, singe, then completely cool it. Slit the goose down the back, from neck to tail. Draw it carefully to avoid harming the liver, which can be used in cooking other dishes.

Remove the fat that surrounds the gizzard and the intestines.

Cut the goose into four pieces: the two breast pieces with the wings attached and the two legs. Leave the carcass bones attached to each quarter.

Rub the pieces of goose inside and out with spiced salt. A large handful of this salt is enough for 1 goose.

After rubbing the goose with salt, put the pieces in a glazed bowl and cover with the remaining spiced salt and a dishcloth. Let marinate in this brine for at least 24 hours.

Then remove the pieces of goose, shake the salt off them, and carefully wipe. Plunge the pieces of goose into a saucepan filled with tepid melted fat—half goose fat from the bird and half pork fat, both clarified and strained.

Gradually bring to a slow boil. The fat should boil but not smoke. At the start of the cooking the fat will be cloudy, but as the goose cooks, it will get clearer. It takes 2 hours to produce a perfect *confit*. The goose will be cooked when the fat is clear; if it has been cooked very slowly, a needle should penetrate the meat easily.

Drain the pieces of goose and remove any loose bones from the carcass or the legs.

Using a glazed earthenware pot, pour in a layer of the cooking fat. Let it harden; then place the goose meat on top, without letting it touch the sides of the pot, in a single layer. Cover with another layer of half-congealed fat. Repeat until all the goose meat is covered.

Two days later pour a new layer of hot fat into the pot to fill any empty spaces. The following day pour on the surface a last layer of pure pork fat, well cooked, which, in turn, will harden.

Cut a piece of wax paper the size of the pot and place it on top of the fat.

1 fat goose
Large handful spiced salt
  made with:
2 pounds sea salt, finely
  crushed
1 teaspoon saltpeter
1 pound sugar
4 cloves
1 bay leaf
Sprig thyme, crushed to
  powder
Melted fat (1 part goose fat
  and 1 part pork fat,
  clarified and strained)

Cover the pot, and keep the *confit d'oie* in a dry, cool place or refrigerate.

Each time you want to use a piece of *confit,* first remove the pork fat, then the cooking fat. After you remove a piece of goose, first replace the goose fat, then the pork fat. This way, the *confit* can be kept for a whole season.

Rillettes are made by using the *confit d'oie* and following the recipe for pork *rillettes* (pages 218–19).

Cassoulet languedocien

CASSOULET LANGUEDOC STYLE (For 8 to 10 people)

Beans

4 cups dry white beans
$^1/_2$ pound lean fresh pork fat
$^1/_2$ tablespoon salt
$^1/_2$ pound fresh pork rinds
1 medium-sized carrot
1 medium-sized onion, stuck with 1 clove
Bouquet garni (parsley, sprig thyme, $^1/_2$ bay leaf, and 3 garlic cloves)

Meat

1$^3/_4$ pounds spareribs
4 pieces *confit d'oie* (page 268)
Salt and pepper
4 medium-sized onions, chopped
3 garlic cloves, crushed
5 tablespoons thick tomato purée
1 uncooked garlic sausage, about $^1/_2$ pound
2 tablespoons fresh bread crumbs

Method. Carefully pick over and wash the beans; soak for 2 hours, drain, and place in a saucepan with 4 quarts cold water and the fresh pork fat. Heat slowly to the boiling point, skim, and boil for 5 minutes; drain.

Rinse the saucepan and return the beans to the saucepan with 2 quarts cold water, the salt, the pork fat, the pork rinds (tied), the carrot, the onion, and the *bouquet garni.*

Cook on a very low flame; the beans should remain whole and be perfectly cooked without being mushy.

In a skillet brown the spareribs on all sides, basting generously with fat from the *confit d'oie,* then season with salt and pepper. When the pork is golden, set aside on a plate and, in the same fat, slowly cook and brown the onions. When the onions are cooked, add the garlic cloves; heat for 2 seconds, add the tomato purée and $^1/_4$ cup of the cooking liquid from the beans. Simmer slowly for 5 minutes.

When the beans are nearly cooked, remove the carrot, the onion, and the *bouquet garni.* Leaving enough liquid to cover them, add the spareribs, the sausage, the *confit d'oie,* and the chopped onions.

Simmer, covered, on a low flame for 1 hour. The dish should barely bubble.

Remove the meat from the beans. Cut the spareribs and the pork fat into slices, the *confit d'oie* into pieces, the pork rinds into julienne, the sausage into thick slices, and remove the skin.

Correct the seasoning of the beans.

Fill a shallow ovenproof earthenware pot first with a layer of beans and a ladleful of their cooking liquid, a couple of tablespoons of pork rinds, then several slices of spareribs and pork fat, pieces of *confit d'oie,* and slices of sausage. Cover with beans, and continue alternating the meats and the beans. Grind some fresh pepper on each layer.

Cover the top layer of the beans with slices of pork fat and sausage. Sprinkle with the bread crumbs and baste with melted goose fat from the *confit d'oie.* Cover.

Cook in a 300° oven for 2 hours. Remove the cover 15 minutes before serving to brown the top. At this point, the juices from the cooking should be quite reduced and slightly thickened by the starch from the beans.

Foie gras

FRESH GOOSE LIVER

Buying fresh *foie gras* requires a certain amount of experience or, at least, minimum information.

In French markets, no differentiation is made between goose liver and duck liver. However, goose liver is superior to duck liver, especially for hot dishes.

Some livers that look fine become gray when cooked; others are marbled with black filaments; others soften and turn into liquid fat when heated.

One must know how to recognize these faults when buying *foie gras.* This is not easy to learn.

When buying fresh goose liver, we suggest that you separate the two lobes of the liver and examine the inside. Absolutely reject livers that do not have a clear pink color or any that are marbled with tiny black veins. To judge the quality cut a tiny piece inside one of the lobes with the point of a knife. Roll this piece slowly between your thumb and forefinger; the heat of your fingers will soften it; a good liver will stay smooth and flexible; a bad one will become oily and fall apart.

Foie gras chaud

HOT GOOSE LIVER

Trim the liver, removing any impurities and the black filaments that held the gall bladder.

Marinate raw truffles for about half an hour in seasoning made with spiced salt (page x) and 1 tablespoon cognac or fine champagne brandy.

Remove the pieces of truffles to another plate. Roll the liver on all sides in the marinade. Then stud it with incisions on the surface of the lobes; in these incisions insert pieces of the marinated truffles.

Then wrap the liver in a piece of fresh pork fat and let stand, covered, for 2 hours in a small bowl; then plunge the liver into boiling water for 2 minutes to coagulate the albumin on the outside.

Meanwhile, prepare 1 pound brioche dough (pages 376–8) or half-flaky dough (page 383). Divide the dough in half and roll each piece into an oval, about $1/16$ inch thick and one-third larger than the surface of the liver. Place one piece of the rolled dough on a pie plate.

Place the *foie gras* on the dough and moisten the edges of the dough with a pastry brush. Cover with the second layer of dough, which should be slightly smaller than the bottom one.

Roll the edges of the bottom dough over the top one and seal by pressing with your fingers. Lightly score the top with the point of a knife; in the center make a small opening to allow the steam to escape. Bake in a 375° oven about 35 minutes for a medium-sized liver.

If it has been properly cooked, the liver will be clearly

pink, although firm. To be certain of that, test with a trussing needle. When you remove the needle and put it against your hand, the needle should be tepid if the liver is cooked.

Cut off the top crust at the table, and serve the liver with a spoon.

Generally, a hot *foie gras* prepared in this way is served with noodles, lasagna, spaghetti, macaroni, or rice cooked according to a standard recipe and dressed with butter or cream.

Foie gras froid au porto

COLD GOOSE LIVER WITH PORT WINE
First Method

2³/₄ cups gelatinous white chicken stock (page 73), made with calf's feet
1 *foie gras*
1 cup cognac or fine champagne brandy
Spiced salt (page x)
Freshly ground pepper
Truffles and peels
Pork fat for barding
Seasoning
1¹/₂ cups port wine

Prepare white chicken stock using calf's feet to make it very gelatinous.

Meanwhile, carefully trim a well-chosen *foie gras* and marinate for 3 hours in cognac or fine champagne brandy with spiced salt, freshly ground pepper, and truffle peels. Steep the liver and the marinade in a tightly closed bowl.

Then wrap the liver in a layer of pork fat, tie with a string, and plunge into boiling stock to which the truffle peels have been added. Correct the stock seasoning.

Simmer on a very low flame, skim, and keep at a slight simmer for 15 minutes for a large liver. Remove the liver from the heat and let cool in the white stock.

To serve, pour off half the stock, degrease it completely, and refrigerate in a bowl to test whether it is gelatinous enough; take into account that port or some other wine will be added and will dilute the stock.

If it is not sufficiently thick, clarify and reduce the stock as necessary. If on the contrary the stock is right, which means that the jelly is trembling but not quite melting, use it as it is, especially if the white stock is clear.

Remove the pork fat from the liver; place the liver in a shallow dish, stud it with quarters of peeled truffles heated and cooled in 1 cup port wine. Coat the liver with a layer of the jellied stock to which ¹/₂ cup port has been added. Repeat the coating operation until the liver is covered by a beautiful, brilliant coat of golden jelly. Garnish the platter by filling it two-thirds full of this delicious jelly.

Keep the liver cool, but do not refrigerate unless the refrigerator can be regulated to 46°.

The *foie gras* cooked this way should be a pink, smooth paste, rare but reached completely by the heat.

A good jelly is, above all, the most rewarding addition.

Second Method

In addition to above ingredients:
Mirepoix made with carrot, onion, and celery stewed in butter

After the livers have been cleaned, trimmed, seasoned, marinated, and wrapped in slices of fresh pork fat (or cheesecloth), place them side by side in a skillet containing a *mirepoix* (a *brunoise* made with finely diced cored carrot, onion, and celery stewed in butter). Cover the livers with port wine, slowly bring to a boil, covered. When the wine boils, remove from the heat and let the livers cool in the cooking liquid.

271

When the livers are cold, remove the pork fat; trim any livers that have become slightly brown because of the port wine, and use the port mixed with a very gelatinous chicken stock to make a jelly.

Finish preparing the liver and serve it as indicated in the first method.

Escalopes de foie gras sautées aux truffes
SCALLOPS OF GOOSE LIVER SAUTÉED WITH TRUFFLES

Slice raw *foie gras* about ¹/₂ inch thick, season with salt and pepper and spices (page x), flour lightly, and cook in butter like calf's liver.

After putting the liver slices on a platter, sauté quartered truffles in the cooking butter; deglaze the coagulated pan juices with Madeira or port wine, and pour over the liver slices.

Mousse de foie gras froide
COLD GOOSE LIVER MOUSSE

Large *foie gras*
White veal stock (page 72)
¹/₄ cup *velouté* sauce (page 77)
1 cup light tasty brown meat jelly (pages 95–6)
2 tablespoons thick *crème fraîche* or heavy cream
³/₄ cup whipped *crème fraîche* or heavy cream
Truffles cut into decorative shapes

Method. Poach a large *foie gras* for 20 minutes in a white veal stock, heated to 195°. Let the liver cool in its cooking liquid, drain, and rub ³/₄ pound of it through a very fine sieve.

Collect the purée in a glazed bowl; place the bowl on top of a bowl of finely crushed ice. Work the *foie gras* with a wooden spatula to make it very smooth.

Next, mix the *velouté* sauce, meat jelly, and *crème fraîche* or heavy cream. Boil to reduce by half; let cool, and strain through a very fine sieve. Add the purée of *foie gras,* then add ³/₄ cup whipped *crème fraîche* or heavy cream. Correct the seasoning.

Presentation. *First method:* Into a 3-cup charlotte mold placed on a bed of crushed ice, pour a little half-set meat jelly. Roll the mold on the ice so that the jelly coats the sides of the mold completely, covering them with a thin layer of transparent glaze.

Decorate the inside of the mold, which means the layer of jelly, with shapes made with truffles arranged artistically. Fill the mold with the prepared mousse.

Refrigerate or put in a cool place.

To serve, dip the mold quickly in hot water, shake it, and turn it upside down on a cold round platter. Remove the mold and surround the base of the mousse with a ring of chopped jelly.

Second method: Pour the mousse into a crystal bowl, decorate the top with truffle decorations, and coat with the half-set meat jelly to cover the mousse with a layer of transparent light-colored jelly about ¹/₈ inch thick. Keep in a moderately cool place until ready to serve.

Terrine de foie gras de canard au naturel
DUCK LIVER TERRINE (For 12 to 15 people)

3 large duck livers, about 1 pound each
4 cups port wine
2 envelopes gelatin
Mixed spices
(³/₄ tablespoon salt, 1 teaspoon pepper, ground very fine, dash grated nutmeg, ¹/₂ teaspoon saltpeter)

Method. Soak the duck livers for 2 hours in tepid water no hotter than 100°.

Drain the livers; open each lobe, breaking them with your hands. Carefully remove any remaining bits of the gall bladder and also all the blood vessels inside the livers.

Place the duck livers in an ovenproof terrine; season with the mixed spices.

Dissolve the gelatin in the port wine and add. Let stand in a cool place for 24 hours.

Cover the terrine and place in a *bain-marie.* Put in an oven preheated to 400°.

Turn off the oven to cook the livers. Cooking time is 40 to 50 minutes.

Set in a cool place.

Serve the duck livers to the guests in the terrine.

Gâteaux de foies de volailles à la bressane
CHICKEN LIVER TIMBALES (For 8 to 10 people):

1 medium onion, chopped
3¹/₂ tablespoons unsalted butter
2 garlic cloves
3¹/₂ tablespoons chopped parsley
2 pounds chicken livers
³/₄ pound fresh pork fat
¹/₂ pound fresh bread, crust removed, soaked in 1 cup milk
6 eggs
1 cup *crème fraîche* or heavy cream
1¹/₂ tablespoons salt
Freshly ground pepper
Nutmeg

For the quality and the success of this dish, the chicken livers must be very fresh and any remaining bits of the gall bladder carefully removed.

Method. Cook the chopped onion in the butter until soft. Place it in an electric blender or food processor with the garlic and the chopped parsley.

Blend for a few seconds. Add the chicken livers, the pork fat, the bread soaked in milk, the eggs, the *crème fraîche,* the salt, the freshly ground pepper, and the nutmeg.

Turn on the machine again and reduce all the ingredients to a fine paste.

Butter 8 to 10 small tart molds. Fill each one with this rich mixture. Cook in a *bain-marie* in a 275° oven. Unmold on a platter or plate.

Serve this dish with a *financière* (pages 157–8), Madeira (page 79), or tomato sauce (page 77).

Quenelles de volaille mousseline
CHICKEN QUENELLES

1 pound chicken meat, without skin or tendons
2 egg whites
³/₄ tablespoon salt
3¹/₂ cups thick *crème fraîche* or heavy cream

Method. Pound the chicken meat very fine in a mortar, adding the egg whites, little by little, and the salt. Rub this paste through a fine sieve into a bowl. Set the bowl in very fine crushed ice and work the mixture with a wooden spoon. Let stand for 2 hours on the ice.

Work the mixture again to smooth it, and make it softer by adding the *crème fraîche* or heavy cream in small quantities. When the consistency seems correct, test by poaching 1 tablespoon of the mixture in boiling water.

Remember that the consistency of the mixture is produced by vigorously crushing the chicken meat and that the only purpose of the egg whites is to bind the creamy mixture. It is best to use as little egg white as possible in proportion to the *crème fraîche.*

To form the *quenelles,* use 2 teaspoons or tablespoons, depending on how large you want the *quenelles* to be, and follow the method used for making floating islands (page 415).

Game

Each year the month of September, with the opening of the hunting season in France, brings a new period of gastronomic abundance.

Hunting for game—ground game, game birds, and wild fowl—provides the table with a variety of unusual and often luxurious dishes.

Cerf (red deer), *daim* (deer), and *chevreuil* (roebuck) are cooked by the same methods. The roebuck has the most delicate meat of the three.

The most sought-after parts of these animals are, in order of quality, the haunch, the saddle, and the chops. The shoulder can be used, boned and rolled, for a roast, but it is usually combined with the neck for a stew.

Lièvre (hare) that is best for cooking is one that is at the most 7 to 8 months old and weighs about 6 pounds. A hare weighing 8 or more pounds is tough and stringy. The gourmet uses it for making pâtés or terrines.

The ordinary *lapin* (rabbit) does not equal the hare; but the young wild rabbit, recognizable by the cartilage of his ears, which tears easily, is delicious sautéed. Older rabbits are better used for making terrines.

Game birds must also be young to make good eating.

The age of the *faisan* (pheasant) can be gauged by the flexibility of the beak and the absence or the weak development of the spurs.

The *gélinotte* (hazel grouse), which is smaller than the pheasant, has very delicate meat.

The *perdrix grise* (gray partridge) is delicious when it is young, which means born in the current year, and it is precisely in the beginning of the *perdrix* season in October that it is at its best. One can tell the bird's age by the gray feet, the pointed ends of the larger wing feathers, and the pliability of the lower beak, which bends when the bird is held suspended by its beak between the thumb and the forefinger.

Caille (quail) must be fresh and fat; then this charming bird becomes a royal dish.

The *bécasse* (woodcock) is one of the best of the game birds. It is not drawn; only the gizzard is removed. The snipe and the young woodcock belong to the same family. The woodcock is the best bird for the lover of salmi.

The *alouette* (lark), which the kitchen transforms into *mauviette* (the name given a cooked lark), is a small bird that is much appreciated in the famous Pithiviers or Étampes pâté.

The *grive* (thrush) appears on French menus during the wine harvest.

There are forty-two varieties in the duck family. Therefore, there is a wide choice in the world of wild ducks; in the kitchen we mainly use a domestic descendant of the ancient Frank duck: the *pilet* (pintail duck), with a long tail; the *souchet* (shoveler duck or river red), with remarkably fine meat but small; the *garrot* (harlequin duck), from Normandy, Picardy, and the Landes.

In addition, there are many other succulent game birds. The *sarcelle* (winter teal), which looks like a duck but is not one and feeds on water cress, wild chervil, and seeds, is extremely fine. The *bécassine* (snipe), common or double, or deaf called *bécot,* fat as a quail in the autumn, is a gourmet's dream. The *bécasseau* (young woodcock) or *cul-blanc,* smaller than the snipe. The *pluvier* (plover), golden or gray, whose emergence over our rivers announces the autumn rainy season, is much sought after. And we will finish this enumeration with the *vanneau* (lapwing), remembering this saying: "No one has eaten well if he has not eaten a woodcock or a lapwing."

Gigot, cuissot ou gigue de chevreuil rôti à la purée de marrons

ROAST LEG OR HAUNCH OF ROEBUCK WITH A CHESTNUT PURÉE

4-pound roebuck haunch
5½ ounces fresh pork fat

Method. Skin the leg of the roebuck, leaving on the foot with its skin. Protect the foot by wrapping it in wax paper before putting the meat into the oven.

Bone the butt end, remove all the tendons from the leg, and lard the meat with the pork fat in narrow rows in the direction of the foot.

Marinate the meat for 24 hours or more.

Marinade
Pinch crushed sea salt
3 shallots, thinly sliced
1 large onion, thinly sliced
1 carrot, thinly sliced
2 sprigs parsley
Sprig thyme
½ bay leaf
Pinch crushed
  peppercorns
¾ cup white wine
4 tablespoons vinegar
4 tablespoons olive oil

Marinating. Place the leg flat in a deep plate. Sprinkle on top sea salt, shallots, an onion, a carrot, parsley, thyme, bay leaf, pepper, white wine, vinegar, and olive oil. Turn the leg from time to time.

Note: Roebuck leg is very tender; avoid making the marinade too acid.

Cooking. Drain the leg and dry it carefully. Place on the rack of a roasting pan and baste with melted butter. Place in a 450° oven to sear rapidly. To prevent the pan juices from burning, place between the oven shelf and the roasting pan a triangle of iron or metal 1 to 1½ inches thick. Baste often with the fatty part of the pan juices.

Cooking time will be about 40 minutes, or 9 to 10 minutes per pound, in an oven; on a spit allow 11 to 12 minutes per pound.

The leg should be rare; let stand for 10 minutes to obtain a nice pink color.

Pepper sauce (page 83)
Chestnut purée (page 346)

Present the leg on a long platter. In a sauceboat serve pepper sauce to which the pan juices have been added. Accompany with a bowl of chestnut purée. Carve as you would a leg of lamb.

Selle de chevreuil Saint-Hubert

ROEBUCK SADDLE SAINT-HUBERT

Proceed as for the leg: remove all the tendons from the filets and lard them in three rows, aiming the *lardons* toward the spine; place in a marinade. Roast following the recipe above, but replace the butter with olive oil.

Serve with a sauceboat of pepper sauce (page 83),

adding a pinch of currants and a pinch of sliced almonds, cut lengthwise and toasted. Accompany with a bowl of boiled red beans.

Côtelettes de chevreuil aux lentilles
ROEBUCK CHOPS WITH LENTILS.

Cut the ribs into chops at least 1¾ inches thick. Trim, flatten slightly, and sprinkle with salt and freshly ground pepper.

In a skillet heat 3 tablespoons oil, and when it is smoking, arrange the chops in one layer. Cook as quickly as possible, turning just once and keeping the meat pink inside.

Place the chops on a large platter in a circle, alternating with heart-shaped croutons fried in butter, the same size as the chops.

Pour pepper sauce (page 83) over the chops and, with them, serve a purée of lentils.

Note: After cooking the chops, drain the oil and with 1 tablespoon pepper sauce deglaze the pan juices sticking to the bottom of the skillet; then add this liquid to the sauce.

Côtelettes de chevreuil à la crème
ROEBUCK CHOPS WITH CREAM

6 roebuck chops sautéed in butter
Pinch paprika
Croutons
¼ cup Madeira
¾ cup thick *crème fraîche* or heavy cream
2 tablespoons unsalted butter
1 teaspoon lemon juice
Chestnut purée (page 346)

Method. Prepare the chops as above, adding a pinch of paprika to the salt and pepper.

Sauté the chops quickly over high heat in butter.

Place on a platter with croutons, as for the chops with lentils.

Into the cooking juice pour the Madeira wine; reduce to 2 tablespoons; add the *crème fraîche;* boil for a few minutes; after thinning, the cream will reduce and thicken.

Off the heat add the butter to the sauce, stirring with a wooden spoon. Finish the sauce with lemon juice. Correct the seasoning, strain through a fine sieve, and serve with chestnut purée.

Côtelettes de chevreuil à la purée de céleri-rave
ROEBUCK CHOPS WITH CELERY ROOT PURÉE

6 roebuck chops
Oil and butter
Croutons, fried in butter
Marinade
1½ cups veal stock (page 72)
Pinch tapioca
2 tablespoons unsalted butter
Seasoning
Celery root purée (page 321)

Method. Cut the roebuck ribs into chops after marinating for 12 hours as indicated for the leg of roebuck (page 277). Sauté quickly in half oil, half butter, smoking hot.

Keep the meat pink. Put chops on a round platter, placing between them heart-shaped croutons fried in butter.

Drain the oil from the skillet; then pour in 4 tablespoons of the marinade; boil to reduce by half, add 1½ cups veal stock and a pinch of tapioca; cook for 10 minutes, reducing again by half. Off the heat add 2 tablespoons butter, correct the seasoning, and strain through a fine sieve over the chops.

Serve with celery root purée.

Note: The tapioca can be replaced by $1/2$ teaspoon cornstarch diluted with a little cold bouillon, or by 1 tablespoon butter mixed with $1/2$ teaspoon flour.

Noisettes de chevreuil à la Berny

SMALL LOIN ROEBUCK STEAKS WITH POTATO CROQUETTES

Take 2 filets from a saddle of roebuck, remove any gristle, and place the filets in a marinade for 12 hours, as for the leg of roebuck (page 277).

Then drain the filets, dry carefully, and cut into slices about $1^3/4$ to 2 inches thick.

Sauté in smoking oil and place each slice on a crouton, fried in butter, about $3/4$ inch thick and the same size as the meat.

In the center of the platter, place a mound of croquettes *à la Berny*, recipe below.

Serve on the side: a sauceboat of pepper sauce (page 83) to which is added a handful of skinned almonds, sliced very thin and toasted; or a sauceboat of red currant jelly.

Potato Croquettes à la Berny

To 2 pounds duchess potatoes (page 358), add $3^1/2$ ounces chopped truffles and $3^1/2$ tablespoons almonds—skinned, chopped, and toasted.

Divide the mixture into balls the size of an egg, about $1^3/4$ ounces each, roll in 1 beaten egg, then in fresh bread crumbs.

Eight minutes before serving, while the chops are cooking, plunge the potato balls into very hot oil.

When golden brown and crusty, drain on paper towels, and sprinkle lightly with a pinch of salt.

Note: These pieces of meat and the leg, saddle, chops, or filet of deer, red deer, or roebuck cooked by the same recipes, can also be served with a purée of Jerusalem artichokes or with applesauce unsweetened or lightly sweetened.

Civet de chevreuil, cerf ou daim

ROEBUCK, RED DEER, OR DEER STEW

Cut the meat into 2-ounce pieces: use the shoulder, neck, and upper part of the ribs. Place in a marinade for 24 hours; drain and wipe dry. Then cook like a hare stew (pages 280–1).

Sanglier ou marcassin

WILD BOAR OR YOUNG WILD BOAR

Use the various recipes for roebuck, increasing the marinating time if the animal is not really young.

Lièvre
HARE

The hare can be cooked still warm, straight from the shotgun. Cold, it should be hung for 2 or 3 days in its skin. To "hang" does not mean to leave it until it is rotten. Rigorously avoid meat that has been hung for longer than is consistent with hygiene and good taste.

Whenever you can, choose a young hare, about 1 year old, with shiny hair and fine paws with the claws barely developed.

Lièvre à la broche
HARE ON A SPIT

After the hare has been barded whole, it can be cooked on a spit. Put a young hare on a spit without marinating it. Sprinkle with salt and pepper. Spice the inside with sprigs of thyme. Brush the hare generously with Dijon mustard. Roast in front of a good wood fire for 35 minutes. During the cooking put 1 tablespoon chopped shallots in the drip pan; before the shallots brown, deglaze with a stream of wine vinegar; add $1\frac{1}{2}$ cups cream. Boil to reduce.

Serve the hare with the sauce on the side, and a bowl of rice pilaf (page 371).

Civet de lièvre
HARE STEW

1 young hare, less than a year old
Salt and pepper
Pinch of thyme and crushed bay leaf
2 large onions
2 tablespoons olive oil
1 tablespoon armagnac
$3\frac{1}{2}$ tablespoons butter
$\frac{1}{4}$ pound fresh pork fat
24 small onions
$\frac{1}{4}$ pound very firm, white mushrooms
2 medium-sized carrots
2 tablespoons flour
2 garlic cloves, crushed
$4\frac{1}{4}$ cups good red Burgundy wine
Bouquet garni
$\frac{1}{2}$ cup cognac
4 tablespoons thick crème fraîche or heavy cream
12 heart-shaped croutons, fried in butter
Chopped parsley

Method. Skin the hare, draw, and carefully collect in a bowl the blood accumulated around the lungs and the throat.

Set aside the liver, with the gall bladder removed.

Cut the hare into pieces, place them on a plate and season with salt and freshly ground pepper, a pinch of thyme and crushed bay leaf; add 1 onion, sliced, the olive oil, and the armagnac.

Mix well, and marinate for 3 hours; turn the hare from time to time.

Heat the butter in a heavy-bottomed skillet big enough to hold the stew. Cut the pork fat into large lardons, soak them in 2 cups of cold water, then boil for 5 minutes, drain, and wipe dry. When the butter is hot, put the lardons into the skillet.

When the lardons are half browned, add the small onions and cook until they are golden; then add the mushrooms, well cleaned and washed rapidly. Season with a pinch of salt; sauté quickly; drain, using a skimmer, and place on a plate.

In the same butter and melted fat, adding more butter if necessary, cook 1 onion and the carrots, quartered, until golden; then sprinkle with the flour. Mix well, and stir continuously with a wooden spoon over a low flame until the flour takes on a dark gold color, if the flour was not already browned.

At this point, add the pieces of hare, drained and wiped dry; sear them in this *roux,* stirring constantly with the wooden spoon. When the meat is seared, sprinkle the crushed garlic on top, mix well, and cover with the red wine. Bring to a boil, stirring, so that the sauce thickens without lumps and is perfectly smooth. Correct the seasoning with salt; add the *bouquet garni,* cover, and place in a 275° to 300° oven for 45 minutes.

Place the stew pot on the kitchen table on a trivet. Next to it place another skillet. Then, with a slotted spoon, remove the pieces of hare and, with the help of a fork, slide them into the other skillet.

Once all the meat has been transferred, place the *lardons,* the small onions, and the mushrooms on top of the hare; pour the sauce onto the meat through a very fine sieve, rubbing the garnish—onions, carrots, *bouquet garni*—through.

Bring the second skillet to a boil, correct the seasoning once more, and cover. Simmer in a 325° oven for 45 minutes.

Rub the liver through a fine sieve onto a plate; mix with the blood; add the cognac and *crème fraîche,* which will dilute the sauce perfectly.

Then proceed to the thickening; when the stew is cooked, remove from the oven and place on the lowest possible heat. While beating with a whisk, slowly pour a ladleful of the stew into the sauce. Heat the mixture slowly, as it will become lumpy if it is cooked too quickly. Strain all the sauce through a very fine sieve and pour it into the stew with one hand, shaking the skillet with the other hand so that the whole stew is evenly coated. Rub through everything that remains in the sieve; nothing should be left. During this time the stew should not boil.

When the sauce is smooth, place the skillet on a very low flame, shaking it until the first signs of boiling. Remove from the heat.

Pour the stew into a shallow dish, place the croutons around the edge, and sprinkle a pinch of chopped fresh parsley in the center.

The sauce should be perfectly thickened, smooth, and black in color, looking almost burned.

Lièvre farci à la Diane

STUFFED HARE DIANE

1 young hare, about 5–6 pounds
1/4 pound larding fat
1 slice pork fat

Method.   Skin the hare, leaving the ears; draw through an opening, as small as possible, made in the skin of the belly. Collect the blood and the liver, removing the gall bladder. Plunge the ears into boiling water and, with a cloth, remove the hair by rubbing firmly.

Remove the tendons from the thighs and the hare filets, exposing them.

Cut the larding fat into small *lardons* as thick as a pencil and about 1 1/2 inches long; place the hare on a cloth to avoid holding it directly with your fingers, and lard the legs and the filets.

**Back and legs of 2 rabbits
Heaping tablespoon salt
Pinch freshly ground
  pepper
Pinch mixed spices
  (page x)
Pinch thyme, bay leaf, and
  marjoram, all pulverized
5¼ ounces ground fresh
  pork fat
5¼ ounces young white
  mushrooms
Large raw truffle
1½ cups white bread,
  crust removed and
  soaked in a little bouillon
  or veal stock (page 72)
1 tablespoon cognac**

Stuffing

When the two rabbits have been skinned and drawn, collect the blood and the livers, removing the gall bladders; put the rabbits' blood with the hare's blood, and set aside the livers.

Cut off the rabbits' hindquarters at the top of the ribs; remove the tendons and bone; cut into pieces, and season with salt, pepper, spices, thyme, bay leaf, and marjoram; mix well and coarsely chop the meat with the livers from the rabbits. Place in a bowl.

Pound the pork fat in a mortar or grate it and add to the chopped meat.

Clean the mushrooms and wash rapidly; coarsely chop the mushrooms and the truffle. Squeeze the soaked white bread and add with the cognac to the other ingredients and the chopped meat.

Mix well with a wooden spatula, and test the seasoning by poaching a small piece of the stuffing in salted boiling water. Correct seasoning if necessary.

Preparing the hare. Place the hare on its back and insert the stuffing into the cavity, evenly distributed. Sew the opening in the belly with thick thread, and place the slices of pork fat over the sewed area. Hold it in place with a string. The barding fat prevents the belly from tearing while cooking and keeps the stuffing in place.

Turn the hare on its belly, and place the paws against the body as if the hare were crouched. Tie the paws in place with a string. Straighten the head in line with the shoulders. Hold it in place with a string tied around the shoulders. Protect the ears by wrapping them with well-buttered paper and tie them together.

Cooking. Use a roasting pan with a rack, big enough to hold the hare comfortably. Arrange the hare, coat with melted butter, sprinkle with a pinch of salt, and place in a 425° oven to sear. Then lower the heat slightly to 400°.

Meanwhile, heat the white wine with the butter and, with a sprig of thyme dipped in it, baste the hare every 7 minutes. Cook it in this way for 1 hour.

Sauce

**2 tablespoons unsalted
  butter
½ cup dry white wine
Sprig thyme
2 large shallots, chopped
  fine and boiled for a few
  minutes
¼ cup thick *crème fraîche*
  or heavy cream
Red currant jelly**

Strain the blood and rub the liver through a fine sieve placed over a soup plate. When the hare is roasted, pour the cooking juices of the hare and the basting juice in the roasting pan through a sieve into a skillet. Degrease this juice, boil to reduce by half, and add the blanched shallots and the cream.

As soon as the mixture starts to boil, pour a few tablespoons of the sauce into the blood, stirring with a whisk; then do the opposite, pour the blood and liver mixture into the sauce, off the heat, stirring continuously with the whisk. Heat again slowly while beating with the whisk; as soon as the sauce starts to boil, remove from the heat. The sauce should not boil.

Correct the seasoning of this thick, rich sauce, which should be spiced with freshly ground pepper.

Presentation. Place the hare on a long platter on its back, remove the bard and the thread, turn it on its stomach, remove the paper from its ears.

On the side serve the sauce in a sauceboat, together with a dish of red currant jelly.

Levraut Chabert
LEVERET CHABERT

1 3–5-month-old leveret, about 3 pounds
Salt and pepper
Pinch of finely crushed bay leaf and thyme
1/4 pound fresh pork fat
3/4 pound onions
3/4 pound St. George's mushrooms or white mushrooms
1/2 cup dry white wine
1 cup veal stock (page 72)
Roux made with 1 1/2 tablespoons butter and 1 tablespoon flour
1 garlic clove, crushed
Sprigs parsley
1/2 cup thick *crème fraîche* or heavy cream
10 heart-shaped croutons, fried in butter

Method. This dish will take 1 1/2 hours to cook. Skin and draw the leveret. Carefully collect the blood that is concentrated around the lungs; then remove the liver, discarding the gall bladder. Cut the young hare into pieces and season with salt, freshly ground pepper, and a pinch of crushed bay leaf and thyme. Mix well and place on a plate.

Remove the skin from the pork fat and chop the fat very fine. Melt in a skillet; then add the pieces of hare and brown on a high flame.

Add the onions cut into fine julienne, mix, and lower the flame; cover, and steam for 15 minutes. The onions should not brown but be well softened.

Meanwhile, prepare the mushrooms. Clean, wash carefully and quickly; cut off the stems and place them on one plate and the caps on another.

When the onions are cooked, pour the white wine on the hare and boil to reduce almost completely over a high flame.

Moisten with the veal stock, and add the *roux* in small amounts; after cooking 15 minutes and cooling, add the mushroom stems, the garlic, and the parsley. The stock should just cover the hare; if there is not enough, add a few tablespoons of water.

Stir until the sauce boils, in order to dissolve the *roux* and blend it completely. Simmer on a low flame, covered, for 25 minutes.

When this is done, drain the pieces of hare with a slotted spoon and, with the help of a fork, place them in a clean skillet.

Sprinkle the mushroom caps on top of the hare. Strain the sauce through a fine sieve, and rub through the onions, so that they are puréed. Using a sieve is an easy way to make a *coulis* of onions. Pour the sauce over the mushrooms.

Bring to a boil, correct the seasoning, and simmer slowly, covered, for 20 minutes more.

When the young hare and the mushrooms are cooked, thicken the sauce: purée the liver through a sieve and mix it. Dilute the mixture with a ladleful of the hot sauce, poured slowly to heat the mixture a little at a time. Remove the hare from the heat, and while shaking the skillet to mix, slowly pour the blood mixture into the sauce.

When the sauce is well mixed, heat slowly again to the boiling point, stirring constantly. Remove from the heat and taste.

To serve, pour the stew into a shallow dish and place the fried croutons around it.

Lièvre à la royale du sénateur Couteaux

ROYAL HARE SENATOR COUTEAUX

You need a male hare, with red fur, of a fine French breed (characterized by its lightness and the nervous elegance of its head and limbs), killed, if possible, in the mountains or in the heather, weighing about 6 pounds, which means past the age of a young hare but still an adolescent. Special requirement for this dish: the animal must be killed neatly in order not to lose a drop of blood.

1 male hare, with red fur, about 6 pounds
3–4 tablespoons goose fat
¼ pound fresh pork fat
¼ pound pork fat, sliced
1 carrot
4 medium-sized onions, between the size of a hen egg and a squab egg
4 cloves
30 garlic cloves
60 shallots
Bouquet garni
Salt and pepper
1 cup good red wine vinegar
2 bottles Chambertin wine, at least 5 years old

Utensils

Oblong copper braising pan, well tinned, 8 inches deep, 20 inches long, and 14 inches wide, with a tight-fitting cover
Small bowl to hold the hare's blood, big enough to whip the blood before incorporating it into the sauce
Chopper
Large shallow platter
Strainer
Small pestle made of boxwood

Method. Skin and draw the hare. Set aside the heart and the lungs. Collect the blood carefully (optional: one can add, following tradition, 2 or 3 small liquor glasses of old and fine Charentes cognac).

First step (preparation time: 1:30 P.M.–5:00 P.M.):
1:30 P.M.—Coat the bottom and the sides of the braising pan with the goose fat and cover the bottom with a layer of sliced pork fat.

Cut off the forequarters of the hare at the shoulders, removing the neck and the head; only the saddle and the paws are left. Then place the animal lying on its back on the pork fat. Cover with a second layer of pork fat. All the sliced pork fat has then been used.

Cut the carrot into quarters, stick 1 clove into each onion. Add, along with 20 garlic cloves, 40 shallots, and the *bouquet garni*.

Pour on the hare 1 cup wine vinegar and a bottle and a half of the Chambertin.

Season with salt and pepper.

2:00 P.M.—Cover the braising pan and place on the flame.

Regulate the heat so that the hare cooks for 3 hours on a low flame.

Second step (to be done during the initial cooking of the hare):
First chop the following four ingredients, separately, very fine: ¼ pound fresh pork fat, the hare's liver and lungs, 10 garlic cloves, and 20 shallots. The garlic and the shallots must be chopped extremely fine. This is one of the most important conditions for the success of this dish.

When the pork fat, the liver, the lungs, the garlic, and the shallots have been chopped separately, put everything into one bowl and mix well until the forcemeat is perfectly blended. Set this forcemeat aside.

Third step (5:00 P.M.–7:45 P.M.):
5:00 P.M.—Remove the braising pan from the heat. Remove the hare carefully; set it on a platter. Then remove all the remaining pork fat, carrot, onions, garlic, and shallots that cling to the hare; put all these condiments back into the braising pan.

Now, using a large shallow platter and a strainer, pour the contents of the braising pan into the strainer placed above the platter; with the small boxwood pestle, rub everything in the strainer, so that all the juices can be extracted. This purée is called the *coulis*.

Mix the *coulis* and the forcemeat. Heat the remaining half bottle of wine. Pour this hot wine into the mixture of *coulis* and forcemeat and mix well.

5:30 P.M.–Put the forcemeat and *coulis* mixture, the hare, along with all the bones from the legs or any other bones that became detached during the cooking, back into the braising pan. Place the braising pan on the stove over a low flame; continue cooking a second time for 1½ hours.

At 7:00 P.M.–Because of the large quantity of fresh pork fat used, it is difficult to check the thickness of the sauce; therefore give it a preliminary skimming. The dish will not be finished until the sauce is sufficiently thickened to have almost the consistency of mashed potatoes, but not quite so thick, because if the sauce became too thick, it would be reduced too much and there would not be enough sauce to moisten the meat of the hare (which is very dry).

The hare, when degreased, can therefore continue to cook slowly until the time when the blood is added to the sauce.

Fourth step (15 minutes before serving):
7:45 P.M.–The thickening of the sauce is nearly completed; a fourth and last step will finish it very rapidly.

Adding the hare's blood: By adding the blood now, not only will the sauce be thickened but it will also take on a nice brown color; the darker the color, the more appetizing the dish.

The blood should not be added more than 15 minutes before serving; furthermore, this should be done after a second skimming of the fat. When this skimming is over, immediately whip the hare's blood with a fork, so that if any part of the blood has curdled, it will become liquid again.

Note: The cognac, which is optional, as was indicated at the beginning of the recipe, helps to prevent curdling.

Pour the blood mixture into the sauce, being careful to shake the braising pan up and down and left to right, in a to-and-fro movement that will cause the blood to penetrate all the corners of the braising pan evenly.

Taste the sauce; then add salt and pepper, if necessary. A little later (about a quarter of an hour maximum) prepare to serve.

Preparation to serve: 8:00 P.M.–Remove the hare from the braising pan; the shape of the meat, naturally, will have altered slightly.

In any case, in the middle of the serving platter, place everything that is still meat—the bones, bare and useless by now, will be discarded—and then, finally, around the stewed hare meat, place all the garnish and pour on the marvelous sauce, so carefully made.

One need not say that, in serving this hare, the use of a knife would be a sacrilege and that a spoon will suffice.

Râble de lièvre sauce poivrade

SADDLE OF HARE WITH PEPPER SAUCE (For 2 people)

The saddle is the part of the hare between the top ribs and the beginning of the thighs.

Method. Choose a nice saddle of hare. After trimming it

1 saddle of hare
3½ ounces fresh pork fat
1 bottle Burgundy wine
2 carrots, sliced
1 medium-sized onion,
  chopped
Thyme and bay leaf
Peppercorns, crushed
Salt
7 tablespoons unsalted
  butter
¼ cup cognac

and removing the tendons, lard it with small strips of pork fat. Place in a bowl for 4 hours in a marinade made with the Burgundy wine, the carrots, the chopped onion, the thyme, bay leaf, and crushed peppercorns.

After marinating, drain the saddle and salt it. Roast in butter in an earthenware pan at 425°; 10 to 15 minutes are enough to cook it. The hare meat, when roasted, should remain pink.

Remove the hare, place on a serving platter, set on the oven door covered with a piece of aluminum foil to keep warm.

Deglaze the roasting pan with the cognac. Boil to reduce by half and add the wine used for the marinade.

Carve the saddle into thin slices. To serve, reshape the saddle, replacing the slices on the backbone.

Serve with pepper sauce (recipe below) in a sauceboat. This dish can be accompanied by a chestnut purée (page 346), a *soubise* (page 86) or celery root purée (page 321), or with fresh noodles in butter.

Pepper Sauce

5 tablespoons oil
1 pound hare trimmings
  and bones
7 ounces *mirepoix* (very
  finely chopped
  vegetables)
5 tablespoons vinegar
Marinade from saddle of
  hare (above)
Salt
½ tablespoon
  peppercorns, crushed
Small *bouquet garni*
3½ tablespoons *beurre
  manié*
Small glass of hare blood

Method. Put the oil in a saucepan, and in it brown the hare trimmings, cut into small pieces, and the bones. Add the *mirepoix* and stew for a few minutes.

Deglaze with the vinegar, and boil to reduce until nearly evaporated. Moisten with the juice from the marinade. Season with salt and the crushed pepper.

After adding the *bouquet garni,* cook on a low flame. Strain the sauce; thicken it with the *beurre manié;* thicken further with the blood.

To finish the sauce, after correcting the seasoning, strain again through a very fine sieve; before using, heat in a *bain-marie.*

Râble de lièvre à la crème
SADDLE OF HARE WITH CREAM

1 saddle of hare
Small fresh pork *lardons*
Salt and pepper
Olive oil
½ cup white wine
½ tablespoon vinegar
9 tablespoons unsalted
  butter
½ cup thick *crème fraîche*
  or heavy cream
Juice of ¼ lemon

Method. With a sharp knife cut open the hare along the stringy muscles that cover the filets. Lard vertically in the direction of the filets with two rows of small fresh pork *lardons*. Break the spine with a blow of your knife, in the middle of the saddle, to avoid contraction.

Season with salt and pepper, and place on a shallow plate; baste with a stream of olive oil and white wine and vinegar. Marinate the saddle for 12 hours, turning it often.

Drain the saddle and wipe dry; roast in 7 tablespoons butter in a 450° oven for 15 minutes. Keep very rare, so that the meat will remain pink after standing over a very low heat for 10 minutes.

Drain off the cooking butter that is left in the roasting pan; replace with *crème fraîche* or heavy cream. Bring to a boil and cook until reduced by half; then off the heat add the lemon juice and the remaining butter cut into small pieces; stir until the sauce thickens. Correct the seasoning, and strain the sauce through cheesecloth or a very fine sieve.

Place the saddle (which has been kept warm) on a long heated platter and baste it with the sauce.

Serve on the side a bowl of chestnut purée (page 346) or a celery root purée (page 321).

Note: It is important to prevent the juices of the hare that gather in the roasting pan from caramelizing while roasting. The deglazing would then be bitter and unusable and the dish would lose most of its flavor.

Train de lièvre rôti
ROAST SADDLE AND LEGS OF HARE

The saddle and legs of a hare in one piece are called the *train de lièvre*.

Carefully remove the tendons from the filets and the legs and lard with several rows of small fresh pork fat *lardons*. If it is a young animal, do not place in a marinade.

Season with salt and pepper on all sides and place on the rack of a roasting pan; baste with melted butter, and roast in a 450° oven for 20 minutes. Baste often with the melted cooking butter, and watch that the juices from the hare do not crystallize at the bottom of the roasting pan; they will caramelize slightly but should not go beyond a pale brown color.

After letting the hare stand for 5 minutes, while the roasting pan is being deglazed with 1/2 cup boiling veal stock (page 72) to dissolve the crystallized juices, place the hare on a long platter and baste it with a little of its juice.

Serve the remaining juice in a sauceboat, along with cooked chestnuts glazed in butter, or mushrooms in cream, or a celery root purée (page 321) or a purée of apples unsweetened or lightly sweetened.

Note: The forequarters of the hare can be stewed.

Lapin de garenne en gibelotte
FRICASSEE OF DOMESTIC RABBIT

3/4 pound lean pork fat
15 small onions
3/4 pound mushrooms
2 tablespoons unsalted butter
1 3-pound domestic rabbit cut into pieces
Salt and pepper
Bay and thyme leaves, crushed
2 scant tablespoons flour
2 garlic cloves, crushed
2 cups dry white wine
Veal stock (page 72) or bouillon or water
Bouquet garni
Chopped parsley

Method. Cut the pork fat into large *lardons;* place them in 2 1/4 cups cold water and boil for 5 minutes. Drain and wipe dry. Peel and scald the onions with boiling water. Drain.

Trim the mushrooms; wash them carefully without letting them stand in the water.

In a skillet big enough to hold the fricassee, heat the butter and half brown the pork fat; add the onions, stir often. When the onions are golden brown, add the mushrooms, and sauté over a high flame for 5 minutes.

Drain the pork fat, onions, and mushrooms with a slotted spoon and set aside on a plate.

In the same butter, adding more if necessary, brown the rabbit (except the liver), and season with salt and pepper, crushed bay and thyme leaves.

Sprinkle with the flour, mix well, and brown slightly. Sprinkle the crushed garlic on the rabbit, mix, add the white wine, and cover with veal stock, or with bouillon or water.

Add the *bouquet garni,* then bring to a boil, stirring continuously; cover, and cook slowly in a 325° oven, for about 30 minutes.

Add the pork fat, onions, and mushrooms; correct the seasoning and continue cooking for 25 minutes. Five minutes before the cooking is over, add the liver, after having removed the gall bladder.

If the sauce seems too thin, because of the gentle boiling, remove the rabbit to a shallow platter and discard the *bouquet garni:* place the sauce over a high flame for a few minutes to boil it down to the necessary consistency.

Pour the sauce over the rabbit, and sprinkle with freshly chopped parsley.

Lapereau de garenne sauté chasseur
SAUTÉED YOUNG DOMESTIC RABBIT

2 tablespoons lard or pork fat
1 domestic rabbit, cut into pieces
Salt and pepper
Thyme
Pinch crushed bay leaf
5¹/₂ tablespoons unsalted butter
4 shallots, finely chopped
¹/₂ pound medium-sized mushrooms, cleaned and thinly sliced
1 cup dry white wine
1 cup lightly salted veal stock (page 72)
2 tablespoons tomato paste
Pinch chopped chervil
Pinch chopped tarragon
Chopped parsley
Croutons

Method. In a skillet heat 2 tablespoons lard or pork fat; when the fat is smoking, brown the pieces of rabbit; set the liver aside.

Season with salt and pepper, thyme, and bay leaf. When the pieces of rabbit are well browned, drain the fat and replace it with 4 tablespoons butter; cover, and stew, in a 325° oven, for 45 minutes. Stir often.

Meanwhile, in a skillet, brown 4 finely chopped shallots in 1¹/₂ tablespoons butter; add the mushrooms.

Sauté the mushrooms on a fairly high flame, and moisten with white wine; boil to reduce almost completely, and add 1 cup lightly salted veal stock and tomato paste. Boil to reduce by one-third; correct the seasoning.

After the young rabbit has been cooked, add the broth and the mushrooms; simmer for 5 minutes; sprinkle with chervil and tarragon; mix carefully, and pour into a shallow dish.

Sprinkle some chopped parsley on top.

Surround the dish with diamond-shaped croutons fried in butter.

Faisan
PHEASANT

Generally, pheasants are prepared like stewing chickens or partridges, in salmis like small ducks, or in any poultry galantine.

Faisan rôti
ROAST PHEASANT

Method. Choose a young pheasant. Pluck, singe, draw, and season it inside with a pinch of salt and pepper; truss and bard to protect the breast, which is extremely delicate.

Place the bird on its side on a rack in a roasting pan, baste with melted butter, and season with salt and pepper.

1 young pheasant
Salt and pepper
Pork fat
Melted unsalted butter
1 rectangular crouton fried
  in butter or cooking fat
1 pheasant and 1 chicken
  liver
Dash mixed spices
  (page x)
1 tablespoon cognac
Water cress
1 lemon
2 tablespoons veal stock
  (page 72), bouillon, or
  water

Place in a 425° oven for 25 to 30 minutes, depending upon the weight.

During roasting, turn carefully so the breast is not exposed to sudden heat; baste often with the cooking butter. Five minutes before the pheasant is cooked, remove the trussing and the pork fat; reserve the fat, keeping it warm, and let the breast brown. Baste often during this last brief step.

The pheasant should be pink when cooked; let stand for a few minutes before serving.

Presentation. Cut a rectangular crouton 10 inches long, 5 inches wide, and ³/₄ inch thick from a loaf of white bread.

Fry it in either butter or the cooking fat from the pheasant roasting pan. This second method will give the crouton a less pleasant color but a better taste.

Spread the following mixture on the crouton:

Cut the pheasant liver and chicken liver into 2 or 3 pieces each, and season with salt and pepper and a dash of mixed spices. Dice an equal quantity of fresh pork fat and melt it in a small skillet; then add the livers, sear, and half cook on a high flame. Remove from the heat; into the skillet pour 1 tablespoon good cognac to dissolve all the liver juices; pour everything into a sieve placed on top of a bowl.

Rub everything through the sieve with a small wooden pestle and collect the purée in a bowl. Work it until smooth with a wooden spatula and spread the paste on the crouton; put the crouton on a hot ovenproof platter in a 450° oven to brown the surface lightly.

Place the pheasant on the crouton, with a bouquet of water cress placed tastefully at either end of the platter. Return the reserved barding fat, which has been kept warm, to the bird; and place 2 half lemons on each side.

Deglaze the roasting pan with 2 tablespoons veal stock, bouillon, or water. If you use water, correct the seasoning. Serve the cooking juice in a sauceboat.

Carve the pheasant at the table after removing the barding fat. First detach the 2 legs, then the 2 wings cut with part of the breast; then cut the breast from the carcass. Place each of the 5 pieces on one-fifth of the crouton. Serve.

If the pheasant has been cooked correctly, the flesh will be pale pink with pink drops of juice oozing out of the meat as the pheasant is carved. If the pheasant is overdone, the meat will be a dull gray, grainy to the teeth. It will have lost its tenderness and succulence.

One generally serves a bowl of potato chips (page 356) or matchstick potatoes (page 355) with this delicious dish.

Faisan en casserole
BRAISED PHEASANT

Prepare a young pheasant as if to roast it, but truss it, also inserting the ends of the drumsticks into incisions in the skin, one on either side of the breast.

Place the pheasant in a pan big enough to hold it comfortably and brown, covered, in 4 tablespoons unsalted butter for 25 to 30 minutes. Remove the barding and the trussing strings a few seconds before the end of cooking.

After cooking the pheasant until pink, pour 1 tablespoon cognac into the pan, cover, and serve immediately in the pan on a plate covered with a folded napkin.

Faisan à la cocotte
PHEASANT IN COCOTTE

Prepare as for the braised pheasant (recipe above) but place it in an ovenproof earthenware pot in a 325° oven. After about 25 minutes add 1 dozen small onions browned in butter and ¼ pound mushrooms, well cleaned, quartered, and sautéed in butter in a skillet. Cook for another 10 to 15 minutes.

Faisan à la crème
PHEASANT WITH CREAM

1 young pheasant, barded
2 tablespoons unsalted
  butter
1 medium-sized onion,
  quartered
¼ pound firm white
  mushrooms
½ cup *crème frâiche* or
  heavy cream
Salt and pepper

Method.   Pan fry the pheasant 25 to 30 minutes in 2 tablespoons butter with an onion.

Meanwhile carefully clean ¼ pound firm white mushrooms without letting them stand in water and cut into medium slices; sauté in butter over a high flame and moisten with ½ cup *crème fraîche*. Season with salt and pepper; bring to a rolling boil, and pour over the pheasant when it is two-thirds cooked. At this point, remove the barding and the trussing strings.

Let the pheasant stay in the oven for 3 minutes, placed on its back to keep the breast out of the boiling *crème fraîche;* then place it on a flat round platter.

Boil to reduce the cream slightly until it has the consistency of a sauce, then pour over the pheasant.

All around the edges, arrange small croutons, cut into points and fried in butter.

Partridge, young guinea fowl, and quail also can be prepared in this way.

Faisan en chartreuse
CHARTREUSE OF PHEASANT

Proceed as for *chartreuse* of young partridges (pages 293–4), but in the cabbage braise an old pheasant; the only role of the pheasant is to give its flavor to the cabbage.

The pheasant that is actually going to be served in the *chartreuse* must be young and tender, roasted or braised.

Salmis de faisan
SALMI OF PHEASANT

There are two methods, both recommended.

1 young pheasant
3 shallots, finely chopped
¹/₃ cup *espagnole* sauce
  (page 76) or *demi-glace*
  sauce (page 76)
1 dozen small mushrooms
20 slices truffles
2 tablespoons cognac or
  champagne brandy
1 tablespoon unsalted
  butter
Croutons fried in butter

1 young pheasant
2 tablespoons unsalted
  butter
1 carrot (core removed),
  finely diced
1 medium-sized onion,
  finely diced
2 shallots, finely diced
Pinch salt, powdered
  thyme, bay leaf
1 heaping tablespoon flour
¹/₂ cup veal stock (page
  72) or bouillon
1 cup dry white wine
1 tablespoon cognac
2 tablespoons unsalted
  butter

First Method

Prepare a young pheasant as if to roast it; set aside the liver.

Roast the bird in a 450° oven for 20 to 25 minutes; while still rare, cut into 6 pieces: the 2 legs, the 2 wings without the tips, and the breast cut into half lengthwise.

Put the pieces in a buttered skillet; cover and keep warm.

While the pheasant is roasting, cook the shallots slowly, without letting them brown, in butter in a small skillet; add ¹/₃ cup *espagnole* sauce, reduced and well degreased, or *demi-glace* sauce. Simmer for 15 minutes.

After the pheasant is carved, pound the remaining carcass in a mortar, along with the wing tips and any other trimmings; add this purée to the *espagnole* sauce.

In the cooking butter in the roasting pan, quickly sauté 1 dozen small mushrooms—firm, very clean, and seasoned with salt and pepper; sear the pheasant's liver, remove it, then add about 20 slices of truffles, cut rather thick; when the truffles are warm, deglaze the skillet with good cognac or fine champagne brandy. Finally, pour everything over the pieces of pheasant.

Rub the liver, which should be rare, through a fine sieve and off the heat add to the *espagnole* sauce, which should then be reduced by half. Mix well with a whisk, heat slowly while stirring, and, as soon as the sauce starts to boil, pour into a very fine sieve placed over the pieces of pheasant. Rub everything through until the sieve is dry. Add 1 tablespoon butter cut into small pieces, shaking gently and heating the sauce without letting it boil until the butter is blended. Correct the seasoning, and pour into a hot dish.

Decorate the dish with diamond-shaped croutons, fried in butter.

At the same time place very hot plates on the table.

Second Method

In a skillet in 2 tablespoons butter slowly stew until completely cooked: the carrot, onion, and shallots; season with a pinch of salt and a pinch of powdered thyme and bay leaf.

Roast a young pheasant as indicated for the first method, above.

Carve the bird, keeping the pieces warm in a covered skillet; pound the carcass in a mortar, rub the liver through a fine sieve or chop it fine to purée it.

Sprinkle the *mirepoix* (carrot-onion-shallot mixture) with flour. Mix and cook this *roux* for 15 minutes until the flour is light brown; moisten with ¹/₂ cup veal stock or bouillon. Mix well to avoid lumps, and simmer for 15 minutes.

Pour dry white wine in the roasting pan used, boil to reduce by two-thirds, and add the sauce above. Add the puréed carcass, bring to a boil for a few seconds; then off the heat finish the sauce by adding the liver purée. Heat slowly, stirring, until the sauce reaches the boiling point; remove from the heat, correct the seasoning, and pass the sauce through a very fine sieve onto the pieces of pheasant, rubbing it through.

Finish the dish with 1 tablespoon good cognac and 2 tablespoons butter. Add the truffles and the mushrooms as for the first method, and present the dish in the same way.

Faisan farci aux marrons et aux truffes
PHEASANT STUFFED WITH CHESTNUTS AND TRUFFLES

1 young pheasant
1 tablespoon olive oil
1 small onion, finely chopped
2 shallots, finely chopped
$^1/_4$ pound mushrooms
$^3/_4$ pound fresh pork fat
$^1/_2$ pound truffles
$^3/_4$ tablespoon spiced salt (page x)
3 tablespoons Madeira
3 tablespoons cognac
12 chestnuts
Slice fresh pork fat

Method.   Pluck the pheasant, draw it through the neck, removing the wishbone. Set aside the liver and the heart; season the pheasant with salt and pepper on the inside.

Heat the oil in a skillet, add the finely chopped onion and shallots, and brown slowly, stirring often. Add the mushrooms—cleaned, washed quickly, and chopped very fine, then dried over high heat while stirring with a wooden spoon. Season with a pinch of salt.

Remove the rind and the membrane from the pork fat; cut it into small pieces and pound it in a mortar; put this paste in a bowl. Put it in a warm place to soften the fat, then rub through a strainer into a bowl.

Add the mushrooms, onion, and shallots; the cleaned truffles, washed carefully and cut into quarters; the spiced salt; the Madeira; the cognac; and the liver chopped into a purée. Work vigorously with a wooden spatula to mix well.

Peel and cook the chestnuts in a little bouillon. Put the stuffing into the pheasant, adding some chestnuts from time to time.

Truss the pheasant and bard with the slice of pork fat; cook together with the heart, following the instructions for braising (page 154), for 20 minutes per pound.

Be sure to protect the breast; finish cooking, and serve following the directions for truffled chicken (pages 242–3).

Note: This recipe can be made without truffles.

Faisan farci au foie gras
dit à la Souvarov
PHEASANT STUFFED WITH FRESH GOOSE LIVER SOUVAROV

Stuff a pheasant with fresh *foie gras* and truffles that have been cut into large cubes, seasoned, and marinated in cognac, then seared in butter. Truss the pheasant, heat it in 3 or 4 tablespoons unsalted butter to sear it, and cook in a 325° oven in a covered pan, sealed with a band of dough (made of a mixture of flour and water) around the lid. This will take about 40 minutes.

Note: Partridge can be cooked in the same way.

Perdreaux
YOUNG PARTRIDGES

All the recipes for pheasant can be used for partridge and vice versa.

Perdreau rôti
ROAST YOUNG PARTRIDGE

Prepare a young partridge as you would a pheasant. However, put a vine leaf on the breast before covering it with the pork fat.

Cook in butter in a 425° oven for 18 to 20 minutes.

As for pheasant, the flesh should still be pink when the cooking is completed.

Garnish like the pheasant with croutons; and serve with the cooking juices thinned slightly with a tablespoon of strong veal bouillon.

Perdreau aux choux
YOUNG PARTRIDGE WITH CABBAGE

1 old partridge
1 good-sized cabbage
Salt and pepper
Lard
1 carrot
1 onion stuck with a clove
1 small *bouquet garni*
1/4 pound unsalted lean
  pork fat
Bouillon or water
1 young partridge

To prepare this very popular dish, an old partridge must be sacrificed to flavor the cabbage; a beautiful young roast partridge is served in its place.

Method. Take a good-sized cabbage, cut it into quarters, remove the core and the thick ribs, and separate the leaves. After washing the leaves well, blanch for a few minutes in boiling water and rinse, then drain. Spread the leaves on the chopping block, season with salt and pepper, and chop coarsely with a knife.

Meanwhile, brown an old partridge in some lard in a stew pot. Cover the browned bird with the cabbage; flavor the dish with a carrot, an onion stuck with a clove, a small *bouquet garni,* and 1/4 pound unsalted lean pork fat. Pour in bouillon or water to reach halfway up. Cover the pot, and simmer for about 1 1/2 hours.

Meanwhile, roast the young partridge in a pan or on a spit.

To serve, pile the cabbage in a mound, place the young partridge in the center, and over the partridge and the cabbage pour the excellent juice from the roasted young partridge. Discard the old bird.

Note: To improve the dish and make it more substantial, one can add a small cervelat sausage and some potatoes, cooked at the last moment with the cabbage.

Perdreaux en chartreuse
CHARTREUSE OF YOUNG PARTRIDGES

Braise 2 or 3 partridges with cabbage, following the recipe above.

Method. Cut the carrots, turnips, and string beans into small sticks as thick as a pencil and 1 1/2 inches long; cook the carrots and turnips separately in a little clear stock. Cook the peas and string beans rapidly in salted water to keep them green.

Choose a charlotte mold big enough to hold the partridge and cabbage and butter it thickly, using about 2 tablespoons.

293

2 or 3 partridges, braised with cabbage
¹/₄ pound carrots (core removed)
¹/₄ pound turnips
¹/₄ pound string beans
¹/₂ cup peas
6¹/₂ tablespoons unsalted butter
Few slices sausage
1 recipe veal forcemeat (page 243)
¹/₄ pound lean fresh pork fat
1 cup veal stock (page 72)

Garnish the bottom of the mold, in a circle, alternating sticks of carrots and turnips; at the edge of the mold put a small pea between each two sticks; in the center put a slice of sausage cut as thick as the sticks.

Decorate the sides of the mold, starting from the bottom with sticks of turnips placed diagonally, a row of carrot sticks placed diagonally in the opposite direction; continue alternating turnips and carrots to the top of the mold, producing a chevron pattern.

Coat the vegetable sticks, being careful not to displace them, with a thin layer of forcemeat, then cover the forcemeat with well-drained cabbage that has been flattened with a skimmer.

Fill the mold with several layers of partridge, quartered; the pork fat, cut into rectangles; and the remaining well-drained cabbage. Finish the top of the mold with a thick layer of veal forcemeat.

Place the mold in a saucepan and fill the saucepan two-thirds up with boiling water. Poach slowly for 40 minutes.

Then let the *chartreuse* stand for 5 minutes; unmold on a hot round platter.

Garnish the top with slices of sausage placed in a circle, inside the circle formed by the sticks of carrots and turnips. In the center, mound the string beans dressed with 1 tablespoon butter.

Around the mold, pour a few tablespoons of the veal stock, reduced and thickened off the heat with 3¹/₂ tablespoons butter.

Perdreaux à la mode d'Isigny

YOUNG PARTRIDGES ISIGNY STYLE

4 ripe cooking apples
7 tablespoons unsalted butter
2 young partridges, trussed and barded
¹/₄ cup *crème fraîche* or heavy cream

Method.   Peel and core the apples and cut them into thick slices; sauté quickly in 3 tablespoons butter without cooking completely; season with a pinch of salt.

Meanwhile, brown the two partridges in 4 tablespoons butter in an ovenproof earthenware casserole. Place the partridges on a plate.

In the casserole spread a layer of the apples and place the partridges on top on their backs, removing the bards and untrussing them; surround the birds with the remaining apples, and pour the *crème fraîche* over the partridges. Place in a 325° oven, uncovered, for 18 minutes. Serve in the casserole, presented on a plate covered with a folded napkin.

Perdreau sauté aux truffes

SAUTÉED YOUNG PARTRIDGE WITH TRUFFLES

Method.   Cut a large partridge into 6 pieces; the 2 legs, the 2 wings, the breast, and the back. Season with salt and pepper.

Heat 4 tablespoons butter in a skillet. When the butter is

1 large partridge, cut into 6
  pieces
Salt and pepper
6 tablespoons unsalted
  butter
12 truffle slices
2 tablespoons Madeira
2 tablespoons veal stock
  (page 72)

hot, place the 6 pieces of partridge flat in the pan, turn them after 7 to 8 minutes, cook them for another 7 to 8 minutes, then place them on a round platter, cover, and keep warm.

In the same butter heat 1 dozen truffle slices, thickly cut, for 2 minutes; sprinkle with a pinch of salt, and add 2 tablespoons Madeira and 2 tablespoons veal stock. Bring to a boil and off the heat add 2 tablespoons butter.

Baste the partridge with this juice, spreading the truffle slices on top.

Perdreaux farcis à la limousine
STUFFED YOUNG PARTRIDGES LIMOUSIN STYLE

2 young partridges
Slices fresh pork fat
Vine leaves
Stuffing
2 tablespoons unsalted
  butter
1 small onion, finely
  chopped
2 shallots, finely chopped
Stems of fresh cèpes
  (taken from the garnish)
2 partridge livers
2 chicken livers
1¾ ounces cooked ham
¾ cup French bread,
  crust removed, soaked
  in milk or bouillon and
  squeezed
1 small egg, beaten
½ teaspoon chopped
  parsley
Pinch salt and pepper
Dash mixed spices
  (page x)
Garnish
¼ pound lean pork fat with
  rind
2 tablespoons butter
½ pound fresh cèpes
2 tablespoons olive oil
2 tablespoons veal stock
  (page 72)
Chopped parsley

Method. In butter in a small skillet brown the onion and the shallots; add the stems of the *cèpes,* chopped fine and seasoned with a pinch of salt; stir over a high flame for 3 minutes. Let cool.

Combine the partridge livers and the chicken livers, seared in butter and kept rare; the ham and stems of the *cèpes*—all finely chopped. Add the bread, the egg, the chopped parsley, salt, pepper, and spices.

Mix well in a bowl. Season the two partridges with salt inside, and stuff them.

Truss the birds; season and bard them, putting a vine leaf under each bard of pork fat.

Remove the rind from the pork fat and cut the fat into small *lardons;* place in 1 quart cold water, boil for 5 minutes, drain, and wipe dry.

Brown the *lardons* in butter in an ovenproof earthenware casserole big enough to hold the 2 partridges. Remove the *lardons* with a skimmer and place on a plate. Put the two partridges in the casserole, and brown them on all sides.

Meanwhile slice the caps of the *cèpes,* season with salt and pepper, brown in a frying pan with very hot oil, and drain; mix with the *lardons* and surround the partridge. Cover the casserole, and bake in a 425° oven for 25 minutes.

Just before the cooking is finished, pour 2 tablespoons of veal stock in the casserole; sprinkle a pinch of chopped parsley on top. Replace the lid; boil for 1 minute on top of the stove, and serve in the casserole, on a plate covered with a folded napkin.

Perdreaux froids Café de Paris
COLD YOUNG PARTRIDGES CAFÉ DE PARIS

Method. Bone 2 good-sized partridges (do not remove the bones from the legs) following the method given for a chicken terrine (page 24).

Spread the partridges on the table, season with salt, freshly ground pepper, and a dash of mixed spices; sprinkle

2 good-sized partridges
Salt, freshly ground
pepper, dash mixed
spices (page x)
Cognac
2 pounds stuffing following
recipe for chicken terrine
(page 24)
2 large truffles
4 pieces raw *foie gras*
Pork fat
1 carrot, sliced
1 onion, sliced
1/2 cup port wine
Gelatinous bouillon

1 cabbage
1/4 pound fresh pork fat
with rind
Sea salt and pepper
2 partridges
1 medium-sized carrot
1 onion stuck with a clove
Bouquet garni
5 1/2-ounce garlic sausage
3 tablespoons chicken fat
or lard
1 quart bouillon
6 long chipolatas

with a thin stream of cognac. Make 2 pounds of stuffing, following the recipe for the chicken terrine. Spread a layer of stuffing inside each bird, as for the chicken terrine; place, lengthwise, in the center, a large truffle, cut in half, and, to the left and right, 2 pieces of raw *foie gras,* as big as half an egg, marinated in cognac and seasonings. Cover with a layer of stuffing not too thick, and shape the partridges again into their natural shape; wrap in pork fat, and tie with a string.

Spread the bones of the carcass, chopped, in a skillet big enough to hold the 2 partridges, add the carrot and onion, and place the partridges on top. Pour over the port wine and bouillon just to cover. Put on the lid, bring to a boil, then lower the flame, and simmer for 30 minutes.

Place the partridges and the liquid in a bowl, letting the birds cool in their cooking juice.

When they are cool, drain and place on a serving platter; clarify the jelly and chill (see pages 95–6); when the jelly is half set, coat the partridges with a shiny coat of jelly. Cover the rest of the platter with 1 inch of jelly.

Perdrix aux choux
PARTRIDGES WITH CABBAGE

This dish will take 2 1/2 hours to cook.

Method. Remove any wilted leaves and the very green leaves of the cabbage; cut out the core and separate the leaves; wash carefully.

Blanch the cabbage by dropping the leaves into a large saucepan of boiling water, then add the piece of pork fat. Boil for 15 minutes, and drain; remove the pork fat, rinse the cabbage, drain again, and squeeze to remove water.

Spread the leaves on a large platter, and season with crushed sea salt and freshly ground pepper.

Meanwhile roast the partridges in a 325° oven with a little bit of fat to start them browning for about 8 minutes.

Prepare a deep casserole, large enough to hold the cabbage, the partridges, and the garnish. In the bottom of the pan, place in this order: the rind from the pork fat, one-third of the cabbage, the partridges, the carrot and the onion, the *bouquet garni,* the second third of the cabbage, the pork fat, the garlic sausage, the remaining cabbage, the chicken fat, and finally enough bouillon so that the cabbage on top is covered. Bring to a boil.

With 3 tablespoons bouillon deglaze the roasting juices from the partridges and pour over the cabbage. Cover with a round of wax paper cut to the diameter of the pan and greased, and then the lid. Bring to a boil on top of the stove; then cook in a 325° oven very slowly for 1 1/2 hours (this is actually braising it).

Remove the sausage after 30 minutes and the pork fat after 45 minutes. Broil the chipolatas.

Presentation. Remove the partridges to a plate; take out the cabbage with a skimmer, draining it well; mound the leaves on a round platter and place the partridges on top, the feet in the air, head to head. Between them, place the chipolatas and the cooked pork fat cut into fairly thin rectangles. Around the edge arrange thick slices of the garlic sausage alternating with slices of the carrot.

Coq de bruyère et gelinotte ou grouse
WOOD GROUSE, HAZEL GROUSE, OR GROUSE

These delicious birds are usually roasted or braised, except for the legs of the wood grouse. If braising, one can deglaze the skillet with a few tablespoons of sour cream mixed with the juice of quarter of a lemon.

Cailles rôties
ROAST QUAIL

Pluck the quail, draw them, and season the insides with salt; truss and bard the birds, and place in a flat pan; baste with melted butter and roast in a 450° oven for 12 minutes.

Remove the trusses and serve the quail immediately on croutons fried in butter.

In a sauceboat, serve the butter and the cooking juices to which have been added 1 tablespoon veal stock or hot water to deglaze the juices sticking to the bottom of the pan.

If the butter-juice mixture were poured directly on the quail, it would be immediately absorbed by the croutons, which would lose their crunchiness.

Cailles aux raisins
QUAIL WITH GRAPES

6 quail
3 tablespoons unsalted butter, melted
Salt and pepper
48 ripe green grapes
Veal stock (page 72)

Method. Prepare 6 quail as for roasting; place in an ovenproof earthenware casserole with 3 tablespoons hot butter.

Season with salt and pepper, and brown the birds quickly on all sides; finish cooking in a 450° oven. These two steps should take 12 minutes.

Meanwhile remove the skins and the pits from ripe green grapes—8 grapes per quail.

When the quail are cooked, add the grapes to the casserole; add a little veal stock to deglaze the pan, cover, bring to a boil, and serve immediately in the casserole, on a plate with a folded napkin.

Risotto de caille
QUAIL RISOTTO (For 1 person)

Method. Roast the quail in a casserole with butter for 12 minutes. When the quail are done, keep warm between two plates. Prepare a risotto with, for each quail, 2 tablespoons rice mixed with 1 teaspoon mushrooms, 1 teaspoon truffles, 1 teaspoon lean ham—all cut into julienne and cooked as described below.

297

1 quail, roasted (page 297)
Unsalted butter
2 tablespoons rice
1 teaspoon mushrooms
1 teaspoon truffles
1 teaspoon lean ham
1 scant tablespoon
  tomatoes, cooked
3 tablespoons veal stock
  (page 72)

In the cooking butter quickly heat first the mushrooms, then the truffles, then the ham. Pour all this mixture into the risotto; mix carefully. Pack the rice into a mold.

To the same skillet add 1 scant tablespoon cooked tomatoes and 3 tablespoons veal stock; bring to a boil for 2 minutes.

Unmold the rice on a hot round plate and place the quail on top, the legs in the air; spoon the chopped tomatoes in the center; baste the quail with the juice.

Cailles froides George Sand
COLD QUAIL GEORGE SAND

6 good-sized quail
2 pieces truffles
2 pieces raw *foie gras*
Salt, pepper, mixed spices
  (page x)
3 tablespoons cognac
Melted unsalted butter
Julienne (1 part carrots, 1
  part truffles, 1 part raw
  mushrooms)
Gelatinous blond stock
  (page 73)

Method. Draw the quail and truss them by making incisions on the flanks of the birds and pushing the foot joints into them, folding the drumsticks back on the thighs.

Season the inside of each quail with a pinch of salt, and then place inside 2 pieces truffles and 2 pieces raw *foie gras* that have been marinated with salt, pepper, mixed spices, and cognac—a dash of all these condiments.

Choose an ovenproof skillet just big enough to hold the 6 quail.

Place the birds in the skillet close to each other; season, baste lightly with melted butter; sear quickly in a 450° oven for 5 minutes.

Drain the fat; pour cognac on the quail, ignite, and smother the flame immediately with the lid. Cover the quail with a julienne of one-third cored carrots, one-third truffles, and one-third raw mushrooms, stewed in butter; cover with a gelatinous blond stock, bring to a boil, and poach slowly for 12 minutes.

Place the quail in a serving bowl; degrease the liquid, and pour it on top of the quail along with the vegetables.

Refrigerate, and serve when the jelly is set.

Note: Since this dish is served in the bowl, the jelly should be less gelatinous than if the dish were to be unmolded.

Grives à la liégeoise
THRUSHES LIÉGE STYLE

6 thrushes
4 tablespoons unsalted
  butter
8 juniper berries, chopped
2 tablespoons dry white
  wine
12 slices French bread,
  fried in butter

Method. Pluck 6 thrushes; through the neck remove only the gizzards; truss the birds by sliding the foot joints into short incisions made on the flanks.

Heat the butter in an ovenproof saucepan, skillet, or earthenware pot. When the butter is hot, quickly brown the thrushes; then cook in a 425° oven for 10 minutes.

Three minutes before the end of cooking, sprinkle the juniper berries, chopped, and dry white wine on the thrushes.

Just before serving, finish the dish with a dozen slices, 1/8 inch thick, of the narrow French bread called flute, fried in butter.

Serve very hot in the pan.

Grives en cocotte aux olives noires
THRUSHES IN COCOTTE WITH BLACK OLIVES

6 thrushes
4 tablespoons unsalted
 butter
¼ pound salt pork fat
3 dozen black olives, pitted
1 dozen garlic cloves
Sprig thyme
1 bay leaf
Croutons

Method. Pluck the thrushes. Do not draw them; remove only the gizzards. Truss the birds, crossing their feet, and stick the beaks into the breastbones.

After seasoning the birds, brown them quickly in butter in a casserole. Then add ¼ pound salt pork fat, diced and boiled for 5 minutes, then drained; 3 dozen black olives, pitted; 1 dozen garlic cloves, unpeeled; 1 sprig thyme; and 1 bay leaf.

Cover the casserole, and simmer on a low flame for about 5 minutes.

To serve, place the thrushes on broiled croutons, cut from country bread; and to complement this dish, serve a good Provençal wine "full of sun."

Poêlon de grives à la provençale
THRUSHES IN A COPPER SKILLET

8 thrushes
5 tablespoons unsalted
 butter
¼ pound salt pork fat
3 dozen black olives, pitted
1 dozen garlic cloves
Sprig thyme
1 bay leaf
Potatoes browned in
 unsalted butter

Method. Pluck the thrushes. Do not draw them; remove only the gizzards. Truss the birds, crossing their feet, and stick the beaks into the breastbones.

After seasoning the birds, brown them quickly in butter in a copper skillet. Add ¼ pound salt pork fat, diced and boiled for 5 minutes, then drained; 3 dozen black olives, pitted; 1 dozen garlic cloves, unpeeled; 1 sprig thyme; 1 bay leaf; and some potatoes browned in butter.

Cover the skillet, and simmer on a low flame for about 5 minutes.

Serve immediately in the skillet.

Grives bonne femme
BRAISED THRUSHES

¼ pound lean pork fat
6 thrushes
4 tablespoons potato balls
4 tablespoons cubed
 croutons, fried in butter
2 tablespoons rich veal
 stock (page 72)

Method. Cut ¼ pound lean pork fat into fine *lardons*, boil 5 minutes, and drain. Heat and brown them in a casserole or an earthenware pot.

When the fat is golden brown, add 6 thrushes and roast in a 375° oven for about 10 minutes.

Just before serving, add 4 tablespoons potato balls cooked separately and 4 tablespoons cubed croutons, fried in butter.

Finish the dish by adding 2 tablespoons rich veal stock.

Alouette ou mauviette
LARK

The lark, when it is fat in the autumn, falls into the hands of the cook and the gastronome. They change its name, calling it *mauviette.*

Mauviettes bonne femme

BRAISED LARKS

Follow the recipe for braised thrushes (page 299).

Mauviettes du Pré-Catelan

LARK WITH POTATOES PRÉ-CATELAN

6 large potatoes
2 tablespoons unsalted
  butter or 1 tablespoon
  cream and 1 tablespoon
  grated gruyère cheese
Pinch salt
Dash grated nutmeg
6 larks, cooked in butter
6 slices Bayonne ham
  (or prosciutto)
Grated gruyère or
  parmesan cheese
Small bouquet parsley

Method. Bake 6 large potatoes, all the same size and un-peeled. When done, cut off a slice from the flattest side of each potato, making an opening. Remove most of the potato pulp, leaving a 1/2-inch layer inside. Put the pulp in a soup plate, and mash with a fork with 2 tablespoons butter or 1 tablespoon cream and 1 tablespoon grated gruyère cheese, a pinch of salt, and a dash of grated nutmeg.

Fill the potato shells with the mixture, leaving a hole in the center of each in which to place a lark that has been cooked in butter; in the same skillet, heat slices of Bayonne ham (or prosciutto) for a few seconds without browning.

Place a lark in each of the potatoes, baste with a little of the cooking butter, cover with a slice of ham, a layer of the mashed potatoes, a layer of grated gruyère or parmesan cheese, and a few drops of the cooking butter; place in a hot oven for a few minutes to heat through and brown the tops.

Place the potatoes in a circle on a round platter on top of a folded napkin.

Place a small bouquet of parsley in the center.

Ortolans

One generally serves 4 ortolans per guest.

Since these birds are extremely fat, it is best to roast them.

Put the birds on a spit, placing in between each pair a half-moon-shaped crouton, as big as the birds and about 1/8 inch thick.

Season the birds with salt; baste them with melted butter; cook them 4 to 5 minutes in a 450° oven.

Serve with the cooking butter.

Ortolans "Caprice d' Eve"

LOUIS PERRIER'S RECIPE (For 4 people)

12 plump ortolans
12 cooking apples
Salt and pepper
Unsalted butter
4 tablespoons applejack
1/2 cup veal stock (page
  72)

Method. Carefully pluck the ortolans. Remove the eyes. Draw the birds delicately, remembering to remove the crops, which are generally full of seeds. As for all small feathered birds, hold the feet after cutting off the claws, and stick the beaks into the breastbones. Peel the apples, and core deeply so that you will be able to insert an ortolan into each of them.

Salt the apples lightly, place them in a buttered ovenproof earthenware pot, and bake them in a 425° oven until half cooked.

300

Meanwhile, season the ortolans with salt and pepper. Sear the birds in butter in a skillet to brown them and to render part of their fat.

Then place each bird in an apple, the head and breast sticking up out of the fruit.

Place the birds in the oven to finish cooking, basting the apples with the fat from the birds.

Deglaze the skillet with the applejack. Add the veal stock. Thicken with 1 tablespoon butter. Correct the seasoning, then coat the birds and apples with this sauce. Serve in the cooking pan.

Becfigues

GARDEN WARBLERS

Garden warblers can be cooked in the same way as ortolans. But more often they are barded and roasted on a spit, 6 at a time. To serve place the birds on a bed of matchstick potatoes (page 355).

Bécasses farcies rôties

ROAST STUFFED WOODCOCKS

3 woodcocks
1 squab
3 large truffles
1 fresh goose liver
Salt and pepper
2 tablespoons Madeira
1 piece stale white French bread
Hot cream
¼ pound unsalted butter
4 egg yolks
Fresh pork fat
6 slices French bread
3 lemons, quartered

This recipe is taken from the *Livre de cuisine des familles.*

"The recipe is for 6 people.

"You need 3 raw woodcocks and 1 squab. Bone one of the woodcocks and remove the best part of the meat; cut the meat into large dice. Clean and peel 3 large truffles, slice them into thick slices that you cut again into squares.

"Take a fresh goose liver, cut it into cubes the same size as the woodcock meat. Place the woodcock meat and the liver in a bowl, add salt and pepper, add 1 tablespoon good Madeira wine, to moisten the mixture.

"Bone the squab, remove all the meat, and, after chopping it slightly, place in a mortar. Pound well. Moisten a piece of stale white French bread as big as a fist, crust removed, with water; squeeze out the water and moisten the bread with a ladleful of hot cream. Add the bread to the mortar along with ¼ pound butter and pound well to mix everything. Finally add to this stuffing 4 very fresh egg yolks. Add salt and pepper.

"Remove from the bowl the pieces of meat and truffles, which are now impregnated with the Madeira. Chop as finely as possible; then take the stuffing from the mortar and place it on the chopping board, and add the meat and truffles to the stuffing, mixing with your fingers and kneading together. It is with this preparation that you will stuff the two woodcocks, which you have not touched as yet.

"The moment has come to take care of the birds.

"After plucking, singe the birds lightly and draw them completely; throw away the crops, the gizzards, and the intestines; keep only the livers of these 2 woodcocks, and set them aside with the liver of the third woodcock. Then, fill the insides of the 2 woodcocks with the stuffing that has been prepared; stuff them well, sew all the openings carefully. When this is done, truss and bard each woodcock, crossing the feet and bringing the head toward the legs, and pass the beak through the jointing of the drumsticks; the bird, this way, seems to be pierced by its long beak. Wrap each woodcock with a thin layer of fresh pork fat. Then, put a metal skewer through it, being careful that each woodcock is pierced on an angle; then place the skewers on a spit.

"Roast over a good fire, which means a clear and lively fire, well tended in the shell-shaped roasting grill. For this roast, the woodcocks should not be rare but, on the contrary, well done; therefore, they must cook 25 to 30 minutes.

"Meanwhile, cut as many slices of French bread as you have guests; first broil them. Place them in the drip pan on a metal rack; they then get the juice dripping from the game, while remaining crunchy. Twelve minutes before the woodcocks have been roasted, remove the slices of bread, spread them with what remains of the stuffing, after mixing the stuffing with the livers of the three woodcocks, well chopped. Your croutons, thus spread, are healthful, contrary to those done by the custom of spreading them with the intestines, the excrement of the game. As soon as the croutons are spread with the stuffing, again place them in the drip pan; the last 10 minutes of cooking are sufficient to cook this garnish.

"Now that the woodcocks are roasted, remove them from the spit, remove their bards and the strings that trussed the birds. Serve the birds on a hot platter, surrounding them with the croutons; accompanied by three lemons, quartered, and a sauceboat with the juice from the drip pan to which you add 1 tablespoon good Madeira.

"Do not forget that the plates should be very warm."

Observation

The next day, with the carcasses of the two roasted woodcocks (what is left from the carving) and with the raw carcass and some of the raw meat left from the third woodcock, which was used for the stuffing, you can make a game soup that will be delicious; you need only cook these leftovers in 1½ quarts bouillon from a *pot-au-feu* for 1 hour, and, after cooking, strain through a fine sieve.

---

1 woodcock
Pinch salt
Slice fresh pork fat
Melted unsalted butter
Crouton, fried in butter
1 tablespoon *foie gras*
Freshly ground pepper
1 tablespoon unsalted
  butter or *foie gras*
1 tablespoon champagne
  brandy
1 tablespoon veal stock
  (page 72) or hot water

Bécasse rôtie
ROAST WOODCOCK

Method.   Pluck the bird just before cooking it. Do not draw it; remove only the gizzard. Singe lightly, remove the eyes, tie the feet together, and stick the beak into the body above the legs.

Season with a pinch of salt.

Wrap the bird in a slice of fresh pork fat.

Roast the woodcock on a spit over a hot fire or bake in a 450° oven, basting with melted butter. Cooking time is 18 to 20 minutes, depending on the weight.

Cook the bird slightly rare.

Place the woodcock on a crouton—4 inches long, 2½ inches wide, and ¾ inches thick—cut from white bread and fried in the cooking butter, if the woodcock is roasted in the oven; spread 1 tablespoon *foie gras,* if available, on the crouton.

Carve the woodcock in front of the guests; put the intestines on a hot plate, grind a little fresh pepper on top, add 1 tablespoon butter or *foie gras;* mash everything together with a fork, adding 1 tablespoon fine champagne brandy.

Spread this purée on the surface of the crouton, which is then divided among the guests. On the side, serve the cooking juice to which you have added 1 tablespoon veal stock or hot water.

Salmis de bécasses à l'ancienne
Christian Bourillot

OLD-FASHIONED SALMI OF WOODCOCK CHRISTIAN BOURILLOT
(For 4 people)

2 good-sized woodcocks
Unsalted butter
***Mirepoix* (page 291)**
Cognac
1½ cups white or red wine
1 cup *demi-glace* sauce (page 76)
Cooking juice from mushrooms
1 tablespoon unsalted butter
Small mushrooms
Slices of truffles
Croutons, fried in butter
Foie gras

Method. After removing the gizzards, truss and season 2 good-sized woodcocks. Roast over a high flame in an oven or on a spit. Cook the meat rare. Carefully separate the legs and the wings from the carcasses, and also the heads. Remove the skin from the wings and the legs and place the meat in a bowl or a shallow covered dish and keep warm. Set aside the intestines.

Meanwhile, chop the carcass and the skin; brown in butter with a finely diced *mirepoix.* As soon as the ingredients are browned, moisten with cognac, ignite, and pour over 1½ cups white or red wine. Boil to reduce by half. Add 1 cup *demi-glace* sauce and boil for a few minutes.

Pass the sauce through a fine strainer, rubbing through all the ingredients to obtain the quintessence of the carcass and the flavorings. The resulting mixture should be more like a *coulis* than a sauce. Thin with reduced mushroom juice, correct the seasoning, and add 1 tablespoon butter to the sauce. When the sauce is done, strain it, very hot, onto the pieces of woodcock to which have been added the 2 heads and a garnish made with small mushrooms and slices of truffles stewed in butter.

To serve, give a final touch to this delicious dish by adding croutons fried in butter and spread with a stuffing made with the intestines and a little bit of *foie gras.*

Note: The recipe for salmi of woodcock *à l'ancienne* can serve as a basic guide for a salmi of numerous other birds: pheasants, partridges, doves, ducks, marsh birds.

Canard sauvage

WILD DUCK

Mallard, pintail duck, shoveler, and teal can all be cooked in the same way.

303

Canard sauvage rôti

ROAST WILD DUCK

Truss the duck after seasoning the inside; do not bard it.
Baste the duck with melted butter and place in a 450° oven for
15 to 20 minutes, depending on its weight. Cook it rare.

Place the duck on a platter with a bouquet of water cress
and half a lemon. Serve with it the cooking juice mixed with
butter and 2 to 3 tablespoons veal stock or hot water added to
deglaze the roasting pan.

Canard sauvage à l'anglaise

WILD DUCK ENGLISH STYLE

Roast the wild duck and serve it with a bowl of unsweetened
or lightly sweetened applesauce.

Salmis de canard sauvage

SALMI OF WILD DUCK

Proceed as for the salmi of pheasant (pages 290–1). Cooking
time will be 18 to 20 minutes. It must be rare.

Canard sauvage à la bigarade

WILD DUCK WITH ORANGE

Follow the recipe for the braised duckling with orange (pages
263–4). Cook it pink.

Sarcelle (gibier maigre)

TEAL (LEAN GAME)

Use any of the recipes given and cook for 12 to 14 minutes.

Pluvier et vanneau (gibiers maigres)

PLOVER AND LAPWING (LEAN GAME)

The best way to cook these birds is to roast them at a high
temperature at the last minute. Cooking time will be 12 to 14
minutes. Cook them pink. Serve with the cooking butter.

Vegetables

The importance of vegetables in cuisine is vast; in addition to their wide variety, the many ways to prepare them, and the wide range of their flavors, they enhance and complete the most elaborate menus.

The major ways of preparing vegetables are cooking in water, steaming, braising, frying, and broiling.

Cooking vegetables in water

Some vegetables, mainly spinach and string beans, are put into large quantities of boiling water in order to cook them thoroughly while maintaining their green color.

The saucepan should be uncovered and placed over a high flame with enough water to cover vegetables completely when they are plunged in, using $1/2$ tablespoon salt to each quart of water. The water should be boiling and should never stop boiling during cooking. It is preferable to use the vegetables as soon as they have been cooked and drained, if they are going to be served plain, à l'anglaise, or with butter.

If the vegetables are rinsed, they must not stay in the water; if they did, they would lose all their flavor—therefore, they must be thoroughly drained.

Some vegetables require special care in cooking, especially artichoke hearts, cardoons, Swiss chard, salsify, etc. Once these vegetables have been peeled or trimmed, they blacken on contact with the air; in order to avoid this problem, they have to be kept in fresh water acidulated by the addition of lemon juice. They are cooked in a liquid called *blanc*.

Blanc à légumes

1 quart water
1 teaspoon salt
1$1/2$ tablespoons flour
Juice of 1 lemon
Fat or oil

The quantity of liquid is determined by the quantity of vegetables to be cooked; for 1 quart water use 1 teaspoon salt; 1$1/2$ tablespoons flour, diluted with cold water; the juice of 1 lemon; and any kind of fat or oil. These ingredients have the effect—in addition to the acidity of the lemon, which kills the tannin—of coating the vegetables so that they do not come in contact with the air while cooking. The vegetables should be cooked in a boiling *blanc*. If the vegetables are not to be used immediately, they should be left to cool in their cooking liquid.

Cuisson à l'étuvée

Also called à l'étouffée, this method requires close attention and continuous surveillance, for it is very delicate. Vegetables cooked à l'étuvée must be young, which means they must be new or spring vegetables. Among those used most often are: carrots, turnips, green peas, string beans, and sorrel. One can also add potatoes, although the cooking method for potatoes is slightly different.

To cook vegetables à l'étuvée, place them in a heavy-bottomed saucepan; salt and butter them lightly. Stir the vegetables over a low flame, making them "sweat." The purpose of this cooking method is to make the vegetables give up some of their water, which is needed to cook them, and, at the same time, to bring out their aroma and flavor. The saucepan should be covered tightly so that when the steam condenses under the lid, it falls back onto the vegetables. The flame should be moderate. If it is too low, the vegetables will disintegrate. If it is too high, because of their sugar content, you risk having them caramelize and stick to the bottom of the saucepan. When cooking is completed, the water from the vegetables should have evaporated without their becoming dry. To sum up, to obtain perfectly cooked vegetables, the cooking must be done slowly; and you should limit the evaporation, so that the liquid needed to produce the steam does not dry up.

Steaming

Cooking by steam is similar to cooking à l'étuvée. The vegetables are enclosed in a steam bath until they are completely cooked. For this you need a saucepan in which the vegetables can be separated from the boiling water by a perforated rack. The water should be salted. It is important that no steam be lost, and so the saucepan should be tightly closed. In order for the vegetables to cook properly the water must be boiling continuously; if not, the steam will not reach the needed pressure and temperature to cook the vegetables.

In England this is the most common way of cooking vegetables. In France we cook mainly potatoes by this method, whereas the English use it for cooking not only their vegetables but even such foods as meats, fish, and shellfish. In England and America, utensils called pressure cookers are used; they are tightly closed steamers in which the steam can reach very high pressures.

Vegetables cooked by steam are eaten plain, with butter.

Broiling

Broiling is one of the first methods ever used by men to cook their food. Although it is very useful to cook meats and fish, it is less so for vegetables. However, for some vegetables, broiling produces good results, giving them a pleasant flavor.

Tomatoes, mushrooms, and most vegetables with a high water content can be broiled very successfully. For broiling, the vegetables should be first seasoned and coated with some fat, preferably olive oil. Place the vegetables on a very hot grill, turn them often, and baste them with oil while they are cooking. The heat must be high so that the exterior of the vegetable will caramelize lightly. The inside pulp is cooked as its water content evaporates.

Broiled vegetables are served most often as a garnish for meats and poultry. The best heat for this method of cooking is produced by charcoal.

307

Frying

Vegetables are fried by immersing them in vegetable or animal fat heated to a specific temperature. This method of cooking requires much experience.

The vegetables that are to be fried must be rich in starch, as is the case with potatoes. If the vegetables do not have starch, you must compensate for this lack by coating them with flour or a frying batter. Zucchini, eggplant, etc., are cooked that way.

What happens during cooking? The vegetables, plunged into the hot oil, are sealed by the high heat; the starch in them forms a thin waterproof skin, enclosing the vegetable's water inside the pulp. The water then boils under this heat and cooks the pulp.

A correctly fried vegetable must be firm, crusty, and a beautiful light-brown color outside, and cooked and soft inside. To obtain these results, it is necessary that the frying oil be sufficiently hot, without, however, reaching too high a temperature; if the heat were too high, the sugar content would caramelize too much and give a bitter taste and too dark a color to the vegetables. The cooking time cannot be determined in advance; it depends on the thickness of the vegetables. One also must not fry too large an amount at one time; the temperature of the frying oil would drop, which would harm the final result. If the temperature drops, the fat will penetrate the vegetable pulp and the pulp will disintegrate instead of permitting the protective skin to form. As soon as they are fried, the vegetables should be drained and dried on a piece of cloth or paper towel, salted, and served immediately, without waiting; otherwise, they will soften.

Frying batter for vegetables

2¹/₂ cups sifted flour
3¹/₂ tablespoons melted
  unsalted butter
2 whole eggs
Salt
Optional
4 egg whites, beaten stiff
Beer

Method.   In a bowl mix the flour with melted butter and 2 whole eggs; add salt, then dilute with enough water to obtain a semiliquid batter. Prepare the batter at least 1 hour before it is to be used.

Vegetables that first have been cooked in water, such as salsify, cauliflower, etc., can be fried. For this type of vegetable, you must prepare a thicker frying batter and, just before using it, add 4 egg whites beaten stiff. One can also make the batter lighter by replacing the water with beer.

Braising

This method is derived from cooking *à l'étuvée*. The vegetables that are going to be braised must first be blanched to reduce their volume and neutralize their bitterness. To do this, plunge the vegetables, cleaned and trimmed, into a kettle of boiling water. The vegetables must be completely submerged in the water. A few minutes of quick boiling are enough. After they have been half cooked, rinse and drain the vegetables.

The chief vegetables that can be braised are: cabbage, celery hearts, lettuce, etc. The braising is done in a heavy-bottomed saucepan on top of a rich *mirepoix*. The vegetables are moistened to a quarter of their height with a fatty bouillon, salted and peppered. The cooking is done in the oven, at a simmer that produces a continuous steam, necessary to the cooking. The braising pan should be covered, and to prevent the surface of the vegetables from drying out, they should be covered with a piece of buttered paper with a hole in the center big enough for the steam to escape and condense on the sides of the braising pan. The cooking time depends on the vegetables being cooked.

For cabbage the braising pan should be lined with slices of fresh pork fat, and in some cases one adds such ingredients as salted pork or breast of game (pheasant, partridge, etc.).

As with celery and lettuce, drain the braised cabbage and place it in a shallow casserole; add some thickened veal stock to the juices in the braising pan. Boil to reduce, correct the seasoning, then strain the sauce onto the vegetables so that they absorb the sauce and are glazed with a shiny coat.

Vegetables can also be stuffed before being braised.

Vegetables à la grecque

VEGETABLES GREEK STYLE (For 2 pounds)

This way of preparing vegetables is not, as one might believe, a Greek specialty. But this method of preparing and cooking was developed and perfected by French cooks on the basis of the original Greek dishes.

Vegetables cooked *à la grecque* are served most often cold as hors d'oeuvre. The most outstanding are artichokes, leeks, small onions, and mushrooms.

1 quart water
1/2 cup virgin olive oil
3/4 tablespoon salt
Juice of 3 lemons
Fennel
Celery
Coriander seeds
Pepper
Thyme
Bay leaf

Method. Whatever vegetables you choose to cook by by this method, the following ingredients are used: water, olive oil, salt, and lemon juice. Season with fennel, celery, coriander seeds, pepper, thyme, and bay leaf, using these spices in proportion to their aromatic strength. In certain cases, part of the water is replaced by a dry white wine.

The vegetables are then cooked in this preparation, and after being cooked, kept in that liquid, which will have reduced in part.

Why and how are vegetables glazed?

Some vegetables, such as carrots, turnips, small onions, etc., are glazed to preserve and accentuate their flavor and to give them a shine, while maintaining their natural color and firmness. Therefore, after being trimmed or rounded on their edges, the vegetables are placed in a shallow heavy-bottomed saucepan, with butter, salt, a pinch of sugar, and water reaching halfway up. The cooking is done by boiling to evaporate the liquid almost completely, reducing it to a syrup. Glazing is done by rolling the vegetables in that syrupy liquid to give them a shiny coating.

309

Glazed vegetables are used as a garnish for meats and poultry. They are also used to make bouquets of vegetables.

The term "glaze" is also used for braised vegetables. However, the glazing of braised vegetables (pages 308–9) differs from the kind of glazing described above.

Cooking dried vegetables

Dried vegetables are mainly leguminous, such as beans, lentils, peas, etc., gathered when ripe. Dried vegetables must not be too old; the best quality are from the current year. Since their water has been partly removed, it is important to soak them for a few hours before cooking them. This immersion in water should not be overdone. If the vegetables are soaked too long, they will germinate and ferment and cause intestinal disorders during digestion. First, the beans must be sorted and washed to eliminate any dirt (bad beans, stones, etc.) that is often found in them.

Unlike fresh vegetables, dried vegetables are started in cold water, in sufficient quantity so that they will cook properly and continue to swell. To be sure of perfect cooking, the liquid must be brought to a boil slowly. Skim the top, spice with an onion stuck with a clove, carrots, garlic, and a *bouquet garni*. Add salt after half an hour, and keep the saucepan covered. The cooking must be slow and regular; under no circumstances should the liquid stop bubbling. If the liquid evaporates, add boiling water—not cold water, which would harden the starch.

Artichauts avec sauces diverses
ARTICHOKES WITH VARIOUS SAUCES

Cook artichokes whole; first cut the stems off close to the leaves; with scissors, remove the pointed ends of the bottom row of leaves and trim the artichokes by one-third; wash them, tie them to keep the leaves together while they are cooking, and plunge them into a saucepan of boiling water, let stand off the heat for 10 minutes, then drain.

Place the artichokes again in boiling salted water, and cook, letting the water boil rapidly.

The artichokes are cooked when they feel soft to a light pressure on the bottom or when a leaf can be detached easily.

To serve artichokes hot drain them well, standing them upside down on their leaves, and place them on a folded napkin. Serve on the side a sauceboat of melted butter, or a hollandaise sauce (page 88), a *mousseline* sauce (page 89), a cream sauce (page 85), or a *velouté* sauce (page 76).

To serve artichokes cold drain them, standing them upside down on their leaves, and let them cool. Place them on a folded napkin after removing the center leaves, and then the chokes. Replace the bouquet of leaves that were removed, with the leaves upside down, the pointed ends inside the center of the artichoke, which will be like a chalice; place a pinch of chopped parsley or chervil on top.

Serve with a cold sauce: vinaigrette (pages 2–3), light mayonnaise (page 90), with or without mustard, a *tartare* sauce (page 91), etc.

Artichauts à la grecque
ARTICHOKES GREEK STYLE

12 small artichokes
3 cups water
3 sprigs parsley
1 celery rib
Sprig thyme
$^1/_2$ bay leaf
Pinch coriander
Pinch fennel
5 crushed peppercorns
Juice of 2 lemons
6 tablespoons oil
$1^1/_2$ teaspoons salt

In April and May small artichokes, called *poivrade,* are available. Choose a dozen, freshly gathered. Quarter them, trim the leaves, and throw into acidulated cold water. Drain.

Method. Blanch the artichokes for 8 minutes by plunging them into boiling water, then drain.

Meanwhile, prepare a marinade with 3 cups water; a bouquet of parsley, celery, thyme, bay leaf, coriander, fennel, and peppercorns; the juice of 2 lemons; 6 tablespoons oil, and $1^1/_2$ teaspoons salt.

Bring the marinade to a boil, and boil quickly for 10 minutes; then add the artichokes; cook on a high flame for 15 to 20 minutes, then pour into a bowl and let cool.

Place the artichokes in a dish with a little of the cooking marinade and serve very cold.

Artichauts à la Barigoule
ARTICHOKES STUFFED WITH MUSHROOMS

6 medium artichokes

Method. Choose 6 medium artichokes of the same size. Cut the stems off close to the leaves and trim the leaves by about $1^1/_2$ inches.

Blanch the artichokes for 15 minutes in boiling water and drain them. When cool enough to handle, remove the center leaves, then all of the choke.

Season lightly, then fill the inside with a large tablespoon of the stuffing.

Stuffing

2 ounces fresh pork fat, grated or cut in tiny dice
2 shallots, finely chopped
$^1/_2$ pound white mushrooms
Salt and pepper
2 ounces sausage meat
1 teaspoon chopped fresh parsley
4 tablespoons unsalted butter
1 carrot, sliced
1 onion, sliced
3 pieces fresh pork rind
Sprig thyme
$^1/_2$ bay leaf
1 cup dry white wine
Blond veal stock (page 72), lightly salted, or bouillon
3 tablespoons reduced *demi-glace* sauce (page 76) or 2 tablespoons unsalted butter

Grate 2 ounces fresh pork fat or cut into tiny dice; slowly heat in a skillet with the shallots.

Meanwhile, quickly chop $^1/_2$ pound white mushrooms, cleaned and washed without letting them stand in the water. Add the mushrooms to the skillet where the pork fat and the shallots are cooking; dry everything on a high flame for 3 minutes, stirring continuously with a wooden spoon; season with salt and pepper.

One can, at this point, add 2 ounces fine sausage meat. Remove from the heat and finish by adding 1 teaspoon chopped fresh parsley and 4 tablespoons butter. Mix well until the butter is completely incorporated. Correct the seasoning. Stuff the artichokes and cover each with a piece of fresh pork fat; tie with strings.

At the bottom of a thickly buttered deep saucepan just big enough to hold the 6 artichokes, place a carrot and an onion, both sliced, 3 pieces fresh pork rind, thyme, and bay leaf; place the artichokes on top, cover, and stew for 10 minutes, simmering; moisten with 1 cup dry white wine and boil to reduce almost completely; add blond veal stock, lightly salted, or some bouillon, to reach halfway up the artichokes. Bring to a boil, cover, and cook in a 325° oven for 45 minutes.

Remove the lid and let the pork fat brown.

Remove the artichokes, take off the strings, and place the artichokes on a hot round platter.

Strain the braising juice into a skillet, degrease it, and boil to reduce it to ¹/₂ cup; correct the seasoning, and add 3 tablespoons reduced *demi-glace* sauce, or off the heat add 2 tablespoons butter.

Pour this sauce on the serving platter with the artichokes or serve in a sauceboat, which is more practical.

Fonds d'artichauts à la bressanne

ARTICHOKE BOTTOMS BRESSE STYLE

12 medium-sized
 artichokes
1 tablespoon flour
2 tablespoons vinegar or
 ¹/₂ lemon
1 quart water
1¹/₂ teaspoons salt
6 tablespoons unsalted
 butter
Salt and fresh pepper
6 tablespoons *crème
 fraîche* or heavy cream
2¹/₂ cups light mushroom
 purée (page 323)

Method.   Remove all the leaves of the freshly gathered artichokes; completely remove the chokes and trim the outsides; rub with a quarter of a lemon to keep them white, and place the artichoke bottoms in cold water.

Meanwhile, prepare a light white *court-bouillon,* made with 1 tablespoon flour, 2 tablespoons vinegar or half a lemon, 1 quart water, and 1¹/₂ teaspoons salt. Moisten the flour with cold water and bring the liquid to a boil, stirring often.

Add the artichoke bottoms and cook, simmering, for 30 to 40 minutes. When the bottoms are cooked, drain and wipe dry; stew in 4 tablespoons butter in a skillet for 15 minutes. Season with a dash of salt and fresh pepper. Raise the heat to brown the bottoms lightly on both sides, turning them carefully with a spatula.

Moisten the artichoke bottoms with 6 tablespoons *crème fraîche,* boil to reduce slowly by half, and add 2¹/₂ cups light mushroom purée.

Remove from the heat as soon as the purée is boiling, and add remaining butter, stirring well. Serve in a bowl.

Fonds d'artichauts farcis

STUFFED ARTICHOKE BOTTOMS

Trim the artichoke bottoms and cook in a white *court-bouillon* following the directions in the recipe for the artichoke bottoms Bresse style above. Drain, season with salt and pepper, and stew in butter for 15 minutes in a skillet; place in a gratin dish, and garnish with a rather thick mushroom purée (page 323); sprinkle with fresh bread crumbs, baste with the cooking butter, and brown in a 425° oven.

Serve with a sauceboat of Madeira sauce (page 79).

Fonds d'artichauts Mornay

ARTICHOKE BOTTOMS WITH MORNAY SAUCE

Proceed as for the stuffed artichoke bottoms above; after the artichoke bottoms are cooked and stewed, put them side by side in a gratin dish, first placing a light layer of Mornay sauce (page 84) at the bottom.

Spoon 1 tablespoon Mornay sauce on each, then sprinkle with some grated parmesan and gruyère cheese, half of each, mixed with a pinch of fresh bread crumbs.

Baste each bottom with a few drops of melted butter, and brown in a 425° oven.

Fonds d'artichauts princesse

ARTICHOKE BOTTOMS WITH ASPARAGUS TIPS

Prepare in the same way as the artichoke bottoms with Mornay sauce above. However, when the bottoms are placed in the gratin dish, garnish them with green asparagus tips, cooked in salted boiling water, drained, stewed for 5 minutes in butter in a skillet, and coated with a few tablespoons of Mornay sauce. Finish the dish as for the artichoke bottoms with Mornay sauce.

Beignets d'artichauts

ARTICHOKE FRITTERS

Prepare artichoke bottoms as directed above, and cook them in a white *court-bouillon* or, even better, steam them; drain and wipe dry. Then cut the bottoms into 4 or 6 pieces each, depending on their size.

Place the artichoke pieces in a bowl and pour over a few drops of lemon juice and a small stream of oil; season with salt and pepper, and add a pinch of chopped parsley and chervil; mix well, and marinate for 20 minutes.

Drain the artichoke pieces and plunge them one at a time into a frying batter (see page 308); then into very hot deep oil. When the fritters rise to the top and are golden brown and crisp, drain them on a paper towel, sprinkle with salt, and place them in bunches on a round platter covered with a folded napkin.

On top of each bunch, place a pinch of fried parsley.

Asperges

ASPARAGUS

Preparing asparagus is very simple. Peel the stems, being careful not to touch the tips; delicately remove the tiny leaves that surround the tips. It is not enough to scrape the stalk because that does not remove the stringy and disagreeable skin.

As the stalks are peeled and the tough part of the stem removed, place the stalks in a bowl of cold water, without leaving them in it too long. Drain them and tie in bunches of about 6 to 10, depending on their thickness; cook by placing the bunches in boiling water, with 1¼ teaspoons salt per quart.

313

The cooking time is 18 to 20 minutes. [*Editor's note:* Directions are for thick white French asparagus; slender green asparagus will take less time to cook.]

The asparagus should not be overcooked; the stalks should remain rather crisp.

If the asparagus is to be served hot, cook it just before serving time. First, remove each bunch with a slotted spoon and dip it in a second pan of boiling water, correctly salted. Washing the asparagus this way will remove the strong taste of the asparagus water and make the stalks more tender and agreeable. Drain the stalks on a paper towel and place on a long platter with a special rack. Place each row of asparagus ³/₄ inch behind the preceding one in order to display the tips well.

If the asparagus is to be served cold, follow the same method but let the stalks cool on a paper towel.

Hot asparagus is served with a hot sauce: hollandaise (page 88), *mousseline* (page 89), or *velouté* sauce (page 76), or melted butter; cold asparagus is served with a vinaigrette sauce (pages 2–3) or a light mayonnaise (page 90), etc.

Asperges au gratin

ASPARAGUS AU GRATIN

After cooking the asparagus as directed above, cut off the tender part 2¹/₄ to 3 inches from the tips. Steam the tips for 10 minutes in butter in a skillet. Season with a dash of salt and freshly ground pepper.

Place the asparagus in a gratin dish and follow the method given for artichoke bottoms with Mornay sauce (pages 312–13)

Asperges à la polonaise

ASPARAGUS POLISH STYLE

Just before serving the asparagus cooked by the directions above, place it, very hot and well drained, on a long platter, putting one row behind the other. Sprinkle the tips with 1 hard-cooked egg yolk (for 15 to 20 asparagus stalks), rubbed through a sieve, and a large pinch chopped parsley, slightly damp.

On the asparagus tips, pour butter cooked until light brown, adding fresh bread crumbs (2 tablespoons crumbs and ¹/₄ pound butter for 3 servings), browned and crunchy.

Serve immediately while the butter is still bubbling.

Points d'asperges vertes

GREEN ASPARAGUS TIPS

Green asparagus is generally used as a garnish; stalks are no thicker than a pencil. Break off the tender part, which is no more than 3 inches long, by bending the asparagus between your fingers; $1/2$ pound green asparagus gives about $3^1/2$ ounces tips.

Tie the tips in small bunches with a string; cut the tender part of the stems into pieces $1/2$ inch long. Place the asparagus in a large quantity of boiling salted water, cook on a high flame, drain well, and prepare according to the recipe chosen.

Aubergines

EGGPLANT

The best eggplant for cooking is the large purple one, which is used in many different ways, either as a vegetable or as a garnish.

It is important to rid the eggplants of their excess water by steeping them in salt for half an hour, when they are to be stewed in butter in a covered saucepan, cooked *au gratin,* or sautéed. In order to remove the water, peel the eggplants, then slice or quarter them, or cut into large sticks or in pieces the shape of an olive, depending upon the dish in which the eggplants will be used. Place the cut eggplants in a bowl, sprinkle with sea salt, mix, and let steep. Drain well, wipe dry, and cook.

In addition to the various ways given here, eggplant can also be sliced thickly, peeled, and sautéed to serve with poached or soft-boiled eggs, with *tournedos, noisettes, grenadins,* etc.

Aubergines au gratin

EGGPLANT AU GRATIN (For 6 people)

3 large eggplants
Salt
Oil for deep frying
1 medium-sized onion
2 shallots
2 tablespoons unsalted butter, plus extra butter
1 tablespoon olive oil
$1/4$ pound white mushrooms
Salt and pepper
1 garlic clove, crushed
2 tablespoons tomato purée
2 tablespoons *espagnole* sauce (page 76) or veal stock (page 72)
2 tablespoons fresh bread crumbs, plus extra bread crumbs
Chopped parsley

Method.   Cut the 3 eggplants in half lengthwise. Score the pulp lightly with the point of a knife and make an incision in each half $1/8$ inch inside the skin around the edge. Let them steep with salt for 30 minutes.

Drain the eggplants, wipe dry, and plunge into very hot oil, cooking just until the pulp can be removed easily with a spoon—about 5 to 8 minutes.

Drain on a paper towel, and remove the pulp with a spoon, being careful not to damage the skins. Spread the skins, side by side, the black side down, on a well-buttered gratin dish; meanwhile, chop the pulp fine and put it in a bowl.

Chop the onion and the shallots, stew them slowly with 1 tablespoon butter and 1 tablespoon olive oil. When they are cooked, raise the heat and brown them. Add the mushrooms, washed and chopped, season with salt and pepper, and cook quickly on a high flame, stirring continuously with a wooden spoon.

When the water from the mushrooms has evaporated, add the garlic, the tomato purée, the *espagnole* sauce or veal stock, and the pulp from the eggplants. Simmer for 5 minutes, stiffening the mixture (it should be like mashed potatoes) by adding some fresh bread crumbs.

Remove from the heat, season, and fill the eggplant skins with this mixture piled in the shape of a dome.

Sprinkle the tops with fresh bread crumbs, moisten with a stream of remaining melted butter (or oil), and brown in a 425° oven. After removing from the oven, pour around each eggplant a border of *espagnole* sauce or veal stock reduced and buttered. Sprinkle each eggplant with a pinch of chopped parsley.

Aubergines à la crème

EGGPLANT WITH CREAM

3 firm eggplants
Salt
9 tablespoons unsalted butter
1½ cups *crème fraîche* or heavy cream
Chopped chervil

Method. Peel 3 firm eggplants; slice ⅛ inch thick; steep in salt for 30 minutes; drain, and wipe dry.

Stew the slices in 7 tablespoons butter in a covered saucepan until completely cooked.

Just before serving, add 1½ cups *crème fraîche* to the eggplants; boil on a high flame to reduce quickly by half, stirring the eggplants but being careful not to crush the slices. When the sauce is sufficiently reduced, correct the seasoning and, stirring, add off the heat 2 tablespoons butter.

Place in a bowl and sprinkle with a pinch of chopped chervil.

Aubergine à la provençale

EGGPLANT PROVENÇAL STYLE (For 1 serving)

3 tablespoons olive oil
½ onion, cut into julienne
1 medium eggplant, cut into ¾-inch cubes
Salt and pepper
1 teaspoon flour
½ garlic clove, crushed
1 tomato, peeled, seeded, juice squeezed out, and coarsely chopped
Chopped parsley

Method. Heat the oil in a skillet, slowly brown the onion until golden; add the eggplant, season with salt and pepper, a pinch of each, and sprinkle with the flour.

Stir often in the skillet to keep the pieces from sticking and to brown everything lightly.

Add the garlic, crushed with a knife blade (never chop garlic); heat for a second, shaking the skillet; then add the tomato.

Correct the seasoning with salt and pepper, and continue to cook slowly. The juice from the tomato changes the cooking process from frying to stewing; the eggplant and the condiments get soft until the moisture has completely evaporated. This step will take about half an hour; then the eggplant, tomato, and oil, well mixed, will look like a marmalade.

To serve, correct the seasoning, pour the compote into a hot bowl, and sprinkle a pinch of chopped parsley on top.

Aubergines frites ou beignets d'aubergines

FRIED EGGPLANT OR EGGPLANT FRITTERS

Peel the eggplants; slice them ⅛ inch thick. Season with salt and freshly ground pepper, sprinkle with 2 tablespoons flour, and mix well.

Shake off the excess flour and plunge the slices into very hot oil.

When they are golden brown and crisp, drain and place on a round platter covered with a napkin. To be delicious, the eggplant must be crisp; the guests, therefore, must wait for this vegetable.

Eggplant slices also can be fried as fritters, dipped in frying batter (page 308).

Cardons
CARDOONS

6 pounds cardoons
Lemon
Vinegar or lemon juice
1 quart water
1 tablespoon flour
2 tablespoons vinegar or juice of ½ lemon
1½ teaspoons salt
¼ pound raw veal fat

Cardoons look like giant artichoke plants; when they reach full growth, the leaves are tied up and the plant is covered to blanch it, that is, to keep it white and tender.

The Tours variety is the best.

Only the tender center stalks are used for the table. A 6-pound plant will yield about 2 pounds of edible parts.

Whatever the recipe, the cardoon stalks need unique preparation.

Method. First remove the tough and wilted branches; then, one by one, cut off the tender branches until you reach the heart. Cut the stalks into pieces 3 inches long, starting from the base, discarding the leafy top part, which is tough and stringy, and keeping only the thick parts, which are tender.

Peel the pieces of stalk, removing all the stringy parts, and rub them with a quarter of a lemon to keep them from darkening. Place the pieces in a bowl of cold water with vinegar or lemon juice.

Prepare a white *court-bouillon* with 1 quart water, 1 tablespoon flour diluted with 2 tablespoons vinegar or the juice of half a lemon, and 1½ teaspoons salt.

Stir until the liquid comes to a boil; add the pieces of cardoon, drained at the last moment.

To protect the pieces of stalk from contact with the air, which would darken them, add to the *court-bouillon* ¼ pound raw veal fat, diced very fine, for each quart water.

Boil slowly, covered, for 2 hours. When the cardoons are cooked, they should give when pressed with your fingers. Pour the cooked cardoons into a glazed bowl and keep them warm until finished for serving.

Cardons à la moelle
CARDOONS WITH MARROW (For 6 people)

1 white cardoon
3 tablespoons flour
1 lemon
Salt and pepper
1½ tablespoons unsalted butter, plus extra butter
1 quart beef bouillon
7 ounces beef marrow
2 ounces gruyère cheese, grated

Method. Cut the tender parts of a cardoon into small sticks 1¼ inches long; trim them and cook in a *court-bouillon* made with 3 quarts water to which are added 1 tablespoon flour diluted in water, the juice of 1 lemon, and 1½ tablespoons salt.

Meanwhile, in a saucepan heat 1½ tablespoons butter. Add the remaining flour and make a *roux*. Into the *roux* pour the beef bouillon, well flavored. After mixing with a whisk, simmer for 20 minutes. Correct the seasoning.

317

When the cardoons are cooked, drain them, mix into the sauce, and place in a buttered gratin dish.

Poach the beef marrow. Slice it. Place the marrow on the cardoons. Sprinkle the grated gruyère on top and brown in the oven.

Serve immediately in the gratin dish.

Cardons au beurre
CARDOONS WITH BUTTER

After cooking the cardoons in a *court-bouillon* (see above), drain them and stew in butter in a covered skillet. Place in a vegetable dish with the cooking butter, and sprinkle a few drops of lemon juice on top.

Cardons frits
FRIED CARDOONS

Cook the cardoons in a white *court-bouillon* (see above), drain, and marinate for 30 minutes with a stream of olive oil, the juice of half a lemon for 2 pounds of cardoons, salt and pepper, and chopped parsley. Drain again.

Dip the cardoon pieces in a light frying batter (page 308), and plunge them, one at a time, into hot deep oil until they are golden brown.

This step should be done at the last moment.

Sprinkle the cardoons with a pinch of salt, and place in bunches on a plate covered with a folded napkin.

Cardons au jus
CARDOONS AU JUS

Stew pieces of cardoons, already cooked by the directions on page 317, in butter in a covered saucepan for 10 minutes.

Then pour in a good lightly salted veal stock (page 72) to cover; simmer for 15 to 20 minutes.

Place in a vegetable dish with the juice, reduced, and buttered off the heat.

Cardons avec sauces diverses
CARDOONS WITH VARIOUS SAUCES

Cardoons, like artichokes, can be served with brown or white sauces: *demi-glace* (page 76), *bordelaise* (page 79), hollandaise (page 88), *mousseline* (page 89), cream (page 85), or *béarnaise* (page 89), etc.; or cold, with a vinaigrette sauce (pages 2–3), rémoulade sauce (page 91), etc.

CARROTS

Cooked alone as a vegetable, or for a garnish, or as a condiment, carrots play an important role in cooking. They can be found in markets all year round; gardeners and truck farmers bring the early forced varieties to the market; these are followed in the fall by the summer crop and the late varieties (which will keep through the winter).

Spring carrots are the best to prepare as vegetables or as a garnish. Short dark orange carrots are the finest of the young spring varieties. They need only be peeled, and the peel should be a very thin film because the nutritive elements, the sugar, and the vitamins are concentrated toward the outside part, which is also the tenderest.

Young carrots should never be blanched, that is, plunged into boiling water. After peeling the carrots, cut them, depending on how large they are, into halves or quarters; round the edges to give each piece the shape of a large olive. Wash in cold water.

Cook the carrot pieces in a saucepan with just enough cold water to cover them; for each 2 cups add a pinch of salt, 1 teaspoon sugar, and 4 tablespoons butter.

Cook, covered, on a moderately high flame, until evaporation is complete. The mixture of the butter, the juices from the vegetables, and the reduced liquid produces a thick syrupy sauce. Sauté the carrots in this mixture until they are covered with a shiny coating.

Cooked this way, the carrots are ready to be served with or without a complementary dish.

When one is obliged to use old carrots, use the dark orange part. The cores, hard and strong in flavor, after being boiled, can be used in moderation as condiments for some cooking stock.

Cut carrots into large pieces, shaped like olives, and cook them in salted water before using in any recipe: this is the only way to remove the strong flavor of old carrots. The carrots can be grated or cut into thin strips and coated with cream and lemon or a mayonnaise (page 90) or any sauce with a mayonnaise base.

CARROTS GLAZED IN BUTTER

The word "glaze" would be senseless if it did not conjure up the image of the shiny envelope that coats the carrots like a varnish when they are cooked.

Prepare by the instructions above and off the heat add some butter, which will mix with the syrupy juice in which the carrots were sautéed.

This vegetable should be cooked just before serving; waiting spoils the fresh sweet taste of the carrots, which then take on an unpleasant reheated flavor.

Carottes à la crème
CARROTS WITH CREAM

Prepare carrots glazed in butter (as directed on page 319); when the sauce is reduced, moisten again, covering the carrots with *crème fraîche* or heavy cream. Boil to reduce by half, correct the seasoning, shake everything to distribute the sauce, and place in a vegetable dish.

Carottes Vichy
CARROTS VICHY

Follow the cooking method for carrots glazed in butter (page 319). Instead of shaping the carrots like olives, they should be thinly sliced; add a pinch of Vichy salt to the cooking water.

Place the carrots in a vegetable dish and sprinkle with freshly chopped parsley.

Purée de carottes
CARROT PURÉE

Slice the carrots very thin, add well-washed rice to equal one-fourth of their weight.

Cook together over high heat, as for carrots glazed with butter (page 319). However, increase the quantity of water. Rub the cooked carrots and rice through a fine sieve, put the purée into a skillet, and dry it on a high flame.

Off the heat add $1/4$ pound butter for each pound of purée, and bring to the proper consistency by adding milk, cream, or boiling bouillon.

Correct the seasoning, place in a vegetable dish, and decorate with diamond- or heart-shaped croutons, fried in butter.

Pieds de céleri et céleri-rave
CELERY STALKS AND CELERY ROOT

These are two different species of the same vegetable. In celery we eat the stalks; in celery root, the root.

Both are eaten raw or cooked. However, they are not prepared in the same ways.

In the chapter on hors d'oeuvre you will find appropriate recipes for each. Here, I will speak of this vegetable as a side dish or garnish.

Trim the celery stalks or heads by removing the green leaves and by slicing off part of the base. Leave enough of the base to hold the trimmed stalks, about 8 inches long, around the heart.

Wash carefully, running cold water between the ribs to remove the dirt and the tiny insects that are sometimes there.

Remove the strings from the outside of the ribs, rinse the celery heads, plunge them into a pot of boiling salted water, and boil for 10 minutes.

Drain and let cool; season the insides with a pinch of salt, and tie the branches with a string.

To braise, place a few slices of carrots and onions and some fresh pork in a buttered saucepan. Place the celery heads on top, side by side; cover them and simmer for 15 minutes. Cover with a good white veal stock (page 72), not degreased, to which is added 3 ounces of chopped fresh pork fat per quart of stock.

Bring slowly to a boil and simmer, covered, in a 275° oven for 2 hours.

If the celery is not to be used immediately, remove to a glazed bowl and pour over the strained juice.

Celery root should first be washed, then peeled, cut into quarters, trimmed or thickly sliced. Rinse in cold water and blanch in salted boiling water for 5 minutes.

Drain and let cool on a paper towel. Stew in butter in a skillet. Season with salt and pepper. After the celery root is cooked, prepare as directed above for celery stalks.

Céleri au jus

CELERY STALKS AU JUS

Drain braised celery stalks (recipe above). Cut the heads in half lengthwise. Place in a skillet and cover with a good veal stock (page 72), lightly salted, adding the braising juices, 1 part braising juice to 2 parts veal stock.

Cover and simmer for 15 to 20 minutes.

Place the celery in a vegetable dish; if the juice has not reduced sufficiently, raise the heat, and boil for a few minutes in order to reduce it to the quantity needed. Off the heat thicken with 3½ tablespoons butter for ½ cup juice. Pour over the celery.

Purée de céleri-rave

CELERY ROOT PURÉE

This purée is made by mixing together 1 part puréed celery root to 1 part puréed potato.

Prepare like mashed potatoes, that is, dry on a high flame to evaporate the moisture; work the purée with a spatula, off the heat, adding 3½ tablespoons butter for 1 pound purée, and bring it back to the proper consistency with hot milk and *crème fraîche* or heavy cream. Spice with a dash of grated nutmeg. Do not let the purée boil. Serve in a vegetable dish.

Les champignons

WHITE MUSHROOMS
First Method

Choose mushrooms that are white, firm, with their gills not visible; cut off the sandy part of the stems. Place the mush-

321

1 pound mushrooms
¹/₂ cup water
2¹/₂ tablespoons unsalted butter
Juice of ¹/₂ lemon
Pinch salt

1 pound mushrooms
¹/₂ lemon
Melted unsalted butter
Pinch salt
2 tablespoons Madeira, veal stock (page 72), or white chicken bouillon

1 pound white mushrooms
10¹/₂ tablespoons unsalted butter
Pinch salt and freshly ground pepper
1 cup *crème fraîche* or heavy cream
Juice of ¹/₄ lemon

rooms in a bowl and pour some cold water over; wash them carefully and quickly in two successive changes of water; drain, and wipe dry immediately.

Trim the mushrooms; cut the stem off, and peel the cap, removing a thin shaving. This way of peeling requires a certain dexterity, for one has to work with one's fingers and a knife while turning the mushroom (page 234).

Meanwhile, prepare a *court-bouillon,* using, for 1 pound mushrooms, ¹/₂ cup water, 2¹/₂ tablespoons butter, the juice of half a lemon, and a pinch of salt. Bring to a boil, and add the mushrooms.

Boil the mushrooms in this prepared liquid for 5 minutes on a high flame, and remove them to a glazed bowl. Cover the mushrooms with a piece of buttered paper to prevent the tops from darkening.

Second Method

As the mushrooms are peeled, rub each one with half a lemon and place them in a skillet with melted butter; add a pinch of salt, 2 tablespoons Madeira, veal stock, or white chicken bouillon. Cover, and stew for 8 minutes. Remove to a bowl, and follow the directions for the first method.

Champignons à la provençale

MUSHROOMS PROVENÇAL STYLE

Follow the recipe for *cèpes à la bordelaise* (page 325); replace the shallots with chopped parsley and garlic, increasing the garlic.

Champignons à la crème

MUSHROOMS WITH CREAM

Method.   Choose mushrooms that are small, firm, and very white. Remove the sandy parts; wash the mushrooms carefully, then drain and wipe dry. If the mushrooms are large or medium, quarter them.

In a skillet large enough to spread out the mushrooms, heat 7 tablespoons butter. When the butter is hot, raise the heat and add the mushrooms; season with a pinch of salt and a few turns of the pepper mill. Sauté on a high flame to evaporate the mushroom liquid quickly and brown the mushrooms lightly.

Add 1 cup *crème fraîche,* the juice of a quarter of a lemon; boil to reduce by half and off the heat thicken with 3¹/₂ tablespoons butter.

Place in a warm vegetable dish.

For this recipe, one must have young mushrooms, well formed and very white; if not, the dish, which should have a beautiful ivory color, may turn gray.

For 2 pounds mushrooms add 1 cup cream; simmer on the stove. After it reduces slightly, correct the seasoning, add a little bit of cream to restore the whiteness to the sauce and to thicken it.

For a large dinner, in order to prevent the cream from curdling, some béchamel sauce (page 78) can be added.

Champignons grillés
BROILED MUSHROOMS

Choose firm, white mushroom caps. After washing and drying them, season and coat with oil or melted butter.

Place them on a hot grill or under a broiler; turn them once and brush with melted butter or oil. Serve the mushroom caps on a plate with *maître d'hôtel* butter (pages 161–2) in their cavities.

They are usually used as a garnish for broiled spring chicken American style, mixed grill, etc.

Purée de champignons
MUSHROOM PURÉE

Carefully wash firm, white mushrooms; rub them through a metal strainer or chop them very fine with a knife. Immediately place the mushroom pulp in a skillet over a high flame and stir with a wooden spoon until the water has evaporated completely.

Finish the purée by adding a béchamel sauce (page 78) made with extra cream. Add salt, pepper, a dash of nutmeg.

Champignons sautés au beurre ou à la Mornay
SAUTÉED MUSHROOMS WITH BUTTER OR MORNAY SAUCE

Slice the mushrooms, if they are large, into 3 to 5 slices. Season with salt and pepper, and sauté in a skillet in butter on a very high flame.

Place the chopped mushrooms in a vegetable dish and sprinkle with chopped parsley.

You can also thicken with Mornay sauce; then pour mushrooms into an ovenproof dish, sprinkle with grated gruyère cheese, and brown.

Duxelles sèche de champignons
DRY MUSHROOM DUXELLES

1 pound mushrooms
Unsalted butter and oil
2 ounces finely chopped shallots and onions
Salt and pepper
Pinch chopped parsley

Method. Finely chop mushrooms; squeeze in a cloth to remove all the juice. In butter and oil in a skillet, sauté 2 ounces finely chopped shallots and onions. Add the chopped mushrooms, salt, and pepper. Cook on a very high flame, stirring with a wooden spoon until the water has evaporated completely. Finish by adding a pinch of chopped parsley.

The dry *duxelles* should be stored in a bowl covered with buttered paper, to be used as needed, especially in stuffings.

Variation

The *duxelles* to stuff some vegetables, such as tomatoes, artichokes, mushroom caps, etc., is prepared in the same way as dry *duxelles;* but toward the end of cooking, add a dash of garlic, a little bit of *demi-glace* sauce (page 76) with tomatoes added and reduced, and fresh bread crumbs, rubbed through a fine sieve.

Champignons farcis
Jean-Paul Lacombe

STUFFED MUSHROOMS JEAN-PAUL LACOMBE

Large mushrooms
Salt and pepper
Melted unsalted butter or olive oil

Method. Choose large mushrooms all the same size.

Clean them, wash, drain, and wipe dry. Remove the stems to make a cavity in each cap.

Place the mushrooms in a well-buttered ovenproof dish, season with salt and pepper, and baste with some melted butter, or olive oil, if you prefer it.

Start the cooking by placing mushrooms in a 450° oven for 5 minutes.

Remove the mushroom caps and in each mound a stuffing made from the stems, chopped and cooked as *duxelles* (see below). Sprinkle with fresh bread crumbs. Baste with melted butter or oil, and brown in a 425° oven.

Duxelles

1 medium-sized onion
1 shallot
7 tablespoons unsalted butter
1 cup *espagnole* sauce (page 76) or veal stock (page 72)
1 tablespoon tomato purée
Grated garlic
1 teaspoon chopped parsley
Few drops of lemon juice
1 heaping teaspoon fresh bread crumbs

For 1/2 pound mushroom stems, finely chop 1 medium-sized onion and 1 shallot and cook them in 3 1/2 tablespoons butter in a skillet without letting them brown. When the onion and shallot are soft, add the finely chopped mushroom stems, heat on a high flame for 3 minutes to evaporate the water, and moisten with 1 cup *espagnole* sauce or a good veal stock and 1 tablespoon tomato purée or the pulp of a fresh tomato. Season with salt and pepper, and flavor with a little grated garlic, chopped parsley, a few drops of lemon juice.

Cook to reduce to the proper consistency for stuffing or thicken with 1 heaping teaspoon fresh bread crumbs. Correct the seasoning, and finish off the heat by adding 3 1/2 tablespoons butter.

Bolets ou cèpes

BOLETUSES OR CÈPES

The boletus is part of the group of polypores. These beautiful mushrooms, some weighing as much as 4 pounds, are called *cèpes* or boletuses in cooking. It is especially in the fall that this mushroom, perfumed with forest essences, is found in abundance. As they grow old, *cèpes* lose a large part of their culinary appeal; sometimes they have parasites, they become spongy, and they can be toxic. Whatever the variety, *cèpes* have a tendency to fall apart in cooking and to become slimy. Here are some basic principles to counteract these drawbacks and some frequently used methods for cooking them.

Cèpes sautés à la bordelaise
(méthode Escoffier)

SAUTÉED CÈPES À LA BORDELAISE (ESCOFFIER'S RECIPE)

1/2 pound cèpes
Salt and pepper
Oil
Unsalted butter
2 tablespoons cèpe
** stems, chopped**
1 teaspoon chopped
** shallots**
Stream lemon juice
Chopped parsley

Preliminary steps.   The *cèpes* should be barely opened or not at all; do not wash but wipe them; however, those that are completely opened must be washed and wiped dry.

Cooking.   Slice the *cèpes,* season with salt and pepper, sauté in very hot oil until they are lightly browned. Drain, replace the oil with butter, and add to the *cèpes* 2 tablespoons *cèpe* stems that have been chopped and set aside and chopped shallots. Sauté the mixture for a few minutes, and put into a bowl; add a stream of lemon juice and some chopped parsley.

Cèpes à la bordelaise

PARISIAN RECIPE

1 pound cèpes
Unsalted butter or oil
1 teaspoon lemon juice
3 tablespoons olive oil
Salt and pepper
3 shallots, chopped
2 tablespoons fresh bread
** crumbs**
1 teaspoon chopped
** parsley**
Lemon juice

Sort 1 pound firm *cèpes;* clean, wash, and stew in butter or oil with lemon juice. Drain the mushrooms, wipe dry; if they are large, slice them, reserving the stems.

In a skillet big enough to hold the mushrooms heat 3 tablespoons olive oil. Toss the *cèpes* into the very hot oil to sear them; season with salt and freshly ground pepper; sauté over a high flame to brown lightly.

Just before serving, add the chopped stems and shallots, fresh bread crumbs, chopped parsley, and a stream of lemon juice.

Cèpes sautés à la provençale

SAUTÉED CÈPES PROVENÇAL STYLE

Prepare the same way as for *cèpes à la bordelaise* (above), but replace the shallots with 1 teaspoon chopped garlic.

Cèpes grillés

BROILED CÈPES

Choose medium-sized *cèpe* caps. Peel and decorate the rounded sides (page 234); salt and pepper.

Brush the caps with oil or melted butter; cook on a very hot grill or under a broiler. Serve with *maître d'hôtel* butter (pages 161–2) inside the caps; they can also be stuffed with the chopped stems, stewed in butter and flavored with chopped parsley and garlic.

Les morilles

MORELS

Gourmets consider morels *(Morchella elata)* the best mushrooms.

Some suggest not washing them; this is wrong because morels have very fine sand in their gills that must be removed. To do this, after removing the sandy part of the stems, place the morels in a large quantity of cold water, then let more cold water run on them. This process is long and painstaking, but it is the only effective way of eliminating the sand.

To cook the morels, cut them into several pieces if they are too large. After cleaning, stew them in a saucepan with salt and pepper, the juice of a lemon, and 3½ tablespoons butter for 1 pound morels.

Cook over a high flame, covered, for 10 minutes.

The juice the mushrooms release is usually sufficient for them to cook in.

Morilles à la crème
MORELS WITH CREAM

After stewing the morels, following the recipe above, add, for 1 pound morels, ½ cup reduced cream; let simmer for a few minutes.

Just before serving, add some fresh cream to thicken and whiten the sauce; correct the seasoning.

Note: This recipe is used frequently to garnish veal or chicken fricassee; morels are also used to fill pies, flaky pastry, *vol-au-vent,* etc.

Girolles appelées aussi chanterelles
CHANTERELLE MUSHROOMS

These excellent mushrooms have a fine, light aroma and do not require any special cooking preparation. After removing the sandy part of the stems, simply wash them well and stew in butter or sauté in oil or butter.

Chanterelles can be cooked *à la bordelaise* or *provençale.* They are also used as a garnish for meats, poultry, or game.

Note: If the *chanterelles* are large, it is advisable to cut them lengthwise; before sautéing them, they can also be blanched for 1 minute in salted boiling water.

Mousserons — roses des prés
ST. GEORGE'S MUSHROOMS

These mushrooms are cooked in the same way as white mushrooms, but they are most popular and appreciated sautéed in butter or used in omelets.

Les truffes
TRUFFLES

In addition to their value as a flavoring, truffles are used as a garnish and for decoration.

Using truffles for decoration is a delicate task; generally, pieces of canned truffles are employed. These truffles are usually large, firm, and very black; they are cut into very thin slices. Placed flat on the counter, the truffles are sliced with a very sharp knife or with truffle cutters into different shapes: crescent, diamond, star, flower, etc. Then the cutouts are placed on a plate with some melted aspic. Once the ingredients are ready, begin decorating by placing each truffle shape on the prepared dish with a larding needle. When the decoration is finished, glaze with a coat of delicious jelly.

To use truffles in cooking, it is better to choose fresh, that is, raw, truffles.

Raw truffles must be cleaned carefully; soak them in tepid water to remove the sand that partly coats them. Then brush each truffle under running water, and with a kitchen knife remove the sand that still remains. Rinse the truffles again and thoroughly dry them. Depending on their use, dice them, cut them into small sticks, slice them, or shape them like olives. The trimmings and the peels, which have a strong perfume, are chopped and used to prepare a Périgueux sauce (page 82) or for stuffings and mousses. Whatever their use, the chopped stems and peels are always stewed in butter, especially if they are raw, before being incorporated in a dish.

Finally, fresh truffles can also be cut into julienne, in sticks, or sliced and used in mixed salads.

Preparing Truffles for Poultry and Game Birds

This procedure is used for capons, large roasting chickens, ducks, turkeys, pheasants, partridges, etc.

First clean and peel the truffles, set aside a few slices; quarter the remaining truffles, trimming the angles.

Then place these quarters in a bowl and marinate them with a little cognac and Madeira. Season with salt, pepper, and mixed spices (page x), in judicious proportions.

Place the reserved slices under the skin of the bird, being careful not to tear it. Remove all the membranes from fresh pork fat and rub it through a fine sieve. Mix with the quartered truffles. Place this stuffing inside the bird, which must be kept cool but not too cold.

The bird must be stuffed with truffles at least 24 hours before cooking. During this time poultry or game birds will soak up the truffle aroma, and this aroma will develop even more during cooking.

The excess fat, melted after cooking, can be used for other purposes.

Preparing Truffles to Stud *Foie Gras*

Truffles for studding fresh *foie gras* must be fresh, peeled, and quartered, seared in cognac on the stove, and cooled in a covered bowl. Use truffles thus cooked to make pâtés, terrines, or galantines.

Canned Truffles

Truffle production is not regular; therefore one must take advantage of an abundant season to can them, for from one year to another the differences in price are very wide. [*Editor's note:* This is practical only if you live in France; Americans must be content with commercially canned truffles.]

Truffles for canning must be sound and all the same size for each can. After cleaning in the usual way, place the truffles in cans or special jars with a little bit of water, Madeira, and salt.

Tightly seal the cans or jars, then place them in cold water, and simmer for about 2 hours.

Sterilized under good conditions, the truffles will retain their properties; the liquid in which they are preserved, usually called truffle juice, is very useful for cooking and improves the flavor of sauces (Madeira, *financière,* etc.) and also of numerous stuffings.

While they are in season, and especially to keep for the holidays at the end of the year, one can use a method for preserving that is much simpler; it consists of immersing the truffles in a terrine of lard or melted salted goose fat.

Truffes sous la cendre (méthode Escoffier)
TRUFFLES COOKED IN EMBERS (ESCOFFIER'S RECIPE)

Choose beautiful fresh truffles; clean them well, but do not peel. Salt the truffles lightly and baste with a stream of fine champagne brandy. Wrap each truffle first with a thin slice of fresh pork fat, then with a double piece of buttered wax paper; dampen the outside piece of paper with water. Bury the wrapped truffles under a layer of burning embers, keeping the top embers glowing.

Allow 3/4 hour cooking for average truffles.

After removing the paper, put the truffles on a napkin placed on a heated plate and serve with fresh butter.

Truffes au champagne
TRUFFLES WITH CHAMPAGNE

1 pound truffles
1/2 cup champagne
1 heaping tablespoon
  mirepoix bordelaise
1/2 cup veal stock
  (page 72)

Method. Season well-cleaned truffles and cook, covered, with 1/2 cup champagne and 1 heaping tablespoon *mirepoix bordelaise,* stewed in butter.

Place the truffles in a silver bowl. Boil the cooking liquid to reduce almost completely; add 1/2 cup veal stock.

Boil for 5 minutes; correct the seasoning, and strain this *mousseline* sauce onto the truffles.

Serve very hot without boiling.

Note: The champagne can be replaced with sherry, port, or Madeira.

Truffes à la crème
TRUFFLES WITH CREAM

1 pound fresh truffles
Salt and pepper
3 1/2 tablespoons unsalted
  butter
Cognac or port
1 1/2 cups cream

Method. Cut 1 pound fresh truffles into thick slices. Season with salt and pepper; stew slowly with butter and a stream of cognac or port.

Moisten with cream and simmer on a low flame without letting the cream separate.

Serve as soon as the sauce is thickened and the seasoning is correct.

Omelette aux truffes fraîches
OMELET WITH FRESH TRUFFLES

Use 3½ ounces truffles for an omelet made with 6 eggs.

Slice the truffles thin. Salt and pepper them and stew them lightly in butter.

Beat the eggs lightly. Season and add three-fourths of the sliced truffles. Make the omelet as usual, well formed, soft, without browning it too much (pages 42–3).

Place the omelet on a long platter, put the remaining truffle slices in a row on top, and serve.

Variation

Instead of mixing the truffles with the eggs, you can stuff the omelet with a truffle stuffing thickened with a reduced *demi-glace* sauce (page 76).

Oeufs brouillés aux truffes
SCRAMBLED EGGS WITH TRUFFLES

Butter small flan molds and place a nice truffle slice at the bottom of each one.

Prepare the scrambled eggs, very soft; add the truffles, diced and stewed in butter.

To 6 scrambled eggs, add 4 raw eggs; mix and season them.

Fill the molds and poach in a *bain-marie* in the oven. Unmold on little round toasts, fried in butter.

Serve with a very light *demi-glace* sauce (page 76) with essence of truffles.

Note: This way of serving scrambled eggs is called molded eggs Verdi.

Rissoles de truffes à la Valromey
TRUFFLE TURNOVERS VALROMEY

Sandwich together, two by two, large thick slices of truffles separated by slices of *foie gras*. Season lightly and baste with a little bit of fine champagne brandy.

Place each sandwiched truffle pair between two layers of flaky pastry (pages 382–3), cut with a cookie cutter into rounds slightly larger than the truffles. Press the pastry edges to make them stick together.

Plunge the turnovers into deep hot oil to brown.

Drain the turnovers and put them on a napkin placed on a heated plate, garnish with fried parsley, and serve immediately with Périgueux sauce (page 82).

Truffes en surprises Roger Roucou
TRUFFLE SURPRISE ROGER ROUCOU

Rub some cooked *foie gras* through a very fine sieve. Put the purée into a silver or stainless-steel bowl and place the bowl on top of shaved ice. With a wooden spoon mix in chopped truffles, cooked in Madeira.

Make small balls of *foie gras* in various sizes. Roll them in finely chopped and dried truffles.

Shape the balls as much as possible like real truffles and place them on a rack in a cool place.

Glaze with a coat of very flavorful aspic (pages 95–6).

Truffle surprise is served on a napkin, in a basket, or in a crystal bowl.

Endives

The variety of chicory called Witloof or Belgian endive, in its second growth, after being blanched by covering with sand, is very white and delicate.

Cooking. Trim 1 pound Belgian endives and wash quickly by placing under running water—endives becomes bitter if permitted to stand in water. Place in a buttered saucepan, sprinkle with salt and 3^1/$_2$ tablespoons butter, cut into pieces; baste with the juice of a quarter of a lemon. Add 3 tablespoons water; cover with buttered paper.

Put the lid on, then bring to a boil; continue cooking for 45 minutes at moderate heat, in the oven, if possible.

1 pound Belgian endives
Salt
3^1/$_2$ tablespoons unsalted butter
Juice of ^{1}/$_4$ lemon
3 tablespoons water

Endives à la crème
ENDIVES WITH CREAM

Stew the endives as described above, then place them in a skillet, cover them with boiling *crème fraîche* or heavy cream, and simmer until the cream has reduced by two-thirds.

Drain the endives and place them in a warm vegetable bowl; correct the seasoning of the cream; off the heat add 3^1/$_2$ tablespoons butter for each ^{1}/$_2$ cup sauce, and pour over the endives.

Endives Mornay
ENDIVES WITH MORNAY SAUCE

Cook the endives as for endives with cream (above) and place them in a gratin dish. Boil the cream to reduce almost completely, then add enough Mornay sauce (page 84) to cover the endives.

Coat the endives with this sauce; sprinkle on top some grated gruyère and parmesan cheese, half of each, mixed with a pinch of fresh bread crumbs. Baste with melted butter and brown in a 375° oven.

Endives à la meunière
BRAISED ENDIVES

Stew the endives as described on page 330 and drain well. Heat some butter in a skillet. When the butter turns a light brown, place the endives in the skillet, in one layer without squeezing them. Cook slowly, turning them one by one to brown on all sides.

Place the endives on a long platter and baste them with the cooking butter.

Choux
CABBAGE

White cabbage, green cabbage, red cabbage, cauliflower, broccoli, Brussels sprouts, rutabagas, and kohlrabi constitute an ample family, each further augmented by the different varieties of each available during each of the four seasons.

Choucroute à la ménagère
SAUERKRAUT HOME STYLE

2 pounds sauerkraut
Coarse salt
Salt and freshly ground
  pepper
Thin slices fresh pork fat
  and fresh pork rind
1 large onion stuck with a
  clove
1 large carrot, quartered
1 teaspoon juniper berries
1 slab smoked salted pork
¼ pound salted bacon
Uncooked garlic sausage
Bouquet garni
Corned beef brisket
  (optional)
Ham knuckle (optional)
3½ ounces lard or goose
  fat
White bouillon or water
Strasbourg frankfurters

Sauerkraut is made with white cabbages with very hard white cores.

Cut the cabbages into shreds, then place the leaves in a small barrel in layers, sprinkling each layer with coarse salt mixed with juniper berries; use ¼ cup salt for each 10 pounds cabbage.

Press the cabbage down with a piece of wood and place a stone on top; the salted vegetable juices will cover the cabbage by the next day.

Kept in a cool place, the sauerkraut will undergo fermentation, which gradually subsides. After three weeks the sauerkraut is ready to be used.

Cooking the sauerkraut. Wash 2 pounds sauerkraut under running water. If it is old, soak it for 2 hours.

Drain the sauerkraut and squeeze it by handfuls. Spread on a dish towel in a thin layer. Season with salt and freshly ground pepper. Adjust the amount of salt depending on the ingredients that are going to be used with it (salt pork) and the liquid for moistening (water or white bouillon). Line a braising pan or an ovenproof terrine with thin slices of fresh pork fat and fresh pork rind. On top first spread a layer of about half the sauerkraut. Place on the sauerkraut a large onion stuck with a clove; a large carrot, cut into quarters; 1 teaspoon juniper berries; a slab of smoked salted pork; ¼ pound salted bacon; an uncooked garlic sausage (prick it a few times with the point of a knife); and a *bouquet garni.*

A piece of corned beef brisket and a ham knuckle can also be added.

Cover with the remaining sauerkraut, and on top spread 3½ ounces lard or goose fat, and finally, slices of fresh pork fat.

Cover with white bouillon or water.

Bring to a boil, cover, and simmer in a 325° oven for 4 hours.

After 1 hour, remove the meat and the sausage, and continue cooking.

When the sauerkraut is cooked, it should be white and slightly acid in taste, due to the fermentation. Place the sauerkraut on a platter, draining it very well; discard the onion, the carrot, and the *bouquet garni.* Cut the bacon, the slab of salt pork, and the garlic sausage into thin slices and place on top; then add Strasbourg frankfurters poached for 5 minutes.

Serve with a bowl of very creamy mashed potatoes or steamed potatoes.

Chou vert
GREEN CABBAGE

The green "full heart" cabbage *(chou vert pommé)* starts its annual cycle in the spring with early varieties. The first one, called "beef heart" *(coeur de boeuf),* appears in the markets in March or April.

New cabbage is nearly always cooked *à l'anglaise,* which means cooked in salted water, after having been quartered and cored.

The cabbage is served, well drained, with the water pressed out with a slotted spoon, accompanied by butter, crushed coarse salt, and freshly ground pepper, with a side dish of boiled potatoes.

This cabbage accompanies the *pot-au-feu* in the spring. It is then blanched for 5 minutes, drained, wrapped in cheesecloth, and cooked with the *pot-au-feu,* at the same time as the other vegetables.

Note: Recipes for green cabbage can also be used to cook white cabbage.

Chou vert braisé
BRAISED GREEN CABBAGE

1 cabbage
Strips fresh pork fat and pork rind
Salt and freshly ground pepper
Dash nutmeg
1 onion stuck with a clove
1 large carrot, quartered
***Bouquet garni* with 2 garlic cloves**
Fatty white bouillon
3 tablespoons lard, goose fat, or fat from a roast
Lean salted bacon, salted pork shoulder, or corned beef brisket (optional)

Method. For braising, use cabbage with a full white heart, which arrives later in the season.

Remove the yellow or very green leaves, quarter the cabbage, remove the core and the thick portions of the stems; wash the leaves carefully and plunge into a saucepan of salted boiling water. Boil for 10 minutes and drain.

Cover the bottom and the sides of a deep casserole, big enough to hold the cabbage, with strips of fresh pork fat and pork rind. In the pan place the cabbage leaves, which have been sprinkled with salt and freshly ground pepper and a dash of nutmeg; in the middle bury an onion stuck with a clove, a large carrot cut into quarters, and a *bouquet garni* with 2 garlic cloves.

Cover just to the top with a fatty white bouillon, add 3 tablespoons lard, goose fat, or fat from a roast. Cover with strips of fresh pork fat and bring to a boil.

Simmer, covered, in a 325° oven for 2 hours.

You can add a piece of lean salted bacon, salted pork shoulder, or corned beef brisket. The amount of salt should be adjusted to compensate for these other ingredients.

Chou vert farci
STUFFED GREEN CABBAGE

1 firm green cabbage
Thin slices pork fat
Stuffing or forcemeat (half fresh pork fat and lean pork, or any other leftover meats, and mushrooms, etc.)
Pork rind
1 medium carrot, sliced
1 onion stuck with a clove
Bouquet garni
Fatty white bouillon, lightly salted

Method. Choose a firm green cabbage. Remove the yellow leaves or those that are too green or faded; remove the core, wash the head, and blanch it, whole, in boiling water for at least 15 minutes.

Drain the cabbage head and place it on a damp towel covered with thin slices of pork fat.

Spread and carefully open each leaf until you reach the heart, and place in the center a ball of stuffing or forcemeat made with equal parts of fresh pork fat and lean pork, or any other leftover meats, mushrooms, etc.

Reshape the cabbage, adding some stuffing or forcemeat between the leaves; season with salt and pepper while closing the cabbage.

Wrap it with strips of pork fat and tie it securely.

In the bottom of a deep casserole just big enough to hold the cabbage, place a layer of pork rind; a medium-sized carrot, sliced; an onion stuck with a clove; and a *bouquet garni.* Add the cabbage and cover with fatty white bouillon, lightly salted.

Bring to a boil, then cover and simmer in a 325° oven for 2 hours.

To serve set the cabbage on a plate, remove the string and the pork fat, and baste with 1 teaspoon of the cooking juice, greatly reduced.

Serve the remaining reduced juice in a sauceboat with a bowl of steamed potatoes.

Chou farci aux marrons
CABBAGE STUFFED WITH CHESTNUTS (For 8 people)

3-pound firm, white cabbage
1 pound chestnuts
6 large onions
1/2 pound unsalted butter
1 tablespoon salt
1/4 teaspoon freshly ground pepper
1 1/2 cups milk, brought to a boil
Broth

This is a Carême dish, robust and delicious, requiring long, slow cooking, at least 5 hours. It is good for a luncheon.

Method. To remove the outside skin of the chestnuts, first soak them in a saucepan of cold water, then cover and bring to a boil, and simmer for 12 minutes.

Remove from the heat; drain a few chestnuts with a slotted spoon and remove their skins; continue to do the same with the remaining chestnuts. Set aside on a plate.

Peel the onions and slice them thinly. Place them in a deep saucepan with 3 1/2 tablespoons butter; heat slowly, then cover and simmer for 15 minutes without letting the onions brown. Then add the chestnuts and 1/4 pound butter. Continue cooking, covered, very slowly. Stir often with a spatula, being careful not to break the chestnuts.

Simmer for $^1/_2$ hour with the same care. The chestnuts will finally take on the color and look of preserved chestnuts.

Sprinkle with half the salt and pepper, then remove everything—onions, chestnuts, and butter—to the plate used for the chestnuts.

Cut out the core of the cabbage and remove any leaves that are too green or withered.

Plunge the cabbage into a big saucepan of boiling water and boil slowly for half an hour.

Drain well, pressing to remove all the water.

Place the cabbage on a dish towel and open the leaves, one by one, until you reach the heart. Replace the heart with 1 heaping tablespoon of the above stuffing. Reshape the cabbage, placing 1 tablespoon stuffing inside each layer of leaves.

Wrap the cabbage twice with string, forming a cross, and tie the ends on top of the cabbage; leave the ends of the string long enough so that you can use them to lift the cabbage out of the saucepan.

Spread the remaining butter in the saucepan. Put in the cabbage, ribs down; sprinkle with the remaining salt and pepper. Cover with the lid, then simmer. As it starts to simmer, the butter melts, the cabbage emits water that produces steam, which in turn condenses on the lid and falls in drops onto the cabbage and the pan. Continue simmering for 5 hours, preferably in a 300° oven.

From time to time, baste the cabbage with its own juice. Do not let the cabbage stick to the saucepan.

After $2^1/_2$ hours of cooking, add the boiling milk, reserving 4 tablespoons; 15 minutes before serving add the remaining milk.

Presentation. Remove the cabbage, lifting it out of the saucepan with the string and a slotted spoon. Place on a serving platter and remove the string.

Dilute the brown juice sticking to the bottom of the saucepan with a little broth. Correct the seasoning, and pour the juice over the cabbage.

Serve as is.

Chou-fleur
CAULIFLOWER

Choose a very white cauliflower with very tight florets.

Generally, one only eats the cauliflower itself; but actually the very pale green leaves that surround the florets and the white ribs can be prepared in the same way as green cabbage. The inside stalk, cut into pieces, and the stems can be prepared *à la grecque* for cold hors d'oeuvre.

To prepare a cauliflower remove the leaves and cut the cauliflower into small bouquets with $^3/_4$-inch stems. Peel the stems and place the bouquets in lightly vinegared cold water.

Cooking. In a saucepan, bring to a boil enough water so that the cauliflower will be completely submerged. Add the florets and boil for 10 minutes. Drain and place them in a

334

second saucepan of salted boiling water. Boil slowly until completely cooked.

Total cooking time is about 25 minutes. Cauliflower cooked this way never has a strong taste.

Drain the florets and place them in a bowl, reshaping the cauliflower; or place them on a plate covered with a folded napkin.

Serve with a sauceboat of hollandaise (page 88), *mousseline* (page 89), white (page 76), or cream sauce (page 85), or melted butter.

Chou-fleur à l'anglaise

CAULIFLOWER ENGLISH STYLE

The cauliflower must be absolutely fresh and ripe, and therefore white, hard, and tight. Remove just enough of the stem not to detach the tender leaves that immediately surround the florets.

Blanch the cauliflower by plunging it into boiling water and boiling for 10 minutes; drain, and cook the cauliflower whole, in salted water, 1¼ teaspoons salt per quart of water; cook slowly until tender.

Serve on a folded napkin with, on the side, a dish of fresh butter and half a lemon or a sauceboat of thick *crème fraîche* flavored with lemon juice.

Chou-fleur à la polonaise

CAULIFLOWER POLISH STYLE

1 cauliflower
10 tablespoons unsalted butter
Salt and freshly ground pepper
Yolk of a hard-cooked egg
1 heaping tablespoon chopped parsley
2 tablespoons fresh bread crumbs

Method. Cook a cauliflower according to the basic recipe above, drain, and lightly brown in a skillet. To do this step correctly, heat 5 tablespoons butter in a skillet large enough so that the florets can be placed flat in it.

When the butter sizzles and starts to turn light brown, add the florets, one at a time. Season with salt and freshly ground pepper, and sauté them over a high flame. Turn the florets with a fork, so that they brown on all sides. When they are golden brown, remove them to a bowl and sprinkle on top the yolk of a hard-cooked egg rubbed through a sieve and mixed with chopped parsley.

Add 5 tablespoons butter to the skillet; when the butter sizzles, add fresh bread crumbs; as soon as the crumbs begin to brown, pour them over the cauliflower.

Serve as is.

Purée de chou-fleur

CAULIFLOWER PURÉE

Prepare a cauliflower according to the basic recipe above. When the florets are stewed and all the water has evaporated, rub them through a fine sieve. Put the purée into a saucepan, and add an equal weight of mashed potatoes. Mix well with a spatula and add cream or boiling water to bring to the proper consistency.

Finish the purée off the heat with 3¹/₂ tablespoons butter. Correct the seasoning. Do not let the purée boil.

Chou-fleur au gratin
CAULIFLOWER AU GRATIN

1 pound cauliflower
Salt and pepper
3¹/₂ tablespoons unsalted
  butter
Mornay sauce (page 84)
1 tablespoon grated
  gruyère or parmesan
  cheese
1 teaspoon fresh bread
  crumbs
Melted unsalted butter

Method. Cook the cauliflower following the basic recipe (page 334); spread the florets on a cloth, season with salt and pepper. In a skillet heat 3¹/₂ tablespoons butter for each pound of cauliflower and stew the florets in the butter for 15 minutes.

Turn them once with a fork, carefully. When the water has completely evaporated and the florets have absorbed the butter, place them in a prepared gratin dish.

At the bottom of the gratin dish spread a layer of Mornay sauce. Place the florets in a circle, the stems facing the center. Cover this first layer with sauce, and continue making layers of cauliflower and sauce until all the cauliflower is used.

Cover completely with Mornay sauce; on top, sprinkle 1 tablespoon grated gruyère or parmesan cheese mixed with 1 teaspoon fresh bread crumbs.

Baste with some melted butter and brown in a 425° oven.

Choux de Bruxelles
BRUSSELS SPROUTS

The recipes that apply to cauliflower can also be used for Brussels sprouts. But the best way to cook the sprouts is to sauté them in a skillet, browning them well.

The leaves of each sprout should be very tight; remove yellow or withered leaves and cut off the stem. Wash the trimmed sprouts and put them in a saucepan of boiling water. Boil for 10 minutes, drain, and cook them again in salted boiling water.

Cook slowly, uncovered, to keep the sprouts green and to hold their shape. If the sprouts boil too quickly, the leaves will fall apart.

Drain hot in a colander; sprinkle with salt, which will help to get rid of the moisture, and place in a skillet with sizzling butter (10 tablespoons butter for 1 pound Brussels sprouts).

Brussels sprouts soak up a lot of fat. They are delicious when sautéed in goose fat, chicken fat, or fat from a lamb or pork roast. Season with freshly ground pepper and a dash of nutmeg.

When the sprouts are well browned, place them in a very hot bowl. Sprinkle a pinch of chopped parsley on top, and serve. Place a hot plate in front of each guest.

Prepared this way, Brussels sprouts are agreeable and easily digestible.

Chou rouge à la mode alsacienne
Paul Haeberlin

RED CABBAGE ALSATIAN STYLE PAUL HAEBERLIN (For 8 people)

1 medium-sized red
  cabbage
¹/₄ pound smoked bacon
20 chestnuts
1 onion stuck with a clove
Bouquet garni
Pinch salt
Dash freshly ground
  pepper
¹/₂ cup bouillon or veal
  stock (page 72), lightly
  salted
3 tablespoons wine
  vinegar
3 heaping tablespoons
  goose fat or roast pork
  fat

Method. Trim off the withered leaves of the cabbage and cut off the stem at the base. Cut the head into quarters, wash, and drain. Remove the core and shred the leaves.

Bring a large saucepan of water to a boil, plunge in the shredded cabbage, and blanch for 6 minutes. Drain in a colander so that all the water can easily run off.

Remove the rind and trim the outside of the bacon, which should be strongly smoked. Cut into rectangles, 4 by 3 inches by ³/₈ inch thick.

Slash the outer skins of the chestnuts, and place them on a pie dish in a 350° oven for 5 to 6 minutes, just long enough to loosen both the outer skin and the thinner inner skin. Remove them from the oven, 3 or 4 at a time, and peel immediately. Set aside on a plate.

Choose a deep casserole, holding about 9 cups. Divide the cabbage into three parts, the bacon and the chestnuts into two.

In the pot first spread a layer of cabbage, then a layer of bacon, then finally a layer of chestnuts. Repeat this step, adding the onion and the *bouquet garni.* Cover with the last part of the cabbage.

Sprinkle with salt and pepper, and moisten with the bouillon or veal stock; add the vinegar, and end with the goose or pork fat.

Cover and bring to a boil. As soon as it starts to boil, place a round piece of buttered paper the size of the casserole on the cabbage. Cover again tightly and simmer in a 325° oven for 2¹/₂ hours.

Presentation. If the braising has been done properly, there should be very little juice in the cabbage, about 4 tablespoons.

Remove the onion and the *bouquet garni,* and pour the vegetables into a bowl, placing the bacon on top. If there is too much juice, boil it to reduce to the necessary quantity and pour over the cabbage.

Chou rouge à la flamande

RED CABBAGE FLEMISH STYLE

1 firm medium-sized red
  cabbage
Salt and pepper
2 teaspoons wine vinegar
Unsalted butter
3 green apples
1 teaspoon sugar

This dish is easy to cook and delicious.

Method. Remove the stem and the withered leaves from a firm medium-sized red cabbage. Cut the cabbage into quarters, wash, remove the core and large ribs, and shred the leaves coarsely.

Season the cabbage with salt and pepper and sprinkle with 2 teaspoons wine vinegar; mix well.

Heavily butter an ovenproof earthenware pan, add the cabbage, then cover tightly, and cook in a 300° oven for 2¹/₂

337

hours. After 2 hours add 3 green apples, peeled, cored, quartered, and sprinkled with 1 teaspoon sugar. Spread the apples on the cabbage. Continue to steam for another half hour; then remove to a bowl.

Chou rouge mariné

MARINATED RED CABBAGE

Trim the cabbage, quarter, wash, remove the core and the large ribs, and thinly shred.

In a large preserving kettle bring 4 quarts water to a boil; plunge the cabbage in and blanch for 5 minutes. Drain well and let cool; salt lightly and place in an earthenware pot or a glass jar containing peppercorns, 1 sprig thyme, $\frac{1}{2}$ bay leaf, and 3 garlic cloves; fill the container with cold boiled vinegar.

Let marinate for 8 days before using the cabbage.

To serve, drain the quantity of cabbage needed and place in a dish or bowl; baste with a stream of olive oil.

Concombres à la crème

CUCUMBERS WITH CREAM

Thinly peel 2 cucumbers and cut them into $\frac{3}{4}$-inch cubes; blanch in boiling water for 5 minutes, drain, and stew in butter in a skillet until all the water has evaporated.

Season with salt and pepper.

Cover the cucumbers with boiling *crème fraîche* or heavy cream, and cook until the cream is reduced by half and the sauce has thickened.

Remove from the heat, and add, stirring, 4 tablespoons butter for each $\frac{1}{2}$ cup cream. Correct the seasoning.

Remove to a bowl.

Épinards

SPINACH

Cooked spinach is a delicious dish. This is true, however, only if the vegetable is extremely fresh, the leaves quite young, and if it is carefully prepared just before serving.

Before the spinach leaves are cooked, remove the stems; wash the leaves in several changes of water, and remove any yellow or withered leaves.

The green color of the spinach is a sign of a healthy plant; this indication of the vegetable's nutritive values is as clear as its flavor.

The spinach should keep its green color until it is eaten. Two steps must be taken to ensure this easy but important result:

1. Cook the spinach quickly.
2. Do not let the spinach stand between the time it is cooked and the time it is served.

Blanching before cooking. In a large enamel (not aluminum) saucepan bring to a boil enough water so that the spinach will be well covered and the water will stop boiling for only a very short time when the spinach is added.

Use 1¼ teaspoons salt for each quart of water, and cook over high heat. When the water boils, add the washed spinach and shake well to distribute.

Note when the water starts to boil again, while pushing down the spinach with a spatula; after 8 minutes of boiling, remove a leaf and see if it is cooked by crushing it between your fingers. If the spinach is young, it should be cooked; if not, continue boiling for a few minutes and check again.

Pour the spinach into a colander; fill the saucepan with cold water, and dump the drained spinach into it. Repeat this step twice, to cool the spinach quickly.

After the spinach is rinsed and drained, squeeze the leaves by handfuls or in a dishcloth to remove all the water; then rub through a fine sieve or chop fine.

If the spinach is not to be used immediately, set aside on an earthenware or an enamel plate large enough to contain it in thin layers: refrigerate or place in a cool spot.

Whenever spinach is not chopped, it is preferable, if one can, to blanch the leaves at the last minute, to drain them, and not to rinse them. It is enough to squeeze the leaves in a dishcloth held at each end and twisted.

When this has been done, place the leaves in a skillet with sizzling butter (3½ tablespoons butter for 1 pound spinach), and dry them rapidly for a few seconds on a high flame. Season following the chosen recipe.

Note: For 1 pound cooked spinach, you need roughly 4 pounds uncooked spinach.

Épinards au beurre

SPINACH WITH BUTTER

Follow the recipe above to prepare the spinach. When it has been dried, add, off the heat, 7 tablespoons butter for 1 pound cooked spinach. Season with a pinch of salt, a pinch of freshly ground pepper, a dash of grated nutmeg, and a dash of sugar, depending on the tartness. Be careful not to sweeten the spinach.

Épinards à la crème

SPINACH WITH CREAM

Follow the recipe for spinach with butter, using, instead of the 7 tablespoons butter, ½ cup cream and 2 tablespoons butter. Season in the same way.

Haricots verts

STRING BEANS

String beans must be cooked as soon as they are gathered. Picked green, they should be eaten green, without adding chemical preservatives, in order to retain their nutritive value and their delicious taste.

First choose beans as nearly equal in size as possible, and string them, which means to snap off the two ends of the bean and strip off the wiry string on the edge.

Wash the beans and drain, shaking them well. Plunge them into a saucepan of boiling salted water, 1¼ teaspoons salt for each quart water. Do not cover, and keep boiling on a high flame.

The best saucepan for cooking string beans is a big enamel bowl used to beat egg whites, or a preserving kettle or large casserole; these utensils must not be aluminum or iron.

After 15 minutes of boiling, pick out a string bean and bite it. If it is slightly crunchy, remove the beans from the heat, and drain.

Sprinkle the string beans with a pinch of salt and shake them in the colander; the water will drain more quickly. Place the beans in a very hot skillet, prepare them following your recipe, and serve.

Serving string beans *à l'anglaise* means simply to serve them with butter on the side.

The beans should be naturally green and delicious.

When they cannot be cooked at the last minute, because of physical or technical reasons, the beans should be rinsed in cold water as soon as they are cooked; then drained and spread on a cloth-covered rack.

If the beans are to be served hot, they are then stewed in a little butter and seasoned.

Haricots verts au beurre maître d'hôtel
STRING BEANS WITH MAÎTRE D'HÔTEL BUTTER

Follow the directions above for cooking string beans; to sauté 1 pound string beans use 7 tablespoons butter cut into pieces.

The string beans should be completely coated with the melted butter.

Put into a bowl and sprinkle a pinch of freshly chopped parsley on top.

Serve on very hot plates.

Haricots verts à la crème
STRING BEANS WITH CREAM

Proceed as for string beans with *maître d'hôtel* butter, above, but instead of coating the beans with butter, cover them just to the top with *crème fraîche* or heavy cream. Bring to a boil and cook until the cream is reduced by half; then off the heat shake to coat the string beans with the cream.

Correct the seasoning.

Note: The cream can be replaced with a *bèchamel* (page 78) or a *velouté* sauce (page 76). Add half as much sauce, and coat the string beans without reducing the sauce.

Haricots verts à la normande
STRING BEANS NORMANDY STYLE

Follow the recipe for string beans with cream; when the reduction is complete, just before serving, take off the heat and add 1 egg yolk (for 1 pound string beans) mixed and diluted with 1 tablespoon cream. The concentrated heat of the string beans and the boiling cream is enough to thicken the egg yolk and partly cook it.

Purée de haricots verts
STRING BEAN PURÉE

After cooking the string beans as in the basic recipe, stew them in 3½ tablespoons butter for 1 pound beans. Rub the beans through a fine sieve and mix with an equal quantity of purée of small green lima beans. Butter off the heat with 7 tablespoons butter or add some *crème fraîche* or heavy cream to bring the purée back to the proper consistency.

Haricots panachés au beurre
MIXED BEANS WITH BUTTER

Mix together equal amounts of string beans and small green lima beans, each cooked separately. Coat with butter as for string beans with *maître d'hôtel* butter.

Haricots blancs frais
FRESH WHITE BEANS

Fresh white beans

1 teaspoon salt for each quart of water
1 medium-sized onion stuck with a clove
2 garlic cloves
½ carrot
Small *bouquet garni*

Unsalted butter
1 onion
1 carrot
1 quart water
2 garlic cloves
Bouquet garni
¾ pound fresh bacon
Fresh white beans

When the beans are ripe but still fresh, gather the pods, spread them in a cool place and shell them just before they are to be cooked.
First Method
Cook the fresh white beans by plunging them into a saucepan of boiling water to which is added 1 teaspoon of salt for each quart of water, an onion stuck with a clove, garlic, carrot, and a small *bouquet garni*.

Skim the top, cover, and boil slowly.
Second Method
The *court-bouillon* should be cooked in advance. In the saucepan where the beans will be cooked, brown the onion and carrot in butter; add 1 quart water, garlic, a *bouquet garni*, and fresh bacon.

Bring to a boil, skim the top, and cook slowly for 20 minutes; add the fresh white beans. Continue cooking, simmering, and finish by following one of the various recipes.

Haricots blancs secs
DRY WHITE BEANS

Dry white beans always should be from the latest harvest; then they need only 2 hours' soaking in cold water.

Before starting this step, one should pick over the beans to remove such waste as tiny stones, etc., and wash them in several different waters to remove the smell of the burlap bag and the dust. [*Editor's note:* Or use the presoaked variety, following directions on the package.]

Dry white beans are cooked exactly like fresh beans (page 341).

However, I do advise proceeding in two steps:

1. Cover the beans with cold water, heat slowly to the boiling point, let boil for 10 minutes, then drain.
2. Place the beans in cold water again, adding 1 teaspoon salt per quart of water; bring to a boil and simmer, covered.

When the beans are cooked, prepare them according to one of the following recipes:

Haricots blancs au beurre
DRY WHITE BEANS WITH BUTTER

For 1 pound beans, use 6½ tablespoons butter.

Drain the beans not quite completely and place them in a skillet with 3 or 4 tablespoons of the cooking bouillon. Add the butter, cut into pieces, and sauté slowly. The butter and the bouillon will mix together, forming a light creamy emulsion that will coat the beans. Grind some pepper on top and mix; correct the seasoning, and pour into a bowl.

Sprinkle a pinch of freshly chopped parsley on top.

Cooked this way, the beans will not be dry; in addition to the butter, the bouillon will add flavor.

Haricots flageolets au beurre
KIDNEY BEANS WITH BUTTER

Use the same method as for the dry white beans, above.

Haricots blancs à la bretonne
DRY WHITE BEANS BRITTANY STYLE

1 pound cooked beans
1 onion
7 tablespoons unsalted butter
½ cup dry white wine
3 large tomatoes
Pinch salt
Grated garlic clove
Freshly ground pepper

Method. Chop the onion fine and brown it slowly in 3½ tablespoons butter that has been heated in a saucepan. Stir often with a wooden spoon; when the onion is cooked but not brown, moisten with dry white wine and boil to reduce to 2 tablespoons. Add the tomatoes, peeled, quartered, and seeded. Do not remove all the juice. Season with a pinch of salt, grated garlic, and a few turns of the pepper mill. Cook for 15 minutes.

If you do not have fresh tomatoes, use ½ cup tomato purée.

Add the drained beans to the onion-tomato mixture and off the heat mix in 3½ tablespoons butter, following the directions for dry white beans with butter, above.

Haricots blancs ménagère

WHITE BEANS HOME STYLE

Cook the beans following the second method for fresh white beans, page 341, adding, besides the fresh bacon, a fresh ham butt, unsalted, or a small ham knuckle, unsalted.

Meanwhile, prepare the sauce as for the dry white beans Brittany style (above), cooking flat sausages called *crépinettes*—1 per guest—along with the chopped onion.

Remove the sausages before adding the white wine, and set aside.

When the beans are added to the sauce, keep the sauce slightly more liquid by adding about ½ cup of the bean cooking liquid; add the fresh bacon and the fresh ham, cut into large dice (the ham should be well cooked, so that the skin is very tender).

Pour the beans into a deep earthenware gratin dish; bury the sausages in them, and sprinkle with fresh bread crumbs.

Baste with 1 tablespoon melted butter, or goose or chicken fat, or the fat from a pork roast; put into a 325° oven and cook for 20 minutes uncovered so that a nice brown crust will form.

Place on a serving platter on a folded napkin.

Haricots mange-tout sautés au beurre

SNOW PEAS SAUTÉED IN BUTTER

This variety of beans, eaten with their pods, are sometimes green and sometimes yellow and in France are called butter beans. They are gathered when half mature, and the pods, still tender, contain young beans, not fully grown.

Cook these beans the same way as string beans, drain, and in a skillet heat 7 tablespoons butter for 1 pound of beans; add the beans, and sauté on a high heat to brown them lightly.

Season with salt and freshly ground pepper and chopped parsley.

Laitues braisées

BRAISED LETTUCE

6 small firm lettuces
1 medium carrot
1 onion
Pork rind
Very small *bouquet garni*
Pinch salt
Well-seasoned fatty veal stock, lightly salted (page 72)
Croutons, fried in butter
4½ tablespoons unsalted butter

Method. Choose 6 small firm lettuces. Remove the yellow or withered leaves and cut out the core in a cone shape. Wash the heads without breaking the leaves and plunge them for 10 minutes into a large saucepan of boiling water, enough water so that the lettuces will be completely covered.

Drain the heads and rinse them; drain them again, then squeeze to remove all the water.

Meanwhile, in the bottom of a well-buttered skillet big enough to hold the lettuces, place 1 medium carrot and 1 onion, both sliced, some pork rind, and a very small *bouquet garni*. On top place the lettuces with the leaves gathered together and tied with string. Sprinkle with a pinch of salt, cover, and simmer for 15 minutes to extract the water, which will evaporate and, after condensing on the lid, will caramelize slightly in the bottom of the skillet.

Cover the lettuces just to their tops with veal stock, well seasoned and fatty, but lightly salted; bring to a boil, top with a buttered piece of paper, and cover with the lid; place in a 325° oven to simmer for 50 minutes.

To serve remove the lettuces one by one; cut each in half lengthwise; fold the halves and place them in a circle on a heated round platter, placing between each pair of lettuces a heart-shaped crouton fried in butter.

Remove the vegetables, pork rind, and *bouquet garni* from the saucepan, reduce the juices to 6 tablespoons; add 4½ tablespoons unsalted butter, sliced; while the reduced cooking juices are still boiling, beat over a high flame. When the sauce is well mixed and thickened, pour it over the lettuce.

Note: One can leave the flavorings in the sauce and cut the pork rind into fine strips.

Laitues farcies et braisées
STUFFED BRAISED LETTUCE

Prepare the lettuce as above. When the heads are boiled and the water has been squeezed out, cut each head in half lengthwise without removing the stem; open the halves and flatten them slightly; stuff each half with a meat stuffing—beef, pork, chicken, etc., mixed with chopped mushrooms—or any other stuffing.

Fold each lettuce half over the stuffing, tie with a string, and braise the bundles as directed for the braised lettuce, above.

To serve remove the strings and place the lettuce halves whole on a round platter in a circle. Baste them with the braising juice, reduced and buttered off the heat.

Lentilles
LENTILS

Lentils are generally sold dry and must be prepared—picked over, washed, and soaked—then cooked like dry beans.

Lentils are used exactly like beans, in soups, as garnishes, or as vegetables, flavored with fat or just with spices.

Le maïs
CORN

Sweet corn, which rarely appears on French menus, is a grain with nutritive values and flavor worth exploring.

The corn should be gathered when the kernels are still milky and therefore very tender.

Cut off the stems and remove the green leaves, leaving the white leaves around the ears, which are then placed in boiling water with milk added, 5 quarts water to 2 cups milk. Do not salt the water.

Cover, and let boil gently for 10 minutes.

Drain the ears; fold back the leaves, and place the corn on a plate covered with a folded napkin.

Serve with a sauceboat of melted butter or with *crème fraîche* or heavy cream and a lemon.

The guests then scrape the cob onto their hot plates and baste the kernels with the melted butter or with the cream and a few drops of lemon juice.

The corn is then mixed and coated like peas English style (page 351).

Maïs au beurre ou à la crème
CORN WITH BUTTER OR CREAM

Poach the corn as described above; shell the ears into a skillet, and coat the kernels with butter, or *crème fraîche* or heavy cream. Add a few drops of lemon juice.

Crêpes au maïs dites à la Marignan
CORN CRÊPES À LA MARIGNAN

Scrape the corn into an unsweetened crêpe batter (see crêpes home style, page 437), add butter or cream, depending on how rich you want to make the crêpes. Make the mixture the right consistency for crêpes, using about equal weights of crêpe batter and corn kernels.

Cook the crêpes, thicker than usual, in butter in a skillet following the classic method.

Marrons
CHESTNUTS

The two ways to peel chestnuts are well known: make a shallow slash in the outer shell and place the chestnuts on a pastry sheet with 3 or 4 tablespoons water; bake in a 425° oven for 8 minutes, or, after making the incision, plunge the chestnuts into boiling oil for 8 minutes. Remove the shells and the inner skins.

Marrons à l'étuvée
STEWED CHESTNUTS

1 pound chestnuts
Fatty white bouillon
1 celery rib
1 lump sugar
3¹/₂ tablespoons unsalted butter

Method. Place the chestnuts, peeled as described above, in a skillet; cover with a fatty white bouillon, add a celery rib, a lump of sugar and 3¹/₂ tablespoons butter.

Cook, covered, for 30 minutes. At this point the bouillon should be reduced to a syrupy liquid. Turn the chestnuts over slowly in the syrup until they are completely coated with a shiny glaze. Serve.

345

Purée de marrons
CHESTNUT PURÉE

Cook the peeled chestnuts as you would for stewed chestnuts (page 345); drain, then pour into a sieve placed above a plate and rub the chestnuts through with a pestle. Put the purée into a saucepan, add a piece of butter, and mix the purée with a wooden spoon. Bring to the proper consistency with milk or boiling cream.

Correct the seasoning, and serve in a bowl.

Soufflé aux marrons
CHESTNUT SOUFFLÉ

1 pound chestnuts
6 eggs, separated
7 tablespoons unsalted butter
Pinch salt
Dash grated nutmeg
Pinch freshly ground pepper
Milk or cream, if necessary

Method. Purée 1 pound chestnuts as in the recipe above. Mix the very hot purée with 6 egg yolks, and add 7 tablespoons butter. Spice with a pinch of salt, a dash of grated nutmeg, and grind a pinch of pepper on top. The purée should have the consistency of thick cream; add some milk or cream, if necessary. Twenty minutes before serving, beat 6 egg whites very stiff and fold into the purée with a spatula, lifting the purée carefully to avoid breaking down the whites.

Fill a buttered 1-quart soufflé dish two-thirds full, and bake in a 350° oven for 20 minutes.

Serve immediately. The soufflé will fall very quickly; any wait would be harmful.

Note: This recipe can be used for a dessert soufflé. In that case, omit the pepper, reduce the quantity of salt, leave in the nutmeg, and add a scant 1/2 cup sugar.

Navets
TURNIPS

Spring turnips and those from other seasons are used mainly for a garnish or for condiments. New turnips are very digestible. Whichever way turnips are prepared, they must be cooked with fat, such as butter, pork, or chicken fat, or even lamb fat, with which they blend very well.

Unlike carrots, which have a thin skin, turnips have a thick and stringy skin, which must be peeled completely.

The young leaves, prepared *à l'anglaise,* are a good vegetable. Turnips can also be prepared following any carrot recipe.

Navets dits glacés
GLAZED TURNIPS
First Method

Peel new turnips and cut them into pieces like large corks. Trim the angles to shape them like olives. Place the turnips in a skillet with 7 tablespoons butter, 1 teaspoon sugar, and a pinch of salt for 1 pound turnips, peeled and trimmed. Cover with water, and simmer until all the water has evaporated.

Add 2 tablespoons butter off the heat and turn over the turnips in the skillet until they are coated and shiny.

Cooking time will be 20 minutes.

This last step should be done just before serving without letting the turnips wait.

Second Method

Peel the turnips, cut and trim them, and sauté in 4 tablespoons butter in a skillet, rather slowly but frying them so that they do not boil but brown and take on a nice golden color. Season with a pinch of salt and, halfway through the cooking, sprinkle with 1 tablespoon sugar.

The sugar will melt, caramelize, and cover the turnips with a clear coating.

Finish cooking by simmering with the juices from the main dish, and serve the turnips as a garnish.

Purée de navets
TURNIP PURÉE

Stew the turnips and rub them through a very fine sieve; add very creamy potato purée (pages 357–8) to equal one-third the weight of the turnips.

A purée of turnips alone has no body or consistency; one must add at least egg yolks and cream and then heat the purée until it thickens. Do not let the purée boil, and finish by adding a little unsalted butter.

Oignons
ONIONS

To blend onions perfectly with uncooked ingredients, do not chop them very fine—which would damage them and remove the juice—but cut them into very small dice or slice and cut into julienne as thin as possible.

Here is a good way to cut an onion:

Cut it in half; place the flat side of one half on the table; cut off the end toward the roots; cut the half onion into very thin slices lengthwise, without, however, cutting completely through the stem; repeat this step horizontally, then crosswise to the other slices. With some experience an onion can be cut into regular dice in less than a minute, without darkening. Use immediately.

Oignons glacés
GLAZED ONIONS
For White Sauces or Garnishes

Choose small onions—as small as marbles—equal in size. You will need 4 or 5 per person. Peel without spoiling their shapes; to make this work easier, blanch the onions for a minute in boiling water or sprinkle them with vinegar.

Place the onions in a skillet large enough so that they will rest evenly in one layer. Cover them with water or, if possible, white bouillon. If you are using water, add a pinch of salt and, in both cases, 1/4 pound butter per quart of liquid.

Bring to a boil, cover, and cook slowly; the stock should be reduced when the onions are cooked. Finish the dish with 2 tablespoons butter cut into pieces; roll the onions in the syrupy juice and coat them with the butter. The onions will be shiny and glazed.

For Brown Sauces or Garnishes

After peeling the onions as described above, brown them slowly in butter in a skillet. Season with a pinch of salt and a pinch of powdered sugar.

The browning and the cooking should be done at the same time. Halfway through the cooking, half cover the onions with white bouillon or water, and proceed to reduce as described above for white sauces or garnishes.

Oignons farcis

STUFFED ONIONS

Use rather large and sweet Spanish onions equal in size.

Peel the onions without spoiling their shapes and make a deep incision around each stem.

Plunge the onions into boiling salted water, 1 1/4 teaspoons salt per quart of water. Boil for 5 minutes, drain.

Guided by the incision, scoop out the onion heart, leaving a hole in the center. Place the onion shells in a thickly buttered skillet.

Sprinkle with a pinch of salt.

Quickly chop the onion hearts that have been removed and stew them slowly in butter for about 15 minutes. Stir often; do not let brown.

Add to this mixture chopped beef, poultry, game, shellfish, or fish; flavor with mushrooms, tomatoes, truffles, etc.

Bring the stuffing to the desired consistency by adding brown or white stock or a brown or white sauce, depending on the chopped meat or fish used. Leftovers lend themselves to this use very well.

Stuff each onion, giving it a dome shape with a spoon or a pastry bag; sprinkle with fresh bread crumbs; baste generously with melted butter, and bake slowly in a 350° oven, uncovered, to brown. Baste often with the cooking butter.

Put 2 or 3 tablespoons spicy blond veal stock on a hot platter, and place the onions on top. Finish the dish by pouring the cooking butter over the onions.

Purée d'oignons ou purée soubise

ONION PURÉE OR PURÉE SOUBISE

Method. Slice the onions, blanch by boiling for 5 minutes in heavily salted water, drain, and place in a saucepan with 7 ta-

1 pound onions
7 tablespoons melted
  unsalted butter
Pinch salt
Pinch white pepper
Pinch sugar
Dash grated nutmeg
2 cups béchamel sauce,
  reduced
4 tablespoons unsalted
  butter
3 or 4 tablespoons *crème
  fraîche* or heavy cream

blespoons melted butter, a pinch of salt, a pinch of white pepper, a pinch of sugar, and a dash of grated nutmeg. Stew slowly without letting them brown until soft.

Mix in 2 cups reduced béchamel sauce (page 78), quite thick. Simmer for 10 minutes, then rub through a very fine sieve. Collect the purée in a saucepan; bring to a boil, boil for a few seconds, and off the heat add 4 tablespoons butter and 3 or 4 tablespoons *crème fraîche,* until the purée reaches the desired consistency. Correct the seasoning.

Note: The consistency of the purée depends upon the use that will be made of it; it can be employed as a purée or as a *coulis.*

Oseille
SORREL

1 pound cooked sorrel
6 tablespoons unsalted
  butter
1 tablespoon flour
Pinch sugar
Freshly ground pepper
1 cup bouillon or white
  veal stock (page 72)
2 eggs or 4 egg yolks
4 tablespoons heated
  crème fraîche or heavy
  cream
Fatty veal stock

Method. Use young sorrel, which is sweeter. Remove the withered or yellow leaves and the stems. Wash very carefully in several changes of water, drain, and place on the stove in a saucepan with a little bit of water.

As soon as the sorrel has become limp, and some juices have collected, drain in a sieve lined with a cloth.

Meanwhile, for 1 pound cooked sorrel, prepare a light-colored *roux* with 3 tablespoons butter and 1 tablespoon flour. Cook the *roux* for 15 minutes, stirring often. Add the sorrel, a pinch of sugar, a few turns of the pepper mill, and 1 cup bouillon or white veal stock.

Mix well with a wooden spatula, letting the sorrel boil; cover, and continue cooking in a 325° oven for 2 hours.

Rub the sorrel through a sieve and place in a saucepan to boil; thicken with whole eggs or egg yolks—2 eggs or 4 egg yolks for each pound of sorrel—then dilute with 4 table-spoons heated *crème fraîche;* strain the eggs through a very fine sieve to remove all the strings which would coagulate into white lumps. Mix the egg and *crème fraîche* into the sorrel off the heat, place back on the stove, and heat, stirring continuously, until the purée starts to boil.

Do not let it boil; remove it immediately. Add the remaining butter—sorrel consumes a great deal of butter—and correct the seasoning before serving with fatty golden veal stock.

Chiffonnade d'oseille
SORREL CHIFFONADE

Gather cleaned and washed sorrel in a bunch and cut the leaves into fine julienne.

Melt butter in a skillet and cook the sorrel until soft with a pinch of salt and a pinch of powdered sugar.

Set the sorrel aside in a glazed bowl to use later for soup, eggs, sauce, etc.

This chiffonade can be kept for quite a long time by pouring a layer of well-cooked lard about 1/4 inch thick on the surface.

349

Poireaux
LEEKS

Leeks are used in cooking more as a seasoning than as a vegetable; however, leeks are excellent for the health when prepared in various ways. This is a vegetable that can be found all year round in the markets in France, and it is generally not too expensive compared to other vegetables.

Poireaux à la grecque
LEEKS GREEK STYLE

Use the white parts of the leeks, blanching for 5 minutes in boiling water; then drain and prepare as for the artichokes Greek style (page 311).

Poireaux à l'étuvée
STEWED LEEKS

12 medium-sized leeks, white part only
Pinch salt and pepper
3 tablespoons unsalted butter
$1/2$ teaspoon lemon juice

Method.   In boiling water blanch 12 medium-sized leeks, white part only, for 5 minutes. Drain completely, sprinkle with a pinch of salt and a pinch of pepper, and place the leeks side by side in a well-buttered skillet. Baste with 3 tablespoons butter and $1/2$ teaspoon lemon juice.

Place buttered paper on top, cover, and stew for 40 minutes in a 275° oven, basting often with the cooking butter.

Poireaux à la vinaigrette
LEEKS VINAIGRETTE (HOT)

Tie the white part of the leeks into bundles and blanch them for 5 minutes in boiling water; drain, and place in a pot of boiling salted water. Cook slowly, drain again completely, and serve with a sauceboat of vinaigrette sauce (pages 2–3) with mustard.

Poireaux à l'italienne
LEEKS ITALIAN STYLE

Steam the white part of the leeks as directed above; after they are cooked, place them in a gratin dish, sprinkle generously with grated gruyère cheese mixed with a large pinch of fresh bread crumbs. Baste with the cooking butter and brown in a 425° oven.

Petits pois
GREEN PEAS

Being very delicate, peas are very demanding. For example, they should be eaten immediately after they have been picked, if you want them to be delicious. If this cannot be done, it is essential to keep the peas in their pods, spread out in a cool place. They should be used, however, within 12 hours; if this is not possible, the peas should be shelled. Then the best way to preserve the peas without heating them—which would be a disaster—is to place them in a bowl with ¼ pound butter for each quart of shelled peas, and mix thoroughly. Then make a well, pushing the peas against the sides of the bowl, where they will stick because of the butter coating them. Keep in a cool place until ready to use.

This technique keeps the peas fresh without any extra expense, for the butter used for this will be used later for cooking the peas.

Last and very important advice: freshly gathered peas are a pale green and will cook in 15 to 20 minutes at the most. They should be cooked just before serving time. The longer the time lapse between the gathering of the peas and the cooking, the longer the cooking will take; however, the care taken to keep them fresh can counteract this.

Petits pois à l'anglaise

PEAS ENGLISH STYLE

3 quarts water
3 teaspoons salt
1¼ cups peas, freshly
  gathered
Pinch salt
Unsalted butter
1 tablespoon chopped
  fresh fennel
1 tablespoon chopped
  fresh mint
1 tablespoon chopped
  fresh savory

Method. Bring 3 quarts salted water (1 teaspoon salt per quart of water) to a boil in a large enamel kettle.

Keep the water boiling, and add 1¼ cups freshly gathered peas. Fifteen minutes later, check for doneness. When they are tender, drain in a large sieve or strainer; sprinkle with a pinch of salt, shake to help the water drain off, and place the peas in a very hot vegetable bowl.

Serve with butter on the side.

Place a very hot plate in front of each guest, letting each dress the peas for himself.

Note: With the peas serve three small dishes: one with 1 tablespoon chopped fresh fennel, another with 1 tablespoon chopped fresh mint, and the third with 1 tablespoon chopped fresh savory.

Petits pois à la menthe

PEAS WITH MINT

Cook the peas *à l'anglaise,* as described above; add some fresh mint leaves to the cooking water.

Drain the peas and pour into a skillet; for each quart shelled peas cut ¼ pound butter into pieces and scatter over the peas; on top sprinkle a pinch of fennel or mint leaves blanched for 1 minute and chopped; off the heat shake to coat the peas.

Add 2 or 3 teaspoons of the boiling cooking water to make the sauce lighter.

Place in a vegetable bowl.

351

5 quarts peas, freshly gathered
12 small spring onions
1 lettuce heart
***Bouquet garni* (parsley root, sprig savory, sprig thyme, 1/2 bay leaf)**
1/4 teaspoon salt
1 1/2 tablespoons sugar
10 tablespoons unsalted butter
2 tablespoons water

Petits pois à la française

PEAS FRENCH STYLE (For 6 people)
Classic Recipe

Method. Shell 5 quarts freshly gathered peas, which will yield about 1 quart shelled peas.

Peel 12 small spring onions.

Separate the leaves of a lettuce heart; wash the leaves, and cut into julienne.

With a string tie a parsley root with a sprig of savory, a sprig of thyme, and 1/2 bay leaf.

Place everything in a bowl with salt, sugar, and 8 tablespoons butter.

Mix well, press down in the bowl, cover with a damp cloth, and refrigerate for about 2 hours, to marinate.

When ready to cook, choose a deep saucepan, not too large. Pour in it 2 tablespoons water, then the pea and lettuce mixture. Cover with a soup plate filled with cold water, to produce condensation of the steam. Cook over medium heat; shake the peas from time to time. The condensation of the water should be enough to cook the peas.

After 20 to 25 minutes, check the peas for doneness, season, remove the *bouquet garni,* and off the heat add 2 tablespoons butter, while stirring.

Note: If the peas have just been gathered, and the cooking has been properly done, the water from the vegetables —the peas and the garnish—reduced and thickened by the butter should provide enough syrupy, lightly foamy sauce to coat the peas without making them too compact or too liquid. The peas and the sauce, placed in a bowl, will mound into the shape of a dome, like a very light mousse. This voluptuous dish is incomparably subtle.

Petits pois à la bourgeoise

PEAS WITH GLAZED CARROTS

Prepare 1 quart green peas, following the recipe for peas *à la française;* and prepare 12 small spring carrots, following the recipe for carrots glazed in butter (page 319), in the same saucepan that will be used for finishing the dish.

When the carrots are nearly done, add the prepared peas with their garnish and continue cooking, raising the heat toward the end to reduce the juice further.

Off the heat mix in 3 tablespoons *crème fraîche* or heavy cream.

Petits pois à la paysanne

PEAS WITH BACON

Follow the recipe above, adding, for 1 quart peas, 1/4 pound bacon, cut into small *lardons,* blanched in boiling water for 5 minutes, and browned in butter in the saucepan in which the peas will be cooked. Omit the carrots and the cream, and let the peas simmer with the bacon; off the heat mix in the butter.

Purée de pois frais
FRESH PEA PURÉE
Preferably, use large sweet peas; cook them *à l'anglaise* or *à la française* (pages 351, 352).

Drain the peas, and if they have been prepared the French way, reserve the cooking liquid; rub the peas through a fine sieve and put the purée into a skillet. For 1 quart peas, add 10 tablespoons butter, and bring to the consistency of a purée by adding some of the cooking liquid.

If the peas are cooked the English way, add some *crème fraîche* or heavy cream.

Piments doux
SWEET PEPPERS
Sweet peppers do not occupy an important place in French cooking. There are three different varieties: red, yellow, and green. The best peppers come from Spain.

Piments farcis
STUFFED SWEET PEPPERS
Use sweet Italian peppers of an even size, half as long as a large carrot; broil the peppers slightly so that they can be peeled; also remove the stem and the seeds; blanch the peppers in boiling water for 2 minutes.

Fill the sweet peppers with a stuffing made with leftovers: lamb, veal, chicken, alone or mixed with rice, using two-thirds meat and one-third creole rice or rice pilaf (pages 370 and 371). Mix with a few tablespoons of veal stock (page 72) or pork stock, not degreased, and thick tomato purée. Season with grated garlic and chopped onion, cooked in butter with freshly ground pepper.

Generously oil a skillet, sprinkle the bottom with chopped onions, and place the sweet peppers side by side. Cover halfway up with a clear tomato *coulis* made with tomato pulp and juice. Bring to a boil, cover, and bake in a 325° oven for 35 minutes.

Place the peppers on a round platter; boil the cooking juice to reduce and add butter off the heat; correct the seasoning. Pour over the peppers.

Note: The reduction of the tomato—pulp and juice—tends to produce a kind of syrup. This sweet juice goes well with the taste of the sweet peppers.

Piments doux à la piémontaise
SWEET PEPPERS PIEDMONT STYLE

Prepare equal amounts of sweet peppers, ripe tomatoes, and a risotto Piedmont style (page 370). Peel, seed, and stew the peppers and tomatoes in butter or olive oil for 15 minutes.

In a gratin dish place alternating layers of the three ingredients, finishing with a layer of tomatoes or sweet peppers. Sprinkle with some grated gruyère cheese, baste with melted butter, and simmer in a 350° oven for 20 minutes until the top browns.

Purée de piments doux

SWEET PEPPER PURÉE
Garnish for Chicken

Peel and seed large red peppers and stew in butter.

Cook rice equal to one-third the weight of the peppers in a white bouillon, as you would for a risotto, but the rice should be cooked until it is softer.

Pound everything in a mortar and rub through a very fine sieve.

Place the purée in a saucepan; heat it well with a wooden spatula, bringing it to the proper consistency by adding *crème fraîche* or heavy cream, milk, or white veal stock (page 72). Bring to a boil, remove from the heat immediately, and add as much butter as desired.

Note: The rice can be replaced, in the same proportions, by a thick béchamel sauce (page 78).

Pommes de terre
POTATOES

In France there are numerous varieties of potatoes, with widely different characteristics. The best are those with yellow flesh: the long Holland potatoes, the *quarantaine,* the Belle de Fontenay, the Belle de Juillet, and the Esterlingen. The long, red sausagelike potato with yellow flesh is excellent for purées and soups.

For potatoes to remain in good condition, they must be carefully cared for and stored properly. They should be kept in an airy, light room, very cool, protected from freezing, and checked often to remove any signs of germination.

Cooking Methods for Potatoes

The various ways of preparing potatoes are:
Frying
Boiling or steaming
Baking in the oven
Browning or stewing in fat

These four ways of cooking are the bases of innumerable recipes. The typical French-fried potato recipe follows:

Pommes frites dites Pont-Neuf

POTATOES PONT-NEUF

Peel, wash, and dry the potatoes; cut them lengthwise into slices ³/₈ inch thick; cut each slice into sticks ³/₈ inch wide.

Never cut the potato sticks thicker, for each stick contains a quantity of starch in the pulp that is not easily digestible and is unpleasant to the palate. The heat must reach and cook it.

Place the potatoes in a frying basket and plunge them into very hot oil or well-clarified beef or veal fat.

The temperature of the fat should be close to 360°; then the potatoes are not fried too much and do not absorb the fat. When cold potatoes are put in, the temperature of the oil drops to 330°. Watch the frying so that when the potatoes start to brown the cooking can be slowed down slightly; the temperature of the fat should ᴜe gradually lowered to 300°, where it should be maintained to prevent boiling.

After 5 minutes of cooking, check for doneness by pressing one fried potato stick between your fingers. If the pulp is easily crushed, drain the potatoes in the frying basket; reheat the oil to the smoking point; the temperature should be raised again to 360°.

At the first contact with the very hot oil, each piece of potato was seared and surrounded by a thin envelope, which encloses some of the water so that it does not completely evaporate during frying.

Suddenly plunge the potatoes, cooled or tepid, a second time into the oil, heated to 360°. The envelope previously formed stiffens, takes on a golden color, and becomes crisp, while the potato stick puffs up because of the expansion of the moisture that has remained inside.

The potatoes are now a beautiful golden color; drain them in the frying basket, sprinkle with a pinch of salt, shake, and turn upside down on a platter covered with a folded napkin. Serve immediately, appetizing and—let us repeat it, because it is the quality and the characteristic that we are looking for—delightfully crisp.

Pommes frites allumettes

MATCHSTICK POTATOES

Cut the potatoes half as thick as potatoes Pont-Neuf, and follow the same recipe. Serve the matchstick potatoes in a heap, golden and very crisp.

Pommes paille

STRAW POTATOES

Cut the potatoes into ¹/₄-inch sticks; wash in cold water and soak for 10 minutes to remove the starch, which might make them stick together; drain and wipe dry. Then fry following the recipe for potatoes Pont-Neuf (above).

355

During the first frying, when they are seared, stir the potatoes with a slotted metal spoon, so that they do not stick to one another. Serve the potatoes in a heap, golden and crisp.

Pommes chips

POTATO CHIPS

Cut the potatoes into very thin slices; soak the slices in cold water for 10 minutes. Rub them with your hands in the water to separate them and to remove the starch, to keep them from sticking to one another while cooking. Drain the slices and dry carefully.

Plunge the potato slices into very hot oil and cook quickly without lowering the temperature. Stir with a slotted metal spoon; then, when the slices are golden brown and very dry, drain them, sprinkle with salt, and serve. They most often accompany roasted game.

Potatoes cooked this way can also be served cold and salted with *apéritifs,* along with salted broiled almonds, olives, etc.

Pommes de terre soufflées

PUFFED FRIED POTATOES

Peel good-quality potatoes with yellow flesh, the Holland variety, if possible.

Dry the potatoes and cut lengthwise into even slices ⅛ inch thick.

Wash the slices in cold water, drain, and wipe dry.

In order to fry these potatoes, it is important to have two saucepans of hot oil, one to use for the first frying and the second for puffing the potatoes.

Heat the first oil to 360°; plunge in the frying basket, moderately filled with potato slices. Continue cooking the potatoes without raising the temperature too much, and shake the saucepan gently back and forth to stir the slices of potatoes. [*Editor's note:* Use great caution—do not spill the oil.]

In 6 or 7 minutes the slices will be golden and soft and will rise to the top.

With a slotted spoon remove the potatoes in small batches, drain them, and plunge them immediately into the second pan of fat heated to a temperature of 375° and smoking.

The phenomenon explained for potatoes Pont-Neuf also takes place here; and because of the shape and the thickness of the slices, each slice puffs up, becoming egg shaped.

The potato slices take on a golden color and dry very quickly; drain them immediately on a paper napkin, sprinkle with salt, and place on a platter lined with a folded napkin; or serve them alongside broiled meat.

Note: Puffed potatoes can be prepared in advance: after the second cooking, drain the slices, place them on a platter, and cover them with a cloth. The potatoes will fall, but this will not spoil them, as they will puff up again when they are plunged into very hot fat a third time.

Pommes de terre cuites par ébullition ou à la vapeur
BOILED OR STEAMED POTATOES

In certain cases boiling is replaced by steaming. This second way of cooking is generally used to cook potatoes *à l'anglaise.*

Pommes de terres à l'anglaise
POTATOES ENGLISH STYLE

Choose potatoes equal in size, as large as a small egg, of a variety that is not too starchy.

Peel them and place them in a steamer; fill the bottom with water. Cover tightly, bring the water to a boil, and simmer for 20 minutes.

If you do not have a steamer, use a soup plate, placed upside down in a saucepan or a small kettle, to hold the potatoes above the water.

Steamed potatoes are served with fish cooked in a *court-bouillon* or poached or with certain other dishes. The potatoes can also be wrapped in foil and cooked in hot coals or baked in the oven.

Pommes en robe des champs
POTATOES BOILED IN THEIR SKINS

Potatoes can also be cooked, unpeeled, in simmering salted water. When they are nearly cooked, pour off the water and dry the potatoes for 10 minutes on a very low flame.

Purée de pommes de terre
POTATO PURÉE OR MASHED POTATOES

Peel, wash, and quarter the potatoes. Place in a saucepan, cover with cold salted water, bring to a boil, and boil until the potatoes are cooked.

From time to time prick a potato with the point of a knife to see if it is done; stop the cooking as soon as the blade penetrates the potato or when the pulp yields to the pressure of your finger. The potatoes should not be overcooked, to keep them from absorbing water.

Drain the potatoes well, put back into the saucepan, and let stand on the lowest possible flame for 8 to 10 minutes to dry.

Place the very hot potatoes in a very fine sieve and push them through with a pestle. To purée the potatoes, push from the top to the bottom. Never mash the pulp by pressing the pestle with a horizontal or circular movement. This will twist the pulp, make it rubbery, and change its taste.

Put the purée back into the saucepan, and set it on a very low flame to keep it hot; add 7 tablespoons butter for 1 pound of purée, beating vigorously with a wooden spatula to make the purée lighter and whiter. Dilute the purée to the desired consistency by adding boiling milk in small quantities. Working with the spatula makes the purée creamier and lighter. Do not boil after this step.

Spice the purée with a dash of grated nutmeg, and correct the seasoning.

You may keep the purée warm in a double boiler; however, any time you can avoid this last step, and serve the purée as soon as it is ready, it will be enjoyed in all its delicacy, which waiting would spoil.

Pommes de terre duchesse
DUCHESS POTATOES

1 pound potatoes
4¹/₂ tablespoons unsalted butter
Pinch salt
Pinch freshly ground white pepper
Dash grated nutmeg
1 whole egg
2 egg yolks, beaten
Unsalted butter

The mixture known as duchess potatoes is used in various garnishes such as croquettes, potatoes *dauphine,* duchess potatoes, etc.

Method. Cook potatoes as directed for purée (above); push through a very fine sieve, put into a skillet, and stir with a wooden spatula over a high flame to evaporate all the moisture.

When the purée is quite dry and is like a compact paste, add, off the heat, 4¹/₂ tablespoons butter, a pinch of salt, a pinch of freshly ground white pepper, and a dash of grated nutmeg. Correct the seasoning and, stirring vigorously, add 1 whole egg and 2 beaten egg yolks.

Butter an enamel or porcelain dish, fill with the purée, and dab the top with a piece of butter on a fork, to prevent a skin from forming.

The mixture is now ready to be used in different recipes, such as duchess potatoes. For this cut the purée into pieces about 2 ounces each, shape them like small brioches; or in squares, circles, or rectangles about ³/₈ inch thick; or in *quenelles,* etc. Place on buttered pastry sheets, then brush with beaten egg, and place in a 400° oven to brown.

Croquettes de pommes de terre
POTATO CROQUETTES

Duchess potatoes
Flour
1 egg
Pinch salt
1 tablespoon olive oil
Fresh bread crumbs

Method. Prepare duchess potatoes (above). Divide into pieces, and on a table dusted with flour roll each piece into the shape of a small sausage; cut each into lengths the size of a long cork.

Dip the croquettes into 1 egg beaten with a pinch of salt and 1 tablespoon olive oil, and roll them immediately in fresh bread crumbs. Plunge the croquettes into very hot oil; as soon as they are golden and crisp, drain on a paper towel and sprinkle with a dash of salt.

Place the croquettes in a heap on a plate covered with a folded napkin.

Gratin dauphinois
POTATO GRATIN DAUPHINOIS (For 6 people)

1 pound medium-large
   yellow potatoes, all the
   same size
2 cups milk
Salt, pepper, and nutmeg
1 egg
¼ pound grated gruyère
   cheese
1 garlic clove
4 tablespoons unsalted
   butter

Method.   Boil the milk and let it cool.

Peel and dry the potatoes; slice them thin; sprinkle with a pinch of salt, grind some pepper on top, add a dash of grated nutmeg, and mix well. Place the potatoes in a bowl.

Beat the egg well, strain it through a fine sieve, and beat in the cooled milk, mixing both well.

Spread two-thirds of the gruyère cheese on the potatoes and mix. Pour the milk-egg mixture over them. The quantity of milk used should just cover the potatoes. Mix well with a spatula; correct the seasoning.

Rub the garlic inside a deep ovenproof gratin dish, and butter it well; pour the potatoes and milk into the dish. The potatoes should not be deeper than 2½ inches. Fill the dish to about ⅜ inch from the top. Carefully wipe the edges. On top. sprinkle the remaining grated gruyère cheese and the butter cut into small pieces.

Bake in a 325° oven for 45 to 50 minutes. The mixture, which can be made richer by adding thick cream, will become thick and succulent, and form a magnificent golden crust.

Gratin de pommes de terre Fernand Point
POTATO GRATIN FERNAND POINT (For 4 to 6 people)

3 pounds yellow potatoes
Salt and freshly ground
   white pepper
1 garlic clove
4½ tablespoons unsalted
   butter, plus extra butter
2 eggs
1 cup milk
2–3 tablespoons *crème
   fraîche* or heavy cream
Grated nutmeg

Method.   Peel, wash, and dry the potatoes. Slice them thin. Place the slices on a cloth. Toss them in salt and pepper.

Take a large gratin dish, rub the inside with a garlic clove, and butter the dish generously.

Spread the potatoes in thin, even layers. Meanwhile, in a bowl combine the eggs, the milk, the *crème fraîche* or heavy cream, and the grated nutmeg. Salt lightly and mix with a whisk.

Cover the potatoes with this mixture. Sprinkle 4½ table-spoons butter, cut into small pieces, on top. Bake in a 350° oven for 45 minutes.

When the gratin is cooked and golden brown, let it stand on the oven door, if necessary.

Serve very hot.

Pommes de terre à la crème
POTATOES WITH CREAM

Cook the potatoes in water; they should remain firm. Peel them while still hot and cut into thick slices; place in a skillet.

Sprinkle the potatoes with salt, a pinch of white pepper, a

Vegetables

dash of grated nutmeg, and cover with boiling milk or cream or mixture of both.

Slowly boil until the milk or cream is completely reduced; just before serving, add off the heat a few tablespoons of *crème fraîche* or heavy cream. Stir to mix, and serve in a bowl.

Pommes de terre rôties au four
BAKED POTATOES

Choose large, long potatoes, all the same size, of a starchy variety. Wash and dry them and bake in a 425° oven for 40 to 60 minutes.

Place the potatoes on a plate covered with a folded napkin, putting them between the napkin folds. Serve with butter.

Pommes de terre rôties dans la cendre
POTATOES ROASTED IN CHARCOAL

Prepare large potatoes as for baked potatoes (above) and bury them in very hot charcoal; some of the coals should still be glowing.

Serve in the same way as baked potatoes.

Other dishes have derived from this way of cooking potatoes, for example:

Pommes de terre mousseline
POTATOES MOUSSELINE

1 pound potato purée
1/4 pound unsalted butter
2 egg yolks
Dash grated nutmeg
Pinch salt
1/2 cup whipped cream
Precooked pie crust
  (optional)

Method. First bake or cook the potatoes in charcoal. Then open and remove the pulp.

Push the very hot pulp through a fine sieve. Put the potato purée into a saucepan, and over a very low flame stir with a whisk, adding, for 1 pound purée, 1/4 pound butter, 2 egg yolks, a dash of grated nutmeg, and a pinch of salt. Do not let the purée boil, but it should be hot enough for the egg yolks to thicken it.

When the purée is smooth and white, add 1/2 cup whipped cream to give it a proper creamy consistency. Serve:

As is, in a bowl, or spread in a buttered gratin dish and baked in a 425° oven, or baked in a precooked pie crust in a 425° oven.

Pommes de terre Macaire
POTATO PANCAKE MACAIRE

1 pound potato purée
9 tablespoons unsalted
  butter
Dash grated nutmeg
Pinch salt and pepper

Method. Remove the very hot pulp of baked potatoes. Put it into a bowl, add, for 1 pound purée, 7 tablespoons butter, a dash of grated nutmeg, a pinch of pepper, and a pinch of salt. Mix well with a fork.

In a skillet heat 1 tablespoon butter; when the butter is light brown, spread the potato purée in a circle about 1¼

360

inches thick. Cook slowly, tilting the skillet as you would in making a crêpe. When the pancake is golden brown, turn the skillet upside down over a plate and transfer the pancake to it. Add 1 tablespoon butter to the empty skillet and slide the pancake back in to brown the other side. Serve very hot.

Pommes sautées à cru
SAUTÉED RAW POTATOES

Cut the potatoes into thin even slices, wash under cold water, drain, dry, and sprinkle with a pinch of salt.

Place the slices in a skillet with very hot butter, and cook, stirring often. The slices should all be golden brown, with crisp brown edges and soft centers.

Place the potato slices in a bowl and sprinkle with a *persillade* (parsley chopped with garlic).

Pommes sautées à la lyonnaise
POTATOES LYONS STYLE

Pommes sautées à la provençale
POTATOES PROVENÇAL STYLE

Pommes sautées à la bordelaise
POTATOES BORDEAUX STYLE

Sauté 1 pound boiled or raw potatoes. Season them after they are browned and a few minutes before serving. For Lyons style, add, in a quantity depending upon one's taste, onion cut into fine julienne and browned lightly in a skillet with butter. For Provençal style, add a dash of grated garlic. For Bordeaux style, add ½ teaspoon finely chopped shallots and 1 tablespoon beef marrow, diced and poached. In all three cases, finish the dish with a *persillade*. Serve as for sautéed raw potatoes (above).

Pommes de terre au beurre dites château ou pommes de terre rissolées
POTATOES IN BUTTER CHÂTEAU OR RISSOLÉ

New potatoes or old potatoes are cooked the same way; only the cooking time is different.

Choose small potatoes; if the only potatoes available are large, cut them into the size of a large walnut. The pieces should be the same size. Peel, wash, drain, and dry the potatoes, and place them in a skillet with sizzling butter. Sprinkle with salt and cook slowly, covered; stir the potatoes from time to time and brown them gradually. When the potatoes are cooked, they should be a uniform golden color, soft and soaked in butter.

The softness of the potatoes results from covering the saucepan tightly in the beginning and during most of the cooking. They should be golden brown when done.

The potatoes can be cooked and browned equally well on top of the stove or in a 350° oven. It is easier to check the progress of the browning when the potatoes are cooked on top of the stove.

Pommes noisettes ou à la parisienne

POTATO BALLS OR POTATOES PARIS STYLE

Choose large potatoes; peel, wash, and drain them. Cut them into round balls with a melon-ball cutter. Give the cutter a circular motion to make the balls; place them in cold water, and continue until all the potatoes have been cut.

Use the remaining pulp in soups.

Potatoes Paris style are prepared the same way, but a smaller cutter is used.

The potatoes are cooked as for château potatoes (above).

Sprinkle with chopped parsley just before serving.

Pommes de terre fondantes

"MELTING" POTATOES

"Melting" potatoes are prepared like château potatoes. However, they are twice as large, and they are cooked, covered, very, very slowly on top of the stove. The potatoes should be placed in one layer in the skillet and turned one at a time as they brown. When they are cooked, the potatoes should be soaked with butter and be very, very soft.

Note: This second series of potato dishes cannot be left waiting after being cooked, if you want to taste them in all their perfection. I do not advise blanching first (placing the potatoes in cold water and boiling for 5 minutes) before sautéing potatoes. That method certainly is faster, and it saves some butter; but naturally it cannot produce the same results.

Pommes de terre Anna

POTATOES ANNA

Choose long, medium-sized potatoes. Peel, wash, and dry; cut into very thin, even slices.

Place the potato slices in cold water; drain, dry in a cloth, and season with salt and pepper.

If you do not have a special mold, use a heavy frying pan or skillet, and butter the inside with clarified butter (page 75).

The water or whey in unclarified butter would make the potatoes stick to the skillet.

Choose the slices that have the same diameter and, starting from the edge of the skillet, cover the bottom completely, placing the slices in circles, each slice overlapping the preceding one, and each circle overlapping the preceding one. Press a circle of potato slices overlapping one another against the sides of the mold. Inside these potatoes place a layer of potato slices ¾ inch thick.

Baste this first layer of potatoes with a few tablespoons clarified butter; start another layer; there is no need to align these slices as carefully as in the circles. Baste again with butter, and continue until you have 5 or 6 layers.

If necessary, add another layer of slices to fill the mold. Finish by basting with butter.

Cover the mold tightly, heat it for a moment on top of the stove, then bake in a 400° oven for 35 to 40 minutes.

With the point of a knife or trussing needle, test the potatoes to see if they are cooked. To serve unmold onto a lid placed on a plate to drain and collect the excess butter. Slide the golden-colored potato cake onto a platter.

Serve immediately.

Pommes de terre à la sarladaise
POTATOES WITH TRUFFLES AND FOIE GRAS

Make layers of potatoes Anna (above) alternating with rows of sliced raw truffles. In the layers sprinkle a few pieces of *foie gras,* diced or sliced. If the liver is raw, sear the pieces quickly in a skillet on a high flame. The dish will be improved if the cooking butter is mixed by half with the fat from the *foie gras.*

Pommes de terre à la boulangère
POTATOES À LA BOULANGÈRE

To 1 pound whole new potatoes or larger potatoes cut to be sautéed, add ¼ pound very small peeled onions.

Cook together very slowly, following the recipe for château potatoes (pages 361–2).

This recipe can be prepared with thin potato slices and small onions or large onions cut into large strips. Spread a thin layer in a thickly buttered earthenware roasting pan, season with salt and pepper, and add a small *bouquet garni.* Place a piece of beef on this bed of vegetables and roast it.

Pommes de terre Lorette
POTATOES LORETTE

Mix well together equal amounts of unsweetened cream-puff pastry (page 397), not too buttery, and of potatoes *dauphine* (page 203).

Take a heaping tablespoonful of this mixture, and with a knife blade dipped in hot water for each fritter, push a piece of the mixture into a saucepan full of very hot oil.

When the fritters rise to the surface and are golden brown, drain them on a paper towel, sprinkle with salt, and place in bunches on a platter on top of a folded napkin.

Salsifis ou scorsonères

SALSIFY OR OYSTER PLANT AND BLACK SALSIFY

These are similar roots, one white, the other black on the outside, from two different plants but both cooked the same way.

Before cooking in a white *court-bouillon,* peel the roots very thinly; they can also be scraped, which is not so satisfactory.

To prevent the roots from turning black, place them in cold water with lemon juice or vinegar as soon as they are peeled. Cut into pieces $2^3/_4$ to 3 inches long.

Meanwhile, prepare a white *court-bouillon* with 1 tablespoon flour, diluted with 1 quart cold water, 2 tablespoons vinegar, and $1^1/_2$ teaspoons salt.

Bring to a boil, stirring often to distribute the flour well. Then add the salsify.

Cover and boil slowly. Cooking time is at least 2 hours.

Check whether the salsify is cooked by pressing a piece between your fingers; it will crush easily if it is done.

Cooked salsify can be refrigerated and kept for several days in the cooking liquid. Once the roots are cooled, place a piece of oiled or buttered paper over the liquid.

Salsifis sautés au beurre

SALSIFY SAUTÉED IN BUTTER

Drain the salsify cooked as directed above, dry, and place in very hot butter in a frying pan. Season with a pinch of salt and freshly ground pepper; sauté and brown as you would for sautéed potatoes. Serve with a *persillade.*

Salsifis sautés à la lyonnaise

SALSIFY LYONS STYLE

Sauté 1 pound salsify in butter, as directed above, then add 1 tablespoon onion cut into thin strips and cooked in butter until soft and golden.

Salsifis au jus de veau

SALSIFY IN VEAL STOCK

After cooking the salsify by the directions above, drain the pieces, then dry them, and place in a skillet, in no more than two layers. Baste with an excellent spicy veal stock, lightly salted and fatty, and stew for 15 minutes.

Place the salsify in a bowl and baste with the juice, reduced, until there is just enough remaining to serve with the salsify.

Salsifis à la crème
SALSIFY WITH CREAM

Cook the salsify by the directions above, drain, and dry. Put the pieces into a skillet in one layer, not too thick. Cover with cream, and simmer slowly. Serve when the cream is reduced by half. Correct the seasoning, grind some pepper on top, and off the heat stir in some butter.

Fritots ou beignets de salsifis
SALSIFY FRITTERS

1 pound salsify
Pinch salt
Pinch freshly ground
  pepper
1 teaspoon chopped
  parsley
Olive oil
1/2 teaspoon lemon juice
Light batter (page 308)
Bouquet fried parsley

Method.   After cooking the salsify by the directions in the basic recipe, drain and dry; put 1 pound salsify to marinate for 30 minutes in a plate with a seasoning made with a strong pinch of salt, a pinch of freshly ground pepper, chopped parsley, a stream of olive oil, and lemon juice. Mix well as for a salad.

A few minutes before serving, dip the salsify pieces in a light batter and drop them, one at a time, into very hot oil.

As soon as the fritters are golden brown and crisp, drain on a paper towel, sprinkle with a pinch of salt, and arrange in bunches on a folded napkin upon a round platter.

On top of the salsify place a bouquet of fried parsley, which has been dipped for 1 second into very hot oil and drained.

Fondue de tomates
TOMATO FONDUE

1 pound ripe tomatoes

Tomato *fondue* is generally used for various garnishes or as a condiment. Depending on its final use, the *fondue* is made *au naturel, à la portugaise, à la niçoise, à la provençale.*

The method of cooking is identical for all of these, but the spices are different.

Au naturel

Salt, pepper, sugar
2 tablespoons oil or 1
  tablespoon oil and 1
  tablespoon unsalted
  butter
3 1/2 tablespoons unsalted
  butter

Cut off the tops of the tomatoes; dip them for 1 second in boiling water; peel. Cut each tomato in half and remove the seeds, leaving as much of the juice as possible; cut into large dice.

Season with salt and pepper and a pinch of sugar.

In a skillet heat 2 tablespoons oil or 1 tablespoon oil and 1 tablespoon butter; add the diced tomatoes and simmer until the juice is completely evaporated.

Off the heat finish by adding 3 1/2 tablespoons butter, cut into pieces, and stir well.

Recipe for *au naturel* **plus**
2 large onions
Persillade

Recipe for *à la portugaise*
plus
1 teaspoon chopped herbs
(parsley, chervil, tarragon,
in equal amounts)
1 teaspoon capers,
chopped
2 tablespoons anchovy
butter

Recipe for *au naturel* **plus**
Persillade
Garlic clove, grated

À la portugaise

Follow the directions above, but at the start of the cooking, cook 2 large onions, thinly sliced, in the oil without letting them brown. Finish with a *persillade*.

À la niçoise

Cook as for tomatoes *à la portugaise,* and finish with 1 teaspoon composed of equal amounts chopped parsley, chervil, and tarragon, and 1 teaspoon chopped capers. Off the heat mix in 2 tablespoons anchovy butter.

À la provençale

Finish the recipe for tomatoes *au naturel* above with a *persillade,* adding another grated garlic clove.

Tomates farcies

STUFFED TOMATOES

Choose medium-sized tomatoes, ripe but firm.

Cut off the tops and stems, and remove the juice and the seeds without destroying the shape of the tomatoes.

Oil or butter a gratin dish; place the tomatoes with the open side on top; sprinkle on each a pinch of salt, a little ground pepper, and a few drops of oil or a pat of butter.

Bake in a 425° oven for 5 minutes.

Collect the juice rendered by the tomatoes and mix it with the prepared stuffing (see below); stuff the tomatoes in a dome shape, sprinkle with fresh bread crumbs, baste with a few drops of oil or melted butter, and bake again in a 425° oven to finish cooking and to brown.

Tomatoes can be served as is or with 1 tablespoon veal stock (page 72), *demi-glace* sauce (page 76), or a light tomato sauce (page 77) poured into the gratin dish.

The tomatoes are usually stuffed with forcemeat made with leftovers or sausage meat cooked with chopped mushrooms, rice pilaf (page 371), sweet peppers, onions, shallots, garlic, etc.

Tomatoes can also be stuffed with *duxelles* (chopped mushrooms, page 324), risotto (page 370) mixed with livers or diced kidneys, etc.

Tomates sautées

SAUTÉED TOMATOES

Remove the stems and cut the tomatoes in half horizontally, squeeze out the juice and the seeds, and place the tomato halves side by side in a skillet in which are sizzling a few tablespoons oil mixed with butter. Season with salt and pepper; cook on a high flame to reduce the remaining juice rapidly and to brown the tomatoes lightly; turn them halfway through the cooking.

To finish sprinkle with a *persillade* mixed with an extra grated garlic clove *(à la provençale).* Or sprinkle with an onion, finely chopped or cut into thin julienne and cooked in butter, and chopped parsley *(à la lyonnaise).*

Or simply sprinkle with chopped parsley *(aux fines herbes).*

Tomates grillées

BROILED TOMATOES

Prepare the tomatoes as you would stuffed tomatoes (above); baste with a few drops of oil or melted butter, season with salt and pepper.

Broil the tomatoes under a low flame. Turn them when they are half cooked.

Note: One can also broil whole tomatoes, after cutting off the stems and tops.

Soufflé de tomates

TOMATO SOUFFLÉ

2 cups tomato *fondue* **(page 365)**
Salt and pepper
Pinch sugar
¹/₂ cup reduced béchamel sauce (page 78)
4 egg yolks, beaten
6 egg whites, beaten very stiff
Unsalted butter

Method. Prepare 2 cups tomato *fondue,* seasoned with salt and pepper and a pinch of sugar, very reduced and strained through a very fine sieve. To the very hot tomatoes, add ¹/₂ cup reduced béchamel sauce, and thicken without boiling with 4 beaten egg yolks. Mix well, correct the seasoning, and add—carefully, to keep them from falling—6 egg whites beaten very stiff.

Butter a 6-cup soufflé dish, fill to ³/₄ inch from the top with this mixture, smooth the surface, and cook in a 400° oven for 15 minutes.

Note: This preparation must be made and cooked at the last moment, then served as soon as it comes from the oven. If not, the soufflé will fall rapidly and lose its character.

This mixture can also be used to stuff tomatoes, or to stuff artichoke bottoms, first cooked and stewed in butter (page 312). Bake them in a 425° oven for 15 minutes.

Pastas

Nouilles fraîches

FRESH NOODLES

5 cups sifted flour
1¹/₂ teaspoons finely crushed salt
6 eggs

Method. Place 5 cups sifted flour in a ring on a table or a pastry marble; make a well in the center of the ring and place in it 1¹/₂ teaspoons finely crushed salt and 6 eggs.

Allow the eggs to absorb the flour little by little, stirring gently, until a very firm dough is obtained. To combine the two ingredients well, knead the dough with your hands, pushing the piece of dough in front of you while crushing it down with the palm of your hand and firmly pushing down against the table surface.

When the dough is very smooth, shape it in a ball; wrap it in a cloth to prevent it from forming a skin, and let stand for an hour or two, depending upon the quality of the flour, until the dough is no longer elastic.

Then divide the dough into pieces the size of a lemon, and roll them into rectangular sheets $1/16$ inch thick.

Fold these sheets in half and place over a stretched string for about an hour to dry them.

Dust the sheets of dough with flour, roll them up, and slice them into strips $1/16$ inch wide.

Spread the strips on cookie pans in thin layers to facilitate drying; do this whenever the fresh noodles are not to be used immediately.

Cooking. For 1 pound fresh noodles, bring 2 quarts water to a boil with $1^1/2$ tablespoons salt. Add the noodles and, when the water starts to boil again, remove from the heat, cover, and poach without boiling from 12 to 15 minutes.

Drain the noodles well to prepare for the next step. Never rinse them. This advice applies to both dry and fresh noodles, whatever the shape.

Macaroni à l'italienne
MACARONI ITALIAN STYLE

Cook $1/2$ pound macaroni, drain well, and place the steaming macaroni back in the still-hot saucepan where it was cooked, adding 2 tablespoons butter, $2^1/2$ ounces grated gruyère cheese, and salt and pepper. Mix well with a wooden spoon. Serve in a bowl.

Macaroni au gratin

Prepare $1/2$ pound macaroni Italian style (above), adding, at the last moment, $1/2$ cup boiling cream.

In a buttered gratin dish, spread the macaroni, sprinkle with grated gruyère cheese mixed with a pinch of fresh white bread crumbs. Baste with 1 teaspoon melted butter.

Brown in a 425° oven.

Macaroni à la napolitaine
MACARONI NAPLES STYLE

To $1/2$ pound macaroni Italian style (above), add 3 tablespoons tomato *fondue au naturel* (page 365) or 3 tablespoons tomato purée.

Macaroni à la milanaise
MACARONI MILANESE STYLE

Method. Prepare $1/2$ pound macaroni Italian style (above). To garnish, use 1 tablespoon truffles, 2 tablespoons lean

½ pound macaroni
1 tablespoon truffles
**2 tablespoons lean cooked
  ham**
2 tablespoons mushrooms
Unsalted butter
1 tablespoon Madeira
**½ cup *demi-glace* sauce
  (page 76)**

cooked ham, 2 tablespoons mushrooms, all cut into julienne. First cook the mushrooms quickly in very hot butter; then, to the mushrooms, add the truffles, the ham, and 1 tablespoon Madeira; reduce by half, and finish with ½ cup *demi-glace* sauce, very rich in tomato. Mix with the cooked macaroni.

Serve in a bowl.

Note: The above macaroni recipes can also be used for noodles, lasagne, and spaghetti.

Ravioli à la niçoise
RAVIOLI NICE STYLE

Roll a rectangular sheet of noodle dough (pages 367–8) about ⅛ inch thick. On top, in rows 2 inches apart, place small pieces of cooked stuffing (recipe below). You may also use any ingredients at hand. If you are using beef, chicken, etc., or if you are using a vegetable stuffing (for instance spinach purée), use an amount the size of an olive.

Moisten the gaps between the stuffings with a feather or a brush dipped into water.

Cover with a second sheet of dough, the same size and thickness.

Stick the two layers of dough together by pressing with your fingers or a ruler on the dampened portions. Then cut with a ravioli cutter or a knife into 2-inch squares.

Plunge the ravioli into salted boiling water and simmer for 6 minutes.

Drain the ravioli in a colander and place on a cloth.

In a gratin dish, spread a few tablespoons veal juice or any other stock. Place the ravioli flat in the dish, baste them with the same stock, and sprinkle with grated gruyère cheese mixed with a large pinch of fresh bread crumbs, which help the cheese to stick to the ravioli. Baste with a few drops of melted butter, and brown in a 425° oven. Serve as is.

Ravioli Stuffing

**Noodle dough (pages
  367–8)**
**½ pound leftover boiled or
  braised beef**
½ pound cooked spinach
1 lamb brain
1 medium-sized onion
2 eggs, lightly beaten
**Salt, fresh pepper, dash
  nutmeg**

Cut ½ pound leftover boiled or braised beef into tiny dice; mix with ½ pound cooked spinach, rubbed through a fine sieve; 1 lamb brain, poached, then mashed with a fork; and 1 medium-sized onion, finely chopped and cooked in butter without letting it brown; then mix all the ingredients together in the skillet used to cook the onion, and add 2 eggs, lightly beaten. Heat slowly, stirring the mixture until completely mixed, without letting it boil. Season with salt, fresh pepper, and a dash of nutmeg.

Rice

Rice has been changed considerably by industrial methods, and the present polished and converted form is generally regarded as a first-class product.

This is a grave mistake, for although it gives the rice a more attractive appearance, this process takes away its vitamins, which means its main nutritive values. Therefore, I advise buying unpolished rice.

Before cooking rice, wash it in cold water and drain well.

There are three main methods for cooking rice: the risotto; Indian or creole rice; and the rice pilaf (or pilau).

Risotto à la piémontaise
RISOTTO PIEDMONT STYLE

1 large onion
4 tablespoons unsalted
  butter
1/2 pound rice
White bouillon (page 73)
  or veal stock (page 72)
2 tablespoons grated
  parmesan or gruyère
  cheese

Method.   Cut a large onion into thin strips and brown lightly and very slowly in 2 tablespoons butter in a skillet. When the onion is cooked, add 1/2 pound rice, washed and drained.

Stir the rice with the onion, leaving the skillet on the lowest possible flame. When the grains of rice have soaked up the butter, cover the rice with twice its volume of white bouillon or veal stock.

Bring to a boil, cover tightly, and cook either in a 325° oven or on the stove over low heat for 25 minutes.

When the rice is cooked, separate the grains with a fork, adding 2 tablespoons butter and 2 tablespoons grated parmesan or gruyère cheese.

Risotto à la milanaise
RISOTTO MILANESE STYLE

1/2 pound risotto
  Piedmont style
4 tablespoons tomato
  purée or pulp of 3 fresh
  tomatoes
1 onion
1 tablespoon lean cooked
  ham
1 large truffle
3 large mushroom caps

Method.   Proceed as for risotto (above). For 1/2 pound rice, add 4 tablespoons tomato purée or the pulp of 3 fresh tomatoes, cooked with an onion and added to the rice after the rice has absorbed the butter.

When the rice is cooked, add 1 tablespoon lean cooked ham, cut into julienne.

Generally, this garnish is completed with 1 large truffle and 3 large mushroom caps, all cut into julienne and added to the rice before the tomato.

Riz à l'indienne ou créole
INDIAN OR CREOLE RICE

Wash the rice, then pour into a saucepan of boiling salted water. Boil for 10 minutes. Drain in a sieve; wash several times in cold water, and drain again.

Pour the rice into a heavy saucepan, cover tightly, and place in a 275° oven for 25 minutes, or in a steamer, until completely cooked. The grains of rice should remain whole and not stick to one another.

Rice, prepared this way, can be seasoned in various ways and served with numerous dishes such as curry, or shellfish *à l'américaine.*

Riz pilaf

RICE PILAF

Soak the rice for 2 hours in cold water before cooking, after having carefully washed it; then drain.

Cook as for the risotto, but increase the quantity of butter to cook the onion and saturate the rice (5 tablespoons butter for 1/2 pound rice).

Cover the rice with twice its volume of white bouillon or veal stock, and cook as for the risotto Piedmont style.

Riz à la Valenciennes

RICE VALENCIENNES STYLE

Cook 1/2 pound rice pilaf, following the recipe above. When the rice has soaked up the butter, add 1 heaping tablespoon small fresh green peas, 1 heaping tablespoon string beans cut into 1-inch pieces, and 1 lettuce heart shredded. Cook for a few minutes before adding the bouillon. Finish cooking as for rice pilaf. Mix well while buttering, and serve.

Riz au beurre

RICE WITH BUTTER

Cook 1/2 pound rice as for the rice pilaf (above) but without the onion. Pour over the rice twice its volume of water. Add salt.

When the rice is cooked, separate the grains carefully, adding 7 to 8 tablespoons butter; the quantity of butter used is determined by one's pocketbook.

Riz à la grecque

RICE GREEK STYLE

1/2 pound rice pilaf (above)
1/4 pound butter
1 medium onion, sliced
1/4 pound chipolatas
1/4 pound shredded lettuce leaves
1/4 pound sweet red peppers, diced
1 cup very fine fresh peas
White chicken bouillon (page 73) or veal stock (page 72)

Method. In a heavy saucepan, melt the butter and brown the onion; then sear the sausage cut into small pieces. Add the rice, washed and drained, and heat until the rice absorbs the butter. Stir carefully to avoid breaking up the sausage, and finish by adding the lettuce, the sweet peppers, and the peas.

Pour white chicken bouillon or veal or any other stock to come up slightly above the rice. Bring to a boil, and cover. Boil slowly on a low flame.

As the rice puffs up and absorbs the liquid, add small quantities of boiling bouillon. Stir in very carefully. Repeat this step several times.

The rice will be cooked when it has absorbed three times its volume in liquid. Cooking time will be 20 minutes.

Although the rice is perfectly cooked, the grains will remain whole and will not stick together, and the rice will be very creamy. Correct the seasoning.

Note: This method of cooking rice is the most advisable and can be used to make risotto.

Riz à l'orientale
ORIENTAL RICE

Cook this like a risotto Milanese style (page 370), but without the ham and flavored with saffron.

Gnocchi

Gnocchi are made either with a starchy paste or with a floury dough. They make a delicious and inexpensive light entrée, which can be varied with accompanying sauces.

Gnocchi à la romaine
GNOCCHI ROMAN STYLE

2 cups boiling milk
³/₄ cup semolina
Salt, pepper, dash nutmeg
1¹/₂ tablespoons unsalted butter
2 egg yolks diluted with 1 tablespoon cold milk
Unsalted butter
Grated gruyère or parmesan cheese

Method. Into 2 cups boiling milk, pour ³/₄ cup semolina, stirring continuously with a wooden spoon.

Season with salt and pepper and a dash of nutmeg; cook very slowly for 20 minutes.

Off the heat, when the mixture has stopped boiling but is still hot, add 1¹/₂ tablespoons butter and mix in 2 egg yolks diluted with 1 tablespoon cold milk.

Correct the seasoning.

Spread this mixture in a layer about ¹/₂ inch thick on a pastry sheet dampened with water. When the mixture is cold, cut it with a circular cutter 2 inches in diameter, or into small squares, diamonds, or rectangles 1¹/₂ to 2 inches long.

Thickly butter a gratin dish, sprinkle it with grated gruyère or parmesan cheese; arrange a layer of gnocchi, sprinkle generously with the grated cheese, baste with melted butter, and brown in a 300° oven.

Serve very hot from the dish.

Gnocchi à l'ancienne
OLD-FASHIONED GNOCCHI

1 cup milk
3¹/₂ tablespoons butter
Pinch salt, plus extra salt
Dash grated nutmeg
1¹/₂ cups flour, sifted
3 eggs
7 tablespoons grated gruyère cheese

This mixture is made with cream-puff pastry.

Method. In a saucepan, combine the milk, the butter, the salt, and the nutmeg. Bring to a boil; as soon as the butter is melted, add the flour, stirring with a wooden spoon. Cook the mixture on a low flame, stirring often, for 5 minutes. Then, off the heat, beat in the 3 eggs, one by one, to obtain a very smooth dough. Stir in the cheese.

In a large saucepan bring salted water to a boil, using 1 teaspoon salt for each quart of water.

Meanwhile, place the dough in a pastry bag with a simple medium tube, and squeeze it with your left hand over the pot of boiling water; using your right hand, with a knife dipped often into hot water, cut the dough as it comes out of the tube into pieces about 2 inches long. Or form pieces of the dough (as large as a small walnut) with a teaspoon, dipped each time into the boiling water, and let the dough slide into the poaching water.

Bring the water back to a boil for about 1 minute, then simmer for 15 minutes.

The gnocchi will rise to the surface when they are cooked. To be sure they are done, drain one and check its elasticity by pressing between your fingers. Drain cooked gnocchi on a cloth. Prepare like the gnocchi Roman style (page 372) or Paris style (below).

Gnocchi à la parisienne

GNOCCHI PARIS STYLE

In a gratin dish, spread a few tablespoons of a light Mornay sauce (page 84). Place the old-fashioned gnocchi on top and cover with more sauce. Sprinkle with grated gruyère cheese mixed with fresh white bread crumbs, 1 part crumbs to 5 parts cheese.

Baste with a few drops melted butter, and brown in a 375° oven.

The gnocchi will puff up to three times their initial volume. Serve very hot.

Gnocchi Belle-de-Fontenay

POTATO GNOCCHI

About 12 potatoes, the long yellow Belle-de-Fontenay variety or any similar spring potatoes (to yield 1 pound potato pulp)
5½ tablespoons unsalted butter
Salt, pepper, grated nutmeg
1 egg yolk
1 whole egg
1¼ cups sifted flour
1½ tablespoons grated gruyère cheese, plus extra cheese

Method.   Wash the potatoes, bake in the oven, remove the pulp while still very hot, and then push the pulp through a fine sieve. Put the purée into a bowl and stir it vigorously with a wooden spoon, adding the butter, a pinch of salt, a dash of pepper, and a dash of nutmeg.

Correct the seasoning when the purée is smooth and white.

Add the egg yolk, and then, in small quantities, the whole egg, lightly beaten.

Finish by adding the flour, then the 1½ tablespoons gruyère cheese.

The dough should be perfectly smooth.

Forming and Poaching the Gnocchi.   Let the dough cool; divide into small balls of about 1 ounce; place the balls on a table dusted with flour and roll them like brioches; then flatten them with a fork, pressing the fork twice in different directions to form a square pattern.

Plunge the gnocchi into a large saucepan of boiling salted water (1 teaspoon salt per quart of water). The gnocchi should move easily in the water.

When the water starts to boil again, lower the flame to maintain a slight simmer; cover, and poach this way for 15 minutes. The poaching is done if when you press the dough with your fingers, it seems elastic. Drain the gnocchi on a cloth.

Thickly butter a round deep gratin dish; sprinkle generously with grated gruyère cheese and arrange one layer of gnocchi. Sprinkle again with grated cheese, and place another layer of gnocchi. Cover the second layer with the cheese.

Meanwhile, in a skillet cook 4½ tablespoons butter until light brown and pour over the last layer of cheese; place in a 425° oven for 7 to 8 minutes to brown, and serve immediately.

Note: The butter can be replaced by a light Mornay sauce (page 84), as for the gnocchi Paris style.

Desserts

Doughs and their derivatives

It is necessary to make a distinction between doughs made with leavening and those that are made by various methods from flour alone, with liquid or fat ingredients.

In the first group are brioche dough, dough for babas and savarins, dough for kugelhopf, etc.

In the second group are flaky dough, dough for cookies, pies, shortbreads, etc.

All these doughs can be made successfully in the home kitchen; the difficulty is in the baking. You must have an oven with heat that is uniform and regular; the bottom of the oven must be able to reach a very high temperature. It is better to take measures to keep the pie crust from burning than to have to try to compensate for insufficient heat.

A brioche cooks and a flaky dough rises because of the heat from below.

You should remember that the oven temperature must be related to the size and the nature of the pastry being baked. For example, the oven should be much hotter to cook a series of small brioches or small puff pastries than it would be for a large brioche or a Pithiviers almond cake. The small pastries need a hot oven to seal them; the large ones should be baked in a moderately hot oven. These general guidelines, although important, cannot replace experience. You can acquire experience very quickly if you are forewarned, for then you are doubly attentive.

Raised doughs

Brioche dough

(For about 2½ pounds dough)

3¾ cups flour
½–1 teaspoon yeast (1 cake fresh yeast is 1 teaspoon or 0.6 ounce), depending upon the temperature
Tepid milk or water
2 teaspoons salt
6–7 whole eggs, depending on size
1½ teaspoons sugar
1 pound unsalted butter
5 tablespoons sugar (optional, may be mixed with flour to produce a beautiful golden crust)
1 egg, beaten (for glazing)

This triple alliance of butter, eggs, and flour, combined by long-established techniques, then allowed to rise properly, will produce the most delicious pastry, with the qualification, however, that the ingredients that make up such a gourmand mixture be of superior quality and impeccably fresh.

Brioche dough can be more or less rich in butter. I will give here an average recipe that will produce excellent results, without increasing the difficulties.

Method. Sift one-third of the flour and place in a circle (called a fountain) on a table or a pastry slab. Make a well in the center, and crumble the yeast into it; the quantity of yeast will depend upon the temperature. On hot summer days, ½ teaspoon will be enough for each pound of flour, while 1 teaspoon will be needed if the day is cold. This difference has important consequences; the yeast produces the leavening of the dough upon which its lightness and its flavor depend. Excessive fermentation gives the dough a bitter, disagreeable taste, destroying its butter-smooth and tasty quality. Too little leavening produces a heavy, indigestible dough; and baking is then difficult because the dough does not rise properly.

Use very fresh yeast and crumble it in the middle of the flour. Dissolve the yeast by pouring in 2 tablespoons tepid water or milk; then little by little mix in the flour, adding more tepid water or milk very gradually until you obtain a dough that is soft but thick enough to be rolled into a ball. Place the ball of dough in a bowl and make a slash across the top. Cover the dough with a cloth, and set in a warm place to activate the fermentation.

The dough will be ready when it has doubled in volume.

While this dough is rising (which will take 20 to 30 minutes), sift the remaining two-thirds of the flour onto the table; pile it in a circle. In the center place the salt dissolved in 2 tablespoons water; break 3 eggs, one by one, into a bowl to check their freshness; old eggs would give the pastry an unpleasant, unappetizing odor (called *à la paille*, "like straw," in French). Add the eggs to the salt in the center of the flour. Meanwhile, cream the butter, mixing it with your hand to make it very malleable and smooth, and set aside on the table. Also prepare the sugar in a bowl, adding 2 tablespoons milk or water to dissolve it. Then start to mix and knead the flour with the salt and 3 eggs.

The dough, stiff in the beginning, will absorb, one by one, 4 more eggs that have been checked and set aside, and then the dissolved sugar. These ingredients should be added slowly, testing the consistency of the dough by pinching it between your thumb and forefinger; work the dough with your fingers, beating it as for an omelet, until it becomes elastic, which means very light but with enough body so that it no longer sticks to the fingers or to the table.

When the dough reaches that point, add the softened butter. This second step will be done less vigorously, and as soon as the butter is mixed into the dough, add the risen dough from the bowl, which should then have doubled its original volume.

Mix the dough again gently, cutting through it with the side of your fingers, held rigid; place one-half of the dough on top of the other. Cut through the stacked dough again and re-stack until the dough is completely mixed. Place the dough in a bowl, sprinkle with flour, and cover with a cloth. Set in a warm place.

The second period of fermentation now begins. It will take 5 to 6 hours.

After this time, place the dough on the table dusted with flour; flatten it with your hands to eliminate the gases; fold several times, roll again in a ball, then place back in the bowl.

This step is called "breaking" the dough; it increases the volume. It precedes the third period of fermentation, which also will last 5 to 6 hours, for a total of 10 to 12 hours.

It is only then that the brioche dough is ready to be used, cut into pieces, and placed in molds.

At this point the dough can be kept for a whole day before it is cooked, provided that you stop the fermentation by refrigerating the dough.

Since this dough is to be used in a home kitchen, we advise baking it immediately.

Correctly fermented brioche dough should be light and moderately elastic. Now divide it into sections and shape it by rolling each small piece of the dough on the table with the palm of your hand (both lightly dusted with flour), the fingers folded around the dough without pressure, and rotating it to the right in a movement in which the dough forms a pivot between the palm of the hand and the table. The dough should not stick to the hand or to the table.

If the dough is going to be used for one large brioche, it is rolled the same way, using both hands this time.

Quickly place the ball of dough in a brioche mold, wide and fluted. It is customary to top each brioche with a "head." This is made of one-fourth of the brioche dough rolled in a ball and then shaped like a pear; attach the pear-shaped piece round end up) to the center of the brioche, punching it halfway in with your forefinger until it is joined.

Cover the small brioches or the one large brioche with a cloth to prevent the dough from forming a skin and set in a warm place so that the dough will rise once more.

When the dough in the mold or molds has increased its volume by one-third, brush with beaten egg, being careful not to flatten the "heads," and make a crosswise slash, using scissors dipped in water, on each top to help the dough to rise. Place the large brioche in a 350° oven; use a 525° over for the small ones.

The cooking time for brioche made with this quantity of dough is 20 to 25 minutes.

To decide when the brioches are done, stick a thin trussing needle or the sharp point of a knife under one of the heads; when you remove the blade or the needle, there should be absolutely nothing sticking to it if the brioche is done.

Do not unmold the brioche immediately, because the hot bread loses its shape rapidly. Unmold after the brioche has cooled.

Brioche mousseline
SPONGE BRIOCHE

Use 1 recipe of brioche dough ready to be placed in molds (see above).

Roll the dough into a thick round; on top spread ¼ pound unsalted butter that has been softened and well creamed; fold the dough over the butter several times until the butter is completely mixed into the dough.

Roll the dough into a ball and place in a tall, narrow, 6-cup cylindrical mold, buttered and lined with a piece of white paper that extends 1¼ inches above the edge. Cut this overlap with scissors into the shape of wolf's teeth.

Allow the brioche to rise in the mold, as described in the recipe for brioche above, then brush it with melted butter, slash across the top with scissors, and place in a 375° oven for 25 to 30 minutes.

Unmold, but leave the paper on until ready to serve in order to keep this superior pastry soft.

Couronne de brioche
BRIOCHE CROWN

This brioche is not put in a mold. Make a ball with 1 recipe brioche dough (pages 376–8); flatten the ball, make a hole in the center with your fingers; pick up the dough through the hole and rotate it as you would a skein of yarn; the hole will increase in diameter until it is about 3¼ inches across; place the ring of dough on a pastry sheet lightly dampened with water; correct the ring shape, cover with a cloth, and let stand for the last fermentation step.

When the dough has increased its volume by one-third, brush with a beaten egg; cut a series of notches around the top with scissors dipped in water, and bake in a 425° oven for 25 minutes.

Pâte à brioche commune
ORDINARY BRIOCHE DOUGH

3¾ cups flour
14–17 tablespoons unsalted butter
4 eggs beaten with milk
½–1 teaspoon yeast (1 cake)
2 teaspoons salt
2 teaspoons sugar

Method. This dough is made with 3¾ cups flour; 14 to 17 tablespoons unsalted butter, depending upon what kind of dough you wish to have; 4 eggs beaten with milk; ½ to 1 teaspoon yeast (1 cake), or less, depending upon the room temperature; 2 teaspoons salt; 2 teaspoons sugar.

Follow the basic recipe for brioche dough (pages 376–8).

This dough is usually used for sandwich breads, for some dishes such as coulibiac (Russian fish pastry) or pastries filled with *foie gras* or other rich stuffing.

Pâte à baba et à savarin
BABA OR SAVARIN DOUGH

3⅓ cups flour
1½–2 teaspoons cake yeast
½ cup tepid milk or water
2 teaspoons salt
7–8 eggs
1½ tablespoons sugar
1⅝ cups unsalted butter, softened
1 tablespoon chopped candied citron

This dough is based on the preceding brioche dough recipe; however, it is fluffier and lighter.

Method. Sift 1⅔ cups flour into a large bowl. Make a well in the center, and place in it 1½ to 2 teaspoons cake yeast, depending upon the season. Dissolve the yeast in ½ cup tepid milk or water, then slowly mix in the flour until the dough is slightly soft, adding more milk or water if needed.

Scrape the sides of the bowl with a spatula and incorporate the scrapings into the dough. Sift 1⅔ cups flour on top of

379

the dough and sprinkle it with 2 teaspoons salt; set in a warm place to rise. When the flour that covers the leavened dough has risen and cracks appear, add 3 eggs and mix well into the flour and the dough, kneading it quickly. The dough should become elastic and detach itself from the palms of your hands; then add, one by one, 4 or 5 more eggs, for a total of 7 or 8 eggs. As the dough softens, beat it lightly with the tips of your fingers.

Finish the dough by adding $1\frac{1}{2}$ tablespoons sugar, which will give it a beautiful color when it is baked; and add $1\frac{5}{8}$ cups softened unsalted butter. Scrape the sides of the bowl again with a pastry spatula, and incorporate the scrapings. Cover with a cloth and set in a warm place; let the dough rise for at least 10 hours. During that time "break" the dough after the first 5 hours, that is, press it down to remove the excess gases and to increase their production. (If you do not have a pastry spatula, use a slice of large potato instead.)

Five hours later, "break" the dough again to make it fall, and add 1 tablespoon chopped candied citron.

Both baba and savarin molds are molds with rounded bases.

Butter the mold with clarified butter; and if you are making a savarin, sprinkle almond slices in the bottom of the mold. Fill the molds two-thirds of the way up, bounce them on a folded cloth so that the dough settles into the molds; let the dough rise again.

When the molds are nearly filled, bake in a 325° oven for about 30 minutes.

As soon as the babas or savarins are done, unmold on a pastry rack, then soak them with syrup.

Note: The above amounts will fill at least three 5-cup molds (the diameter of an ordinary plate).

Pâte à baba
BABA DOUGH

Some cooks differentiate between baba dough and savarin dough on the basis of the quantity of butter. For the baba use less butter: $\frac{1}{2}$ pound instead of $\frac{3}{4}$ pound for each $3\frac{3}{4}$ cups flour; replace the chopped citron with Smyrna raisins and currants—$\frac{1}{3}$ cup each.

Take the stems off the raisins, shake in a cloth with a pinch of flour, then rub through a coarse sieve, and add to the dough just before placing it in the molds.

The preparation, kneading, fermentation, molding, and baking are the same as for the baba or savarin dough above.

Savarin au rhum ou baba au kirsch
SAVARIN WITH RUM OR BABA WITH KIRSCH

Prepare a sugar syrup (see pages 452–3) by boiling 5 cups sugar with $4\frac{1}{3}$ cups water for a few minutes in a saucepan with a diameter larger than the savarins. Remove from the heat and lower the temperature to 175°. Add a flavoring such as rum, kirsch, or another liqueur, and plunge the baba or the savarin into the syrup.

Remove the cake carefully, place it on a rack over the top of a bowl, and baste with a few tablespoons of the syrup to moisten the cake all the way to the center. Finish basting with 1 tablespoon kirsch or rum or whatever flavor you have chosen.

Note: The small savarins or babas are baked in small molds shaped like crowns or bowls, following the instructions above.

Savarins au rhum Maurice Bernachon

SAVARINS WITH RUM MAURICE BERNACHON (For 8 people)

5 ounces Smyrna raisins
Old rum
2½ cups sifted flour
1 teaspoon cake yeast
4 eggs
10 tablespoons unsalted butter
½ tablespoon salt
1½ tablespoons sugar
Apricot sauce (optional)

1 quart water
1 cup old rum
2½ cups sugar

Method. The night before, macerate 5 ounces Smyrna raisins in old rum.

In a bowl place 2½ cups sifted flour, 1 teaspoon cake yeast dissolved in a little tepid water, and 4 eggs. Knead the dough and cover with 10 tablespoons unsalted butter without mixing it in; let it rise for 2 hours. Then mix in the butter and ½ tablespoon salt, 1½ tablespoons sugar, and the raisins. Fill a 5-cup savarin mold. Let rise for 1 hour, and cook about 30 minutes in a 325° oven; unmold.

Syrup

Combine 1 quart water and 1 cup old rum; boil with 2½ cups sugar. Soak the savarin in the syrup, then drain on a rack; decorate with fruits, and serve with apricot sauce (page 417), if desired; the savarin syrup can also be made with a good-quality maraschino.

Pâte à kouglof

KUGELHOPF DOUGH

Toward the middle of the seventeenth century this Alsatian pastry seems to have introduced into France the use, in pastry making and then in bread making, of dry brewer's yeast, which had been in use for a long time in Poland and Austria.

Kugelhopf dough resembles brioche and baba dough in its composition and its consistency. It has more sugar than baba dough, and it is softer than brioche dough, but not so soft as savarin dough.

The rising, molding, and baking are the same. The kugelhopf mold is special; it is very deep, with fluted sides and a hollow tube in the center. Butter the mold and sprinkle the bottom with chopped almonds; you should also include ⅓ cup currants. Unmold as soon as the cake is baked. Serve like a brioche.

Flaky pastry doughs

Le feuilletage

FLAKY OR PUFF PASTRY (For about 2³/₄ pounds dough)

Pastry cooks have known how to make flaky dough since the thirteenth century, but it was during the eighteenth and nineteenth centuries that this pastry was brought to a high level of perfection.

The recipe is simple but the technique is difficult for someone with no experience.

Since flaky pastry plays an important role in the making of desserts, I am going to try to describe as clearly as possible the method of making it.

Method.   Sift the flour and place in a circle on a pastry board or preferably on a piece of marble. Make a well in the center, and put the salt and half the water in it.

Dissolve the salt by stirring the water with your fingers; then gradually mix in the flour, adding part or all the remaining water to give the dough a medium consistency.

The quantity of water used depends upon:
1. The nature of the flour.
2. The hardness of the butter, which will always have to be adjusted—in winter, by placing it in a warm place; in summer, by placing it in a cool place—then, in both cases, by kneading it in a cloth.

This kneading is to soften the butter, to make it smooth, and to prepare it to be mixed later with the paste of flour and water called *détrempe*.

The flour-water mixture should be combined without working the dough too much; it is sufficient to gather the dough into a ball; avoid giving it too much elasticity.

The reader must understand that it would not be possible to blend hard dough and soft butter or vice versa with a rolling pin. This faulty technique would make the butter stick to the rolling pin, the pastry would be impossible to "turn" correctly, and then the dough would separate from the butter while baking, producing a pastry that was not flaky but very hard.

Gather the dough, neither too soft nor too hard, in a homogeneous mass, wrap in a cloth, and set in a cool place for 20 minutes. This rest will enable the dough to lose any elasticity it may have acquired, and will make it more or less inert.

Dust the board or marble with flour, and place the rested dough on it. Spread the dough with the palm of your hand, shaping it in an even circle about 1 inch thick.

Place the kneaded butter in the center and spread it uniformly on the dough in a square about 1¹/₂ inches inside the edges. Then take, one by one, the four flaps of the dough not

5 cups unbleached sifted flour
2²/₃ teaspoons very fine salt
1–1¹/₂ cups cold water
1 pound unsalted butter

covered with the butter and fold them up over the butter, covering it completely. The dough now has the shape of a square, which then is called a *pâton*.

"Turning" is done to mix the butter and the dough by combining them in superimposed leaves.

You can understand better now why the consistency of the dough and that of the butter must be similar, since they are going to be mixed together.

Cooling the *pâton* too much would be a mistake because the butter would harden and become lumpy and it would be impossible to mix the two ingredients.

We are now assuming that the two ingredients are well matched; the *pâton* is then ready to be "turned" twice.

Dust the marble or the board and the dough with flour, and roll the dough with a rolling pin into a symmetrical rectangle about 24 inches long and 1/2 inch thick; always roll away from yourself.

Take the lower short edge of the rectangle and fold one-third of it toward the top edge. Press the folded edge lightly with the rolling pin; fold over it the other third of the dough that is above. Seal the three-layered dough with the rolling pin.

This first "turn" is followed by a second one. But before you fold or roll, the dough will be given a quarter of a turn, which will place the folded edges to your right and left; roll the dough away from you again, making it the same size (24 inches long) and repeat the folding and rolling of the second turn. Then put the folded dough in a cool place and cover with a cloth to prevent the top from drying out.

After letting the dough stand for 20 minutes, give the third and fourth turns, being careful, at each turn, always to roll the dough with the folded edges to your right and left, never facing you.

After letting the dough stand for another 20 minutes, or more if the flour is of good quality, give the fifth and sixth turns. The flaky dough is then ready to be used. Shape and bake in a 375° oven without waiting.

The dough will rise and will be very light if the various steps have been made correctly; it will have 729 layers, which explains why it rises very high.

The bottom of the oven must be quite hot.

Demi-feuilletage
HALF-FLAKY PASTRY

Half-flaky pastry is the leftover trimmings of the dough. Gather the pieces into a ball; then give it two "turns."

The dough for small cookies is also given this name.

Pâte pour galettes
COOKIE DOUGH

The dough for cookies is a less rich flaky dough. It is prepared exactly the same way as the flaky pastry (above), but the quantity of butter is different: $^1/_2$ pound instead of 1 pound for 1 pound flour, and the number of "turns" is four instead of six.

Gâteau aux amandes dit Pithiviers
PITHIVIERS ALMOND CAKE (For 8 servings)

Make 1 recipe of flaky pastry with all its turns completed (pages 382–3).

Roll out $^3/_8$ inch thick; place a plate upside down on it, or use the bottom part of an 8-inch flan pan, and with the point of a knife cut a circle. Remove the trimmings, gather them, and give them two "turns"; make a second circle with this dough, the same size as the first one but half as thick.

Place the second circle on a pastry sheet slightly dampened with water; press the dough down with your fingers and prick with a fork three or four times. Moisten the edges with water on a pastry brush. On top, $1^1/_2$ inches inside the edge, spread a layer of almond cream (recipe below) about 1 inch thick. Place the first pastry circle on top. Press the edges with your thumbs to stick them together. Crimp the edges, brush the top with beaten egg, and cut a rosette with the point of a knife.

Bake in a 375° oven until golden brown.

A few minutes before removing the cake from the oven, sprinkle confectioners' sugar on the top; this will give it a nice dark gold color.

One variation on this delicious cake called Pithiviers consists of sprinkling the top, after the cake is baked, with a light layer of confectioners' sugar and baking again for 2 minutes in a 500° oven. In that case the glazing with the beaten egg is omitted. While cooking, the sugar melts, caramelizes slightly, and gives a very nice taste to this pastry.

Serve tepid.

Almond Cream

1 pound almonds
$2^2/_3$ cups sugar
12 eggs
1 pound unsalted butter
1 teaspoon vanilla sugar
1 tablespoon rum

Method. Boil the almonds for 2 minutes, drain, and remove the skins by pressing each almond between your thumb and forefinger. This is called blanching; the almond is forced away from you by the pressure of your fingers and the skin stays behind.

Place the almonds in a mortar, and pound and crush them into a paste with cube sugar in preference to granulated sugar; add the eggs, one by one, then the slightly softened butter. Make the paste very light by working the pestle in the mortar. From time to time scrape the sides of the mortar with a pastry scraper. When the almond paste is white and creamy, place it in a bowl and add the vanilla sugar and the rum.

The paste will be extremely fine and ready to use.

Note: If you do not have a mortar, grate the almonds or crush them in some other way. Combine the nuts with powdered sugar in a bowl and continue working the paste with a wooden spatula following the method above. This method is not so good as the one above.

384

Petits Pithiviers
SMALL PITHIVIERS ALMOND CAKES

The small Pithiviers are made by the same recipe as the large one (above) but formed into small, individual cakes. Cut the rectangular flaky dough, rolled very thin, into circles with a fluted cookie cutter 3 to 3³/₄ inches in diameter. Use the trimmings, gathered and "turned," to make the bottom crusts, which are placed on a slightly dampened pastry sheet, then filled with ¹/₂ tablespoon of almond cream each. Dampen the edges and cover with the first series of small circles. Stick the layers of dough together with a smaller pastry cutter; brush the tops with beaten egg, and make a design with the point of a knife in each one. Bake in a 375° oven for 10 to 15 minutes. Two minutes before removing from the oven, sprinkle with confectioners' sugar.

Jalousies aux amandes
ALMOND SQUARES

Roll a piece of flaky dough into a rectangle 7 inches wide, 11 to 15 inches long, and ³/₁₆ inch thick.

Roll a second piece of flaky dough the same dimensions, but thinner and made with the dough trimmings.

Place the second sheet of dough on a slightly dampened pastry sheet and prick it with a fork to prevent bubbles from forming. Moisten the edges with water and spread a layer of almond cream (page 384) ³/₄ inch thick and 3 inches wide, along its length. On top of the cream place the first sheet of pastry; stick the edges together by pressing with your fingers and trim the edges in a straight line with a knife. Crimp the two sides with the point of a knife; brush the top with beaten egg or sprinkle with granulated sugar. With the point of a knife score the dough in 2¹/₂- to 3-inch squares; make a crisscross pattern on each square; bake in a 375° oven for 12 to 15 minutes.

If the dough has been brushed with egg, glaze the cake before you remove it from the oven by sprinkling it with confectioners' sugar.

When the cake is cold, cut it along the scored squares to serve it.

Gâteau des rois
TWELFTH NIGHT CAKE

Use half-flaky pastry or cookie dough (pages 383–4), about ¹/₂ cup per serving. Fold the angles toward the center to form a ball; flatten the ball, then roll with a rolling pin to make dough ⁵/₈ inch thick and absolutely round, which can be done by turning the dough slightly each time you roll it.

Crimp the edges of the dough by pressing with the point of a knife; place the dough on a slightly dampened pastry sheet, brush with a beaten egg, make a crisscross design on top with the point of a knife, prick two or three times, and bake in a 375° oven until golden brown.

Hide a bean in the dough before putting it on the pastry sheet.

[*Editor's note:* The French bake a dried bean into the cake; the person who finds the bean becomes the king or queen and chooses a consort; the guests drink to their health.]

Pie dough and short pastry

This dough is used to make pies, timbales (filled pastries), various other pastries such as *gâteau* Saint-Honoré, etc.

Fine dough

5 cups flour
1¹/₂ teaspoons salt
1 teaspoon sugar
21 tablespoons unsalted butter
1 egg
2–3 tablespoons milk

Note: The amount of liquid—egg, water, or milk—depends upon the quality of the flour rather than a rigorous mathematical rule. While making the dough, you will be aware of how much liquid to add (often only a couple of drops sprinkled in with the fingers) to obtain the right consistency; the dough should always be slightly firm.

Ordinary dough

The ingredients are the same as above, except for the butter: 17 tablespoons instead of 21; omit the egg and replace it with ¹/₂ cup water.

Very fine dough or sablée (short)

3³/₄ cups flour
1¹/₂ teaspoons salt
1 tablespoon sugar
26 tablespoons unsalted butter
2 eggs
2–3 tablespoons milk

Do not make the dough too firm.

This is a delicious dough for small fruit tarts, such as strawberry tarts.

Royal dough or sablée (short)

This dough is delicate to make. Do not work or knead it. Mix slowly and gather into a ball. Do not make too firm.

3³/₄ cups flour
1¹/₂ teaspoons salt
1 tablespoon sugar
1 pound unsalted butter
4 egg yolks
6 tablespoons milk or,
even better, *crème
fraîche* or heavy cream

Method. These four doughs are usually made the same way, except where otherwise indicated.

Sift the flour and make a circle with it on a table or a piece of marble; in a well in the center place the salt, the sugar, and the butter (previously kneaded in a cloth dusted with flour), the egg yolks or the egg, and the milk or the *crème fraîche* or water.

Dissolve the salt and slowly mix in the butter and the liquids, pushing the flour with your fingers from the outside of the well to the center; if necessary, sprinkle some small quantities of water with your fingers; the dough should not be too firm. To finish the dough, work it twice, except in making royal dough, when it should not be worked at all.

Working these doughs is not ordinary kneading; it is, on the contrary, a method that permits all the ingredients to mix perfectly without making the dough elastic, which must be avoided because it would contract during cooking.

Here is the description of this method, called *fraisage:*

After all the ingredients have been coarsely mixed in 2 or 3 minutes during the first step, then the procedure called *fraisage* begins: with the heel of your hand, press down on small pieces of dough on the pastry table or marble, pushing away from you; when all the dough has been pressed, gather the pieces into a ball, and start this step over again. This double working mixes the butter and the flour together very well.

Fraisage is not advisable for dough that is rich in butter, for this working would break down the combination of the eggs and butter, which is the main ingredient of the mixture. Furthermore, because of the quantity of butter used, the mixing can be done easily without having to work the dough.

Sweet dough

5 cups sifted flour
Pinch salt
1¹/₄ cups sugar
9–14 tablespoons unsalted
butter, depending on the
fineness of the dough
3 eggs

Method. Mix the dough as you would for pie dough (above). Flavor with 1 tablespoon orange-blossom water or any other flavor.

Pâte à petits gâteaux sucrés pour le thé
DOUGH FOR SMALL SWEET TEA CAKES (For 100 small cakes)

Method. Prepare the dough as you would for pie dough (above). Gather the dough into a ball, wrap it in a cloth, and let it stand in a cool place for 1 hour before using it.

5 cups sifted flour
Pinch salt
1¹/₂ cups sugar
21 tablespoons unsalted
butter
1 whole egg
4 egg yolks
3 tablespoons *crème
fraîche* or heavy cream
1 tablespoon
orange-blossom water

387

5 cups sifted flour
1 teaspoon salt
1 teaspoon sugar
21 tablespoons unsalted
  butter melted with 1 cup
  very hot *crème fraîche* or
  heavy cream, or hot milk

Pâte à petits gâteaux salés pour le thé

DOUGH FOR SMALL SALTED TEA CAKES (For 100 small cakes)

Method. Prepare the dough following the recipe for flaky pastry (pages 382–3). Let the dough stand for 1 hour before using it.

Cutting, molding, preparing, and baking pastry

Croûte à vol-au-vent

LARGE PATTY SHELL (For 6–8 people)

Method. Roll out 1/2 a recipe of flaky pastry (pages 382–3) after having done the six "turns"; roll it 1 inch thick.

Place a plate upside down (or the bottom part of an 8-inch flan pan) on that thick layer of dough and with the point of a knife cut a circle around the edge of the plate, cutting through all the thicknesses of dough. Remove the trimmings and then the plate, turn the dough over and place it on a slightly dampened pastry sheet. Press the dough lightly to make it stick to the pan. With the dull edge of a knife, make a series of indentations all around the edge of the dough, 1 1/2 inches apart. This step is called "crimping."

Place an upside-down dessert plate (or any other 5-inch round) on this disk of flaky pastry; cut a circle around the edge of the plate with the point of a knife, making an incision 1/16 inch deep. That inside disk will become the cover.

Brush the surface of the pastry with a beaten egg using a pastry brush or a goose feather. Be careful not to put too much egg along the incision, or to brush the edges of the dough, or to dribble any excess egg with the pastry brush, which would prevent the dough from rising uniformly. With the point of a knife make a crisscross design on the disk that will serve as the cover. Bake in a 375° oven for 20 minutes.

It is important to have an oven with heat that is regular, preferably with a bottom made of cast iron; the quality of the oven bottom determines, in great part, the success of flaky dough, which rises because of heat coming from below.

When the *vol-au-vent* is lightly browned, remove from the oven; with the point of a knife, cut around the cover, remove the top layers, and scoop out from the shell most of the soft inside dough.

The *vol-au-vent* is ready to be served; keep it warm, and fill it at the last minute.

PIE OR TART

The pie or tart—which can be used for either a main dish or a dessert—dates from the ancient days of cookery.

Served as an entrée, the pie is prepared and baked with its filling or baked unfilled, like a *vol-au-vent,* and filled later.

If the pie shell is cooked unfilled, take a *pâton* of flaky pastry dough (pages 282-3) after it has been given six turns, following the method given for flaky pastry, and roll it into a long band 1 inch thick and as long as the circumference of the pan you are using. With a knife cut the dough to make a band 1½ inches wide and as long as the dough. Reserve this band.

Gather the trimmings, give them two "turns" (page 383) and make a ball with the dough; then roll the dough ¹/₁₆ inch thick; cut a circle of dough to fit the pie pan. Dampen the pie pan with water, and place the circle of dough in the bottom. Prick the dough generously with a fork.

If the pie is to be cooked with its filling, divide the filling into pellets and arrange in the center of the dough. Cover the top with another layer of dough ¹/₁₆ inch thick, made with the trimmings of the flaky dough. Dampen the edges of the bottom layer of dough and press down the top layer with your thumb all around the edges to stick them together.

If the shell is to be baked empty, cover the bottom with a wad of paper domed in the center, and put the second circle of dough over it.

In both cases, moisten the edges of this last circle of dough lightly with a pastry brush or a cloth and on top place the strip of flaky pastry prepared earlier. Press the ends of the dough together, cutting them on the bias where they meet, and crimp the edge coarsely with the point of a knife.

Brush with a beaten egg on the surface of the strip of dough and the cover only. Make a crisscross design with the point of a knife on the cover.

Bake in the oven like the *vol-au-vent* (page 388).

When the pie shell is cooked empty, cut around the cover while it is still hot, lift it up, and remove the wad of paper.

Fill the shell the same way you would a *vol-au-vent*.

If it is a dessert pie, the preparation is identical. The filling will be made of pastry cream (page 410), frangipane cream (page 410), or almond cream (page 384), cooked or uncooked fruit, or fruit jam.

Sweet pies can be made without a cover. One must then be careful that there is no contact between the strip of dough and the filling; the filling would hamper the rising of the dough.

Bake for 35 to 45 minutes, depending upon the thickness and the filling, in a 325° oven. Five minutes before removing from the oven, sprinkle the pie generously with confectioners' sugar, raise the heat to 475° to produce the beginning of caramelization; the melting sugar will become light brown.

One can also spread on the fruit, after the pie is baked, a light coat of fruit purée or jam.

Bouchées
SMALL PUFF PASTRIES

Bouchées are small individual *vol-au-vent*.

Roll ½ recipe flaky pastry (pages 382–3) with a rolling pin, making it ⅙ inch thick; then, with a scalloped cookie cutter 3¼ inches in diameter, cut 20 circles, about ¾ to 1 ounce each.

Turn these circles of dough over and place on a lightly dampened pastry sheet.

Brush the circles with beaten egg on the top only; do not brush the edges—that would prevent the dough from rising. With a plain cookie cutter 1¼ inches in diameter, cut the top covers by pressing about 1/16 inch into the circles. Dip the cutter into tepid water before each use.

Make a crisscross design with the point of a knife on each cover.

Bake in a 425° oven for 12 to 15 minutes. Remove the covers as soon as you take the pastries out of the oven, and press the inside dough down lightly to make room for the filling.

Timbale dough

Method.   Make 1½ recipes pie dough (pages 386–7) and divide into thirds. Combine two of the thirds.

Make each piece of dough into a ball and roll the larger out in a circle 8 inches in diameter. Turn the pastry circle over and dust it lightly with flour, fold it in two, and bring together both ends of this half circle in the center to produce a pointed cap. You can extend the points of the dough by rolling once on the left side, once on the right side.

When it is about ⅛ inch thick all around, open the cap and slide it point down into a buttered 6-cup charlotte mold.

Press the inside of the cap against the mold, using a small ball of dough, so that the dough will stick very well to the sides and the bottom of the mold. Cut off the excess dough ⅜ inch from the edge.

Prick the bottom of the pastry with a fork, and line the dough with fine white paper; then fill with dry beans up to the edges of the mold. On top of the dry beans, place a dome of crushed paper and cover it with a thin layer of dough cut from the reserved dough. Stick this circle of dough to the dampened edges of the bottom layer. Then, pressing with the thumb and the forefinger, give the edge of the top dough the shape of a crest. Pinch this crest front and back with a pastry crimper or with your fingers.

Decorate the lid, placing on top tiny pieces of pastry dough in the shape of very thin rosettes, cut with a fluted cookie cutter; mark the petals with the back of a knife blade. Overlap these tiny rosettes, starting from the edge of the lid, to form a crown. Make a decoration as big as a marble by pressing two or three small pieces of dough into a ball shape, gathering the edges toward the center as for a top. Place over the crown and then lightly mark a cross on top.

Brush well with beaten egg and bake in a 325° oven for 40 minutes. When the shell is baked, remove the lid carefully and set aside. Remove the dry beans from inside the timbale; carefully remove the paper; brush the inside with beaten egg, and place the shell in the oven again for 5 minutes to dry the inside and give it a golden color.

Unmold the timbale; brush the outside with beaten egg and return to the oven for a few seconds. As soon as it is a nice golden color, remove from the oven and set aside to be filled.

Petites timbales individuelles
SMALL INDIVIDUAL TIMBALES

Make small timbales following the technique above. Use the same pie dough, and roll the cap of dough until it is $1/8$ inch thick. Mold in small baba molds or any other molds of the same dimensions.

Croûte à tarte cuite à blanc
PIE CRUST BAKED BLIND (UNFILLED)

Butter the inside of a 10-inch flan ring, and place it on a cookie sheet slightly dampened with water.

Make a ball of $1/2$ recipe pie dough, using any of the four types on pages 386–7, depending on how delicate you wish to make the dessert; roll in a circle 12 inches in diameter.

Fold the dough in half and place it on the ring, with the fold across the center line of the flan ring; open the pastry circle and lower it, pressing it against the sides of the ring to make it stick. Fold the excess dough down over the edge and sides and cut the excess off by running the rolling pin over the top. This last step will form a fold of dough around the edge. Take the fold of dough with both hands between your thumbs and index fingers and squeeze it to make a crest $3/8$ inch high, turning the ring with your right hand toward your left hand. Then crimp the outside of the crest with a pastry crimper held on the bias.

Prick the bottom of the dough with a fork to prevent bubbles from forming during cooking. Line the inside of the pastry with fine buttered paper; fill to the top with dry beans (which can be reused endlessly for this purpose); bake in a 325° oven for 25 minutes.

Remove from the oven; take out the dry beans, the paper, and the ring; brush the sides of the tart shell with beaten egg and replace in the oven for 2 or 3 minutes to dry and brown the crust, which is then ready to be filled with raw or cooked fruit.

Croûtes pour tartelettes cuites à blanc
CRUSTS FOR SMALL TARTS BAKED BLIND (UNFILLED)

Small tarts can be made with any of the pie doughs (pages

391

386–7) or trimmings from flaky pastry (pages 382–3) or cookie dough (page 383).

Roll the chosen dough in a rectangular shape not more than $1/16$ inch thick; cut the dough with a fluted cookie cutter of a diameter slightly larger than the molds that will be used. Butter each mold and place a small circle of dough in it. Press it with a small ball of dough, lightly floured, so that each circle of dough will take the shape of the mold. Prick the bottom of each pastry and put a circle of buttered paper and dry beans or dry cherry pits inside it; bake in a 325° oven for 10 to 12 minutes; finish the tarts as indicated in the recipe for pie crust.

Croûte pour pâtés en croûte

CRUST FOR PÂTÉS IN A CRUST

The molds used for pâtés in a crust are usually deep, decorated, and round or oval; they can have the shape of a timbale, which is the type used for *pâté de foie gras*.

The crust is generally made with ordinary pie dough. Sometimes brioche dough is used.

The method is absolutely identical to that used for making a timbale (pages 390–1). The cap of dough should be $3/8$ inch thick. Prick the dough several times. Fill with the desired ingredients, following the directions in the recipes; cover with a thin circle of dough; stick the two layers together and form a crest around the edge; pinch the crest, as explained in the recipe for a timbale, then on top of the pâté place a second layer made with the trimmings of flaky pastry, "turned" twice (page 383), about $1/8$ inch thick.

Brush the surface with beaten egg, score it, forming rosettes or leaves, with the point of a knife; make a hole in the center (or make two holes for an oval mold) and in the hole put a cone of buttered paper, which works like a tiny chimney to allow the steam to escape; bake in a 325° oven, following the individual recipe for the cooking time.

Tarts and flans

Flan aux pommes Jérôme

APPLE FLAN JEROME (For 6 people)

Method. Butter a 10-inch flan ring and place on a pastry sheet.

Prepare $1/2$ recipe pie dough (pages 386–7); gather the dough in a ball and roll it $1/4$ inch thick. To make this dough perfectly round, follow the steps described for the Twelfth Night cake (pages 385–6). The dough should be at least 13 inches in diameter.

Place the dough on the flan ring and ease it down little by little so that the dough takes the exact shape of the inside of the ring. Then tamp the crust against the ring using a small ball of slightly floured dough.

Fold the excess dough over the edge and cut it by running a rolling pin over it. This method will form a rim of dough. Take the rim of dough in your two hands between your thumbs and index fingers and squeeze to form an even crest. Pinch the crest with a pastry crimper to imitate a little rope.

Prick the bottom of the dough with a fork.

Meanwhile cook 2 pounds apples into applesauce. Choose firm and well-flavored apples.

First wash and peel the apples. Cook the peels, uncovered, in 1/2 cup water for 15 to 20 minutes; drain with a slotted spoon, and remove 3 tablespoons of the juice, reserve; add 1 heaping tablespoon sugar to the remaining juice and cook this syrup 4 to 5 minutes; pour into a bowl. In the same saucepan, with the reserved juice, cook the apples (set aside the most beautiful one), quartered and seeded. Cover the saucepan, and cook slowly for 20 to 30 minutes. The apples should then be applesauce; add 2/3 cup sugar. Continue cooking for about 10 minutes to reduce this mixture, which will become slightly liquid when the sugar is added.

Rub through a fine sieve or mash the apples with a sauce whisk. Cool.

When ready to fill the pie, stir 1 tablespoon kirsch into the applesauce; then fill the pie crust two-thirds of the way up, smooth the applesauce, and cover with slices of the reserved apple.

To do this, peel the apple set aside, cut it into quarters; seed each quarter and cut into thin slices. These thin slices of fruit will be arranged as half-moons, overlapping slightly, in circles starting against the flan ring, with each succeeding circle going in the opposite direction and partly overlapping the preceding one; continue until you reach the center. Sprinkle the top with 1 tablespoon sugar.

Bake in a 325° oven for 30 to 35 minutes.

Take the tart out of the oven, remove the flan ring, brush the crust with beaten egg all around the vertical edge; place in the oven again for 3 minutes; then cover the top of the apples with the reserved 3 tablespoons of juice cooked to a jelly.

Note: This recipe can be used to make small individual tarts in the same way.

Flans aux fruits, mirabelles, abricots, quetsches, reines-claudes

FLANS WITH FRUIT, SMALL GOLDEN PLUMS, APRICOTS, PURPLE PLUMS, GREENGAGE PLUMS

Make a pie dough (pages 386–7) in a flan ring as for the apple flan (above).

Sprinkle the bottom of the crust with 1 teaspoon sugar and make circles to fill with halves of one of the above fruits.

393

First, pit the plums or cut the apricots or greengages in two and remove their pits.

Arrange the fruit halves in circles, cut sides up, each overlapping the preceding one slightly and reversing the direction of the fruit for each new circle.

Cook in a 325° oven with strong heat coming from the bottom to sear the bottom crust so that the fruit juices do not soak into the dough.

After removing the flan from the oven, take off the ring, and sprinkle the surface of the fruit with confectioners' sugar.

Cover the fruit with apricot jam, slightly melted, which will cool into a jelly.

Tarte aux cerises
CHERRY TART

Follow the same method as for the preceding tart. Pit sweet cherries and fill the bottom of the tart, placing them close together.

After the pie is baked, sprinkle with confectioners' sugar or coat with red currant jelly.

Tarte aux fraises
STRAWBERRY TART

1 pound strawberries, cleaned and hulled
½ recipe sweet dough (page 387)
6 tablespoons red currant jelly
Kirsch

Method. Prepare the dough following the recipe for sweet dough; gather into a ball and roll in a circle.

Place the dough in a flan ring on a slightly dampened pastry sheet; press the dough down so that it takes the exact shape of the ring. Bake blind (unfilled), as directed on page 391.

After baking, let cool; remove the ring when the crust is nearly cold.

A few minutes before serving, arrange the hulled strawberries attractively in the tart. Glaze the surface of the berries with red currant jelly slightly diluted with kirsch.

Tarte à l'alsacienne
ALSATIAN TART

Place a flan ring on a slightly dampened pastry sheet and line it with fine or very fine dough (page 386). Form a crest around the edge, prick the bottom, and fill halfway up with pastry cream (page 410).

Cut apples or pears into quarters, core, then slice lengthwise and arrange the slices on top of the cream in tight circles. Sprinkle with 1 tablespoon sugar, and bake in a 325° oven for 20 minutes.

As soon as the tart is baked, remove the ring; brush the vertical edge with beaten egg and place in the oven again for 2 to 3 minutes to finish baking.

Spread 1 tablespoon apple jelly or apricot jam, slightly reduced, on the apples or pears.

Tarte normande
NORMANDY TART

Follow the recipe for Alsatian tart (above); but replace the pastry cream with a frangipane cream (page 410) using 1 part frangipane cream to 5 of *crème fraîche* or heavy cream.

After baking, finish the tart with a layer of *crème* Chantilly (page 411) about ³/₄ inch thick.

Decorate the surface of the whipped cream with a design traced with the point of a knife or press the *crème* Chantilly through a pastry bag with a large fluted tube.

Tarte aux cerises à la crème
CHERRY CREAM TART

The method used is nearly identical to the preceding one. After lining the flan ring with dough, fill the bottom with a layer of pastry cream, made light by adding about one-fifth *crème fraîche,* or custard cream (see the section on cream fillings, pages 410–13); then cover with pitted sweet cherries that have been macerated in a little sugar and 1 tablespoon kirsch; cover the cherries with another layer of light pastry cream or custard cream.

Bake in a 325° oven for 25 to 30 minutes.

Tarte aux pommes pâte brisée
APPLE TART WITH PÂTE BRISÉE

Pâte brisée
3³/₄ cups flour
1 tablespoon salt
26 tablespoons unsalted butter
3 whole eggs
       or
Pâte sablée
3³/₄ cups flour
2 teaspoons salt
1 cup sugar
21 tablespoons unsalted butter
3 whole eggs

Method.   Place a flan ring on a pastry sheet and line with *pâte brisée* or *pâte sablée* (see page 387 for method). Let stand for 2 hours. Make a compote with 2 lightly sugared apples that have been puréed. Pour the compote into the tart. Peel 4 large apples, core and slice them, and place in the tart. Sprinkle the apples with granulated sugar and place on top 14 tablespoons butter, diced very small.

Bake in a 350° oven for 30 minutes.

Tarte à la crème
CREAM TART

Place a flan ring on a slightly dampened pastry sheet and line with pie dough (page 386); do not prick; fill with a custard made as for *crème renversée* (page 414).

Bake in a 325° oven for 15 minutes. The surface of the tart should be a nice golden color. Do not let the custard boil while baking.

Tarte aux poires
PEAR TART

Line a flan ring with *pâte brisée*. Peel and slice ripe pears and place them in the pie shell.

In a bowl combine 2 cups heavy cream, 4 eggs, ½ cup sugar, and a pinch of salt. Stir well and pour over the pears. Bake for 30 minutes in a 325° oven.

Tarte Tatin

1½ cups unsalted butter
½ cup sugar
2 pounds apples
2 scant cups flour
1 egg
Pinch salt

Method. Take a large *génoise* pan (9 inches in diameter) and butter the bottom generously (using 7 tablespoons butter), then sprinkle with half the sugar.

Peel the apples, dry with a cloth, core, cut into quarters or thick slices. Arrange the apple pieces together tightly to cover the bottom of the pan. Sprinkle the remaining sugar on top. Add 1½ tablespoons melted butter. Place the mold on the stove over high heat for about 20 minutes; the sugar should caramelize but remain light brown.

Meanwhile mound the flour on a pastry board. In the center form a well and in it place the egg, the salt, and the remaining butter, softened. Mix all the ingredients together. Add some water, if necessary, to produce a soft dough that can be rolled in a circle, as thin as possible.

Cover the pan with this dough, pushing the edges inside the mold. Bake in a 325° oven for 30 minutes.

Invert the *tarte* Tatin on a serving platter. Let it cool before serving.

Cream-puff pastry

This dough is used for main dishes as well as for desserts. Depending upon its use, the ingredients for the dough will vary. Whatever the use, the preparation of the dough is the same.

Pâte à choux fine

FINE CREAM-PUFF PASTRY

2 cups water
Pinch salt
½ pound unsalted butter
2 scant cups flour
7–8 eggs, or use 6–7 eggs
  plus 6 tablespoons milk
  or *crème fraîche*
1 tablespoon orange-
  blossom water
1 scant tablespoon sugar

Method. Pour the water into a large heavy-bottomed saucepan; add the salt and the butter cut into small pieces; heat to the boiling point, stirring the boiling mixture with a wooden spatula; then add the flour.

Work the dough with the spatula over a high flame. The water will evaporate little by little until the dough is completely dry; at this point the butter will sizzle.

Now remove the dough from the heat, and beat the dough without stopping, adding the eggs, one by one, then the milk or *crème fraîche.*

The quantity of eggs needed depends upon their size and on whether or not you add milk, which, while saving an egg, makes the dough softer.

Flavor the dough with orange-blossom water and sugar.

The dough should be vigorously beaten with a spatula until it is smooth and light.

The dough should not have too soft a consistency. It should be stiff enough to squeeze through a pastry bag while still hot. The dough will flatten slightly on the pan.

It is then ready to use.

Pâte à choux ordinaire
ORDINARY CREAM-PUFF PASTRY

2 cups water
¼ pound unsalted butter
Pinch salt
2 scant cups flour
7–8 eggs
1 scant tablespoon sugar

Method.   Proceed as for the fine cream-puff pastry (above).

If the dough is to be used for main dishes, omit the sugar.

Pâte à beignets soufflés
BATTER FOR PUFFED FRITTERS

2 cups water
Pinch salt
7 tablespoons unsalted butter
3 cups sifted flour
7–8 eggs, depending upon their size
1 level tablespoon sugar
1 tablespoon orange-blossom water

Method.   Proceed as for ordinary cream-puff pastry (above).

Since these fritters are fried in oil, less butter is used in the dough.

Pâte à ramequin et à gougère
DOUGH FOR RAMEKINS AND GOUGÈRE

Make ordinary cream-puff pastry (above), but replace the water with milk and omit the sugar; when the dough is finished, stir in 3½ ounces grated gruyère cheese.

Éclairs au café ou au chocolat
COFFEE OR CHOCOLATE ECLAIRS

For 12 regular-sized eclairs, prepare 1 recipe cream-puff pastry (pages 396–7); put the dough into a pastry bag with a plain ⅝-inch tube.

Press the pastry bag with the hand that holds it and guide it with the other hand; pipe onto a pastry sheet strips of dough about 3½ inches long, placing them 2 inches apart. Each eclair uses about 1 ounce of dough.

To cut the dough when each strip is the correct length, stop pressing the bag and raise the tube with a sharp gesture of the guiding hand.

Brush the dough strips with a pastry brush dipped into beaten egg and bake in a 275° oven. Let cool.

When the eclairs are cooled, split each one on the side, open like a box, and fill the cavity with cream flavored with coffee or chocolate.

One can also fill the eclairs with frangipane cream, pastry cream, Saint-Honoré cream, or *crème* Chantilly (pages 410–13).

Close the eclairs, and cover the lids with lukewarm coffee or chocolate icing (pages 453–4).

Place them on a board.

When the icing has hardened, remove any drips, and serve the eclairs on a plate.

Choux à la crème
CREAM PUFFS

Proceed as for the eclairs (above), but, instead of making strips of dough, make small balls of dough the size of macaroons, spacing them 3 inches apart. Brush the tops with beaten egg and bake in a 325° oven for 15 to 20 minutes.

When the puffs are cool, cut off the tops, turn the cut-off pieces upside down, and put them inside the puffs; cover the top, in a dome shape, with Saint-Honoré cream (pages 412–13) or *crème* Chantilly (page 411).

Choux grillés
"BROILED" PUFFS

These puff pastries are identical to cream puffs; however, after brushing the tops with egg, flatten them slightly and coat each top with a pinch of chopped almonds covered with a pinch of powdered sugar. Press lightly to make the nuts stick.

Bake in a 325° oven for 15 to 20 minutes and serve after the puffs cool.

Gâteau Saint-Honoré

(For 6 servings)

Fine dough (page 386)
1 cup water
1 scant cup flour
1/4 pound unsalted butter
3 eggs
1 egg, beaten
Saint-Honoré cream
 (pages 412–13) or *crème*
 Chantilly (page 411)
Sugar syrup (optional)
Granulated sugar or
 chopped toasted almonds
 (optional)

The *gâteau* Saint-Honoré is an example of the pastries made by the old Pâtisserie Chiboust, near the Palais Royal or, more exactly, on the rue Saint-Honoré, which gives this exquisite cream cake its name; the cake was created by this renowned bakery in the era when all fashionable Paris visited the Palais Royal.

Method. Roll a piece of fine pie dough, making it the diameter of an ordinary plate (about 10 inches) and about 5/8 inch thick.

Pierce the dough several times with a fork and cut out a circle with the point of a knife, using a plate turned upside down on the dough to guide you.

Place the circle of dough on a pastry sheet slightly dampened with water.

Make fine cream-puff pastry with 1 cup water, 1 scant cup flour, 1/4 pound unsalted butter, and 3 eggs (see pages 396–7 for method).

Using a pastry bag fitted with a 5/8-inch plain tube, pipe a roll of cream-puff pastry all around the edge of the circle of dough and spiral it toward the center, leaving a space between the coils.

On another pastry sheet, make 30 small puffs the size of small walnuts.

Brush all the cream-puff pastry with beaten egg and bake in a 325° oven for 15 to 20 minutes.

When they are golden brown, place the circle of dough and the puffs on a rack; let cool.

Meanwhile, prepare the Saint-Honoré cream, or just before serving, prepare *crème* Chantilly. Now fill the circle of dough with the cream, spreading it 1½ inches thick right up to the edge of the cream-puff pastry. Then with a tablespoon, drop spoonfuls of the cream side by side on top of the cream layer, giving each one the shape of an elongated egg. Drop each spoonful of cream with an abrupt movement; this gives it a ridge on the top.

Remove the tops of the tiny cream puffs and with the pastry bag give each one a squirt of cream filling. Then place the tiny cream puffs around the top of the roll of cream-puff pastry, like a string of large pearls.

Stick the filled puffs to the rolls of cream-puff pastry by attaching them to the cream piled on the Saint-Honoré.

You can, but this is more complicated, dip the tops of the tiny puffs in sugar syrup (pages 452–3), which will form a solid transparent coating. The tops of alternate puffs are then dipped into granulated sugar or into chopped toasted almonds. With the same sugar syrup, still very hot, stick the puffs to the rolls of cream-puff pastry, turning the tops up.

If this method is used, put the tiny puffs in place before filling the circle with cream.

Croque-en-bouche

PASTRY THAT CRUMBLES IN YOUR MOUTH (For 10 servings)

2 cups cold milk
½ pound unsalted butter
2 teaspoons salt
1½ tablespoons sugar
About 3 cups flour
12 eggs

Method. Place milk, butter, salt, and sugar in a saucepan. Bring to a boil, add the flour, dry the dough on the heat for about 4 minutes, beat in the eggs, one at a time. Butter the pastry sheets, put the dough into a pastry bag, and pipe 60 small puffs onto the sheets. Bake in a 400° oven for about 20 minutes.

Cream Filling

1 vanilla bean
Pinch salt
4½ cups milk
8 egg yolks
3 cups sugar
⅔ cup flour
Caramelized almonds
Caramelized orange slices

Steep a vanilla bean with a pinch of salt in 4½ cups milk; in a bowl, mix the egg yolks with 1½ cups sugar and then add the flour; stir into the milk with a whisk and cook over a low flame for a good 5 minutes; use to fill the puffs.

Heat 1½ cups sugar until it melts and turns caramel color. Oil the inside of a cone-shaped mold. Dip the puffs into the caramel. Starting from the point, stuff the whole mold with puffs, each one dipped into caramel. Let cool. Unmold. Decorate with caramelized almonds and caramelized orange slices.

2¹/₂ cups sugar
16 eggs
3¹/₃ cups flour
14 tablespoons unsalted butter, clarified (page 75)

Génoise, madeleine, plum cake, spongecake

Génoise ordinaire

PLAIN GÉNOISE

Note: These proportions can be altered; if the flour is limited to less than 3 cups, the dough will be lighter; if the butter is reduced or omitted, then the cake will be less fine and less soft.

Flavor with vanilla sugar, various kinds of liqueur, or the grated rind of lemon or orange crushed with a lump of sugar.

Method.   Place the sugar in a deep copper bowl, which will make the egg whites mount; if you do not have such a bowl, use an ordinary bowl, which is of course less effective. Add the eggs, breaking them one by one into another bowl, to check their freshness before adding them to the sugar. Mix well with a whisk, and beat as you would beat eggs for an omelet. The mass will increase in volume, become lighter in color and creamy, until the consistency is such that it coats the wires of the whisk. The cream is ready when, if you lift the whisk, the mixture falls slowly in ribbons.

This beating with the whisk will take about 30 minutes. This time can be shortened by placing the bowl over a very low flame or on hot coals. That method is quicker but more risky, and the dough will fall more easily when the flour and the butter are added.

If you adopt this second method, remove the bowl from the heat when it is lukewarm, and continue to beat until the mixture is completely cooled.

Whatever the method chosen, when the mixture forms a ribbon, remove the whisk and replace it with a wooden spatula or a spoon; then sift the flour into the bowl, stirring the mixture with your right hand with a spatula while from time to time you rotate the bowl in the opposite direction with your left.

After adding the flour, add the flavoring and pour in the clarified butter in a stream, mixing it in the same way as the flour.

Pour the batter into round, square, or oval molds, plain or decorated, buttered carefully with clarified butter, dusted with flour, and well shaken. Fill each mold two-thirds full; bake in a 350° oven for 20 to 25 minutes, with the oven door slightly ajar.

You will know that the cake is done when it resists slightly when pressed lightly with your finger; unmold immediately onto a rack and let cool naturally without permitting the steam of the cake to condense.

The batter can be baked in 2 large rectangular pans about

1¼ inches deep (such as jelly-roll pans). After baking, the cake can be cut up in various ways depending upon its use.

Génoise au chocolat

CHOCOLATE GÉNOISE CAKE

8 eggs
1¼ cups superfine sugar
2 cups well-sifted flour
⅓ cup cocoa
7 tablespoons ground almonds
10½ tablespoons unsalted butter, melted
Ganache à truffes (page 455)

Method. In a bowl, beat the eggs with the sugar; then add the well-sifted flour, cocoa, and ground almonds. Mix well, and add the melted butter. Pour into a mold, set in a shallow pan of hot water, and bake in a 275° oven for 35 minutes.

Cut the cake in half horizontally and fill with *ganache à truffes* (semisweet chocolate mixed with heavy cream).

Gâteau du Président

PRESIDENT'S CAKE (Maurice Bernachon's recipe)

4 eggs
1¼ cups sifted flour
⅔ cup sugar
7 tablespoons unsalted butter
2 cups cream
1¼ pounds semisweet chocolate
Glazed cherries

Method. Make a *génoise* (page 400) with 4 eggs, 1¼ cups sifted flour, ⅔ cup sugar, and 7 tablespoons butter. Beat the eggs with the sugar as directed. As soon as the batter forms a ribbon, add the flour, then the melted butter. Cook over a low flame for 20 minutes; butter an 8-inch mold and dust it with flour before pouring in the batter. Meanwhile, cook 2 cups cream with 1¼ pounds semisweet chocolate for 10 minutes. Remove from the heat, beat with a stainless-steel whisk until completely cool. Add some glazed cherries and use this chocolate cream to fill and frost the cake. Then with a knife make curls of chocolate to cover the cake.

Madeleine

(For 48 madeleines)

2⅔ cups sugar
12 eggs
5 cups sifted flour
1 pound unsalted butter
1 teaspoon vanilla sugar

Method. Proceed as for the *génoise* (page 400), but mix the ingredients cold. When the mixture forms a ribbon, add first the flour, then the butter, melted and clarified (page 75). Be careful not to include the whey, which would sink to the bottoms of the molds during cooking and cause the dough to stick to them, making unmolding quite difficult. The cakes would not have their nice shape.

Fill the madeleine molds, pouring the batter in with a pastry scraper or a tablespoon, placing a little of the batter in each of the madeleine molds, which come 6 to 12 in a tin; butter the molds first, not excessively but carefully, with clarified butter; dust with flour, and then shake the molds.

Bake in a 325° oven for about 25 minutes; unmold as soon as they are done.

Plum cake

Method. Fill a large bowl with boiling water and let stand until the bowl is lukewarm. Empty the water, wipe the bowl,

½ pound unsalted butter
8 eggs
1⅓ cups sugar
Sultanas or currants
Candied peels of orange
  and citron (2 ounces
  each)
½ cup rum
1 teaspoon vanilla sugar
2½ cups sifted flour

and put in the butter, which has been softened by kneading it in a cloth and cut into pieces. Work the butter with a wooden spoon until it becomes smooth and white.

Add the eggs, one by one, continuing to work the mixture with a wooden spoon. The volume of the mixture increases as the eggs are added, but it is also the long beating that makes the mixture light, white, and completely creamy. At this point add the sugar and beat the batter until all the sugar is absorbed.

As soon as the mixture forms a ribbon when you lift it with the spatula, add the sultanas and currants, cleaned by dusting them with flour and rubbing them in a sieve that will let the stems through. Then add the candied orange and citron peels cut into tiny dice, the rum, the vanilla sugar, and then the sifted flour.

Adding these ingredients should not weigh down the egg-butter mixture.

Fill the special deep loaf cake pans, which are rectangular in shape, 4¾ inches high, 4 inches wide at the top, and 3¼ inches wide at the base. Butter the pans with clarified butter (page 75) and line with buttered white paper. Cut the paper ¾ inch higher than the mold and zigzag the top like wolf's teeth.

Spoon the batter into the pans. Fill only two-thirds of the way up. Tap down the top with a folded dishcloth so that it is level.

Bake in a 325° oven for about 1 hour.

This cake, which originated in England, on the other side of the Channel, is cooked with 1 teaspoon ammonium carbonate. Under the action of this baking powder, the top of the cake cracks and rises in a point. If one omits this ingredient, it is necessary to split the top of the cake lightly lengthwise with a knife during baking. This helps the cake to rise and keeps it light.

After removing the cake from the oven, unmold it but leave it wrapped in the paper, and cool on a rack.

In order to cut the cake easily into ⅜-inch slices, keep it a day or two before serving.

This is one of the finest cakes.

Biscuit de Savoie
SAVOY SPONGECAKE

2⅔ cups sugar
12 eggs, separated
5 cups sifted flour
1 teaspoon vanilla sugar
Clarified butter (page 75)

Method. Place the sugar and the 12 egg yolks in a large bowl.
Beat the egg whites very stiff.

Mix with a spatula and beat the mixture vigorously until it has tripled in volume and is white, creamy, and slides from the spatula in a thick, consistent ribbon.

At this moment add the flour, folding it into the batter with the spatula; add the vanilla sugar and one-quarter of the beaten egg whites. Mix very well; finish by folding in the remaining beaten egg whites, but this time fold very gently to keep the mixture from becoming heavy.

Molds for this cake are round and deep with a central tube and generally decorated. Butter three 8-cup molds carefully with clarified butter and turn them upside down to let them drain. Dust the inside with a mixture of equal parts of flour or cornstarch and superfine sugar or confectioners' sugar.

Fill the pans two-thirds full and smooth the tops with a folded cloth.

Bake in a 275° oven for 40 minutes.

The Savoy spongecake should be a pale golden color.

The dusting of sugar inside the mold forms a fine fragile wrapping.

After removing the cakes from the oven, let them stand for 5 minutes before unmolding.

Biscuits à la cuiller
LADYFINGERS

2²/₃ cups sugar
16 eggs, separated
4 cups sifted flour
1 tablespoon vanilla sugar
Powdered sugar

Method. Follow the directions for the Savoy spongecake, above.

Put the batter into a pastry bag with a plain tube 1 inch in diameter. Close the bag, and follow the steps described in the recipe for eclairs (pages 397–8).

Make strips about 5 inches long on a buttered pastry sheet dusted with flour or covered with wax paper. Leave a 2-inch space between each.

Sift some powdered sugar on top of the strips, let them stand for 2 minutes, then lift the pan or the paper and shake off the excess sugar.

Using a paintbrush dipped in water and shaken to remove the excess, sprinkle small drops of water on the sugar left on the ladyfingers. These drops of water, mixed with the sugar while cooking, will be transformed into little pearls.

Place the pastry sheet in a 225° oven for 25 minutes. When they are done, the ladyfingers should be just barely browned. When they have cooled, detach the ladyfingers from the paper or the pastry sheet and pair them two by two, back to back. Place in a tightly closed box where they can be kept extremely soft.

Biscuit manqué
MIXED-UP SPONGECAKE

1 pound sugar, about 2 ²/₃ cups
18 egg yolks
Vanilla
3 tablespoons rum
4 cups sifted flour
21 tablespoons unsalted butter
12 egg whites, beaten very stiff

Method. Proceed as for Savoy spongecake above, adding to the beaten sugar and egg yolks, the vanilla, the rum, the flour, the butter, and the egg whites, in that order.

403

14 tablespoons unsalted
  butter
1½ cups sugar
½ pound almonds and 1
  bitter almond, blanched
  (skins removed after
  boiling for 1 minute), all
  finely ground
8 eggs
2 teaspoons curaçao
8 tablespoons flour

½ pound almonds and 1
  bitter almond, blanched
  (skins removed after
  boiling for 1 minute)
6 eggs
1⅝ cups sugar
8 tablespoons flour
¼ pound unsalted butter,
  melted
1 teaspoon anisette

Pain de Gênes

GENOA CAKE

The Genoa cake is one of the best cakes of this type. It is
somewhat difficult to make it perfectly; but with care and experience, you can surmount the problems even if you are not
a professional cook. Two methods can be used to make this
cake, depending upon the equipment you have.

First Method

Soften the butter in a bowl by working it with a spatula; add
the sugar; mix well, beating vigorously with the spatula to
lighten and whiten the mixture. Add the ground almonds
and, one at a time, 4 whole eggs and 4 yolks.

The batter will become lighter, creamier, and increase in
volume. At this point, carefully add the curaçao, the flour,
and the 4 egg whites, beaten stiff. Fold the mixture with a
spatula, lifting the batter very gently.

Second Method

Pound the almonds in a mortar. When they form a paste, beat
in, one at a time, the 6 eggs, then the sugar; work the batter
vigorously to make it creamy and light. When it is ready, add
the flour and the melted butter, folding them very carefully into
the batter with a spatula.

Flavor with anisette.

[*Editor's note:* Bake following the instructions for Savoy
spongecake (pages 402–3).]

*Petits fours: small
cakes and cookies*

Petits gâteaux feuilletés

SMALL CAKES MADE WITH FLAKY PASTRY

Roll a piece of flaky dough (pages 382–3) with a rolling pin
until you have a sheet about ⅜ inch thick. Cut this dough
into small diamonds, rectangles, or squares, 2½ to 3¼ inches
on each side, or similar-sized rounds or ovals cut with a fluted
cookie cutter.

Place each small cake, turning it upside down, on a
slightly dampened pastry sheet. Brush only the top surface
with beaten egg, decorate using the point of a knife, and bake
in a 400° oven for 12 to 14 minutes.

Just before the cakes are done, remove from the oven,
sprinkle confectioners' sugar on the top; place back in the
oven for 1 minute, long enough to melt the sugar, which will
give a pleasant taste and a nice color.

Palmiers
PALM LEAVES

Use a piece of flaky pastry that has had four "turns" (page 383); let stand for 15 minutes, then give the fifth and sixth turns but, instead of sprinkling the table with flour, sprinkle generously with sugar.

When the dough has had six turns, fold it, then roll out the dough as if you were going to give it another turn until it is about 16 inches long and $3/8$ inch thick. Fold each end of the dough toward the center so that the ends touch; then fold one half on top of the other, like a wallet.

The rectangle of dough should be 4 inches long and $1^1/2$ inches thick. With a knife cut slices $3/8$ inch thick and put them, cut side down, on a slightly dampened pastry sheet, placing them 5 to 6 inches apart. Bake in a 400° oven for about 15 minutes, watching carefully. While baking, the cakes will open like palm leaves, and the sugar in them will caramelize quickly.

Palets au sucre
SUGAR COOKIES

With a fluted cookie cutter cut some flaky pastry or trimming from flaky pastry (pages 382–3) into circles about $1/4$ inch thick.

Dust the table with sugar; and with a rolling pin, roll each circle in the sugar until it becomes oval.

Turn the thin ovals over and place them on a slightly dampened pastry sheet, the sugared surfaces on top.

Bake in a 400° oven for 10 to 12 minutes, watching carefully because the sugar will caramelize quickly.

Sacristains
TWIST CAKES

Use trimmings of flaky pastry (page 383) pressed into a ball. Roll the dough on sugar until it is $3/8$ inch thick, giving it a rectangular shape; trim with a knife to make it 6 inches wide.

Brush with beaten egg, cover with chopped almonds, and sprinkle generously with sugar. Stick the almonds and the sugar to the dough by pressing lightly with the flat part of a knife blade.

Turn the strip of dough over, placing it almond side down on the table sprinkled with sugar. Repeat the steps: brush with egg, cover with almonds, sprinkle with sugar, and press down with a knife blade.

Then cut crosswise into small strips $1^1/4$ inches wide; take these little strips, one by one, and give each one a double twist before placing it on a slightly dampened pastry sheet.

Bake in a 400° oven for 10 to 12 minutes. Check while baking, because the sugar caramelizes very quickly.

Note: The above flaky cakes can be made very small to be served as *petits fours*.

3/4 pound unsalted butter
2 eggs
3³/4 cups flour
1¹/3 cups sugar
1/2 pound almonds,
  crushed or finely ground
1 or 2 egg yolks (optional)
1 teaspoon vanilla sugar
  or 1 tablespoon rum

Gâteaux sablés fins
SMALL SAND CAKES

Method. Mix together ³/4 pound butter and 2 eggs with 3³/4 cups flour combined with 1¹/3 cups sugar and ¹/2 pound crushed or finely ground almonds.

Knead the dough quickly. If the dough is too firm and breaks, add 1 or 2 egg yolks.

Flavor with 1 teaspoon vanilla sugar or 1 tablespoon rum.

Wrap the dough in a cloth and let stand for 20 minutes.

Then roll with a rolling pin into a sheet ³/16 inch thick, and cut into small squares using a fluted rolling pastry cutter. Place each cake on a pastry sheet, prick with a fork to avoid bubbles, and bake in a 400° oven for 15 to 20 minutes.

These delicious crumbly cakes should be a nice light brown color when done.

Keep the cookies in a tightly closed box.

¹/4 pound almonds, skinned
  and finely pounded in a
  mortar, dried, and ground
1 teaspoon cornstarch
³/4 cup sugar
1 tablespoon vanilla sugar
2 egg whites and 1 yolk
Sliced almonds

Tuiles aux amandes
ALMOND TILES

Method. In a bowl, work the pounded or grated almonds with a wooden spatula, adding the cornstarch, the sugars, and 1 egg white. When the mixture is smooth and creamy, add the egg yolk and, a few seconds later, the other egg white.

This mixture should be soft and spread slightly; if it is too thick, add more egg white.

Using a pastry bag with a ³/8-inch tube or a teaspoon, make small balls of dough as big as walnuts on a buttered pastry sheet. Place them about 2¹/2 inches apart, since the dough will spread. Sprinkle a few slices of almonds on each small cookie and bake in a 225° oven until they begin to brown on the edges.

To make the tiles curved, while they are still hot, place each one on the side of a rolling pin. While they are warm, they are very pliant and will take the shape of the rolling pin, which they will hold when they cool and become very crisp and crunchy.

Keep them dry in a tightly closed box.

²/3 cup sugar
1 teaspoon vanilla sugar
1 egg
¹/2 cup light cream or milk
⁷/8 cup flour

Langues de chat
CATS' TONGUES
Ordinary Recipe

Method. In a bowl, combine the sugars, the egg, and the cream or milk; add the flour, sifted. Mix well.

Place the batter in a pastry bag with a plain ³/8-inch tube and pipe small strips about 3¹/4 to 4 inches long on a lightly buttered pastry sheet.

Keep the strips about 2¹/2 inches apart so that the dough can spread.

Bake in a 375° oven for 7 to 8 minutes. The cats' tongues

should be a light golden-brown color, edged with a darker brown.

Remove the cats' tongues from the pastry sheet when they are completely cold, and keep them very dry, in a tightly closed box, so that they will remain crisp.

Langues de chat
CATS' TONGUES
Special Recipe

¹/₄ pound fine butter
¹/₂ cup sugar
3 eggs, separated
1 cup sifted flour
2 tablespoons vanilla
  sugar

Method.   Warm a small bowl with boiling water, pour out the water, and dry the bowl; put in the butter, cut into pieces, and work with a wooden spatula until it is soft and smooth. Then add the sugar, beating vigorously until the mixture is creamy; and finish by beating in the egg yolks, one by one. Add the flour, then the 3 egg whites, beaten stiff. Put the dough into a pastry bag and pipe strips onto a buttered pastry sheet and bake as described in the preceding recipe.

Palets aux raisins
CURRANT COOKIES

¹/₄ pound dried currants
2 tablespoons rum
¹/₄ pound unsalted butter
²/₃ cup sugar
3 eggs
⁷/₈ cup flour

Method.   Pick over the dried currants and rub them with a pinch of flour in a sieve coarse enough to let the stems through. Macerate in the rum.

In a slightly warmed bowl, soften the butter, cut into small pieces, and work it with a spatula to make it creamy. Add the sugar, and work the mixture again; add the eggs, one by one, the flour, and the currants, beating after each addition. Flavor with rum.

Fill a pastry bag with a plain tube and pipe small balls of dough onto a buttered pastry sheet. Place them about 2 inches apart so that the cookies do not stick to one another as they spread when they are baked.

Bake in a 325° oven and keep in a tightly closed box, like the cats' tongues.

Pastry desserts

Most pastry desserts combine cake and cream, cake and jam, or cake and icing.

Any type of cake can be used as a foundation for a dessert. The most delicate one is the dough for madeleines (page 401), baked in the pans for mixed-up spongecake (page 403) or *génoise* cake (page 400).

These cakes can be filled with a variety of creams: butter

cream in any of a number of flavors; or frangipane cream, pastry cream, *crème* Chantilly, or Saint-Honoré cream.

A cake can be coated with sugar, chopped pistachio nuts, chopped or sliced almonds, sugared or toasted almonds, grated chocolate. Icings are almost always flavored with coffee, chocolate, kirsch, anisette, maraschino, rum, etc.

Moka
MOCHA CAKE

2²/₃ cups sugar
16 eggs
5 cups sifted flour
1 tablespoon vanilla sugar
Mocha cream (pages 411–12)
Sugar

This is a cake that despite its birth date, 1857, has not grown old. It has kept all the freshness of Normandy or Charentais butter allied with the exquisite taste of mocha.

Besides the advice given above on a suitable dough, here is a supplementary recipe for a light cake that is better to use for mocha cakes and generally for all cakes to be filled with butter cream.

Method. Beat the sugar in a large bowl with the eggs. Place the bowl on charcoal or on the lowest possible heat of the stove. When the batter forms a ribbon, add the sifted flour, mixing carefully with a spatula. Flavor with 1 tablespoon vanilla sugar. Pour into a 2-quart pan, and bake in a 275° oven. Unmold on a rack, and let cool completely before filling with butter cream.

Serving. When the cake is cold, with a long thin knife cut it horizontally into three parts. Spread a layer of mocha cream about ¹/₄ inch thick on the bottom layer; place the second layer of cake on top, then spread with a second layer of mocha cream; and place the third layer of cake on top. Then coat the cake on the sides and the top with a thick layer of mocha cream. This last step is done by placing the cake on a rack slightly smaller than the cake, which will allow you to smooth the cream evenly on the sides of the cake.

Finish the sides by pressing on some sugar. Do this step over a sheet of paper to catch the sugar that will inevitably spill.

With a small pastry bag fitted with a very fine fluted tube decorate the top of the cake with 2 tablespoons mocha cream; make a design of rosettes, garlands, and tiny roses, which can easily be done by giving the fluted tube a circular movement. Refrigerate until ready to serve.

Chocolatine pralinée
CHOCOLATE CAKE WITH SUGARED ALMONDS

Make this like the mocha cake (above), using butter cream flavored with cocoa or chocolate.

Cover the sides with chopped almonds that have been coated with sugar and browned; and decorate the top with chocolate cream in the same way as the mocha cake.

Gâteau mascotte

MASCOT CAKE

Frost several round or square layers of *génoise* cake (page 400) or any other cake with mocha cream (pages 411–12) or chocolate butter cream. Follow the steps for the mocha cake (above), but serve the cake as it was in the pan, which means with the rounded surface on top. Frost it more in the center, so that it curves slightly on the top. Cover the sides with cream as for the mocha cake; on the top and sides, sprinkle generously with sliced almonds, sugared and browned. Finally, dust with vanilla-flavored confectioners' sugar.

Bûche de Noël

CHRISTMAS LOG

The Christmas log is a mocha cake traditionally made at Christmas time.

The *génoise* batter (page 400) or any other batter is baked in a long semicylindrical mold. If you do not have a special mold, bake a sheet of cake, spreading it in a very flat pan lined with a piece of wax paper or simply on a piece of paper on a pastry sheet. Once the cake is baked and cooled, remove the piece of paper and spread a layer of mocha (pages 411–12) or chocolate cream about $1/2$ inch thick on top of the cake; then roll the cake to make a log. Whatever method you use for making the cake, the bottom of the cake should be iced with mocha cream and then stuck to a base of cooked *sablée* pastry (pages 486–7), or any other pastry, with a layer of cream; this base should be about $1^1/4$ to $1^1/2$ inches larger than the cake. Then cover the top of the cake with rows of cream from a pastry bag fitted with a fluted flat tube. These rows of cream should imitate the rough bark of a log.

With a little skill you can make the stumps of one or two cut branches from a piece of cake with rough edges that is covered with cream. Cover the cut ends with plain butter cream; and, here and there, place a small amount of chopped almonds, tinted green, to imitate moss. Meringue mushrooms, imitation leaves, and other such trimmings can also be used. The decoration of the cake is mostly a matter of imagination and taste.

Creams, Bavarian creams, charlottes, puddings, and rice desserts

CREAMS

Crème frangipane
FRANGIPANE CREAM

4¹/₂ cups milk
1 vanilla bean
1¹/₃ cups flour
1 cup sugar
Pinch salt
4 eggs
6 egg yolks
7 tablespoons unsalted butter
4 tablespoons macaroon crumbs

Method. In a heavy-bottomed saucepan holding about 2 quarts, boil 4¹/₂ cups milk with a vanilla bean.

Meanwhile, in a bowl, mix the flour with the sugar and salt; then stir in the eggs and egg yolks.

While the milk is still very hot, pour it slowly into the egg mixture, beating with a whisk, and pour the mixture back into the saucepan; heat to the boiling point, stirring continuously. Remove from the heat, and add the butter and the macaroon crumbs.

Pour the frangipane cream into a bowl, and stir it with a wooden spoon until completely cold. This last step prevents the formation of a skin on top of the cream that would eventually produce lumps. A skin can also be avoided by dabbing the surface with a piece of butter. Keep refrigerated until ready to use.

Crème pâtissière
PASTRY CREAM

4¹/₄ cups hot milk
2²/₃ cups sugar
1 scant cup flour
Pinch salt
12 egg yolks
Vanilla

Method. Proceed as for frangipane cream (above), changing the quantities of the ingredients in this way: 4¹/₄ cups very hot milk poured slowly into a mixture of 2²/₃ cups sugar, 1 scant cup flour, pinch of salt, and 12 egg yolks.

When mixture reaches the boiling point, pour into a bowl and stir often with a wooden spoon until completely cold.

This cream should be flavored with vanilla, but you also can add essence of coffee, cocoa, orange or lemon rind—steep the rind in the boiling milk, covered.

Note: When these creams are cold, scrape the sides of the bowl to incorporate whatever has stuck to them while stirring; after each stirring, smooth the top surface of the cream and cover with buttered white paper.

Crème Chantilly

The base of this cream is very thick fresh cream from milk. Keep it on ice or in the refrigerator during the hot season.

Pour the cream into a bowl, and whip, beginning slowly, with a small, flexible whisk. The cream will slowly increase in volume until doubled. When cream reaches that point, whip faster; and stop only when the cream stands in peaks and stays in the whisk when you lift it, as egg whites do when beaten stiff.

Be careful not to beat too much, because butter will start to form; you need only 2 or 3 minutes more to make whipped cream into butter.

Carefully add $^2/_3$ to $1^1/_3$ cups sugar for each $4^1/_4$ cups whipped cream, depending on its use.

Note: Since this cream can be beaten quickly, we advise whipping it just before serving.

Crème anglaise

CUSTARD CREAM (For 1 quart cream)

This cream is the base for, or is served with, many hot or cold desserts and some ice creams called parfaits.

2³/₄ cups boiled milk with a split vanilla bean steeped in it, covered, after milk has boiled
1¹/₃ cups sugar
8 egg yolks

Method. In a bowl mix the sugar and the egg yolks; beat this mixture with a wooden spoon until it is frothy, thick, and nearly white. Then slowly add the milk.

Pour the mixture back into the saucepan, and cook on a low flame; stir continuously with the spatula, moving it all around the bottom of the pan to prevent the egg yolks from coagulating.

As the sauce heats, the egg yolks will thicken the cream. As soon as the cream starts to coat the spoon, which is as soon as it reaches the boiling point, remove from the heat and pour into a bowl to hasten the cooling and to stop the egg yolks from further cooking, which would harden them into tiny particles and destroy their ability to smooth and thicken the mixture.

Making this cream requires some experience. It is possible to compensate for insufficient practice by adding 1 teaspoon cornstarch to each quart of milk.

Note: If you want to increase the fineness and the smoothness of the custard, you can increase the number of egg yolks to about 20 for 1 quart milk and add, after the cream has cooled, 1 cup thick *crème fraîche* or heavy cream.

Crème moka

MOCHA CREAM

Among pastry creams, this cream is the supreme mixture of sugar, egg yolks, and butter. There are various good methods for making this cream, but the two following recipes are recommended because they are simpler to make in the home kitchen.

411

First Method

In a saucepan, mix 1 cup sugar and 8 egg yolks; beat the mixture with a wooden spatula to make it white and creamy. Then slowly add 1 cup strong coffee and heat slowly, stirring continuously as in making a custard cream. As soon as the cream reaches the boiling point, thickens, and coats the back of the spatula, stop the boiling at once and remove quickly from the heat, pouring it into a bowl to cool it and stop the egg yolks from cooking.

When the cream is lukewarm, add 3/4 pound fine unsalted butter, cut into small pieces about the size of half a walnut, and mix with a whisk into a smooth paste; then whip vigorously with a sauce whisk.

When it has been mixed, the cream becomes smooth and shiny. The color is light brown, the flavor like tasty mocha coffee.

Use the mocha cream immediately without refrigerating, which would harden it and make it difficult to use.

Second Method

Prepare 1 cup custard cream (page 411); when it is still tepid, add, following the first method, 1/2 pound unsalted butter. Finish the cream by adding 1 teaspoon coffee essence.

Or replace the custard cream with 1 1/2 cups pastry cream (page 410), which is not so fine, and finish the cream as above.

Note: It is an invariable rule that equal amounts of butter and cream must be used. Not enough butter causes the two ingredients to separate, which is easy to correct by readjusting the proportions.

Crème moka délice
DELICIOUS MOCHA CREAM
(In memory of Master Chef Urbain Dubois)

8 egg yolks
1 tablespoon confectioner's sugar
1/2 cup sugar syrup made with strong fresh coffee instead of water (pages 452–3)
28 tablespoons unsalted butter

Method. With a whisk beat, in an unlined copper bowl over charcoal, 8 egg yolks with 1 tablespoon confectioners' sugar; slowly add syrup made with sugar and fresh strong coffee. [*Editor's note:* Today, unlined copper is not considered healthful, but such utensils were favored by past generations of French chefs.]

When the cream coats a wooden spoon like custard, remove from the heat and continue to whip until the cream is lukewarm. Then pour the cream on the butter, first softened into a paste in a bowl.

Work the mixture vigorously with a whisk.

Crème à Saint-Honoré
SAINT-HONORÉ CREAM

Pastry cream (page 410)
2/3 cup sugar
6 egg whites
1/2 teaspoon vanilla sugar
2 envelopes gelatin, softened in water

Method. Follow the recipe for pastry cream. When the cream is cooked, add the gelatin off the heat; then, while the cream is still hot, add the egg whites, beaten stiff with the sugar.

Here are two ways to mix the cream and the egg whites:
Either slowly pour the boiling cream into the beaten egg

whites, folding carefully with a spatula, lifting the mixture to prevent the whites from falling, or first pour the very hot cream into a bowl and fold in the beaten egg whites, in small quantities, as above.

This second method is preferable.

Saint-Honoré cream should be used right away, before it sets and hardens.

Crème à la purée de marrons
CHESTNUT PURÉE CREAM

Prepare a butter cream, following the second method for mocha cream (page 412) but omitting the coffee essence, and, when it is finished, add chestnut purée equal in weight to the sugar used in the cream.

To make the purée, rub broken candied chestnuts through a sieve, or remove the double skins from fresh chestnuts, cook, and rub them through a sieve. Mix with a little sugar syrup or milk.

This purée should be creamy and rather firm.

Blancs d'oeufs en neige
BEATEN EGG WHITES

To make whites of eggs frothy, smooth, and white, two utensils are needed: an unlined copper bowl for beating eggs (see *note*, page 412), a wooden-handled whisk with tinned-steel wires. To this day no electric appliance has been able to replace the wrist, except a machine made for laboratories, run by a motor, with armatures that reproduce exactly the movements of the arm and wrist.

Very fresh egg whites have a tendency to granulate and to separate at the end of the whipping. This problem can be overcome by adding a pinch of salt at the beginning of the whipping and a couple of tablespoons of superfine sugar— 1 or 2—at the end.

In the beginning, beat slowly as for an omelet—with the bowl held slightly inclined and the whites at the bottom. As the albumin coagulates and increases in volume, it is important to increase the speed of the whipping and finally to change the movement of the whisk, moving it quickly and pushing against the sides of the bowl. The egg whites are sufficiently beaten when they become firm and can be lifted by the wires of the whisk. If you notice the egg whites separating, add the sugar.

When the egg whites are firm, they should be used immediately.

To mix beaten egg whites with other ingredients, use a spatula and fold them in, lifting the mass carefully to keep the whites from falling.

Crème pour bavaroises, plombières, puddings, charlottes glacés

CREAM FOR BAVARIAN CAKES, ICE CREAMS, PUDDINGS, COLD CHARLOTTES

Prepare a custard cream (page 411), with at least 12 egg yolks for each quart of milk.

Add 2 envelopes of gelatin, softened in cold water, per quart of mixture. Add the gelatin after the milk is mixed into the egg yolks.

After cooking, strain through a fine sieve, pour into a bowl, and stir until completely cool to prevent the formation of a skin or lumps.

Crème renversée

1 quart boiled milk
1 cup sugar, dissolved in the milk
4 whole eggs and 8 egg yolks or 8 whole eggs

Method. The function of the egg whites in this custard is to coagulate the cream under the effect of the heat. The role of the yolks is to make the cream smooth. Therefore, the higher the proportion of egg yolks and the lower the proportion of egg whites, the finer the cream will be. However, 4 egg whites are the minimum quantity reasonable to use for a cream stiff enough to unmold properly.

Crème renversée is flavored by steeping a vanilla bean in the milk; using orange or lemon rind; melting chocolate in the milk or using cocoa; adding to the milk a chosen flavor such as coffee or tea or any other liquid, being careful to subtract an equal amount of milk from the liquid used.

Combine the sugar and the eggs in a bowl and beat the mixture with a wooden spoon for a few minutes; pour the boiling milk into it, stirring constantly; strain through a fine sieve, remove the froth that floats on top, and pour into a mold: a cake pan with a tube in the center, a *génoise* pan, or any other low pan or small individual molds.

Cooking. Place the mold in a shallow baking pan and fill the baking pan two-thirds up with nearly boiling water; bake in a 325° oven for at least 1 hour.

The water should never boil, because boiling would partially separate the cream, which then would have small pockets of water sprinkled through it. In case the water should start to boil, stop it by adding a few tablespoons of lukewarm water.

Check the cooking by touching the surface and insert a fine needle or a thin knife blade; if it comes out clean, the cream is baked.

Let cool in the mold. Unmold just before serving.

Crème renversée au caramel

Dissolve 4 cubes sugar or 2 tablespoons sugar in 3 tablespoons water. Cook this mixture slowly until the water has completely evaporated and the sugar starts to dissolve; remove from the heat when its color is light brown.

Rapidly plunge the bottom of the saucepan or frying pan into cold water to prevent the sugar from burning or the taste will become bitter; or pour the caramel immediately into the mold in which the cream will be baked and spread it, tipping the mold in all directions in order to give it a coating of caramel about ⅛ inch thick.

If you wish to serve a caramel syrup with the cream, double the quantity of sugar and water, pour half the finished caramel into the molds and add ½ cup water to the remaining syrup in the saucepan; cook to a syrup, and set aside to serve with the cream.

Meanwhile, prepare the custard; pour it into the mold coated inside with caramel and bake in a *bain-marie* in a 325° oven for at least 1 hour. It is preferable to prepare this dessert 6 hours before serving. While it stands, the moisture of the cream will dissolve the caramel, which will soak into the cream producing a beautiful color when the dish is unmolded.

Oeufs à la neige Gisou

FLOATING ISLANDS GISOU

This family dessert is always successful. The quality of the dessert depends on the freshness of the eggs.

8 extremely fresh eggs, separated
1⅓ cups sugar
2 cups boiled milk with a split vanilla bean steeped in it, covered, after milk has boiled

Method. In a saucepan, combine 8 egg yolks with half the sugar; beat cold with a whisk until mixture forms a ribbon.

Add the milk. Place the saucepan on the stove and heat, stirring with a wooden spoon. As soon as the cream thickens and coats the spoon, remove from the heat. Do not let the cream boil. Immediately strain through a fine sieve into a bowl; stir until completely cold.

Place 8 egg whites in a large stainless-steel bowl. With a whisk, start to stir them and whip them slowly. Beat faster until the whites are quite firm. They will form a light froth that sticks to the wires of the whisk. At that point add the remaining sugar, a little at a time, in order to keep the egg whites very light.

Take a large low saucepan, fill it three-quarters up with water. Bring the water to a boil.

Using a wooden spoon preferably, form the egg whites in large ovals to resemble eggs.

Place each spoonful on the surface of the simmering water, giving a little bang on the edge of the saucepan to detach the egg white from the spoon.

Poach about 6 at once. With a slotted spoon turn them over after a minute or two to poach them on all sides.

Drain the egg whites on a cloth or a fine sieve placed over a bowl. Let cool.

Place the cold cream in a large deep dish. Place the "floating" egg whites on top, overlapping them slightly.

You can sprinkle the eggs with slices of toasted almonds or pour a stream of caramel over them or even dust them with powdered chocolate.

415

This delicious dessert is eaten cold but not iced.

Note: To get more volume into the egg whites, add a pinch of salt or a drop of lemon juice.

Pots de crème

CUSTARD IN SMALL POTS

Of all the cooked custard creams, the most delicate to prepare is that for *pots de crème.* These creams are served in their own cooking pots, not unmolded, which allows you to omit the whites of eggs completely. The quantities are easy to adjust. Use 1 egg yolk or less per pot (if the pots hold about 1/2 cup of liquid). Let us consider that the combined volume of the egg yolks and the sugar equals one-quarter of the capacity of the pots, and calculate the quantity of milk or, even better, fresh cream, needed on the basis of these figures and the number of pots to be used. Measure the quantity of egg yolks, adding 2 tablespoons sugar for each 1/2-cup pot; then add three times this amount of milk or cream. Beat well and pour into the pots. After filling the pots, let them stand for a few minutes, then carefully remove the foam that rises to the tops.

Cooking.   Poach the covered pots of cream in a *bain-marie* in the oven very carefully, because of the extreme sensitivity of the custard. Being covered, the tops of the cream will not brown; if flavored with vanilla, they will be yellow or gold; if with chocolate, the color of chocolate and shiny.

Les sabayons

(For 1 quart)

The *sabayons* are served as an accompaniment to hot or cold desserts.

They are always prepared in the same way, and with the same combination of ingredients; only the flavoring element changes, depending on the dessert they are to be served with.

Method.   In a saucepan combine the egg yolks and the sugar, and beat the mixture as for *génoise* cake (page 400). When the mixture is nearly white and forms a ribbon from the wires of the whisk, add the white wine; then while still beating, heat the mixture in a *bain-marie* until it is like a light cream and just hot enough so that the egg yolks are beginning to cook, as you would for a custard cream (page 411); this will keep the mixture from losing its lightness and homogeneity.

At this point, pour into a bowl and let cool, whipping often, or pour into a special *bain-marie* for sauces, and keep the *bain-marie* warm.

Flavor just before serving with one of these flavorings or liqueurs: vanilla, orange, or lemon sugar; 1/2 cup rum, kirsch, kümmel, maraschino, Grand Marnier, or Marie Brizard apricot liqueur.

If the flavoring is to be wine (Madeira, port, sherry, Samos, or champagne), omit the white wine in the cream and replace with the chosen wine.

10 egg yolks
2 cups sugar
2 cups dry white wine
Flavoring or liqueur (see below)

An easy method that gives very good results: rub 1 or more cubes of sugar on the skin of the fruit until all the surfaces of the sugar are covered with rind from the fruit. Then scrape the sugar with a knife and rub the rind again until you have the quantity of sugar needed; stop while the fruit still has some colored skin left, which is the part that is flavored.

SAUCES TO ACCOMPANY DESSERTS

Sauce crème au chocolat
CHOCOLATE CREAM SAUCE

½ pound sweet chocolate or ¼ pound cocoa
½ cup water
1 cup *crème fraîche* or heavy cream
2 tablespoons unsalted butter

Method. For 15 minutes slowly cook sweet chocolate or cocoa with ½ cup water, stirring from time to time. Just before serving, add off the heat the *crème fraîche* and the butter. Whip vigorously for 2 minutes.

Note: If cocoa is used, add ⅔ cup sugar when it is dissolved.

Sauce aux abricots
APRICOT SAUCE (For 1 quart)

3½ cups apricot jam
1 cup water
¼ cup sugar

Method. Boil the ingredients slowly for 5 minutes, skim, and strain through a fine sieve, pushing through the pieces of fruit. Keep warm in a double boiler.

Before using, flavor the sauce with kirsch or maraschino and vanilla.

For other sauces follow the method above, substituting the corresponding jam: for strawberry sauce, flavor with kirsch; for raspberry sauce, flavor with maraschino; for currant sauce, flavor with kirsch; for orange sauce, flavor with curaçao and add one-third apricot sauce.

Sauce crème pralinée
CREAM SAUCE WITH CARAMELIZED NUT POWDER

To 1 quart custard cream (page 411) or *sabayon* made with champagne (page 416), add 3 tablespoons caramelized almonds (page 454) of filberts or pistachios, finely crushed.

Sauce Montmorency

½ pound Montmorency cherries
½ pound currant and raspberry jelly
Juice of ¼ pound raspberries (optional)
Juice of 2 oranges
Pinch ginger
2 ounces candied cherries
2 tablespoons kirsch

Method. Crush the Montmorency cherries (slightly bitter) to get the juice. Put the juice into a bowl with partially melted jelly made with raw currants and raspberries. Add the juice of ¼ pound raspberries, if the jelly was not made with half raspberries. Then add the orange juice, ginger, and candied cherries macerated in kirsch mixed with 1 tablespoon tepid water so that they will puff up.

BLANCMANGE

This dish, which is a very old recipe, remains among the most delicious of desserts. Simple and French in its taste, it seems to be forgotten more and more by modern cooks, which is very regrettable. I wanted it to keep its place in this book, remembering that it is the delicate ancestor of our puddings, Bavarian creams, and ice creams.

½ pound sweet almonds mixed with 2 bitter almonds
2 cups light *crème fraîche*
½ cup sugar, loose or in cubes
½ teaspoon vanilla sugar
2 envelopes gelatin

Method. Boil and skin the almonds, rinse; soak for 1 hour in cold water to make them very white, drain, and dry; then pound in a mortar, moistening them, in the beginning, with 2 tablespoons water; slowly add the *crème fraîche,* in small quantities, as you pound. Pour this mixture into a dishcloth or linen towel and squeeze by twisting the ends in opposite directions over a bowl.

Dissolve the sugar in the cold almond milk. Add ½ teaspoon vanilla sugar, then the gelatin softened in a little of the cold almond milk and heated to dissolve.

Pour the almond milk into a mold, and refrigerate exactly like a Bavarian cream. It is served in the same way.

BAVARIAN CREAMS

The Bavarian cream and all the other chilled desserts that derive from it take the place of ice cream or ice cream with fruits in making up a menu.

The advantage these chilled desserts have over ice cream is that they can be made with limited kitchen equipment.

Furthermore, these desserts are very popular.

Bavarian cream base

1⅓ cups sugar
8 egg yolks
2 cups boiled milk with a split vanilla bean steeped in it, covered, after milk has boiled
2 envelopes gelatin, softened in cold water

Method. Follow the recipe for custard cream (page 411); while hot, add the gelatin, stir until dissolved, and strain through a fine sieve into a glazed bowl.

Let the cream cool, stirring often. When it is nearly cold and starts to jell, carefully add 2 cups *crème fraîche,* thick and whipped, and sweeten with 2 tablespoons confectioners', preferably, or superfine sugar. At the same time, add the flavoring and the chosen garnish.

Molding. Bavarian creams are nearly always made in a mold with a hollow center tube. If you do not have such a mold, you can use a charlotte, savarin, or *génoise* mold, or the mold for a Breton cake. Or even more simply, a crystal bowl or a nice silver bowl. In that case do not unmold the cream; the gelatin can be reduced by half, which increases the delicacy of the dessert's texture.

If the Bavarian cream is to be unmolded, oil the mold lightly with almond oil before filling it, or coat the mold with caramel, very light in color, which is much better.

When the mold is filled with the cream mixture, tap it lightly on a folded cloth so that the contents settle into the shape of the mold; place the mold in a bowl of crushed ice or refrigerate for at least 3 hours.

To unmold dip the mold for one second into warm water, wipe it, and turn it over onto a serving platter.

The Bavarian cream can be served with a plate of small, soft vanilla and chocolate macaroons.

Bavaroises aux liqueurs
BAVARIAN CREAMS WITH LIQUEURS

Grand Marnier, Cointreau, Marie Brizard apricot liqueur, kirsch, maraschino, rum, fine champagne brandy, plum brandy, etc.; almonds, filberts, nuts, caramelized powdered almonds, lemon, orange, coffee, chocolate, port, Marsala, Frontignan—all may be used to flavor a base of Bavarian cream.

In the springtime Bavarian creams can be prepared with flowers such as violets, rose petals, acacia flowers, orange blossoms, elder flowers, or carnations; gather them fresh and choose those with the strongest scent.

The simplest method is to steep the flowers, covered, in the boiling syrup prepared for this dessert. When they have steeped, strain the syrup through a very fine sieve, and continue as for a Bavarian cream with fruit (below).

Bavaroises aux fruits
BAVARIAN CREAMS WITH FRUIT

Bavarian creams based on fruit purées are made with equal parts of fresh fruit purée and sugar syrup. Combine 5$\frac{1}{4}$ cups sugar and 4$\frac{1}{3}$ cups water for the syrup, and follow the instructions on pages 452–3). For 1 quart fruit and syrup, add the juice of 3 lemons or 3 oranges, 4 envelopes gelatin softened in cold water and dissolved in the hot syrup, and 2 cups whipped cream.

The method is the same as for the basic Bavarian above: When the sugar syrup has cooled and is close to solidifying because of the gelatin, add the fruit purée, the lemon or orange juice, and then the whipping cream.

The best fruits to use are: strawberries, raspberries, blackberries, pineapple, peaches, apricots, bananas, cherries, and melon. All these fruits must be very ripe to obtain the maximum flavor. Here is another simple recipe:

Bavaroise nectarine
NECTARINE BAVARIAN CREAM

30 ripe nectarines
1$\frac{1}{3}$ cups superfine sugar
** or 1$\frac{1}{2}$ cups lump sugar**
5 envelopes gelatin
2 tablespoons kirsch
1$\frac{1}{2}$ cups *crème fraîche* or
** heavy cream, whipped**
$\frac{1}{2}$ cup light sugar syrup
30 strawberries, hulled
Currant jelly

Method.   Remove the skins and the pits of the nectarines; put the fruit into a large bowl with $\frac{2}{3}$ cup superfine sugar or, preferably, $\frac{3}{4}$ cup lump sugar. Mix carefully, cover with a cloth, and place in a cool place to macerate for 30 minutes. Stir from time to time.

Then pour the fruit into a fine sieve placed over a bowl and rub through to make a purée, to which you add, again, $\frac{2}{3}$ cup superfine or $\frac{3}{4}$ cup lump sugar.

419

Soften 5 envelopes gelatin in cold water and then dissolve in ¼ cup hot water and add, stirring, to the nectarine purée. Mix continuously until the gelatin starts to set.

At this point, add to the mixture 1 tablespoon kirsch and the whipped *crème fraîche.* Mold following the directions given above, and refrigerate.

While the mold is chilling, bring the light sugar syrup to a boil; remove from the heat, pour in 1 tablespoon kirsch and add the strawberries. Stir to coat the fruit, cover, let cool, and refrigerate immediately.

To serve, unmold the Bavarian cream, following the instructions above, onto a round platter. Surround it with a circle of the glazed strawberries. Coat everything with currant jelly, made with raw fruit, partially melted and diluted with a few tablespoons of the syrup from the strawberries. Serve with a tray of almond tiles (page 406).

Rêverie Candice et Stéphanie

CANDICE AND STEPHANIE'S DREAM

1 *génoise* cake, about 10–12 inches in diameter (page 400)
Maraschino
1 cup heavy cream
²/₃ cup sugar
1 teaspoon cornstarch
4 egg yolks
3 envelopes gelatin
Cube sugar rubbed on an orange skin
¼ pound strawberries
2 ounces raspberries
2 ounces wild blackberries
2 cups confectioners' sugar
1 tablespoon maraschino or kirsch
3 tablespoons hot light sugar syrup
1 cup *crème fraîche* or heavy cream, whipped and sugared like *crème* Chantilly (page 411)
Crystallized violets (page 454)

Method. Prepare a *génoise* cake about 10 to 12 inches in diameter; soak the *génoise* with maraschino. Refrigerate.

Make a custard cream (for method see page 411) with 1 cup heavy cream, ²/₃ cup sugar, 1 teaspoon cornstarch; 4 egg yolks, and 1 envelope softened gelatin; cook until the cream coats a spoon and then strain through a very fine sieve into a bowl. Stir until completely cool. Flavor with a cube of sugar rubbed on an orange skin.

At this point it will begin to set. Pour the cream into a Bavarian cream mold at least 2½ inches smaller than the diameter of the *génoise* cake. Cool the cream on a bed of crushed ice, turning and tipping the mold so that the cream sticks to the mold and coats the inside completely. Refrigerate.

Pick over and hull ¼ pound strawberries, 2 ounces raspberries, and 2 ounces wild blackberries, freshly gathered. Collect the berries in a bowl and sprinkle with confectioners' sugar. Moisten with 1 tablespoon maraschino or kirsch. Mix with a silver spoon, cover with a cloth, and macerate in the refrigerator for 15 minutes. Pour into a fine sieve placed above a large bowl and rub all the fruit through the sieve.

Mix this fruit-flavored *coulis* with:

2 envelopes gelatin softened in cold water, then dissolved in 3 tablespoons hot light sugar syrup, and at the moment when the gelatin is setting, add 1 cup whipped *crème fraîche,* sugared like *crème* Chantilly.

Pour this fruit cream into the mold coated with the custard cream and refrigerate for at least 3 hours.

To serve place the *génoise* cake on a round platter large enough to accommodate the garnish; dip the Bavarian mold into hot water, wipe, and turn over on the *génoise* cake. At the base of the Bavarian cream place a row of crystallized violets;

and around the edge of the *génoise* cake place a row of blackberries rolled in sugar.

Serve with a bowl of red currant jelly partially melted, and a plate of small sand cakes (page 406).

Pudding glacé du prélat

ICED PUDDING (For 6 people)

2 cups boiled milk with a split vanilla bean steeped in it, covered, after milk has boiled
5 egg yolks
1¹/₃ cups sugar
3 envelopes gelatin
1³/₄ ounces candied fruits
¹/₄ pound ladyfingers (page 403)
¹/₄ pound Malaga grapes
Macaroons
Rind of ¹/₄ lemon
Raspberry sauce

Method. While the vanilla bean is steeping in the hot milk (for 15 minutes), combine the egg yolks and the sugar in a bowl and beat the mixture with a wooden spoon until it is white and creamy; beat in the hot milk. Return to the saucepan, and heat slowly, stirring, to the boiling point; do not let boil. The mixture will thicken, becoming smooth, and coat the wooden spoon. Add the gelatin, softened in cold water; as soon as it has dissolved, strain the cream through a very fine sieve and set aside in a bowl.

Choose a 1¹/₂-quart charlotte mold or a mold with a hollow tube in the center. Oil the inside with almond oil or very pure olive oil that is absolutely tasteless.

Arrange the preserved fruit, quartered or diced, on the bottom of the mold in an attractive pattern; on top arrange the ladyfingers, each cut into 6 pieces; then, over the whole, sprinkle the grapes dipped in lukewarm water, seeded, and dried; then macaroons, crumbled into small pieces; on top of them, a pinch of chopped lemon rind. Repeat these layers until all the ingredients are used, pouring in the hot custard, in small quantities, in order to soak the pieces of cake and the pieces of macaroon, which, as they slowly absorb the custard, will settle in the mold and not rise to the top. It is important that the custard, the cake, and the fruit should be equally distributed in the mold all the way up.

Let the mold cool, then refrigerate or place it in crushed ice for 7 hours.

Unmolding the pudding is quite easy: slide the blade of a knife all around the edges of the mold or dip the mold into a bowl of hot water. Turn the mold over onto a large platter and cover the pudding completely with some of the following raspberry sauce.

Raspberry Sauce

¹/₂ pound very ripe raspberries
6 tablespoons sugar
1 teaspoon lemon juice
1 tablespoon kirsch
¹/₂ cup thick *crème fraîche* or heavy cream, whipped

Rub very ripe raspberries through a fine sieve, removing the stems; put the juice and the pulp in a glazed bowl; avoid letting them touch metal or tin, which would darken the juice.

In a saucepan combine 6 tablespoons sugar, 3 tablespoons water, and 1 teaspoon lemon juice and bring to a boil; skim and continue cooking until a drop of the syrup put on a plate will harden without running, keeping its round shape. Then pour the raspberry pulp into the syrup, mix with a silver spoon, and remove from the heat immediately without boiling the raspberries, which would lose their flavor.

Pour into a glazed bowl, cool, then refrigerate.

When the sauce is quite cold, add kirsch and *crème fraîche.*

421

Serve the extra raspberry sauce in a glass bowl; it should be a strong, beautiful red.

This recipe for iced pudding finishes the series of Bavarian creams, to which it really belongs rather than to the true puddings.

CHARLOTTES

Charlotte reine du Canada
CHARLOTTE QUEEN OF CANADA

2 pounds very fragrant apples
3 tablespoons sugar
4½ tablespoons butter, plus melted butter
1 vanilla bean
Zest of ½ lemon
2 tablespoons dry white wine
1 loaf white bread, crust removed
4 tablespoons apricot jam, rubbed through a sieve

Method. Peel the apples, quarter, core, and place in a saucepan; sprinkle the sugar and butter, cut into pieces, on top; bury the vanilla bean, quartered, and the lemon zest among the apples, and add the white wine. Cook slowly, stirring often, on a high flame to produce a thick applesauce; remove from the heat, mix in the strained apricot jam, and cool.

Thickly butter the bottom and sides of a charlotte mold. Cut part of the bread into slices ¼ inch thick, and from these slices cut a dozen triangles so that they will completely cover the bottom of the mold. Dip one side of each triangle into melted butter and place the triangles to form a rosette in the bottom of the mold, putting the buttered side down against the bottom of the mold.

Then cut most of the remaining bread into slices ⅜ inch thick and cut the slices into rectangles 1½ inches wide and at least ¾ inch longer than the height of the mold, unless the mold is very deep—in that case, cut them to fit.

Proceed as for the bottom of the mold; dip each rectangle of bread into melted butter and apply them, overlapping, to the sides of the mold.

Fill the mold with the applesauce, removing the vanilla bean and the lemon zest, and cover the top with a round slice of bread about ¼ inch thick dipped into melted butter, placing the buttered side of the bread toward the applesauce. This round covering of bread can be made in two pieces.

Place the charlotte in a 425° oven to brown the bread immediately and keep it from getting soggy. Cook for 40 minutes.

Let stand at least 15 minutes before unmolding; then serve immediately.

Charlotte de la Saint-Jean

¼ pound strawberries mixed with 1 tablespoon raspberries
2 tablespoons sugar
2 tablespoons kirsch
1 cup milk
⅔ cup sugar
4 egg yolks
½ vanilla bean
1 envelope gelatin
½ pound ladyfingers (page 403)

Method. Remove the stems from the berries and place them in a bowl with the sugar and the kirsch; mix carefully, and let stand for 45 minutes.

With the milk, sugar, egg yolks, and vanilla bean, prepare a custard cream (page 411).

As soon as the custard coats a wooden spoon, strain through a fine sieve into a glazed bowl, add the gelatin softened in cold water, and stir until completely cool.

While the cream cools, trim the ladyfingers so that the sides and the ends are cut neatly; cover the bottom of a char-

1 cup *crème fraîche* or
  heavy cream, whipped
Large strawberries and
  raspberries all the same
  size, for garnish
Candied angelica

lotte mold with a round piece of buttered paper, and on it place ladyfingers, cut into triangles, to form a rosette. Line the sides of the mold with the ladyfingers, placed side by side, very close together. The curved side of the biscuits should be placed against the mold, so it will show when unmolded.

When the custard is cold and starts to stiffen because of the gelatin, fold in the whipped *crème fraîche,* lightly sweetened, then the fruit.

Pour the custard into the mold; sprinkle the trimmings from the ladyfingers on top, and refrigerate for at least 4 hours.

To serve unmold the charlotte at the last moment onto a round platter covered with a fine linen doily; remove the paper and around the base of the charlotte place strawberries and raspberries, like a ring of large rubies. In the center of the charlotte, stick three diamond-shaped leaves cut from a piece of candied angelica.

Charlotte de la Saint-Martin

1²/₃ cups sugar
3 eggs
1 cup sifted flour
3¹/₂ tablespoons unsalted
  butter, melted
1 teaspoon vanilla sugar
3 macaroons, crushed
10 ounces *marrons glacés*
  pieces
2 tablespoons unsalted
  butter
2 cups thick *crème fraîche*
  or heavy cream, whipped
  and sugared like *crème*
  Chantilly (page 411)
Vanilla
Large *marrons glacés*

Method. Prepare a madeleine dough (for method see page 401) with ²/₃ cup sugar, 3 eggs, 1 cup sifted flour, 3¹/₂ tablespoons melted butter, and 1 teaspoon vanilla sugar. Add 3 crushed macaroons at the same time as the flour. Bake this cake in a square 8- or 9-inch *génoise* mold, buttered and floured. Let stand at least 2 days.

With 1 cup sugar and 1 cup water, make a syrup and boil for 2 minutes.

With pieces of *marrons glacés* and one-third of the syrup, make a purée, first softening the chestnuts, then mashing them with 2 tablespoons butter.

Molding. Place a round piece of white paper in the bottom of a 1-quart charlotte mold.

Cut the cake into rectangles the height of the mold and 1¹/₄ inches wide by ¹/₄ inch thick.

Line the sides of the mold, overlapping the pieces. The mold should be completely lined with the cake.

Whip 2 cups thick *crème fraîche;* add sugar as for *crème* Chantilly, and flavor with vanilla.

When the cream is stiff and has doubled its volume, put one-third into the refrigerator.

Beat the chestnut purée with a wooden spatula and add the remaining syrup to thin it. When the purée is smooth, add the remaining two-thirds of the whipped cream. This mixture should be folded in carefully, always lifting the purée.

Pour the purée into the mold, sprinkle 1 tablespoon cake crumbs on top, and refrigerate for at least 3 hours.

To serve, place a fine linen doily on a round platter and unmold the dessert a few minutes before serving.

Remove the round piece of paper; and in its place pipe a decoration with the refrigerated whipped cream, using a pastry bag with a fluted tube.

At the edge of the charlotte, make a circle of large *marrons glacés,* set in small fluted paper cups.

Note: This very rich dessert sets because of the butter mixed with the chestnut purée.

20 ladyfingers (page 403)
½ cup sugar
4 egg yolks
1 cup milk or ½ cup milk
  and ½ cup *crème frâiche*
  or heavy cream
1 vanilla bean
2 teaspoons gelatin
1½ cups whipped cream
2 tablespoons sugar
½ teaspoon vanilla sugar

Charlotte à la russe

Method. The outside of this dessert is the same as for the charlotte de la Saint-Jean (pages 422–3).

A 1½-quart charlotte mold will require about 20 ladyfingers.

Before placing the ladyfingers, it is a good idea to line the sides and the bottom of the mold with white paper, a round piece at the bottom and a strip for the sides.

The ladyfingers that line the sides should be ½ to ¾ inch higher than the mold. They should all be cut the same length so that the charlotte balances when unmolded.

Fill the inside of the mold with the following cream:

Prepare a custard cream (for method see page 411) with ½ cup sugar, 4 egg yolks, 1 cup milk, or ½ cup milk and ½ cup *crème fraîche,* and a vanilla bean.

When the custard coats a wooden spoon, remove immediately from the heat and add 2 teaspoons gelatin, softened in cold water; stir until dissolved.

Strain the mixture through a fine sieve into a glazed bowl as soon as the gelatin is completely mixed.

Let the custard cool on ice or refrigerate, stirring often. As soon as it starts to set, carefully add 1½ cups whipped cream flavored with 2 tablespoons sugar and ½ teaspoon vanilla sugar.

Pour the mixture into the lined mold, filling it to the top. Smooth the surface with a knife blade and sprinkle with a pinch of cake crumbs; refrigerate for at least 2 hours.

To serve unmold on a round platter covered with a fine linen doily.

Note: The above custard can be replaced by a Saint-Honoré cream (pages 412–13).

Charlotte Antonin Carême

Follow the recipe for the charlotte *à la russe* (above), and add to the custard ½ cup raspberry purée before adding the whipped cream.

Select large raspberries all the same size; macerate in kirsch, drain on a plate, and one by one sprinkle heavily with superfine sugar, which will give the fruit a crystallized coating. Unmold the charlotte on a round silver platter and surround the base with a row of the raspberries.

Charlotte Chantilly

This recipe has the advantage of being prepared quickly. Line the charlotte mold the same way as for the charlotte *à la russe* (above). This part can be done in advance.

A few minutes before serving the dessert, in a glazed bowl set in a bowl of ice, whip 2½ cups thick *crème fraîche* or heavy cream, adding ⅔ cup superfine sugar and 1 teaspoon vanilla sugar.

Fill the mold to the brim and sprinkle a large pinch of cake crumbs on top; unmold the dessert on a round platter lined with a lace doily. Serve immediately.

PUDDINGS

Pudding soufflé Victoire

14 tablespoons unsalted butter
10 egg yolks
1 cup sugar
3 tablespoons peach purée
3 tablespoons raspberry purée
6 egg whites, beaten stiff
Champagne biscuits
Banyuls or Frontignan wine
Raspberries
Red currant jelly
1 tablespoon champagne brandy

Method. Soften the butter to a paste, then add the egg yolks one by one, beating the mixture until each is absorbed; then add the sugar; continue working with a wooden spatula until the cream is frothy and white.

At this point add very fine peach purée and raspberry purée; finish by adding the egg whites. For this last step fold the egg whites into the batter, lifting with the spatula each time. The difficulty, easily eliminated with a little experience, is to get a well-blended mixture without allowing the egg whites to fall.

Thickly butter a mold with a hollow tube in the center, and fill it with the batter, in layers. In between each two layers, sprinkle some pieces of champagne biscuits (which may be bought in tins) dipped into a few tablespoons of very good-quality Banyuls or Frontignan dessert wine.

Place the mold in a *bain-marie* and poach in a 325° oven for 25 to 30 minutes. When the pudding is done, it is slightly resistant to a light pressure with the back of a spoon or any other utensil.

Unmold on a round platter, garnish the center of the pudding with raspberries coated with partially melted red currant jelly flavored with 1 tablespoon Banyuls or Frontignan wine mixed with 1 tablespoon fine champagne brandy.

Pudding de l'Aiglon

10½ tablespoons unsalted butter
¾ cup sugar
1 teaspoon vanilla sugar
1½ cups sifted flour
2 cups boiled milk with a split vanilla bean steeped in it and cooled
Pinch salt
9 eggs, separated

Method. In a heavy, slightly heated saucepan, soften the butter; with a wooden spoon, work in the sugar and vanilla sugar; then add the sifted flour. Moisten this dough with the vanilla milk. Add a pinch of salt, heat slowly, stirring constantly with a wooden spatula. The dough should be very smooth. Keep on the flame until the dough dries up and detaches itself from the pan, as for cream-puff pastry.

Remove the saucepan from the heat, let cool; then beat in the egg yolks one by one. Then following the recipe for a soufflé omelet (page 443), add the egg whites, beaten stiff.

Pour the mixture into a well-buttered soufflé dish or a charlotte mold and poach in a *bain-marie* in a 325° oven for 30 to 35 minutes.

Check whether the pudding is done by pressing the top lightly.

During the baking be careful not to subject the pudding to high heat in the beginning: a crust would form on top that would prevent the heat from penetrating inside the pudding. Protect the top from the heat, if necessary, with a piece of buttered paper.

Unmold on a warm round platter; then coat the pudding with a hot chocolate cream (page 417) mixed with the same amount of *crème* Chantilly or with the sauce in the recipe below.

Serve on the side the remaining chocolate cream in a silver sauceboat, and a plate of some fine cats' tongues (pages 406–7).

Chocolate Sauce for Dessert

**¹/₂ pound milk chocolate
¹/₂ cup thick whipped cream
Vanilla, vanilla sugar, or a vanilla bean**

Break the milk chocolate into small pieces; melt with 2 to 3 tablespoons water. Make an absolutely smooth thin paste, then add 1 cup water.

Cook slowly for 15 minutes to produce a syrup with the consistency of a custard cream; just before serving, add the whipped cream. Flavor with vanilla or vanilla sugar, or by cooking a vanilla bean with the chocolate.

Pudding Henry Clos-Jouve

(For 8 people)

**2³/₄ ounces sweet almonds and 1 bitter almond, freshly skinned
1 cup *fleurette* (fresh light cream) or milk
Zest of 1 lemon
5¹/₂ tablespoons tapioca
Pinch salt
6 eggs, separated
3¹/₂ tablespoons fine unsalted butter
¹/₂ cup sugar
Caramel (pages 414–15)
Sabayon sauce
Powdered caramelized almonds (page 454)
Macaroons
Red sugared almonds**

Method.   Make almond milk by soaking the almonds in water so they become very white. Then drain, dry, and crush in a mortar, moistening from time to time with a few drops of water so that they do not become too oily. To this paste add the *fleurette* or milk. Collect the thinned paste in a cheesecloth and squeeze all the liquid into a saucepan. Heat the almond milk, and steep the zest of 1 lemon in it for 5 minutes. Remove the zest, boil the milk, and in a stream add the tapioca, stirring with a wooden spoon. Add the salt. After boiling for 3 minutes remove from the heat. The mixture should then be a thick paste; pour it into a large bowl.

Immediately add the 6 egg yolks, one by one, then the butter and the sugar, beating the dough vigorously with a wooden spoon. The dough should soften, becoming lighter and smooth like baba dough.

Just before cooking the dessert, beat the 6 egg whites until stiff and fold them into the dough, following the classic recipe for soufflé omelet (page 443).

Immediately pour the batter into a charlotte mold lined with very pale caramel. The mold should be half filled with batter.

Place the mold in a deep *bain-marie* so that the water reaches three-quarters of the way up the mold. Poach in a 325° oven for 45 minutes. The pudding should not be subjected to very high heat; protect the top of the dessert with paper while baking.

To serve unmold on a hot round platter.

Pour all around a few tablespoons of *sabayon* sauce (page 416), very creamy and made with half almond milk, half champagne, and 1 tablespoon caramelized powdered almonds or crushed macaroons. Serve the remaining *sabayon* in a crystal bowl; and serve with it a plate of soft macaroons glazed with vanilla icing.

Just before serving, sprinkle a good pinch of red sugared almonds, coarsely crushed, on the pudding; and on top of the bowl of *sabayon,* sprinkle 2 additional tablespoonfuls. Just before serving the first guest, mix the sugared almonds with the pudding before the sugar has time to melt. It is delightful to crunch the pleasantly flavored sugar while eating the pudding.

Pudding mousseline de la vieille Catherine

(For 8 people)

1 ounce almonds, plus 1 bitter almond
1½ cups boiled milk with a split vanilla bean steeped in it, covered, for 20 minutes after milk has boiled
¼ pound butter
½ cup sugar
⅝ cup cornstarch
6 egg yolks
***Sabayon* sauce (page 416) or cream (recipe below)**

Method. Skin the almonds by plunging them into boiling water; let stand in the water for 5 to 6 minutes, drain, spread on a cloth, and taking them one by one between your thumb and forefinger, squeeze each almond, which will be forced out of its skin. Then wash the almonds in cold water, drain, and dry in a dishcloth. Sort out the larger ones, and cut them into thin slices lengthwise. Spread the almond slices in a pie tin.

Chop the remaining almonds very fine and spread them also in a pie tin. Place both almond pans in a hot oven, leaving the door ajar. Watch the almonds closely: they will first dry, then toast. Stir often and remove from the oven as soon as the nuts are uniformly light brown. Set aside.

Meanwhile, soften the butter, kneading it in a dishcloth. Use 1 tablespoon to butter the mold, and place the remaining butter, exactly 7 tablespoons, in a 3-quart saucepan. In a warm place work the butter to a paste with a wooden spoon. Add the sugar; beat the paste again until it becomes white and creamy, add the cornstarch, then dilute the paste, little by little, with the vanilla milk.

Put on the stove; heat slowly, stirring continuously; it will thicken little by little up to the boiling point; remove from the fire and beat in, one by one, 6 egg yolks. Then add the toasted chopped almonds. Spoon into the mold, filling it two-thirds full. Shake the pudding to level the top.

Place the mold in a deep *bain-marie,* cover the mold with a lid, and bake in a 425° oven for 40 minutes. Remove the lid toward the end of the cooking time.

Remove from the oven; let stand for 5 minutes in the *bain-marie,* then unmold onto a warm round platter, wiping the mold before this last step. Coat the pudding with the following cream or with a *sabayon* and sprinkle with sliced toasted almonds.

Cream

1½ cup milk boiled with a vanilla bean
⅓ cup sugar
3 egg yolks
1 tablespoon cornstarch
1 teaspoon kirsch or rum

Boil the milk flavored with vanilla; when cool, pour in slowly, stirring, a mixture of the sugar, 3 egg yolks, and 1 tablespoon cornstarch. Heat slowly, stirring constantly, and as soon as the custard starts to boil, remove from the heat immediately.

Just before using the cream, flavor with 1 teaspoon kirsch or rum.

Pudding Gaston Lenôtre

(For 8 people)

2 cups milk
Zest of 1/2 lemon
3/4 cup cornstarch
1/4 cup sugar
Pinch salt
1 1/2 tablespoons unsalted
  butter
3 eggs
3 tablespoons Malaga
  raisins
3 tablespoons currants
1 tablespoon rum
Sauce
1 teaspoon cornstarch
1/2 cup water
3 tablespoons sugar
6 tablespoons red currant
  jelly

Method. Boil the milk, steeping the lemon peel in it and being careful the bitter white pith is removed.

When the milk is cooled, remove the lemon peel and mix the liquid with the cornstarch, the sugar, and the salt. Add the butter, cut into pieces, and heat to the boiling point, stirring constantly with a wooden spatula.

The mixture will thicken until it forms a dough similar to cream-puff pastry. Continue cooking until the dough is dry enough to detach itself easily from the sides of the saucepan and the spoon.

Remove from the heat, and after waiting a couple of minutes for the dough to cool slightly, add the eggs, one by one, beating the dough vigorously after each addition to make it very smooth and light.

Then add the raisins, washed in tepid water, drained carefully, and dried; then the rum.

Beat the dough for another few minutes, as for baba dough, to aerate it completely. Thickly butter a charlotte mold; dust with flour, and shake out the excess. Pour in the batter, filling the mold two-thirds of its capacity; shake the mold to settle the dough; place in a deep *bain-marie* in a 325° oven, avoiding any sudden rise in heat. Cook for about 1 hour.

To serve unmold the pudding on a hot round platter and pass the following sauce, prepared 8 to 10 minutes before serving:

In a flameproof porcelain or enamel pan, mix 1 teaspoon cornstarch in 1/2 cup water; add 3 tablespoons sugar and 6 tablespoons red currant jelly.

Heat slowly, without boiling, to produce a mixture with the consistency of syrup; remove from the heat, add rum, and serve in a sauceboat.

Pudding Ile-de-France

3/4 cup wheat semolina
1 cup milk
1 cup *fleurette* (fresh light
  cream)
1/4 cup sugar
Pinch salt
8 tablespoons unsalted
  butter
4 egg yolks
1 tablespoon chopped
  pistachios
3 egg whites, beaten stiff
Macédoine of fruit
Apricot jam flavored with
  maraschino

Method. Pour the semolina in a stream into a boiling liquid made with milk, *fleurette* (fresh light cream), sugar, and salt. Heat, stirring with a wooden spoon until the mixture reaches the boiling point; add 1 tablespoon butter, cover with a lid, then cook in a 300° oven for about 30 minutes.

When cooked, dump the semolina into a bowl, without scraping the saucepan. Thicken with 4 egg yolks, adding them one by one, and 7 tablespoons butter, cut into small pieces. Work the mixture with a spatula to make it smooth; add chopped pistachios, and fold in 3 egg whites, beaten stiff.

Butter a mold with a hollow tube in the center, fill two-thirds full with the batter, and bake in a *bain-marie* in a 325° oven for 20 minutes.

Unmold when ready to serve on a warm round platter, and place in the center of the pudding a macédoine of fruit cooked in syrup and mixed with a few tablespoons of apricot jam flavored with maraschino.

Serve with a sauceboat of *sabayon* sauce (page 416) made with 1 part apricot jam flavored with maraschino to 4 parts *sabayon*.

Pudding au citron ou à l'orange
LEMON OR ORANGE PUDDING

1/2 pound unsalted butter
3/4 cup sugar
1 1/2 cups sifted flour
2 cups boiled milk, lukewarm
2 cubes sugar
1 orange or lemon
8 egg yolks
6 egg whites
***Sabayon* sauce (page 416)**

Method. In a saucepan, near the heat, soften the butter, working it with a wooden spoon; beat in the sugar and the flour. Dilute with the milk. Bring the mixture to a boil, stirring, then dry the dough as for cream-puff pastry.

Remove from the heat, and immediately add 2 cubes sugar that have been rubbed on the rind of a lemon or an orange, to soak the sugar with the flavor of the fruit; beat in the yolks, one by one, then fold in the whites, beaten very firm.

Pour the batter into a charlotte or a savarin mold, thickly buttered, and bake in a *bain-marie* in a 325° oven for 30 to 35 minutes.

Unmold onto a warm round platter; serve with a *sabayon* sauce flavored with lemon or orange and a plate of almond tiles (page 406).

Pudding de Noël à la française
FRENCH CHRISTMAS PUDDING

1 pound *marrons glacés* pieces, crushed fine and flavored with vanilla
7 tablespoons unsalted butter
Few tablespoons *crème fraîche* or heavy cream
8 egg yolks
6 egg whites, beaten very stiff
Chocolate cream sauce (page 417)
Chocolate macaroons with apricot jam

Method. Crush the *marrons glacés* fine, flavor with vanilla, and work in the butter. Dilute this paste with a few tablespoons *crème fraîche,* until it is like cream-puff pastry.

Pour this purée into a sieve placed on top of a bowl and rub the chestnuts through with a pestle. Beat with a wooden spatula, add 8 egg yolks, and fold in 6 egg whites, beaten very stiff.

Fill a well-buttered charlotte mold two-thirds, and bake in a *bain-marie* in a 325° oven for 30 minutes.

Unmold to serve, and coat the pudding with a chocolate cream sauce.

Serve with a sauceboat of chocolate sauce and a plate of soft chocolate macaroons sandwiched together with a little thickened apricot jam.

Pudding au porto
PUDDING WITH PORT WINE

Follow the recipe for the pudding Ile-de-France (page 428); before folding in the stiffly beaten egg whites, add 1 tablespoon port. Fill a buttered savarin mold one-third; sprinkle small pieces of cake soaked in port over the batter, cover with an equal quantity of batter, and bake in a *bain-marie* in a 325° oven for 20 minutes.

Just before serving, unmold the pudding and coat with a

sabayon sauce (page 416) flavored with port wine and with cubes of sugar rubbed on an orange skin; add one-fourth of its volume of *crème* Chantilly (page 411). Serve with the pudding the remaining *sabayon* sauce and a plate of currant cookies (page 407).

Note: The port can be replaced with a French wine: Frontignan, Banyuls, Château-Yquem, etc.

Pudding à la crème
CREAM PUDDING

1½ tablespoons sultanas and 1½ tablespoons currants, washed in lukewarm water
3 tablespoons candied fruit cut into small dice
½ cup kirsch, rum, or Grand Marnier
Angelica and candied cherries
6 ladyfingers (page 403), cut in half lengthwise, then in half horizontally, and soaked in the same liqueur
Apricot jam
2 cups *crème renversée* (page 414)
Sabayon sauce (page 416) or custard cream (page 411)

Method. Macerate the sultanas and currants and the candied fruit in the kirsch, rum, or Grand Marnier. Carefully butter a savarin mold and decorate the inside with angelica and candied cherries. Spread the ladyfingers on top, then sprinkle on some raisins and fruit macerated and well drained. Place teaspoons of apricot jam here and there, and continue, alternating the ladyfingers and the fruit.

Pour in the prepared *crème renversée,* a little at a time, so that the ladyfingers will soak it up and not dislodge the garnish.

When the mold is full, bake in a *bain-marie* in a 325° oven for about 40 minutes, guarding against boiling as for the *crème renversée.*

Let stand for 10 minutes before unmolding, and serve hot with a *sabayon* sauce flavored with vanilla or port or with a custard cream.

Pudding à l'allemande
GERMAN PUDDING

6 ounces rye bread, crusts removed
2 cups Moselle or Rhine wine or beer
⁵⁄₈ cup brown sugar
2 eggs and 3 egg yolks
Large pinch cinnamon
7 tablespoons melted unsalted butter
3 egg whites, beaten stiff
Bread crumbs
Apricot syrup (page 468)

Method. Soak the bread in the wine or beer with the sugar, then rub through a sieve. Collect the mixture in a bowl, and slowly add the whole eggs, the yolks, the cinnamon, the butter, and then fold in the beaten egg whites.

Butter a kugelhopf mold, line with fine bread crumbs, fill with the mixture, and bake in a *bain-marie* in a 325° oven for 35 minutes.

Unmold on a hot round platter and serve with apricot syrup.

Note: I have already mentioned a French pudding in the section on Bavarian creams, under the name iced pudding (page 421).

Pudding à l'anglaise
ENGLISH PLUM PUDDING
Traditional

½ cup candied orange peel, diced
½ cup candied lemon peel, diced
½ cup candied citron, diced

Method. Macerate all the fruits in the rum for 2 hours.

Combine all the ingredients in a bowl and mix well.

Pack this mixture into special earthenware pudding bowls. Or grease a dishcloth soaked in cold water, dust it with flour,

430

2 tablespoons candied ginger, diced
1 cup peeled, chopped apples
1 pound Malaga raisins, sultanas, and currants
¹/₂ cup rum, plus extra rum
¹/₂ pound white bread, crusts removed
1¹/₄ cups sifted flour
1 pound chopped beef suet
1³/₄ cups brown sugar
¹/₂ cup chopped blanched almonds
Juice of ¹/₄ lemon
Juice of ¹/₄ orange
¹/₂ teaspoon chopped lemon and orange peel
Strong pinch mixed spices (page x) with extra cinnamon and nutmeg
2 eggs
¹/₂ cup Madeira
¹/₂ cup cognac
1¹/₂ teaspoons salt
1 cup beer
Custard cream (page 411), flavored with rum (optional)

and wrap it around a ball of the mixture; close the dishcloth, gather the ends, and tie securely, bringing the string around the ball, which will be tightly held by it.

Whether the mixture is tied in a ball, put into a pan, or cooked in the special bowls, handle in the same way but cover the mixture with a white paper before wrapping in the cloth.

Place the bowl or ball in boiling water and simmer for 3 hours.

Take out the pudding and let it drain and cool; remove from the molds or dishcloth, cut into ¹/₄-inch slices, and place them on a very hot platter; set in a hot oven for a few minutes, sprinkle with sugar, and pour on some heated rum; ignite the rum at the table to flame it, or serve with a hot custard cream flavored with rum.

Serve on very hot plates.

Note: English plum pudding is prepared many days in advance; it is also served whole; in that case, it is reheated in its cooking mold in simmering water for 20 minutes.

RICE DESSERTS

In desserts rice can be the main ingredient or one of the lesser ingredients. In either case it is cooked in the same way.

Use long grain rice such as Carolina or Patna rice; wash it in several changes of cold water until it drains clear; blanch it by placing it in boiling water, then drain and wash it again in lukewarm water, and drain completely; then cook it.

First Method

2 cups milk
1 vanilla bean
Zest of orange or lemon
Pinch salt
⁵/₈ cup rice
3 egg yolks
1 tablespoon cream or boiled milk
1¹/₂ tablespoons unsalted butter
¹/₃ cup sugar

Boil the milk with the vanilla bean, the orange or lemon zest, and salt; boil for 10 minutes, remove the bean and zest, add the rice in a stream, and stir with a wooden spoon; when the water boils again, cover. Bake in a 325° oven for 35 minutes. Do not stir the rice. Remove from the oven, and let cool slightly; then add the yolks, diluted with the cream or boiled milk, and mix in the butter, cut into small pieces. Mix the yolks and butter into the rice carefully with a fork, in order not to break the grains of rice.

The sugar can be sprinkled on the rice when it is removed from the oven before adding the eggs; but if placed in the milk in the beginning, it will not permit the rice to poach perfectly.

Second Method

Only the manner of cooking is different from the first method. The rice is first blanched, washed, and drained, as explained above. Pour in ¹/₂ cup boiling milk with 1 tablespoon butter and a pinch of salt. Stir and continue boiling slowly, covered. When all the milk is absorbed and the rice puffs out with liquid, add a second ¹/₂ cup boiling milk, and continue in the same way until all the milk is used. Stir the mixture each time, carefully, with a fork.

After the rice is cooked, add the sugar and thicken with the egg yolks as explained in the first method.

This second method of cooking rice will give a creamier dessert and is preferable to the first method. It is inspired by the common Italian practice in making desserts in the family kitchen.

Gâteau de riz

RICE CAKE

Prepare dessert rice, cooked and thickened as described above; add ¼ cup mixed sultanas and currants, cleaned by rubbing them in a cloth dusted with flour and then in a coarse sieve to rub off the stems and shake away debris.

Beat 3 egg whites very stiff, then fold in the rice. The flavoring (orange, lemon, or kirsch, rum, etc.) is added at the same time as the sultanas and currants.

Pour the rice into a 1-quart charlotte or *génoise* mold lined with a very thin layer of pie dough (page 386), or lined with caramel (pages 414–15), or simply buttered carefully.

Bake in a 325° oven for 45 minutes.

Protect the top of the cake from the heat either with the lid of the mold or with buttered paper. Test to see if the cake is done by inserting a needle, which should come out clean and very hot.

Remove from the oven and let stand for about 10 minutes before unmolding on a round plate.

Serve this dessert lukewarm rather than hot, with a syrup or a cream.

Gâteau de riz au caramel

RICE CAKE WITH CARAMEL

Follow the recipe above. Line the mold with caramel; flavor the rice with vanilla and lemon peel. Serve with a caramel syrup or with a custard flavored with caramel syrup.

Gâteau de riz au sabayon

RICE CAKE WITH SABAYON SAUCE

Follow the recipe above. Line the mold with fine pie dough (page 386); flavor the rice with kirsch. Serve with a *sabayon* sauce (page 416), made with kirsch and vanilla.

Gâteau de riz à la crème

RICE CAKE WITH CREAM

Follow the recipe above. Butter the mold; flavor the rice with maraschino and lemon peel or curaçao and orange peel;

432

make custard cream (page 411) with maraschino and add one-fourth its volume of whipped cream. When the dessert is unmolded coat it with this mixture and serve the remaining cream on the side.

Fritters, waffles, crêpes, omelets, and soufflés

FRITTERS

We must head this group of sweet desserts with a recipe for frying batter. The batter may be made at the last minute and used immediately, or it can be prepared in advance.

In the first case the batter must be lightly beaten, to prevent its becoming rubbery, which would keep it from penetrating and sticking to the ingredients that will be dipped into it. In the second case beating the dough will warm it and hasten the start of fermentation, which will make it lighter. Letting the dough stand breaks down the stiffness produced while beating it.

Frying batter

(For 1 quart)

2½ cups sifted flour
Pinch salt
2 eggs, separated
1 cup beer
1 cup water or milk
2 tablespoons melted
  butter or olive oil

Method. In a bowl combine the flour, salt, and egg yolks; dilute little by little with the beer and the water or milk, then the butter or oil.

Let the batter stand for at least 2 hours in a warm place to start the fermentation. Just before using, add 2 egg whites beaten stiff.

The frying batter should be like a light, slightly fluffy cream.

Note: This recipe can be used for frying all kinds of foods. The fermentation can be increased by adding a pinch of yeast or a spoonful of frying batter a few days old and well fermented.

Frying batter for fruit fritters

To the above ingredients add 1 teaspoon sugar and follow the same procedure.

Beignets de reinettes

APPLE FRITTERS

With the point of a knife or with a corer, remove the cores of large apples (1 per serving). The seeds and the casings that surround them should be carefully removed. Then peel the apples and cut them into slices $3/16$ inch thick.

Spread these slices on a large plate or on several plates; sprinkle each slice with sugar and baste generously with cognac, rum, or kirsch; macerate for 20 minutes covered with an upside-down plate or plates.

Eight minutes before the fritters are to be served, dip the apple slices one by one in the batter, then plunge each immediately into very hot oil.

The fritters should be seared immediately, so that they will fry and not boil, to keep the dough from soaking up oil, which would give a disagreeable taste and make them indigestible.

Fried quickly, the batter will be transformed into a crunchy protective coating of a golden brown.

Drain the fritters on a paper towel, wipe them carefully; sprinkle with confectioners' sugar and place them flat on a pastry sheet. Slide under the broiler for 1 minute to caramelize the surface lightly. Serve on a warm round platter.

Beignets d'ananas marquisette

PINEAPPLE FRITTERS MARQUISETTE

1 fresh pineapple
Rum
1 cup milk
4 heaping tablespoons
  sifted flour
2 heaping tablespoons
  sugar
1 egg and 2 egg yolks
1 vanilla bean steeped in
  milk
$1^{1}/_{2}$ tablespoons unsalted
  butter
1 tablespoon blanched,
  chopped pistachios
Confectioners' sugar
Light frying batter (page
  433)
Frying oil

Method. Peel a fresh pineapple, cut in half lengthwise and cut each half in $3/16$-inch slices. Remove the center core from each slice.

Place the pineapple slices on a plate, sprinkle with sugar, and baste with rum. Cover with an upside-down plate and macerate for 20 minutes.

Meanwhile, prepare $1^{1}/_{2}$ cups frangipane cream: mix 1 cup milk with 4 heaping tablespoons sifted flour, 2 heaping tablespoons sugar, 1 egg, 1 vanilla bean steeped in milk almost at the boiling point. Stir with a whisk without stopping until the custard starts to boil; remove from the heat, and finish by adding $1^{1}/_{2}$ tablespoons butter and 2 egg yolks. Stir the cream while it is cooling to prevent the formation of lumps; then add the pistachios.

Drain the slices of pineapple, dip them one by one into the lukewarm cream, being careful to coat each one well, and place them on a plate dusted with confectioners' sugar.

Let the slices stand until the cream solidifies.

When the cream is firm, follow the recipe for frying fritters, just 8 minutes before serving.

At that time, separate the slices of pineapple, being careful not to dislodge the cream; and dip them, one by one, in a light frying batter; then plunge them, one by one, into hot oil to sear them perfectly.

Drain the fritters and wipe dry; sprinkle with confectioners' sugar, place under the broiler to glaze them, and serve in a circle on a platter.

Beignets d'ananas

PINEAPPLE FRITTERS

Choose a large pineapple to make about 2 dozen fritters.

If the pineapple is fresh, peel, remove the hard core, and cut into 3/16-inch slices; spread the slices on a plate, sprinkle with sugar, and baste with kirsch; macerate, covered, for 20 minutes.

Then follow the recipe for apple fritters (page 434).

Beignets de poires

PEAR FRITTERS

With the harvest comes a succession of different pears, offering the possibility of a changing menu of fritters: fritters made with Williams pears (August), fritters made with Louise Bonne (September), fritters made with Doyenné (October), fritters made with Comice (October), fritters made with Beurré d'Aremberg (winter months).

Follow the recipe for the apple fritters exactly; however, to remove the seeds easily, peel the fruit and cut into thin slices, then remove the core from each slice with a cookie cutter. Sprinkle the slices with sugar and macerate in a liqueur: maraschino, Grand Marnier, etc.

Note: The pears must be very ripe.

Beignets de bananes

BANANA FRITTERS

Peel the bananas; cut each in half lengthwise and place on a plate; sprinkle with sugar, and baste with cognac or fine champagne brandy. Macerate for 20 minutes.

Then cook following the recipe for apple fritters (page 434), frying in very hot oil.

Glaze and serve them in the same way as the apple fritters.

Beignets soufflés

SOUFFLÉ FRITTERS

2 cups water
7 tablespoons unsalted butter
1/2 teaspoon salt
1 1/2 teaspoons sugar
3 cups sifted flour
6–7 eggs
Rum or other alcohol or liqueur
Frying oil
Confectioners' sugar

Method. The batter for soufflé fritters is an ordinary cream-puff pastry: 2 cups water, 7 tablespoons butter, 1/2 teaspoon salt, 1 1/2 teaspoons sugar.

In a saucepan combine all these ingredients; bring to a boil, and off the heat add 3 cups sifted flour. Mix over a high flame to dry the dough, stirring vigorously with a wooden spatula.

The dough is ready when it detaches itself from the side of the saucepan in one mass.

Remove from the heat, then add, one at a time, 6 to 7 eggs, depending on their size, beating the dough vigorously during this last step.

435

The batter should be smooth and medium thick; flavor with rum or any other alcohol or liqueur.

With a tablespoon and a knife drop the batter in pieces the size of a small walnut into hot deep oil.

This step is easy to do: Fill the tablespoon with batter, then with the blade of a knife, dipped each time into hot water, push the dough out by sliding the end of the knife along the bowl of the spoon. The dough will gather into a ball the size of a walnut and will fall from the damp blade into the oil.

Increase the heat of the oil slowly as the fritters start to cook and double their volume, at least; cook until golden brown and dry.

Drain on paper towels; sprinkle with confectioners' sugar, and place in bunches on a folded napkin.

Beignets soufflés à la créole
CREOLE SOUFFLÉ FRITTERS

Prepare the soufflé fritters (recipe above) and stuff each one, using a pastry bag with a plain 1/8-inch tube filled with whipped cream with chocolate added (kept on ice before using).

This step should be done just before serving; the very hot fritters are served stuffed with ice-cold cream.

Place the fritters in a circle with a mound of the same cream, decorated with a fluted tube, in the center.

WAFFLES
Gaufres de grand-mère Bocuse
GRANDMOTHER BOCUSE'S WAFFLES

5 cups flour
Pinch salt
Pinch yeast
3 teaspoons sugar
1 cup milk
3 cups cream
8 egg yolks
1 tablespoon rum
21 tablespoons melted
  unsalted butter
4 egg whites, beaten stiff

Method.   In a bowl, mix the flour with the salt, the yeast, and the sugar.

Moisten the mixture first with the milk, then the cream, the egg yolks, and the rum. After this has been done carefully, add the melted butter and fold in the egg whites, whipped very stiff.

Heat and butter a waffle iron; pour a quantity of batter on one side, covering all the squares.

Close the waffle iron and turn it over, so that the batter will sink into the pattern on the other half.

Cooking this way, you will produce a very crisp waffle.

The waffles can be eaten sprinkled with powdered sugar or filled with *crème* Chantilly (page 411) or any excellent homemade jam.

CRÊPES

Tradition calls for eating crêpes during Lent. But in reality, this delicious dessert occupies a permanent place in menus, since there are so many different kinds of crêpes, from the thick homemade crêpe that is served not only on holidays to the delicate lacy crêpe that is often served with a frozen dessert.

Whether the batter used for the crêpes is ordinary or very fine, the method for preparing them is always the same.

Method. In a bowl combine the flour, the sugar, and the salt. Add the eggs, one at a time, beating to produce a perfectly smooth, homogeneous batter. Continue by adding the milk, in small quantities, beating it into the mixture.

It is important to prepare this batter at least 2 hours before using it; keep it in a warm place to produce an almost imperceptible fermentation.

Finish the batter by adding a flavoring, just before using it.

Cook the crêpes in a very hot pan lightly brushed with clarified butter (page 75). The crêpes should be thin, light, and golden brown on both sides. Turning them over—flipping them—is also part of the French tradition; it requires more dexterity than explanation.

Sprinkle the crêpes with sugar as you make them, and place them on a napkin.

Here are some variations.

Crêpes ménagères

CRÊPES HOME STYLE

Method. Follow the recipe above for cooking and serving.

2¹/₂ cups sifted flour
Pinch salt
¹/₂ cup sugar
1¹/₂ cups boiled milk
3 eggs
Flavoring: orange-blossom water, rum, kirsch, or orgeat

Crêpes châtelaines à la crème de marrons

CRÊPES WITH CHESTNUT CREAM
Crêpe Batter

Mix together all the ingredients. Let the batter rest for a while if possible.

Cook following the basic recipe (above). As the crêpes are made, spread each one with the frangipane cream (recipe below).

Fold the crêpes in four with the cream inside and place them on a long platter, overlapping them; sprinkle with superfine sugar and place them for 1 minute in a 475° oven to melt the sugar and glaze the crêpes.

Frangipane Cream

Make a frangipane cream (for method see page 410), with sugar, flour, egg yolks, milk, and a vanilla bean. As soon as the cream boils, remove from the heat and add the butter and the *marrons glacés,* well crushed.

2¹/₂ cups sifted flour
10¹/₂ ounces sifted chestnut flour
Pinch salt
¹/₂ cup sugar
3¹/₂ cups boiled milk
6 eggs
Flavoring: orgeat and cognac

¹/₂ cup sugar
¹/₂ cup flour
6 egg yolks
2 cups milk
1 vanilla bean
3¹/₂ tablespoons unsalted butter
¹/₄ pound *marrons glacés*

2½ cups sifted flour
Pinch salt
½ cup sugar
4 tablespoons melted
  unsalted butter
2 tablespoons *crème
  fraîche* or heavy cream
6 eggs and 2 egg yolks
Light brown sugar
Flavoring: cognac (2
  tablespoons), few drops
  orange-blossom water

Crêpes à l'eau de fleur d'oranger

CRÊPES WITH ORANGE-BLOSSOM WATER

Method. Follow the basic crêpe recipe (pages 436–7). Do not make the crêpes too thin, and cook them in 2 large well-buttered frying pans, so they can be served to people without waiting.

Before turning them, prick each one with a fork; the moisture will evaporate immediately.

When the crêpe is cooked, slide onto a hot plate sprinkled with brown sugar; also sprinkle the crêpe with brown sugar and with a few drops of orange-blossom water; slide a second crêpe on top of the first one, sugar it, then sprinkle with the orange-blossom water and serve right away.

While the guests are enjoying these, make a new batch of crêpes.

2½ cups sifted flour
Pinch salt
½ cup sugar
1½ teaspoons yeast
½ cup boiled milk
6 eggs, separated
2 cups whipped cream

Crêpes légères

LIGHT CRÊPES

Method. Make a batter following the recipe for crêpes (pages 436–7), using 6 egg yolks. Let the batter rise for 2 hours in a warm place; then fold in 6 egg whites, whipped stiff, and 2 cups whipped cream.

Let stand for 10 minutes.

Spread 2 or 3 tablespoons batter in a well-buttered frying pan of the proper size, and cook as in the recipe for crêpes.

Sprinkle the crêpes with confectioners' sugar and place in a 450° oven for 1 minute to glaze.

2½ cups sifted flour
Pinch salt
5 tablespoons sugar
3 eggs and 3 egg yolks
2 cups boiled milk
1 cup *crème fraîche* or
  heavy cream
7 tablespoons unsalted
  butter
Flavoring: maraschino

Crêpes Vatel

Mix and cook following the recipe for crêpes on pages 436–7.

2½ cups sifted flour
4 eggs plus 2 egg yolks
Pinch salt
1 tablespoon granulated
  sugar
2 cups milk
½ pound unsalted butter,
  melted, plus extra butter

Crêpes flambées au Grand Marnier

CRÊPES FLAMED WITH GRAND MARNIER

Method. In a bowl, combine the flour, the eggs, the egg yolks, the salt, and the granulated sugar.

Pour in the milk slowly, stirring, in order to get a smooth batter without any lumps; finally add the melted butter and the Grand Marnier.

Heat the crêpe pan and pour in a full tablespoon of the batter. As soon as the crêpe detaches from the pan, shake it and flip it, and cook the second side.

¼ cup Grand Marnier
2 tablespoons con-
fectioners' sugar

Slide the crêpe onto a buttered ovenproof dish; sprinkle with confectioners' sugar, and brown the sugar under the broiler.

Serve the crêpes basted generously with Grand Marnier and flame in front of the guests.

Serve 3 or 4 crêpes per guest.

Note: Since this batter is made with butter, there is no need to grease the crêpe pan for each crêpe. The thinner the crêpes, the better they are.

PANCAKES

This dessert is made with a variety of crêpes filled with infinitely varied stuffings.

All the various crêpe batters, more or less fine, can be used to make pancakes. Here is one that is excellent:

2½ cups sifted flour
8 eggs, separated
2 cups milk
½ cup *crème fraîche* or
heavy cream
¼ cup sugar
Pinch salt
¼ pound unsalted butter,
melted
2 crushed bitter almonds
1 teaspoon vanilla sugar

Mix the sifted flour in a bowl with the yolks, adding them to the flour one at a time; stir in the milk, *crème fraîche,* sugar, salt, and melted butter.

Flavor with 2 crushed bitter almonds and 1 teaspoon vanilla sugar.

Let the batter stand for 2 hours; just before making the pancakes, fold in the egg whites, beaten very stiff.

Make the crêpes very thin, in special crêpe pans, thickly buttered. Be careful to spread the batter thinly and evenly in the pan.

When they are cooked, keep the crêpes warm, piling one on top of the other, while finishing them.

Pannequets soufflés

SOUFFLÉ PANCAKES

The crêpes are cooked very thin; in the center of each crêpe, place 1 tablespoon kirsch soufflé batter (pages 451–2); fold the crêpe to enclose the batter completely, giving the pancake a rectangular or semicircular shape, like an apple turnover.

Place the pancakes on a round ovenproof platter; sprinkle some confectioners' sugar on top and place in a 425° oven for 3 minutes, just to glaze the sugar and to make the soufflé batter puff.

Serve immediately, accompanied by a bowl of kirsch-flavored *sabayon* sauce (page 416).

Pannequets à l'impératrice

EMPRESS PANCAKES

Make the pancakes following one of the recipes for crêpes (pages 436–8). Fill each pancake with 1 tablespoon hot poached dessert rice (page 431), folded into 1 tablespoon whipped cream flavored with maraschino. Finish each with 1 tablespoon diced pears poached in syrup and macerated in maraschino.

Fold the crêpes like apple turnovers and place them on a round ovenproof platter in a circle, overlapping slightly; sprinkle with confectioners' sugar, then bake for 1 minute in a 450° oven, just long enough to glaze them.

Decorate the center with beautiful pear halves poached in syrup flavored with maraschino and well drained. Stand them upright leaning on each other, serving one for each guest.

Coat the pears with a few tablespoons of chocolate sauce to which the reduced poaching syrup has been added.

Serve the remaining chocolate sauce in a sauceboat on the side.

Pannequets aux confitures
PANCAKES WITH JAM

Any kind of jam can be used to stuff pancakes made from one of the recipes for crêpes (pages 436–8).

The jam must be quite thick, so that it does not liquefy into a syrup as soon as it comes in contact with heat. Coat the pancakes on one side with a layer of jam, then fold them as directed in the recipes above.

Place the folded pancakes in a circle on a plate, sprinkle with confectioners' sugar, and bake in a 450° oven just long enough to glaze them.

You can fill the center of the dish with a mound of fruit of the same variety as the jam, poached in a syrup, whole, cut in half, or diced.

If you do that, baste the fruit with a little sauce made with the fruit used, flavored with kirsch; serve the same sauce on the side.

Pannequets tonkinois
TONKIN PANCAKES

Make the pancakes by one of the recipes for crêpes (pages 436–8).

Prepare diced cooked pineapple in an apricot syrup thickened with apple jelly, reduced, and flavored with maraschino.

Fill the pancakes, fold them, and arrange in a circle on a plate; sprinkle with confectioners' sugar and glaze in the oven. In the center of the ring of shiny golden pancakes, place a pyramid of stewed pineapple in an apricot syrup, considerably reduced to coat the fruit and flavored at the last moment with maraschino.

Serve apricot sauce (page 417) on the side.

Pannequets à la crème frangipane
PANCAKES WITH FRANGIPANE CREAM

Make the pancakes by one of the recipes for crêpes (pages 436–8). Fill each pancake with 1 tablespoon frangipane cream (page 410), place the pancakes on a plate, sprinkle with confectioners' sugar, and glaze in a 425° oven.

Pannequets à la crème de marrons
PANCAKES WITH CHESTNUT PURÉE

Prepare a chestnut purée with pieces of candied chestnuts (page 413); make it light and smooth by adding whipped cream. Make the pancakes by one of the recipes for crêpes (pages 436–8). Fill them with this purée as explained.

Serve the same way. They will be enhanced if accompanied by a bowl of *sabayon* sauce (page 416) flavored with maraschino.

Pannequets aux fruits
PANCAKES WITH FRUIT

All kinds of fruit make an exquisite filling for pancakes. Make the pancakes by one of the recipes for crêpes (pages 436–8). Pears, apples, pineapples, bananas, or peaches should be poached in syrup, diced, drained, and coated with pastry cream (page 411) flavored with a few drops of *pastis.* Pit cherries, poach, and coat in the same way.

Strawberries and raspberries, picked small and coated in the same way, are also good choices.

The preceding recipes show what considerable resources dessert pancakes offer. There is vast scope for anyone with imagination.

DESSERT OMELETS

There are three different types of dessert omelets: sweet omelets, omelets with liqueurs, omelets with jams, as well as soufflé omelets.

Omelette au sucre
SWEET OMELET (For 2 people)

6 eggs, or 4 eggs plus 3 egg yolks
Pinch salt
1/2 teaspoon sugar
2 tablespoons *crème fraîche* or heavy cream, or 2 tablespoons boiled milk
Confectioners' sugar

Method. Whatever the name, the basic preparation is the same: 6 eggs, or 4 eggs plus 3 egg yolks, beaten moderately with a pinch salt, 1/2 teaspoon sugar, and 2 tablespoons whipped *crème fraîche*—if you wish to be economical, the *crème fraîche* can be replaced by 2 tablespoons boiled milk.

Make the omelet (following the recipe on pages 42–3), turn it out on a hot plate, and sprinkle it with confectioners' sugar.

Heat a stainless-steel twisted skewer until red hot and apply to the omelet, making a dark gold crisscross design by caramelizing the sugar.

Omelette aux liqueurs
OMELET WITH LIQUEUR

Make an omelet as you would a sweet omelet (page 441), being careful to turn it out onto a very hot plate. After sprinkling it with confectioners' sugar, pour on any chosen liqueur or spirits, previously heated.

Serve the omelet immediately; ignite the liqueur, and let flame on the omelet until it burns itself out.

The best liqueurs or spirits to use for an omelet are: rum, kirsch, fine champagne brandy or cognac, armagnac, calvados, mirabelle, quetsche, raspberry or blackberry brandy, Grand Marnier, Cointreau, anisette, Pernod, Izara, or chartreuse.

Omelette aux confitures diverses
OMELET WITH JAM

This type of omelet differs from the two sweet omelets above only in that the filling is added before rolling it. Before rolling it, in the center spread 3 tablespoons of the chosen jam or fruit marmalade, both quite thick.

Finish the omelet, turn it out on a plate, sprinkle with confectioners' sugar, and decorate with a red-hot skewer (see sweet omelet, page 441).

Omelette tahitienne
TAHITIAN OMELET

3 slices pineapple, fresh or canned
3 tablespoons apricot jam, melted
2 tablespoons maraschino
Sweet omelet (page 441) made with 6 eggs and 2 egg yolks
Confectioners' sugar

Method. Dice 3 slices fresh or canned pineapple, removing the core. Place in a skillet with 3 tablespoons melted apricot jam, bring to a boil, and stew slowly for 15 minutes. Off the heat flavor with 2 tablespoons maraschino. Prepare a sweet omelet with 6 eggs and 2 egg yolks, fill it with the diced pineapple; fold the omelet, sprinkle with confectioners' sugar, and glaze in a 425° oven or under the broiler just long enough so that the sugar melts and takes on a golden color.

Surround the omelet with some of the apricot syrup used to stew the pineapple.

Omelette aux griottes
OMELET WITH CHERRIES

Remove the stems from $1/2$ pound cherries and cook one-quarter for 15 minutes in a syrup made with $1/2$ cup water and 4 tablespoons sugar. Crush the remaining three-quarters of the cherries, with their pits, very fine and cook the *coulis* with equal its weight in sugar. When the *coulis* has the consistency of a marmalade, remove it from the heat, strain through a fine sieve and then through cheesecloth. Put into a bowl, flavor with 1 teaspoon kirsch, and add the stewed cherries, pitted.

Make a sweet omelet (page 441) and fill with this delicious purée.

Sprinkle the omelet with confectioners' sugar and flame with kirsch.

Omelette de la belle Aurore
BELLE AURORE OMELET

Prepare 4 tablespoons frangipane cream (page 410), replacing the macaroons with 1 heaping tablespoon caramelized almonds and pistachios (half of each) crushed to a very fine paste. Flavor with 1 teaspoon of any fruit-pit liqueur.

Lighten the mixture with 2 tablespoons whipped *crème fraîche* or heavy cream. Fold it into the frangipane cream carefully and fill a sweet omelet (page 441), made with extra cream to keep it moist.

Sprinkle lightly with sugar, and make a design with a red-hot skewer.

Omelette Côte-d'Ivoire
IVORY COAST OMELET

2 large bananas, sliced into ⅛-inch slices
Pinch sugar
Unsalted butter
2 tablespoons sweet almonds, freshly skinned
1 blanched bitter almond
1 heaping tablespoon sugar
2 tablespoons *crème fraîche* or heavy cream
Sweet omelet (page 441)

Method.   Sprinkle the bananas with a pinch of sugar. Melt a large piece of butter in a skillet; when it is very hot, add the sliced bananas and cook quickly.

Meanwhile, in a mortar pound the almonds, add the sugar and, gradually, the *crème fraîche*. Strain quickly through a fine sieve, or leave the almond cream as it is, and use to coat the warm sliced bananas.

Make a sweet omelet and fill with the bananas.

Sprinkle the omelet with sugar and glaze in a 425° oven, or under the broiler, turning it once.

Make a ¾-inch slash on top of the omelet, and through this opening pour 1 tablespoon almond cream; pour the remaining cream around the omelet.

Omelette soufflée

SOUFFLÉ OMELET

The method for making a soufflé omelet is always basically the same, and it can also be used for a long list of omelet surprises.

I recommend the recipe below for vanilla soufflé omelet; you can vary it to make all the omelet surprises.

Omelette soufflée à la vanille

VANILLA SOUFFLÉ OMELET (For 2 or 3 people)

Method.   In a bowl, combine ¾ cup sugar and 4 egg yolks. Beat this mixture with a wooden spatula for at least 15 to 20

443

³/₄ cup sugar
4 egg yolks
Cube sugar rubbed on an
    orange skin
1 teaspoon vanilla sugar
6 egg whites, whipped very
    stiff
Confectioners' sugar

minutes, which means until the mixture is thick and creamy, and is pale yellow.

Rub all the sides of a sugar cube on the skin of an orange. When the sugar is soaked with the rind, crush it and add to the mixture with 1 teaspoon vanilla sugar.

Then when the batter has reached the point described above, whip 6 egg whites until very stiff and fold them in carefully in the following way: First add one-fourth of the egg whites into the egg-sugar mixture; mix until smooth and light. Then fold in the remaining whites, lifting the batter with the spatula held in your right hand while your left hand rotates the bowl opposite to the direction in which you are turning the spatula. You must not allow the batter to fall; it must keep its lightness, which is its most important property.

Butter a long ovenproof platter generously, then sprinkle it with sugar. On the platter place the batter in a mound, smooth it with a pastry spatula or a knife; in the center make a hole on the top to permit the steam to escape, and decorate the omelet by making designs with the point of a knife or with some of the egg mixture piped through a pastry bag with a fluted tube.

Cooking.   Bake immediately in a 350° oven; look at it after about 20 minutes. You must be careful that it does not brown too rapidly or get too dark. The cooked omelet should be a pale *café au lait* color.

After baking for about 20 minutes, sprinkle the omelet with confectioners' sugar; the sugar will melt in a few seconds. Watch the dessert continuously. The sugar melts and caramelizes very quickly. A beautiful glaze will then cover the omelet. It must be served immediately; and the guests must wait for it. If the opposite is allowed to happen, it will be a great disappointment; the least wait is detrimental to this sweet, which will fall and become heavy and very unappetizing.

When such a dessert is part of your menu, you should time the length of the dinner so that you can fix exactly the time to start the soufflé omelet, taking into account the time to prepare (15 to 20 minutes), to decorate (5 minutes), and to cook (25 minutes).

Omelette soufflée au Grand Marnier

SOUFFLÉ OMELET WITH GRAND MARNIER (For 2 or 3 people)

1 cup sugar
4 egg yolks
1 cube sugar
1 orange peel
1 teaspoon vanilla sugar
1 tablespoon Grand
    Marnier
6 egg whites
Butter
Confectioners' sugar

Preparation.   In a bowl beat the sugar and the egg yolks with a wooden spatula for at least 15 to 20 minutes.

Rub all the surfaces of the sugar cube on the skin of an orange. When the sugar is soaked with the rind, crush it and add to the mixture with the vanilla sugar and the Grand Marnier. Mix well.

Next, whip the egg whites until stiff and fold in carefully in the following way: First add one-fourth of the egg whites and mix quickly, making the batter smooth and light; then fold in the remaining whites, lifting the batter with the spatula held in your right hand while your left hand rotates the bowl opposite to the direction in which you are turning the spatula. The mixture must not fall; it must remain light.

Butter a long ovenproof platter and sprinkle it with sugar. Pile the omelet mixture in the center in an oval mound and smooth with a spatula. Make an opening in the center so that the heat can penetrate.

Cooking. Bake immediately in a 350° oven; look at it after about 20 minutes.

The cooked omelet should be a pale *café au lait* color. After baking for about 20 minutes, sprinkle the omelet with confectioners' sugar; the sugar will melt and caramelize very quickly. Serve immediately.

Omelette soufflée aux liqueurs
SOUFFLÉ OMELET WITH LIQUEUR

This dessert derives from the vanilla soufflé omelet (pages 443–4) and is prepared in the same way, using the same ingredients, but adding to the batter, when it is creamy, 2 teaspoons of rum, kirsch, maraschino, curaçao, raspberry liqueur, or the like.

When the omelet is cooked and glazed, through the top opening pour 4 tablespoons of the liqueur used in the omelet (first heated), and light it, presenting the flaming dessert to the guests.

OMELET SURPRISES

The surprise effect of these omelets comes from the contrast between the cold and hot ingredients.

All follow the same pattern: a cake bottom, forming a base for an ice cream, covered with a soufflé-omelet batter, baked in the usual way and served hot.

Omelette norvégienne
NORWEGIAN OMELET OR BAKED ALASKA (For 6 to 8 people)

1/2 cup sugar
3 egg yolks
1 cube sugar rubbed on a lemon or orange skin until soaked with the oil, then finely crushed
1 teaspoon vanilla sugar
5 egg whites
8-inch *génoise* cake (page 400), baked in or cut to an oval shape
1–2 tablespoons liqueur (choice depends on the flavor of the ice cream)
1 pint ice cream

Method. Prepare a batter for a soufflé omelet (pages 443–4) using 3 egg yolks and 5 whites.

Lightly moisten the *génoise* cake, which should not be more than 1 1/2 inches high, with a few tablespoons of the chosen liqueur.

Unmold the ice cream or spoon it onto the cake and completely cover it with the thick batter for the soufflé omelet. Smooth with a pastry spatula and decorate by piping the same batter through a pastry bag with a large fluted tube.

This is baked very much like an ordinary soufflé omelet. Here, however, one must not brown the omelet too much. In a 325° oven a protective crust immediately forms, which shields the ice cream from the heat.

The baking time for a Norwegian omelet, and all the others that derive from it, is less than for a soufflé omelet; 6 to 7 minutes is enough.

445

For all these recipes the omelet should remain very creamy because, if it is not cooked very much inside, it will keep the ice cream firm.

These desserts must be served as soon as they are removed from the oven. Waiting would be detrimental to the omelets.

You must time the length of your lunch or dinner exactly to know when to start preparing the dessert.

Omelette princesse Élisabeth
PRINCESS ELIZABETH OMELET

Follow the recipe for Norwegian omelet (page 445), replacing the *génoise* cake with a Genoa cake (page 404); moisten the cake lightly with kirsch; place on top, in layers parallel to the cake, strawberry ice cream and vanilla ice cream; into the omelet batter, flavored with kirsch, mix 1 tablespoon crystallized violets (page 454).

After removing the dish from the oven, put a few crystallized violets on top of the dessert.

Omelette surprise aux pêches
PEACH SURPRISE OMELET

Pit and peel several small, quite ripe peaches, all the same size. Poach in a maraschino syrup and refrigerate.

It is important to prepare in advance a long platter that is big enough so that the peaches can be placed between the ice-cream omelet and the rim of the platter.

Follow the recipe for Norwegian omelet (page 445); moisten the *génoise* cake (page 400) with a few tablespoons of any fruit-pit liqueur; fill with two ice creams, one made with a custard for ice-cream *bombe* (pages 460–1), flavored with maraschino and powdered caramelized almonds (page 454), and the other a strongly flavored, creamy peach ice cream. Flavor the omelet batter with maraschino.

When the omelet is baked and glazed, surround it with a row of peaches. Coat each peach with 1 tablespoon red currant jelly, partially melted.

Omelette moscovite
MOSCOW OMELET

Follow the recipe for Norwegian omelet (page 445); moisten the cake base with a few tablespoons of kümmel; top the cake with the ice cream. Cover with a soufflé-omelet batter lightly flavored with Pernod or anisette liqueur. Flavor very creamy vanilla ice cream (page 459) with kümmel. Stir in some preserved, semisweet cherries, macerated in kümmel.

Drain brandied cherries and dip in fondant (page 453) flavored with kümmel. Set aside in the refrigerator. After baking and glazing the omelet, place each cherry in a fluted pastry case. Put a row of them around the edges of the omelet.

Omelette soufflée merveilleuse
MARVELOUS SOUFFLÉ OMELET

6–7 pears, peeled, stems on, cored from bottom
Maraschino
Norwegian omelet (page 445), made with madeleine batter (page 401)
4 heaping tablespoons finely crushed macaroons
Vanilla-flavored ice-cream *bombe* (page 460–1)
Pear ice cream, colored pink
Champagne *sabayon* (page 416)
Whipped Cream

Method. Poach the pears in a light pink syrup flavored with maraschino. Set aside in the syrup and refrigerate.

Proceed according to the recipe for a Norwegian omelet, using for the cake base a madeleine batter, with 4 heaping tablespoons finely crushed macaroons added. On the cake sprinkle drops of maraschino and cover with 1¼ inches of vanilla-flavored ice-cream *bombe;* then add a second layer, 2½ inches thick, of pear ice cream, colored pink, and cover with a third layer, identical to the first one.

Cover the cake and the ice cream with a fine soufflé omelet flavored with maraschino and decorated by piping the batter with a pastry bag with a large fluted tube; bake in a 425° oven. Meanwhile, drain the pears.

When the omelet is baked and glazed, in various spots around the omelet and inside the edges of the platter (which should be large enough to hold the ice cream and the garnish) arrange the pears.

To finish the dessert coat each pear with 1 tablespoon champagne *sabayon* flavored with maraschino and mixed with one-fourth its volume of whipped cream. It should have the consistency of a custard cream. This consistency can be adjusted by mixing in 1 or 2 tablespoons of the poaching syrup. Serve on the side a crystal bowl of very cold *sabayon* sauce.

SOUFFLÉS

There are two kinds of soufflés, one based on cream or milk thickened with egg yolks and the other based on sugar syrup cooked to the hard-crack stage, to which a fruit purée is added. In both cases the egg whites are beaten very stiff before being folded into the batter.

Soufflé à la crème
CREAM SOUFFLÉ OR VANILLA SOUFFLÉ (For 6 people)

2 tablespoons flour or cornstarch
1 cup milk
4 heaping tablespoons sugar
Vanilla bean
4 egg yolks
1½ tablespoons butter
Flavoring
5 egg whites

Method. Moisten the flour first with a little cold milk. Boil the milk with the sugar and the vanilla bean; steep the bean for 5 minutes, remove, and mix the still-warm milk with the flour. Heat gently, stirring, just to the boiling point. Remove from the heat; the mixture should be very smooth. Off the heat add the egg yolks, the butter, and the flavoring. Then fold in the stiffly beaten egg whites.

The whites must be folded in very gently so that they do not fall.

While whipping the egg whites, you may often notice that just as they start to get stiff, the albumin separates. A

447

cook may say: "The whites are grainy." This description is more expressive than accurate but it describes a problem that you must surmount. As soon as you notice the problem, add 1 tablespoon sugar, and continue beating. This graininess often occurs in very fresh eggs.

Add 1 tablespoon beaten egg whites to the prepared batter and mix well with a wooden spatula. This first tablespoon will lighten the batter, making it easier to fold in the remaining egg whites. Folding, as explained before in this book, consists in cutting the batter with a spatula in a movement from the bottom to the top, starting from the center and going toward the left. At the same time, the bowl is rotated in the opposite direction. The batter thus becomes well mixed, while the whites keep their fluffy consistency.

Molding and Cooking.   Soufflés are always served in the molds in which they are baked: special silver molds or ovenproof porcelain soufflé dishes, round and no deeper than 7 to 8 inches; the diameter of the base is quite large and can stand easily in the oven.

Butter a 6-cup soufflé mold and sprinkle the inside with confectioners' or granulated sugar.

Fill the mold to three-quarters its capacity, smooth the surface of the batter with a knife, make a rosette design on the surface with a knife.

Place the mold for 1 minute on the floor of a 325° oven to heat the bottom and to prepare the contents to rise; then place the mold in the center of the oven. Watch the cooking attentively; rotate the mold often; this series of steps must be done quickly to avoid leaving the oven door open too long.

After 18 to 20 minutes, the soufflé should have risen 3 to 4 inches above the edges of the mold and started to take on a dark golden color; begin then to glaze the soufflé. With a quick gesture, sprinkle the surface with a cloud of confectioners' sugar and replace the mold in the center of the oven; in 2 seconds the sugar will melt; sprinkle again with sugar; do this at least 6 times.

You will get a transparent glazed coating, with a beautiful color and drippings like large golden pearls that will remind you of the enamel tears that decorate stoneware sculptures.

Then place the mold on a platter on top of a delicate lace doily and immediately show it to the waiting guests.

Although this wait is essential, it should be limited to the absolute minimum; be careful to time the dinner accurately.

Two Last Pieces of Advice

1. The cook who watches the soufflé must not be distracted from the work; it requires complete attention.
2. I caution the reader against the temptation to serve the soufflé as soon as it has risen. To be delicious, a soufflé must also be cooked; the heat must penetrate the soufflé so that the egg whites lose the raw albumin taste one often encounters. This is a technical and gastronomic mistake that must be avoided.

If you study and understand these explanations, it is impossible not to make a soufflé correctly and to cook it perfectly; all the following recipes are based on the explanations above.

Soufflé au citron

LEMON SOUFFLÉ

This is a soufflé batter (pages 447–8) flavored with lemon zest. Rub a couple of sugar cubes over the rind, then dissolve them in the milk, with 2 tablespoons candied lemon rind, cut into tiny dice, and add to the batter before folding in the whites.

Soufflé à l'orange

ORANGE SOUFFLÉ

Follow the directions for the lemon soufflé (above), replacing the lemon with orange.

Soufflé aux pralines

SUGARED ALMOND SOUFFLÉ

Add to the soufflé batter (pages 447–8), 2 tablespoons caramelized almonds (page 454) or almond brittle, pounded into a powder; add 6 caramelized almonds, coarsely chopped, to the batter while folding in the egg whites, then sprinkle 5 or 6 caramelized almonds on the top of the soufflé just before it is baked.

Soufflé Martine

SOUFFLÉ MARTINE

Garnish the orange soufflé (above) with small ladyfingers (page 403) or champagne biscuits (sold in tins) soaked in Grand Marnier. Place these pieces of cakes between two layers of batter when filling the mold.

Soufflé au chocolat

CHOCOLATE SOUFFLÉ

Follow the soufflé recipe (pages 447–8); omit the starch and add 3 ounces sweet chocolate; break up the chocolate, melt, and cook for 10 minutes with 2 tablespoons water; add it to the milk, cook to reduce to the consistency of a thick syrup, and off the heat thicken with egg yolks. Continue following the directions given in the basic recipe.

Soufflé au café

COFFEE SOUFFLÉ

Flavor the basic recipe (pages 447–8) with 1 tablespoon strong fresh coffee or 1 teaspoon coffee essence.

Soufflé dame Blanche

LADY BLANCHE SOUFFLÉ

Follow the basic recipe (pages 447–8); replace the milk with almond milk (see page 426). Before folding in the egg whites, add 2 tablespoons chopped toasted almonds, slightly sugared, to the batter.

Soufflé aux avelines

HAZELNUT SOUFFLÉ

Follow the recipe for Lady Blanche soufflé (above), using the almond milk, but replacing the sugared almonds with hazelnuts.

Soufflé Palmyre

Follow the basic recipe (pages 447–8), and add pieces of ladyfingers (page 403) or champagne biscuits (sold in tins) soaked in kirsch. Place in layers in the batter when filling the mold.

Soufflé Rothschild

Make the basic batter (pages 447–8), adding 3 tablespoons candied fruit, diced and macerated in kümmel. When the soufflé is baked, around the edge quickly place a row of strawberries or candied cherries.

Fin soufflé de bonne-maman

GRANDMA'S FINE SOUFFLÉ (For 6 people)

½ cup sugar
1 teaspoon vanilla sugar
6 eggs, separated
3 tablespoons coarsely
 chopped walnuts
1 teaspoon fruit-pit liqueur
½ cup whipped cream

Method. In a bowl combine the sugars and add the egg yolks, one at a time, beating the mixture with a wooden spatula. Mix well for about 10 minutes, so that the batter whitens and becomes light. At this point add the walnuts, the liqueur, and the whipped cream; then fold in the 6 egg whites, beaten stiff.

To fold in the whites, follow the explanation given for the basic recipe (pages 447–8).

Fill a well-buttered soufflé mold and bake following the basic recipe.

Note: This soufflé has no flour or starch; it is thickened only by the whipped cream, which contributes its fat and gives the sought-after softness. This is an exquisite batter of great delicacy and lightness.

Soufflé aux fleurs

SOUFFLÉ WITH FLOWERS

Make the basic soufflé batter (pages 447–8), adding 2 tablespoons crystallized flowers (page 454), coarsely chopped:
Soufflé de Parme (candied Parma violets)
Spring Soufflé (candied acacia flowers)
France Soufflé (candied petals of France roses)

Soufflés aux fruits

SOUFFLÉS WITH FRUIT (For 6 people)

This series of soufflés is related to the preceding group by the manner of presentation and by the sugar and the egg whites they contain.

1¹/₃ cups sugar
⁷/₈ cup fresh fruit purée
5 egg whites

Method. Prepare the fruit purée, rubbing it through a fine sieve. Set aside in a bowl.

Place the sugar in a heavy skillet; sprinkle with 4 tablespoons water. After dissolving the sugar, heat and boil; skim carefully, and cook until the sugar cracks (about 280°).

At this point, add the fruit purée; do not let boil unless the addition of the fruit lowers the temperature of the sugar below the hard-ball stage (about 250°).

While the mixture is still very hot, pour the fruit purée in a stream onto the very stiffly beaten egg whites, lifting them with a spatula to mix well.

The molding and baking are the same as for a cream soufflé (page 448).

The best fruits for these soufflés are strawberries, raspberries, apricots, peaches, melons, blueberries, red currants, and pineapple; these must be ripe and uncooked. Apples, pears, and quince should all be cooked to a marmalade, then puréed.

It is important to add a few cubes of sugar rubbed on the rind of an orange or a lemon to give more flavor to the fruit used.

Then you should add a small quantity of liqueur to these batters, about 2 teaspoons of kirsch, maraschino, any fruit-pit liqueur, or rum. The liqueur is added to the batter at the point when the fruit and the sugar are mixed into the egg whites.

Soufflés aux liqueurs et vins

SOUFFLÉS WITH LIQUEUR AND WINE

Rum, curaçao, Grand Marnier, Marie Brizard apricot, Cointreau, anisette, kümmel, chartreuse, kirsch, crème d'abricots, crème de cacao, Marsala, port, Frontignan, Madeira—all can be used to flavor the soufflé in which milk and cream remain the basic ingredients; the liqueur is added to the starch, cornstarch, or flour and eggs.

Use the basic recipe (pages 447–8), taking into account the quantity of liqueur or wine added. The consistency of the cream will depend upon the quantity of liqueur added.

Note: To finish this series of desserts let us add that, in the basic recipe, you can substitute half pastry cream (page 411) or frangipane cream (page 410). It is possible to replace the starch with flour and to make a quick white *roux* with the given amount of butter.

I prefer to use starch or cornstarch or, even better, the recipe for Grandma's fine soufflé (page 450).

Oranges soufflées

(For 4 people)

4 large oranges
1/3 cup sugar
4 eggs, separated

Method. Cut off the top third of each orange and scoop out the pulp with a spoon. Reserve the removed tops. Rub the pulp through a fine strainer. In a skillet boil the pulp to reduce it; add 1 tablespoon finely chopped boiled orange rind, made with the reserved tops.

Add the sugar, and cook for a few minutes. Cook off the heat, and thicken with the egg yolks. Beat the egg whites very stiff, and fold a little at a time into the batter.

Fill the emptied orange shells with this batter. Bake in a 325° oven like any other soufflé, for 15 to 18 minutes.

Serve on a platter, immediately.

Sugar, chocolate, meringues, frozen desserts

SUGAR

Cooking sugar

The instructions that follow are designed to explain the principles of cooking and storing sugar syrups and jams.

They also make it easier to accomplish feats of candymaking with the limited means of the home kitchen.

Making sugar syrup

In a saucepan, combine the quantity of sugar, granulated or in cubes, and water specified in the recipe, using, for example, 2½ cups sugar and ½ cup water.

Put it on the fire, heat slowly, stirring now and then until the sugar is dissolved and almost at the boiling point.

As the syrup heats, impurities will rise to the surface; skim carefully. Then add 1 teaspoon corn syrup to keep the sugar from becoming grainy during the cooking.

Boiling makes the water in the syrup evaporate and thickens it; when this is complete, the syrup is soon covered with tiny bubbles very close to one another. The temperature will be about 180°.

Thereafter the pan must be watched attentively, for the syrup changes very rapidly, and easily caramelizes or burns. From this point on it is essential to use a candy thermometer and be vigilant. The syrups should be boiled for at least 3 minutes at 200° to 210°. The temperature must be kept below 220°, which is the point at which sugar caramelizes.

Consult the individual recipes for the proportions for specific syrups.

Sirop de framboises au naturel
FRESH RASPBERRY SYRUP

Rub 2 pounds beautiful, ripe raspberries through a fine sieve. Add an equal weight of sugar to the raspberry pulp, and stir until dissolved. Raspberry syrup is used mainly to top dishes of ice cream with fruit.

Glace
GLAZE

At a low temperature mix confectioners' sugar with a flavored syrup and a piece of glucose (or a spoonful of light corn syrup) until it reaches the consistency of a thick cream. It is then ready to use.

Fondant ou glacé
FONDANT OR SUGAR ICING

In a heavy stainless-steel skillet melt 2⅔ cups sugar with a few tablespoons water. Place on the stove and cook to the soft-ball stage (234° to 240°). Skim carefully while cooking. Pour on a piece of marble in a frame made with 4 steel bars (the marble and the bars—sold at confectioners' suppliers—should be oiled). When the sugar is lukewarm, remove the bars and work the mixture with a spatula, throwing back the edges toward the center. During this step, the sugar will become white and harden, and then be transformed into a smooth paste, pliable and creamy.

Place in a bowl and cover with a fresh cloth for later use.

The flavor is added when the fondant is used. Heat the fondant gently to expand it and make it slightly liquid while preserving its shine. A piece of glucose, as big as a filbert, can then be added. [*Editor's note:* A spoonful of light corn syrup can replace the glucose.]

Nougat aux amandes

ALMOND BRITTLE

Place 1 cup sugar in a heavy stainless-steel pot; heat slowly, stirring constantly with a spatula.

Sugar melts, dry, at a temperature of 320°. It then has a light golden color. As soon as the sugar reaches the syrup stage, pour in 7 ounces almonds, skinned, chopped, and dried, which have been kept warm. Off the heat mix the two ingredients and pour onto a lightly oiled platter. Keep the mixture warm. Mold it on a piece of marble into small, thin pieces, which are then put into oiled molds to harden.

Unmold when hard.

Praliné

POWDERED CARAMELIZED ALMONDS

Combine equal amounts of sugar, chopped skinned almonds, and chopped skinned filberts. Follow the recipe for almond brittle (above); after the brittle has cooled, crush in a mortar or in some other way.

Keep in a jar covered with oiled paper.

Fleurs pralinées

CRYSTALLIZED FLOWERS

[*Editor's note:* Crystallized flowers are lovely for decorating cakes and desserts. They may be bought in specialty shops, but the recipe is delightful to read.]

Violets and acacias and petals of roses and lilies are most commonly utilized for crystallized decorations.

Measure 5¾ cups sugar and an equal amount of flowers (stems removed). Place the sugar in a heavy stainless-steel skillet, pour over 4⅓ cups water, and cook as directed on pages 452–3).

At this point plunge the flowers into the syrup. Bring to a boil, and with a slotted spoon drain the flowers onto a plate; continue cooking the syrup to the soft-ball stage (234° to 240°), remove from the heat, and stir the sugar with a spatula; it will slowly become white and grainy. Return the flowers and mix until the flowers are coated with the sugar. Spread in the top pan of a double boiler. Cook for 10 hours over medium heat; then sift carefully, gathering only the flowers coated with sugar.

The sugar can be dyed the same color as the flowers used.

Marrons confits

Peel large chestnuts without breaking them. Cook slowly in a white *court-bouillon* (water mixed with a small quantity of flour). Drain and place in a glass or glazed earthenware jar with a vanilla bean, and cover with boiling sugar syrup made according to the instructions on pages 452–3), using 4 cups sugar to $4^{1}/_{3}$ cups water. After 48 hours the chestnuts will have absorbed this liquid. Replace it with new syrup with $4^{1}/_{2}$ cups sugar and the same quantity of water. After another 48 hours add more boiling syrup, made with 5 cups sugar and the same quantity of water. Repeat in another 48 hours, increasing the sugar to $6^{1}/_{4}$ generous cups, while the amount of water remains the same. After 48 hours more pour in the final glazing, using a syrup made with $6^{1}/_{2}$ generous cups sugar and as always $4^{1}/_{3}$ cups water. This last syrup should be worked with a spatula until it is white.

CHOCOLATE

Truffes

TRUFFLES

4¹/₄ cups very heavy cream
3 pounds semisweet
chocolate, melted
14 tablespoons very good
quality unsalted butter
Cocoa

Boil the cream, then add it to the chocolate, melted in a double boiler; this is a *ganache*. Let it stand in the refrigerator overnight. The next morning, with the *ganache* still in the double boiler, heat slightly, adding the butter. Put the mixture into a pastry bag, form into pieces, and roll them in cocoa.

MERINGUES

Batter for meringues can be made in four ways:

> Ordinary meringue
> Italian meringue
> Cooked meringue
> Swiss meringue

The first meringue is a cold mixture of 8 egg whites beaten very stiff with $2^{2}/_{3}$ cups sugar poured on the whites in a stream while they are being whipped. The proportion of whites varies from 6 to 12 for this quantity of sugar, depending upon how the meringue will be used. The quantity of 8 whites is an average, frequently used in various pastries.

The second meringue is a mixture of $2^{2}/_{3}$ cups sugar in syrup cooked to the soft-ball stage (234° to 240°) and poured into 6 to 8 egg whites whipped very stiff; it is used for desserts.

The third meringue is made with the egg whites whipped with confectioners' sugar, this time over low heat, until the consistency of a very thick cream is reached. It is used for *petits fours*, ladyfingers, etc.

The fourth meringue is made by beating with a spatula

3½ cups confectioners' sugar, 2 egg whites, and a few drops of acetic acid (or ½ teaspoon lemon juice). When the mixture is thick, firm, and creamy, add the remaining egg whites, whipped very stiff. This is used for decorations and glazing with or without sugared almonds.

Meringues ordinaires
ORDINARY MERINGUES

Make the batter by the first method above and flavor with vanilla; pour into a pastry bag with a ½-inch plain tube; on a buttered and floured pastry sheet pipe meringue shells into oval puffs about the size and shape of an egg; bake in a 225° oven for at least 1 hour to dry the meringues and give them an ivory color.

Before baking, proceed as for ladyfingers, by sprinkling the meringue shells with a sugar mixture containing 1 part granulated sugar and 4 parts confectioners' sugar. Shake off the excess sugar and keep it for later use; then sprinkle the meringues with drops of water to "pearl" them. When you take the shells from the oven, press down the inside of each one lightly, using an egg.

Once cooled, the meringue shells will remain crisp for a very long time if kept in a tightly closed tin box.

Meringues garnies
FILLED MERINGUES

Meringue shells (recipe above) are generally used in pairs joined with *crème* Chantilly (page 411), with which they are also garnished, or with ice cream or fruit, as there will be a space of 1¼ inches between the top and the bottom meringues, which should be filled with cream. Saint-Honoré cream (pages 412–13) can also be used.

This is a very delicate dessert and can be used in many different ways; it is a question of a gourmand's fertile imagination, for example:

Mousselines au marasquin
MARASCHINO FLOATING ISLANDS

Prepare ordinary meringue (above), flavored with vanilla. Boil milk with sugar and vanilla in a skillet; add the meringue, molded with a tablespoon, and poach the egg shapes in the simmering milk.

A few minutes later, turn the meringues over so that they cook on both sides. When the meringue eggs are firm to the touch, drain on a cloth, then place in a large bowl. With the cooking milk, make a custard cream (page 411), thickened with 10 egg yolks for 1 quart milk.

When the custard is cool, flavor with maraschino and pour over the meringues. Serve very cold with a plate of small sand cakes (page 406) or a sponge brioche (page 378).

Bouchées exquises
EXQUISITE MOUTHFULS

Arrange pairs of meringue shells (recipe above) filled with *crème* Chantilly (page 411) colored pink with a few table-spoons of strawberry purée with a dash of maraschino. Stick each pair of filled shells together and coat with a very light, white fondant (page 453) flavored with kirsch that is transparent enough to let the pink tint of the cream show. Place the meringues on a pastry platter lined with a linen doily.

Zéphirs antillais
WEST INDIAN BREEZES

These are meringues filled with vanilla ice cream flavored with rum. Pile to look like rocks.

Accompany with a light chocolate *sabayon* (page 416), served very cold in a crystal bowl, and a plate of cats' tongues (pages 406–7).

FROZEN DESSERTS

In this group are: frozen desserts made with cream, fruit ices, custard for ice-cream *bombes*, batter for mousses and parfaits, and sherbets.

To make a frozen dessert four main steps must be followed:
1. Prepare the mixture.
2. Pack the ice-cream freezer.
3. Turn the mixture until frozen.
4. Mold and freeze again.

The packing of the ice-cream freezer consists of placing the ice-cream container on its pivot and surrounding it with crushed ice mixed in layers with coarse salt and saltpeter, 3 pounds salt and 5¼ ounces saltpeter for 20 pounds of crushed ice. Pound down the ice to pack it tightly and lower its level to about two-thirds the height of the freezer. Cover the salted ice with a cloth.

Freezing. Depending on the nature of the dessert, the mixture is either first frozen in an ice-cream freezer, then molded, and frozen again; or directly molded and frozen.

In the first case the custard, prepared and cooled, is poured into the container after the container has been put in place in the freezer, all set to go.

Whether turned by hand or electrically, the container must first be closed tightly to prevent the salt getting into the ice cream.

Open the container and fill it about half full with the ice-cream custard or other mixture, close tightly, and start the machine. The old-fashioned freezer was simple. You can use it today if you do not have a modern electric freezer.

The container itself has not changed since Procope (a Sicilian who introduced ice cream to France in 1660): it is a deep tinned cylinder with a bottom made like a cap; it is closed with a tightly fitting lid, which has a strong handle.

Only the handle has disappeared from modern ice-cream freezers turned by motor. Years ago the cook, after having half-filled the container, would bury it in salted crushed ice. Then, holding the handle of the lid, he would turn the container, left to right, in a rotating movement that would throw the custard against the sides of the container, where it would freeze. The cook would open the container frequently, scrape the sides and mix the frozen part with the remaining custard. He would continue churning until all the custard had become ice cream.

I describe this method, which is not so successful as using a hand or an electric machine, only to let the reader know that it is possible to make an ice-cream dessert even if you do not have an ice-cream freezer.

A modern ice-cream freezer has a dasher, attached to the cover of the container, that mixes the custard.

The continuous rotation of the dasher throws the custard against the sides of the container, where it freezes in thin layers, which are immediately scraped off by the dasher and thrown back into the custard, which, continuously whipped, becomes very light. The custard thickens, becoming smooth and homogeneous.

The frozen mixture can then be served immediately in small bowls or piled in a mound on a folded napkin, using a tablespoon dipped in warm water.

Generally, ice cream is shaped in simple molds or in special decorated ones. The ice cream is then spooned into the mold, which should be tapped on the table to fill any cavities. When the mold is filled to the brim, cover with a piece of white paper with a diameter slightly larger than that of the mold; butter the edges of the lid, place it on the mold and place the mold in a container filled with crushed ice, mixed with salt and saltpeter as for freezing the ice cream.

Leave the molds in the bucket of ice for at least 1 hour before serving if the ice cream is going to be unmolded without being glazed. Using the above method, the ice cream can be kept on ice for 2$\frac{1}{2}$ hours after being molded.

Serving. At the last moment remove the molds from the salted ice, wash each one, and dip it for a second in warm water. Wipe, remove the lid, and turn the mold over onto a folded napkin placed on a serving platter.

Serve with a plate of cookies or small cakes.

Note: The use of ice to make ice cream will soon belong to the past; it was first replaced by dry ice, which now can be found in stores. The advantage of dry ice over regular ice with salt and saltpeter is that it eliminates these three ingredients and their dampness. Dry ice goes from the solid state to a gas very slowly.

But dry ice itself has been quickly overtaken by the increasing use of electric freezers with very low temperatures (at 5°, −4°, or even −22°); an ice cream, unmolded after a certain time in such a freezer, will be so hard that it cannot be eaten until it has been out of the freezer a few hours. This process represents scientific progress and practicality, but it adds nothing to—even detracts from—the high quality of the ice cream made with methods that some may consider quite old-fashioned.

Glaces à la crème

ICE CREAMS (For 8 to 10 people)

3 cups milk
1 vanilla bean
1¹/₂ cups sugar
8 egg yolks

Method. Boil the milk with the vanilla bean; steep for 5 minutes.

Meanwhile, in a bowl combine the sugar and the egg yolks; beat with a wooden spatula until the batter is light and slowly forms a ribbon when poured from the spatula.

Slowly beat the milk into the mixture; after they are blended, pour back into the saucepan, heat slowly, avoid boiling, and as soon as the mixture thickens like a light cream (coating the spatula), remove from the heat and pour it into a bowl through a fine sieve. Stir to accelerate the cooling process.

Cooking this custard is a rather delicate step and requires either experience or a great deal of attention. Readers should understand that the smoothness comes from the egg yolks, which, if they are cooked too quickly, will harden into tiny grains and lose their softness and their thickening and enriching properties. The number of egg yolks can be increased up to 16 yolks for 4¹/₄ cups of milk and the sugar increased gradually to 2 cups, to obtain a finer, richer custard.

The milk can be replaced in part or totally by fresh light cream.

Glace au café

COFFEE ICE CREAM

Use the same proportions as for ice cream (above). To flavor steep 3¹/₂ tablespoons freshly ground coffee in the boiling milk. Cover the saucepan. Strain through a fine sieve.

Glace au chocolat

CHOCOLATE ICE CREAM

Replace the coffee with a chocolate syrup made by melting ¹/₂ pound semisweet chocolate with ¹/₂ cup water. Decrease the quantity of sugar by about ¹/₂ cup. Boil slowly for 10 minutes. You may use unsweetened cocoa; reduce the amount of cocoa to ¹/₃ pound and do not change the amount of sugar.

Glace pralinée
ICE CREAM WITH SUGARED ALMONDS

To each quart of ice cream (page 459), add ¼ pound caramelized almonds or filberts (page 454) pounded in a mortar and then rubbed through a sieve.

1³/₄ pounds ripe red currants
¹/₂ pound white currants or 3 cups juice
2 cups sugar syrup, made with 1²/₃ cups sugar and 1¹/₄ cups water (see pages 452–3)

Glace à la groseille
RED CURRANT ICE

Method.   Squeeze the currants in a dish towel to extract the juice. Mix the syrup with the currant juice.
   Freeze, following basic instructions, mold, and harden.

1 pound strawberries (*fraises des bois* or any other fragrant variety)
2 cups sugar syrup, made with 1²/₃ cups sugar and 1¹/₄ cups water (see pages 452–3)
Juice of 1 lemon or orange

Glace aux fraises
STRAWBERRY ICE

Method.   Mash the washed and hulled strawberries into a purée and rub through a fine sieve.
   Mix the fruit purée and the syrup in equal quantities (2 cups each), add the lemon or orange juice, and freeze, following instructions on pages 457–8.

2 cups water
2²/₃ cups sugar
Juice and rind of 4 oranges or equivalent amount of tangerine juice
Juice and rind of 1 lemon

Glace à l'orange ou à la mandarine
ORANGE OR TANGERINE ICE

Method.   Boil the sugar and water, steeping the rind of the oranges and the lemon; strain, and let cool. Then add the orange or tangerine juice and the lemon juice. Freeze, mold, and harden, following instructions on pages 457–8.

4 cups milk
1 vanilla bean
Rind of 3 lemons
2 cups sugar
10 egg yolks

Glace aux citrons
LEMON ICE
First Method
Follow the recipe for ice cream (page 459) and the instructions for freezing on pages 457–8.
Second Method
Follow the recipe for orange ice (above), and replace the 4 oranges with 4 lemons.

Appareils à bombe glacée
CUSTARD FOR ICE-CREAM BOMBE

Method.   Combine the syrup and the egg yolks in a large stainless-steel bowl.

4¹/₄ cups sugar syrup, made with 2¹/₂ cups sugar and 2 cups water (see pages 452–3)
32 egg yolks
6¹/₂ cups *crème fraîche* or heavy cream, whipped

Place over a very low flame and whip it like a *génoise* cake (page 400) until the egg yolks are partially cooked as for a custard cream (page 411) or a *sabayon* (page 416). The mixture will expand and form a ribbon as for the *génoise* batter. At this point remove the bowl from the heat and continue to whip until completely cold.

Add the chosen flavor, then the whipped *crème fraîche*. Fold carefully.

Mold.

This custard is not frozen in an ice-cream freezer but molded directly.

Generally the inside of a *bombe* mold is first lined with a thin layer of ice cream of a different flavor from the *bombe* mixture—vanilla ice cream, for example—which acts as a support for the very delicate *bombe* batter.

Close the mold following the directions on page 458 and pack in ice and salt; leave it in the container filled with ice for at least 2 hours; just before serving unmold on a folded napkin, and serve with a plate of cookies or small cakes.

Les pâtes à mousse, biscuits et parfaits

BATTER FOR MOUSSES, FROZEN CAKES, AND PARFAITS

There are two kinds of mousse, one with syrup and one with cream.

The syrup mousses are easy to make, provided you have a candy thermometer. Generally, one can, with no problem, use the following proportions: For 4¹/₄ cups sugar syrup, combine 2¹/₂ cups sugar with 2 cups water, and follow the directions on pages 452–3).

Cold Mousse with Syrup

Combine 4¹/₄ cups syrup (see recipe above) with 4¹/₄ cups strained fruit purée, and 8¹/₂ cups stiffly beaten *crème* Chantilly (page 411).

This quantity will fill 4 molds of 1 quart each and would serve about 35 people.

It is therefore easy to make less or more, as needed.

Mold (not too deep), and pack in ice and salt to freeze for 2¹/₂ to 3 hours, following the method described on page 458. The molds can also be placed in an electric freezer compartment for 4 hours.

Cold Mousse with Cream

2²/₃ cups sugar
16 egg yolks
2 cups milk
2 cups *crème fraîche* or heavy cream
3 envelopes gelatin
2 cups strained fruit purée

Using 2²/₃ cups sugar, 16 egg yolks, and 2 cups milk, prepare a custard cream (for method see page 411). When the cream is cold, add 2 cups *crème fraîche,* 3 envelopes gelatin, and 2 cups strained fruit purée.

Place the bowl containing this custard on crushed ice and whip the mixture vigorously to make it frothy and very light.

Mold and close tightly, pack in ice and salt to chill as directed for ice cream (page 458), or place in the refrigerator for 4 hours; the mousse should be set but not frozen.

Soufflé glacé aux cerises
COLD CHERRY SOUFFLÉ

Prepare 2 cups cold-mousse batter (page 461) with cherries cooked in syrup flavored with maraschino.

With a string tie a strip of paper around a soufflé mold so that the dish can be filled 1½ inches above the brim.

Fill the mold with the batter to ½ inch from the top of the paper, smooth the surface, and cover completely with whole pitted sweet cherries, their stems removed, poached and cooled in a maraschino-flavored syrup.

Refrigerate for 3 hours.

Just before serving, remove the strip of paper and coat the cherries lightly with a *coulis* of fresh raspberries (see the recipe for fresh raspberry syrup, page 453). Serve with a brioche crown (page 379), cut in ½-inch slices; sprinkle each slice with vanilla confectioners' sugar and place under a hot broiler for a few seconds—just long enough to color the sugar.

Appareils à biscuits glacés
BATTER FOR FROZEN CUSTARD CAKES

2⅔ cups sugar
12 egg yolks
4 egg whites, beaten very stiff
⅔ cup sugar
4¼ cups whipped cream

Method. Prepare and whip the batter with a whisk as for a *génoise* cake (page 400), beaten hot and partially cooked like a custard or *sabayon* in a double boiler. The proportions are 2⅔ cups sugar to 12 egg yolks. When the batter expands and forms a ribbon, remove from the hot water and continue whipping until completely cold.

Make an Italian meringue (for method see page 455) with 4 egg whites, beaten very stiff, into which, while beating, you pour in a stream ⅔ cup sugar cooked to a syrup at the soft-ball stage (234° to 240°). Finish by adding the Italian meringue and 4¼ cups whipped cream to the batter.

The molding is done in special square or rectangular molds with two deep lids. These molds make it possible to use three layers of batter with different flavors and color, since the lids are filled as well as the mold itself.

Pack in a container of ice and salt to set, following the directions on page 458, or place in a refrigerator as for the mousses.

Parfaits

4¼ cups sugar syrup
32 egg yolks
4¼ cups whipped cream
Coffee essence

A parfait was originally fine coffee ice cream.

The batter is made like a custard cream (see page 411) in which the milk has been replaced with syrup made with 5 cups sugar and 4⅓ cups water (see pages 452–3). The parfait proportions are 4¼ cups syrup, 32 egg yolks, and 4¼ cups whipped cream.

When the custard cream, heated slowly, coats the spatula, strain it through a very fine sieve into a bowl, and whip it until completely cold. Then place the bowl on top of crushed ice and continue to whip for at least 15 minutes. Finish by adding the whipped cream.

Flavor with coffee essence.

Mold in a *bombe* mold and pack in ice and salt as directed on page 458.

Modern cuisine has added different flavors to this batter. I will limit my suggestions to adding 3 tablespoons strained powdered caramelized almonds (page 454) for $4\frac{1}{4}$ cups of parfait ice cream.

Note: Innumerable combinations of flavors can be employed in the recipe given above. I am always careful to give the essential proportions for a basic custard that will work for any cook, provided that the techniques of preparation are followed strictly. It is easy to follow them, for making ice cream requires some attention to minute details but presents no great difficulty.

Among the flavors that can be chosen, I mention especially:

Coffee, chocolate, vanilla, and tea

Almonds, filberts, pistachios, walnuts, and caramelized almonds

Oranges, tangerines, and lemons

Red currants, raspberries, strawberries, cherries, and apricots (for all red fruits add a few tablespoons orange juice or lemon juice to give tartness to the flavor)

Bananas, pineapples, and melons

Crystallized violets and rose petals

Maraschino, Benedictine, Grand Marnier, Pernod or any other anise liqueur, Cointreau, Marie Brizard apricot, chartreuse, etc.

Rum, kirsch, raspberry liqueur, Izara, etc.

Parfaits can be served without molding; for example, pineapple ice can be put into the shell of the fruit just before serving and decorated with pineapple leaves. An orange, tangerine, or lemon ice can fill the carefully emptied fruit shells and be covered with the tops of the fruit used, which will still have some leaves.

Give your imagination free rein, as long as the rules of good taste and the harmony of the flavors are not forgotten.

The names of some ice creams indicate that they are made with more than one flavor, but the ingredients are not always evident from the name. For example:

AIDA: Line the mold with raspberry ice cream, filled inside with vanilla ice cream; after unmolding, decorate with a pastry bag with a fluted tube filled with *crème* Chantilly (page 411).

AIGLON: Line the mold with pineapple ice; fill the inside with tangerine ice cream.

AMBASSADEUR: Line the mold with strawberry ice cream; fill the inside with *crème* Chantilly (page 411) sprinkled with strawberries macerated in a little kirsch.

ARCHIDUC: Line the mold with apricot ice cream; fill with vanilla ice cream with fresh walnuts, peeled and pounded.

CENDRILLON: Line the mold with cherry ice cream; fill the inside with a vanilla mousse custard sprinkled with fresh or candied fruits macerated in maraschino.

MIREILLE: Line the mold with apricot ice cream; fill the inside with maraschino ice.

NELUSKO: Line the mold with vanilla ice cream; fill the inside with chocolate ice cream.

VICTOIRE: Line the mold with red currant ice cream; fill the inside with a raspberry mousse, sprinkled with strawberries macerated in raspberry liqueur.

This list could contain a hundred or more combinations involving different molds and decorations.

Sorbets
SHERBETS

Sherbets are classified into four categories similar to light ices: *granités, marquises,* punches, and spumes.

In fact, these are derivatives of the liqueur ices made only with syrup; in this case make a syrup with 3 scant cups sugar and 4½ cups water (see pages 452–3). Add the liqueurs, about ½ cup liqueur for 4⅓ cups syrup.

If wine is used—champagne, port, Madeira, Samos, sauternes such as Château-Yquem—make a syrup with 3¾ generous cups sugar and 4⅓ cups water. Mix 2 cups wine with 2 cups syrup, and add the juice of 2 lemons and 1 orange.

Fruit juices can also be used but are limited to red currant, raspberry, strawberry, pineapple, melon, cherry; use half juice and half syrup. The syrups should be made with 4⅓ cups water and 3 scant cups sugar or 3¾ generous cups sugar, depending on the fruit.

When the mixture is ready, freeze it in an ice-cream freezer just before serving, not freezing it too hard; its consistency should be nearly that of a drink. Sherbets are served in small fruit dishes or glasses.

For 12 people, you will need 4 cups sherbet mixture.

Granités

Granités are made only with acid fruit juices: oranges, lemons, red currants, or cherries mixed with a syrup made of 2 cups sugar and 4⅓ cups liquid (juices plus water; see pages 452–3).

Because this syrup is very light, freezing produces a grainy texture that gives the ice its name.

Marquises

This sherbet is made only with pineapple juice with kirsch or with puréed strawberries, using a sugar syrup made with 2½ generous cups sugar and 4⅓ cups water (see pages 452–3).

After freezing in an ice-cream freezer, the mixture is made stiffer than an ordinary sherbet by the addition of 2 cups whipped cream for 4^1/$_2$ cups sherbet.

Punchs
PUNCHES

Make a syrup of 3^3/$_4$ generous cups sugar and 4^1/$_3$ cups water (see pages 452–3). Steep the zest (thin yellow part of the rind without the white pith) of 1 lemon and 1 orange in the syrup. In an ice-cream freezer, freeze a mixture made with 2 cups syrup, and 2 cups champagne brut, the juice of 2 oranges and 2 lemons, and the zest.

After freezing, add 2 egg whites, beaten stiff with ^{1}/$_2$ cup sugar (Italian meringue, page 455), and finish by adding ^{1}/$_2$ cup rum in a stream. Fill the glasses or fruit dishes as for sherbets.

Spooms
SPUMES

Of all the four sherbets, spumes are the thickest. They are prepared with a sugar syrup made with 4 cups sugar and 4^1/$_3$ cups water (see pages 452–3). They nearly always are made with champagne, muscatel, or sauternes. They are exceedingly light and frothy. To reach that point, the mixture is frozen in an ice-cream freezer and then combined with an equal amount of Italian meringue (page 455) folded in carefully. This is also served in fruit dishes.

L'orange à l'orange
ORANGE SHERBET IN ORANGES (For 6 people)

12 large oranges
1 cup grenadine syrup

Method. With a knife, peel the zest (the rind without the white pith) of 6 of the oranges; cut the zest into fine julienne and cook for a few minutes in 1 cup water with the grenadine syrup.

Trim the remaining pith from the 6 oranges that have been peeled. Cut the pulp into thin slices. Place the orange slices in a deep dish and sprinkle them with 1 generous tablespoon of the sauce made with the grenadine.

Meanwhile, scoop out each of the remaining 6 oranges to form a bowl and keep the shells cold; reserve the pulp and juice of the oranges to make the sherbet (below). Then fill each orange shell with some of the sherbet, the slices of oranges, and the zest, drained and cooled.

Orange Sherbet

4^1/$_2$ cups orange juice
Juice of 2 lemons
1 cup sugar

Turn in the ice-cream freezer as for ordinary ice cream.

Fruit desserts

APRICOTS

Compote d'abricots

STEWED APRICOTS

3/4 cup sugar
2 cups water
1 vanilla bean
12 large, ripe apricots
1 tablespoon kirsch or
 fruit-pit liqueur

Method. Make a light syrup with 3/4 cup sugar, 2 cups water, and a vanilla bean. Plunge apricots for a moment into boiling water, and peel at once. Cut in two, pit them, and break four of the pits. Cut the inside kernels in two, and add to the syrup, along with the apricots.

Bring the apricots slowly to a boil and poach, simmering, for 8 minutes. Cook gently, so that the apricots do not become soft or lose their shape.

Keep in the syrup in a glazed bowl until time to use.

Flavor the syrup when it is lukewarm with 1 tablespoon kirsch or fruit-pit liqueur.

Abricots compotés au marasquin

BAKED APRICOTS WITH MARASCHINO

Spread 2 tablespoons thick *crème fraîche* or heavy cream on an ovenproof porcelain plate. Side by side on the cream, arrange apricot halves peeled as for stewed apricots, above.

Sprinkle with confectioners' sugar and bake in a 325° oven.

After baking, baste with 1 tablespoon maraschino and serve warm in the baking dish.

Abricots Condé

RICE RING WITH APRICOTS

First stew 10 apricots by the recipe above and prepare 1/4 pound rice (5/8 cup) for dessert (see pages 431–2). As soon as the rice is cooked (tender and fluffy), add beaten egg whites and flavor with kirsch; pour into a ring mold—a savarin mold with a curved bottom. Poach, then unmold on a round platter. Drain the apricot halves, which have been kept warm in the syrup, and place 16 of them on the rice, overlapping them around the curved top of the ring. Decorate the apricots with designs in angelica and candied fruits, sugared cherries, citron, etc.

Baste everything with a sauce made by boiling the syrup to reduce it to a scant cup. Rub the 4 remaining apricot halves through a fine sieve and mix with the syrup. Flavor the sauce with 4 teaspoons kirsch.

Note: Out of season, use canned apricots in syrup and thicken the syrup with apricot jam.

466

Abricots Bourdaloue

APRICOTS BOURDALOUE

Poach 12 apricots as for stewed apricots (page 466). Flavor with 4 inside kernels.

Prepare 2 cups frangipane cream (page 410). Pour the cream into a fine flan crust made with *sablée* dough and baked unfilled (see page 391).

Carefully drain the apricot halves and arrange them on the cream. Sprinkle generously with crushed dry macaroons; dust lightly with confectioners' sugar and bake in a 425° oven for a few minutes to caramelize the sugar and to form a fragrant crust.

Serve with a bowl of apricot sauce flavored with kirsch, adding the poaching syrup, reduced.

Abricots Colbert

APRICOTS COLBERT

3½ ounces wheat
  semolina for desserts
1 cup boiling milk,
  sweetened, flavored
  with vanilla
Pinch salt
2 egg yolks
2 tablespoons unsalted
  butter
12 apricots
1 egg
Fresh bread crumbs
Frying oil
Confectioners' sugar
Apricot sauce (page 417)
  flavored with kirsch or
  maraschino

Method.   Cook wheat semolina, pouring it in a stream into boiling milk, sweetened and flavored with vanilla and a pinch of salt.

Poach, covered, in a 325° oven for 30 minutes. After removing from the oven, separate the grains with a fork and thicken with the egg yolks and 1 tablespoon butter (a piece as big as a small egg).

Poach the apricots, whole, following the recipe for stewed apricots (page 466), keeping them rather firm. Drain and half open each one to remove the pit and replace it with an equal quantity of the cooked semolina.

Close the apricots and dip them, one at a time, into 1 egg beaten with 1 tablespoon melted butter, then roll each one in fresh bread crumbs.

Plunge the coated apricots in a deep fryer with very hot oil, 8 minutes before serving.

Drain on a cloth, sprinkle lightly with confectioners' sugar, and place in bunches on a linen doily.

Serve with a bowl of apricot sauce flavored with kirsch or maraschino.

Abricots flambés au Grand Marnier

APRICOTS FLAMED WITH GRAND MARNIER

12 whole apricots
1 tablespoon chopped
  almonds
2 inside kernels from
  apricot pits
Vanilla sugar
Pinch cornstarch
1 tablespoon Grand
  Marnier per serving

Method.   Poach whole apricots (see recipe for stewed apricots, (page 466) and place on an ovenproof porcelain platter.

Remove the pits from the apricots and keep the fruit warm in the syrup, which should be as thick as possible.

Sprinkle the tops of the apricots with chopped almonds with which you have included 2 inside kernels from the apricot pits, then sprinkle with vanilla sugar and brown the tops lightly in a 400° oven.

6 ripe apricots
1 cup sugar syrup
Liqueur
**Large piece of unsalted
 butter (optional)**

In the bottom of the plate pour a few tablespoons of the poaching syrup thickened slightly with a pinch of cornstarch.

Heat to boiling before serving; then, when ready to present the dish to the guests, pour 1 tablespoon Grand Marnier per serving on the apricots and ignite.

Apricot Sauce

Rub 6 ripe apricots through a fine sieve. Mix the pulp with 1 cup sugar syrup; place the mixture in a heavy skillet and cook like jam. Flavor with the chosen liqueur when the sauce is tepid or cold.

If used warm, add off the heat a large piece of butter.

Abricots meringués Clairette

APRICOTS WITH MERINGUE CLAIRETTE

**8-inch Genoa cake (page
 404)**
Fruit-pit liqueur
**$1/2$ cup dessert rice (pages
 431–2)**
Vanilla
**12 large apricots, stewed
 whole (page 466)**
Crushed macaroons
Unsalted butter
2 egg whites
$2/3$ cup sugar
Pinch vanilla sugar
**Ordinary meringue
 (page 456)**
Red currant or apricot jelly

Method.   Prepare:

A Genoa cake soaked with fruit-pit liqueur.

Dessert rice flavored with fruit-pit liqueur and vanilla.

Stewed apricots, pits removed; replace them with small
  balls made with 1 part crushed macaroons and 1 part butter
  flavored with few drops of fruit-pit liqueur.

Egg whites (reserved from the yolks used in the rice), whipped
  stiff with $2/3$ cup sugar and a pinch of vanilla sugar.

Place the Genoa cake on a large platter, spread the rice on top in an even layer; arrange the apricots, carefully closed, on top and cover everything with a meringue, following the method for a Norwegian omelet (see page 445).

Smooth the meringue with a spatula, and decorate with rosettes, roses, etc., made with a pastry bag fitted with a fluted tube.

Bake in a 325° oven, sprinkle with sugar, and remove from the oven when the meringue is a light brown color.

In the centers of the rosettes or roses, etc., place a little red currant or apricot jelly.

This dessert is excellent served cold. In that case, make sure that the meringue is completely cooked or use a meringue made with a sugar syrup.

Abricots Robert d'Ardeuil

APRICOTS ROBERT D'ARDEUIL

1 cup water
$2/3$ cup sugar
2 envelopes gelatin
20 ripe apricots
Juice of 1 orange
Juice of $1/2$ lemon
10 apricots
$7/8$ cup sugar
1 cup water
**$1^1/2$ ounces sweet almonds
 with 1 bitter almond**
$1/2$ cup light cream or milk

Method.   Prepare an unclarified jelly by heating 1 cup water with $2/3$ cup sugar and 2 envelopes gelatin soaked in cold water.

Pit 20 apricots and reserve the pits. Make a purée with the apricots, rubbing them through a fine sieve; put into a bowl.

Break the apricot pits, remove the kernels, skin them after blanching them for 1 minute in boiling water, and slice thin.

Combine the fruit purée, the apricot kernels, and the jellied syrup before it is set. Add the juice of 1 orange and $1/2$ lemon.

Oil a bowl or a bowl-shaped mold and fill with the mixture just before it starts to set.

Refrigerate for 3 hours before serving.

While the purée is refrigerated, slowly poach 10 apricots, pitted carefully to keep the fruit intact, in a syrup made with $^7/_8$ cup sugar and 1 cup water.

Poach in barely simmering syrup just until the fruit is barely tender.

Drain onto a plate and refrigerate.

Boil the syrup to reduce by half.

Skin 1$^1/_2$ ounces sweet almonds with 1 bitter almond, and soak in cold water. Pound them in a mortar.

Moisten the almonds slowly, as they are being pounded, with $^1/_2$ cup light cream or milk.

Place the paste in a dishcloth or linen towel and squeeze out the milk. Mix the almond milk, off the heat, into the syrup; strain through cheesecloth into a bowl. Refrigerate.

To serve unmold the apricot mold by dipping it for a second into hot water, shake, and turn over onto a large plate. Surround the base with the poached apricots and baste with the almond syrup. Serve on the side a bowl of the remaining syrup, everything very cold.

PINEAPPLE

Because it contains rare substances that promote digestion, which, like its flavor, are impaired by cooking, pineapple should always be eaten fresh and uncooked. It can be prepared in marvelous ways.

MOLDED RICE WITH PINEAPPLE

Peel a pineapple; cut it in half lengthwise and remove the very hard core; or leave the fruit whole and remove the center core.

Cut into $^3/_8$-inch slices, sprinkle with powdered sugar, and place on a plate to macerate with a few tablespoons kirsch.

Prepare some dessert rice (pages 431–2); mold it in a *génoise* mold, poach, and unmold on a round platter; while the rice is very hot, arrange the slices of pineapple, well drained, on top in a rosette.

Coat the rice with apricot sauce (page 417) flavored with kirsch and the macerating juice from the pineapple.

Ananas meringué

PINEAPPLE WITH MERINGUE

Follow the recipe for apricots with meringue Clairette (page 468) except that the pineapple is peeled, sliced, then cut into large dice, macerated as for molded rice with pineapple (above), and spread in one layer on the rice. Cover with the meringue, decorate, and bake.

1 very ripe pineapple
Sugar
1 tablespoon Marie Brizard
  apricot liqueur or
  Cointreau
1½ ounces wheat
  semolina
4 egg yolks
4 egg whites
Pinch vanilla sugar
⅔ cup sugar
2 large apples, peeled,
  seeded, quartered
1 tablespoon unsalted
  butter
1 tablespoon sugar
1 teaspoon water
Vanilla
Crème Chantilly (page 411)
Apricot sauce (page 417),
  flavored with Marie
  Brizard apricot liqueur or
  Cointreau
Candied cherries

Ananas et zéphirs normands

NORMANDY PINEAPPLE BREEZES

Method. Peel a very ripe pineapple and cut in half lengthwise after removing the core. Then slice the pulp into ⅜-inch slices. Dice 3 slices in ⅜-inch cubes, sprinkle with sugar, and pour over 1 tablespoon Marie Brizard apricot liqueur or Cointreau. Macerate the remaining slices with sugar and liqueur in another bowl.

Prepare 1½ ounces wheat semolina as for apricots Colbert (page 467) but thicken with 4 egg yolks and add 2 egg whites, whipped very stiff.

Flavor, after adding the yolks but before adding the whites, by adding the macerated diced pineapple. Add the vanilla sugar.

Pour into a buttered mold shaped like a half sphere. Poach in a *bain-marie* in the oven.

Whip 2 egg whites with ⅔ cup sugar into ordinary meringues (page 456), and, with a pastry bag or a tablespoon, form small meringue shells as large as pullets' eggs on a pastry sheet and bake.

Cook the apples in a skillet with 1 tablespoon butter, 1 tablespoon sugar, and 1 teaspoon water. Stew slowly until all the pulp is soft. Mash with a fork, add vanilla, and mix with half its volume of *crème* Chantilly.

Make apricot sauce flavored with liqueur.

Presentation. Carefully put the meringue shells together in twos, with a filling of the apple Chantilly marmalade.

Unmold the cake on a large round platter. On the domed top place the half slices of pineapple, overlapping.

In the spaces between the pineapple slices and around the edges of the plate, pour the apricot sauce to contrast with the golden color of the fruit.

Then, around the pineapple slices and at the base of the plate, place a row of the pairs of meringues.

Between the meringues place a candied cherry. On the top group three meringues and one cherry.

Coat the pineapple very lightly with the apricot sauce, and serve the remaining sauce on the side. Add the liqueur and juice from the pineapple to the reserved sauce.

Ananas aux liqueurs

PINEAPPLE WITH LIQUEUR

Follow the method given for Normandy pineapple breezes (above), until the sliced fruit has been macerated.

Place the pineapple slices on a hot platter sprinkled with confectioners' sugar, then sprinkle the slices with the same sugar, and pour on them the chosen liqueur, heated beforehand.

Ignite the liqueur, and present to the guests while still burning. Baste the slices until the flames are extinguished naturally.

1 large sweet-smelling
  pineapple
Thick sugar syrup
Kirsch
2 cups Bavarian cream
  (page 418)
4 tablespoons strawberries
1 tablespoon sugar
1 slice *génoise* cake (page
  400), 1½ inches thick
Whole strawberries
Juice of ½ blood orange

Method. Choose a large sweet-smelling pineapple with a beautiful golden color. Cut off the top, leaving about ½ inch attached to the leaves.

Remove the fruit from the shell, cutting it all around, ½ inch from the skin, with a long thin blade, turning it so that the pineapple is removed in one piece.

Cut the pulp into two equal parts lengthwise and remove the hard core. Then cut half the pineapple pulp into ⅜-inch slices, and the other half into ⅜-inch dice.

Poach the two batches of cut fruit separately in a thick sugar syrup. Pour into two bowls, flavor with kirsch, and refrigerate.

Prepare 2 cups Bavarian cream, flavor with kirsch, and add the poaching syrup from the pineapple. Just as the cream is about to set, add the diced pineapple and 4 tablespoons strawberries macerated in kirsch with 1 tablespoon sugar.

Before the mixture sets, pour it into the pineapple shell. Pack in crushed ice or refrigerate for 3 hours.

Presentation. On a large platter place a thick slice of *génoise* cake with a circle cut out in the center to hold the pineapple standing up.

On top of the pineapple and around the edges of the cake place circles of macerated strawberries; and on the very top place the pineapple top with its leaves.

At the base of the cake arrange the half slices of pineapple in scallops against the side of the cake. Fill the center of each half slice with a strawberry.

Squeeze the juice of ½ blood orange into the poaching syrup and add 2 tablespoons kirsch; pour on the pineapple slices. The excess syrup will be absorbed by the cake. After serving the Bavarian cream, cut the cake into small wedges and serve.

BANANAS

Bananas, peeled and poached in syrup, can be prepared *à la Bourdaloue* (page 467), with dessert rice (pages 431–2), with meringue (page 456); you can also make excellent banana cream soufflés; in that case, slice the bananas in half and cook slowly in butter in a skillet; sprinkle with sugar, and purée before adding the basic soufflé cream (pages 447–8).

Instead of baking and serving the banana soufflé in a soufflé dish, you can make a delicious fantasy called soufflé bananas with caramelized almonds. When you peel the fruit, be careful not to spoil the peels of half the bananas; place the skins in their natural shape in a circle on an ovenproof dish. Add 1 tablespoon crushed caramelized almonds (page 454) or crushed macaroons to the banana soufflé batter. Using a pastry bag with a large tube, fill the banana skins with the batter. Sprinkle the powdered almonds on top of each banana, then dust with confectioners' sugar. Bake in a 425° oven for 5 minutes and serve as is.

CHERRIES

Cerises flambées

FLAMING CHERRIES

Remove the pits and the stems from sweet cherries and poach them in a syrup flavored with fruit-pit liqueur. Follow the method for apricots flamed with Grand Marnier (pages 467–8).

STRAWBERRIES

Fraises mignonnes glacées

ICED STRAWBERRIES

2 pounds strawberries
3 tablespoons sugar
4 teaspoons vanilla sugar
1/2 cup curaçao
1/2 cup champagne
1 quart lemon ice
3 1/2 ounces crystallized violets (page 454)
2 cups light cream
20 crystallized orange flowers (page 454)
1/2 tablespoon candied orange rind

Method.   Place the strawberries in a bowl, sprinkle with 3 tablespoons sugar and 1 teaspoon vanilla sugar; baste with curaçao and champagne. Refrigerate for 30 minutes, stirring the fruit from time to time so that the berries are completely soaked in the liqueur syrup.

Prepare 1 quart lemon ice, not frozen too hard. It should be somewhat soft.

Coarsely crush 3 1/2 ounces crystallized violets. Sweeten 2 cups light cream with 3 teaspoons vanilla sugar and keep refrigerated.

Prepare 20 crystallized orange flowers and 1/2 tablespoon candied orange rind cut into tiny dice.

Just before serving, spread the lemon ice in a crystal fruit bowl or a silver bowl, then, in one layer, on top, the strawberries, drained and basted with syrup strained through cheesecloth. Coat everything with the sweetened cream and on the cream sprinkle the crushed violets mixed with the diced candied orange peel.

Decorate here and there with the 20 crystallized orange flowers.

This presentation should be done very quickly.

Fraises aux fruits d'or

STRAWBERRIES WITH GOLDEN FRUIT

1 medium-sized pineapple, very ripe and sweet-smelling
Sugar syrup flavored with kirsch
2 golden yellow bananas
1 pound sweet-smelling strawberries
3 tablespoons sugar
Juice of 1 orange

Method.   Peel the pineapple, cut it in half lengthwise, and remove the center core; cut the thickest part of the pineapple into 12 half slices and dice the remaining pineapple in 3/8-inch cubes.

Place the half slices in a deep dish and baste them with a few tablespoons sugar syrup flavored with kirsch; refrigerate.

Peel the bananas, dice them like the pineapple, and add them to the pineapple.

Wash the strawberries quickly in cold water, remove the stems, and add the berries to the pineapple and bananas. Sprinkle the fruit with 3 tablespoons sugar and baste with the juice of 1 orange and 1 tablespoon kirsch. Refrigerate to macerate; mix the fruit carefully from time to time.

In a fruit bowl place the half slices of pineapple in a circle on the edge; then in a mound in the center, the pineapple, strawberries, and bananas. Baste everything with the macerating juice strained through cheesecloth.

CHESTNUTS

Mont-Blanc aux marrons
CHESTNUT MONT-BLANC

Push candied chestnuts (page 455) through a fine sieve over a savarin mold. The chestnuts will fall into the mold in the shape of vermicelli. Finish filling the mold by spooning up the chestnuts that fall around it.

Turn the molded chestnuts out on a serving platter and with a spoon fill the center of the ring with a mound of *crème* Chantilly (page 411) flavored with chartreuse.

MELONS

Melon royal
ROYAL MELON

Use 2 ripe melons with good flavor.

Rub the pulp of one of the melons, seeded and strings removed, through a fine sieve and with it prepare a light sherbet (page 464) flavored with curaçao.

Cut the top off the other melon to make a hole big enough to remove the seeds and the strings; then scoop out the pulp with a silver tablespoon—each piece of pulp removed should be as big as a small egg.

The skin of the melon should remain intact. To keep it firm, refrigerate.

Place the pieces of melon in a bowl, sprinkle with confectioners' sugar, and baste with 1 part curaçao and 2 parts fine champagne brandy. Let macerate for 1 hour.

To serve place the melon shell on a base of crushed ice and fill with layers of melon sherbet and macerated melon. Cover with the top part of the melon.

Melon de la bonne auberge
THE GOOD INN MELON

Choose small melons, of the Charentais variety, which are especially fragrant and never disappointing to those who know how to select them.

Have 1½ melons per guest; 9 melons for 6 servings, for example.

Scoop out 6 melons following the method for royal melon (above), keeping the skins intact; peel the other 3, and reserve their pulp along with that removed with a tablespoon.

Refrigerate the shells, and place the pieces of pulp to macerate in a bowl with some very old port wine and, for each

473

melon, 1 tablespoon fine champagne brandy. Cover the bowl tightly and refrigerate. Maceration time will be 30 minutes.

To serve fill the empty melon shells with the macerated pulp, dividing the port wine among the 6 melons.

Place the melon shells on a bed of crushed ice, cover the top of each melon with the cut-off piece, and serve.

The guests will appreciate this royal dish, with each spoonful enjoying pieces of melon, rosy colored from their sumptuous bath, and some of the liqueur.

PEACHES

You should always remove the skin of peaches; to get a clean, velvety fruit, dip them for a second or two, depending upon how ripe they are, into boiling water.

Poach peaches in sugar syrup, either whole or cut in half.

Prepare peaches following any of the apricot recipes.

Pêches archiduc
PEACHES ARCHDUKE

¼ pound semolina
2 cups boiling milk
Vanilla
Pinch salt
³/₈ cup sugar
2 cups pastry cream (page 411)
***Crème* Chantilly (page 411)**
2 tablespoons kümmel
¹/₂ cup sugar
1 cup water
1 vanilla bean
6 large peaches
3 egg yolks
Italian meringue (optional, page 455)
Light cream
12 teaspoons strawberry or raspberry purée

Method.   Cook ¼ pound semolina, pouring it in a stream into 2 cups boiling milk flavored with vanilla, seasoned with a pinch of salt, then sweetened with ³/₈ cup sugar.

Cover, and bake in a 325° oven, without stirring, for 30 minutes.

While the semolina is cooking, prepare 2 cups pastry cream with one-quarter of its volume of *crème* Chantilly, flavored with 1 tablespoon kümmel.

In a syrup made with ¹/₂ cup sugar, 1 cup water, and 1 vanilla bean, poach 6 large peaches, peeled, cut in half, and pitted. Set aside in a bowl in the refrigerator.

When the semolina is cooked, while it is still very hot, separate it with a fork, adding 3 egg yolks. Cool in a bowl. Separate the grains from time to time, so that the mixture does not become too compact. When very cold, add another tablespoon kümmel and one-quarter of the semolina's volume of *crème* Chantilly or Italian meringue made with 3 egg whites, whipped stiff, and cooked sugar.

Presentation.   Lightly oil a savarin mold with sweet almond oil; fill with the semolina and let stand for 15 minutes in the refrigerator; unmold on a round platter after dipping the mold for a second in hot water and wiping it.

In the center pour half the pastry cream; on top arrange peach halves in a circle. Thin the remaining pastry cream with fresh light cream, and pour some of this cream mixture over the semolina. Serve the remaining portion in a bowl with the dessert.

Complete the dish by coating each peach half with a teaspoon of strawberry or raspberry purée lightly sweetened and flavored with kümmel.

Sprinkle a pinch of coarsely chopped macaroons on the edge of the plate.

12 large peaches
Sugar syrup made with 5¼
  cups sugar and 4⅓ cups
  water (see pages 452–3)
1 tablespoon calvados
6 large apples, peeled,
  cored, sliced
2 tablespoons sugar
2 tablespoons unsalted
  butter
Piece of lemon zest
Peach purée
Strawberries
Wild blackberries

Pêches du bocage

PEACHES FROM THE ORCHARD

Method. Dip the peaches in boiling water for a few seconds, and remove the skins and then the pits by cutting down from the stem ends, being careful not to hurt the fruit.

Poach the peaches, keeping them slightly firm, in a sugar syrup. Do not let them boil. Remove from the heat, drain, and place in a bowl. Baste them with 1 tablespoon calvados; then add the poaching syrup and refrigerate.

Meanwhile, prepare some applesauce with sweet-smelling apples, stewed with 2 tablespoons sugar, 2 tablespoons butter, and a piece of lemon zest.

Keep this purée quite thick and rub it through a fine sieve; place in a bowl, and refrigerate.

When the apple purée is very cold, add equal its volume of good-quality uncooked peach purée, made by peeling and pitting peaches and pushing them through a sieve.

Pile the purée in a dome in the center of a fruit bowl; around its base place the 12 poached peaches, drained.

Coat the peaches with a *coulis* of uncooked red fruit, half strawberries and half wild blackberries, sugared with a couple of tablespoons of poaching syrup, reduced and iced. Serve the remaining *coulis* in a bowl.

Serve a plate of very crunchy and tender *crêpes dentelles* with this dessert.

Pêches glacées au sirop

CHILLED PEACHES WITH SYRUP

Choose good-quality peaches all the same size; remove the skins without blanching if the peaches are quite ripe. One at a time plunge them into sugar syrup made with 5½ generous cups sugar and 4⅓ cups water (see pages 452–3).

Poach the peaches slowly, keeping them firm; then place them in a crystal bowl with the syrup, which should barely cover them.

When the peaches are cold, baste them with 1 tablespoon kirsch, maraschino, or fruit-pit liqueur, and refrigerate for 1 hour. Serve as is.

Pêches Melba

MELBA PEACHES
Created by Chef Auguste Escoffier in Honor of the Famous Singer on a Visit to London

Poach large peaches in syrup (see above); when they are cold, let them stand in the syrup in the refrigerator.

Fill a crystal bowl with vanilla parfait (pages 462–3). On top arrange the fruit, well drained and with the pits carefully removed. Coat the peaches with raspberry purée lightly sweetened and flavored with kirsch.

Pêches sultane
SULTAN PEACHES

Proceed as for Melba peaches, replacing the vanilla parfait with pistachio ice cream and coating the fruit with the poaching syrup made with 5½ generous cups sugar and 4⅓ cups water (see pages 452–3). This should be very cold and flavored with essence of roses.

Pêches déesses
GODDESS PEACHES

Peel and poach large peaches as for Melba peaches. Let them cool in the syrup; and when cold, flavor with liqueur Vieille Cure de Cenon.

Meanwhile, prepare a light frangipane cream (page 410), using 2 cups for 12 peaches, rather thick and flavored with macaroons.

In a fruit bowl large enough to hold them easily, place the peaches in a circle, stem side down. In the center pile the frangipane cream in a mound, coat the peaches with shiny, partially melted red currant jelly prepared with uncooked fruit, and sprinkle a few petals of sugared roses like rain on the cream.

Serve with a crystal bowl of red currant jelly prepared with raw fruit.

Les pêches de mon moulin
PEACHES FROM MY MILL

12 spring peaches
Sugar syrup made with 5½ generous cups sugar and 4⅓ cups water (pages 452–3)
Sherry
1 pound strawberries
3 tablespoons sugar
1 tablespoon kirsch
Vanilla-flavored whipped cream

Method. Dip the peaches in boiling water, peel them, and poach in syrup. Place in a bowl with the syrup and refrigerate; flavor with sherry and let macerate.

Macerate 1 pound strawberries with 3 tablespoons sugar and 1 tablespoon kirsch.

Drain the peaches; remove the pits carefully, and replace each one with a macerated strawberry of the same size; arrange the stuffed peaches in a circle in a fruit bowl.

Coat the remaining strawberries with vanilla-flavored whipped cream and place in a mound in the center of the circle of peaches.

Baste the peaches with a teaspoon of the poaching syrup with sherry.

Pêches Astoria
ASTORIA PEACHES

Prepare 12 large peaches as for Melba peaches (page 475). When they are chilled, drain and remove the pit from each fruit without spoiling the shape of the peach and replace the pit with an equal volume of powdered caramelized almonds (page 454) crushed in butter, 1 part butter to 1 part almonds.

Fill a crystal fruit bowl with orange ice (page 460) made only with orange juice (add no lemon); place the very cold poached peaches on the ice and coat the fruit with fresh *cassis* juice, adding some confectioners' sugar to the cold juice and lightly flavoring it with kirsch.

Sprinkle the dessert with a light rain of crystallized rose petals.

Note: The *cassis* juice is made by squeezing the ripe fruit in a cloth and mixing the cold juice with confectioners' sugar, 4 cups sugar for each 2 pounds of fruit. Crush a piece of clove and add it to the fruit before squeezing it in the cloth.

Serve very cold with palm-leaf cookies (pages 405).

PEARS

Soft, ripe pears should be peeled and poached in a flavored syrup. Use the same recipes as for apricots and apples.

Flan de poires flambées

FLAMING PEAR FLAN

1 flan crust of very fine dough (page 386), 12–14 inches in diameter
6 apples
Cinnamon
1 tablespoon green walnuts
6 ripe pears
2 cups old red wine
1⅓ cups sugar
Piece cinnamon stick
½ lemon rind
12 red sugared filberts
½ cup old marc or calvados
Unsalted butter

Method. Prepare:
One flan crust of very fine dough, baked unfilled (page 391). Applesauce made following the recipe for exquisite apples (page 481); flavor with cinnamon and mix with 1 tablespoon green walnuts, coarsely chopped, lightly sugared, and toasted. Pears poached in a syrup made with red wine, sugar, cinnamon, and lemon rind.

With all the ingredients warm, pour the applesauce into the crust; cut each pear in half and scoop out the core with a spoon, filling the hole with a red sugared filbert. Arrange the pear halves on top of the applesauce, stems toward the center. Over the fruit pour ½ cup old marc or calvados (first heated); ignite and serve to the guests immediately, with the poaching syrup reduced to ½ cup and lightly buttered on the side.

Poires à la beaujolaise

PEARS WITH BEAUJOLAIS WINE

6 large pears
1 bottle Beaujolais wine
¾ cup sugar
1½ teaspoons powdered cinnamon
1 clove
2 slices orange
2 slices lemon
5 black peppercorns (indispensable)

Method. Peel the pears, leaving the stems on, and cook them in a Beaujolais syrup made with the remaining ingredients.

They will take about 15 minutes to cook.

Serve this dessert cold.

Poires Félicia
FELICIA PEARS
Crème renversée with caramel

2 cups milk
1 vanilla bean, steeped in the milk
1/2 cup sugar
4 egg yolks
2 whole eggs
3 tablespoons caramel syrup
6 medium-sized ripe pears
12 small pears, the size of an egg, all the same size
2 cups vanilla sugar syrup made with a vanilla bean, 1 1/3 cups sugar, and 1 1/4 cups water (see pages 452–3)
1 cup old red Burgundy wine
Pinch cinnamon
1/2 cup sugar
1 1/2 cup thick *crème fraîche* or heavy cream
1 tablespoon sugar
1 teaspoon vanilla sugar
5 red sugared almonds, crushed
Red currant jelly, partially melted

Prepare the *crème renversèe* following the recipe on page 414; pour it into a ring mold lined with sugar cooked to a dark caramel color and bake in a *bain-marie* in a 325° oven for at least 1 hour. After it is cooked, let the custard cool in the mold.

Pears

Peel the pears; remove the cores from the bottoms and prepare a poaching syrup by simmering 1 1/3 cups sugar with 1 1/4 cups water and a vanilla bean.

Divide the syrup in half; to one part add the red wine, a pinch of cinnamon, and 1/2 cup sugar.

Poach the 6 pears, cut into quarters in the plain syrup; cook the 12 small pears in the syrup with the Burgundy wine.

After poaching, pour the pears with their syrups into two fruit bowls; cool and refrigerate or place over crushed ice.

Presentation. Before unmolding and assembling the dish, drain the small pears, poached in wine, on a rack.

Unmold the *crème renversée* onto a round platter with a diameter 4 inches larger than that of the mold.

In the center place the quartered pears, well drained, in a pyramid; whip the *crème fraîche* and sweeten it with 1 tablespoon sugar and 1 teaspoon vanilla sugar and completely cover the pear pyramid. Sprinkle coarsely crushed sugared almonds on top.

Just before serving dip the small pears in partially melted red currant jelly to coat and place them in a circle around the *crème renversée.*

Serve with a tray of small sand cakes (page 406).

Poires Rose-Marie
PEARS ROSE-MARIE

Fine dough for Genoa cake flavored with maraschino, baked in an 8-inch *génoise* mold
6 large ripe pears
2 cups sugar syrup made with 5 1/2 generous cups sugar and 4 1/3 cups water (see pages 452–3)
Maraschino
Half an egg (1 tablespoon) of powdered caramelized almonds (page 454)
Half an egg (1 tablespoon) of unsalted butter
Kirsch
Jelly made with fresh red currants and raspberries
1 1/2 cups *crème* Chantilly (page 411) flavored with vanilla
Crystallized rose petals

Method. Bake a Genoa cake following the recipe on page 404.

Peel the pears, cut them in two, remove the pits, and poach the pears in the syrup. Place in a bowl; when cooled, flavor with maraschino. Refrigerate.

Mash the almonds with the butter; set aside on a plate.

Unmold the Genoa cake onto a round platter or shallow fruit bowl; soak the cake with kirsch, then cover it with a thick layer of red currant jelly. Return to the refrigerator for 10 minutes so that the jelly sets.

Arrange the pear halves, drained, in a rosette on top, and fill the cavities in the pear halves with nut-sized balls of the caramelized almond butter.

Using a pastry bag with a fluted tube filled with *crème* Chantilly, pipe a braid between the pears; also color some of the *crème* Chantilly pale rose by adding partially melted red currant jelly, and with the pastry bag pipe a beautiful rose in the center of the dessert.

Sprinkle the edge of the plate with crystallized rose petals. Serve with a plate of cats' tongues (pages 406–7).

Note: All the recipes for peaches can be applied to pears.

Marmelade de poires

FLAMING CRÊPES WITH PEAR MARMALADE (For 6 people)
Crêpe Batter

5 cups sifted flour
6 egg yolks
3 cups milk, boiled and cooled
Pinch salt
1 tablespoon sugar
1 teaspoon vanilla sugar
7 tablespoons unsalted butter, softened

Mix 5 cups sifted flour with 6 egg yolks and 3 cups milk, boiled and cooled; add a pinch of salt, 1 tablespoon sugar, 1 teaspoon vanilla sugar; then, when the dough is smooth and fluid, add 7 tablespoons softened butter.

The mixture should not be too light; watch the quality of the flour and reduce, if necessary, the quantity of milk. Let the bowl of dough stand at least 3 hours in a warm place, covered with a cloth. Fermentation will start while the dough stands, and the flour will lose the body that it may have acquired during the mixing.

Pear Purée

Sugar syrup made with 5½ generous cups sugar and 4⅓ cups liquid (2 parts water, 1 part Anjou white wine, see pages 452–3)
3 large ripe pears, peeled
2 tablespoons thick *crème fraîche* or heavy cream
Cointreau
Champagne brandy

Meanwhile, make the sugar syrup. In it poach the ripe, sweet-smelling pears. Place the pears in a bowl and let them cool in the syrup. As soon as the fruit is cold, rub the pears through a fine sieve and put the purée in a bowl. Thicken with 2 tablespoons thick *crème fraîche* and a little of the poaching syrup, reduced to the soft-ball stage (234° to 240°). Store in the refrigerator.

Make the crêpes (following the cooking method on pages 436–7); spread each one with a layer of very cold pear purée, fold in four. Place the crêpes in a circle on a large, very hot platter and baste them with Cointreau mixed with an equal quantity of fine champagne brandy, heated without boiling, and ignite, presenting the flaming crêpes to the guests.

APPLES

Apples can be prepared by any of the recipes for apricots. However, some recipes are designed especially for apples.

Pommes bonne femme

OLD-FASHIONED APPLES

Wipe several large apples; cut out the cores with a knife or an apple corer, making a cylindrical hole in each center about ¾ inch in diameter from the stem to the bottom of the apple, and removing all the seeds. With the point of a knife make an incision about ¹⁄₁₆ inch deep at the midpoint of each apple, going all around it. Place the fruit in an ovenproof baking dish; in the bottom of the dish pour a few tablespoons water or white wine; fill the hole in each apple with sugar and place a piece of butter on top. Bake in a 325° oven for 30 to 60 minutes.

While the apples are baking, prepare a ⅜-inch-thick bread crouton for each apple; fry them in butter (or make small cakes with *génoise* dough (page 400) or Genoa dough (page 404) or madeleine dough (page 401), and place them on a serving platter; set a cooked apple on each one.

Pour the cooking juice around the croutons; sprinkle the holes with confectioners' sugar or pour on some half-melted red currant jelly, flavored with kirsch.

Mousseline de reinettes aux noix
APPLE FLUFF WITH NUTS

11 medium-sized apples
4 tablespoons unsalted butter
3 tablespoons sugar
1 teaspoon vanilla sugar
Piece of lemon rind, very finely chopped
1½ cups water
⅔ cup sugar
1 vanilla bean
1½ cups thick *crème fraîche* or heavy cream, whipped
3 whole eggs, lightly beaten
3 egg yolks
2 tablespoons green walnuts, coarsely chopped
Fruit-pit liqueur

Method. Peel, core, and slice 8 apples; stew them with 2 tablespoons butter, 3 tablespoons sugar, 1 teaspoon vanilla sugar, and a piece of lemon rind, very finely chopped.

Cut the remaining apples into 8 pieces each, and poach them in a syrup made with 1½ cups water, ⅔ cup sugar, and 1 vanilla bean. This poaching should be done very slowly, and at the end the fruit should be barely tender.

Remove 15 pieces of apple at this point, and let the remaining 9 pieces cook until they are soft; then drain. Reserve the syrup.

With a fork mash up the apples in the first sauce as soon as they are cooked, and boil to reduce the sauce over a high flame, stirring with a spatula until all the water has evaporated and you are left with a real fruit paste.

At this point remove from the heat.

While the apple paste is still hot, stir in ½ cup thick *crème fraîche,* whipped; 3 eggs, lightly beaten; 3 egg yolks; 2 tablespoons green walnuts, coarsely chopped; and, to finish, the 15 lightly poached apple pieces.

Butter a 6-cup charlotte mold and pour the apple mixture into it; tap it slightly to remove the bubbles and bake in a *bain-marie* in a 325° oven for 40 minutes.

Check to see if the baking is done by pressing lightly with your finger. The mixture should have the consistency of a baked custard.

To serve let the mold stand for about 10 minutes after taking from the oven; then unmold onto a warm round platter.

Make a sauce by boiling down the syrup in which the 9 apple slices were cooked until it is reduced to ½ cup; rub the syrup and the 9 slices through a fine sieve and cook to make a purée, then off the heat add 1 tablespoon butter and 1 cup whipped *crème fraîche.* Flavor with fruit-pit liqueur. Coat the dessert with the sauce.

Serve with a plate of cats' tongues (pages 406–7) or any other crisp, delicate small cakes.

Pommes à la limousine
APPLES LIMOUSIN STYLE

Method. Poach the apples in a light syrup made with 3 cups water, 1⅓ cups sugar, and a vanilla bean.

**6 large apples, peeled and
  cored
3 cups water
2²/₃ cups sugar
3 vanilla beans
4 cups chestnuts
Milk
Few tablespoons *crème
  fraîche* or heavy cream
Handful of almonds
3 egg yolks
1 heaping tablespoon flour
2 cups hot boiled milk
Unsalted butter**

Watch the poaching, which must be done very slowly so that the apples keep their shape perfectly.

While the apples are poaching, prepare the chestnuts: make a slash in each one, and put them in a pot of cold water; bring to a boil and boil for 5 minutes. You will be able to remove both the outer and inner skins easily while they are still hot.

Put the peeled chestnuts into a deep saucepan, add a pinch salt and a vanilla bean, cover with milk, and cook for 40 minutes.

When chestnuts are cooked, rub them through a sieve and put the pulp into a skillet with ²/₃ cup sugar; bring to a boil, and thin to the consistency of a light purée with a few tablespoons of *crème fraîche*.

Blanch a handful of almonds by boiling them for 1 minute and slipping the skins off; slice the nuts and sprinkle them on a pie plate, mixed with a pinch sugar, and brown them lightly in the oven.

In a bowl mix ²/₃ cup sugar with 3 egg yolks. Beat this mixture with a wooden spoon for 15 minutes; it should become white and creamy. Add 1 heaping tablespoon flour, then slowly dilute with 2 cups hot boiled milk; finish with a vanilla bean. Pour into the saucepan used to boil the milk and bring to a boil, beating without stopping.

As soon as the cream starts to boil, remove from the heat and finish with a piece of butter the size of an egg.

To serve, spread the chestnut purée on a serving platter; place the 6 apples in a circle on top; coat with the prepared cream, and sprinkle with the browned almonds.

Pommes exquises

EXQUISITE APPLES

**¼ pound Carolina or Patna
  rice
Kirsch
Light caramel sugar
  (pages 414-15)
6½ tablespoons unsalted
  butter
8–9 apples
4 tablespoons sugar
½ pound red currant jam
6 caramelized almonds
  (page 454), coarsely
  crushed**

Method. Cook ¼ pound rice as for a rice cake (page 432), flavoring it with kirsch. Pack into a ring mold, after coating the mold with a light caramel sugar.

Melt a piece of butter as large as an egg (2 tablespoons) in a skillet, and add 4 to 5 apples, peeled, cored, and sliced; sprinkle with 2 tablespoons sugar. Cook the apples until they are soft and mash them into a fine purée. Off the heat add 3½ tablespoons butter.

Peel 4 nice apples, core, and cut into slices about ⁵/₈ inch thick; put them into a bowl, sprinkle with sugar, pour on 1 tablespoon kirsch, and macerate for at least 15 minutes.

Partially melt ½ pound red currant jam made with uncooked fruit or, in the spring, jam made with the last apples and the first strawberries. Strain the jam and put this ruby-colored *coulis* in a bowl with 2 tablespoons sugar and 1 tablespoon kirsch. If you are using red currant jam, also flavor it with kirsch.

Unmold the ring of rice on a warm round platter. Drain the apple slices well and sprinkle them lightly with flour; brown on both sides in a skillet where a good tablespoon of butter is sizzling. These slices should be barely tender and gold colored. Place the sautéed apple slices on top of the rice ring, overlapping them. In the center pile the applesauce in a mound.

Coat the apple slices with either the red currant jelly or the *coulis* of strawberries.

Decorate the top of the mound with 6 coarsely crushed caramelized almonds.

Pommes belle angevine

BEAUTIFUL APPLES WITH ANJOU WINE

6 large baking apples
Unsalted butter
Anjou wine
6 teaspoons sugar mixed with 1 teaspoon vanilla sugar
6 small savarins (pages 380–1)
Sugar syrup made with 5$\frac{1}{2}$ generous cups sugar and 4$\frac{1}{3}$ cups water (see pages 452–3)
Cointreau
6 green walnuts
1 tablespoon sugar
Crème Chantilly

Method. Choose 6 large baking apples, well shaped and fragrant. Wipe them with care; make an incision about $\frac{1}{16}$ inch deep with the point of a knife all around each apple at the midpoint, and core them with an apple corer or a knife, removing the seeds, their casings, and the stem. Place the apples on an ovenproof porcelain plate, buttered and moistened with $\frac{1}{2}$ cup rich Anjou wine, such as wine from the hills of Layon.

Inside each apple pour 1 teaspoon vanilla-sugar mixture. On top of each apple place a piece of butter; then bake in the oven as for old-fashioned apples (page 479).

Baste the apples often, adding tablespoons of Anjou wine as it evaporates and reduces. When the apples are cooked, they should retain their shape and have a nice golden color topped by a circle of dark brown from the caramelizing of the vanilla sugar and the fruit sugar in the wine. The Anjou wine will be almost all absorbed by the apples; what remains will make a thick, rich syrup.

Let the dish cool, then set in the refrigerator or in a very cool place.

Prepare 6 small savarins baked in small ring molds used for individual cakes.

Soak the cakes in the sugar syrup flavored with Cointreau. Drain on a pastry rack and keep in a cool place.

Coarsely chop 6 green walnuts; if they are fresh, remove the thin skin that protects them, which is very bitter in the first weeks after the harvest; spread the nuts on a pie tin, sprinkle with 1 tablespoon sugar, and place them in a 425° oven for a few minutes to glaze them to a light brown color. Let cool.

Presentation. In a circle on a large platter—a beautiful silver one if possible—arrange the 6 small savarins; soak each one again with 1 teaspoon Cointreau.

Place a baked apple on each of the savarins and sprinkle the chopped sugared walnuts on top.

In the center of the ring of apples spoon a mound of *crème* Chantilly flavored with the juice from the apples cooked in Anjou wine, which has been scrupulously gathered in the cooking pan and barely warmed (place the plate for only 1 second on a hot surface).

The *crème* Chantilly can be replaced, although it will not be so good, with frangipane cream (page 410) or a Saint-Honoré cream (pages 412–13).

Pommes au four Martiniquaise

BAKED APPLES MARTINIQUE STYLE

Choose large equal-sized apples of good quality that will not lose their shape when cooked.

Peel the apples and core from the stem to the eye with a corer ³/₄ inch in diameter; bake as for old-fashioned apples (page 479).

When the apples are baked, place each one on a Genoa cake (page 404) molded in a small tart mold and lightly soaked with rum; fill the empty hole with chopped pineapple macerated in rum and mixed with 1 or 2 tablespoons frangipane cream (page 410).

Coat the apples generously with frangipane cream lightened and flavored with rum; sprinkle with crushed macaroons; scatter a few pieces of butter on top and brown quickly in a 425° oven.

PRUNES

Pruneaux au vin de Bourgogne

PRUNES COOKED IN BURGUNDY WINE

2 pounds dried prunes
6 cups red Burgundy wine
³/₄ cup sugar
1¹/₂ tablespoons cinnamon
  stick
1 orange, sliced
1 lemon, sliced

Method. Soak the prunes in cold water for a couple of hours. Drain and place them in a saucepan. Moisten with the red wine. Add the sugar, the cinnamon stick, and the slices of orange and lemon.

Bring to a boil; remove the saucepan from the heat at once and let cool.

Serve the prunes in a bowl with their syrup and the slices of citrus fruit.

FRESH FRUITS OR MACÉDOINES OF FRUITS

Various kinds of ripe raw fruit can be cleaned, peeled, pitted, and cut into small dice, or sliced or left whole—and washed if necessary in water with lemon juice added. Macerate this fruit salad for at least 3 hours with sugar and kirsch, maraschino, or any other liqueur or wine, such as champagne, in a cool place.

Mix from time to time so that the ingredients of the fruit salad are well blended. Place in a bowl 15 minutes before serving and set on crushed ice. Serve as is.

OTHER COLD DESSERTS WITH FRUIT

Riz à l'impératrice

EMPRESS RICE

Method. Wash the rice in several changes of water until the water comes out clear; then boil for 5 minutes. Drain and

1/4 pound Carolina or Patna
  rice
2 cups boiling milk
1 vanilla bean
Pinch salt
Unsalted butter
6 tablespoons sugar
3 tablespoons apricot
  marmalade
1/4 pound candied fruit
4 tablespoons kirsch,
  maraschino, or Grand
  Marnier
2 1/2 cups custard cream
  (page 411)
1 envelope gelatin
1 1/2 cups whipped cream
Fruit sauce

rinse again; then pour the rice in a stream into 2 cups boiling milk with a vanilla bean and a pinch of salt. Add a good piece butter, cover, and bake in a 275° oven for 35 minutes without stirring.

Remove from the oven and sprinkle with 4 tablespoons sugar; mix carefully with a fork, adding 3 tablespoons apricot marmalade and 1/4 pound candied fruit, diced and macerated in 4 tablespoons kirsch, maraschino, or Grand Marnier.

While the rice is still hot, add 2 1/2 cups custard cream, also hot, and stir in the gelatin softened in cold water; stir until it dissolves. Refrigerate the mixture, but before it sets, add 1 1/2 cups whipped cream sweetened with 2 tablespoons sugar.

Using almond oil, lightly coat a mold with sides decorated or not, or a tube baking pan, and fill it with the rice mixture.

Bury the mold in crushed ice or refrigerate to set the rice without hardening it.

Unmold on a round platter and decorate the edge with candied fruit. Serve with a fruit sauce made with cherries, apricots, red currants, etc., flavored with kirsch.

Fruits divers à l'impératrice

EMPRESS RICE WITH FRUITS

The rice mixture above can be served alone, but it is usually served with a fruit poached in syrup. For example, empress peaches, pears, apples, apricots, or bananas.

Peel, seed, and cut the fruit (except the apricots) in half. Poach in a syrup made with 5 1/2 generous cups sugar and 4 1/3 cups water (see pages 452–3). Cool in the poaching syrup flavored with liqueur.

Mold the rice mixture In a ring mold with straight sides. Unmold and garnish with the halved fruit either on the edge or in the center.

Then coat everything with a fruit sauce (page 417) or with *sabayon* sauce (page 416).

Empress rice enables you to make a variety of delicious desserts with fruit that is either fresh or preserved in syrup.

Diplomate aux fruits

DIPLOMAT PUDDING WITH FRUIT

Virtually any fruit is suitable for this dish.

Method.   Prepare a bottom layer with madeleine batter baked in a Genoa cake mold (see pages 401 and 404).

Make a Bavarian cream with fruit (page 419), and mold in a ring mold 3 to 4 inches smaller in diameter than the madeleine cake.

Poach fruit in a syrup of the chosen flavor.

Presentation.   All the ingredients must be very cold.

On the madeleine cake spread an apricot marmalade somewhat reduced and flavored with fruit-pit liqueur. Place the cake on a serving platter and unmold the Bavarian cream on top of it.

Place the poached fruit, drained, all around the base of the Bavarian cream. Cover everything with a fruit sauce (page 417), a creamy *sabayon* sauce (page 416) made with champagne, or a custard cream (page 411) made with port.

Déjeuner

offert par

Monsieur le Président de la République

et

Madame Valéry Giscard d'Estaing

à l'occasion de la réception

de

Monsieur Paul Bocuse

dans le grade de Chevalier de la Légion d'Honneur

25 février 1975

Montrachet 1970
en magnum du Domaine de la Romanée-Conti

Château Margaux 1926

Morey Saint-Denis 1969
en magnum du Domaine Dujac

Champagne Roederer 1926
en magnum

Grand Bas-Armagnac Laberdolive 1893

Grande Fine Champagne
(âge et origine inconnus)

Soupe de truffes
Paul Bocuse

Escalope de saumon de Loire à l'oseille
Pierre et Jean Troisgros

Canard Claude Jolly
Michel Guérard

Les petites salades du Moulin
Roger Vergé

Fromages

Les desserts
Paul Bocuse

Le Président de la République
et Madame Valéry Giscard d'Estaing

prient Monsieur et Madame Paul BOCUSE

de leur faire l'honneur de venir
déjeuner au Palais de l'Élysée
le Mardi 25 Février 1975 à 12 heures 45

Tenue de ville

Paul Bocuse was born February 11, 1926, in Collonges-au-Mont-d'Or; his restaurant is in that same house today. In the intervening years Bocuse has been around the world countless times, teaching and practicing the fine art of cooking. But the Bocuse family has lived in this part of France since 1634, as millers and restaurant proprietors, and Bocuse always returns to his beloved market in nearby Lyons.

Bocuse's father, also a chef, made the grand tour as well, serving as an apprentice in many of the most celebrated restaurants in France before settling in Collonges and taking over the restaurant from his grandfather.

In 1942 his son, young Paul, was apprenticed to one of his father's friends, Claude Maret, in Lyons. But Paul was soon caught up in the Second World War and wounded. When the war ended, he quickly won a place at a three-star restaurant, the renowned establishment of La Mère Brazier, outside Lyons. From there he moved to another three-star restaurant, the Pyramide, run by another of his father's friends, Fernand Point, and then to still another three-star post, at the Restaurant Lucas Carton, where he completed his education.

Finally, in 1959 he succeeded his father at Collonges, and in only two years he won his first star, and at the same time the accolade of Meilleur Ouvrier de France cuisinier. A second star followed in 1962 and a third in 1965. In February of 1975 Bocuse was made a member of the Légion d'honneur by President Valéry Giscard d'Estaing in recognition of his services as an ambassador of French cuisine. On that occasion Bocuse prepared the official dinner at the Élysée Palace.

Bocuse has won numerous other awards, including the Gault-Millau "Chef of the Year" for 1986, and he is a culinary consultant to Air France and Pan Am. His efforts at spreading the fine art of cooking around the world include several restaurants in Japan, a cooking school in Osaka, international teaching tours, a range of wine and gourmet products bearing his name, and a new restaurant at Epcot Center in Orlando, Florida.